CAROLINGIAN CIVILIZATION

A READER

EDITED BY PAUL EDWARD DUTTON

broadview press

Canadian Cataloguing in Publication Data

Carolingian civilization: a reader

ISBN 1-55111-003-2

1. Carolingians. I. Dutton, Paul Edward, 1952-

DC70. C37 1993 944'.014 C93-093162-9

Broadview Press
Post Office Box 1243, Peterborough, Ontario, Canada K9J 7H5

in the United States of America:
3576 California Road, Orchard Park, NY 14127

in the United Kingdom:
B.R.A.D. Book Representation & Distribution Ltd.,
244A, London Road, Hadleigh, Essex. SS7 2DE

Broadview Press gratefully acknowledges the support of the Canada
Council, the Ontario Arts Council, and the Ministry of Canadian Heritage.

PRINTED IN CANADA

CAROLINGIAN CIVILIZATION

for Charles Hamilton
on his retirement

Contents

INTRODUCTION

MUCH TALK AT THE START OF A BOOK OF READINGS RISKS UNDERMINING the very purpose of the reader, which is to take students away from the secondary chatter that surrounds history and towards the primary documents upon which historical knowledge rests. But talk I must, since even source books are subjective compilations and want a word or two of explanation.

My own fascination with the Carolingians was born twenty years ago when I first chanced to read the opening pages of Eriugena's masterpiece, the *Periphyseon*. Not only was I struck by its comprehensive, syzygial definition of Nature, but also by the boldness and inventiveness of Carolingian thought. What I wanted to understand then, as I do today, is the intricate world of events and economics, politics and war that encircled and informed the lives and thoughts of Carolingian men and women. Eriugena led me to Einhard, Einhard to Boniface, and Boniface to Dhuoda and others.

The documents themselves are both plentiful and engaging, whether they be polyptyques or capitularies, polemics or saucy poems. Indeed, the period between 770 and 880 experienced what can fairly be called an explosion of words. Though not subject to sure and scientific quantification, Migne's *Patrologia Latina* can give us a rough indication, for it contains six volumes of writings from the seventh century (two of these house the works of Isidore of Seville) and fourteen from the eighth (six of those by the venerable Bede), thirty-five from the ninth, and seven from the tenth. Perhaps, it is not rash, in light of this outpouring of ninth-century words, to claim that the Carolingian age represents the documentary reawakening of western civilization. Though the tenth century may not have maintained the same literary and documentary pace, it preserved the written remains of the ninth century. One only needs to look at the library of Cluny in the early twelfth century; it was crammed full of Carolingian books and was even more heavily indebted to Carolingian scribes who had copied and so saved the monuments of the ancient world.

The phrase 'Carolingian Civilization' may strike readers as unexpected, perhaps even as a contradiction in terms. "Civilization," claims one textbook definition, "is a form of human culture in which many people live in urban centers." Indeed a colleague of mine, a distinguished historian of Islam, went so far as to assert that without cities and a vibrant urban life there could be no civilization. If that were true, then surely the Carolingians never had a civilization since their world was dominated not by cities, but by the countryside, the royal palace, monasteries, and cathedrals. Cities with ancient foundations still existed, but they had shrunk in size, falling well back within the territory enclosed by their old Roman walls. Nor were they any longer at the center of things. We do not find Carolingian writers lingering over street scenes, bazaars, or bookshops, but they did not want for places to gather or for a sense of community. At Aachen in his palace Charlemagne collected together family and friends in gatherings as rich and stimulating as those achieved by many courtly societies.

Despite the title, then, readers are left to decide whether the Carolingians achieved a civilization and, if so, of what sort. There are several fine readers that document Charlemagne's reign, but here I propose to present a broader selection of documents that ranges chronologically from Pepin the Short's inaugural reign in the middle of the eighth century to Charles the Fat's demise late in the ninth and that is not confined to politics alone, but also speaks of theology and philosophy, economics and literature, social history and daily life. Though the collection has been arranged chronologically, as far as that is possible, the reader will find at the end an Index in which the documents are sorted by topics. Thus a reader wishing to investigate a specific topic such as constitutional documents or women should begin by consulting the Index.

The great issue that all students face when studying Carolingian civilization is one of assessing the formative elements that went into producing it and of determining what impact it had on the direction taken by the Middle Ages. To put it more simply: what went in and what came out? If continental Europe in the age of the Merovingians had contained Roman, Christian, and Germanic elements, these had often remained isolated from each other. The seventh century may have been a crucible, as Barraclough once suggested, but the fire was far from hot enough to melt and mix stubborn metals and there was no sure-handed smith to tend the flame. The cultural synthesis achieved by Pepin the Short and his line may have been slow to take hold and shallow in its effect, losing strength the further away from the royal palace one was, but it did exist and Alfred the Great, Cluny, and the Ottonians were not to be untouched by it. To the readers of this volume must fall the task of trying to assess the importance of Carolingian civilization. Was it, indeed, the eye through which the disparate parts of western civilization were threaded? If so, then the ninth century represents the fundamental beginning of European history, at least in so far as it directly matters to us today. If not, was Carolingian civilization a dead end for the Middle Ages, an empire that was premature and bound to fail, taking its court culture down with it?

These were the kinds of fundamental questions that I put to the students in a senior seminar at Simon Fraser University three years ago. I soon realized that my students could not make a judgment on those and other questions without wider exposure to the literary and historical documents of the Carolingian age. Though many of these had been translated by dedicated medievalists over the last century, no systematic reader of them had ever been collected together. And so with my photocopy card, the assistance of Helen Davies and Ian Fell, the diligence of the Inter-Library Loan staff of my university, and the financial support of Jerald Zaslove and the Institute for the Humanities, I set out to make this reader.

Some license has been taken in updating older translations whose Victorian cadence must now strike the modern student as odd and off-putting. I have also attempted to check most of the older translations against the original documents, but many mistakes must remain. Inconsistencies in the citation of names and places will also be found, though an effort was made to standardize them. The square brackets throughout this collection represent insertions for clarity or explanation by the editor and some of the translators. In order to help students who are stuck for things to ask or tests to put to a text, I have placed some basic questions at the end of each document. These may be safely ignored by most readers.

Since all translation is, at some level, an interpretation, the prudent student will try not to rest an entire argument on a single turn of phrase or a particular word since it might belong to the translator rather than the text itself. Translators must be the humblest of all scholars, since they know how many compromises they have been forced to make, how often they have failed to understand the full meaning of a medieval thought, how frequently they have been unable to express in their own language the spirit of a foreign text.

Putting aside all these cautions and these regrets, my fondest hope is that this book of readings will encourage students and their teachers to find a fitting place for the Carolingians in their study of the Middle Ages. They are invited here to be my fellow investigators of the Carolingian age, to explore the general patterns and particular delights to be found in the writings of the poets, historians, and polemicists of a lost world. But they should not stop here, for there are many fine texts in translation now available or forthcoming. The Manchester Medieval Sources Series has under the guidance of Janet L. Nelson, for instance, undertaken to provide translations of the major annals.

As I worked on this reader, I could not but think of Charles Hamilton with whom I have taught an introductory course on western civilization for the last ten years. Throughout this time it was not only his unwavering commitment to undergraduate teaching and his love of historical learning that inspired me, but his fundamental decency as a colleague and friend. Alcuin too must have smiled as he left Aachen for Tours so long ago:

Est nam certa quies fessis venientibus illuc.

CHAPTER ONE

THE TIME OF PEPIN THE SHORT

(741–768)

The Carolingian Image of Christ

A nineteenth-century drawing [after Woltmann and Woermann] of the painting of Christ in the Godescalc Evangelistary, a manuscript created by the Court School of Charlemagne *circa* 781-783. The manuscript survives today in Paris (B.N. lat 1203).

1. A List of Superstitions and Pagan Practices

By the middle of the eighth century missionaries and reformers such as Boniface had begun, with the support of the mayors of the Merovingian palace, Charles Martel, Pepin the Short, and his brother Carloman, to try to cut back the tangled jungle of pagan religious beliefs and customs that still predominated in northern Europe, mixing with and compromising orthodox Christianity. The following is a precious, if rather strange and unexplanatory hand-list of pagan practices that may have been written down by a church official in the 740s.

Source: trans. J.T. McNeill and H.M. Gamer, Medieval Handbooks of Penance (New York: Columbia University Press, 1938), pp. 419-21; reprinted with permission.

1. Of sacrilege at the graves of the dead.
2. Of sacrilege over the departed, that is, "dadsisas."
3. Of the swinish feasts in February.
4. Of the little houses, that is, sanctuaries.
5. Of sacrilegious acts in connection with churches.
6. Of the sacred rites of the woods which they call "nimidas."
7. Of those things which they do upon stones.
8. Of the sacred rites of Mercury and of Jupiter.
9. Of the sacrifice which is offered to any of the saints.
10. Of amulets and knots.
11. Of the fountains of sacrifices.
12. Of incantations.
13. Of auguries, the dung or sneezing of birds or of horses or of cattle.
14. Of diviners or sorcerers.
15. Of fire made by friction from wood, that is, the "nodfyr."
16. Of the brains of animals.
17. Of the observance of the pagans on the hearth or at the inception of any business.
18. Of undetermined places which they celebrate as holy.
19. Of the bed-straw which good folk call Holy Mary's.
20. Of the days which they make for Jupiter and Mercury.
21. Of the eclipse of the moon—what they call, "Triumph, Moon!"
22. Of storms, and horns, and snail shells.
23. Of furrows around villas.
24. Of the pagan course which they call "yrias," with torn garments or footwear.
25. Of this, that they feign for themselves that dead persons of whatever sort are saints.
26. Of an idol made of dough.
27. Of idols made of rags.
28. Of an idol which they carry through the fields.
29. Of wooden feet or hands in a pagan rite.
30. Of this: that they believe that women command the moon that they may be able to take away the hearts of men, according to the pagans.

Questions: Why does the document exist in this particular form and for whom was it likely made? What model of religious conversion would best explain these practices? Has Christianity, in other words, been penetrated by pagan practices or has it, in the countryside of northern Europe, grafted itself onto an existing set of beliefs?

2. The Correspondence of Boniface, Missionary and Martyr

Boniface was born in the third quarter of the seventh century near Exeter in England and was called Winfred. He was a contemporary of Bede, but was encouraged in Rome by the pope to spread the word of Christ among the unenlightened peoples of northern Europe. For the last thirty years of his long life Boniface established ecclesiastical administration in Frankish territories and forged links between the papacy and the house of Charles Martel (from whom the term Carolingian derives). Indeed Boniface was a central player in the negotiations that led to the creation of the Carolingian monarchy. He died in Frisia in 754 while preaching to pagans. If one visits Fulda today one can see the tomb of Saint Boniface. The surviving collection of Boniface's correspondence is an extremely important source for understanding both the religious and political events of his time. Through the letters we can examine the role played by the papacy in the conversion of northern Europe, the function of a missionary, and the nature of the attack on paganism.

Source: trans. E. Emerton The Letters of Saint Boniface (New York: Octagon Books, 1973), pp.43-45, 47, 78-83, 157-79; reprinted with permission.

1. Pope Gregory II Recommends Bishop Boniface to the Frankish Peoples, December 722

Gregory, bishop and servant of the servants of God, to his best-beloved sons, both lay and clerical, living in Thuringia, greeting in the Lord.

We have made haste to comply with your praiseworthy desire by ordaining our brother and now fellow bishop Boniface as your prelate. We have laid our commands upon him that he shall never presume to confer unlawful ordinations, that he shall not admit to the sacred office one who has married a second time, or who has married a woman not a virgin, or who is illiterate, or is defective in any part of his body, or is under penance or a court order, or is known to be subject to any liability. If he shall find such persons already in office he shall not advance them. Africans who dare to apply for admission to ecclesiastical orders he may not accept upon any terms whatsoever; some of these are Manichaeans and others have often been shown to be rebaptized.

The offices and adornment of the churches and whatever endowment they have he shall strive not to diminish but to increase. The revenue of the church and the offerings of the faithful he is to divide into four parts: one for himself; one for the clergy according to the diligence with which they perform their duties; a third for the poor and for strangers; a fourth to be set aside for the maintenance of ecclesiastical buildings, and of these he is to render an account in the day of God's judgment. Ordinations of priests or deacons are not to take place except on the fast days of the fourth, seventh, and tenth months and also at the beginning of Lent and on the evening of the Saturday after Mid-Lent. The sacrament of baptism is to be administered only during Easter and Pentecost, except to those who are in peril of death lest they perish eternally.

As long as he shall observe the decrees of our see you are to obey him with devout hearts that the body of the church may be at peace and without reproach through Christ our Lord who lives and reigns with God the Father almighty and the Holy Spirit forever and ever.

May God preserve you from all evil, my best-beloved sons.

Given on the Kalends of December [25 November] in the seventh year of our most pious and august Lord Leo [722], crowned emperor by God, in the seventh year of his consulship, and in the fourth year of the Emperor Constantine his son, in the sixth indiction.

2. Pope Gregory II recommends Boniface to Charles Martel, December 722

Pope Gregory to his son, the glorious duke Charles.

Knowing, best beloved in Christ, that you have shown a religious spirit upon many occasions, we notify your highness beloved of God that the bearer of these presents, our brother Boniface, a man of approved faith and character, consecrated bishop by us, well instructed in the traditions of the holy Apostolic See over which we preside for the general welfare of the church, has been sent by us to preach to the German peoples dwelling on the eastern side of the Rhine, fettered by pagan errors, many of them still lost in the darkness of ignorance.

For their sakes we warmly commend him to your high favor and pray you to help him in every need, to defend him against every enemy over whom you may prevail in the Lord's name, bearing in mind that whatever support you solicitously give to him will be given to God, who said that those who received his holy apostles, sent forth as a light to the Gentiles, would be receiving Himself. This prelate, instructed by us in the apostolic doctrine, goes forth to undertake this missionary work.

3. Charles Martel extends his support to Boniface in 723

To the holy and apostolic bishops, our fathers in Christ, and to the dukes, counts, vicars, palace officials, all our lower agents, our circuit judges [*missi*] and all who are our friends, the noble Charles, mayor of the palace, your well-wisher, sends greetings.

Be it known to you how that the apostolic man in Christ, father Boniface, a man of apostolic character and a bishop, came to us with the request that we should take him under our guardianship and protection. Know that we have acquiesced with pleasure and, hence, have granted his petition before witnesses and commanded that this written order signed by our own hand be given him, that wheresoever he may choose to go, he is to be left in peace and protected as a man under our guardianship and protection to the end that he may render and receive justice. If he shall be in any need or distress which cannot be remedied according to law, let him and those dependent upon him come in peace and safety before our presence, so that no person may hinder or do him injury, but that he may rest at all times in peace and safety under our guardianship and protection.

And that this may the more surely be given credit, I have signed it with my own hand and sealed it with our ring.

4. Boniface to Pope Zacharias
on the condition of the Frankish church in 742

To our best beloved Lord Zacharias, the apostolic man wearing the insignia of the supreme pontificate, Boniface, a servant of the servants of God.

We must confess, our father and lord, that after we learned from messengers that your predecessor in the apostolate, Gregory of reverend memory, pontiff of the Apostolic See, had been set free from the prison of the body and had passed on to God, nothing gave us greater joy or happiness than the knowledge that the Supreme Arbiter had appointed your fatherly clemency to administer the canon law and to govern the Apostolic See. We gave thanks to God with uplifted hands. And so, just as if we were kneeling at your feet, we most earnestly pray that, as we have been devoted servants and willing disciples of your predecessors under the authority of Saint Peter, so also we may be worthy to be the obedient servants of your holiness under the canon law. It is our earnest desire to maintain the Catholic faith and the unity of the Roman church. As many hearers or learners as God shall grant me in my missionary work, I will not cease to summon and urge them to render obedience to the Apostolic See.

We have also to inform your paternity that by the grace of God we have appointed three bishops over those peoples in Germany who have been to a certain extent won over and converted and we have divided the province into three dioceses. The bishoprics of these three towns or cities where they were ordained we beg you to confirm and establish by your authority in writing. We have appointed one episcopal see in the fortress called Würzburg, another in the town of Buraburg, and a third in a place called Erfurt, which was formerly a city of heathen rustics. The choice of these three places we earnestly pray you to strengthen and confirm by your own charter and by authority of your apostolic office, so that, God willing, there may be in Germany three episcopal sees founded and established by apostolic order and under the authority and direction of Saint Peter. And may neither the present nor any future generation presume to break up these dioceses or to defy the orders of the Apostolic See.

Be it known also to your paternity that Carloman, duke of the Franks, summoned me to him and requested me to bring together a council in the part of the Frankish kingdom which is under his rule. He promised that he would do something toward reforming and reestablishing the ecclesiastical discipline, which for a long time, not less than sixty or seventy years, has been despoiled and trampled upon. If, therefore, he is really willing, under divine inspiration, to carry out this purpose, I should have the advice and direction of your authority—that is, the authority of the Apostolic See. The Franks, according to their elders, have not held a council for more than eighty years, nor have they had an archbishop or established or restored anywhere the canon law of the church. For the most part the episcopal sees in cities are in the hands of greedy laymen or are exploited by adulterous and vicious clergymen and publicans for secular uses. If, then, I am to undertake this business by your order and at the instance of the aforesaid duke, I desire to have at once the command and the suggestions of the Apostolic See, together with the church canons.

If I find among these men certain so-called deacons who have spent their lives since boyhood in debauchery, adultery, and every kind of filthiness, who entered the diaconate with this reputation, and who now, while they have four or five concubines in their beds, still read the Gospel and are not ashamed or afraid to call themselves deacons—nay rather, entering upon the priesthood, they continue in the same vices, add sin to sin, declare that they have a right to make intercession for the people in the priestly office and to celebrate Mass, and, still worse, with such reputations advancing from step to step to nomination and appointment as bishops—may I have the formal prescription of your authority as to your procedure in such cases so that they may be convicted by an apostolic judgment and dealt with as sinners? And certain bishops are to be found among them who, although they deny that they are fornicators or adulterers, are drunkards and shiftless men, given to hunting and to fighting in the army like soldiers and by their own hands shedding blood, whether of heathens or Christians. Since I am the recognized servant and legate of the Apostolic See, my word here and your word there ought to agree, in case I should send messengers, as I have done in the past, to learn the decision of your authority.

In another matter, also, I have to ask your advice and permission. Your predecessor of reverend memory directed me in your presence, to name, God willing, a [certain] priest as my heir and successor in the service of the church in case of my death. If this be the will of God, it is agreeable to me. But now I am in doubt and do not know whether it can be done, because since then a brother of that priest has killed an uncle of the duke of the Franks and up to the present time we do not know how and when that quarrel will be settled. I pray you, therefore, to give me your authority to act in this choice, with the approval of the servants of God, as may seem best to us all for God and for the advantage and spiritual profit of the church and the protection of religion. May I have your consent to act in this matter as God shall deign to inspire me, since it does not seem possible to accomplish it against the wishes of the prince?

I have further to seek the advice of your paternity in regard to a certain perplexing and scandalous report which has come to us recently and has greatly disturbed us, filling with confusion the priests of our churches. A certain layman of high station came to us and said that Gregory of sainted memory, pontiff of the Apostolic See, had granted him permission to marry the widow of his uncle. She had formerly been the wife of her own cousin but had left him during his lifetime. She is known to be related in the third degree to the man who now desires her and who declares that permission was granted him. She formerly made a vow of chastity before God and took the veil but laid it aside and was married.

The aforesaid man declares that he has a license form the Apostolic See for such a marriage as this! But we do not believe this to be true; for a synod of the church of the Saxons beyond the sea, in which I was born and reared, namely the synod of London [in 605], convoked and directed by disciples of Saint Gregory, the archbishops—Augustine, Laurentius, Justus, and Miletus—declared such a marriage union, on the authority of Holy Scripture, to be a heinous crime, an incestuous and horrible offense, and a damnable sin. Wherefore, I beg your paternity to deign to enlighten us as to the true doctrine in this case, that scandals and schisms or new errors may not arise and increase there from among the clergy and the Christian people.

Some of the ignorant common people, Alemannians, Bavarians, and Franks, hearing that many of the offenses prohibited by us are practiced in the city of Rome imagine that they are allowed by the priests there and reproach us for causing them to incur blame in their own lives. They say that on the first day of January year after year, in the city of Rome and in the neighborhood of Saint Peter's church by day or night they have seen bands of singers parading the streets in pagan fashion, shouting and chanting sacrilegious songs and loading tables with food day and night, while no one in his own house is willing to lend his neighbor fire or tools or any other convenience. They say also that they have seen there women with amulets and bracelets of heathen fashion on their arms and legs, offering them for sale to willing buyers. All these things, seen by evil-minded and ignorant people, are a cause of reproach to us and a hindrance to our preaching and teaching. It is of such things that the Apostle says reprovingly: "Ye observe days and times; I fear I have labored with you in vain." And Saint Augustine said: "He who believes in such evil things as incantations or diviners or soothsayers, or amulets, or any kind of prophecies, even though he fast, or pray, or run to church continually, and though he give alms generously, or torment his body with all kinds of tortures, it shall profit him nothing so long as he does not abandon these sacrilegious rites." If your paternity would prohibit these heathen practices at Rome, it would bring rewards to you and the greatest advantage to us in our teaching.

Some bishops and priests of the Frankish people who were adulterers and fornicators of the worst kind, whose children born during their episcopate or priesthood bear witness against them, now declare, on returning from the Apostolic See, that the Roman pontiff has given them permission to carry on their episcopal service in the church. Against this we maintain that we have never heard that the Apostolic See had ever given a decision contrary to canonical decrees.

All these things, beloved master, we made known to you that we may give an answer to these people upon your authority and that under the guidance of your instruction the sheep of the church may not be led astray and that the ravening wolves may be overcome and destroyed.

We are sending you some trifling gifts, not as being worthy of your paternity, but as a token of our affection and our devoted obedience: a warm rug and a little silver and gold.

May God's hand protect your Holiness and may you have health and length of days in Christ.

> May God enthroned on high for long preserve
> In his holy temple the ruler of the Apostolic See,
>   May the honey-sweet doctrine visit the grateful earth
> And make it worthy of God for Christ's blessed sake,
>   May the blooming mother rejoice,
> And may the house of the Lord be joyful with abundant offering!

5. Boniface to Pope Zacharias
on the foundation of the monastery of Fulda in 751

To the most reverend and beloved lord and master to be revered in fear and honor, Zacharias, endowed with the privilege of the apostolic office and raised to the dignity of the Apostolic See, Boniface, your humble and most unworthy servant, but your most devoted legate in Germany, sends hearty greetings of unfailing love.

I beseech your fatherly and gracious Highness with earnest prayer that you will kindly and favorably receive this priest of mine and bearer of my letter, by name Lullus. He brings certain confidential messages for your gracious hearing only, partly by word of mouth, partly in writing. He will also make certain inquiries of importance to me and bring me the answers and the advice of your fatherly kindness for the comfort of my old age under authority of Saint Peter, prince of the Apostles. When you have heard and considered all these matters, if they meet with your approval I shall strive with God's help to enlarge upon them; but if, as I fear, they may not altogether please you I shall follow your apostolic precept and either crave your indulgence or do penance as is fitting.

Your second predecessor, Gregory [II] of reverend memory, when he ordained me—unworthy as I was—and sent me to preach the word of faith to the Germans, bound me by an oath to be the aid and supporter of regular and right-minded bishops and priests in word and deed, and this, by divine grace, I have tried to do. False priests, however, hypocrites, misleading the people, I would either restore to the way of salvation or reject and refrain from communion with them; this I have in part accomplished but in part have not been able to maintain and carry through. In spirit I have kept my vow, because my soul has not consented to their counsels. But in the body I have not been able absolutely to keep apart from them when I have gone to the Frankish court on business of the church and have found there persons of whom I could not approve. Nevertheless, I have not partaken with them in the holy communion of the body of Christ.

The same apostolic pontiff required me also to report to the pontiff of the Apostolic See upon the customs and way of life of the peoples whom I visited, and I trust in God that I have done this.

In regard to the question of the archbishop and the palliums to be requested from the Roman church according to the promise of the Franks which I called to the attention of your holiness some time since: I have to ask the indulgence of the Apostolic See because after long delay they [the Frankish princes] have not fulfilled their promises, the affair is still being discussed and postponed, and no one knows what they may be willing to do. If it had depended upon me, the promise would have been kept.

There is a wooded place in the midst of a vast wilderness and at the center of the peoples to whom we are preaching. There we have placed a group of monks living under the Rule of Saint Benedict, who are building a monastery. They are men of strict abstinence, who abstain from meat and wine and spirits, keeping no servants, but content with the labor of their own hands. This place I have acquired by honorable effort, through the help of pious and God-fearing men, especially of Carloman, formerly prince of the Franks, and have dedicated it in honor of the holy Savior. Here I am proposing, with your kind permission, to rest my age-worn body for a little time and after my death to be buried here. The four peoples to whom we have spoken the word of Christ by the grace of God dwell, as is well known, round about this place, and as long as I live and retain my faculties, I can be useful to them with your support. It is my desire, upheld by your prayers and led by God's grace, to continue my close relations with you, to remain in your service among the German people to whom I was sent, and to follow your directions, as it is written: "Beloved sons, hear the judgments of your father, and so do that you may be saved." And elsewhere: "He who honors his father lengthens his life." And again: "Honor thy father, that blessing from God may be upon you, and the blessing of the father shall strengthen the house of the sons."

Questions: What light does Boniface's correspondence cast on the nature of the alliance between the papacy and the Carolingian house? Who benefited and in what ways? From whom did Boniface's practical and official powers derive? How did Boniface conceive of his role in northern Europe?

3. The Coronation of Pepin the Short

In the middle of the seventh century Grimoald I, a mayor of the palace and member of the family from which the Carolingian house descended, did try to install his son as king of Austrasia, but rival aristocrats cut short his premature attempt to replace the Merovingian line with the Pippinid. In 737 when King Theuderic IV died Charles Martel, the mayor of the palace, chose not to set up another Merovingian figurehead king, but ruled on his own until his death in 741. In the disputed mayoral succession that followed between Pepin the Short and his brothers Carloman and Grifo, Childeric III was elevated to the kingship. Whether he was the do-nothing king portrayed so effectively by Einhard (see doc.7.1-2 below) or not, by 750-751 Pepin the Short had decided once and for all to usurp the Frankish throne. He could not do this, however, without some sanction. The Royal Frankish Annals, the official house history of the Carolingians, later recalled the important sequence of events in this way.

Source: trans. P.E. Dutton, from Annales regni Francorum, ed. G.H. Pertz and F. Kurze, Monumenta Germaniae Historica: Scriptores Rerum Germanicarum in Usum Scholarum (Hanover, 1895), pp.8-11.

750

Burchard, the bishop of Würzburg, and the chaplain Fulrad were sent to Pope Zacharias to ask him whether it was good that at that time there were kings in Francia who had no royal power. Pope Zacharias informed Pepin that it was better for him who [really] had the royal power to be called king than the one who remained without [effective] royal power. By means of his apostolic authority, so that order might not be cast into confusion, he decreed that Pepin should be made king.

751

Pepin was, according to the custom of the Franks, chosen king and was anointed by the hand of Archbishop Boniface of blessed memory and was lifted up to the kingship by the Franks in the city of Soissons. Childeric, who was falsely called king, was tonsured and sent to a monastery.

754

With holy oil Pope Stephen confirmed Pepin as king and joined with him as kings his two sons, the Lord Charles [Charlemagne] and Carloman. The archbishop, Lord Boniface, preaching the word of the Lord in Frisia was martyred.

Questions: Why was Childeric not murdered? Was Pepin not worried about the return of the Merovingian line? Why or how had Pepin been 'chosen' by the Franks?

4. The Reanointing of Pepin in 754

The so-called Clausula de unctione Pippini, added to the end of a copy of Gregory of Tours's book of miracles, is another report of the reanointing of Pepin by Pope Stephen and the anointing of Charlemagne and Carloman. Scholars have long speculated on the reasons why a new royal dynasty wished not only papal sanction, but also to demonstrate its legitimacy through holy oils and royal symbols such as crowns and scepters.

Source: trans. B. Pullan, Sources for the History of Medieval Europe from the Mid-Eighth to the Mid-Thirteenth Century (New York: Barnes & Noble, 1966), pp.7-8; reprinted with permission.

If, reader, you wish to know when this little book was written and issued in precious praise of the holy martyrs, you will find that it was in the year of the Lord's incarnation 767, in the time of the most happy, serene, and catholic Pepin, king of the Franks and patrician of the Romans, son of the late Prince Charles [Martel] of blessed memory, in the sixteenth year of his most happy reign in the name of God, indiction five, and in the thirteenth year of his sons, kings of the same Franks, Charles [Charlemagne] and Carloman, who were consecrated kings with holy chrism by the hands of the most blessed lord Pope Stephen of holy memory together with their father, the most glorious lord King Pepin, by the providence of God and by the intercession of the holy apostles Peter and Paul.

This most prosperous lord and pious King Pepin had, three years previously, been raised to the throne of the kingdom by the authority and commandment of the lord Pope Zacharias of holy memory, and by unction with the holy chrism at the hands of the blessed priests of Gaul, and election by all the Franks. Afterwards he was anointed and blessed as king and patrician in the name of the holy Trinity together with his sons Charles and Carloman on the same day by the hands of Pope Stephen, in the church of the blessed martyrs Denis, Rusticus, and Eleutherius, where, as is well known, the venerable Fulrad is archpriest and abbot. Now, in this very church of the blessed martyrs, on the same day, the venerable pontiff blessed with the grace of the sevenfold Spirit the most noble and devout and most assiduous devotee of the holy martyrs Bertrada, wife of this most prosperous king, clad in her robes. At the same time he strengthened the Frankish princes in grace with the blessing of the Holy Spirit and bound all, on pain of interdict and excommunication, never to presume in future to elect a king begotten by any men other than those whom the bounty of God has seen fit to raise up and has decided to confirm and consecrate by the intercession of the holy apostles through the hands of their vicar, the most blessed pontiff.

We have inserted these things briefly, gentle reader, on the very last page of this little book so that they may become known by common report to our descendants in subsequent pages.

Questions: If Pepin was already king of the Franks, why was he reanointed by a new pope? Why would an author writing around 767-768 have taken the trouble to remember this incident?

5. The Donation of Constantine

The Donation is one of the most famous and controversial documents in western history. Though it pretends to be a decree of the Emperor Constantine issued in 317, it was probably composed by a papal cleric in the 750s, in part to support papal property and constitutional claims. The overthrow of the Merovingian line, the rise to monarchy of the papally sanctioned Carolingian house, the Lombard threat to Rome, and the pope's desire for the military intervention of Pepin are some of the background events that likely inform the Donation.

Source: trans. E.F. Henderson, Select Historical Documents of the Middle Ages (London: George Bell and Sons, 1892), pp.319-329; revised.

1. In the name of the holy and indivisible Trinity of the Father, Son, and Holy Spirit. The emperor Caesar Flavius Constantine in Christ Jesus, the Lord God our Savior—one of that same holy Trinity—faithful, merciful, supreme, beneficent ruler of the Alemannians, Goths, Sarmatians, Germans, Britains, Huns, pious, fortunate, victorious, triumphant, and always august: to the most holy and blessed father of fathers Sylvester, bishop of the city of Rome and pope, and to all his successors, the pontiffs who are about to sit upon the chair of Saint Peter until the end of time, and to all the most reverend and beloved catholic bishops, subjected by this our imperial decree throughout the whole world to this same holy Roman church, who have been established now and in all previous times. May grace, peace, charity, rejoicing, and long suffering mercy be with you all from God the Father almighty and from Jesus Christ his Son and from the Holy Ghost.

2. Our most gracious serenity desires, in clear discourse, through the page of this our imperial decree, to bring to the knowledge of all the people in the whole world what things our Savior and Redeemer the Lord Jesus Christ, the Son of the most high Father, has most wonderfully seen fit to bring about through the intervention of his holy apostles Peter and Paul and through our father Sylvester, the highest pontiff and universal pope. First, indeed, putting forth, with the inmost confession of our heart, for the purpose of instructing the mind of all of you, our creed which we have learned from the aforesaid most blessed father and our confessor, Sylvester the universal pontiff; and then at length announcing the mercy of God which has been poured upon us.

3. For we wish you to know, as we have signified through our former sacred imperial decree, that we have departed from the worship of idols, from mute and deaf images made by hand, from devilish contrivances, and from all the pompous displays of Satan; and have arrived at the pure faith of the Christians, which is the true light and everlasting life. We believe what that revered supreme father and teacher, the pontiff Sylvester has taught us: in God the Father, the almighty maker of heaven and earth, of all things visible and invisible; and in Jesus Christ, his only Son, our Lord God, through whom all things are created. And we believe in the Holy Spirit, in such a way that,

in the perfect Trinity, there shall also be a fullness of divinity and a unity of power. The Father is God, the Son is God, and the Holy Spirit is God, and these three are one in Jesus Christ.

4. There are, therefore, three forms but one power. For God, wise in all previous time, gave forth from himself the word through which all future ages were to be born; and when, by that sole word of his wisdom, he formed the whole creation from nothing, he was with it, arranging all things in his mysterious secret place.

Therefore, the virtues of the heavens and all the material parts of the earth having been perfected, by the wise nod of his wisdom first creating man from the clay of the earth in his own image and likeness, he places him in a paradise of delight. Him the ancient serpent and envious enemy, the Devil, through the most bitter taste of the forbidden tree, made an exile from these joys; and, he being expelled, did not cease in many ways to cast his poisonous darts; in order that, turning the human race from the way of truth to the worship of idols, he might persuade it, namely, to worship the creature and not the creator; so that, through them [the idols], he might cause those whom he might be able to entrap in his snares to be burned with him in eternal punishment. But our Lord, pitying his creature, sending ahead his holy prophets, announcing through them the light of the future life—the coming, that is, of his Son our Lord and Savior Jesus Christ—sent that same only begotten Son and Word of wisdom: in him descending from heaven on account of our salvation, being born of the Holy Spirit and of the Virgin Mary, the word was made flesh and dwelt among us. He did not cease to be what he had been, but began to be what he had not been, perfect God and perfect man: as God, performing miracles; as man, sustaining human sufferings. We so learned Him to be very man and very God by the preaching of our father Sylvester, the supreme pontiff, that we can in no way doubt that He was truly God and truly man. And, having chosen twelve apostles, he shone with miracles before them and before an innumerable multitude of people. We confess that this same Lord Jesus Christ fulfilled the law and the prophets; that he suffered, was crucified, on the third day arose from the dead according to the Scriptures; was received into heaven, and sitteth on the right hand of the Father. Whence he shall come to judge the quick and the dead, whose kingdom shall have no end.

5. For this is our orthodox creed, placed before us by our most blessed father Sylvester the supreme pontiff. We exhort, therefore, all people, and all the different nations, to hold, cherish and preach this faith; and, in the name of the Holy Trinity, to obtain the grace of baptism; and, with devout heart, to adore the lord Jesus Christ our Savior, who, with the Father and the Holy Spirit, lives and reigns through infinite ages; whom Sylvester our father, the universal pontiff, preaches.

6. For he himself, our Lord God, having pity on me a sinner, sent his holy apostles to visit us, and caused the light of his splendor to shine upon us. And do rejoice that I, having been withdrawn from the shadow, have come to the true light and to the knowledge of truth. For, at that time a mighty

and foul leprosy had invaded my entire body. Though I was tended by many physicians who collected by my side, not one of them was able to cure me. Then the priests of the Capitol gathered, saying to me that a font should be made on the Capitol, and that I should fill this with the blood of innocent infants; and that, if I bathed in it while it was warm, I might be cleansed. And many innocent infants were rounded up in response to their words, whom the sacrilegious priests of the pagans intended to slaughter in order to fill the font with their blood. Our serenity, however, perceived the tears of their mothers, and I was at once shocked by the demanded deed. Pitying the mothers, I ordered their sons to be restored to them; and, giving them vehicles and gifts, I sent them off rejoicing to their homes.

7. When that day had passed and the silence of the night and sleep had come upon us, the apostles Peter and Paul appeared, saying to me: "Since you have put an end to your vices, and have rejected the shedding of innocent blood, we have been sent by Christ the Lord our God, to give to you a plan for restoring your health. Hear, therefore, our warning, and do what we tell you. Sylvester, the bishop of the city of Rome, is on Monte Soratte, fleeing your persecutions; there he clings in caves to the darkness with his clergy. This one, when you have called him to yourself, will show you a pool of piety. Once he has immersed you in it for the third time, the power of that leprosy will disappear. When this has been done, make this promise to your Savior, that by your order churches may be restored throughout the whole world. Purify yourself, moreover, in this way, so that, leaving behind all superstitious belief in idols, you may adore and cherish the living and true God, who stands alone and true, and that you may commit yourself to carrying out his will."

8. Rising, therefore, from my sleep, I immediately did what I had been advised to do by the holy apostles; and, having summoned that excellent and benignant father and our enlightener—Sylvester, the universal pope—I told him all the words that had been taught to me by the holy apostles; and asked him who were those gods Peter and Paul. But he said that they were not really called gods, but apostles of our Savior the Lord God Jesus Christ. And again we began to ask that same most blessed pope whether he had some clear image [a painting] of those apostles, so that, from that likeness, we might learn if they were those whom the revelation had shown to us. Then that same venerable father ordered the images of those apostles to be shown to us by his deacon. And, when I had looked at them, and recognized in those images the images of those whom I had seen in my dream, with a great noise, before all my satraps, I confessed that those were the very faces that I had seen in my dream.

9. Hereupon, that same most blessed Sylvester our father, bishop of the city of Rome, imposed upon us a time of penance to be served in our Lateran Palace, in the chapel, in a hair garment, so that I might obtain pardon from our Lord God Jesus Christ our Savior by vigils, fasts, tears and prayers, for all the things that I had impiously done and unjustly ordered. Then through the imposition of the hands of the clergy, I came to the bishop himself; and

there, renouncing the pomps of Satan and his works and all idols made by hands, of my own will before all the people I confessed: that I believed in God the Father almighty, maker of heaven and earth, and of all things visible and invisible; and that I believed in Jesus Christ, his only Son our Lord, who was born of the Holy Spirit and of the virgin Mary. And, the font having been blessed, the wave of salvation purified me there with a triple immersion. For there I, being placed at the bottom of the font, saw with my own eyes a hand from heaven touching me. You should know that once I rose up clean from the font I was cleansed entirely of the squalor of leprosy. Rising from that venerable font and putting on white raiment, the pope administered to me the sign of the sevenfold holy Spirit, the unction of the holy oil, and he traced the sign of the holy cross upon my brow, saying: "God seals you with the seal of his faith in the name of the Father, the Son, and the Holy Spirit, to symbolize your faith." All the clergy replied: "Amen." The bishop added, "peace be with you."

10. And so, on the first day after receiving the mystery of the holy baptism, and after the cure of my body from the squalor of the leprosy, I recognized that there was no other God save the Father, Son, and Holy Spirit—whom the most blessed Sylvester the pope preaches about—a trinity in one, a unity in three. All the gods of the nations, whom I have worshipped up to this time, are proved to be demons; they are works made by the hand of men. That same venerable father told us most clearly how much power in heaven and on earth our Savior conferred on his apostle Saint Peter, when discovering how faithful he was after questioning him, the Lord said: "Thou art Peter, and upon this rock I shall build my church, and the gates of hell shall not prevail against it." Listen you powerful ones, and bend the inner ear of your hearts towards that which the good Lord and Master said to his disciple: "I will give you the keys of the kingdom of heaven, and whatever you shall bind on earth shall be bound also in heaven, and whatever you shall loose on earth shall be loosed also in heaven." This is very wonderful and glorious, to bind and loose on earth and to have it bound and loosed in heaven.

11. And with the blessed Sylvester preaching these things, I perceived them and learned that by the kindness of Saint Peter himself I had been entirely restored to health: I and all my satraps and the whole senate and the nobles and all the Roman people, who are subject to the glory of our rule, considered it advisable that, as on earth he [Peter] is seen to have been constituted vicar of the Son of God, so the pontiffs, who are the representatives of that same chief of the apostles, should obtain from us and our empire greater power of supremacy than the earthly goodness of our imperial serenity is seen to have. We choose that same prince of the apostles, or his vicars, to be our constant intercessors with God. And, to the extent of our earthly imperial power, we decree that his holy Roman church shall be honored with veneration. And that the most sacred seat of Saint Peter shall be more gloriously exalted than our empire and earthly throne, we give to it imperial power, the dignity of glory, vigor and honor.

12. And we ordain and decree that he [the pope] shall have the supremacy

as well over the four chief seats—Antioch, Alexandria, Constantinople and Jerusalem—as also over all the churches of God in the whole world. And he who for the time being shall be pontiff of that holy Roman church shall be more exalted than, and chief over, all the priests of the whole world; and everything which is to be provided for the service of God or the stability of the faith of the Christians is to be administered according to his judgment. It is, indeed, just, that there the holy law should have the seat of its rule where the founder of holy laws, our Savior, told Saint Peter to take the chair of the apostleship; where also, sustaining the cross, he blissfully took the cup of death and appeared as imitator of his Lord and Master; and that there the people should bend their necks in confession at Christ's name, where their teacher, Saint Paul the apostle, extending his neck for Christ, was crowned with martyrdom. There, until the end, let them seek a teacher, where the holy body of the teacher lies; and there, prone and humiliated, let them perform the service of the heavenly king, God our Savior Jesus Christ, where the proud were accustomed to serve under the rule of an earthly king.

13. Meanwhile we wish all the people, of all races and and nations throughout the whole world, to know that we have constructed within our Lateran Palace, to the same Savior our Lord God Jesus Christ, a church with a baptistery. And know that we have carried on our own shoulders, from its foundations, twelve baskets weighted with earth, according to the number of the holy apostles. Which holy church we command to be spoken of, cherished, venerated and preached of, as the head and summit of all the churches in the whole world, as we have commanded through our other imperial decrees. We have also constructed the churches of Saints Peter and Paul, the chief apostles, which we have enriched with gold and silver; where also, placing their most sacred bodies with great honor, we have constructed their caskets of electrum, against which no force of the elements prevails. And we have placed a cross of purest gold on each of their caskets, and fastened them with golden keys. And on these churches, in order to provide light, we have conferred estates, and have enriched them with different objects; and, through our sacred imperial decrees, we have granted them our gift of land in the east as well as in the west; and even on the northern and southern coast: namely in Judea, Greece, Asia, Thrace, Africa, Italy, and various islands. All shall be administered by the hand of our most blessed father the pontiff Sylvester and his successors.

14. Let all the peoples and nations of the whole world rejoice with us. We exhort all of you to give unbounded thanks, together with us, to our Lord and Savior Jesus Christ. For he is God in Heaven above and on earth below, who, visiting us through his holy apostles, made us worthy to receive the holy sacrament of baptism and health of body. In return for which, to those same holy apostles, my masters, Peter and Paul, and through them also to Saint Sylvester, our father and the chief pontiff and universal pope of the city of Rome, and to all the succeeding pontiffs, who until the end of the world shall sit on the seat of Saint Peter, we concede and, by this present, do confer, our imperial Lateran Palace, which is preferred to, and ranks above,

all the palaces in the whole world; then a diadem, that is, the crown of our head, and at the same time the tiara; and, also, the shoulder band, that is, the collar that usually surrounds our imperial neck; and also the purple mantle, and crimson tunic, and all the imperial raiment; and the same rank as those presiding over the imperial cavalry; conferring also the imperial scepters, and, at the same time, the spears and standards; also the banners and different imperial ornaments, and all the advantages of our high imperial position, and the glory of our power.

15. And we decree, as to those most reverend men, the clergy who serve, in different orders, the holy Roman church, that they shall have the same advantages, distinctions, powers and excellence by the glory of which our most illustrious senate is adorned; that is, that they shall be made patricians and consuls. We also command that they be decorated with the other imperial dignities. And even as the imperial soldiery, so, we decree, shall the clergy of the holy Roman church be adorned. And even as the imperial power is adorned by different offices—by the distinction, that is, of chamberlains, and door keepers, and all the guards—so we wish the holy Roman church to be adorned. And, in order that the pontifical glory may shine forth more fully, we decree this also: that the clergy of this same holy Roman church may use saddle cloths of linen of the whitest color, namely that their horses may be adorned and so be ridden, and that, as our senate uses shoes with goats' hair, so they may be distinguished by gleaming linen, in order that, as the celestial beings, so the terrestrial may be adorned to the glory of God. Above all things, moreover, we give permission to that same most holy one, our father Sylvester, bishop of the city of Rome and pope, and to all the most blessed pontiffs who shall come after him and succeed him in all future times—for the honor and glory of Jesus Christ our Lord—to receive into that great catholic and apostolic church of God, even into the number of the monastic clergy, any one from the whole assembly of our nobles, who, in free choice and of his own accord, may wish to become a clerk. No one should presume for this reason to act in a haughty manner.

16. We also decreed that this same venerable one, our father Sylvester, the supreme pontiff, and all his successors might use and bear upon their heads—to the praise of God and for the honor of Saint Peter—the diadem, that is, the crown of purest gold and precious gems, which we have granted him from our own head. But he, the most holy pope, did not at all allow that crown of gold to be used over the clerical crown which he wears to the glory of Saint Peter; but we placed upon his most holy head, with our own hands, a tiara of gleaming splendor representing the glorious resurrection of our Lord. And, holding the bridle of his horse, out of reverence for Saint Peter we performed for him the duty of groom, decreeing that all the pontiffs, his successors, and they alone, may use that tiara in processions.

17. Behold that, in imitation of our own power, so that the supreme pontificate might not deteriorate, but rather be adorned with even more power and glory than the dignity of an earthly government, we are handing over to that blessed pontiff, our father Sylvester, the universal pope, our palace, the city

of Rome and all the provinces, districts and cities of Italy or of the western regions. We are relinquishing them, by our inviolable gift, to the power and sway of himself and his successors. We do decree this by our sacred charter and imperial constitution, that it shall be so arranged, and do concede that these [properties and rights] shall lawfully remain with the holy Roman church.

18. Wherefore we have perceived it to be fitting that our empire and the power of our kingdom should be transferred and changed to the regions of the east, and that, in the province of Byzantium, in a most fitting place, a city should be built in our name; and that our empire should there be established. For, where the supremacy of priests and the head of the Christian religion has been established by a heavenly ruler, it is not just that there an earthly ruler should have jurisdiction.

19. We decree, moreover, that all these things which, through this our imperial charter and through other godlike commands, we have established and confirmed, shall remain uninjured and unshaken until the end of the world. Wherefore, before the living God, who commanded us to reign, and in the face of his terrible judgment, we conjure, through this our imperial decree, all the emperors, our successors, and all our nobles, the satraps also, and the most glorious senate, and all the people in the whole world now and in all times previously subject to our rule, that no one of them, in any way, allow himself to oppose or disregard, or in any way seize, these things which, by our imperial sanction, have been conceded to the holy Roman church and to all its pontiffs. If any one, moreover—which we cannot believe—should prove a scorner or despiser in this matter, he shall be subject and bound over to eternal damnation, and shall feel that the holy chiefs of the apostles of God, Peter and Paul, will be opposed to him in the present and in the future life. And, being burned in the nethermost hell, he shall perish with the Devil and all the impious.

20. This page of our imperial decree, we, confirming it with our own hands, did place above the venerable body of Saint Peter, chief of the apostles. There we promised to that same apostle of God that we would preserve inviolably all its provisions, and would leave directions for all our successors to preserve them. Thus did we hand it over, to be enduringly and happily possessed, to our most blessed father Sylvester, the supreme pontiff and universal pope, and, through him, to all the pontiffs, his successors, with the consent of God, our Lord and our Savior Jesus Christ.

And the imperial subscription: may God preserve you for many years, you most holy and blessed fathers.

Given at Rome on the third day before the Kalends of April, our master the august Flavius Constantine, for the fourth time, and Gallicanus, being consuls and illustrious men.

Questions: What did the author of the Donation hope to accomplish and in what ways, if any, was royal power compromised by the existence of this document? Also, are there any elements to the Donation that might have suggested, even to the Carol-

ingians, that it was not what it pretended to be? Why did learned Carolingians not suspect the document was fraudulent? Would Pepin the Short or Charlemagne have been troubled by the existence of this document?

CHAPTER TWO

THE TIME OF CHARLEMAGNE

(768–814)

The Equestrian Statue of a Carolingian King

A nineteenth-century drawing [after Vétault] of the small bronze statue of a ninth-century king long thought to be Charlemagne. It is more likely a statue of Charles the Bald. The short hair and mustache were typical features of the new royal style of the Carolingians who wanted to distinguish themselves from the hairy Merovingians whom they had overthrown. The statue survives today in the Louvre.

6. Pope Stephen Scolds Charlemagne and Carloman

After the death of Pepin the Short in 768, his two sons held separate kingdoms in Francia. Their mother Bertrada tried to preserve the peace between them, though relations between the brothers were tense. Bertrada also seems to have arranged for Charlemagne to marry a woman whom scholars have called Desiderata. She was the daughter of Desiderius, the king of the Lombards. The papacy was understandably worried, since it had tried to use the Franks as defenders and counterweights to the Lombards in northern Italy. Within a short time, the marriage was dissolved, not because of the pope's criticism, but because Desiderata may have been infirm and barren (at least, according to Notker) or perhaps because Charlemagne's political needs had changed. When Carloman died in 771, his wife fled to Desiderius for protection.

Source: trans. J.I. Mombert, A History of Charles the Great (Charlemagne), (London: Kegan, Paul, Trench & Co., 1888), pp. 79-80; revised.

It has come to our attention and with sadness we have learned that Desiderius, the king of the Lombards, has persuaded one of you to marry his daughter. The Devil alone could have suggested such a thing, since this would not be a marriage, but a shameful association. It was madness to attempt a union of the most noble race of the Franks and that fetid brood of the Lombards, a brood hardly human, that had brought leprosy into the land.... You should remember that, by your father's explicit order, you were [already] united in marriage to beautiful Frankish women, to whom you ought to hold tight in love. It is unbecoming and unlawful for you to repudiate your wives and to take up the strangers of another race; that would be sinful and heathenish.... You should remember that the representative of Saint Peter has anointed you and sanctified you with the blessing of heaven; ...that your father had been prevented by the remonstrances of his [the pope's] predecessor from divorcing your mother; remember, moreover, your father's promise to Saint Peter to be the friend of his friends, and the enemy of his enemies. He had kept his promise, and how could you...dare to make common cause against the Apostolic See with that treacherous race of Lombards? ...Wherefore, Saint Peter himself, the pope [Stephen III], the clergy and people of Rome, adjure you by all that is lawful, by the living and true God, the judge of the quick and the dead, by the ineffable omnipotence of divinity, by the tremendous day of judgment, by all the divine mysteries, and by the most sacred body of Saint Peter, that neither of you presume to wed the daughter of Desiderius, or give your God-beloved sister Gisela in wedlock to his son....

We have laid this exhortation and adjuration on the tomb of the apostles, presented it in sacrifice to God, and from that sacred spot have now sent it to you.

Should either of you, contrary to his expectation, presume to disregard it, then by the authority of Saint Peter you will be placed under the ban of the most fearful anathema, will become an alien from the kingdom of God, and will be doomed, with the Devil and his most wicked ministers, and all impious men to eternal flames. But he who shall obey and observe this exhortation shall be worthy of divine enlightenmnet with all heavenly blessings, and of exaltation to everlasting glory with all the saints and elect of God.

Questions: How much did Stephen know about the marriage when he wrote this letter. Did he, in fact, have any power other than moral suasion over Carolingian marriage arrangements?

7. Einhard's *Life of Charlemagne*

Widely considered to be the jewel of early medieval biography, the Life of Charlemagne was written around 826, twelve years after Charlemagne's death and in the shadow of the recent troubles of his successor. Einhard, who had served in a variety of roles at the late court of Charlemagne, was certainly influenced by the structure and language of Suetonius's biographies of the Caesars, but his portrait of the great king strikes a different tone, being more laudatory and intimate. Whether this emphasis was a comment on Louis the Pious's difficulties or a true reflection of Charlemagne's reign is a matter for the reader to weigh.

Source: trans. S.E. Turner, in Einhard, Life of Charlemagne (New York: Harper & Brothers, 1880); revised.

[Preface]

Since I have taken it upon myself to narrate the public and private life, and no small part of the deeds, of my lord and foster-father, the most excellent and most justly renowned King Charles, I have condensed the matter into as brief a form as possible. I have been careful not to omit any fact of which I was aware or could learn, but at the same time not to offend by a prolix style those minds that despise everything modern. Can one possibly avoid offending by a new work men who seem to despise also the masterpieces of antiquity, the works of most learned and brilliant writers? But I do not doubt that there are many people devoted to learning and quiet study who must feel that the affairs of the present generation ought not to be entirely neglected. Nor do they believe that everything done today is unworthy of mention and fit to remain in silence and oblivion. Nevertheless these people, seduced by a desire for immortality, celebrate the glorious deeds of other times in their compositions, rather than deprive posterity of the mention of their own names if they wrote nothing.

Be that as it may, I see no reason why I should refrain from taking up a challenge of this sort, since no one can write with more accuracy than I can of the events that took place around me, and of the things I saw with my own eyes. Moreover, I have no way of knowing whether or not anyone else will ever relate these things.

In any event, I would rather commit my story to writing, and hand it down to posterity in partnership with others, so to speak, than to allow the most glorious life of this most excellent king, the greatest of all the princes of this day, and his wonderful deeds, difficult for people of later times to imitate, to slip into the darkness of oblivion.

But there are still other reasons, not without warrant and explanation, in my opinion, that compel me to write on this subject, namely, the care that King Charles bestowed upon me in my childhood, and my constant friendship with himself and his children after I began living at court. In this way he strongly endeared me to himself, and made me his debtor in death as well as in life, so that were I, forgetful of the benefits conferred upon me, to keep silent concerning the most glorious and brilliant deeds of a man who was so good to me, and suffer his life to lack proper eulogy and written memorial, as if he had never lived, I would rightly be considered ungrateful. Still my powers are feeble and scanty, next to nothing indeed, and not at all well suited to writing and publishing an account of a life that would tax the eloquence of [Cicero himself].

Thus I submit this book [to you]. It contains the history of a very great and distinguished man, but there is nothing in it to be amazed by beyond the deeds themselves, except for the fact that I, who am of German stock and little trained in Latin, should have imagined myself capable of writing gracefully and respectably in the language of the Romans. Thus, with impudence, I ignored the advice of Cicero, as given in the first book of his *Tusculan Disputations*. Of Latin authors, he said: "It is an outrageous waste of time and materials for people to commit their thoughts to writing when they lack the ability to arrange and elucidate them, or to attract readers by the charm of their style." This dictum of the famous orator might have deterred me from writing if I had not made up my mind that it was better to risk the wrathful opinion of the world and to subject, by writing [this book], my own insignificant reputation to criticism, than to neglect the memory of so great a man.

[Family History]

1. The Merovingian family, from which the Franks used to choose their kings, is commonly said to have lasted until the time of Childeric, who was deposed, shaved and thrust into the cloister by command of the Roman Pontiff Stephen [II]. But although, to all outward appearances, the family ended with him, it had long since been devoid of vital strength, and was conspicuous only because it bore the empty epithet 'royal'. The real power and authority in the kingdom lay in the hands of the chief officer of the court, the so-called mayor of the palace, and he was in charge of affairs. There was nothing left the king to do but to enjoy the name of king and to sit on his throne, his hair long, his beard lavish, and play the ruler, giving ear to the ambassadors that came from all over and dismissing them, as if on his own responsibility, in words that were, in fact, suggested to him or even imposed upon him. He had nothing that he could call his own beyond the empty title of king and the precarious support provided by the mayor of the palace at his discretion, except a single country seat that brought him a very small income. There was a house connected to that place and a small number of servants attached to it who were sufficient to perform the necessary tasks. When he had to go out from there, he used to ride in a cart that was drawn, in rustic fashion, by yoked oxen driven by a plowman. He was conveyed in this way

to the palace and to the general assembly of the people that met once a year for the welfare of the kingdom. He returned in the same way. The mayor of the palace took charge of the government and everything that had to be planned or executed at home and abroad.

2. At the time of Childeric's deposition, Pepin, the father of King Charles, held the office [of mayor of the palace], as if by hereditary right; for Pepin's father Charles [Martel] had received it at the hands of his father Pepin, and filled it with distinction. It was this Charles who crushed the tyrants who claimed to rule the whole Frank land as their own, and it was he who utterly routed the Saracens when they attempted to occupy Gaul, in two great bat- tles—one in Aquitaine near the city of Poitiers and the other on the River Berre near Narbonne—and compelled them to return to Spain.

The title [of mayor] was usually conferred by the people only upon men who stood out because of their illustrious birth and their ample wealth. For some years ostensibly under King Childeric, Pepin, the father of King Charles, shared the duties inherited from his father and grandfather most amicably with his brother Carloman. The latter, then, for reasons unknown, re- nounced the heavy cares of wearing an earthly crown and retired to Rome. Here he exchanged his wordly garb for a cowl, and built a monastery on Monte Soratte near the church of Saint Sylvester, where he enjoyed for several years the seclusion that he desired, in company with other men who had the same object in view. But so many distinguished Franks, who were making the pilgrimage to Rome to fulfill their vows, insisted upon paying their re- spects to him as their former lord, along the way, that the repose which he so much loved was broken by these frequent visits, and he was driven to change his residence. Accordingly, when he found that his plans were frus- trated by his many visitors, he abandoned the mountain, and withdrew to the monastery of Saint Benedict on Monte Cassino, in the province of Sam- nium, and passed the rest of his days there in religious life.

3. Pepin, however, was raised, by decree of the pope of Rome, from the rank of mayor of the palace to that of king, and ruled alone over the Franks for fifteen years or more. At the close of the war in Aquitaine, which he waged against Waifar, the duke of Aquitaine, for nine successive years, he died of dropsy in Paris. He left two sons, Charles and Carloman, upon whom, by the grace of God, the succession devolved.

The Franks in a general assembly of the people, made them both kings, on the condition that they should divide the whole kingdom equally between them, Charles to take and rule the part which his uncle, Carloman, had [once] governed. The conditions were agreed upon, and each took possession of the share of the kingdom that fell to him by this arrangement. But peace was maintained between the brothers with the greatest difficulty, because many of Carloman's party kept trying to disturb their good relations, and there were some even who plotted to entangle them in a war with each other. The outcome of things, however, showed that this danger was more imaginary than real, for at Carloman's death his widow fled to Italy with her sons and her husband's chief nobles. There without [good] cause, having spurned her husband's brother, she put herself and her children under the protection of

Desiderius, the king of the Lombards. Carloman had succumbed to disease after ruling two years in common with his brother and at his death Charles was unanimously elected king of the Franks.

[Charlemagne's Childhood and Einhard's Plan]

4. It would be a mistake, I think, [for me] to write anything about Charles's birth and infancy, or even his boyhood, since nothing has ever been written on the subject, and there is no one alive now who can supply information on it. I have, therefore, decided to treat that as if it were unknown, and to proceed at once to describe his character, his deeds, and the other facts of his life that are worth telling and setting forth, and shall first give an account of his deeds at home and abroad, then of his character and pursuits, and lastly of his reputation and death, omitting nothing worth knowing or necessary [for the reader] to know.

[Wars]

5. His first military undertaking was the war in Aquitaine, which was begun by his father but not brought to a close. Because he thought that it could be soon concluded, he took it up while his brother was still alive and called upon him to render aid. Once the campaign had begun, he conducted it with the greatest vigor, despite his brother's failure to provide the assistance he had promised. But Charles did not give up or back off from his self-imposed task until, with determined persistence, he had completely accomplished his goals. He compelled Hunold, who had attempted to seize Aquitaine after Waifar's death and to resume a war that was almost over, to abandon Aquitaine and flee to Gascony. Even here he allowed Hunold no retreat, but crossed the River Garonne, and sent messengers to Lupus, the duke of Gascony, to demand the surrender of the fugitive, threatening to take him by force unless he were promptly given up to him. Thereupon Lupus chose the wiser course, and not only surrendered Hunold, but submitted himself, with the province which he ruled, to Charles's power.

6. After bringing this war to an end and settling matters in Aquitaine—and with [Carloman], his fellow-ruler, now dead—he was induced, by the prayers and entreaties of Hadrian [I], the bishop of the city of Rome, to wage war on the Lombards. His father before him had undertaken this task at the request of Pope Stephen [II], but with great difficulty, since some prominent Franks, from whom he usually received advice, had so vehemently opposed his plan as to declare openly that they would desert the king and go home. Nevertheless, the war against the Lombard King Haistulf had been taken up and very quickly concluded. Now, although Charles seems to have had almost identical grounds for declaring war as his father, the war itself differed from the earlier one both in Charles's vigorous pursuit of it and in its successful oucome. Pepin, to be sure, after besieging King Haistulf for a few days in Pavia, had compelled him to grant hostages, to restore to the Romans the cities and castles that he had taken, and to give an oath that he would not attempt to seize them again. But Charles did not cease, after his declaration

of war, until he had exhausted King Desiderius with a long seige and forced him to surrender. He drove his son Adalgis, the last hope of the Lombards, not only from his kingdom, but also from Italy, and restored to the Romans all that they had lost. He also subdued Rotgaud, the duke of Friuli, who was plotting an uprising, and he reduced all Italy to his power, and set up his son Pepin as king over it.

At this point I should describe Charles's difficult passage over the Alps into Italy, and the hardships that the Franks endured in climbing trackless mountain ridges, lofty cliffs, and jagged peaks, but it is not my intention in this work to record the details of his wars. Rather I want to set out the manner of his life. Suffice it to say that the war ended with the subjection of Italy, the banishment of King Desiderius for life, the expulsion of his son Adalgis from Italy, and the return of the lands conquered by the Lombard kings to Hadrian, the head of the church of Rome.

7. At the conclusion of this struggle, the Saxon war, which had been laid aside for a time, was taken up again. No war undertaken by the Frankish people was ever carried on with such persistence and bitterness, or involved such great commitment, because the Saxons, like almost all the tribes of Germany, were a fierce people, given to the worship of devils and hostile to our religion. They did not consider it dishonorable to transgress and violate either human or divine laws. Never a day seemed to pass without some incident designed to shatter the peace. Except in a few places, where large forests or mountain ridges intervened and made the border certain, the line between ourselves and the Saxons passed almost for its entire length through open country, so that there was no end to murders, theft, and arson on both sides. In this way the Franks became so embittered that they resolved at last to make reprisals no longer, but to declare open war on the Saxons. Accordingly the war against them broke out and was waged for thirty-three successive years with great fury; more, however, to the disadvantage of the Saxons than to that of the Franks. It could doubtless have been brought to an end sooner, had it not been for the faithlessness of the Saxons. It is hard to say how often they were beaten, and, humbly submitted to the king, promising to do what was asked of them, giving without hesitation the required hostages, and receiving the legates sent to them by the king. They were sometimes so much weakened and reduced that they promised to renounce their worship of devils and to adopt Christianity, but they were as quick to break these terms as they had been prompt to accept them, so that it is impossible to tell which came easier to them. Scarcely a year passed from the beginning of the war until its end without such about-faces on their part. But the king did not suffer his high purpose and steadfastness—firm both in good and evil fortune—to be turned aside from the task at hand; to the contrary, he never allowed their faithless behavior to go unpunished, but either took the field against them in person or sent his counts with armies to wreak vengeance and exact righteous satisfaction. At last, after conquering and subduing all who had offered resistance, he took ten thousand of those that lived on the banks of the Elbe River and settled them with their wives and children in many different groups here and there in Gaul and Germany. The war that had lasted so many years was at length ended when the Saxons

acceded to the terms offered by the king, which were that they would renounce their worship of devils and the religious rites of their ancestors, that
they would accept the sacraments of the Christian faith and religion, and
would unite with the Franks to form one people.

8. Charles himself fought only two pitched battles in this war, although it
was a long and protracted contest—one on Mount Osning, at the place called
Detmold, and again on the bank of the River Haase; both battles occurred
in the space of little more than a month. The Saxons were so routed and
overthrown in these two battles that they never afterwards ventured to take
the offensive or to resist the attacks of the king, unless they were protected
by a strong and fortified enclosure. A great many Franks as well as many
Saxon nobles, men occupying the highest positions of honor, perished in this
war, which only came to an end after the lapse of thirty-two years. So many
and so serious were the wars that were declared upon the Franks in the
meantime, and so skilfully were they conducted by the king, that one might
reasonably wonder which, his determination or his good fortune, is to be
more admired. The Saxon war began two years before the Italian war, but,
although it went on without interruption, business elsewhere was not neglected. Nor was there any shrinking from other equally arduous contests.
This king, who excelled all the princes of his time in wisdom and greatness
of soul, allowed no difficulty to deter him or danger to daunt him from
anything that had to be taken up and achieved, for he had trained himself
to bear and endure whatever came his way, without yielding to adversity or,
in times of prosperity, listening to the false promises of [good] fortune.

9. In the midst of his vigorous and almost uninterrupted struggle with the
Saxons, he established garrisons at important points along the frontier and
marched over the Pyrenees into Spain at the head of all the forces that he
could muster. All the towns and castles that he attacked surrendered and
up to the time of his homeward march he sustained no loss whatsoever. But
on his return through the Pyrenees he experienced the treachery of the
Basques. That region is particularly well suited to ambushes, since it is covered by thick forests. As his army was advancing in a long line of march,
made necessary by the narrowness of the road, the Basques, who lay in waiting
on the top of a high mountain, attacked the rear of the baggage train and
the guard that was protecting it and the column [marching] ahead of it. The
Basques drove them down into the lower reaches of the valley. In the struggle that ensued, they slaughtered them down to the last man. Then they
plundered the baggage and dispersed with great haste in every direction under cover of approaching night. The lightness of their armor and the nature
of the battle ground stood the Basques in good stead on this occasion,
whereas the Franks were at a considerable disadvantage, because of the weight
of their armor and the unevenness of the ground. Eggihard, the king's steward, Anselm, the count of the palace, and Roland, the lord of the March of
Brittany, and many others, fell in this engagement. This ambush could not
be avenged immediately, because the enemy scattered so widely after carrying
out their attack that no clue as to their whereabouts could be discovered.

10. Charles also subdued the Bretons, who live on the sea coast, in the extreme western part of Gaul. When they refused to obey him, he sent an army against them, and compelled them to give hostages and to promise to do his bidding. He afterwards entered Italy in person with his army and passed through Rome on his way to Capua, a city in Campania, where he pitched his camp and threatened the Beneventans with hostilities unless they submitted themselves to him. Their duke, Areghis, escaped the danger by sending his two sons, Rumold and Grimoald, with a great sum of money, to greet the king, begging him to accept them as hostages, and promising for himself and his people compliance with all the king's commands, on the single condition that his personal attendance should not be required. The king, considering the welfare of his people rather than the stubborn nature of the duke, accepted the proffered hostages, and, in view of the handsome gift, released him from the obligation to appear before him. He retained only the younger son as a hostage, and sent the elder back to his father. Then he returned to Rome, leaving commissioners with Areghis to exact the oath of allegiance and to administer it to the Beneventans. He stayed in Rome several days in order to pay his devotions at the holy places and then came back to Gaul.

11. Suddenly at this time the Bavarian war broke out, but it came to a speedy end. This war was caused by the arrogance and folly of Duke Tassilo. His wife, a daughter of King Desiderius, was desirous of avenging her father's banishment through the agency of her husband, and thus induced him to make a treaty with the Huns, the neighbors of the Bavarians on the east, and not only to leave the king's commands unfulfilled, but to challenge him to war. Charles's spirited nature could not abide Tassilo's insubordination, for it seemed to him to pass all bounds. Thus, he at once summoned his troops from all sides for a campaign against Bavaria and appeared in person with a great army on the River Lech, which forms the boundary between the Bavarians and the Alemannians. After pitching his camp upon its banks, he determined to test the duke's intentions by sending an embassy to him before he entered the province. Tassilo did not think that it was in his own or his people's best interests to persist, and so surrendered himself to the king, turned over the hostages demanded, among them his own son Theodo, and promised by oath not to give ear to anyone who should attempt to turn him from his commitment. Hence, this war, which threatened to be so harmful, came very quickly to an end. Tassilo, however, was afterward summoned into the king's presence and not allowed to depart. The government of the province which he had held was no longer entrusted to a duke, but to a number of counts.

12. After these uprisings had been so put down, war was declared against the Slavs who are commonly known among us as the Wiltzi, but properly, that is to say in their own tongue, are called Welatabi. The Saxons served in this campaign as auxiliaries among the tribes that followed the king's standard at his summons, but their obedience lacked sincerity and devotion. War was declared because the Slavs kept harassing the Obodrites, old allies of the Franks, by continual raids, in spite of all commands to the contrary.

A gulf of unknown length, but nowhere more than a hundred miles wide, and in many parts narrower, stretches off towards the east from the western Ocean. Many tribes have settlements on its shores: the Danes and Swedes, whom we call Northmen, live along its northern shore and all the adjacent islands, while the southern shore is inhabited by the Slavs, Esthonians, and various other tribes. The Welatabi, against whom the king now made war, were the chief of these tribes, but in a single campaign, which he conducted in person, he so crushed and subdued them that they did not think it wise thereafter to refuse obedience to his commands.

13. The war against the Avars, or Huns, followed, and, except for the Saxon war, was the greatest that was waged [by Charles]. He took it up with more spirit than any of his other wars, and made far greater preparations for it. He conducted one campaign in person in Pannonia, of which the Huns then had possession. He entrusted all subsequent operations to his son, Pepin, to the governors of the provinces, and to the counts and their legates. Although they most vigorously prosecuted the war, it only came to a conclusion after seven years of struggle. The utter depopulation of Pannonia and the deserted and destroyed site of the khan's palace, where now not a trace of human habitation is visible, bear witness to the many battles that were fought in those years and to just how much blood was shed. The whole of the Hun nobility perished in this contest, along with all their glory. All the riches and treasure that they had spent years amassing were seized, and no war in which the Franks have ever engaged within the memory of man brought them such wealth and booty. Indeed, up until that time the Franks had passed for a poor people, but so much gold and silver was found in the khan's palace, and so much valuable spoil taken in battle, that one might well say that the Franks had taken justly from the Huns what they had taken unjustly from other peoples in earlier times. Only two prominent Frankish nobles died in this war—Eric, the duke of Friuli, who was killed in Tersatto, a town on the coast of Liburnia, by the treachery of its inhabitants, and Gerold, the governor of Bavaria, who was killed (no one knows by whom) in Pannonia along with the two men who were escorting him as he was readying his forces for battle against the Huns and riding up and down the line encouraging his men. This war was otherwise almost a bloodless one so far as the Franks were concerned, and ended most satisfactorily, although by reason of its magnitude it was long and protracted.

14. Next the Saxon war came to a successful end, [an end] that matched its long duration. The Bohemian and Linonian wars that came next did not last long, and both were conducted expeditiously under the leadership of the younger Charles [Charlemagne's son]. The last of his wars was the one declared against the Northmen known as the Danes. They began their careers as pirates, but afterwards took to ravaging the coasts of Gaul and Germany with their large fleet. Their king, Godefrid, was so puffed up with vain aspirations that he expected to seize control of all Germany. He looked upon Saxony and Frisia as his provinces. He had already subdued his neighbors, the Obodrites, and made them a tributary people. Soon, he boasted, he would appear with an immense army at Aachen where Charles held his court.

Some credence was given to his words, empty as they might sound, and it is believed that he would have attempted something of the sort if he had not been prevented by a premature death. He was murdered by one of his own bodyguards, and so ended at once his life and the war that he had started.

15. Such are the wars, most skilfully planned and successfully fought, which this most powerful king waged during the forty-seven years of his reign. He so substantially increased the Frankish kingdom, which was already great and strong when he received it from his father, that he doubled its territory. The authority of the Franks was originally confined to that part of Gaul included between the Rhine and the Loire, the Atlantic Ocean and the Balearic Sea, along with that part of Germany which is inhabited by the so-called eastern Franks, which is bounded by Saxony and the Danube, the Rhine and the Saal—this stream separates the Thuringians from the Sorabians—and [finally] to the country of the Alemannians and Bavarians. By the wars described here he made tributary lands out of Aquitaine, Gascony, and the whole of the region of the Pyrenees as far as the River Ebro, which rises in Navarre, and flows through the most fertile districts of Spain, and empties into the Balearic Sea beneath the walls of the city of Tortosa. He next reduced and made tributary all Italy from Aosta to southern Calabria, where the border separates the Beneventans and the Greeks, a territory more than a thousand miles long. Then [he subdued] Saxony, which constitutes no small part of Germany, and is reckoned to be twice as wide as the country inhabited by the Franks, while about equal to it in length. In addition, he added both Pannonias, Dacia beyond the Danube, and Istrai, Liburnia, and Dalmatia, except the cities on the coast, which he left to the Greek emperor for friendship's sake and because of the treaty that he had made with him. Then he vanquished and made tributary all the wild and barbarous tribes dwelling in Germany between the Rhine and Vistula rivers, and the ocean and the Danube, all of which speak very much the same language, but differ widely from one another chiefly in customs and dress. The chief among these are the Welatabi, the Sorabians, the Obodrites, and the Bohemians, and he had to make war upon these. The rest, though even greater in number, submitted to him of their own accord.

[Foreign Relations]

16. He also added to the glory of his reign by gaining the goodwill of other kings and peoples. So close, indeed, was the alliance that he established with Alfonso [II], the king of Galicia and Asturias, that the latter, when sending letters or ambassadors to Charles, invariably styled himself his man. His munificence won the kings of the Irish also to pay such deference to his wishes that they never gave him any other title than lord, or called themselves other than his subjects or slaves. There are letters from them which survive in which these feelings towards him are expressed. His relations with Harun-al-Raschid, the king of the Persians, who rules over almost the whole of the east with the exception of India, were so friendly that this prince preferred his favor to that of all the kings and potentates of the earth, and considered

that only Charles deserved honor and munificence. Thus, when the ambassadors sent by Charles to visit the most Holy Sepulcher and place of resurrection of our Lord and Savior presented themselves before him with gifts, and made known their master's wishes, he not only granted what was asked, but gave possession of that holy and blessed spot. When they returned, he sent his own ambassadors back with them, and sent along magnificent gifts, including robes, perfumes, and other wonderful works of eastern lands. A few years before this, Charles had asked him for an elephant, and he sent the only one he had. The emperors of Constantinople, Nicephorus [I], Michael [I], and Leo [V], made advances to Charles, and sought friendship and alliance with him by means of several embassies. And even when the Greeks suspected him of designing to wrest the empire from them, because of his assumption of the title emperor, they still maintained a close alliance with him, that he might have no cause for offense. In fact, the power of the Franks was always viewed by the Greeks and Romans with a jealous eye, whence the Greek proverb "Have a Frank for your friend, but never for your neighbor."

[Building Projects]

17. This king, who showed how great he was by extending his empire and subduing foreign nations, and who was constantly preoccupied by military plans, also undertook other works calculated to adorn and benefit his kingdom. He brought several of these [building projects] to completion. Among them, the most deserving of mention are the basilica of the Holy Mother of God at Aachen, which is constructed in a wonderful way, and a bridge over the Rhine River at Mainz, which is half a mile long, the breadth of the river at this point. This bridge was destroyed by fire the year before Charles died, but, owing to his death so soon afterwards, it could not be repaired, although he had intended to rebuild it in stone. He began building two palaces of beautiful workmanship—one near his manor at a place called Ingelheim, not far from Mainz, the other at Nijmegen, on the Waal, the stream that runs along the south side of the island of the Batavians. But, most important of all, he devoted special attention to sacred buildings throughout his whole kingdom. Whenever he found them falling into ruin from age, he commanded the bishops and abbots who were in charge of them to repair them, and made sure by means of his investigators that his instructions were obeyed. He also fitted out a fleet for the war with the Northmen. The vessels required for this purpose were built on the rivers that flow from Gaul and Germany into the northern sea. Moreover, since the Northmen continually overran and laid waste to the Gallic and German coasts, he set up stations large enough to admit vessels, in order to prevent, by these military fortifications, the enemy from departing. In the south, in Gaul and Septimania, and along the whole coast of Italy as far as Rome, he took the same precautions against the Moors, who had recently commenced their piratical practices. Hence, Italy suffered no great harm in his time at the hands of the Moors, nor Gaul and Germany from the Northmen, except that the Moors took possession of the Etruscan town of Civitavécchia by treachery, and sacked it, and the Northmen harried some of the islands in Frisia off the German coast.

[His Domestic Life]

18. Thus Charles not only defended and expanded his kingdom, but he beautified it, as everyone knows. Now I must speak of his intellectual gifts, of his great inner strength, which showed in good times and bad, and of other characteristics that belong to his private and domestic life.

After his father's death, while sharing the kingdom with his brother, he bore his petty quarrels and jealousy most patiently, and, to the wonder of all, could not be provoked to anger by him. At the insistence of his mother he married a daughter of Desiderius, the king of the Lombards, but he repudiated her at the end of a year for some unknown reason and married Hildegard, a woman of high birth and of Swabian origin. He had three sons by her—Charles, Pepin, and Louis—and as many daughters—Rotrude, Bertha, and Gisela. He had three other daughters besides these—Theoderada, Hiltrude, and Rothaide—two of these by his third wife, Fastrada, a woman of east Frankish (that is to say, German) origin, and the third by a concubine, whose name for the moment escapes me. At the death of Fastrada, he married Liutgard, an Alemannic woman, who bore him no children. After her death he had three concubines—Gersvinda, a Saxon, by whom he had a daughter named Adaltrude, Regina, who was the mother of Drogo and Hugh, and Adallinda, by whom he had Theoderic. Charles's mother, Bertrada, passed her old age with him in great honor and he held her in the greatest veneration. There was never any disagreement between them except when he divorced the daughter of King Desiderius, whom he had married to please her. She died soon after Hildegard, after living to see three grandsons and as many granddaughters in her son's house, and he buried her with great pomp in the church of Saint Denis, where his father lay. He had only one sister, Gisela, who had been delivered up to the religious life while a girl, and he cherished as much affection for her as for his mother. She also died a few years before him in the convent where she had passed her life.

19. The plan that he adopted for his children's education was, first of all, to have both boys and girls instructed in the liberal arts, to which he also turned his own attention. As soon as their years admitted, in accordance with the customs of the Franks, the boys had to learn horsemanship, and to practice war and the chase, and the girls to familiarize themselves with cloth-making, to handle distaff and spindle, that they might not grow indolent through idleness, but might learn the value of virtuous work.

He only lost three of his children while he was alive, two sons and a daughter: Charles, who was the eldest, Pepin, whom he had made king of Italy, and Rotrude, his eldest daughter, whom he had betrothed to Constantine, emperor of the Greeks. Pepin left one son, named Bernard, and five daughters, Adelhaid, Atula, Gundrada, Berthaid, and Theoderada. The king gave striking proof of his fatherly affection at the time of Pepin's death: he appointed his grandson [Bernard] to succeed Pepin and ordered his granddaughters to be reared with his own daughters. When his sons and his daughter died, he was not so calm as might have been expected from his remarkably strong mind, for his affections were no less strong, and they moved him to tears. Again, when he was told of the death of Hadrian, the Roman pontiff, whom he had loved most of all his friends, he wept as much as if he had lost a brother or a very dear son. He was by nature very keen to make friendships, and not only made friends easily, but clung to them persistently and cherished most fondly those with whom he had formed such ties.

He was so attentive in the training of his sons and daughters that he never took his meals without them when he was at home, and never made a journey without them. His sons would ride at his side, and his daughters would follow him, while some members of his bodyguard, assigned for their protection, would bring up the rear. Although his daughters were beautiful women, and he loved them very dearly, it is remarkable that he was never willing to marry any of them to a man of their own people or to a foreigner, but kept them all at home until his death, saying that he could not dispense with their presence. Hence, though otherwise happy, he experienced bad luck as far as they were concerned, but he ignored the rumors that circulated about his daughters and paid no heed to the doubts about their reputations.

20. By one of his concubines he had a son, handsome in face, but hunchbacked, named Pepin, whom I neglected to mention in the list of his children. When Charles was at war with the Huns, and was wintering in Bavaria, this Pepin shammed sickness and plotted against his father in company with some of the leading Franks, who seduced him with the vain promise of a kingdom [of his own]. When this deceit was discovered, and the conspirators punished, Pepin was tonsured and was allowed to devote himself to the religious life in the monastery of Prüm, a life for which he had a calling.

A serious conspiracy against Charles had previously been attempted in Germany, but all the traitors were banished, some of them without mutilation, others after their eyes had been put out. Three of them lost their lives, because they had drawn their swords and resisted arrest. After killing several men, they themselves were cut down, because they could not be overpowered in any other way. It is supposed that the cruelty of Queen Fastrada was the primary cause of these plots, since they were both due to Charles's apparent acquiescence to his wife's cruel conduct and to his deviation from the usual kindness and gentleness of his nature. All the rest of his life he was regarded by everyone with the utmost love and affection, so much so that not the least accusation of unjust rigor was ever made against him.

21. He liked foreigners, and was at great pains to take them under his protection. There were often so many of them that they might reasonably have been considered a drain on [the resources of] both the palace and the kingdom, but he, with his magnanimous nature, was little concerned, because he felt himself more than repaid and compensated for the huge inconvenience by the praise of his generosity and the reward of a good reputation.

[His Physical Nature]

22. Charles was large and strong, and of a lofty stature, though not disproportionally so since his height is known to have been seven times the length of his foot. The upper part of his head was round, his eyes very large and animated, his nose a little long, his hair fair, and his face cheerful and fre-

quently full of laughter. Thus his appearance was always stately and dignified, whether he was standing or sitting, and this despite the fact that his neck was thick and somewhat short, and his belly rather prominent. But the symmetry of the rest of his body concealed these defects. His gait was firm, his whole carriage manly, and his voice clear, but not so strong as his size led one to expect. His health was excellent, except during the four years preceding his death, when he was subject to frequent fevers; at the end he even limped a little with one foot. Even in those years he trusted his own instincts rather than the advice of physicians, who were almost despised by him, because they wanted him to give up roasts, to which he was accustomed, and to eat boiled meat instead.

In accordance with the national custom, he took frequent exercise on horseback and in the hunt, accomplishments in which scarcely any people in the world can equal the Franks. He enjoyed natural warm springs, and often practiced swimming, at which he was so good that no one could surpass him. Hence it was that he built his palace at Aachen, and lived there constantly during his latter years until his death. He used not only to invite his sons to his bath, but his nobles and friends, and now and then a troop of his retinue or bodyguard, so that a hundred or more persons might bathe with him.

[His Dress]

23. He used to wear the national dress of the Frank: next to the skin a linen shirt and linen breeches, and above these a tunic fringed with silk, while hose fastened by bands covered his lower limbs, and shoes his feet. He protected his shoulders and chest in winter by a close-fitting coat of otter or ermine skin. Over these he flung a blue cloak and he always had a sword girt about him, usually one with a gold or silver hilt and belt. Sometimes he carried a jewelled sword, but only on great feast days or at the reception of ambassadors from foreign lands. He despised foreign costumes, however handsome, and never allowed himself to be robed in them, except twice in Rome, when he donned the Roman tunic, chlamys [a Greek mantle], and shoes; the first time was at the request of Pope Hadrian, the second to gratify Leo, Hadrian's successor. On great feastdays he made use of embroidered clothes and shoes bedecked by a golden buckle, and he appeared crowned with a diadem of gold and gems, but on other days his dress varied little from the dress of the common people.

[Food and Drink]

24. Charles was temperate in eating, and particularly so in drinking, for he hated to see anyone inebriated, and would not tolerate it of himself or those of his household. But he could not easily abstain from food, and often complained that fasts injured his health. He very rarely gave banquets, and then only on great feastdays to large numbers of people. His meals ordinarily consisted of four courses, not counting the roast, which his huntsmen used to bring in on a spit; he was more fond of this than any other dish. While at table, he listened to reading or music. The subjects of the readings were

the stories and deeds of ancient times and he was fond of Saint Augustine's books, especially the one entitled *The City of God*. He was so moderate in the use of wine and all sorts of drink that he rarely allowed himself more than three cups in the course of a meal. In summer, after the midday meal, he would eat some fruit, drain a single cup, pull off his clothes and shoes, just as he did at nighttime, and rest for two or three hours. He was in the habit of awaking and rising from his bed four or five times during the night. While he was dressing and putting on his shoes, he not only met his friends, but if the count of the palace told him of any suit in which his judgment was necessary, he had the parties brought before him immediately, listened to the case, and gave his decision, just as if he were sitting at a [normal] tribunal. This was not the only business that he transacted at this time, but he performed any duty of the day whatever, whether he had to attend to the matter himself or to give commands concerning it to his officers.

[Learning]

25. Charles had the gift of ready and fluent speech, and could express whatever he had to say with great clarity. He was not satisfied with knowing his native tongue, but paid attention to the study of foreign ones and, in particular, was such a master of Latin that he could speak it as well as his native language. But he could understand Greek better than he could speak it. He was so eloquent, indeed, that he might have passed for a teacher of eloquence.

He zealously cultivated the liberal arts, holding those who taught them in great esteem and conferring great honors upon them. He took lessons in grammar from the deacon Peter of Pisa who was at that time an aged man. Another deacon, Alcuin of Britain, surnamed Albinus, who was a man of Saxon extraction, was the greatest scholar of the day. Alcuin was his teacher in the other branches of learning; the king spent a good deal of time and labor with him studying rhetoric, dialectic, and especially astronomy. He learned mathematics and used to investigate the motions of the heavenly bodies with curiosity and intelligent scrutiny. He also tried to write, and used to keep wax-tablets and notebooks under the pillows on his bed, so that when he had spare time he might train his hand to form letters. However, as he did not begin his efforts early in life, but late, they met with little success.

[Piety]

26. He cherished with the greatest fervor and devotion the principles of the Christian religion, which had been instilled into him from infancy. Hence it was that he built the beautiful church at Aachen, which he adorned with gold and silver, with lamps, and with rails and doors of solid brass. He had the columns and marbles for this structure brought from Rome and Ravenna, for he could not find any that were suitable elsewhere. He was a constant worshipper at this church as long as his health permitted, going morning and evening, even after nightfall, as well as attending mass. He took care that all the services conducted there should be administered with the utmost

possible propriety, very often warning the sacristans not to let any improper or unclean thing be brought into the building or remain in it. He provided it with a great number of sacred vessels of gold and silver and with such a quantity of clerical robes that not even the doorkeepers who fill the humblest office in the church were obliged to wear their everyday clothes when performing their duties. He was at great pains to improve the church reading and psalmody, for he was well skilled in both, although he neither read in public nor sang, except in a low tone and with others.

27. He was very keen to help the poor and practiced that form of undemanding charity which the Greeks call alms, so much so that he not only made a point of giving in his own country and his own kingdom, but when he discovered that there were Christians living in poverty in Syria, Egypt, and Africa, at Jerusalem, Alexandria, and Carthage, he had compassion for their needs, and used to send money over the sea to them. The reason that he zealously strove to make friends with the kings beyond the sea was so that he might help and give relief to the Christians living under their rule. He cherished the church of Saint Peter the Apostle at Rome above all other holy and sacred places, and heaped its treasury with a vast amount of gold, silver, and precious stones. He sent great and countless gifts to the popes, and throughout his whole reign the wish that he had nearest at heart was to reestablish the ancient authority of the city of Rome under his care and by his influence, and to defend and protect the church of Saint Peter, and to beautify and enrich it out of his own store above all other churches. Although he held it in such veneration, he only went to Rome to pay his vows and make his supplications four times during the whole forty-seven years that he reigned.

[The Imperial Title]

28. When he made his last journey there, he also had other things on his mind. The Romans had injured Pope Leo [III], tearing out his eyes and cutting out his tongue, so that he was forced to call upon the king for help. Thus, Charles traveled to Rome in order to straighten out the affairs of the church, which were in great confusion. He passed the whole winter there. It was then that he received the titles of emperor and augustus, to which he at first had such antipathy that he declared that he would not have set foot in the church the day that they were conferred, although it was a great feast-day, had he foreseen the plan of the pope. He bore very patiently the jealousy that the aggrieved Roman [that is, Greek] emperors demonstrated when he received these titles. By dint of frequent embassies and letters, in which he addressed them as brothers, he made their haughtiness bend to his magnanimity, a quality in which he was unquestionably much their superior.

[Law and Translations]

29. After becoming emperor, Charles realized that the laws of his people were defective in many things. For the Franks have two law codes which differ in many respects. Therefore, he determined to supply what was want-

ing, to reconcile the discrepancies, and to correct what was vicious and wrongly cited in them. However, he went no further in this matter than to supplement the laws with a few new chapters, but left even that work unfinished. He did, however, order the unwritten laws of all the tribes that came under his rule to be compiled and set down in writing.

He also had the old [Germanic] songs that celebrate the deeds and wars of ancient kings written down so that they might be preserved for posterity. He began a grammar of his native language. He gave the months names in his own tongue, in place of the Latin and barbarian names by which they were formerly known among the Franks. He likewise designated the winds by twelve appropriate names; there were hardly more than four distinctive ones in use before. He called January *Wintarmanoth*, February *Hornung*, March *Lentzinmanoth*, April *Ostarmanoth*, May *Winnemanoth*, June *Brachmanoth*, July *Heuuimanoth*, August *Aranmanoth*, September *Witumanoth*, October *Windumemanoth*, November *Herbistmanoth*, December *Heilagmanoth*. He named the winds as follows: Subsolanus *Ostroniwint*, Eurus *Ostsundroni*, Euroauster *Sundostroni*, Auster *Sundroni*, Austro-Africus *Sundwestroni*, Africus *Westsundroni*, Zephyrus *Westroni*, Caurus *Westnordroni*, Circius *Nordwestroni*, Septentrio *Nordroni*, Aquilo *Nordostroni*, Vulturnus *Ostnordroni*.

[Succession and Death]

30. Toward the end of his life, when he was broken by ill-health and old age, he called for his only surviving son by Hildegard, Louis, the king of Aquitaine, to come to him. He assembled all the chief men of the whole kingdom of the Franks in a solemn gathering and there, with their unanimous consent, established Louis to rule with himself over the whole kingdom and he constituted him heir to the imperial name, placing the diadem upon his son's head, and ordered that he be called emperor and augustus. This act was hailed by all present with great support, for it truly seemed as if God had prompted him to this measure for the kingdom's good. It increased the king's dignity, and struck no little terror into foreign nations. After dispatching his son back to Aquitaine, he proceeded to hunt, although he was weak from age. He returned about the first of November. While wintering there, he was seized in the month of January, with a high fever, and took to his bed. As soon as he had taken sick, he prescribed for himself abstinence from food, as he always used to do when he had a fever, thinking that the disease could be driven off, or at least weakened, by fasting. Besides the fever, he suffered from a pain in the side, which the Greeks called pleurisy, but he still persisted in fasting, and in keeping up his strength only by taking a draught once in awhile. He died on 28 January [814], seven days after he took to bed, at nine o'clock in the morning, after partaking of holy communion. This was the seventy-second year of his life and the forty-seventh of his reign.

31. His body was washed and cared for in the usual manner, and was then carried into the church, and interred amid great wailing by everyone. There was some question at first where to lay him, because in his lifetime he had given no directions as to his burial, but at length all agreed that he would

nowhere be more honorably entombed than in the very cathedral that he had built in Aachen, at his own expense, for the love of God and our Lord Jesus Christ and in honor of His Mother, the Holy Eternal Virgin. He was buried there the same day that he died, and a gilded arch was erected above his tomb with his image and an inscription. The words of the inscription were as follows:

> IN THIS TOMB LIES THE BODY OF CHARLES, THE GREAT AND ORTHODOX EMPEROR, WHO GLORIOUSLY EXTENDED THE KINGDOM OF THE FRANKS, AND REIGNED PROSPEROUSLY FOR FORTY-SEVEN YEARS. HE DIED AT THE AGE OF MORE THAN SEVENTY, IN THE YEAR OF OUR LORD 814, IN THE SEVENTH INDICTION, ON THE TWENTY-EIGHTH DAY OF JANUARY.

[Portents]

32. Many omens had portended his approaching end, a fact that he had recognized as well as others. Eclipses both of the sun and moon were very frequent during the last three years of his life, and a black spot was visible on the sun for the space of seven days. The gallery between the basilica and the palace, which he had built at great pains and labor, fell in sudden ruin to the ground on the day of the Ascension of our Lord. The wooden bridge over the Rhine at Mainz, which he had ordered to be constructed and which took ten years of hard work to complete, was so well built that it seemed as if it might last forever, but it caught fire and was so completely consumed in three hours that not a single splinter of it was left, except what was under water. Moreover, one day while on his last campaign in Saxony against Gode-frid, the king of the Danes, Charles himself saw a fiery meteor that shone with a great light fall suddenly from the sky, just as he was leaving camp before sunrise to set out on the day's march. It flashed across the clear sky from right to left, and everyone wondered what its meaning was, when the horse on which he was riding suddenly collapsed, head first, throwing Charles to the ground so heavily that his cloak buckle was broken off and his sword belt shattered. His attendants hastened to the king, who lay without his arms and needed help to rise. The javelin that he had been holding was found lying twenty feet away from the spot where he fell.

The palace at Aachen frequently suffered earthquakes, and the roofs of whatever buildings he stayed in kept up a continual crackling noise. The cathedral in which he was afterwards buried was struck by lightning, and the gilded ball that adorned the pinnacle of the roof was shattered by that thunderbolt and hurled upon the bishop's house that stood beside it. In this same cathedral, on the edge of the cornice that ran around the interior, between the upper and lower tiers or arches, a legend was inscribed in red letters, stating the name of the architect of the cathedral. The year that he died it was remarked by some, that a few months before his death the letters of the word PRINCEPS were so faded that they were no longer legible. But Charles despised, or feigned to despise, all these omens, as if they had no reference whatsoever to his life.

[The Division of his Treasure]

33. It had been his intention to make a will, that he might give some share of the inheritance to his daughters and to the children of his concubines, but it was begun too late and could not be finished. Three years before his death, however, he made a division of his treasure, money, clothes, and other moveable goods in the presence of his friends and servants, and called them to witness it, that their voices might insure the ratification of the disposition thus made. He had a summary drawn up of his wishes regarding this distribution of his property, the terms and text of which are as follows:

In the name of the Lord God, the almighty Father, Son, and Holy Ghost. This is the inventory and division dictated by the most glorious and most pious Lord Charles, emperor and augustus, in the 811th year of the Incarnation of our Lord Jesus Christ, in the 43rd year of his reign in France and 37th in Italy, the 11th of his empire, and in the 4th Indiction.

Considerations of piety and prudence have determined him, and the favor of God enabled him, to make a division of his treasures and the money ascertained this day to be in his treasure chamber. In this division he is especially desirous to provide not only that the largesse of alms which Christians usually make of their possessions shall be made for himself in due course and proper order from his wealth, but also that his heirs shall be free from all doubt, and know clearly what belongs to them, and be able to share their property by suitable partition without litigation or strife. With this intention and to this end he first divided all his substance and the moveable goods ascertained to be in his treasure chamber on the day aforesaid in gold, silver, precious stones, and royal ornaments into three lots, and has subdivided and set off two of the said lots into twenty-one parts, keeping the third intact. The first two lots have been thus subdivided into twenty-one parts because there are in his kingdom twenty-one recognized metropolitan cities, and in order that each archbishopric may receive by way of alms, at the hands of his heirs and friends, one of the said parts, and that the archbishop who shall then administer its affairs shall take the part given to it, and share the same with his suffragans in such manner that one-third shall go to the church, and the remaining two-thirds be divided among the suffragans. The twenty-one parts into which the first two lots are to be distributed, according to the number of recognized metropolitan cities, have been set apart from one another, and each has been put aside by itself in a box labelled with the name of the city for which it was destined. The names of the cities to which this alms or largesse is to be sent are as follows: Rome, Ravenna, Milan, Aquiliea, Grado, Cologne, Mainz, Salzburg, Trier, Sens, Besançon, Lyons, Rouen, Rheims, Arles, Vienne, Moutiers-en-Tarantaise, Embrun, Bordeaux, Tours, and Bourges.

The third lot, which he wishes to be kept intact, is to be bestowed as follows. While the first two lots are to be divided into the aforesaid parts, and set aside under seal, the third lot shall be employed for his own daily needs, as property which he shall be under no obligation to part with in order to fulfill any vow, and this as long as he shall be in the flesh, or consider it necessary for his use. But upon his death, or voluntary renunciation of the affairs of this world, this said lot shall be added to the aforesaid twenty-one parts; the second shall be assigned to his sons and daughters, and to the sons and daughters of his sons, to be distributed among them in just and equal partition; the third, in accordance with the custom common among Christians, shall be devoted to the poor; and the fourth shall go to the support of the male and female servants on duty in the palace. It is his wish that to this said third lot of the whole amount, which consists, like the rest, of gold and silver, shall be added all the vessels and utensils of brass, iron, and other metals, together with the arms, clothing, and other moveable goods, costly and cheap, adapted to diverse uses, as hangings, coverlets, carpets, woollen stuffs, leather articles, pack-saddles, and whatsoever shall be found in his treasure chamber and wardrobe at that time, in order that thus the parts of the said lots may be augmented, and the alms distributed reach more persons.

He ordains that his chapel—that is to say, its church property as well as that which he has provided and collected and that which came to him by inheritance from his father—shall remain intact, and not be divided by any partition whatsoever. If, however, any vessels, books, or other articles be found therein which are certainly known not to have been given by him to the said chapel, whoever wants them shall have them on paying their value at a fair estimation. He likewise commands that the books which he has collected in his [personal] library in great number shall be sold for fair prices to such as want them, and the money received therefrom given to the poor.

It is well known that among his other property and treasures there are three silver tables, and one very large and massive golden one. He directs and commands that the square silver table, upon which there is a representation of the city of Constantinople, shall be sent to the church of Saint Peter the Apostle at Rome, with the other gifts destined for that place; that the round one, adorned with a delineation of the city of Rome, shall be given to the episcopal church at Ravenna; that the third, which far surpasses the other two in weight and in beauty of workmanship, and is made in three circles, showing the plan of the whole universe, drawn with skill and delicacy shall go, together with the golden table, the fourth mentioned above, to increase that lot which is to be devoted to his heirs and to alms.

This deed, and the dispositions thereof, he has made and appointed in the presence of the bishops, abbots, and counts able to be present, whose names are added below: bishops—Hildebald, Richolf, Arn, Wolfar, Bernoin, Leidrad, John, Theodulf, Jesse, Heito, Waltgaud; abbots—Fridugis, Adalung, Angilbert, Irmino; counts—Wala, Meginher, Otulf, Stephen, Unruoc, Burchard, Meginhard, Hatto, Rihwin, Edo, Ercangar, Gerold, Bero, Hildigern, Hroccolf.

Charles's son Louis, who by the grace of God succeeded him, after examining this summary, took pains to fulfill all its conditions most religiously as soon as possible after his father's death.

Questions: What limitations did Einhard have as a biographer? What might he not have seen or understood? What does he try to hide or excuse? How does he portray Charlemagne as a warrior? Why did Charlemagne refuse to allow his daughters to marry? What was Charlemagne's attitude towards religion and the church? At what points does Einhard seem to possess special and personal knowledge? If the structure of the biography came from Suetonius's imperial biographies, did this force Einhard to describe some parts of Charlemagne's life in unsuitable terms and to talk about things that had little place in his life?

8. Pepin's Victory over the Avars

This rough-hewn poem celebrates the Carolingian conquest of the Avars. The war had begun in 782 and was still going on in the first few years of the ninth century, but the poem is directly concerned with the events of 795-796 when Pepin of Italy, Charlemagne's son, concluded the conquest of the Avars that earlier that year Eric of Friuli had achieved when he had seized the Avar Ring with its bountiful treasure. Einhard had noted that before that conquest the Carolingians had been a poor people. Also the reader might like to notice that this boastful poem celebrates a bloodless and battle-free encounter.

Source: trans. P.E. Dutton from Monumenta Germaniae Historica: Poetae Latini Aevi Karolini, vol. 1, ed. E. Dümmler (Berlin, 1881), pp. 116-117.

O Christ, the Son of God, who made all peoples,
All lands, waters, rivers, mountains, and shaped humankind,
You have in recent days converted the Avars.

From ancient times they have done many evil things,
Sacking the sanctuaries and monasteries of God,
Stealing sacred golden, silver, and clay vessels.

They contaminated the holy cloths of the most sacred altars.
The linen garments of our deacons and nuns were handed over,
At the urging of their devil, to their own women.

God sent Saint Peter, the prince of the Apostles,
To aid Pepin, the son of our great king,
And to protect his path and that of the Frankish forces.

King Pepin, a catholic king encircled by the power of God,
Set up his camp on the clear flowing Danube River,
Placing fortifications all around the camp against the enemy.

Unguimer, from the race of the Avars, being badly frightened,
Spoke to the king and his wretched wife Catuna,
in strong terms: "You are beaten, O Kagan,"

"Your kingdom is done with; you shall no longer reign,
Your old kingdoms have been handed over to Christians,
They were demolished by Pepin that Catholic prince."

"King Pepin with a huge army draws near
To occupy your lands and slaughter your people,
To place fortifications on your mountains, woods, and slopes."

"Get up at once! Take an abundance of gifts with you.
To live a while longer, humble yourself before this king.
Give him gold and jewels, lest he order your death."

Hearing this, Kagan, the king, was overwhelmed with fear and
Immediately climbed up on a mule and, with his Tarchan chiefs,
He came to humble himself before the king and to offer him gifts.

He said to Pepin: "Greetings, O prince! Be my lord!
I give you my kingdom with all its straw and greenery,
With all its woods, mountains, and slopes and with everything growing
    thereon.

"Take my children with you; let them offer obedience to you.
Nor should you spare my nobles. Turn your army around,
For I give to you my children and my very life."

Let us faithful Christians give thanks to God,
Who confirmed the kingdom of our king over the kingdom of the
    Huns,
And who gave us victory over pagan peoples.

Let King Pepin live and rule in fear of the Lord!
May his father reign and grow old and beget sons,
Who will preserve his palaces while he lives and after he dies!

The force that enclosed the great, wide, most powerful realm,
Was not that of Caesar or the pagans, who did not make
The present earthly kingdoms, but divine grace.

Everlasting glory to the Father and to his Son.

Question: What function would a poem such as this have served at court?

9. Epitaphs and Eulogies

Writers at the royal court often went to some trouble to compose epitaphs and eulogies for members of the royal family.

1. Theodulf of Orléans, An Epitaph for Queen Fastrada

Fastrada, who had been blamed, according to Einhard, for the cruelty of Charlemagne, was doubtless blameless, a mere scapegoat for contemporaries who feared to attack Charles himself. Charlemagne once sent her a mildly affectionate letter while he was away on campaign. Fastrada was troubled, apparently, by poor teeth and ill health. She died in 794. The average life expectancy of Carolingian noble women was slightly less than thirty-five years. Hildegard, the "mother of kings," who bore Charlemagne nine children, married him when she was twelve and died when she was twenty-five years old.

Source: trans. P.E. Dutton from Monumenta Germaniae Historica: Poetae Latini Aevi Karolini, vol. 1, ed. E. Dümmler (Berlin, 1881), p. 483.

Here rest the glorious remains of Queen Fastrada,
    Whom frigid death stole away in the full bloom of her life.
That noble woman was united in marriage to her mighty husband,
    But now she is even nobler, being married to the King of Heaven.
The better part of her soul, King Charles himself, remained behind,
    To whom let gentle God grant a longer life.

2. Alcuin's Letter to Charlemagne on the Death of Liutgard

Charlemagne may have decided after Liutgard's death in 800 not to marry again in order not to complicate the matter of his succession, since he still had three sons alive. By 800 he may also not have needed the political alliance that a new marriage would have represented.

Source: trans. J.I. Mombert, A History of Charles the Great (Charlemagne), (London: Kegan Paul, Trench & Co., 1888), pp. 227-228; revised.

I cannot lament the good luck of one who has finished the thorny path of earth and winged her way to Him who made her. For...this is the condition of our frailty: we are born to die, and we die to live. Is it not better to enter upon life than upon death?

It is said that one [that is, Anaxagoras], whom others sought to comfort concerning the death of his son, replied, "I knew that I was born mortal." Why should we bewail that which we cannot avoid? Time often soothes our sorrow better than reason.

Let the gifts of our love follow our loved ones. Let us offer the gift of our salvation for them. Let us be merciful that we may obtain mercy. Whatever we do in faith for them, will profit ourselves.

O Lord God Jesus, gentle and merciful, have mercy upon her whom thou hast taken away from us. Heal us through your medicine for our wounds [Jesus Christ], who hung upon the Cross, and sitting at your right hand, now intercedes for us. For I know your mercy, which desires for all men to be saved. Remit unto her such sins as she may have contracted after the water of salvation [that is, after baptism]. Remit them, O Lord, we pray, remit them. Enter not into judgment against her. Let mercy exalt itself above judgment. For all your words are true, even the mercy you did promise to the merciful; that such as they were, so will you give unto them. You who are merciful to the merciful, O Lord, have mercy upon your creature, that your creature may praise and evermore extol your mercy. And the soul that triumphs eternally, will say world without end; "In my life I shall praise the Lord; I shall sing to my God as long as I shall be."

Oh, may this daughter of mine, so dear, abide for evermore in happiness, I earnestly desire, and let her be dear to God too, I pray.

3. An Epitaph for Adalhaid, an Infant Daughter of Charlemagne

Infant mortality struck the royal family almost as often as it must have struck commoners. Indeed, Louis the Pious was the twin of a brother who died not long after birth. Adalhaid was the daughter of Hildegard and Charles and was born in Italy in 773 while the king was waging his campaign against Desiderius and the Lombards. If the poem is to be taken literally, the baby was separated from her father and mother and sent back to Francia, but died before she reached Lyons. Hildegard seems to have remained with Charlemagne on his campaign. One of the king's Italian scholars wrote this epitaph for the parents of the dead child.

Source: trans. H.M. Jones, in P.S. Allen, The Romanesque Lyric: Studies in its Background and Development from Petronius to the Cambridge Songs, 50-1050 (Chapel Hill: University of North Carolina Press, 1928), p.240; revised.

Within this sepulcher a little girl lies buried;
    She was called at baptism Adalhaid.
Charles was her father, Charles the Great, noble in wit,
    Intrepid in the midst of war, the bearer of the two diadems.
While her powerful father conquered the Italian kingdom,
    She was born near the high walls of Pavia.
Nearing the Rhône, she was snatched from the threshold of life.
    From afar her mother's heart was stricken with sorrow.
She died, never to behold the triumphs of her father,
    Now she obtains the blessed kingdoms of the eternal Father.

4. The Tombstone Inscription of Pope Hadrian I

This inscription, carved in Square Capital script into a large piece of black marble quarried in northern Europe, can still be seen in Saint-Peter's today. The verses may well have been written by Alcuin himself, since some of its language resembles the technique and language of his poetry. What does the inscription suggest about the relationship between Charlemagne and the pope?

Source: trans. J.I. Mombert, A History of Charles the Great (Charlemagne), (London: Kegan Paul, Trench & Co., 1888), pp.337-338; revised.

Here sleeps the famous chief, and ornament of Rome
The father of the church, Pope Hadrian, the blessed;
Whom God gave life, the law his virtue, Christ his glory.
An apostolic father to goodness always prompt;
Of grand ancestral line a noble scion,
More noble than them all, through holiness he became

A faithful pastor with untiring zeal who strove
The temples of his God in beauty to array.
The church with choicest gifts, with sacred love the flock
Imbued, and unto all the way beyond the stars he traced.
His bounty blessed the poor, his goodness passed by none,
In ceaseless vigils for the flock his prayers arose.
With learning, wealth, and walls thy battlements he reared,
Thrice honor'd Rome!, chief city through the world renowned.
Grim death, by that of Christ redeemed, could hurt him naught.
And proved to him but gateway to the better life.
O father, thee beweeping, I Charles these lines have writ,
For thee, sweet love and father mine, with sorrow bowed.
Remember me, whose mind forever follows thee,
When thou with Christ the blissful realms above shalt sway.
The clergy, all the church, in love did thee enshrine,
O best of pontiffs, who to all was all their love.
Illustrious man, our names and titles now I join,
O Hadrian and Charles the king, the pontiff thou.
Kind reader of these lines, with loving heart for both
In prayer engage, and gently Miserere say.
This tomb, O dearest friend, thine earthly frame doth hold,
The while thy happy soul with saints of God delights,
Until the final trump within thy ears shall sound:
"Awake! with princely Peter rise thy God to see;"
When sure, I know, the Judge with loving voice will call:
"Into thy Lord's surpassing joy now enter thou."
Then best of fathers all, thy son bear thou in mind;
"A son should join his father," say, "And this is mine."
To Christ's celestial realms, blest father, lead the way,
With intercessions thence thine orphaned flock to aid,
The while his fiery locks the sun resplendent shakes,
Thy praises, Holy Father, throughout the world shall sound.

This pope of blessed memory filled the pontifical chair for twenty-three years, ten months, and seventeen days, and died on the seventh Kalends of January [16 December 795].

5. An Epitaph for Eggihard who Died at Roncesvalles

Even in the ninth century, the legend of Roland and Roncesvalles began to take shape. Long before the Chanson de Roland was written down, nobles were already naming their sons Roland. Here an anonymous poet remembered one of the other fallen warriors whose name was listed by Einhard but destined to be forgotten by the Chanson tradition.

Source: trans. P.E. Dutton from Monumenta Germaniae Historica: Poetae Latini Aevi Karolini, vol. 1, ed. E. Dümmler (Berlin, 1881), pp.109-110.

His pale limbs are covered by this shallow grave,
But his spirit seeks the lofty stars of heaven.
This son of noble roots, born with Frankish blood in his veins,
A little while ago was [our] glory in all things on earth.
The dewy down [of youth] had hardly encircled his rosy cheeks
When, alas, this beautiful young man died.
Eggihard was his name, as his father too was known,
He had risen to the highest heights at the court of the king.
Insatiable death met him in the shadows with a piece of iron,
But the everlasting light conveyed him to the stars.
When Charles trampled the wastelands of Spain under his feet,
Eggihard died to the world, but he lives to God.
Italians cry for him, as do all the Franks,
Aquitaine moans for him, and so does Germany.
You now, therefore, O Vincent, greatest of martyrs,
Look after him on the highest with God.
His corpse lies in a tomb, but only his flesh is buried there.
He took the red road; now he lives at the court of God.
But you Christians, who cross the threshold of this holy church,
Implore Christ who came from the heart of his Father:
"God in your mercy," all should say,
"Take away the sins of your servant, Eggihard."

He died on the eighteenth Kalends of September [that is, August 15]. May he rest in peace.

Questions: Whose eyes were the poets trying to catch with epitaphs? Would these have been commissioned or voluntary compositions? Are the sentiments expressed ever personal or do they remain formal and predictable?

10. The Equestrian Statue of Theoderic

When Charlemagne passed through Ravenna, in 800, if not much earlier, he must have seen a monumental equestrian statue of the Ostrogothic king, Theoderic the Great, which he ordered transported back to Aachen. What he meant to signify by it is difficult to say, though even Einhard noted that he had loved to hear stories of ancient Germanic kings and their wondrous deeds. After his death, however, the court of Louis the Pious took a different and disapproving view of the statue. Walahfrid Strabo wrote a critical poem in which he spoke of Theoderic as a hell-bound and avaricious king. Louis the Pious must have thought much the same about the great Ostrogoth. Agnellus of Ravenna writing in the 830s and early 840s recalled how the statue was removed from his beloved city.

Source: trans. P.E. Dutton from Agnellus, Liber Pontificalis ecclesiae Ravennatis, 94, ed. O. Holder-Egger, Monumenta Germaniae Historica: Scriptores rerum Langobardicarum et Italicarum, saec. VI-IX (Hanover, 1878), p.338.

[On a base] almost ten feet high stands a horse made of bronze washed with yellow gold and his rider is King Theoderic who carries on his left arm a shield and holds in his raised right arm a lance. From the flaring nostrils and from the mouth of the horse fly birds that have built nests in its stomach. Who could believe such a thing? Anyone doubting it should make a trip to Francia to see [the statue].

...To that incredible equestrian statue made of bronze, but embellished with gold, Theoderic affixed his own name. It has been almost 38 years now since Charles, king of the Franks, conquered every kingdom and received from Pope Leo III the empire of the Romans. After he made an offering to Saint Peter, he began to return to Francia, but stopped at Ravenna. There he saw that beautiful statue whose like he had never seen before. He ordered it to be transported to Francia and to be set up [outside] his palace at Aachen.

Questions: Could there be other reasons why Charlemagne wanted to possess the statue? How does Agnellus know so much about a statue removed from Ravenna long before his day?

11. The Lateran Palace of Pope Leo III

One of the problems with trying to imagine the wider physical world of the Carolingians is that so many of the major monuments (such as the statue of Theoderic and ninth-century cathedrals such as those of Rheims, Sens, and Milan) are now gone or seriously compromised. They were often destroyed, built over, or replaced during subsequent ages, especially in other ages of grand renewal such as the twelfth, thirteenth, and fifteenth centuries. Hence art and cultural historians of the ninth century are frequently forced to study Carolingian prose descriptions of lost buildings and works of art, and to search out early-modern drawings and accounts of Carolingian ruins.

Source: trans. C. Davis-Weyer, Early Medieval Art, 300-1150, in Sources & Documents in the History of Art, ed. H.W. Janson (Englewood Cliffs, New Jersey: Prentice-Hall, 1971), pp.88-92; reprinted with permission.

1. The Account in the *Liber Pontificalis*

Pope Leo III not only crowned Charlemagne emperor in 800, but spent lavishly on the churches of Rome. To his Lateran Palace he added two state halls (triclinia) which are described in the so-called Book of the Popes. What allowed Pope Leo to build so richly was doubtless Charlemagne's patronage, and Carolingian cash would continue to flow to Rome and Saint-Peter's throughout the ninth century. Charlemagne's division of his moveable property at the end of his life is an example of that commitment to the papal see.

Leo III built in the Lateran Palace a triclinium that bears his name, richly decorated, and larger than any other triclinium. He built it over very firm foundations and decorated it throughout with marble. He also paved it with a variety of marble and adorned it with finely hewn columns of porphyry and white marble, with bases and capitals and [its doors] with jambs and lintels. He decorated the main apse and its vault with mosaic and the two other apses with paintings of different stories, likewise placed above the marble revetment.

He also made in the Lateran Palace a triclinium of marvelous size decorated with an apse mosaic, and he made ten other apses on both sides and different paintings of the apostles as they preach to the Gentiles, adjoining the basilica of Constantine. In the triclinium he also installed couches. In the center he placed a fountain in the form of a porphyry shell. He also covered the floor with multi-colored marble.

2. A Sixteenth-Century Account of Leo III's State-Halls

An antiquarian named Panvinio saw the two triclinia; the smaller one–the Aula Leonina–that would have been standing when Charlemagne visited Rome in 800 was already in ruins, but the larger one was still in use early in the sixteenth century.

As soon as one enters the Lateran Palace and climbs a flight of stairs, one sees a large hall with three apses, which in the old days was called "aula

Leonina" after its founder Leo III. Its interior was covered with mosaics and marble incrustation. Of the old decoration there remains only a mosaic around the arch of the main apse...in which Saint Peter is shown seated, while handing a banner to Charlemagne with his left hand and a pallium to Leo III, both of whom kneel before him. It contains these inscriptions: OUR HOLY LORD POPE, LEO III and also OUR LORD KING CHARLES. Under Saint Peter's feet is written: HOLY PETER GIVE...TO POPE LEO AND VICTORY...TO KING CHARLES. This hall, as I said, was formerly called the smaller "Basilica Leonina" in order to distinguish it from the larger one, which is also called "The Large House." It [the smaller hall] was built adjoining the papal rooms. In it the pope used to eat with the cardinals on certain feasts, such as the second and third day of the Easter week. Public assemblies and consistories used also to be held in this place. Its roof and its pavement are destroyed; what stands are the remains of the very high walls, adorned with some precious columns.

...On the side of the Lateran Basilica is a door from which by marble stairs one ascends to a large and spacious hall, which today is called "The Council Room." Apart from a main apse it has ten smaller apses on both sides, a brick floor, and a wooden roof, covered with tiles. On its north side the aula is supported by several arcades and extremely heavy pillars. The main apse is decorated by mosaics, done by very inept artists, representing Christ, the Holy Virgin, the holy apostles Peter and Paul, and several other saints. On the wall which precedes the apse are the twenty-four seniors and some of the signed 144 thousand in the Apocalypse and four angels depicted in mosaic by an unskilled artist. On the arch of the apse is this monogram:

P
LOE
A

that is, Leo Papa. The smaller apses all have a central window. Between the apses and the pilasters flanking them are twenty-two other windows which were restored by [Pope] Julius II [who died in 1513] during the Lateran Council. At the entrance wall toward the pulpit of Boniface VIII [who died in 1303], that is, toward the north, there are six arches, three above and three beneath, carried by four supports, the two above being of porphyry. After this comes a second wall with three doorways from which one reaches the loggia of Boniface VIII. This hall we now refer to as "The Council Room" because here, as I believe, Eugene IV [who died in 1447] decided to celebrate a council and here Julius recently celebrated another. Formerly it was called "The Large House" on account of its size or the "Basilica of Leo" on account of its founder, Leo III [who died in 816], who built and adorned it to be used by the popes.

At that time, on certain feast days such as Easter and Christmas, the Roman bishops customarily dined with a solemn ritual. The basilica was renovated by Leo IV [who died in 855] as Anastasius the Librarian writes: "Leo III built from its foundations the large dining hall and endowed it with the necessary furnishings. When these had been lost on account of time and the neglect of his papal successors, Leo IV generously and swiftly restored everything that had been taken away..." All this seems to be in agreement with the prayer that is written underneath the main apse: LORD, WHOSE RIGHT HAND SUSTAINED THE BLESSED PETER WALKING ON THE WATER LEST HE SHOULD SINK AND LIBERATED HIS CO-APOSTLE PAUL THREE TIMES SHIPWRECKED FROM THE DEEP SEA, MAY YOUR HOLY RIGHT HAND PROTECT THIS HOUSE AND THE FAITHFUL DINING IN IT, WHO ENJOY HERE THE GIFTS OF YOUR APOSTLE.

3. The Aula Leonina in 1617

Another antiquarian, the papal librarian J. Grimaldi, later desribed in greater detail the mosaics of the Aula Leonina.

In the [Lateran] Palace, the Aula Leonina, built by Leo III is still visible. It has been made into a garden. Of its three apses, only the one in front stands with its mosaics intact; the others are half destroyed. In the center of the apse vault stands the Savior on a mountain from which the four rivers of paradise spring. He blesses with his right hand, with his ring finger and his thumb touching each other. In his left hand he holds an open book. He wears purple clothes and has five apostles on each side, of whom the one standing closest to the Savior's right is old and carries a long cross. None of the others carries an attribute. Over the Savior's head there is, as it were, a cloud, fiery with lightning. All the figures are nimbed. Where the frieze ends, the border of the mosaic, consisting entirely of various flowers, appears. Springing from a vessel it encircles the entire arch and bends down into a second vase. In the center of this border, over the Savior's head, is the monogram of Leo III. It is formed like this:

L

PEA

O

A second exterior border encircles the arch, bearing the inscription cited below. At the feet of Christ and the apostles runs a frieze with an inscription. On the triangular wall left of the apse is a picture of Saint Peter, Leo III and Charles the Great, described below.

On the above mentioned border, which encircles the arch, is written...GLORY TO GOD IN THE HIGHEST: AND ON EARTH PEACE TO MEN OF GOOD WILL.

In the frieze of the apse...[is written] GOING THEREFORE, TEACH YE ALL NATIONS, BAPTIZING THEM IN THE NAME OF THE FATHER AND THE SON AND THE HOLY GHOST. AND BEHOLD I AM WITH YOU ALL DAYS, EVEN TO THE CONSUMMATION OF THE WORLD.

In the vault of the apse are the ten apostles, and the eleventh, the prince of the apostles, is in the triangle of the apse wall. This was actually the number of apostles present when Christ uttered those words, according to Matthew, Chapter 28. In the angle to the right of the apse was probably an image of Saint Paul. But it is completely gone and the wall is rough....

On the triangular wall to the left of the apse a mosaic has survived showing Saint Peter enthroned, dressed in chasuble and pallium, an old man with a nimbus. To his right appears Leo III, round-faced and black haired, with the top of his head shaven, seemingly in his sixties. Around his head he has a rectangular nimbus, the sign of the living. He wears pallium and chasuble. He receives the stole, namely the episcopal pallium, from Peter's right hand. Next to the Pope one reads the inscription: OUR MOST HOLY LORD POPE LEO. To his left kneels Charlemagne, the august emperor, receiving a tall standard from Saint Peter's left hand. It shows six red roses in a blue field. Charles wears the imperial crown and the square nimbus. He wears the imperial cloak or mantle and has a sword on his side. His face is that of an old man. His chin is shaven. On the upper lip he has two twisted mustaches in the fashion of Turks or Franks. His eyes are large. At Saint Peter's feet is the salutation in which Leo augurs for Charles the crown, life, and victory, as he had been acclaimed at his coronation in the basilica of Saint Peter's...: BLESSED PETER GIVE CHARLES THE CROWN, LIFE, AND VICTORY.

Next to Charles is his name likewise written in Roman majuscules: OUR LORD KING CHARLES.

...This mosaic...which should be treasured because of its antiquity and its connection with Leo III and Charlemagne, is now exposed to the inclemency of the skies.

4. Early Modern Drawings of the Lateran Mosaics

There are a number of drawings of the Lateran mosaics, the details of which are much discussed. Of greater interest may be the iconography. Both Leo and Charles kneel before Saint Peter, the pope to receive the pallium, the symbol of his spiritual authority, and the king to accept the standard representing his divinely sanctioned temporal authority. But if the pope was another Peter and in possession of his constitutive powers, then surely there is in the mosaic a claim for papal precedence. Perhaps it was because of subtle, but persistent claims like this that Charlemagne came later to regret that he had allowed Leo to orchestrate and handle his imperial coronation on Christmas Day 800.

Following page: The Lateran Palace Mosaics: Early modern drawings [after Mont-faucon].

Questions: Why did Leo build so lavishly in Rome? What impression would such buildings have made upon Carolingian kings? What does the icononography of the mosaics suggest about the relations between Charlemagne and the papacy?

SCS
PETRVS

☩S CSSIMVS
DN
LE
O PP

☩ ON CARVLO REGI

BEATE PETRE DONA
VITA LEONI PP E BICTO
RIA CARVLO REGI DONA

Y

12. Charlemagne and Pope Leo

This epic poem written in the early ninth century gives part of the Carolingian court view of how Charlemagne rose to the imperial title. Unfortunately only its third book, which highlights the assault upon Pope Leo III by Roman plotters, survives today. The poem probably concluded with an elegant account of Charlemagne's march to Rome and his imperial coronation. It has been argued that Einhard is the most likely author of the verses. What the reader should especially notice is the Virgilian tone of the piece, not only in its vocabulary and borrowed imagery, but also in its imperial ideology, which Einhard promoted. Thus, when he later wrote his biography of Charlemagne he took the structure and some of his language from Suetonius's biographies of the Caesars; here, if he was indeed the author, he imitated Augustus's own poet and his most imperial poem, the Aeneid. The poet describes Pope Leo, bloodied and blinded in the king's dream, just as Virgil had described the wounded Hector sending Aeneas on his fateful voyage towards a new home. The journey that awaited Charlemagne, of course, was the march to Rome to restore the pope. But if Aeneas was Augustus or the model for a new Roman hero, then in the sophisticated allusion of this Carolingian poem Charlemagne too becomes both an epic wanderer and an emperor waiting upon his moment in the imperial sun.

Source: trans. P.E. Dutton from Monumenta Germaniae Historica: Poetae Latini Aevi Carolini, vol.1, ed. E. Dümmler (Berlin, 1881), pp.366, 374, 377-379.

Once again my burdened anchor wishes me to get moving,
To set sail in unpredictable winds on an unknown course.
My feeble limbs have survived two storms [the two previous books]
Only to repair now their exhausted muscles for this new strain,
To ready my accomplished hands to row with these heavy oars
Out to where the gentle breezes call; where ships test a still
And flat sea with soft winds blowing behind them.
I would sail rapidly over the seas to unknown lands
And on my voyage even risk ramming into rocky promontories.
Now the gentle east wind, with powerful puffs, sets me sailing,
And forces me swiftly on my difficult way
Towards Europe where a lighthouse with a brilliant light flashes forth.
King Charles casts the light of his great name all the way to the stars.
Just as the sun illumines with its rays, so this David
Lights up the world with the great light of his kindness.

There follows after this opening of the third book a long panegyric, full of the imagery of light and radiance, on Charlemagne's many accomplishments and his perfection. Next the poet imagines Charlemagne ordering the construction of a new Rome, with a forum and senate, in Aachen, and then, in the company of his assembled family, preparing for a great hunt. After its exertions, the king lays down to sleep.

While the sun falls and night shadows and locks up the light,
His tired limbs long for quiet sleep.
But in his dreams the king sadly sees an awful
And horrifying sight, for there stands Leo,

The supreme pontiff of the city of Rome, shedding sad tears,
His eyes are wounded, his face covered with blood,
His tongue is mutilated and he bears many frightening wounds.
A cold fear now steals over the restless limbs of the emperor.
[Awaking] he orders three agents to travel rapidly to Rome,
To learn if Leo, the good pastor of his flock, were indeed well.

The agents of the king discovered that there had, in fact, been an attempt upon the pope's life, but that he had somehow survived. They accompanied the pope to Paderborn in the summer of 799 where he was royally received by Charles.

Charles, [having heard of the pope's actual fate] recalled his dreams,
And recognizing from their account the vestiges of his vision,
Did not doubt that this had happened, that he had seen,
In his dream, the pope shed sad tears.
Hence, without delay, he ordered [his son] Pepin to go out
To meet the pope, conveying wishes of peace and well-being.
Carrying out the orders of his father, Pepin readied to go;
He gladly went out with a great throng of troops.
King Charles, ever just, sat on his high throne
Giving laws to his many lands, and confirming royal treaties.
On a huge wide field, the apostolic pastor sees noble Pepin
And his great crowd of men come towards him;
He stretches both his hands to the sky
And prays from his heart for the [Frankish] people.
The entire army prostrates itself three times before the pope,
And the suppliant throng three times pays its respects.
Pope Leo with generous and open heart welcomes Pepin,
Embracing him with his holy arms,
And in this embrace, the pope kisses Pepin [in welcome].
Prince Pepin walks and talks with the pope,
Discussing a number of different problems.
  Meanwhile kind King Charles, [our] great hero,
Raises himself up on his throne and addresses the people:
"O you warriors, rouse yourselves and put on your weapons.
You are to go [as if] to war, to tempt harsh contests,
And to be confident in bloody battles.
We shall soon in a speedy manner meet the good pontiff."
Scarcely does [our] hero say this, when the crowd breaks out in a
        clamor;
The throng assembles with its javelins, leather breastplates,
Broad shields, helmets, and arrows.
Bronze shields rattle; the cavalry seems ready to charge;
Clouds of dust darken the sky;
And horns from a hill blast the troops below.
Battle signals sound; the fields are covered with troops;
The whole army, plumed, marvelously shines.
Javelins sparkle in the light, standards flutter in the wind,
Armed young men are afire [with passion] and confident youth

Rejoices on horseback; a firm ardor grows as they listen [to their king.]
Charles at the front and center of his troops shines in joy:
A golden plume encircles his brow and, outfitted in arms,
He stands out, the best general astride an immense horse.
Before the camp stand lines of priests divided into three choirs;
They are dressed in long vestments
And hold up the sacred standards of the holy cross.
The priests and the joyful people await the pope's advent.
Now father Charles sees his troops arrayed on the wide field;
He knows that Pepin and the highest pastor are fast approaching;
He orders his people to wait for them.
He divides his troops into a ring-like shape,
In the center of which, he himself, that blessed one, stands,
Awaiting the advent of the pope, but higher up than his comrades
On the summit of the ring; he rises above the assembled [Franks].
Now Pope Leo approaches and crosses the front line of the ring.
He marvels at the many peoples from many lands whom he sees,
At their differences, their strange tongues, dress, and weapons.
At once Charles hastens to pay his reverent respects,
Embraces the great pontiff, and kisses him.
The two men join hands and walk together, speaking as they go.
The entire army prostrates itself three times before the pope,
And the suppliant throng three times pays its respects.
The pope prays from his heart for the people three times.
The king, the father of Europe, and Leo, the world's highest pastor,
Walk together and exchange views,
Charles inquiring as to the pope's case and his troubles.
He is shocked to learn of the wicked deeds of the [Roman] people.
He is amazed by the pope's eyes which had been blinded,
But to which sight had now returned,
And he marveled that a tongue mutilated with tongs now spoke...
When the church service was over,
Charles invited Leo to his great palace.
His gorgeous court-hall shines inside with colorful tapestries,
And its chairs are covered in purple and gold.
The joyful company sits down at table and enjoys a variety of delights.
In the middle of the high hall they celebrate a great banquet.
Golden bowls overflow with Falernian wine.
King Charles and Leo, the highest prelate in the world,
Dine together and quaff sparkling wine from their bowls.
After the joyful repast and much drinking,
Kind [King] Charles gives many gifts to great Leo.
Then the king returns to his private chambers in the palace
And the pope retires to his own quarters.

*Questions: How is the relationship between the pope and Charlemagne portrayed?
Who has, in the eyes of the court poet, predominance? How did court figures such
as the poet and Alcuin convince Charlemagne to take up the imperial title?*

13. Capitularies

The author of the epic poem, Charlemagne and Pope Leo, conceived of Charlemagne not only as a warrior, but also as a law-giver. Einhard had noted in his biography that Charles ordered collections of the Germanic law codes to be compiled, but he neglected to explain the king's chief legal activity which was to issue laws of his own orally and in public. These laws seem to have had legal force because the king "said" them, often in response to specific questions from his agents, the missi dominici, or to address some general problem. Versions of these oral statements must have been written down and were kept at court and spread by the missi as they made their judicial inquiries throughout the kingdom. They are called capitularies because they consist of a series of sections or chapters of laws. Although his heirs would also issue laws, no Carolingian king laid down as impressive or fundamental a set of laws as Charlemagne himself.

1. The Capitulary on the Saxon Territories

As described by Einhard, the conquest of Saxony proved particularly difficult for Charlemagne because of the persistent paganism of the Saxons. For the Carolingians, conquest and conversion to Catholicism were to be almost equal parts in an overall policy of integrating new territories into the kingdom. Thus, the protracted Saxon conflict forced the king, at some point between 775 and 790, to think about how to institute and legally enforce the Carolingian and Christian control of Saxony.

Source: trans. D.C. Munro in Translations and Reprints from the Original Sources of European History, vol. 6.5: Laws of Charles the Great (Philadelphia: The University of Pennsylvania, 1899), pp.2-5; revised.

1.   It was pleasing to all that the churches of Christ, which are now being built in Saxony and consecrated to God, should not have less, but greater and more illustrious honor, than the temples of the idols had had.
2.   If anyone shall have fled to a church for refuge, let no one presume to expel him from the church by violence, but he shall be left in peace until he shall be brought to the judicial assemblage; and on account of the honor due to God and the saints, and the reverence due to the church itself, let his life and all his members be granted to him. Moreover, let him plead his cause as best he can and he shall be judged; and so let him be led into the presence of the lord king, and the latter shall send him where it shall have seemed fitting according to his clemency.
3.   If anyone shall have entered a church by violence and shall have carried off anything in it by force or theft, or shall have burned the church itself, let him be punished by death.
4.   If anyone, out of contempt for Christianity, shall have despised the holy Lenten fast and shall have eaten flesh, let him be punished by death. But, nevertheless, let it be taken into consideration by a priest, lest perchance anyone from necessity has been led to eat flesh.
5.   If anyone shall have killed a bishop or priest or deacon, let him likewise be punished capitally.
6.   If anyone deceived by the Devil shall have believed, after the manner of

the pagans, that any man or woman is a witch and eats men, and on this account shall have burned the person, or shall have given the person's flesh to others to eat, or shall have eaten it himself, let him be punished by a capital sentence.

7. If anyone, in accordance with pagan rites, shall have caused the body of a dead man to be burned and shall have reduced his bones to ashes, let him be punished capitally.

8. If anyone of the race of the Saxons hereafter concealed among them shall have wished to hide himself unbaptized, and shall have scorned to come to baptism and shall have wished to remain a pagan, let him be punished by death.

9. If anyone shall have sacrificed a man to a devil, and after the manner of the pagans shall have presented him as a victim to the demons, let him be punished by death.

10. If anyone shall have formed a conspiracy with the pagans against the Christians, or shall have wished to join with them in opposition to the Christians, let him be punished by death; and whosoever shall have consented to this same fraudulently against the king and the Christian people, let him be punished by death.

11. If anyone shall have shown himself unfaithful to the lord king, let him be punished with a capital sentence.

12. If anyone shall have ravished the daughter of his lord; let him be punished by death.

13. If anyone shall have killed his lord or lady, let him be punished in a like manner.

14. If, indeed, for these mortal crimes secretly committed anyone shall have fled of his own accord to a priest, and after confession shall have wished to do penance, let him be freed by the testimony of the priest from death.

15. Concerning the lesser chapters all have consented. To each church let the parishioners present a house and two *mansi* of land, and for each one hundred and twenty men, noble and free, and likewise *liti*, let them give to the same church a man-servant and a maid-servant.

16. And this has been pleasing, Christ being propitious, that whencesoever any receipts shall have come into the treasury, either for a breach of the peace or for any penalty of any kind, and in all income pertaining to the king, a tithe shall be rendered to the churches and priests.

17. Likewise, in accordance with the mandate of God, we command that all shall give a tithe of their property and labor to the churches and priests; let the nobles as well as the freemen, and likewise the *liti*, according to that which God shall have given to each Christian, return a part to God.

18. That on the Lord's day no meetings and public judicial assemblages shall be held, unless perchance in a case of great necessity or when war compels it, but all shall go to the church to hear the word of God, and shall be free for prayers or good works. Likewise, also, on special festivals they shall devote themselves to God and to the services of the church, and shall refrain from secular assemblies.

19. Likewise, it has been pleasing to insert in these decrees that all infants shall be baptized within a year; and we have decreed this, that if anyone shall have despised to bring his infant to baptism within the course of a year,

without the advice or permission of the priest, if he is a noble he shall pay 120 *solidi* to the treasury, if a freeman 60, if a *litus* 30.

20. If anyone shall have made a prohibited or illegal marriage, if a noble [he shall pay] 60 *solidi*, if a freeman 30, if a *litus* 15.

21. If anyone shall have made a vow at springs or trees or groves, or shall have made any offering after the manner of the heathen and shall have partaken of a repast in honor of the demons, if he shall be a noble [he shall pay] 60 *solidi*, if a freeman 30, if a *litus* 15. If, indeed, they have not the means of paying at once, they shall be given into the service of the church until the *solidi* are paid.

22. We command that the bodies of Saxon Christians shall be carried to the church cemeteries and not the mounds of the pagans.

23. We have ordered that diviners and soothsayers shall be handed over to the churches and priests.

24. Concerning robbers and malefactors who shall have fled from one county to another, if anyone shall receive them into his power and shall keep them with him for seven nights, except for the purpose of bringing them to justice, let him pay our ban. Likewise, if a count shall have concealed him and shall be unwilling to bring him forward so that justice may be done and is not able to excuse himself for this, let him lose his office.

25. Concerning a pledge: that no one shall in any way presume to pledge another, and whosoever shall do this shall pay the ban.

26. That no one shall presume to impede any man coming to us to claim justice; and if anyone shall have attempted to do this, he shall pay our ban.

27. If any man shall not have been able to find a fidejussor [one who gives security], his property shall be sequestrated until he shall present a fidejussor. If, indeed, he shall have presumed to enter into his own dwelling in defiance of the ban, he shall forfeit either ten *solidi* or an ox for the violation of the ban itself, and in addition he shall pay the sum for which he was in debt. If, indeed, the fidejussor shall not observe the day fixed, then he shall suffer as much loss as his proportion of the guarantee was; moreover, he who was debtor to the fidejussor shall restore double the loss which he has permitted the fidejussor to incur.

28. Concerning presents and gifts: let no one receive gifts to the detriment of an innocent person; and if anyone shall have presumed to do this, he shall pay our ban. And if perchance the count shall have done this (may it not happen!) he shall lose his office.

29. Let all the counts strive to preserve peace and unity with one another; and if perchance any discord or disturbance shall have arisen between them, they shall not on this account neglect either our aid or profit.

30. If anyone shall have killed or shall have aided in the murder of a count, his property shall go to the king, and he shall become the serf of the latter.

31. We have granted the authority to the counts within their jurisdiction of inflicting the ban of 60 *solidi* for revenge [*faida*] of the greater crimes; for the lesser crimes, on the other hand, we have fixed the ban of the count at 15 *solidi*.

32. If anyone owes an oath to any man whatsoever, let him duly make his oaths to that one at the church on the day appointed; and if he shall have despised to take the oath, let him give a pledge, and let him who was con-

tumacious pay fifteen *solidi,* and afterwards let him fully compound for his act.

33. Concerning perjuries, let it be according to the law of the Saxons.

34. We have forbidden that all Saxons shall hold public assemblies in general, unless perchance our *missus* shall have caused them to come together in accordance with our command; but each count shall hold judicial assemblies and administer justice in his jurisdiction. And this shall be cared for by the priests, lest it be done otherwise.

Questions: How successful by this time had the Carolingians been in converting the Saxons? What problems persisted? How were they being dealt with?

2. The General Capitulary for the *Missi* from 802

The reader should first notice the need Charlemagne felt to have his people swear a new oath to him as emperor. Whether he believed that some might feel that the old oaths sworn to him as king were now without force or that he required a clearer statement of allegiance to him as emperor can be debated, but what is certain is that the imperial title had altered the constitutional character of his rule. Students might also like to think here as well about the extent to which Charlemagne's government was theocratic or the church monarchic.

Source: trans. D.C. Munro in Translations and Reprints from the Original Sources of European History, vol. 6.5: Laws of Charles the Great (Philadelphia: The University of Pennsylvania, 1899), pp.16-27; revised.

First chapter. Concerning the embassy sent out by the lord emperor. Therefore, the most serene and most Christian lord Emperor Charles has chosen from his nobles the wisest and most prudent men, both archbishops and some of the other bishops also, and venerable abbots and pious laymen, and has sent them throughout his whole kingdom, and through them by all the following chapters has allowed men to live in accordance with the correct law. Moreover, where anything which is not right and just has been enacted in the law, he has ordered them to inquire into this most diligently and to inform him of it; he desires, God granting, to reform it. And let no one, through his cleverness or astuteness, dare to oppose or thwart the written law, as many are wont to do, or the judicial sentence passed upon him, or to do injury to the churches of God or the poor or the widows or the wards of any Christian. But all shall live entirely in accordance with God's precept, justly and under a just rule, and each one shall be admonished to live in harmony with his fellows in his business or profession; the canonical clergy ought to observe in every respect a canonical life without heeding base gain, nuns ought to keep diligent watch over their lives, laymen and the secular clergy ought rightly to observe their laws without malicious fraud, and all ought to live in mutual charity and perfect peace. And let the *missi* themselves make a diligent investigation whenever any man claims that an injustice has been done to him by anyone, just as they desire to deserve the grace of omnipotent God and to keep their fidelity promised to Him, so that entirely in all cases everywhere, in accordance with the will and fear of God, they shall administer the law fully and justly in the case of the holy churches of God and of the poor, of wards and widows and of the whole people. And if there shall be anything of such a nature that they, together with the provincial counts, are not able of themselves to correct it and to do justice concerning it, they shall, without any ambiguity, refer this, together with their reports, to the judgment of the emperor; and the straight path of justice shall not be impeded by any one on account of flattery or gifts from any one, or on account of any relationship, or from fear of the powerful.

2. Concerning the fidelity to be promised to the lord emperor. He commanded that every man in his whole kingdom, whether ecclesiastic or layman, and each one according to his vow and occupation, should now promise to him as emperor the fidelity which he had previously promised to him as king; and all of those who had not yet made that promise should do likewise, down to those who were twelve years old. And that it shall be announced to all in public, so that each one might know, how great and how many things are comprehended in that oath; not merely, as many have thought hitherto, fidelity to the lord emperor as regards his life, and not introducing any enemy into his kingdom out of enmity, and not consenting to or concealing another's faithlessness to him; but that all may know that this oath contains in itself this meaning:

3. First, that each one voluntarily shall strive, in accordance with his knowledge and ability, to live wholly in the holy service of God in accordance with the precept of God and in accordance with his own promise, because the lord emperor is unable to give to all individually the necessary care and discipline.

4. Secondly, that no man, either through perjury or any other wile or fraud, on account of the flattery of gift of anyone, shall refuse to give back or dare to abstract or conceal a serf of the lord emperor or a district or land or anything that belongs to him; and that no one shall presume, through perjury or other wile, to conceal or abstract his fugitive fiscaline serfs who unjustly and fraudulently say that they are free.

5. That no one shall presume to rob or do any injury fraudulently to the churches of God or widows or orphans or pilgrims; for the lord emperor himself, after God and his saints has constituted himself their protector and defender.

6. That no one shall dare to lay waste a benefice of the lord emperor, or to make it his own property.

7. That no one shall presume to neglect a summons to war from the lord emperor; and that no one of the counts shall be so presumptuous as to dare to dismiss thence any one of those who owe military service, either on account of relationship or flattery or gifts from any one.

8. That no one shall presume to impede at all in any way a ban or command of the lord emperor, or to dally with his work or to impede or to lessen or in any way to act contrary to his will or commands. And that no one shall dare to neglect to pay his dues or tax.

9. That no one, for any reason, shall make a practice in court of defending another unjustly, either from any desire of gain when the cause is weak, or by impeding a just judgment by his skill in reasoning, or by a desire of oppressing when the cause is weak. But each one shall answer for his own

cause or tax or debt unless anyone is infirm or ignorant of pleading; for these the *missi* or the chiefs who are in the court or the judge who knows the case in question shall plead before the court; or if it is necessary, such a person may be allowed as is acceptable to all and knows the case well; but this shall be done wholly according to the convenience of the chiefs or *missi* who are present. But in every case it shall be done in accordance with justice and the law; and that no one shall have the power to impede justice by a gift, reward, or any kind of evil flattery or from any hindrance of relationship. And that no one shall unjustly consent to another in anything, but that with all zeal and goodwill all shall be prepared to carry out justice.

For all the above mentioned ought to be observed by the imperial oath. [Also]:

10. That bishops and priests shall live according to the canons and shall teach others to do the same.

11. That bishops, abbots, and abbesses, who are in charge of others, with the greatest veneration shall strive to surpass their subjects in this diligence and shall not oppress their subjects with a harsh rule or tyranny, but with sincere love shall carefully guard the flock committed to them with mercy and charity or by the examples of good works.

12. That abbots shall live where the monks are and wholly with the monks, in accordance with the rule, and shall diligently learn and observe the canons; the abbesses shall do the same.

13. That bishops, abbots and abbesses shall have advocates, vicars and *centenarii* who know the law and love justice, who are pacific and merciful, so that through these great profit or advantage may accrue to the holy church of God; because we are entirely unwilling to have in the monasteries harmful and greedy provosts and advocates, from whom greater blasphemy or injury may arise for us. But they shall be such as the canonical or regular institution orders them to be, submissive to the will of God and always ready to render justice to all, fully observing the law without malicious fraud, always exercising a just judgment in the case of all, such provosts indeed as the holy rule teaches that they should be. And let them wholly observe this, that they shall in no way deviate from the canonical or regular norm, but shall exhibit humility in all things. If, moreover, they shall have presumed to do otherwise, let them feel the discipline of the rule; and if they shall have been unwilling to amend their ways they shall be removed from the provostship, and those who are more worthy shall be appointed in their places.

14. That bishops, abbots and abbesses, and counts shall be mutually in accord, following the law in order to render a just judgment with all charity and unity of peace, and that they shall live faithfully in accordance with the will of God, so that always everywhere through them and among them a just judgment shall be rendered. The poor, widows, orphans and pilgrims shall have consolation and defense from them; so that we, through their goodwill, may deserve the reward of eternal life rather than punishment.

15. We will and command in every way that abbots and monks shall be subject to their bishops in all humility and obedience, just as is commanded by the canonical constitution. And all the churches and basilicas shall remain

in the defense and power of the church. And no one shall dare to divide or to cast lots concerning the property of the basilicas. And what has once been offered shall not be taken back, and shall be sanctified and shall be claimed as legal property. But if any one shall have presumed to do otherwise he shall pay and make good our ban. And the monks shall be corrected by the bishops of their province; but if they do not amend their ways then the archbishop shall summon them to the synod; and if even then they shall not have amended their ways, then they shall come together with their bishop into our presence.

16. Concerning choosing men for ordination, just as the lord emperor had formerly granted it, by the law of the Franks, to the bishops and abbots, so he has also now confirmed it; nevertheless, in this manner, so that neither a bishop nor an abbot in a monastery shall prefer the more worthless to the better, and he shall not desire to advance any one before his betters on account of relationship or any flattery, and that he shall not lead such a one to us to be ordained when he has a better concealed and kept back; we are in no way willing that this should be done, because it seems to be a mockery and deceit of us. But in the monasteries men of such a character are to be prepared for ordination that reward and profit may accrue both to us and to those who recommend them.

17. Moreover, that the monks shall live firmly and strictly in accordance with the rule, because we know that any one whose goodwill is lukewarm is displeasing to God, as John bears witness in the Apocalypse: "I would that thou wert cold or hot. So then, because thou art lukewarm, and neither cold nor hot, I will spue thee out of my mouth." Let them in no way usurp to themselves secular business. They shall not have leave to go outside of their monastery at all, unless compelled by a very great necessity; but nevertheless the bishops, in whose diocese they shall be, shall take care in every way that they do not get accustomed to wandering outside of the monastery. But if it shall be necessary for anyone to go outside in obedience to a command, and this shall be done with the counsel and consent of the bishop, persons of such character shall be sent out with a certificate, that there may be no suspicion of evil in them and that no evil report may arise from them. For the property and business outside of the monastery the abbot, with the permission and counsel of the bishop, shall ordain who shall provide, not a monk, but another of the faithful. Let them wholly shun secular gain or a desire for worldly affairs, because avarice or a desire for this world ought to be shunned by all Christians, but especially by those who seem to have renounced the world and its lusts. Let no one presume in any way to incite strifes and controversies, either within or outside of the monastery. But if anyone shall have presumed to do so, he shall be corrected by the most severe discipline of the rule and in such a manner that others shall fear to commit such actions. Let them entirely shun drunkenness and feasting, because it is known to all that from these men are especially polluted by lust. For a most pernicious rumour has come to our ears that many in the monasteries have already been detected in fornication and in abomination and uncleanness. It especially saddens and disturbs us that it can be said, without a great mistake, that some of the monks are understood to be sodomites, so that whereas the greatest hope of salvation to all Christians is believed to

arise from the life and chastity of the monks, damage has been incurred instead. Therefore, we also ask and urge that henceforth all shall most earnestly strive with all diligence to preserve themselves from these evils, so that never again such a report shall be brought to our ears. And let this be known to all, that we in no way dare to consent to those evils in any other place in our whole kingdom; so much the less, indeed, in the persons of those whom we desire to be examples of chastity and moral purity. Certainly, if any such report shall have come to our ears in the future, we shall inflict such a penalty, not only on the guilty but also on those who have consented to such deeds, that no Christian who shall have heard of it will ever dare in the future to perpetrate such acts.

18. Monasteries for women shall be firmly ruled, and the women shall not be permitted to wander about at all, but they shall be guarded with all diligence, and they shall not presume to arouse litigations or strife among themselves, nor shall they dare to be disobedient or refractory in any way toward their rulers and abbesses. Where, moreover, they have a rule, let them observe it in every respect; let them not be give to fornication or drunkenness or lust, but let them live justly and soberly in every respect. And into their cloisters or monasteries let no man enter, except when the priest enters with a witness to visit the sick, or for the mass alone; and let him immediately go forth. And let no one from another place enroll his daughter in the congregation of the nuns without the knowledge and consideration of the bishop to whose diocese that place pertains; and the latter shall diligently inquire why she desires to remain in the holy service of God, and shall confirm her residence or profession in that place. Moreover, maid-servants belonging to other men, or such women as are [not] willing to live in the holy congregation in accordance with its manner of life, shall be wholly cast out from the congregation.

19. That no bishop, abbots, priests, deacons, or other members of the clergy shall presume to have dogs for hunting, or hawks, falcons and sparrow-hawks, but each shall observe fully the canons or rule of his order. If anyone shall presume to do so, let him know that he shall lose his office. And in addition he shall suffer such punishment for it that the others will be afraid to usurp such things for themselves.

20. That abbesses, together with their nuns, shall live within the cloisters in concord and watchfully, and shall never presume to go outside of their cloister. But if the abbesses wish to send any nuns out of the cloisters, they shall not do this without the consent and advice of their bishops. Likewise, also, when there ought to be any ordinations or receptions in the monasteries, they shall previously discuss these fully with their bishops; and the bishops shall announce to the archbishop what seems the safer or more useful way, and with his advice they shall perform what ought to be done.

21. That priests and the remaining canonical clergy, whom they have as associates in their minister, shall be wholly subject to their bishops, and just as the canonical institution orders let them consent to be taught the sacred discipline fully by their bishops, if they desire to have our favor or their own offices.

22. Moreover, the canonical clergy shall observe fully the canonical life, and shall be instructed at the episcopal residence or in the monastery with all

diligence according to the canonical discipline. They shall not be permitted to wander outside at all, but shall live under strict guardianship, not given to base gain, not fornicators, not thieves, not homicides, not robbers, not quarrelsome, not wrathful, not proud, not drunken, but with a chaste heart and body, humble, modest, sober, merciful, pacific, that as sons of God they may be worthy to be promoted in the sacred order; not in the villages or villas near to or adjoining the churches, without a master and without discipline, like those who are called sarabaites, living in luxury or fornication or other iniquity, to consent to which is absurd.

23. The priests shall carefully watch over the clerks whom they have with them, that the latter live according to the canons; that they are not given to vain sports or worldly convivialities or songs or luxuries; but that they live chastely and healthfully.

24. If, moreover, any priest or deacon shall presume hereafter to have with him in his house any women except those whom the canonical license permits, he shall be deprived of both his office and inheritance until he be brought into our presence.

25. That counts and *centenarii* shall compel all to do justice in every respect, and shall have such assistants in their ministries as they can securely confide in who will observe the law and justice faithfully, who will oppress the poor in no manner, who will not dare under any pretext, on account of flattery or reward, to conceal thieves, robbers, murderers, adulterers, magicians, wizards or witches, and all sacrilegious men, but instead will give them up that they may be punished and chastised in accordance with the law, so that, God granting it, all of these evils may be removed from the Christian people.

26. That judges shall judge justly in accordance with the written law, and not according to their own will.

27. And we command that no one in our whole kingdom shall dare to deny hospitality to rich or poor or pilgrims, that is, no one shall deny shelter and fire and water to pilgrims traversing our country in God's name, or to anyone traveling for the love of God or for the safety of his own soul. If, moreover, any one shall wish to serve them farther, let him expect the best reward from God, who Himself said: "And whoso shall receive one such little child in my name, receiveth me," and elsewhere: "I was a stranger and ye took me in."

28. Concerning embassies coming from the lord emperor. That the counts and *centenarii* shall provide most carefully, as they desire the grace of the lord emperor, for the *missi* who are sent out, so that they may go through their departments without any delay; and he commands to all everywhere that they ought to see to it that no delay is encountered anywhere, but they shall cause them to go on their way in all haste and shall provide for them in such a manner as our *missi* may direct.

29. Concerning the poor to whom in his mercy the lord emperor has granted the ban which they ought to pay, that the judges, counts or our *missi* shall not, for their own advantage have the power to compel them to pay the fine which has been granted to them.

30. Concerning those whom the lord emperor wishes, Christ being propitious, to enjoy peace and protection in his kingdom, namely, those who are hastening to his clemency, either Christians or pagans, because they desire to announce some news, or seeking his aid on account of their poverty or

hunger, that no one shall dare to constrain them to serve him, or to seize them or alienate or sell them; but wherever they may wish to remain voluntarily, there under the defense of the lord emperor they shall be aided in his mercy. If anyone shall have presumed to act contrary to this, let him who has so presumptuously despised the commands of the lord emperor, know that he shall suffer the loss of his life for it.

31. And against those who announce the justice of the lord emperor, let no one presume to plot any injury of damage, or to stir up any enmity. But if any one shall have presumed, let him pay the imperial ban or, if he deserves a heavier punishment, it is commanded that he shall be brought into the emperor's presence.

32. Murders, by which a multitude of the Christian people perishes, we command in every way to be shunned and to be forbidden; God himself forbade to his followers hatred and enmity, much more murder. For in what manner does anyone trust to placate God, who has killed his son nearest to him? In what manner truly does he, who has killed his brother, think that the Lord Christ will be propitious to him? It is a great and terrible danger also with God the Father and Christ, Lord of heaven and earth, to stir up enmities among men: it is possible to escape for some time by remaining concealed, but nevertheless by accident at some time he falls into the hands of his enemies; moreover, where is it possible to flee from God, to whom all secrets are manifest? By what rashness does anyone think to escape his anger? Wherefore, lest the people committed to us to be ruled over should perish from this evil, we have taken care to shun this by every means of discipline; because he who shall not have dreaded the wrath of God, shall find us in no way propitious or to be placated; but we wish to inflict the most severe punishment upon any one who shall have dared to murder a man. Nevertheless, lest sin should also increase, in order that the greatest enmities may not arise among Christians, when by the persuasions of the Devil murders happen, the criminal shall immediately hasten to make amends and with all celerity shall strike an accommodation for the evil done with the relatives of the murdered man. And we forbid firmly, that the relatives of the murdered man shall dare in any way to continue their enmities on account of the evil done, or shall refuse to grant peace to him who asks for it, but having given their pledges they shall receive a suitable accommodation and shall make a perpetual peace; moreover, the guilty one shall not delay to achieve an accommodation. When, moreover, it shall have happened on account of sins that anyone shall have killed his brethren or his neighbor, he shall immediately submit to the penance imposed upon him, and just as his bishop arranges for him, without any ambiguity; but by God's aid he shall desire to accomplish his atonement and he shall compound for the dead man in accordance with the law, and shall make peace in every way with his relatives; and the pledge being given, let no one dare thereafter to stir up enmity against him. But if anyone shall have scorned to make the fitting accommodation, he shall be deprived of his property until we shall render our decision.

33. We prohibit in every way the crime of incest. But if anyone shall have been contaminated by sinful fornication, he shall by no means be released without severe punishment, but for this he shall be corrected in such a manner that others shall fear to do likewise and that uncleanness shall be wholly

removed from the Christian people, and the guilty man shall fully atone for this by penance, just as his bishop shall arrange for him; and the woman shall be placed in the hands of her parents until we render our judgment. But if he shall have been unwilling to consent to the judgment of the bishops concerning his amendment, then he shall be brought to our presence, mindful of the example which was made concerning the incest which Fricco perpetrated with the nun of God.

34. That all shall be fully and well prepared, whenever our order or proclamation shall come. But if anyone shall then say that he was unprepared and shall have neglected our command, he shall be brought to the palace; and not only he, but also all who dare to transgress our ban or command.

35. That all shall wholly venerate their bishops and priests with all honor in the service and will of God. That they shall not dare to pollute themselves and others by incestuous nuptials; that they shall not presume to be married until the bishops and priests together with the elders of the people have inquired diligently into the consanguinity of those marrying; and then they shall be married with a benediction. Let them shun drunkenness, avoid greed, commit not theft; let them wholly shun strifes and contentions and blasphemies, both at feasts and assemblies, but let them live in charity and concord.

36. And that all shall be entirely of one mind with our *missi* in performing justice in every respect. And that they shall not permit the use of perjury at all, for it is necessary that this most evil crime shall be removed from the Christian people. But if anyone after this shall have been proved a perjurer, let him know that he shall lose his right hand; and they shall be deprived of their property until we shall render our decision.

37. That those who shall have been guilty of patricide or fratricide, or who shall have killed a maternal or paternal uncle or any other relative, and shall have been unwilling to obey and consent to the judgment of the bishops, priests and other judges, our *missi* and counts, for the safety of their own souls and in order to bring about a just judgment, shall be kept in such custody that they may be safe and may not infect other people until they are led into our presence; and from their own property in the meantime they shall have nothing.

38. And let this likewise be done with those who have been seized in illegal and incestuous unions and corrected, and who are not willing to amend their ways nor to obey their bishops and priests, and who presume to despise our ban.

39. That in our forests no one shall dare to steal our game, which we have already many times forbidden to be done; and now we again strictly forbid that anyone shall do so in the future; just as each one desires to preserve the fidelity promised to us, so let him take heed to himself. But if any count or *centenarius* or our *bassus* or anyone of our ministerials shall have stolen our game, he shall be brought into our presence without fail to render account. But if anyone of the remaining people shall have stolen our game, let him without fail pay what is just; let no one hereafter be released from this on any account. But if anyone knows that this has been done by another, let him not dare to conceal this, in order that he may preserve the fidelity which he has promised to us and which he now has to promise.

40. Lastly, therefore, we desire all our decrees to be known in our whole kingdom through our *missi* now sent out, either among the men of the church, bishops, abbots, priests, deacons, canons, all monks or nuns, so that each one in his ministry or profession may keep our ban or decree, or where it may be fitting to thank the citizens for their good will, or to furnish aid, or where there may be need still of correcting anything. Likewise also to the guardianship of the holy churches or of widows and orphans and the weaker; or the robbing of them; or the arrangements for the assembling of the army; or any other matters; how they are to ban, or how each one strives in all things to keep himself in the holy service of God; so that all these good things may be well done to the praise of omnipotent God, and we may return thanks where it is fitting. But where we believe there is anything unpunished, we shall so strive to correct it with all our zeal and will that with God's aid we may bring it to correction, both for our own eternal glory and that of all our faithful. Likewise we desire all the above to be fruitfully known by our counts or *centenarii*, our ministerials.

Questions: How far down did Charlemagne's control of the church penetrate? Indeed, did he not have more direct control over the church in northern Europe than Pope Leo III did from distant Rome? How was the church in Francia organized and how did Charlemagne enforce his control over it? What were the principal forces of corruption, according to the king?

3. Relating to the Army

Despite Einhard's account of Charlemagne's extensive conquests, Charlemagne was not, it must be said, a Roland, a warrior who risked all in heroic and reckless combat. In fact, the king was exactly the opposite. He conquered his enemies by superior organization, by cleverly planning his campaigns, and by wearing down his enemies. Indeed, the Carolingians were like Republican Romans a thousand years earlier in that they fought on a seasonal basis, the army marching out from Francia in the spring as soon as there was sufficient fodder on the ground to support their horses and returning in November when the fodder and their supplies were exhausted. Because of his superior planning, Charlemagne was often able to put more men into the field than his enemies, who promptly retreated, whereupon Charlemagne's troops would destroy their crops and wait for the enemy to surrender. Some evidence of the deliberate and rational nature of Carolingian warfare is to be found in the capitularies.

Source: trans. D.C. Munro in Translations and Reprints from the Original Sources of European History, vol. 6.5: Laws of Charles the Great (Philadelphia: The University of Pennsylvania, 1899), pp.6-12; revised.

Capitulary of Herstal, 779

14. Let no one presume to gather an armed following.
20. Let no one dare to sell any coats of mail outside of our realm.

Capitulary of the *Missi*, 803

7. Shields and coats of mail shall not be given to merchants.

Italian Capitulary, 801

2. Concerning the payment of the host. If any free man, out of contempt for our command, shall have presumed to remain at home when others go to war, let him know that he ought to pay the full *heribannum* according to the law of the Franks, that is, sixty *solidi*. Likewise, also, for contempt of individual capitularies which we have promulgated by our royal authority, that is, anyone who shall have broken the peace decreed for the churches of God, widows, orphans, wards, and the weak, shall pay the fine of sixty *solidi*.
3. Concerning deserters. If anyone shall have shown himself so contumacious or haughty as to leave the army and return home without the command or permission of the king, that is, if he is guilty of what we call in the German language *herisliz*, he himself, as a criminal, shall incur the peril of losing his life, and his property shall be confiscated for our treasury.

Double Capitulary of Thionville for the *Missi*, 805

6. Concerning the equipment in the army the same shall be observed as we have previously commanded in another capitulary, and, in particular, every man who possesses twelve *mansi* shall have a coat of mail; he who has a coat of mail and shall not have brought it with him shall lose his whole benefice, together with the coat of mail.
7. Concerning those merchants who go to the countries of the Slavs and Avars, whither they ought to go on their business; that is, in the country of the Saxons as far as Bardowiek, which is under the charge of Hredi; and to Schesel, which is under the charge of Madalgaudus; and to Magdeburg, which is under the charge of Aito; and to Erfurt, which is under the charge of Madalgaudus; and to Halazstat, which is under the charge of the same Madalgaudus; to Forchheim and to Pfreimt and to Regensburg, which are under the charge of Audulfus; and to Lorsch, which is under the charge of Warnarius. And they shall not carry arms and coats of mail for sale; but if they shall have been discovered carrying any, all their property shall be taken from them; half shall go to the royal treasury, the other half shall be divided between the above-mentioned *missi* and the discoverer.
19. Concerning the payment of the host (*heribannum*) we decree that our *missi* ought to exact it faithfully this year in accordance with our command, without indulgence for any person, either from favors or terror; that is, that they shall receive the lawful fine, namely, three pounds, from each man who has six pounds in gold, silver, coats of mail, bronze utensils, clothing, horses, oxen, cows, or other live stock; but the women and children shall not be deprived of their garments for this fine. Those who do not have the aforesaid property to the value of more than three pounds shall pay thirty *solidi*; he who has not more than two pounds, ten *solidi*; if indeed, anyone has not more than one pound, five *solidi*, so that he may be able again to prepare himself for the service of God and for our need. And our *missi* shall take

care and inquire diligently, lest through any evil action any defraud our justice by transferring or commending their property to others.

Memorandum concerning Calling Out the Army in Western Gaul, 807

1. In the first place, all who seem to have benefices shall come to the army. 2. Each free man who seems to hold five *mansi* shall likewise come to the army; and he who holds four *mansi* shall do the same, and he who seems to have three shall likewise go. Moreover, wherever two have been found of whom each seems to have two *mansi*, one shall equip the other, and the one of them who shall be better able shall come to the army. And where two shall have been found of whom one has two *mansi* and the other has one *mansus*, they shall join together in the same way and one shall equip the other, and the one who shall be better able shall come to the army. Wherever, moreover, three shall have been found of whom each has one *mansus*, two shall equip the third, the one of them who is better able shall come to the army. Of those who have half a *mansus*, five shall equip the sixth. And of those who shall have been found so poor that they have neither serfs nor their own property in lands, and yet have personal property to the value of [100] *solidi*, five shall prepare a sixth [and where two, a third from those who seem to have small possessions in land]. And to each one of those who go in the army five *solidi* shall be paid by the aforesaid poorer ones who seem to have no property in land. And let no one abandon his lord on this account.

Capitulary on a Variety of Subjects, circa 807

2. If it shall be necessary to furnish aid against the Saracens of Spain or the Avars, then five of the Saxons shall equip a sixth; and if it shall be necessary to bear aid against the Bohemians, two shall equip a third; if, indeed, there is need of defending the native country against the Sorbs [that is, Slavs], then all shall come together. 3. From the Frisians we will that the counts and our vassals, who seem to have benefices, and all the horsemen in general, shall come well prepared to our assembly; of the remaining poorer men six shall equip a seventh, and thus they shall come well prepared for war to the aforesaid assembly.

Capitulary for the *Missi* on Mobilizing the Army, 808

1. Every free man who has four *mansi* of his own property, or has a benefice from anyone, shall equip himself and go to the army, either with his lord, if the lord goes, or with his count. He who has three *mansi* of his own property shall be joined to a man who has one *mansus*, and shall aid him so that he may serve for both. He who has only two *mansi* of his own property shall be joined to another who likewise has two *mansi*, and one of them, with the aid of the other, shall go to the army. He who has only one *mansus* of his own shall be joined to one of three who have the same and shall aid him, and the latter shall go alone; the three who have aided him shall remain at home.

4. From the men who have been enfeoffed by the counts the following are to be excepted and are not commanded to pay the ban: two who shall have been left behind with the wife of a count and two others who shall have been commanded to remain to guard his territory and to perform our service. In this case we command, however, that each count shall leave at home two men to guard each separate territory which he has, in addition to those two who remain with his wife; all the others, without any exception, he shall take with him, or if he remains at home, he shall order them to proceed with the one who goes to the army in his stead. A bishop or abbot shall leave at home only two of those who are enfeoffed and laymen.

The Capitulary of Bologna, October 811

3. If any man holding an office under us shall have been summoned to the host and shall not have come to the appointed muster, he shall abstain from meat and wine for as many days as he shall have been proved to be late in coming to the appointed muster.

4. If anyone, without the license or permission of the prince, shall have deserted from the army, the Franks call this *herisliz*, we wish the ancient law to be preserved, that is, he shall be punished by a capital sentence.

5. If anyone of those who holds a royal benefice shall have abandoned his peer proceeding in the army against the common enemies, and shall have been unwilling to go or stay with him, he shall lose his office and benefice.

6. That in the host no one shall ask his peer or any other man to drink. And if any drunken person shall have been found in the army, he shall be so excommunicated that in drinking he shall use nothing but water until he acknowledges that he has acted wrongly.

7. Concerning the royal vassals who serve in the household at the present time and yet are known to have benefices, it has been decided that those who remain at home with the lord emperor shall not retain their vassals in the household with themselves, but shall permit the vassals to go with the count to whose district they belong.

8. It has been enacted that the preparation for serving in the army shall be defined and continued in accordance with the ancient custom, namely, victuals for a three months' march and arms and clothing for a half-year. But, nevertheless, it has been decided that this shall be observed in the following manner, so that those who march from the Rhine to the Loire shall compute the beginning of their provision from the Loire; those, indeed, who make their journey from the Loire to the Rhine shall compute their victuals for the three months from the Rhine; those moreover, who dwell across the Rhine and proceed through Saxony shall know that the Elbe is their boundary; and those who remain across the Loire and ought to go to Spain shall know that the Pyrenees are their boundary.

9. If it shall have been learned that any free man has not been, during the present year, in the army with his lord, he shall be compelled to pay the full *heribannum*. And if his lord or count shall have permitted him to remain at home, the former shall pay the same fine on his account; and as many *heribanni* shall be demanded as he has allowed men to remain at home. And because in the present year we have allowed each lord to leave two of his

men at home, we will that these shall be shown to our *missi*, because we have granted the *heribannum* to these alone.

10. It has been enacted that no bishop or abbot or abbess, or any rector or guardian of a church, shall presume without our permission to give or sell a coat of mail or sword to any man outside, except only to his own vassals. And if it shall happen that he has in any church or sacred place more coats of mail than are needed for the men who guard the same church, then the same rector of the church shall ask the king what ought to be done with these.

Capitulary of Aachen, 802-803

9. Concerning going to the army; the count in his country under penalty of the ban, and each man under penalty of sixty *solidi* shall go to the army, so that they come to the appointed muster at that place where it is ordered. And the count himself shall see in what manner they are prepared, that is, each one shall have a lance, shield, bow with two strings, and twelve arrows. And the bishops, counts, and abbots shall oversee their own men and shall come on the day of the appointed muster and there show how they are prepared. Let them have breast-plates or helmets, and let them proceed to the army, that is, in the summer.

10. That the equipment of the king shall be carried in carts, also the equipment of the bishops, counts, abbots and nobles of the king: flour, wine, pork and victuals in abundance, mills, adzes, axes, augers, slings, and men who know how to use these well. And the marshals of the king shall add stones for these on twenty beasts of burden, if there is need. And each one shall be prepared for the army and shall have plenty of all utensils. And each count shall save two parts of the fodder in his county for the army's use, and he shall have good bridges and good boats.

Letter Calling for the Mobilization of an Abbot's Troops

In the name of the Father, Son, and Holy Ghost. Charles, most serene, august, crowned by God, great pacific emperor, and also, by God's mercy, king of the Franks and Lombards, greetings to Abbot Fulrad.

Be it known to you that we have decided to hold our general assembly this year in the eastern part of Saxony, on the river Bode, at the place which is called Stassfurt. Therefore, we have commanded you to come to the aforesaid place, with all your men well armed and prepared, on the fifteenth day before the Kalends of July [17 June], that is, seven days before the festival of Saint John the Baptist. Come, accordingly, so equipped with your men to the aforesaid place that thence you may be able to go well prepared in any direction whither our summons shall direct; that is, with arms and gear also, and other equipment for war in food and clothing, so that each horseman shall have a shield, lance, sword, dagger, bow and quivers with arrows; and in your carts utensils of various kinds, that is, axes, planes, augers, boards, spades, iron shovels, and other utensils which are necessary in an army. In the carts also supplies of food for three months, dating from the time of the assembly, arms and clothing for a half-year. And we command this in general, that you cause it to be observed that you proceed peacefully to the aforesaid place, through whatever part of our realm your journey shall take you, that is, that you presume to take nothing except fodder, wood and water; and let the men of each one of your vassals march along with the carts and horsemen, and let the leader always be with them until they reach the aforesaid place, so that the absence of a lord may not give an opportunity to his men of doing evil.

Send your gifts, which you ought to present to us at our assembly in the middle of the month of May, to the place where we then shall be; if perchance your journey shall so shape itself that on your march you are able in person to present these gifts of yours to us, we greatly desire it. See that you show no negligence in the future if you desire to have our favor.

Questions: What was the procedure for calling up the army and who had to go? How did Charlemagne enforce his military rights? Why were the Carolingians worried about the spread of mail coats?

4. Relating to Vassalage

When the Carolingian family had served the Merovingians as mayors of the palace, it had employed the bonds of vassalage as a means of securing the allegiance of subordinates. In 757, in fact, Tassilo, the duke of the Bavarians, came to King Pepin at Compiègne and commended himself with his hands into vassalage to the king. While placing his hands on saints' relics, the duke swore oaths of allegiance and faithfulness to Pepin and his sons. Still vassalage was an institution in flux throughout the ninth century and one that often as not compromised royal power rather than enhanced it. Yet it was also a social fact, one that the Carolingian royal house had pioneered, but could not completely control despite all its legal attempts to do so.

Source: trans. D. Herlihy in The History of Feudalism (New York: Harper & Row, 1970), p.87; reprinted with permission.

No. 64, in 810

17. Let every [lord] compel his dependants to obey better and better and consent to the imperial commands and orders.

The Capitulary of Aachen, 802-803

16. Let no man abandon his lord after he has received from him the value of a single *solidus*, unless the lord wishes to kill him, or to beat him with a stick, or to violate his wife or daughter, or to deprive him of his inheritance.

No. 104, circa 801-813

8. If any vassal should wish to abandon his lord, he may do so only if he can prove that the lord has committed one of these crimes:
  1. if the lord should have unjustly sought to enslave him.

2. if the lord plotted against his life.
3. if the lord committed adultery with the wife of his vassal.
4. if the lord willingly attacked him with drawn sword in order to kill him.
5. if after the vassal commended his hands into his, the lord failed to provide defense when he could have done so.

If the lord has committed any of these five offenses against his vassal, the vassal may abandon him.

Questions: What did Carolingian vassalage consist of? What rules governed conduct? Why did the king wish to enforce what were essentially private contracts?

5. Sample Inventory of a Royal Estate

Though not a capitulary itself, the following is one of a series of inventories included in the capitularies as examples of the form and content such inventories should take. But the figures provided are an indication of the problems faced by a subsistence agricultural economy. The ratio of the harvest that had to be sown to produce the next year's crop is very high: 100% of the rye and 54% of the spelt. Thus Asnapius, in the year of the inventory, seems to have suffered a particularly poor harvest, since its old grain supplies almost equal the previous year's production. These percentages are repeated in the other sample inventories for that year. What they seem to testify to is an agricultural economy that often experienced cycles of good and bad harvests and needed to balance the two in order to achieve subsistence levels. Though the Carolingians had cerealized northern Europe and were heavily dependent on wheat, their economy was still diversified. They produced a wide range of foodstuffs, some of which—such as wild pigs roaming in the forests and nuts and berries—were available in seasons when there were wheat shortages.

Source: trans. R.P. Falkner in Translations and Reprints from the Original Sources of European History, vol. 3.2: Statistical Documents of the Middle Ages (Philadelphia: University of Pennsylvania, 1907), pp.4-5; revised.

We found on the royal estate of Asnapius a royal house built of stone in the best manner with 3 rooms; the whole house surrounded with balconies, with 11 rooms for women; beneath, 1 cellar; 2 porticoes; 17 other houses built of wood within the courtyard with as many rooms and other appurtenances, well built; 1 stable, 1 kitchen, 1 mill, 2 granaries, 3 barns.

The yard surrounded carefully with a hedge and stone gateway and above a balcony from which to make distributions. An inner yard, likewise enclosed within a hedge, arranged in a suitable manner, and planted with various kinds of trees.

Linen: coverings for 1 bed, 1 table cloth, 1 towel.

Utensils: 2 bronze vessels, 2 drinking cups, 2 bronze cauldrons, 1 iron one, 1 frying pan, 1 gramalmin, 1 pair of andirons, 1 lamp, 2 hatchets, 1 chisel, 2 augers, 1 axe, 1 knife, 1 large plane, 1 plane, 2 scythes, 2 sickles, 2 spades tipped with iron. Enough wooden utensils for use.

Farm produce: old spelt from last year, 90 baskets which can be made into 450 measures of flour; 100 measures of barley. From the present year,

110 baskets of spelt, of which 60 baskets have been planted, the rest we found; 100 measures of wheat, 60 sown, the rest we found; [some] measures of rye, all sown; 1800 measures of barley, 1100 sown, the rest we found; 430 measures of oats, 1 measure of beans, 12 measures of peas. At the 5 mills, 800 measures, 200 of which were given to those from the home farm who worked. At the 4 breweries, 650 small measures, 240 given to the prebendaries, the rest we found. At the 2 bridges, 60 measures of salt and 2 shillings. At the 4 gardens, 11 shillings, 2 measures of honey, about 1 measure of butter (for dues), from last year 10 sides of bacon, 200 sides of new bacon, as well as fragments and fats, 43 measures of cheese from the present year.

Of cattle: 51 older horses, 5 three-year-olds, 7 two-year-olds, 7 yearlings; 10 two-year-old colts, 8 yearlings, 3 stallions; 16 oxen; 2 donkeys; 50 cows with calves, 20 young bullocks, 38 yearling calves, 3 bulls, 260 hogs, 100 pigs, 5 boars, 150 ewes with lambs, 200 yearling lambs, 120 rams, 30 goats with kids, 30 yearling kids, 3 male goats, 30 geese, 80 chickens, 22 peacocks.

Also concerning the dependencies which pertain to the above demesne. In the villa of Grisio we found domain buildings, where there are 3 barns and a yard surrounded by a hedge. There is 1 garden with trees, 10 geese, 8 ducks, 30 chickens.

In another villa we found demesne buildings and a yard surrounded by a hedge and within 3 barns, 1 arpent of vines, 1 garden with trees, 15 geese, 20 chickens.

In a third villa, [we found] demesne buildings. It has 2 barns, 1 granary, 1 garden, 1 yard well enclosed by a hedge.

We found all the dry and liquid measures just as in the palace. We did not find any goldsmiths, silversmiths, blacksmiths, huntsmen or persons engaged in other services.

The garden herbs which we found were lily, putchuck, mint, parsley, rue, celery, lovage, sage, savory, juniper, leeks, garlic, tansy, wild mint, coriander, shallotes, onions, cabbages, kohlrabi, betony. Trees: pears, apples, medlars, peaches, filberts, walnuts, mulberries, and quinces.

Questions: What problems were there with the Carolingian manorial economy? Are there certain items in these inventories that seem unnecessary?

6. Articles from the Capitulary on the Maintenance of Royal Estates (De Villis)

Charlemagne, like his father before him, was extremely interested in proper and careful estate management. In part this was because, in a subsistence economy, his large court was an expensive operation to run. Hence it was necessary for his royal estates to produce a surplus with which to supply his palace with food and material resources. But it was also the case that his court, especially in the early years, was peripatetic and so his scattered estates needed to support the king and his retinue when they arrived for a short stay. Indeed Pepin the Short and the young Charlemagne may have moved so frequently from palace to palace, because no single estate could long support the presence of the king and his party.

Source: trans. R.P. Falkner in Translations and Reprints from the Original Sources of European History, vol. 3.2: Statistical Documents of the Middle Ages (Philadelphia: University of Pennsylvania, 1907), pp.2-4; revised.

62. That each steward shall make an annual statement of all our income: an account of our lands cultivated by the oxen which our plowmen drive and of our lands which the tenants of farms ought to plow; an account of the pigs, of the rents, of the obligations and fines; of the game taken in our forests without our permission; of the various payments; of the mills, of the forest, of the fields, of the bridges, and ships: of the free-men and the hundreds who are under obligations to our treasury; of markets, vineyards, and those who owe wine to us; of the hay, fire-wood, torches, planks, and other kinds of lumber; of the waste-lands; of the vegetables, millet, panic; of the wool, flax and hemp; of the fruits of the trees, of the nut trees, larger and smaller; of the grafted trees of all kinds; of the gardens; of the turnips; of the fish-ponds; of the hides, skins, horns; of the honey, wax; of the fat, tallow and soap; of the mulberry wine, cooked wine, mead, vinegar, beer, wine new and old; of the new grain and the old; of the hens and eggs; of the geese; the number of fishermen, smiths [workers in metal], sword-makers, and shoe makers; of the bins and boxes; of the turners and saddlers; of the forges and mines, that is iron and other mines; of the lead mines; of the people giving tribute; of the colts and fillies; they shall make all these known to us, set forth separately and in order, at Christmas, in order that we may know what and how much of each thing we have.

23. On each of our estates our stewards are to have as many cow-houses, piggeries, sheep-folds, stables for goats, as possible, and they ought never to be without these. And let them have in addition cows furnished by our serfs for performing their service, so that the cow-houses and plows shall be in no way weakened by the service on our demesne. And when they have to provide meat, let them have steers lame, but healthy, and cows and horses which are not mangy, or other beasts which are not diseased and, as we have said, our cow-houses and plows are not to suffer on account of this.

34. They must take the greatest care, that whatever is prepared or made with the hands, that is, lard, smoked meat, sausage, partially salted meat, wine, vinegar, mulberry wine, cooked wine, garum, mustard, cheese, butter, malt, beer, mead, honey, wax, flour, all should be prepared and made with the greatest cleanliness.

40. That each steward on each of our domains shall always have, for the sake of ornament, swans, peacocks, pheasants, ducks, pigeons, partridges, turtle doves.

42. That on each of our estates, the chambers shall be provided with counterpanes, cushions, pillows, bed-clothing, coverings for the tables and benches; vessels of brass, lead, iron and wood; andirons, chains, pot-hooks, adzes, axes, augers, cutlasses and all other kinds of tools, so that it shall never be necessary to go elsewhere for them, or to borrow them. And the weapons, which are carried against the enemy, shall be well cared for, so as to keep them in good condition; and when they are brought back they shall be placed in the chamber.

43. For our women's workshops they are to provide at the proper time, as has been ordered, the materials, that is the linen, wool, woad, vermillion, madder, wool-combs, teasels, soap, grease, vessels and the other objects which are necessary there.

44. Of the food-products other than meat, two-thirds shall be sent each year for our own use, that is of the vegetables, fish, cheese, butter, honey, mustard, vinegar, millet, panic, dried and green herbs, radishes, and in addition wax, soap, and other small products; and they tell us how much is left by a statement, as we have said above; and they shall not neglect this as in the past; because from those two-thirds, we wish to know how much remains.

45. That each steward shall have in his district good workmen, namely, blacksmiths, gold-smiths, silver-smiths, shoemakers, turners, carpenters, sword-makers, fishermen, foilers, soap-makers, men who know how to make beer, cider, berry and all other kinds of beverages, bakers to make pastry for our table, net-makers who know how to make nets for hunting, fishing and fowling, and other [occupations] that are too numerous to be named.

51. Our stewards must beware that dishonest men do not hide our seed from us, either beneath the ground or in some other place, thus making the harvest seem less plentiful than it is. Likewise let them beware that other types of mischief do not happen.

Questions: What were the essential characteristics of material culture in the Carolingian world? What was most valuable? What was least valuable? What system of manorial management did the royal family promote?

7. On Education

Charlemagne may have been imperfectly educated himself, as Einhard suggested, but his commitment to learning was profound. We may judge this not only from his capitularies, where his emphasis may seem somewhat rudimentary to the modern student, but also from the learned foreigners, men such as Alcuin of York and Theodulf from Spain, whom he brought to the continent and to his court to teach the Franks. Nevertheless one should not slight the fundamental nature and enduring importance of Charlemagne's educational reform, for from his promotion of correct reading and writing in monastery and cathedral schools would rise a vibrant literary culture in his son's time. Moreover, the fundamentalism of this educational reform led to the invention or perfection of a new script called Caroline Minuscule; it is in that script of small, evenly spaced, discrete letters that this very page is essentially written. Manuscripts for three hundred years after Charlemagne would continue to be written in Caroline Minuscule and it was the script to which Italian Renaissance humanists would return. For when they read the oldest manuscript copies of Cicero and Lucan, they found that they were written in Caroline Minuscule and assumed that was the very style of handwriting once used by Cicero himself. Indeed without the fundamental nature of Charlemagne's educational enterprise, a majority of the texts of the ancient Latin world would not have survived at all, for they would not have been copied and kept in monastic and royal libraries.

Source: trans. D.C. Munro in Translations and Reprints from the Original Sources of European History, vol. 6.5: Laws of Charles the Great (Philadelphia: The University of Pennsylvania, 1899), pp.12-16; revised.

[A Letter of Charles on the Cultivation of Learning, 780-800.]

Charles, by the grace of God, king of the Franks and Lombards and patrician of the Romans, to Abbot Baugulf and to all the congregation, also to the faithful instructors entrusted to you, we send a loving greeting through our ambassadors in the name of omnipotent God.

Be it known, therefore, to your devotion, which is most pleasing to God, that we, together with our faithful, have considered it to be useful that the bishoprics and monasteries entrusted by the favor of Christ to our control, in addition to the manner of monastic life set out in their rule and their practice of holy religion, ought also to be zealous in the cultivation of learning and in teaching those who by the gift of God are able to learn, according to the capacity of each individual. Thus just as the observance of the rule imparts order and grace to their conduct, so also zeal in teaching and learning may do the same for their sentences, so that those who desire to please God by living rightly should not neglect to please him also by speaking correctly. For it is written: "Either from thy words thou shalt be justified or from thy words thou shalt be condemned." For although correct conduct may be better than knowledge, nevertheless knowledge precedes conduct. Therefore, each one ought to study what he desires to accomplish, so that so much the more fully the mind may know what ought to be done, as the tongue hastens in the praises of omnipotent God without the hindrances of errors. For since errors should be shunned by all men, so much the more ought they to be avoided as far as possible by those who are chosen for this very purpose alone, so that they ought to be the special servants of truth. For when in the past few years letters were often sent to us from several monasteries in which it was stated that the brethren who dwelt there offered upon our behalf sacred and pious prayers, we have noticed in most of these letters both correct thoughts and uncouth expressions; because what pious devotion dictated faithfully to the mind, the tongue, uneducated on account of the neglect of study, was not able to express in the letter without error. Whence it happened that we began to fear lest perchance, as the skill in writing was less, so also the wisdom for understanding the Holy Scriptures might be much less than it rightly ought to be. And we all know well that, although errors of speech are dangerous, far more dangerous are errors in understanding. Therefore, we exhort you not only to avoid neglecting the study of literature, but also with most humble mind, pleasing to God, to study earnestly in order that you may be able more easily and more correctly to penetrate the mysteries of the divine Scriptures. Since, moreover, images, tropes and similar figures are found in the sacred pages, no one doubts that each one in reading these will understand the spiritual sense more quickly if previously he shall have been fully instructed in the mastery of letters. Such men truly are to be chosen for this work as have both the will and the ability to learn and a desire to instruct others. And may this be done with a zeal as great as the earnestness with which we command it. For we desire you to be, as it is fitting that soldiers of the church should be, devout in mind, learned in discourse, chaste in conduct and eloquent in speech, so that whosoever shall seek to see you out of reverence for God, or on account of your reputation for holy conduct, just as he is edified by your appearance, may also be instructed by your wisdom, which he has learned from your reading or singing, and may go away joyfully giving thanks to omnipotent God. Do not neglect, therefore, if you wish to have our favor, to send copies of this letter to all your suffragans and fellow-bishops and to every monastery.

From the General Letter of Charlemagne, before 800

Charles, confiding in the aid of God, king of the Franks and Lombards, and patrician of the Romans, to the religious lectors subject to our power.

Since the divine clemency always guards us at home and abroad, in the issues of war or in the tranquility of peace, though human significance is in no way able to pay back his benefits, nevertheless, because our God is inestimable in his mercy, He approves benignly the goodwill of those devoted to his service. Therefore, because we take care constantly to improve the condition of our churches, we have striven with watchful zeal to advance the cause of learning, which has been almost forgotten by the negligence of our ancestors; and, by our example, also we invite those whom we can to master the study of the liberal arts. Accordingly, God aiding us in all things, we have already corrected carefully all the books of the Old and New Testaments, corrupted by the ignorance of the copyists.

Incited, moreover, by the example of our father Pepin [the Short], of venerated memory, who by his zeal decorated all the churches of the Gauls with the songs of the Roman church, we are careful by our skill to make these churches illustrious by a series of excellent lectionaries. Finally, because we have found the lectionaries for the nocturnal offices, compiled by the fruitless labor of certain ones, in spite of their correct intention, unsuitable because they were written without the words of their authors and were full of an infinite number of errors, we cannot suffer in our days discordant solecisms to glide into the sacred lessons among the holy offices, and we propose to improve these lessons. And we have entrusted this work to Paul the Deacon, our friend and client. We have directed him to peruse carefully the sayings of the Catholic fathers and to choose, so to speak, from the most broad meadows of their writings certain flowers, and from the most useful to form, as it were, a single garland. He, desiring to obey devoutly our highness, has read through the treatises and sermons of the different Catholic fathers, has chosen from each the best, and has presented to us in two volumes lessons suitable for the whole year and for each separate festival, and free from error. We have examined the text of all these with our wisdom, we have established these volumes by our authority, and we deliver them to your religion to be read in the churches of Christ.

The General Admonition, 789

72. And we also demand of your holiness that the ministers of the altar of

God shall adorn their ministry by good manners, and likewise the other orders who observe a rule and the congregations of monks. We implore them to lead a just and fitting life, just as God Himself commanded in the Gospel. "Let your light so shine before men that they may see your good works and glorify your Father who is in heaven," so that by their example many may be led to serve God; and let them join and associate to themselves not only children of servile condition, but also sons of free men. And let schools be established in which boys may learn to read. Correct carefully the Psalms, the signs in writing (notas), the songs, the calendar, the grammar, in each monastery or bishopric, and the catholic books; because often some desire to pray to God properly, but they pray badly because of faulty books. And do not permit your boys to corrupt them in reading or writing. If there is need of writing the Gospel, Psalter and Missal, let men of mature age do the writing with all diligence.

Capitulary for the *Missi*, 803

2.   Priests shall not be ordained without an examination. And excommunications shall not be ordered at random and without cause.

Capitulary for the *Missi*, 802-813

2.   [We will and command] that laymen shall learn thoroughly the creed and the Lord's prayer.

Questions: Why was Charlemagne interested in promoting sound education? How would his family have gained from the rise of better educated ecclesiastics and nobles? Does his letter to Baugulf actually constitute the outline of an educational reform? Where were boys to be educated? How would the women associated with court have been educated?

14. An Exhortation to the Faithful

Charlemagne's reign was disturbed by few doctrinal controversies, in part because his own orthodoxy was so simple and straightforward, but also because the educational reform he had begun had not yet produced the clever readers and debaters who would in the middle of the ninth century argue over such complex topics as predestination and the nature of the eucharist. The following text was printed by Baluze and later G. H. Pertz as a statement of faith by the emperor himself. More likely it is the dogma or creed of the higher ecclesisatics of his realm, but as such it must also contain the official doctrines upheld by Charlemagne himself.

Source: trans. J.I. Mombert in A History of Charles the Great (Charlemagne), (London: Kegan Paul, Trench & Co., 1888), pp.322-325.

Dearly beloved brethren,

We are sent hither for your benefit in order that we might admonish you to lead a righteous and good life in the eyes of God, and pursue justice and mercy in this world.

First I admonish you to believe in one almighty God, the Father, the Son, and the Holy Spirit, the perfect Trinity and true unity; the creator of all things visible and invisible in whom we have salvation, and who is the giver of all the good things we enjoy.

Know that the Son of God was made man for the salvation of the world, and that He was begotten of the Holy Spirit out of the Virgin Mary; that for our salvation He suffered death, on the third day rose from the dead, ascended into heaven, and sits now at the right hand of God; that He shall come to judge the quick and the dead and give to each of us according to our works.

Believe in this one church, that is, the congregation of the good throughout this earthly sphere; and know that they only can be saved and belong to the kingdom of heaven, who in the faith, communion, and the charity of this church persevere until the end, while those who for their sins are excommunicated from this church and fail penitently to return to the same, cannot in this world render acceptable service to God.

Be assured that in baptism you have received forgiveness for all your sins.

Expect that from God's mercy through confession and penitence your daily sins are forgiven.

Believe in the general resurrection of the good to eternal life, and of the evil to eternal punishment.

This then is your faith, through which you will be saved, if you firmly cling to it and flourish in good works, for faith without works is dead, and works without faith, though they should be good, cannot please God.

First then, love God the Almighty with all your heart and with all your prayers, and whatever pleases him, do that always, with him as your helper and according to your ability; shun what you know displeases him; for the one that says that he loves God, and does not keep his commandments, is a liar. Love your neighbor as yourself; give alms to the poor as you are able. Entertain strangers; visit the sick; be merciful to prisoners. Do ill to no one, nor consent to those who do such, for the receiver is as bad as the thief; forgive as you hope to be forgiven; redeem the captive, help the oppressed, defend the cause of the widow and orphan; render righteous judgment; do not consent to any wrong; persevere not in wrath; shun excess in eating and drinking.

Be humble and kind to one another; serve your lord faithfully; do not steal, do not perjure yourselves, nor let others do so. Envy, hatred, and violence separate people from the kingdom of God.

Be swift to reconciliation; for to sin is human, to amend is angelical, but to persevere in sin is diabolical.

Defend the church and promote her cause, so that the priests of God may pray for you. Remember what you did promise God in baptism; you promised to renounce the Devil through all his works; do not return to what you renounced, but remain faithful to God as you vowed, and love him who created you, and from whom you have all the good things you have.

Let every person in whatsoever station he [or she] be, serve God faithfully.

Let the wife be subject to her husband in all goodness and purity; let them abstain from fornication, rewards, and avarice, for those who do such things go against God.

Let them bring up their children in the fear of God, and give him alms, as they are able, with cheerfulness and a good will.

Let the husband love his wife, and call her not by improper names; let him rule his house well, and in all goodness frequent church.

Let people render unto each other what they owe without begrudging it, and unto God what is due to him with a good will.

Sons should love their parents and honor them, and not be disobedient; let them beware of theft, murder, and fornication; when they are of lawful age, let them marry a lawful wife, unless they prefer to enter the service of God.

Let clerics, and canons, diligently obey their bishops; let them not wander from place to place. Let them abstain from the entanglements of secular pursuits, maintain their chastity, study the Holy Scripture, and discharge the duties of their sacred ministry. Let monks be true to their calling, obey their abbot, and avoid filthy lucre. Let them remember and faithfully observe [Saint Benedict's] Rule, knowing that it is better not to vow a thing, than to break a vow once made.

Dukes, counts, and judges, I ask you to judge the people righteously; be compassionate to the poor, abhor bribery, and let not personal considerations lead you to punish the innocent.

Always remember the words of the Apostle: "We must all appear at the judgment-seat of Christ, that each man may receive according to that which he has done, be it good or bad." Even as our Lord has said: "With what judgment ye judge, even so shall ye be judged." That is, be merciful, that you may obtain the mercy of God. "There is nothing hidden that shall not become known, and nothing concealed that shall not be revealed." And "for every idle word we must give account on the day of judgment."

Whatever we do, let us endeavor in all things to please God, that after this present life we may enjoy with the saints of God that which is everlasting.

This life is short, and the time of our death is uncertain; it is wise to be always prepared.

Let us remember that it is a fearful thing to fall into the hands of God. If we confess our sins, show penitence, and give alms, the Lord is merciful and kind.

If we turn to him with all our heart, He will be very merciful, and grant us in this life prosperity, and in that which is to come, everlasting happiness with his saints. God bless you, dearly beloved brethren!

Question: How would you characterize Charlemagne's religious outlook? What were the normal doctrines of the Frankish church?

15. The Iconodule Controversy in Francia

The doctrinal controversies that disturbed Charlemagne's reign came chiefly from the outside. One of these was the Adoptionist heresy of Felix of Urgel and Elipandus of Toledo who claimed that Christ in his human nature was not the true son of God, but adopted. At Frankfurt in 792 Felix debated with Angilbert of Saint-Riquier, Alcuin, and other Carolingian scholars and, for a time, recanted his unorthodox position on the Trinity.

Meanwhile, at Nicaea in 787, the eastern church formally approved the veneration of images, thus dramatically reversing the iconoclastic position held previously by official Byzantium. Pope Hadrian, who had representatives at the council, sent an imperfect translation of its acts to Charlemagne who responded by asking his scholars, particularly Theodulf of Orléans, to condemn the iconodule position. The so-called Caroline Books denied that images were worthy of veneration, since all things made by humans were inferior and that God was best understood through the literal truths of the Bible. But if pictorial art was, therefore, deemed not divine by the Carolingians, it was also freed from having to confine itself exclusively to the treatment of the divine and the devotional. The principles of Carolingian aesthetics were, therefore, to be very different. Theodulf thinks that artists express at best imperfect representations of things and events which writers are better able to express. Still, he cannot help being impressed with skillful artistry, its rich imaginings, and striking objects.

Source: trans. C. Davis-Weyer, Early Medieval Art, 300-1150, in Sources & Documents in the History of Art, ed. H.W. Janson (Englewood Cliffs, New Jersey: Prentice-Hall, 1971), pp.100-103; reprinted with permission.

Truth persevering always pure and undefiled is one. Images, however, by the will of the artist seem to do many things, while they do nothing. For, since they seem to be men when they are not, to fight when they do not fight, to speak when they do not speak, to hear when they do not hear, to see when they do not see, to beckon when they do not beckon, to touch when they do not touch and other things like this, it is clear that they are artists' fictions and not that truth of which it is said: "And the truth will make you free." That they are images without sense and reason is true; that they are men, however, is false. And if someone affirms that images according to a logical trick can be called men, as for example, "Augustine was a very great philosopher," and, "Augustine ought to be read," and "a painted Augustine stands in the church," and "Augustine is buried there," let him realize, that although all these things come from one source, that is, from Augustine, he alone is the true Augustine who is called "a very great philosopher." Of the others, however, one is a book, one is an image, one is a buried corpse. The principal difference between a true and a painted man is that one is true and the other false, and they have nothing in common except the name. For since he is true of whom it can be said that he is an animal, rational, mortal, capable of laughter and pain, then one must necessarily consider him false who has none of these attributes, and if he who lacks all these things is not false then neither is he who possesses all of them true...

And when somebody says: "Images are not contrary to Holy Scripture," while many things are being painted by painters about which Scripture says nothing and which can be shown to be completely false not only by learned but also by unlearned men, must one not grant, that what he says is not only extremely ridiculous but downright false? Does he not know that it is contrary to Scripture to fashion the sea as a man pouring forth a large stream of water? And is it not certainly contrary to Scripture if the earth is depicted in human form, either as arid and sterile or as overflowing with fruits? And is it not obvious that it is contrary to Scripture if one depicts rivers and streams and their confluence as men pouring water out of urns? And if the sun and the moon and the other adornments of the sky are depicted in human form, their heads crowned with rays, does not all of this run quite contrary to Holy Scripture? And if one credits each of the twelve winds with a different shape according to its strength or gives a different appearance to each of the months according to the time of year, so that some appear naked, others half naked, others clad in various garments, or if one depicts the four seasons as four different figures—either verdant with flowers as spring, or scorched by the heat and loaded with grain as summer, or bent under the load of wine vats and grapes as autumn, or now freezing in the cold, now warming himself at a fire, or feeding animals or catching birds, which are exhausted by the cold, as winter—does one not recognize that these things, are contrary to Scripture, which does not contain any of them?

How is it, then, that Scripture is not contradicted by painters, who frequently follow the vain fables of the poets? They sometimes fashion events which have actually happened, but also incredible inanities on other occasions. What neither has happened nor can ever happen they depict: what is understood mystically by the philosophers, venerated superstitiously by the pagans, and rejected rightfully by the Catholics. And although all these things are contained in pagan literature they are nevertheless utterly alien to Scripture.

Is it not alien to Scripture that they paint how the three-headed Chimaera is killed by Bellerophon, although he did not overthrow a monster, as some pretend, but made the mountain habitable as others rightly understand? Or is it not alien to Scripture if one pretends that Erichthonius is the son of the limping Vulcan and the earth and that he heats his iron in Mount Aetna and has his oven in Vesuvius, a mountain of Campania, which is known to burn perpetually? Or is it not alien to Scripture if one paints how Scylla is girded with the heads of dogs, or how Phyllis because of someone's love was changed into a tree, or how Itys because of his aunt's defilement by his father and the murder his mother and aunt committed against him was together with his parents and his aunt changed into a bird, or if one paints how the Sirens are in part young women and in part birds, or if one paints how Ixion deceived by Juno embraces a cloud and generates the centaurs, or if one paints how Neptune with his trident governs the sea tides? Or is it not alien to Sacred Scripture if one fashions how Perseus kills the three Gorgons with Minerva's help or how he flies toward Medusa backwards, or if one paints how out of Medusa's blood Pegasus is born, the winged horse that breaks open with his hoof the fountain of the Muses? Or is it not contrary to Divine Scripture, that they depict Prometheus making lifeless men out of clay and the same Prometheus being lifted up among the guardians of heaven and, while he beholds the heavenly beings, touching the wheels of Phoebus with his fennel stalk, stealing fire, and touching the breast of the man he had fashioned, thereby giving him life? Or is it not contrary to Sacred Scripture that they depict Tantalus, placed in a lake in Hades, his lips trembling with greed at the false water, and at fruit appearing above, hanging down by his face, and turning to ashes at a touch, furnishing him a rich sight but a poor meal? Or is it not alien to Holy Scripture when the blind Phineas is depicted, and the Harpies stealing his food and fouling his meals with their excrement, those Harpies whom Zetes and Calais, the sons of the Northwind, are supposed to have driven away? Or is it not contrary to Holy Scripture to paint how Admetus, the king of Greece, had to hitch a lion and a stag together to a cart with the aid of Apollo and Hercules, in order to satisfy his father-in-law and enjoy marriage with Alcestis, or if Hercules is depicted as slaying Cerberus, the three-headed dog of Hell? And is it not contrary to Holy Scripture that they depict a certain hunter, named Actaeon, changed into a stag because he saw Diana bathing, and, so disguised, being devoured by the bites of his own dogs? Or is it not contrary to Divine Scripture, that they depict how Cybele loved the very beautiful youth Attis and incensed by vanity and jealousy castrated him and made him a half-man? Or is it not contrary to Divine Scripture to depict Orpheus, loving Euridice and winning her as his wife with his cithar, and also Euridice, flying from Aristeus the shepherd, since she could not bear his pursuit, and being killed by a serpent she stepped on, and her husband following her descending into Hades and accepting the rule that he should not turn around to look at her and turning around and losing her again? Or is it not alien to Divine Scripture, that Venus is represented embracing Mars, and being discovered by the Sun and caught by Vulcan and bound by him together with Mars in adamantine chains?

These and similar things, to us painful to recount, but to the poets and the philosophers of the Gentiles sweet to sing and recondite to expound, and to the painters suitable for their compositions, are utterly alien to Holy Scripture. For, to be silent about other matters, if any painter dares to paint two heads on one body or one head on two bodies, or the head of one creature on the body of another, like a centaur, who has the body of a horse and the head of a man, or the Minotaur, who is half bull and half man, is not this admittedly contrary to Scripture?

And what does it mean if one says: "Painters do not contradict Scripture," if not that they cannot paint anything that would seem opposed to Holy Scripture? In Holy Scripture, however, nothing vicious, nothing unsuitable, nothing impure, and nothing false can be found, except where Scripture records what the wicked said and did. But in painting, much that is false, wicked, foolish, and unsuitable can be found, and to pass over specific examples, almost everything either possible or impossible has been depicted by learned painters. By establishing these facts we have exposed the babbling of John the priest and eastern legate on this subject, as on others. Let the prudent reader take note of how false and inane is this declaration of the same priest: "Whatever Scripture treats, painters can represent." For how can all the commands of Divine Law, given by God through Moses, like that, "Hear O Israel, the Lord thy God is one God," and other things of this sort, in which there is nothing that can be painted, be represented by painters? For is painting in its vanity able to represent all the words of the prophets in which doctrines, exhortations, arguments, considerations, warnings or other like things are contained? In them one often finds, "This says the Lord," or, "God commanded," or things similar to these which may be expressed by writers rather than by painters. For which single word of the Lord and the apostles can be represented by painters? Painters therefore have a certain ability to remind one of things that have happened. Such things, however, as are understood by reason and expressed in words can be expressed not by painters, but by writers through verbal discourse. Therefore it is absurd to say, "Painters do not contradict Scripture and whatever Scripture treats, they can represent."

Questions: Why was the western attitude towards images more moderate than in the east? Why would the issue have interested Charlemagne and his court? Is Theodulf at all iconoclastic? How would he have learned so much about mythology?

16. Theodulf and the Antique Vase

Despite his seeming rejection of pagan art and ancient mythology, one can not help but sense that these things must have fascinated Theodulf of Orléans and his contemporaries. Indeed even kings such as Charles the Bald collected ancient artifacts and objets d'art such as the Cup of the Ptolemies with its rich Bacchic imagery. Perhaps the final implication of Theodulf's aesthetics was that such art, since it could have no transporting religious significance, could be appreciated for what it was, a human creation, and not an icon. In a poem written by Theodulf to counsel the missi on how to avoid corruption, he described how people tried to bribe judges with precious artifacts. Thus, Theodulf once again returns us to his preoccupation with art and mythology.

Source: trans. P.E. Dutton from Monumenta Germaniae Historica: Poetae Latini Aevi Carolini, vol. 1, ed. E. Dümmler (Berlin, 1881), pp.496, 498-499.

Too often I see that our judges relinquish the law to those
  Who bribe them with gold, fine food, and delicious drink.
Often I am keen to prevent those who wish to accept bribes,
  But there are many wishing to take, few willing to say no.

As the missi arrive in a town on their judicial tour, the crowds come out seeking satisfaction over this or that dispute.

Great crowds in gathering after gathering sought us out,
  Every age and every sex was represented there:
Small ones, old and young ones, fathers, unmarried women and men,
  Elders, youths, old women, husbands, wives, and children.
Why do I hold back? These people immediately offered us gifts,
  Thinking that if they gave, they would receive what they wanted in
    return.

They tried hard to smash our resistance with this assault,
  So that our will would collapse before the intense pressure.
One of them promises me eastern gems and a crystal
  If I can get for him the lands belonging to another.
Another showed me a huge number of golden coins,
  Some of which bore Arabic lettering,
Some, these silver, bearing Latin inscriptions;
  All to help him obtain estates, fields, and houses.
In a hushed voice yet another whispered to my assistant,
  That he should carry the following message to me:
"I possess a vase decorated with ancient figures.
  Its metal is pure and it is heavy to hold.
On its sides are engraved the crimes of Cacus:
  The skulls of men stuck on stakes and rotting flesh,
His rocks chained down and evidence of rapine and theft,
  The fields colored with the blood of men and cattle.
There Hercules in fury smashed the bones of Vulcan's son,
  Who spits out his father's fire from his beastly jaw,
As Hercules knees him in the stomach and kicks his abdomen,
  Shattering with his club the beast's smoldering throat and face.
There you can see the bulls emerging from the cave,
  Afraid that they might be dragged back again.
On the inner mouth of the vase, on a thin band,
  Can be seen a series of small figures:
The Tirinthian infant [Hercules himself] slaying the two snakes,
  And his ten labors shown in their proper sequence.
The outer surface of the vase, however, is well worn from handling,
  And a scene that once existed there is rubbed down.
There Alceus, the river Calydon, and the centaur Nessus
  Fight over the beauty of Deianira.
The poisonous robe laced with the blood of Nesseus is depicted,
  Along with the frightening fate of wretched Lichas.
As well Antaeus is seen losing his life in the powerful arms of Hercules,
  For he is prevented from touching the ground as he needed to.
This vase I shall bring to your lord—for he was calling me his lord—
  If he heeds my requests.
There are a great many people—mothers, fathers,
  Children and youths of both sexes—
Whom my father and mother left behind as free,
  And from that fact they remain free.
If I could falsify their records, the lord would own the ancient vase,
  I would own those people, and you would soon receive gifts."
Another said, "I own a rug dyed in a variety of colors,
  Which I believe a wild Arab sent.
On it a young calf can be seen following its mother and a heifer
    trailing a bull.
  The colors of the calf and heifer are alike, while those of the cow and
    the bull are the same.
You can see the beauty of the piece, and the artistic use of color,

And how a small circle is artistically joined to larger ones.
I am involved in a dispute with another man over some nice cows,
   On behalf of which I am ready to give suitable gifts:
A calf for the calves, a bull for the bulls,
   One cow for the cows, and one ox for the oxen."
Another man promises to give me some beautiful cups,
   If I grant that he need not hand over what another demands...

Oh this foul plague [of bribery] which is found everywhere,
   Oh this crime, this madness, this too savage habit,
Which lays claim to and evilly captures the whole world,
   There is no one who does not give and no one who does not take
      bribes.

Questions: Do the stories told by Theodulf sound like the real experiences of a missus, a judge traveling about the countryside and hearing cases? What did he hope to achieve with this poem?

The Cup of the Ptolemies

An eighteenth-century drawing [after Félibien] of an ancient cup carved with Bacchic images that once belonged to Charles the Bald. The king apparently donated the cup to Saint-Denis for it was Abbot Suger in the twelfth century who added the inscription to the golden base. Many ancient objects—cameos, silver plates, and stone sculptures—must have been owned by Carolingian kings and their nobles. This one survives today in the Cabinet des médailles of the Bibliothèque Nationale in Paris.

17. Six Short Poems by Theodulf

Theodulf was not only a bishop, judge, and controversialist, but one of the greatest poets of his time. Even here, however, his combative nature appears, since he sometimes used poetry as a way of attacking his rivals. In the first poem below, he seems to be attacking some unnamed poet whose sincerity and intelligence he doubted. At the court of Charlemagne such poems would have been recited and passed around for the amusement and chagrin of various parties. But Theodulf, when he wanted, could also be witty as one can see from his poem on the stolen horse.

Source: trans. P.E. Dutton from Monumenta Germaniae Historica: Poetae Latini Aevi Carolini, vol. 1, ed. E. Dümmler (Berlin, 1881), pp.464-465, 488, 551-552, 555-556.

1. On the Folly of Hypocrites and Fools Who Will Not Be Swayed from their Depravity by Sound Exhortation

Neither wit nor wisdom corrects the hypocrite and the fool,
  Teaching can not overcome the fool, nor wit the hypocrite.
It is worthless to apply learning to the fool's brain,
  The more you teach him, the stupider he becomes.
Likewise, if anyone tries to wash a rough brick,
  The more he washes, the dirtier he makes it.
How do fine words help, where there is no good will,
  Why would one sow seeds among thorny weeds?
Why would one pour golden honey into a foul pond,
  Why would one mix olive oil with excrement?
What use is a lyre, if it is played by a long-eared ass,
  Or a trumpet, if it be blown skillfully for a horned bull?
As much as the vision of the blind man improves with the rising sun,
  So too does the intelligence of the fool after good advice.
Poetry can accomplish much, but not everything,
  Though both profane and sacred literature say that it can.
It is said that Circe transformed the friends of Ulysses
  Into various wild beasts through her skillful songs.
While poetry can accomplish much, it can not heal mange,
  Nor can its gentle murmur cure one of worms.
As poetry is of no help to one who has a hernia,
  And while they are sung the whole exercise is useless,
So that work will be useless to you, you infamous hypocrite,
  If you attempt to slip in something good.
The wise king, [Christ,] has said many things about this,
  And by way of example I shall set down one:
"Though a stupid man be crushed in a mortar like a grain
  Of wheat, his indolence will not leave him."
Thus the words of our Lord; now let me set down what
  The rural folk often say so wisely about this kind of thing:
"You can not by practice or punishment make an owl into a hawk
  That will attack cranes with its talons."
Nor can a vulture take up your place, falcon,

91

Because it is slow, given to gluttony, and ponderous in flight.
The hypocrite does not desire to learn good things, but only bad,
Do you want to know why? He is [also] a fool.
Being worse than Judas, he wants to seem better than you, [Saint]
    Peter;
Fate covers over many evils with a false dress.
He thinks small things important, and many evil things to be nothing:
While he wants to deceive others, the fool deceives himself.

2. About a Stolen Horse

Often cleverness supplies what strength can not,
And often he who lacks power makes up for it with skill.
Listen to how a soldier using his brains recovered his horse,
Which was stolen in the confusion of a military camp.
Sad over the loss of the horse, he yelled at the crossroads:
"Whoever has my horse should return it immediately,
Or I will be forced, because of this, to do
What my father once did while he was in Rome."
This statement frightened everyone, and the thief, being afraid
Of what would happen to him and the people, let the horse go.
When the owner regained his horse, he was extremely happy;
Those who had been afraid before, now congratulated him.
Then they asked what he would have done if the horse had not been
    returned,
Or rather what his father had once done in Rome.
He answered, "My poor father tied the bridle and saddle
Together around his own neck and so weighed down with things, off
    he walked.
With nothing now to prod, he [still] wore spurs on his heels.
Thus once a rider, my father returned a walker.
You may believe me. I would have sadly done the same,
Had my horse not been returned to me [at once]."

3. Over the Entrance to a House

Those who wish to see crowds of people coming and going from
    Rome and Tours,
Should get up and go to Rome and Tours.
Here [on the other hand] you will see crops, vines, and pens for
    animals,
Rivers, meadows, roads, and orchards full of fruit.
When you look upon these things and take delight in them,
Remember God, who is the creator of all of them.

4. While Sitting on the Bishop's Throne

May Theodulf's presence on this throne and his every act
Be pleasing to you, merciful God, who are pleased by all good things.

For without you no good can be done, but with you much good can
    be done.
I beg you to give me the will and the power to do good here.

When great ones come before this throne, let the people stand, with
    young ones by its side,
Address those around you with pious speech.
May your mind remain humble, your heart prudent, your acts pure:
    Trust in God with constant attention, you who sit upon this throne.

Whoever you are who stand here, do not impugn any person.
    It is a crime to slander the lives of those not present.
Those of you who stand here, stop your idle chatter,
    Lest the one who sits here be forced to order you outside.

5. Sign above a Bar

May he who once changed water into the benefit of wine,
    And he who made the likeness of water into wine,
Bless our cups with his kind touch,
    And may he let us have [today] a delightful day.

6. Wide Wibod

*A wicked characterization of a certain count at court, taken from a longer poem
meant for the amusement of court and king.*

Perhaps big-boned Wibod, our hero, may hear this poem,
    And shake his thick head three or four times,
And gazing fiercely try to frighten with a look and a mutter,
    And overwhelm me with his threats, even though I am not there.
If, however, the king in all his majesty should summon him,
    Wibod would go with faltering step and knocking knees.
And his huge gut would go before him and his chest;
    He would resemble Vulcan in his feet, Jove in his voice.

*Questions: What functions would poetry have served at the Carolingian court and
how would it have bound together the intellectual and social dimension of the court
even when its members were absent, perhaps on campaign or home to church and
monastery?*

18. Theodulf of Orléans:
Precepts for the Priests of his Diocese

Theodulf was also a responsible and attentive bishop, who tried to raise the standard of learning and behavior among his priests and his flock. There is much interesting social information in the following text, including talk of schools and learning, the role of women, popular religious practices, the condition of the parish church, sin and confession, merchants, and daily diet.

Source: trans. G.E. McCracken with A. Cabaniss in Early Medieval Theology, vol. 9 of The Library of Christian Classics (Philadelphia: Westminster Press, 1957), pp.382-399; reprinted with permission.

Theodulf to Our Brothers and Fellow Presbyters, the Priests of the Diocese of Orléans

1. I beg you, my most beloved brothers, to labor with the most watchful care with regard to the progress and improvement of the people subject to you, so that, by showing them the way of salvation and instructing them by word and example, we shall bring back fruitful harvests to our Lord Jesus Christ with his aid, you from their progress, and ourselves from yours. I beg your brotherhood, also, that you read carefully these chapters which I have briefly laid down for the improvement of life, and commit them to memory, and that by reading them and the Holy Scriptures you may regulate the morals and improve the life of the people put under you, and with them, the Lord being your helper, you may strive to reach the heavenly kingdom. You ought to know truly and always to remember that we, to whom the care of governing souls has been entrusted, will render an accounting in regard to those who perish through our neglect, but in regard to those whom by word and example we shall have gained, we shall receive the reward of eternal life. For to us the Lord has said, "You are the salt of the earth." Because if a faithful people is God's food, we are the spice of his food. Know that your rank is second to our rank and is almost joined to it. For as the bishops hold in the church the place of the apostles, so the presbyters hold the place of the other disciples of the Lord. The former hold the rank of the chief priest Aaron, but the latter the rank of his sons. For this reason you ought to be mindful always of so great authority, mindful of your consecration, mindful of the holy unction which you have received in your hands, that you do not lower this authority, nor nullify your consecration, nor defile with sin the hands besmeared with holy oil, but preserving purity of heart and body, offering to the people an example of proper living, you may offer to those over whom you are in charge guidance to the heavenly kingdoms.

2. You ought to be continually reading and constantly at prayer, because the life of the righteous man is taught and equipped by reading, and by constantly reading a person is fortified against sin, according to him who said, "In my heart have I hidden thy word that I might not sin against thee." For these are the arms, namely, reading and prayer, by which the Devil is defeated; these are the means by which eternal blessedness is obtained; with these arms

vices are suppressed; upon these foods virtues are nourished.

3. But, also, if there by any interruption in reading, the hands should then be used, because "idleness is the enemy to the soul" and the ancient enemy easily carries off to vices the one whom he finds free from reading or praying. By the use of reading you will learn how you should live and how to teach others; by the use of prayer you will be able to be of value both to yourselves and to those united with you in love. By the operation of the hands and the chastisement of the body, you will both deny nourishment to the vices and will supply your own needs and have something to offer for the needs of sufferers.

4. When you come, according to custom, to a synod, carry with you clothing and books, and holy utensils, with which to perform your ministry and the office united with it. Bring with you some two or three clergy with whom you may celebrate the solemnities of the Masses, in order that it may be proved how carefully, how zealously, you perform God's service.

5. Let the bread which you offer to God for sacrifice be baked either by yourselves or by your servants in your presence, in clean and careful manner, and let it be carefully observed that the bread and the wine and the water, without which Masses cannot be celebrated, be kept very clean and handled with care, and that nothing be found in them of poor quality, nothing not approved, according to the passage of Scripture which says, "Let the fear of the Lord be with you and do everything with diligence."

6. Let women never approach the altar when the priest is celebrating Mass, but let them stand in their own places and there let the priest receive their offerings as he will offer them to God. For women ought to be mindful of their weakness and of the infirmity of their sex, and therefore fear to touch anything holy in the ministry of the church. These even laymen ought to fear, lest they undergo the punishment of Uzzah, who was willing to touch in an unusual fashion the ark of the Lord but, struck by the Lord, died.

7. Let a priest never celebrate Mass alone, because as it cannot be celebrated without the salutation of a priest, the response of the people, the admonition of the priest, and, again the response of the people, thus it ought never to be celebrated by one man alone. For there should be people to stand around him, to receive his salutation, to give responses to him, and to recall to him that saying of the Lord: "Wherever two or three shall be gathered in my name, there also am I in their midst."

8. We frequently see in churches harvested crops and hay piled up, and for this reason we wish it to be thoroughly observed that nothing should be stored in a church except ecclesiastical vestments and holy vessels and books, lest by chance if businesses are being carried on other than should be, we may hear from the Lord, "My house shall be called a house of prayer, but you have made it a brigands' cave."

9. In these regions in olden times use was made of the church for burying the dead, and often places set apart for divine worship and prepared for offering sacrifices to God were made into cemeteries or *polyandria*. For this reason I want this practice henceforth to be abandoned and no one to be buried in a church, unless perchance such a person be a priest, or some righteous man, who on account of the merit of his life acquired by living in such a way a place for his dead body. Let bodies, however, which in olden times were buried in churches never be cast out, but let the tombs which are visible be lowered more deeply into the earth, and, a paving being built over them, and no trace of the tombs being visible, let the respect for the church be preserved. Where, however, there is such a great number of corpses that this is hard to do, let this place be considered a cemetery and the altar be taken hence and set up where sacrifice can be offered to God reverently and purely.

10. You ought not to gather in the church for any other cause except for praise of the Lord and for carrying on his service. Controversies, however, and tumults, and vain speaking, and other proceedings should be entirely forbidden in that holy place. For where the name of God is invoked, sacrifice is offered to God, and as without doubt angels congregate there in great number, it is dangerous to say anything or do anything there which is not fitting to the place. For if the Lord cast out from the temple those who bought and sold the victims which were to be offered to himself, with how much greater anger will he cast out thence those who defile with lies, vain speaking, jokes, and trifles of this sort, the place set for divine worship?

11. The celebrations of Masses ought never to take place elsewhere than in a church, not in just any houses or in mean places, but in a place which the Lord shall choose, according to the passage of Scripture: "See that you do not offer your burnt offerings in any place which you see, but in a place which the Lord shall choose to place his name there."

12. Let no woman live with a presbyter in a single house. Although the canons permit a priest's mother and sister to live with him, and persons of this kind in whom there is no suspicion, we abolish this privilege for the reason that there may come, out of courtesy to them or to trade with them, other women not at all related to him and offer an enticement for sin to him.

13. You should take care to refrain from drunkenness, and to preach that the people under your care should refrain, and that you should never go through the taverns eating and drinking, nor travel around through houses and villages out of curiosity, nor attend feasts with women or with any impure persons, unless some head of a household, perhaps, shall invite you to his home and, with his wife and children, wishes to rejoice with you in spiritual joy, and to receive the refreshment of your words and to offer you carnal refreshments in the duty of love, for it is fitting that, if at any time any of the faithful gives you the refreshment of carnal foods, he should be given spiritual refreshment by you.

14. Let no presbyter persuade the faithful of the holy church of God belonging to the parish of another presbyter to leave their own church and come to his church and give their tithes to him, but let each one, content with his own church and people, never do to another what he would not wish to be done to himself, in accordance with the passage in the Gospel: "Whatsoever you wish men to do to you, do these same things to them." Moreover, whoever shall contravene these established principles, or shall attempt to struggle against these warnings of ours, let him know that he will lose his rank or that he ought to be kept in prison for a long time.

15. This we absolutely forbid, that none of you attempt to entice over or receive a cleric subordinate to another, because there is a heavy punishment for this act in the sacred canons.

16. If any presbyter shall be found to be giving a bribe or to have given one to any man, cleric or lay, so that he may steal away the church of another presbyter, let him know that for this theft and keen covetousness, either he will lose his rank or he ought to be kept in toils of prison a long time doing penance.

17. If a sick infant shall be brought to any presbyter for baptism from the parish of another, let the sacrament of Baptism by no means be denied him. Should anyone refuse to grant this office upon request, and the infant should die without the grace of Baptism, the one who did not baptize him shall know that he shall render an accounting for his soul.

18. Let no presbyter presume to employ for other purposes a chalice or a paten or any sacred utensils set apart for divine worship. For whoever drinks from a consecrated chalice anything other than the blood of Christ which is received in the sacrament, and holds a paten for any other function than for the ministry of the altar, must be deterred by the example of Belshazzar, who, when he took the vessels of the Lord for common purposes, lost his life and his kingdom as well.

19. If any of the presbyters wishes to send his nephew or other relative to school, in the church of the Holy Cross, or in the monastery of Saint Aignan, or of Saint Benedict, or of Saint Lifard, or in others of those monasteries which it has been granted us to rule, we grant him permission to do so.

20. Let the presbyters keep schools in the villages and hamlets, and if any of the faithful desires to entrust his small children to them to be taught their letters, let them not refuse to receive and teach them, but let them teach them with the greatest love, noticing what is written: "They, however, who shall be learned shall shine as the splendor of the firmament, and they who instruct many to righteousness shall shine as the stars forever and ever." When, therefore, they teach them, let them demand no fee for this instruction, nor take anything from them, except what the parents shall offer them freely through zeal for love.

21. Since, therefore, the pages of all the Holy Scriptures are crammed full of the instruments of good works, and on the fields of the Holy Scriptures can be found the arms with which vices may be suppressed and virtues nourished, it has pleased us to insert into this our prescript the opinion of a certain father [Benedict] about the instruments of good works which contains with great brevity what ought to be done and what avoided:

In the first place, to love the Lord thy God from the whole heart, the whole soul, and the whole power, then, thy neighbor as thyself. Then, not to kill; not to commit adultery; not to steal; not to covet; not to give false testimony; to honor all men, and what anyone does not want to be done to himself, not to do to another. To deny himself to himself that he may follow Christ. To castigate the body, not to embrace pleasures; to love fasting; to restore the poor; to clothe the naked; to visit the sick; to bury the dead; to be helpful in tribulation; to comfort the sorrowing. To keep oneself separate from the doings of this life. To place nothing before the love of Christ; not to execute anger; not to reserve a time for wrath; not to hold treachery in the heart; not to give false peace; not to cease loving. Not to swear, lest perchance you swear falsely. To utter truth from the heart and lips; not to return evil for evil; to do no wrong, but to suffer one done to oneself in patience. To love enemies, not to curse those who curse you, but rather to bless. To bear persecution in return for justice. Not to be proud, drunken, gluttonous, drowsy, lazy, grumbling, a disparager. To place one's hope in God. When he sees something good in himself, let him connect it with God, not himself, but let him always know that the bad has been done by himself and let him attribute it to himself. To fear the Day of Judgment; to dread hell; to desire life eternal with every spiritual desire; to keep death daily before one's eyes. To guard the actions of one's life at every hour. To know that in every place God is certainly watching. To dash at once evil thoughts as they come into one's mind to Christ and to lay them before one's spiritual elder. To guard one's mouth from evil or wicked speech; not to love to speak much; not to speak vain words or those fit to laugh at; not to love much laughter or hilarity. Gladly to hear sacred readings, to dwell continually in prayer, to confess daily in prayer to God one's own past misdeeds with tears and groans. To reform from the very misdeeds themselves of another, not fulfill the desires of the flesh. To hate one's own will, to obey the teachings of the priest and teacher in all things, even if he himself does otherwise—which God forbid—mindful of that precept of the Lord: "Do what they say, but do not do what they do." Not to wish to be called holy before one is, but first to be it so that it may be said more truly. To fulfill daily with deeds the teachings of God, to love purity, to hate no one, not to have jealousy or envy, not to love strife, to avoid self-exaltation, to respect those older and to love those younger. In love of Christ to pray for enemies. To return to peace with those who disagree before the sun sets, and never to despair of God's mercy.

See, these are the tools of the spiritual art which, when they have been employed by us unceasingly, night and day, and on the Day of Judgment are marked again, we shall be recompensed by the Lord with that reward which he himself has promised: "Which eye has not seen, nor ear heard, nor has it ascended into the heart of man, which God has prepared for those who love him."

22. The faithful must be reminded that all of them together, from the least to the greatest, should learn the Lord's Prayer and the Creed, and they must be told that upon these two propositions the whole foundation of the Christian faith rests and unless anyone shall remember these two propositions and believe them with his whole heart, and repeat them very often in prayer, he cannot be catholic. For it has been established that none shall be anointed, nor baptized, nor be lifted up from the water of that fountain, nor can he hold anyone before the bishop to be confirmed, unless he has committed to memory the Creed and the Lord's Prayer, save only those whose age has not yet taught them to speak.

23. They must be told that every day he who cannot pray more often should at least pray twice, that is, in the morning and evening, saying the Creed or the Lord's Prayer or the "O Thou who hast fashioned me," or even, "God, be merciful to me a sinner," and, "Thanks be to God," in return for the provisions of daily life and because He has deigned to create him after his own image and distinguish him from the beasts. When this has been done and God the sole creator has been adored, let him call upon the saints that they may deign to intercede on his behalf with the divine majesty. Let those near a church do this in a church; he who, however, is on a journey or for some reason is in the forests or the fields, wherever the morning or evening hour itself finds him, let him do so, knowing that God is present everywhere, as the Psalmist says: "In every place of his dominion" and "If I should ascend into heaven, thou art there."

24. On the Lord's Day, however, because on it God established light, on it rained manna in the desert, on it the Redeemer of the human race voluntarily for our salvation rose again from the dead, on it he poured forth the Holy Spirit upon his disciples, there should be so great an observance that besides prayers and the solemnization of the Masses, and those things which pertain to eating, nothing else should be done. For if there should also be need of sailing or traveling, permission is given provided that on these occasions the Mass and prayers are not passed by. Each Christian must come on the Sabbath Day to church with lights; he must come to the night vigils or to the morning office. He must come also with offerings for the solemnization of Masses. And while they come to church, no case should be pleaded or heard, no lawsuits may be held, but the time must be free for God alone, namely, in the celebration of the holy offices, and in the offering of alms, and in feasting spiritually on praise of God with friends, neighbors, and strangers.

25. They must be exhorted to love hospitality and to refuse to furnish shelter to no one, and if by chance they should supply shelter to anyone, not to take pay from him, unless perhaps the recipient gives something of his own accord. They must be told how many have pleased God through the duty

of hospitality, as the apostle says: "For by this some have pleased God, having received angels under their roof." And again, "Hospitable without grumbling." And the Lord himself will say at the Judgment, "I was a stranger and you made me your guest." Let them know also that whoever loves hospitality receives Christ in the guests. For that limitation of hospitality is not only inhuman but even cruel, in which a guest is never received unless the one who gives the hospitality is first paid, and what the Lord has bidden to do in regard to receiving the heavenly kingdom, let this be done in regard to receiving earthly possessions.

26. You must preach also that the faithful beware of perjury and to refrain from it absolutely, knowing that this is a great crime both in the Law and the Prophets, and prohibited in the Gospels. For we have heard that some people think this crime of no importance and somehow place upon perjurers a small measure of penance. They ought to know that the same penance should be imposed for perjury as for adultery, for fornication, for homicide, and for other criminal vices. If anyone, however, who has committed perjury or any criminal sin, and, being afraid of the pain of long penance, is unwilling to come to confession, he ought to be expelled from the church, from both Communion and association with the faithful, so that no one eats with him, nor drinks, nor speaks, nor takes him into his house.

27. They must be told to abstain from false testimony, knowing that this is also a very serious crime, and forbidden by the Lord himself on Mount Sinai, when the same Lord said: "Thou shalt not give false testimony," and, "A false witness will not be unpunished." Let whoever has done this know that he must be purified by such penance as was stated above concerning perjury, or he must be condemned by the same condemnation and excommunications as was stated. They must be told that it is the highest—I shall not say stupidity but—wickedness, to incur guilt for so great a crime on account of a desire for silver and gold, or clothing, or any other thing, or, as very frequently happens, because of drunkenness, so that he be kept in close confinement for seven years, or be expelled from the church, as the Lord says, "What does it profit a man if he shall gain the whole world and cause the loss of his soul?" Although he may seem more cruel to others, let him really be cruel to himself.

28. We exhort you to be ready to teach the people. He who knows the Scriptures, let him preach the Scriptures, but he who does not know them, let him at least say to the people what is very familiar, that they "turn from evil and do good, seek peace and pursue it, because the eyes of the Lord are upon the righteous and his ears are turned to their prayers," etc. No one can therefore excuse himself because he does not have a tongue which he can use to edify someone. For when he shall see anyone in error, he can at once, to the best of his ability and powers, by arguing, pleading, reproving, withdraw him from his error, and exhort him to do good works. But when, with the Lord's help, we assemble together for a synod, let each man know how to tell us how much he has accomplished. And if any man perhaps needs our aid, let him tell us this in love, and we with no less love will not

postpone bringing aid to him as we are able.

29. You ought to admonish the faithful to be constant and zealous in prayer. The prayer, however, ought to be of this kind that, when the Creed has first been said, as if the constant foundation of his faith, let him say, whoever he is, three times the "O Thou who hast fashioned me, have mercy upon me" and three times the "O God be merciful to me a sinner," and let him complete the Lord's Prayer. If, therefore, the place and time should permit, let him pray to the holy apostles and martyrs to intercede for him, and, having armed his forehead with the sign of the cross, let him lift up his hands and eyes with his heart and give thanks to God. But if the time should be insufficient to do all this, let so much suffice: "O Thou who hast fashioned me, have mercy upon me," and "O God, be merciful to me a sinner," and the Lord's Prayer, but with groaning and contrition of heart.

30. For every day in our prayer to God, either once or twice or more often as we can, we ought to confess our sins, as the prophet says: "I have acknowledged my sin to thee, and my unrighteousness I have not hid. I said, 'I shall confess against myself my unrighteous acts to the Lord,' and Thou didst forgive the guilt of my sin." For when confession has been made to the Lord in prayer with a groan and tears, the fiftieth or the twenty-fourth or the thirty-first Psalm should be recited, or others pertaining to the same subject, and so the prayer should be completed. Because the confession which we make to priests brings us also this support that, having received from them salutary advice, we wash away the stains of sins by the most wholesome observance of penance, or by silent prayers. But the confession which we make to God alone is helpful in that in so far as we are mindful of our sins, so far does the Lord remember, and, on the other hand, so far as we forget them, so far does the Lord forget them, as the prophet says: "And thy sins shall I not remember." You, however, be mindful of what David the prophet is recorded as having done, when he said, "Since I know my iniquity and my sin is ever against me."

31. Confessions should be made concerning all sins committed in either deed or thought. There are eight chief vices, from which hardly anyone can be found free. The first is gluttony, that is, voracity of the belly; second, fornication; third languor or sadness; fourth, avarice; fifth, vainglory; sixth, envy; seventh, anger; eighth, pride. When, therefore, anyone comes to confession, he should be diligently asked how or when he has committed the sin which he confesses he has done, and according to the measure of the deed ought the penance to be indicated to him. He ought also to be directed to make his confession of the eight principal vices, and the priest ought to mention each one of them by name and to receive confession about it.

32. The hungry should be filled, the thirsty should be given drink, the naked covered, the sick and those in prison visited, and the strangers taken in, as the Lord says: "For I was hungry and you gave me to eat; I was thirsty and you gave me to drink," etc. For all these things, each one ought to do spiritually in himself and fulfill them bodily in others, because all these are

almost of no value for gaining life eternal, if anyone lives lustfully, proudly, enviously, and, not to repeat each of them individually, in vice and without control, and lacks other good works. Therefore, he who sees that he does not possess Christ who said, "I am the living bread which came down from heaven," and does not have love, which is the food of the soul, is hungry indeed, but if by good works he unites himself with Christ and fills himself with the sweetness of love, he has fed his hungry self completely. He who lacks the flowing water of the teaching of the Holy Spirit and the Holy Scriptures, is thirsty, but if he waters himself on the stream of God's Word, and saturates his soul on the sweetness of the spiritual cup, he gives his thirsty self to drink. He who sees himself bare of righteousness or of other evidences of good works, and puts on righteousness or other virtues, clothes his naked self without a doubt. If he lies on the bed of his vices, and labors with the sickness of his iniquity, he is sick, indeed, but if from the mire of vices he goes to confession and through the laments of penance he is freed from the bonds of sins, and goes to the light of good works, he visits his sick self and himself in prison without a doubt. If on the highway of this life he sees himself laboring and beset with the inclemency, as it were, of the stormy weather of his vices, and that he does not have a shelter of good works, let him know that he is a man on a journey in need of shelter, but if he leads himself to a house of virtues, and betakes himself to the shelter of their protection, he receives a stranger indeed. Since he shows all these kindnesses to himself in spiritual fashion, in himself he feeds, gives to drink, clothes, visits Christ, whose member he is.

33. The faithful of God's holy church should be warned that they teach their sons and daughters to show obedience to their parents, as the Lord says: "My son, honor thy father"; for the parents also themselves ought to act moderately toward their sons and daughters, as the apostle says: "And you, parents, do not provoke your sons to wrath." For they should be told this, that if they wish to be sparing in parental affection to the hurt of their sons, the Lord does not permit these things to go unpunished unless, perhaps, worthy penitence is shown and because it is easier for the sons to accept a flogging from the parents than to incur God's anger.

34. The people should be admonished that it is true love which loves God more than oneself and a neighbour as oneself, and which does not wish to do to another except what one wishes to be done to oneself, and more things which would be long to recount. For whoever thinks love is only in drink and in food, and in the giving of aid and the receiving of things, makes an error of no moderate proportions, as the apostle says: "The kingdom of God is not food and drink." For when they do these very things with love, they are good, and to be accounted among virtues.

35. They who are intent upon business and trade are to be admonished not to desire earthly gain more than eternal life. For he who thinks more of earthly matters than about the salvation of his soul wanders far from the path of truth, and according to a certain wise man, in his lifetime has destroyed his innermost parts. Here as elsewhere must be followed the apos-

tolic saying, "And let no man transgress and wrong his neighbor in business," for God is the protector from all these things. For as by those who are excessively concerned with labor in fields and other toil to acquire food and clothing and the other things necessary for human needs, tithes and alms must be given, so this also must be done by those who engage in commerce involving these necessities. For to each man God has given skill by which he may be fed, and each man, of his skill, from which he derives the necessary support of his body, ought to supply support to his soul which is the more necessary.

36. One week before the beginning of Lent confessions should be given to the priests, penance received, quarrels reconciled, and all disputes settled, and from their hearts they ought to forgive debts, so that they may freely say, "Forgive us our debts as we also forgive our debtors." And so, entering upon the blessed Lenten season, they may, with clear and purified minds, approach the holy Easter, and through penitence may renew themselves, which is a second baptism. For as Baptism cleanses sins, so does penitence. And because after Baptism the sinner cannot be baptized again, this remedy of penitence has been given by the Lord that through it in place of Baptism sins committed after Baptism may be washed away. For the Holy Scriptures show that sins can be forgiven in seven ways: First, in Baptism, which has been given on account of the forgiveness of sins. Secondly, by martyrdom, according to the words of the psalmist: "Blessed is he to whom the Lord imputes no sin," because according to what the same David says, "Blessed are those whose iniquities are forgiven and whose sins are covered." Sins are forgiven through Baptism; they are covered through penitence; they are imputed not through martyrdom. Thirdly, by alms, according to Daniel, who says to the heathen king Nebuchadnezzar, "Redeem thy sins with alms in mercies to the poor," and this: "Water quenches burning fire and alms quench sin." And the Lord in the Gospel: "But give alms and behold, all things pure are yours." Fourthly, if anyone forgives the sins of the one who sins against him, according to this: "Forgive and it will be forgiven to you," and this: "So also your Father will forgive you your sins, if you forgive anyone from your hearts." Fifthly, if through his preaching anyone should, by the exercise of good works, convert others from their error, in accordance with what the apostle says: "If anyone should make a sinner to turn from the error of his way, he will save his soul from death, and will cover a multitude of sins." Sixthly, through love, according to this: "The love of God covers a multitude of sins" through Jesus Christ our Lord. Seventhly, through penitence, according to what David says: "I turned in my affliction, while it is transfixed with a thorn."

37. Lent itself, however, ought to be kept with highest observance, so that in it the fast never be broken except on the Lord's Days, which are excepted from fasting, because those days are the tithes of our year, which we ought to pass through with all devotion and sanctity. Let there be in them no occasion for breaking the fast because at another time it is customary to dispense with the fasting for the sake of love, but this should not be then. Because at another time, whether to fast or not is based on the wish and

judgment of the individual, but at this time a failure to fast is to transcend the will of God. And to fast at another time is to get a reward for the one who fasts, but at this time, except for the sick and the little children, whoever does not fast shall gain punishment for himself because these same days the Lord has consecrated to holy fasting through Moses and through Elijah and through himself.

38. On the days of the fast, alms should be given, so that anyone, if he does not fast as he ought, may distribute food and drink to the poor, because to fast and to keep the food for lunch until dinner is an increase, not of recompense, but of foods.

39. Many who think they are fasting have the habit of eating as soon as they hear the bell for nones, but they should not believe that they are fasting if they should eat before the office of vespers. For one must go to Masses, and hear the solemnization of Masses and office of vespers, and also give alms, before approaching food. If anyone should be so limited of necessity that he cannot attend Mass, he should break his fast having shown respect to the vesper hour and having completed his prayer.

40. On those days there should be abstention from every pleasure and they must live soberly and chastely. He who can abstain from eggs, cheese, fish, and wine, gains great credit for virtue; he, however, who cannot abstain from them, either because some illness comes or some sort of work, may make use of them. Only let the fasting continue until the celebration of vespers; and let him take wine, not to get drunk, but to restore his body. To abstain, however, from cheese, milk, butter, and eggs, and not to fast [on wine], is foolishness to the highest degree, and bereft entirely of rationality. For getting drunk on wine and profligacy are forbidden, not milk and eggs. The apostle does not say, "Do not take milk and eggs," but "Do not get drunk on wine in which there is profligacy."

41. On each Lord's Day in Lent the sacraments of the body and blood of Christ should be taken by all except those who are excommunicated, and on the Lord's Supper, and on the day of preparation, on the eve of the Passover, and on the day of the Lord's resurrection, should be communicated to absolutely all, and all those days of the Passover week should be kept with equal sanctity.

42. On these days of fasting there should be no lawsuits, no quarrels, but one should continue in the praise of God and doing necessary work. For the Lord reproves those who engage in quarrels and lawsuits in the time of Lent and who demand debts from debtors, speaking through the prophet: "Behold, on the day of your fasting your pleasures are to be found, and you keep looking for all your debtors. Behold, you fast for lawsuits and for quarrels, and you strike wickedly with your fist."

43. One should abstain from wives on these most consecrated days, and live chastely and piously, so that these holy days be passed with heart and body

made holy, and so arrive at the holy day of Pascha because fasting is of little value if defiled by the marital act, and what prayer, vigils, and alms do not recommend.

44. The people must be admonished to approach the most sacred and holy sacrament of the Lord's body and blood with no delay and never to refrain from it, but with all diligence to choose a time when for a little they abstain from the marital act and cleanse themselves from vices, adorn themselves with virtues, be continually in alms giving and prayers, and so approach so great a sacrament. Because, as it is dangerous for an impure person to approach so great a sacrament, so also it is dangerous to abstain from it for a long time. Except for the list of those who are excommunicated, let them take Communion, not when they please but at specified times, and for those who live devoutly and in holy fashion let them do this almost every day.

45. Let it be ordained that when special Masses are celebrated by priests on Lord's Days, they should not take place in public in such a way that the people can hear them and particularly so that they do not draw themselves away from the public solemnization of Masses according to the canon at the third hour. For some people have a very bad practice in that when, on Lord's Days or on other holy days, they look to hear Masses—they may be Masses for the dead or for other purposes, which are privately celebrated by priests—and then from early morning through the whole day they give themselves to drunkenness and feasting and vain speaking, rather than to serving God.

46. On account of which care must be taken that all come together in public to holy mother church to hear the solemnization of Masses and preaching. Likewise, it is decreed that in a city in which a bishop has been established, all the presbyters and people, both of the city and of its environs, in vestments, should stand with devout heart at that Mass itself until the benediction of the bishop and Communion, and afterward, if they wish, they may with permission revert to their own rank, after the benediction and Communion have been received. And the priests should diligently watch out that neither in the oratories nor the monasteries in the countryside, nor in churches in the countryside, should they presume to celebrate Masses before the second hour except with great caution, and with the doors locked, so that the people may not at all be able to take occasion to absent themselves from the public solemnities, from the Mass or preaching of the bishop, but all of them, the priests of the suburbs as well as those assigned to the city, and all the people, as we said above, may come together with them for the public celebration of Masses, and nobody except little children and the sick, though they may have heard a Mass, both in the cities and in the parish churches, may presume to eat and drink before the completion of the public office.

If anyone should try to transgress these statutes, let him be brought before the canonical judges until he give satisfaction.

Questions: Is this text an example of the way in which Charlemagne's interest in the fundamental reform of society penetrated downwards? What would have hindered and compromised that reform movement? What is the basic thrust of Theodulf's treatise and what standard of conformity could he hope to achieve?

19. Letters of Alcuin

Alcuin was born just a few years before Bede died and was in many ways his intellectual heir. While Charles Martel and Pepin the Short were undercutting and overthrowing the Merovingian house, Alcuin was successively a student, teacher, and librarian of York. In 781 at Parma Alcuin chanced to meet Charlemagne who invited him to take charge of his palace school. Alcuin thus became the central figure in Charlemagne's drive for educational reform. In 796 he was made the abbot of the great monastery of Saint Martin at Tours, where in his last years he became involved in a dispute with Theodulf and the royal court. Alcuin died in 804. Over three hundred of his letters survive, most dating from the last decade of his life when he had a stable of secretaries and a thriving and influential scriptorium at Tours.

Source: trans. S. Allott in Alcuin of York, c. A.D. 732 to 804 (York: William Sessions, 1974), pp.11-13, 36-38, 72-73, 78, 80-82, 91-92, 120-121, 123-126; reprinted with permission.

1. To the King on Books, Learning, and Old Age (796)

Alcuin was particularly energetic in promoting the interests of Saint-Martin's and in the following letter he may be reminding the king of the understanding they had reached. For around 795 Alcuin had begun to talk of returning to Britain, but had been talked out of it by Charlemagne with the offer of the abbacy of Saint-Martin. In this letter, Alcuin may be suggesting to the king that his students should be allowed to travel to Britain to copy the books that he would have seen had he gone home himself. He is also not slow to remind Charles of what he had accomplished on the continent.

To the most virtuous, excellent and honorable King David [the nickname for Charles], Flaccus [Horace's name served as a nickname for Alcuin] Albinus sends good wishes for eternal joy in Christ.

The sweetness of your affection fully restores the longing of my heart every hour and minute; your gracious appearance, which I looked upon so often with love, happily fills all the veins of my memory with great joy, and the name and sight of your goodness is laid up like a treasure in my heart.

So it is a great joy to me to hear the happiness of your good fortune. I sent this boy, my little retainer, as you know, for the news, so that I might praise the mercy of our Lord Jesus Christ for his acts of grace in your majesty's recovery. Not only should I, the most insignificant servant of our Savior, share the joy in your majesty's welfare, but the whole church of God should give thanks to almighty God in a united hymn of love, since he has in his merciful generosity given one so good, wise and just to rule and protect the Christian people in this last dangerous period of history, who is to make every effort to correct the wrong, strengthen the right and raise the holy, rejoicing in spreading the name of the Lord God of heaven, through many areas of the earth and trying to light the lamp of the catholic faith in distant parts. This, most sweet David, is your glory, praise and reward in the judgment of the great day and in the eternal company of the saints, that you diligently strive to correct those entrusted to you by God and lead souls long blinded by the darkness of ignorance to the light of the true faith. God will always reward goodwill and effort, but he who labors more in God's work will receive more reward in God's kingdom. This life passes quickly, and once gone does not return; but God's ineffable goodness has provided for the human race to work briefly and be crowned forever. So we should value our time, and not carelessly lose what we can possess forever through the practice of a good life. Nor shall we be able to love anything as much on earth as blessed rest in heaven. He who wishes for that should strive to deserve it by his good works now. The door of the kingdom of heaven is open to all equally, but it is those who hurry to enter with a harvest of goodness who are allowed in.

I, your Flaccus, am busy carrying out your wishes and instructions at Saint-Martin's, giving some the honey of the holy Scriptures, making others drunk on the old wine of ancient learning, beginning to feed others on the fruits of grammar, while to some I propose to reveal the order of the stars, like the painted roof of a great man's house. I become many things to many men, in order to train many for the advance of the holy church of God and the honor of your imperial kingdom, that the grace of almighty God may not be idle in me nor your generosity unavailing.

But I, your servant, need some of the rarer learned books which I had in my own country [Northumbria] through the devoted efforts of my own teacher and also through some labor on my own part. I say this that you may agree to send some of our students to get everything we need from there and bring the flowers of Britain back to Francia, that as well as the walled garden in York there may be off-shoots of paradise bearing fruit in Tours, and the south wind may come and blow through the gardens by the Loire and waft their fragrance abroad....

Philosophers tell us that nothing is more necessary for ruling a people, nothing better for developing a life on the best principles than philosophy, discipline, and education....

My lord king, encourage all the young men of the palace to [take up] earnest study and the daily practice of wisdom, that while in the bloom of life they may so advance as to bring honor upon their grey hairs and come to eternal happiness. I shall not be slow to sow seeds of wisdom among your servants in these parts, as far as my poor talent allows.... In the morning [of my life], at the height of my powers, I sowed the seed in Britain, now in the evening, when my blood is growing cold, I am still sowing in Francia, hoping both will grow, by the grace of God.

In my broken state of health I am comforted by what Jerome said in his letter to Nepotianus: "Almost all the physical powers change in the old, wisdom alone increasing while the others decrease." A little later he says: "Those who have studied liberal arts in youth and meditated day and night on the law of the Lord become more learned in old age, gaining experience and

wisdom as time passes and gathering the sweet fruits of their old studies."
He who wishes can read more in this letter in praise of wisdom and the
study of the ancients and understand how eager the ancients were to flourish
in the accomplishment of wisdom....

2. To the King on the State of Learning in His Day (799)

*Readers might like to compare Alcuin's desire for right reading and writing with
Charlemagne's own program. Indeed Tours was to be one of the chief scriptoria
from which the reformed script, Caroline Minuscule, was to spread over northern
Europe. One also sees here how men like Alcuin were called upon to seek out rare
books and have them copied.*

To the most religious and excellent lord, King David, greetings from Flaccus,
whom love's dart has wounded.

I thank you, good lord, for having the book which I sent you on your instructions read in your hearing and its errors noted and sent back for correction. Yet you could have corrected it better; a second opinion is so often
more valuable than that of the author.

You have not done all that love required, as you have not noted unschol-
arly statements or unorthodox expressions; for I have a suspicion that your
letter hints that you do not approve of all that you read, since you have
ordered a defense of the work to be sent to you, though my poor words
could have no more suitable defender or reviser than yourself. The sponsor
of the work should defend the writer.

Speed of thought often results in spelling and punctuation being less ac-
curate than the rules of grammar demand, while the reader's concentration
anticipates his eyes. Nor, when I am weary with headaches, can I weigh the
words which pour out in dictation—he who would not take the blame for
someone else's carelessness, should not blame them for it.

I have not read the debate of Felix with the Saracen, nor can we find it
here; in fact I have not heard the title before. But when I made further
inquiries if any of our people had heard of it, I was told that Bishop Leidrad
of Lyons might have a copy. So I sent a messenger in haste to the bishop
in the hope that it may be found there and sent to you with all speed.

When I went to Rome as a young man and spent some days in the royal
city of Pavia, a certain Jew called Lull had a debate with Master Peter [of
Pisa], and in the same city I heard that there was a written record of the
debate. This was the Peter who made his name as a teacher of grammar in
your palace. Perhaps your Homer [the nickname for Angilbert of Saint-Ri-
quier] has heard something about it from him.

I have sent you some forms of expression supported by examples from
the Fathers and also some arithmetical curiosities to amuse you on the empty
sheet you sent me, that what appeared before me naked should return
clothed, for I thought it proper for my writing to grace a sheet honored by
your seal. Our friend and helper, Beselel [the nickname for Einhard], will
be able to supply further examples of the expressions from the Fathers, if
required, and can also look up the problems in an arithmetic book.

Punctuation adds greatly to the style of sentences, but its use has almost been lost by copyists owing to their lack of education. It seems to need restoring in the work of copyists, just as fine scholarship and sound learning in general are beginning to be revived through your noble efforts.

I too, however ill-equipped, battle daily against ignorance in Tours. Do you have the boys at court taught to record as elegantly as possible the clear and eloquent thought you express, that the documents that circulate in the king's name may display the quality of the king's learning?

3. On the Sack of Lindisfarne by the Northmen in 793

When the Northmen attacked the coastline of Northumbria in the 790s Alcuin was deeply shocked. His analysis of the Sack of Lindisfarne is interesting, in part because of its incomplete and perhaps contradictory character. He suspected that some sin of the monks (hence all the talk about dress, drink, and right behavior) might explain why God and the saints had allowed the monastery to be pillaged, but he also wanted to argue that all disasters in this life belonged to the world of transitory things. Thus he hoped to lift the minds of the suffering brothers above this troubled world to the kingdom of heaven. It must have been at about this time that Charlemagne began to set up coastal defenses on the continent.

To Bishop Higbald and the whole community of the church of Lindisfarne, good sons in Christ of a most blessed father, the holy Bishop Cuthbert, Alcuin, a deacon, sends greeting and blessing in Christ.

When I was with you your loving friendship gave me great joy. Now that I am away your tragic sufferings daily bring me sorrow, since the pagans have desecrated God's sanctuary, shed the blood of saints around the altar, laid waste the house of our hope and trampled the bodies of the saints like dung in the street. I can only cry from my heart before Christ's altar: "O Lord, spare thy people and do not give the Gentiles thine inheritance, lest the heathen say, 'Where is the God of the Christians?'"

What assurance can the churches of Britain have, if Saint Cuthbert and so great a company of saints do not defend their own? Is this the beginning of the great suffering, or the outcome of the sins of those who live there? It has not happened by chance, but is the sign of some great guilt.

You who survive, stand like men, fight bravely and defend the camp of God. Remember how Judas Maccabaeus cleansed the Temple and freed the people from a foreign yoke. If anything needs correction in your way of gentleness, correct it quickly. Recall your patrons who left you for a season. It was not that they lacked influence with God, but they were silent, we know not why.

Do not glory in the vanity of dress; that is cause for shame, not boasting, in priests and servants of God. Do not blur the words of your prayers by drunkenness. Do not go out after the indulgences of the flesh and the greed of the world, but stand firm in the service of God and the discipline of the monastic life, that the holy fathers whose sons you are may not cease to protect you. May you remain safe through their prayers, as you walk in their footsteps. Do not be degenerate sons, having such fathers. They will not cease protecting you, if they see you following their example.

Do not be dismayed by this disaster. God chastises every son whom he accepts, so perhaps he has chastised you more because he loves you more. Jerusalem, a city loved by God was destroyed, with the Temple of God, in Babylonian flames. Rome, surrounded by its company of holy apostles and countless martyrs, was devastated by the heathen, but quickly recovered through the goodness of God. Almost the whole of Europe has been denuded with fire and sword by Goths and Huns, but now by God's mercy is as bright with churches as the sky with stars and in them the offices of the Christian religion grow and flourish. Encourage each other, saying, "Let us return to the Lord our God, for he is very forgiving and never deserts those who hope in him."

And you, holy father, leader of God's people, shepherd of a holy flock, physician of souls, light set on a candle-stick, be a model of all goodness to all who can see you, a herald of salvation to all who hear you. May your community be of exemplary character, to bring others to life, not to damnation. Let your dinners be sober, not drunken. Let your clothes befit your station. Do not copy the men of the world in vanity, for vain dress and useless adornment are a reproach to you before men and a sin before God. It is better to dress your immortal soul in good ways than to deck with fine clothes the body that soon rots in dust. Clothe and feed Christ in the poor, that so doing you may reign with Christ. Redemption is a man's true riches. If we loved gold we should send it to heaven to be kept there for us. We have what we love: let us love the eternal which will not perish. Let us love the true, not the transitory, riches. Let us win praise with God, not man. Let us do as the saints whom we praise. Let us follow in their footsteps on earth, to be worthy to share their glory in heaven. May divine goodness keep you from all adversity and bring you, dear brothers, to the glory of the heavenly kingdom with your fathers.

When our lord King Charles returns from defeating his enemies, by God's mercy, I plan to go to him, and if I can then do anything for you about the boys who have been carried off by the pagans as prisoners or about any other of your needs, I shall make every effort to see that it is done.

Fare well, beloved in Christ, and be ever strengthened in well-doing.

4. Advice to the King on Converting the Saxons

Alcuin spoke against the forcible conversion of the Saxons and other peoples in 796. Like Boniface, he believed that conversion, if sincere, should be a slow and thoughtful process of acceptance. Charlemagne's experience with Saxon conversion and Saxon treachery was, however, not at all gentle and not always thoughtful; in 782 he had 4500 Saxon rebels hung at Verden.

To Charles, king of Germany, Gaul, and Italy, the most excellent and devout lord, and to the holy preachers of God's word, Albinus, a humble son of mother church, sends Christian greetings.

Glory and praise to God the Father and our Lord Jesus Christ, that through your good intent and devoted service to the faith by the power of the Holy

Spirit he has spread the kingdom of Christianity and the knowledge of the
true God and brought many peoples far and wide from the errors of irreligion
to the way of truth! What glory will be yours, most blest king, when all
these, who have been turned from the worship of idols to know the true
God by your good care, follow you as you stand in happy case before the
judgment seat of our Lord Jesus Christ and your reward of eternal joy is
increased through them all!

With what generous devotion to the spread of Christ you have worked to
soften the hardness of the unhappy Saxon people with counsel on true salvation! But divine election does not seem yet to have been accorded them,
so many of them still remain in the filth of their evil ways, to share the
Devil's damnation.

But it has pleased Christ to reward your good purpose with greater glory
and praise. He has brought the Hun peoples, who have long been feared
for their ferocity and might, beneath your warlike scepter to his honor, and
with prevenient grace has bound their necks, so long haughty, to the yoke
of faith, pouring the light of truth on minds that have been blind from
ancient times.

Now in your wise and godly concern may you provide good preachers for
the new people, sound in conduct, learned in the faith and full of the teaching
of the Gospel, intent on following the example of the apostles in the preaching of the word of God. For they gave their hearers milk, as the apostle
Paul said: "I fed you milk to drink, not meat, as babies in Christ...", meaning
that new converts to the faith must be fed on gentler teaching as babies on
milk, lest minds too weak for harder teaching vomit what they have imbibed....

Therefore you should consider in your wisdom whether it is right to impose the yoke of tithes upon a simple people who are beginners in the faith,
making a full levy from every house. We should ask if the apostles, who
were taught by the Lord himself and sent out to preach to the world, required
the payment of tithes in any place. We know it is good for our property to
be tithed, but it is better to lose the tithe than destroy the faith. Even we
who have been born and brought up in the catholic faith find it hard to
agree to a full tithing of our property; how much harder it is for their tender
faith, their infant will and greedy spirit. When their faith is strengthened
and they are established in the Christian life, they may, as adults, be given
harder teaching, which minds soundly based in Christianity will not reject.

Careful thought must also be given to the right method of preaching and
baptizing, that the washing of the body in baptism be not made useless by
lack in the soul of an understanding of the faith... The Lord told his disciples
in the Gospel, "Go, teach all nations, baptizing them in the name of the
Father, Son, and Holy Spirit." The blessed Jerome in his commentary on
Saint Matthew's Gospel explained the order of this commandment as follows:
"First they teach all nations, and then dip them in water. The body cannot
receive the sacrament of baptism if the soul has not first received the truth
of the faith...." So infants who have not the use of reason but are guilty
through the sins of others, can be saved in the rite of baptism through the
faith and confession of others, if they keep the faith that has been professed
for them, when they come of age....

So I believe we should be careful to keep the order in teaching adults which Saint Augustine laid down in his book, 'On Teaching the Catechism to the Uneducated.' A man must first be taught about the immortality of the soul and the future life and rewards for good and evil and both kinds of eternity, later the particular sins for which he must suffer eternal punishment with the Devil and the good deeds for which he may enjoy everlasting glory with Christ. Then belief in the Holy Trinity must be carefully taught and the coming of the Son of God, our Lord Jesus Christ, into the world for the saving of mankind must be expounded, with the mystery of his passion, the truth of his resurrection and ascension into heaven and his coming to judge all nations; also the resurrection of our bodies and the eternity of punishment for the wicked and reward for the good must later be instilled in the novice's mind. After this preparation and strengthening in the faith he should be baptized. The teaching of the Gospel must be given in preaching frequently at suitable times, till he grows into the perfect man and is made a worthy dwelling for the Holy Spirit and a perfect son of God in works of mercy, as our heavenly Father is perfect, who lives and reigns in the perfect Trinity and blessed unity, God and Lord, world without end, amen. The grace of our Lord Jesus Christ be always with you.

5. To the King on the Meaning of Swords in Scripture

One of the many duties of client-scholars was to supply the king with answers to a wide variety of questions, for Charlemagne was not a disinterested patron. He wanted to improve education within his kingdom in part so that he might cultivate the administrative service of learned men. Here Charlemagne seems to have passed along to Alcuin a question sent to him by some noble about the meaning of certain references to swords by Christ. Alcuin suspected that the question was one that interested Charlemagne himself. How does Alcuin steer the question in another direction?

To his lovingly respected and respectfully loved lord, King David, Flaccus Albinus, sends his greetings in loyalty and affection.

On receiving your letter telling of your good health so dear to us and your prosperity so necessary to the whole Christian empire, I poured forth the feelings of my heart in thankfulness to Christ, the most merciful King, earnestly praying his goodness with all who share our spiritual labors that he guard, guide, and extend your peaceful and loving power to the advancement of his church and give lasting prosperity to the government of the holy empire.

In your learned letter I see your intention is to rouse me from my idleness by shrewd questions, as is your custom. I realize that your questions are more to teach than to learn, for I see you write, "To ask good questions is to teach," and after a similar statement of this truth you add, "Dear teacher in Christ, I must tell you the question about the Gospel put to us not by a cleric, but by a layman. We have postponed answering him for the present, not that we could not answer his point," etc.

I am really very thankful that laymen sometimes produce questions on the Gospel, though I once heard a certain wise man say that it was not for laymen but for clergy to learn the Gospel. Yes, but all things have their time, and often a later hour allows what an earlier hour could not. This layman, whoever he is, is wise in heart, though he has a soldier's hands. Your majesty should have many like him.

But let us turn our pen to answer the question to the satisfaction of the questioner, if our poor ability can satisfy so distinguished a mind. The problem as set in your excellency's letter was as follows, to quote the actual words: "There is a place in the Gospel of Luke where the Lord, being about to go to his passion, told his disciples to sell his tunic and purse and buy a sword. When he was told they had two swords, he said it was enough. We think Peter used one of them in cutting off Malchus's ear. Then the Lord said to him, 'Put your sword back in its sheath, for all who take the sword will perish by the sword.' How is it consistent to say those who take the sword will perish by the sword, when he has just told them to sell their tunic and buy a sword? If the sword is the word of God, and the Lord meant the word of God when he told them to buy a sword, how is it reasonable that all who receive the word of God should perish by the word of God?"

The solution is easy if the context of the passage in each evangelist is considered and different meanings of 'sword' are understood. For 'sword' does not have the same meaning everywhere.... It means 'division' when he says: "I have not come to bring peace but a sword," that is, to separate the good from the bad. But it means punishment where we read: "He does not carry a sword in vain, for he punishes whose who do evil"....

The sword in Matthew means the vengeance of our injuries. He who follows this will die in his wickedness.... So he tells us to put it back in the sheath of our hearts, that there each may forgive his brother from his heart....

But let us see what the sword in Luke could mean, which was the original question. This is surely the word of God which we must buy, selling all the baggage of the worldly life, and fight manfully with it against all the plots of the old serpent.... But the question proposed raises another.... If the sword is, as we said, the word of God, why did it cut off an opponent's ear, when the word of God usually comes by hearing to the secret couches of the heart?.... This simply means that the ear of infidelity is cut off, that it may be healed anew by the touch of divine grace.... Why did the Lord himself heal his persecutor, but because every preacher in the church of Christ does not cease to heal his enemies by the word of goodness?....

I hear that a certain reprehensible practice exists among the churches of Christ which your wise authority can easily correct.... For they say the bishops have forbidden priests and deacons [Alcuin himself remained a deacon, never becoming a priest] to preach in the churches.... Let them cease to keep as a special right what can be for the greater profit of the souls of very many.... Why in churches everywhere are homilies read by clergy of every rank? What is a homily but preaching? It is strange to allow reading but not interpretation to enable all to understand. Thus those who hear will have no profit and Virgil's words will come true, "He gives sound without sense."

We have seen in some places the altars of God carelessly left unroofed and fouled with the droppings of birds and the urine of dogs. This you can easily correct through the bishops, that the table of the Lord may be treated with due reverence or be removed to a greater church....

6. To his Patron with Advice on a Hostile Duke (800-801)

Many of Alcuin's letters cover a number of topics. Often he was a go-between for petitioners who believed that he could put in a good word for them with the king.

...I have already made my humble entreaty through your servant Candidus, which I beg you to receive in a spirit of mercy. I have entrusted my suggestions to his safe keeping and he will pass them on faithfully to you.

But new events urge me to write anew in love. I have heard news that I cannot speak of without grief and tears, that my very dear friend, your faithful Megenfrid, has died in Benevento. So I have been asked by the brothers of Saint-Peter's [in Tours] to send a letter on behalf of the chapels that have an ancient connection with this church, that you may earn merit from some of them, if you approve, and similarly for the porch within the city walls, from which a decent dwelling-place could be built for the brothers of Saint-Peter. You will decide on all this what is pleasing to God and in keeping with your name and goodness.

But a much more important reason arises for Christians to offer up their humble entreaties before you: first, that you should not be angry with my loyal affection, for I recognize sincerely how much I owe to your generosity; secondly, and I ask this in heart-felt conviction, that you should reflect on what is pleasing to God and profitable to the Christian people over the invasion of Benevento, lest greater loss be suffered there by your faithful subjects. You know well how divine providence fought for you, carrying off the father [Duke Archisus of Benevento] and brother [Ramualdus, both of whom died in 787] of this wicked man [Duke Grimoald] in a moment of time. He will suffer in the same way, we believe, if it is His holy will that he should perish, and that without any loss of your loyal servants. Such things may well happen in time, and better by diplomacy than by open attack. The more a man humbles himself beneath the hand of almighty God, the quicker He avenges the injuries of His servants—for he says, "Vengeance is mine, I will repay."

7. On the Famous March to Imperial Rome (799)

The degree of Alcuin's role in the promotion of imperial ideals in the period between 798 and 800 has always been difficult to judge. Still this letter suggests that he was kept well informed about the drift of events and that he was not opposed to Charlemagne's flirtation with the idea of empire. Indeed he thought it Charlemagne's duty to restore the assaulted pope to full dignity. Yet Alcuin himself wanted nothing to do with marching off to Rome, despite Charlemagne's apparent invitation.

...Spare your Christian people and defend the churches of Christ, that the blessing of the heavenly King may strengthen you against the pagans. We read that one of the old poets [Virgil], in writing in praise of the ideal rulers of the Roman Empire, said, if I remember rightly, "To spare his subjects and defeat the proud," a line which Saint Augustine expounded with much praise in his *City of God*. Yet we should heed the teaching of the gospel more than the poetry of Virgil. Our Lord said, "Blessed are the merciful, for they shall obtain mercy," and elsewhere, "Be merciful, as your heavenly father is merciful."

It was so like your Christian goodwill to inform me of the remarkable recovery of the pope. Every Christian people should rejoice in this mercy of divine protection and praise the holy name of our God, who never deserts those who hope in him; for he has restrained the hands of the wicked from carrying out their evil will, though they wished in the blindness of their hearts to put out their own light and wickedly plotted to deprive themselves of their true head.

You will consider in your wisdom what should be done about them, knowing well what punishment is appropriate to each for what he has done and how the good shepherd, freed from the hands of his enemies by divine protection, can serve Christ safely in his see.

As to the strictures in your kind letter on Flaccus's silence, it is the heat of August that has made him sluggish, not any intended laziness.

About our boys whom you command to go to Rome in their father's place, please tell me when, where and with what companions they should meet your majesty. I see you write in your letter, "They can perform your service for you while you are resting." I grant that with your bidding and help they are equal to the burden of my work, but I do not yet yield to them the remuneration which you used to give me so generously. For Moses, whom you quote to me as an example, divided the spoils among the people himself after the battle was over and the Amalekites routed, and when Syria had been conquered under Joab's generalship David dedicated the gold and jewels in the temple and set the crown of the king of the Ammonites on his own head, though Joab had borne the heat of the battle.

As to your wish to reproach me for preferring the sooty roofs of Tours to the gilded citadels of Rome, I know you have read Solomon's proverb: "It is better to sit in the corner of a loft than in a house shared with a quarrelsome woman." And if I may say so, swords hurt my eyes more than soot. For Tours with its sooty roofs remains at peace through God's grace and your kindly foresight. But Rome is in the grip of fratricidal strife and incessantly poisoned by feuds, so that your majesty has had to leave your pleasant home in Germany to check this ruinous infection.

We bewail your absence and follow your journey with unceasing prayers, humbly beseeching divine mercy that he may lead you and yours in health with all success and bring you back rejoicing. I do not at all think that you would forget to write to me. But write more often to comfort me and I will kiss your letters and read them again and again and keep them ever fresh in the treasury of my heart.

Beloved David, may Christ grant to you
A happy reign and happiness in heaven.

8. He Explains his Involvement in the Case of an Escaped Convict

When, in 802, Alcuin became involved in an ugly incident at Tours, he wrote to two of his former students who were at the court in the hope that they might explain his side of the story to the emperor. The conflict brought Alcuin and his old nemesis Theodulf into direct conflict, but Charlemagne seems to have sided with the bishop of Orléans.

To Candidus and Nathanael, his dear sons in Christ, Albinus sends greetings.

...The venerable father, Bishop Theodulf, is in dispute over an escaped prisoner with some of your brothers of Saint-Martin's, who pray for you faithfully. This prisoner, after many different punishments, suddenly escaped from jail and sought sanctuary in the church of Saint Martin, an outstanding confessor of Christ; he confessed his sins, begged for reinstatement, appealed to Caesar, and demanded access to his holy presence. We surrendered him to the men sent by the said bishop. But on their departure they let him go as he stood before the doors of the church, apparently because an ambush had been laid on their route. After this a large number of men belonging to the same bishop came in a hostile manner, as we have discovered. Eight leaders entered the church with our bishop [Archbishop Joseph] on a Sunday. They...seized the prisoner, profaned the house of God, and insulted Saint Martin the confessor of Christ, actually breaking in past the altar rails. The brothers drove them out from before the altar. If they say otherwise, they lie. Not one of them bowed his head before the altar of God at that time.

It was noised in the city that enemies had come from Orléans to profane the sanctuary of Saint Martin, for they knew the fellows lodging in the hamlets had come from there. Immediately the beggars gathered from every part of the city, ready to defend their protector; everywhere was panic and uproar. Our brothers rescued the aforesaid bishop's men from their hands, so that they should come to no harm, and drove the people out of the church.

I know the above-named prelate [Theodulf] will bring many accusations against our brothers, exaggerating what happened and adding much that did not happen, as his letters say. So I urgently lay it upon you, my dear sons, to prostrate yourselves before the feet of my lord David, the most just and serene emperor, begging that when the bishop comes you may make our defense and dispute with him whether it be just for a prisoner to be forcibly haled from a church to face the very punishment from which he sought sanctuary, and whether it be right for one who appeals to Caesar not to be brought to Caesar, and whether it be lawful for a penitent who confesses his misdeeds to be robbed of his goods to his last bootlace, and whether the saying of the Lord, "Mercy is exalted over justice," is being observed.

In such action, on the contrary, justice is exalted over mercy. Yet mercy is many times praised by our Lord Jesus Christ himself, as in the beatitudes in the Gospel: "Blessed are the merciful, for they shall obtain mercy." ...We should remember we are servants of one who prayed for his crucifiers when he was led to the cross.

How can the venerable father say that a prisoner who is a sinner should not be received in church? If sinners are not to enter church, perhaps no priest will be found to say Mass or sing the responses, except one who has just been baptized; for the apostle John says, "If we say we have no sin, we deceive ourselves and the truth is not in us."

Again we find in the good bishop's letter that the same prisoner is called a devil, not a man. Think of the apostle's words, "Do not judge before the time."

9. He Defends Himself to the Emperor in the Same Case

Alcuin was caught between several competing forces and probably could not win in this incident. On the one side stood Charlemagne and Theodulf who cannot have been happy at the idea of prisoners fleeing from one city to another; on the other stood a group of Turonian citizens who may have had personal or family connections with the escaped man (why else would he have run there?) and who were certainly offended by the violation of their church and city by armed men from Orléans. And so Alcuin backtracked, all the while claiming that he was in the right and that his actions had all along been above reproach.

To the most excellent and honorable lord Charles, king and emperor, the most victorious, great, good and serene Augustus, his pensioner Albinus wishes present prosperity and future joy forever in our Lord God Christ.

My letter must at once give whole-hearted thanks to our Lord God for your health and safety which is so necessary to me and to all Christians. Next I must beg the mercy of your great goodness upon my knees with contrite heart and tears for the brothers of Saint-Martin, to whose service you appointed me in the kindness of your heart, unworthy though I am.

I call God to witness that I have never known them to be as they are described by some, who are more ready to accuse than to help. As far as can be told, they perform the offices in church worthily, and I can truly testify that I have not seen other men anywhere worshipping more correctly or praying more conscientiously for your preservation and the security of the Christian empire. You can hear of their manner of life from Wido who is a sound man, an honest judge, and a loyal emissary. He has examined all their affairs and knows what they have done and how they have lived. Nor have I been slow to counsel them on faithfulness in the monastic life, as they themselves bear witness, if anyone thinks their word is to be trusted. I do not know what they have done to their accusers, to make them show such hatred towards them. I wonder why they wish to interfere with another's harvest, contrary to the law. The eminent teacher too forbids this, when he says: "Who are you to judge another's servant? He will stand or fall by his own master; indeed he will stand, for God is mighty to set him up." The city of Tours has a pastor [Archbishop Joseph] of high character devoted to preaching, who knows well how to give Christ's household their portion of food. Each shepherd should watch over his own flock, that none lack the grace of God, so that when the Shepherd of all comes he may find them worthy of the eternal reward.

With regard to the disturbance which occurred in Saint Martin's church and outside in the porch, I declare in the sight of Him who knows each man's heart that it happened without any support or knowledge or wish of mine. I confess that I have never been in greater stress over the sins of others than I was then. Nor was anything done purposely by the brothers, as far as I can gather. I have found no indication that they wished it; no one who fears God and cares for his own salvation should think of such a thing, still less do it.

Did not the venerable Teotbert, who was sent on your authority, spend nineteen days among us on this inquiry, and our accusers were with him by turns. He flogged whom he wished; he put in chains whom he wished; he put on oath whom he wished; he summoned whom he wished into your presence.

I have served my Lord Jesus Christ in vain all this time, if his mercy and wisdom have so far deserted me that I have come to such wickedness in the days of my old age. But I confess in all honesty that I would not take all the gold in Francia to be responsible for causing so dangerous a disturbance in the church of Christ by my advice or action. But I, a needy pilgrim in this world, fear God and take some little care for the salvation of my soul, though this has shown far from perfectly in my life. And now especially in the days of my old age and infirmity I know I must beware of such a terrible burden of wickedness, for I know well that the judgment of my life is drawing near. In fear of this judgment I have freed myself of the tumult of this world on the advice of your majesty, that I might serve God alone in quietness and, in return for all the good you have done for me through God's favor, pray for you each day with tears.

I am not ashamed to explain to your excellency the true reason for the disturbance, as far as I can understand it, and I shall spare no one in declaring the truth. I feel that the chief offender in this scandalous affair was the prisoner's guard—his carelessness has resulted in so much trouble. If those who hear this letter read will allow me to say so, I think it would be fairer for him who carelessly let the prisoner escape to be imprisoned himself than that the prisoner who sought the protection of our God Christ and his saints should be dragged out of church back to the same prison. This is not just my opinion, but is supported by the word of God who bade the prophet say to the king of Israel who let the king of Syria go, "Thus says the Lord, since you let go a man who deserved to die, you shall give your life for his."

Secondly I understand that the disturbance was created by the armed men who came from Orléans to Tours in unnecessarily large numbers, especially as the rumor spread through the people that they had come to take by force one who had sought sanctuary at the church of Christ and Saint Martin. It is the natural thing anywhere to resent disrespect to one's saints. It is possible too that the poor fellow encouraged drunken yokels who came to his lodging to defend the church of Saint Martin, and prevent him being carried off by force.

The third cause of the disturbance was when the holy father, our archbishop, went into the church at an unfortunate moment in the presence of the people with the men who were thought to have come to carry off the prisoner. He may have done this in the simplicity of his heart, not thinking any harm could come of it. Seeing this the ignorant mob, which always acts without thought or propriety, shouted out and ran for their clubs. Some active men ran in when they heard the bell ring. They were set going by ignorant hands, as was established by your envoys and even by our accusers themselves. (For the holy Gospel was brought out in their presence, with wood from the cross, and all the brothers who were told to took the oath.) When the brothers heard the bells, they ran from the refectory to find out why they rang. On arriving they calmed the uproar as much as they could, so I am told; but some lads who were at fault in the disturbance have been traced and brought before you. They will tell you what they did, and they have sworn that no one prompted them but they acted on their own foolish impulse. None of the vassals of Saint-Martin was there except one called Amalgarius who was with me at that hour. I sent him at once with the other brothers to allay the disturbance and to save the bishop's men from being harmed by the people. As soon as the uproar died down they were taken into the monastery where they could be safe. They were so virulent against me that they took in bad part a kindness I ordered to be done for them, saying that I had sent them food as an insult, which was quite false, as they did not know I was inspired by our Lord's command, "Do good to those who hate you."

Consider these points, my good lord, and learn the truth, showing kindness to your servants in the love of almighty God and respect for Saint Martin who prays for you, for he has always been honored in this kingdom by the kings of Francia.

In confessing our sins we say to God, "If you mark our sins, Lord, who will stand?" Let us say to you also, as we know you are the most eminent member of that Head, "if you mark our sins, lord emperor, who will stand," especially as the particular virtue, goodness, and praise of emperors is mercy towards their subjects—so much so that the eminent Emperor Titus said that no one should leave an emperor's presence sad. Gladden the hearts of your servants by the high gift of your mercy; let mercy be exalted over justice. You have shown praiseworthy goodness in pardoning the worst traitors against your authority: forgive our misfortune in the noble goodness of your holy purpose, which I have always known to be remarkably powerful in the wisdom of your thought. We read that David, the ancestor of Christ, was praised for that greatness of his mercy and the justice of his judgments: so we know that you are always worthy of praise and honor for these merits, by the grace of Christ.

May almighty God, the Father, through his only son our Lord Jesus Christ enlighten, fill and rejoice your heart with all blessing and wisdom in the Holy Spirit and deign to grant to your noble sons perpetual prosperity for the salvation of our Christian people, most dearly loved lord, and best and most august father of our fatherland.

> King David's glorious majesty
> In wisdom, virtue, triumphs, thrive!

Questions: How are Carolingian letters different from modern ones? To what ends did Alcuin employ his correspondence? What was the nature of his defense to the emperor over the matter of the escaped convict? Would he have convinced him? How much influence had Alcuin lost by leaving the court?

20. Five Poems of Alcuin

Though not the poet that Theodulf was, Alcuin was even more prolific. In his poems, he on occasion captures a mood of pacific tranquility and elevating spirituality that Theodulf rarely achieved.

Source: trans. P.E. Dutton from Monumenta Germaniae Historica: Poetae Latini Aevi Carolini, vol. 1, ed. E. Dümmler (Berlin, 1881), pp.243-244, 269-270, 321, 350.

1. Lament for the Cuckoo

Cuckoo and Daphnis were nicknames for Dodo, one of Alcuin's disciples, who was too fond of wine. Alcuin was deeply influenced in form and language in this poem by Virgil's fifth eclogue where two shepherds, Menalcas and Mopsus, sing songs about the death of their fellow shepherd Daphnis.

"We lament the loss of our cuckoo, our dearest Daphnis,
  Whom a wicked step-mother [wine] suddenly seized from us.
We lament his loss with our complaining song;
  Begin first, I beg you, elder Menalcas [that is, Alcuin]."
"Oh cuckoo that used to sing to us,
  What wicked season has now taken you away from us?
Oh cuckoo, our cuckoo, wherever you are,
  It is an unhappy time for us here.
Everyone everywhere laments the loss of our cuckoo,
  [They claim] he is gone for good, that he is dead.
Our cuckoo is not dead, he will come back in the spring,
  And returning to us he will be full of song.
Who knows if he will come back? I still worry that he has been
  Lost at sea, trapped and drowned by swirling liquids.
Woe to me, if Bacchus [the god of wine], who seizes the young,
  Has cast him into waves, into some noxious whirlpool.
If he still lives, let him return to our kind nest.
  Let not the raven rip at our cuckoo with his wild talons.
Who snatches you from your father's nest, cuckoo?
  He [Bacchus] stole you; I do not know if you will return.
If you care for songs, cuckoo, come quickly,
  Oh, I beg you, please come at once.
Do not delay, I beg you, my cuckoo, while you still can fly,
  Our young ones long to have their Daphnis return.
Spring is upon us, arise now from your slumber, cuckoo,
  Your father, old Menalcas, wants you back.
Our youngsters are browsing on the leaves of books,
  Only our cuckoo is wanting. Who is feeding him, I ask?
It is Bacchus, that wretch, I think, who feeds him evil food,
  It is Bacchus who wants to turn everyone to evil.
Lament for our cuckoo now as we always have;
  Full of joy he left us, but full of tears he will return.
I hope our cuckoo will come crying, that we might be reunited,

That we might wail together tear for tear.
Lament with weeping your frequent falls, my dear boy,
Pour out your woeful innards [to us]."

2. A Prayer in a Dormitory

Much of Alcuin's poetry was written for books, monuments, and buildings. The dedicatory nature of his poetic work suggests that he might have been, almost, the poet laureate of his world.

You who still great waves and the stormy sea,
You who watch over Israel and who will never sleep,
Give sweet sleep to the brothers in this royal court.
A dark power releases terrors to disturb our sleep,
I ask the merciful right hand of God [Christ] to suppress them.
He who created the day so that we might work in the light,
Also allows us rest at night for our exhausted bodies,
And, to his great praise, he causes us to rise up refreshed.

3. A Sign in a Latrine

It is not impossible that Alcuin was here once again thinking of his wayward and sodden disciple Dodo, since he once wrote to him "What you ate and drank yesterday is today shit, which I do not wish to speak of, but which even you tremble to see." Alcuin may have meant the following sign to catch the attention of those who were hung over.

O reader, understand the rankness of your devouring belly,
  For it is that which you now smell in your putrid shit.
Therefore, leave off feeding the gluttony of your belly,
  And in good time let the sober life return to you.

4. A Prayer Before Falling Asleep

This poem, composed in elegiac couplets, is found in the Prayerbook of Charles the Bald, a book of hourly prayers that the king carried with him on his travels. Once again Alcuin remembered the image of Christ stilling the storm at sea.

With calm heart, Christ snatched some sleep in the stern,
  Arising he commanded the wind and the sea [to still].
Although my limbs rest here, weighed down with profound fatigue,
  Grant that my heart may keep watch with you.
O gentle lamb of God who took away all the sins of the world,
  Guard my sleep from the enemy [the Devil].

5. My Little Cell

Many scholars long believed that this poem was written by Fridugis, Alcuin's disciple and successor as abbot of Saint-Martin's, but Peter Godman recently returned to the older view of Dümmler and others that the poem is in fact Alcuin's own lament. Cut off from the company of his fellow poets at court and now distant from Aachen, which may be the cell referred to, Alcuin could only lament his deep loss, which reminded him that he was now old and reaching the end of his life. In this poem he was, as well, influenced by the lugubrious exile poetry of ~~Ovid~~. Virgil

O beloved little cell, to me [you were] a sweet place to live,
    Farewell forever my little cell.
On all sides trees surround you with rustling branches,
    A comely little woods full of wild flowers.
All your fields bloom with life-giving herbs,
    Which the doctor's hand searches out for the work of healing.
Rivers surround you everywhere with flowering banks,
    There the happy fisher spreads his nets.
Your walls, hard by the gardens, smell of fruit trees,
    And [of] white lillies mixed with red roses.
There every kind of bird sings its morning chorus
    And praises God, the creator, in song.
In you the kind voice of the master once resounded,
    In pious speech he handed down the books of wisdom.
In you at specified times the holy praise of God
    Rose up from voices and minds that were at peace.
O my little cell, I now, with sad song, weep for you,
    Crying I lament from deep within my loss,
Seeing that you have suddenly shunned the songs of the poets,
    And a completely unfamiliar hand now holds you tight.
Neither Flaccus [Alcuin] nor the poet Homer [Angilbert] will now have
    you,
    Nor will the boys sing their songs below your roof.
And so all the beauty of the world is quickly upturned,
    And all things in their time are transformed.
For nothing remains forever and nothing is immutable,
    Dark night obscures even the clear[est] day.
A freezing winter cold strikes down gorgeous flowers,
    And a bitter wind unsettles calm seas.
On fields where the pious boy once hunted deer,
    A tired old man now stoops with his walking stick.
Why do we wretched ones love you, O fleeing world?
    Always crashing down, you still flee from us.
May you flee, fugitive world; let us always love Christ.
    May the love of God always grip our hearts.
May kind Christ defend his servants from a dreaded enemy,
    Carrying our hearts upwards to the heavens.
Let us praise and love him fully with our hearts,
    He, ever kind, is our glory, our life, our salvation.

Questions: Did Alcuin use poetry for the same ends as Theodulf? Is there a difference in tone? In 'My Little Cell' what is it that Alcuin most misses at court? Is his regret caused by his removal from court or from old age? How does he regard old age? What game is he playing in the 'Cuckoo' when he turns poor sodden Dodo into a bird?

21. Alcuin's Dialogue with Young Prince Pepin

Alcuin was not the author, but the adapter of the following text which he seems to have pulled together from at least three different sources, one of which was a supposed conversation between the Emperor Hadrian and the Stoic philosopher Epictetus. That borrowing, however, suggests an interesting parallel since it would make of Alcuin another wise man instructing another imperial son, Pepin [the son of Charlemagne who died in 810], in the ways of the world. Readers might like to look for an arrow, bells, an egg, and an echo, among the dialogue's more difficult riddles.

Much of Alcuin's voluminous work—in theology, grammar, and biblical commentary—was derivative, but for some scholars this makes it more interesting, not less. For it connects Alcuin to the intellectual world of Isidore and Bede that was shortly to be surpassed in the ninth century by the likes of Walahfrid Strabo and Eriugena. Alcuin was certainly a transitional figure in the intellectual history of western civilization. He was also just the kind of teacher that the first generation of the Carolingian renaissance needed, for he was energetic, demanding, and learned. His mind was one given to meticulous organization and administrative acumen. Charlemagne cannot, in the end, have been disappointed that he chose Alcuin to teach his sons and lead his educational reform.

Source: trans. P.E. Dutton from L.W. Daly and W. Suchier, Altercatio Hadriani Augusti et Epicteti philosophi (Urbana: University of Illinois Press, 1939), pp.137-143.

Pepin: What is a letter?
Alcuin: The guardian of history.
Pepin: What is a word?
Alcuin: The betrayer of the mind.
Pepin: What produces a word?
Alcuin: The tongue.
Pepin: What is the tongue?
Alcuin: The whipper of air.
Pepin: What is the air?
Alcuin: The guardian of life.
Pepin: What is life?
Alcuin: The joy of the blessed, the sorrow of the wretched, the expectation of death.
Pepin: What is death?
Alcuin: An unavoidable event, an uncertain pilgrimage, the tears of the living, the final confirmation of a will, the thief of mankind.
Pepin: What is a human being?
Alcuin: A slave of death, a passing traveler, a stranger to [this] place.
Pepin: What is a human [homo] like?

Alcuin: An apple [pomo; this is a pun].
Pepin: How is a human situated?
Alcuin: Like a lamp in the wind.
Pepin: Where is a human situated?
Alcuin: Within six walls.
Pepin: Which ones?
Alcuin: Above, below, before, behind, right, and left.
Pepin: What companions does a human have?
Alcuin: Four.
Pepin: Who are they?
Alcuin: Hot, cold, dry, wet.
Pepin: In how many ways does he change?
Alcuin: Six.
Pepin: What ways are those?
Alcuin: Between hunger and satiety, rest and work, wakefulness and sleep.
Pepin: What is sleep?
Alcuin: The image of death.
Pepin: What is freedom for a human?
Alcuin: Innocence.
Pepin: What is a head?
Alcuin: The pinnacle of the body.
Pepin: What is the body?
Alcuin: The dwelling place of the soul.
Pepin: What is hair?
Alcuin: The clothing of the head.
Pepin: What is a beard?
Alcuin: A difference between the sexes, a token of age.
Pepin: What is the brain?
Alcuin: The preserver of memory.
Pepin: What are eyes?
Alcuin: The guides of the body, dishes of light, spies of the mind.
Pepin: What are nostrils?
Alcuin: Conveyors of odor.
Pepin: What are ears?
Alcuin: Collectors of sound.
Pepin: What is the forehead?
Alcuin: An image of the mind.
Pepin: What is the mouth?
Alcuin: The feeder of the body.
Pepin: What are teeth?
Alcuin: The mill-stones of our biting.
Pepin: What are lips?
Alcuin: The folding-doors of the mouth.
Pepin: What is the throat?
Alcuin: The swallower of food.
Pepin: What are hands?
Alcuin: The workers of the body.
Pepin: What are fingers?
Alcuin: The pickers of chords.

Pepin: What is the lung?
Alcuin: The preserver of air.
Pepin: What is the heart?
Alcuin: The receptacle of life.
Pepin: What is the liver?
Alcuin: The guardian of heat.
Pepin: What is the gall-bladder?
Alcuin: The awakener of anger.
Pepin: What is the spleen?
Alcuin: The holder of joy and laughter.
Pepin: What is the stomach?
Alcuin: The cooker of food.
Pepin: What is the belly?
Alcuin: The guardian of the weak.
Pepin: What are bones?
Alcuin: The strength of the body.
Pepin: What are hips?
Alcuin: Cross-beams that rest on columns.
Pepin: What are legs?
Alcuin: The columns of the body.
Pepin: What are feet?
Alcuin: A moveable foundation.
Pepin: What is blood?
Alcuin: The humor of veins, the food of life.
Pepin: What are veins?
Alcuin: The fountains of flesh.
Pepin: What are the heavens?
Alcuin: A spinning sphere, a vast summit.
Pepin: What is light?
Alcuin: The visage of all things.
Pepin: What is the day?
Alcuin: The impetus to work.
Pepin: What is the sun?
Alcuin: The light of the world, the adornment of the heavens, the grace of nature, the splendor of the day, the dispenser of hours.
Pepin: What is the moon?
Alcuin: The eye of night, the bringer of dew, the foreteller of storms.
Pepin: What are stars?
Alcuin: A painting of the heavens, guides for sailors, ornaments of the night.
Pepin: What is rain?
Alcuin: A reservoir of the earth, the begetter of crops.
Pepin: What are clouds?
Alcuin: Night in the day, work for the eyes.
Pepin: What is wind?
Alcuin: A disorder of the air, changeableness of water, dryness of land.
Pepin: What is the earth?
Alcuin: The mother of growing things, nurse of the living, the pantry of life, she who consumes all things.
Pepin: What is the sea?

Alcuin: The way of the bold, the end of land, the divider of regions, the home of rivers, the source of rain, a refuge in danger, the grace of satisfaction.

Pepin: What are rivers?

Alcuin: An unending flow, the repairing of [the work of the] sun, the irrigation of the earth.

Pepin: What is water?

Alcuin: The helper of life, the cleanser of dirt.

Pepin: What is fire?

Alcuin: Excessive heat, the warmer of growing things, the ripener of crops.

Pepin: What is cold?

Alcuin: A shivering of limbs.

Pepin: What is frost?

Alcuin: The killer of plants, destroyer of leaves, the imprisonment of the land, the source of water.

Pepin: What is snow?

Alcuin: Dry water.

Pepin: What is winter?

Alcuin: The banishment of summer.

Pepin: What is spring?

Alcuin: The adorner of the earth.

Pepin: What is summer?

Alcuin: The readornment of the earth, the ripening of the crops.

Pepin: What is autumn?

Alcuin: The granary of the year.

Pepin: What is a year?

Alcuin: The four horsed chariot of the world.

Pepin: Who drives it?

Alcuin: Night and day, cold and heat.

Pepin: Who is its driver?

Alcuin: The sun and moon.

Pepin: How many palaces do they have?

Alcuin: Twelve.

Pepin: Who are the keepers of the palace?

Alcuin: Aries, Taurus, Gemini, Cancer, Leo, Virgo, Libra, Scorpio, Sagittarius, Capricorn, Aquarius, Pisces.

Pepin: How many days do they spend in each palace?

Alcuin: The sun spends thirty days, ten and one-half hours; the moon spends two days, eight and one-half hours.

Pepin: Master, I fear to go higher.

Alcuin: What led you this high?

Pepin: Curiosity.

Alcuin: If you are afraid, let us descend. I shall follow you wherever you go.

Pepin: If I knew what a ship was, I would ready it so that you might come to me.

Alcuin: A ship is a wandering home, a resting place wherever it is, a wanderer leaving no tracks, a neighbor to beaches.

Pepin: What is sand?

Alcuin: A wall of earth.
Pepin: What is grass?
Alcuin: The clothing of the earth.
Pepin: What are vegetables?
Alcuin: The friends of physicians, the joy of cooks.
Pepin: What is it that makes bitter things taste better?
Alcuin: Hunger.
Pepin: What is it that people never grow tired of?
Alcuin: Money.
Pepin: What is sleep for those who are wide awake?
Alcuin: A hope.
Pepin: What is hope?
Alcuin: A cooling off after work, uncertain success.
Pepin: What is friendship?
Alcuin: A similarity of minds.
Pepin: What is faith?
Alcuin: Certainty in what is unknown and wonderful.
Pepin: What is a wonder [or riddle]?
Alcuin: I recently saw a person standing, working, and walking, who never was.
Pepin: How can it be? Explain [what you saw].
Alcuin: A reflection on the water.
Pepin: Why did I not understand this myself, since I have so often seen this person myself?
Alcuin: Since you are a young man with a keen interest and natural cleverness, I will set some other wonders [riddles] before you. See if you can unravel them by yourself.
Pepin: I shall do it, but if I say something incorrect, you must correct me.
Alcuin: As you wish. Some man spoke to me without using his tongue or his voice; he never existed before nor will he exist afterwards; and I did not hear him, nor did I know him.
Pepin: Master, perhaps a dream overcame you.
Alcuin: That's it, my boy. Now here's another [riddle]. I saw the dead beget the living, but the dead were consumed by the violence of the living.
Pepin: Fire arises from rubbing sticks together, thus consuming the wood.
Alcuin: That is true. I have heard the dead saying many things.
Pepin: Never very well, unless they were suspended in the air.
Alcuin: Right. I saw an unextinguishable fire go out in water.
Pepin: I believe you are thinking of a flint in water.
Alcuin: I saw the dead sitting upon the living and the living are dying in ridicule of the dead.
Pepin: Our cooks have long known this.
Alcuin: They have known it, but put a finger to your mouth, lest the boys hear about it. I was on a hunt with some people, on which, when we began, we carried nothing with us; what we could not catch we carried home with us.
Pepin: That is the hunt of peasants?
Alcuin: It is. I saw something born before it was conceived.

Pepin: You saw and you ate it.

Alcuin: I ate it. What is it that is not, but has a name and answers to one speaking?

Pepin: Put the question to books in the woods.

Alcuin: I saw a host running with his home; that one was quiet, but his home spoke.

Pepin: Prepare a snare for me and I will explain it to you.

Alcuin: What is it that can only see with its eyes closed?

Pepin: The one who snores showed that to you.

Alcuin: I saw a man having eight in his hand and when, suddenly, he took seven from the eight, six remained.

Pepin: Boys in school know [the answer].

Alcuin: What is that which, if you remove the head, rises up again even taller?

Pepin: Go to bed and there you will discover the answer.

Alcuin: There were three: one never born and ever dead; another ever born and never dead; and the third ever born and twice dead.

Pepin: The first is our ambiguous birth and death on earth; the second to our Lord; the third into a condition of poverty.

Alcuin: Give me the first letters of their names.

Pepin: I, V, XXX.

Alcuin: I saw a flying female, having an iron beak, wooden body, feathered tail, and bearing death.

Pepin: She is the companion of soldiers.

Alcuin: What is a soldier?

Pepin: The wall of the empire, a threat to enemies, glorious service.

Alcuin: What is that which is and is not?

Pepin: Nothing.

Alcuin: How can it both be and not be?

Pepin: It exists in name, but not in fact.

Alcuin: What is a quiet messenger?

Pepin: The one I hold in my hand.

Alcuin: What do you hold in your hand?

Pepin: Your letter, master.

Alcuin: Read it with profit, my boy.

Questions: What does the dialogue tell us about the first stage of Charlemagne's educational reform? Does it tell us anything in particular about the way in which boys were taught, or is this form a mere literary artifice?

22. Charlemagne's Division of his Kingdoms

In February 806, when he was in his mid-60s, Charlemagne announced the formal division of his properties between his three sons, Charles, Pepin, and Louis. The Carolingian royal house, like the Merovingian before it, believed its territory to be partible; that, indeed, the kingdom was a personal holding of the king that should be rightfully divided between sanctioned and supportable sons upon the king's death. By this principle of Germanic partition, Charlemagne himself and his brother Carloman had inherited portions of Pepin the Short's kingdom. Yet Charlemagne, who was never one to follow traditions blindly or to allow fortune to look after what he might better plan himself, must have foreseen future problems between his heirs if he did not formally and specifically set out how his lands were to be partitioned. The reader should notice, however, that, though Charlemagne gave a portion of the kingdom to each son, he granted young Charles, his eldest son, the vast heart and prosperous center of Francia, while his two younger sons were granted peripheral kingdoms.

Source: trans. D.C. Munro in Translations and Reprints from the Original Sources of European History, vol. 6.5: Laws of Charles the Great (Philadelphia: University of Pennsylvania, 1899), pp.27-33; revised.

In the name of the Father and Son and Holy Ghost. Charles, the most serene augustus, the great and pacific emperor crowned by God, governing the Roman Empire, and also by the mercy of God king of the Franks and Lombards, to all the faithful of the holy church of God and to our subjects present and future.

As we believe it is known to all of you and hidden from none of you how the divine clemency, by whose will earthly tendencies to decay are checked through successive generations, has of his great mercy and kindness richly endowed us by giving to us three sons, because through them in accordance with our vows and our hopes He has strengthened the kingdom and reduced the chance of oblivion in the future. Therefore, we wish to make this known to you, namely, that we desire to have these our sons by the grace of God as associates in the kingdom granted to us by God as long as we live, and after our departure from this life we desire to have them as heirs of the empire and of our kingdom preserved and protected by God, if this is the will of the divine majesty. So that we might not leave it to them in confusion and disorder or provoke strife and litigation by giving them the whole kingdom without division, we have caused to be described and designated the portion which each one of them ought to enjoy and rule in this way, so that each one of them, content with his own portion in accordance with our ordination, may strive with the aid of God to defend the frontiers of his kingdom and preserve peace and charity with his brothers.

1. It has pleased us to divide the empire, preserved and protected by God, and our kingdom so that to our beloved son Louis we have assigned: the whole of Aquitaine and Gascony (except the province of Tours) and whatever is beyond to the west and towards Spain and from the city of Nevers, which is situated on the river Loire, with the province of Nevers, the province of

Avallon and Auxois, Chalon[-sur-Saône], Mâcon, Lyons, Savoy, Maurienne, Tarantaise, Mont-Cenis, the valley of Susa to the mountain passes and thence from the Italian mountains to the sea. These provinces with their cities and whatever is beyond these on the south and west as far as the sea or Spain, that is to say this portion of Burgundy, Provence, Septimania, and Gothia, [we have allotted to Louis].

2. To our beloved son Pepin [we give] Italy, which is also called Lombardy, and Bavaria, just as Tassilo held it (with the exception of the two villas of Ingolstadt and Lauterhofen which we formerly gave to Tassilo as a benefice and which belong to the district which is called the Nordgau), and from Alemannia the part which is on the south bank of the river Danube, and from the source of the Danube in a direct line as far as the river Rhine on the boundary of the districts of Kletgau and Hegau at the place which is called Engen, and thence up the river Rhine to the Alps. Whatever is within these limits and extending to the south or east, together with the duchy of Chur and the canton of Thurgau, [we give to Pepin.]

3. To our beloved son Charles moreover we have granted all of our kingdom that is outside of these limits, that is to say, Francia and Burgundy (except that part which we have given to Louis), Alemannia (except the portion which we have assigned to Pepin), Austria, Neustria, Thuringia, Saxony, Frisia, and the part of Bavaria which is called the Nordgau. Thus Charles and Louis may be able to go into Italy to bear aid to their brother, [Pepin,] if such a necessity should arise, Charles by the valley of the Aosta which is in his kingdom and Louis by the valley of the Susa; Pepin also has a means of entance and exit by way of the Norican Alps and Chur.

4. Moreover we have arranged this disposition [of territory] in such a manner that if Charles, who is our eldest son, should die before his other brothers, the part of the kingdom which he held shall be divided between Pepin and Louis, just as formerly it was divided between us and our brother Carloman, in such a way that Pepin may have that portion which our brother Carloman had, and Louis may receive that part which we [ourselves] obtained in that division.

But if during the lifetime of Charles and Louis, Pepin should die, Charles and Louis shall divide between them the kingdom which he had, and this division shall be made in such a manner that from the entrance to Italy at the city of Aosta, Charles shall receive Ivrea, Vercelli, Pavia, and thence along the river Po, following its course to the territory of Reggio and Reggio itself, and Cittanuova and Modena up to the boundary of the territory of Saint Peter. These cities with their suburbs and territories and the counties which belong to them, and whatever is beyond towards Rome on the left, from the kingdom which Pepin had, together with the duchy of Spoleto, let Charles receive this portion just as we have described it. But of the aforesaid kingdom whatever (from the aforesaid cities or counties) lies on the right as one goes towards Rome, that is, the portion which remains from the region beyond the Po, together with the duchy of Tuscany as far as the southern sea and Provence, Louis shall receive to increase his kingdom.

But if Louis shall die during the lifetime of the others, Pepin shall receive that part of Burgundy which we have joined to the kingdom of Louis together with Provence and Septimania or Gothia, as far as Spain; and Charles shall receive Aquitaine and Gascony.

5. But if a son shall have been born to any one of these three brothers, whom the people wish to elect so that he may succeed his father in his kingdom, we wish that the uncles of the boy shall consent to this and shall permit the son of their brother to rule in the portion of the kingdom which his father, their brother, held.

6. After this disposition by our authority it has pleased us to decree and command in the case of our aforesaid sons, for the sake of the peace which we desire to be perpetual among them, that no one of them shall presume to invade the frontiers or boundaries of his brother's kingdom, or fraudulently enter to disturb his kingdom or to diminish his territory, but each of them shall help his brother and shall bear aid to him against his enemies, either within the country or against foreign peoples, so far as the occasion may demand and he may be able.

7. Nor shall any one of them receive a vassal of his brother, who may flee to him for any cause or crime whatsoever, nor shall he intercede for that one, because we desire that any man who sins and needs intercession shall flee either to the holy places or to official men within the kingdom of his lord, and thence shall receive [from them] fitting intercession.

8. Likewise we command that if any free man shall have deserted his lord against the will of the latter and shall have gone from one kingdom into another, the king himself shall not receive him nor consent to his vassals receiving the man or daring unjustly to retain him.

9. Wherefore it seems fitting to us to command that after our departure from this life the vassals of each one of them shall receive benefices only in the kingdom of his lord and not in the kingdom of another, lest perchance, if it was otherwise, some trouble might arise. But each one of their vassals shall have, without contradiction, any inheritance that may fall to him in whatsoever kingdom he may happen to hold it lawfully.

10. And each free man, after the death of this lord, shall be allowed to commend himself within these three kingdoms to whomsoever he chooses; likewise the same goes for those who have not yet commended themselves to anyone.

11. Concerning gifts and sales, such as are wont to be made, we command that none of these three brothers shall acquire, by gift or purchase from any individual, real estate in the kingdom of another, that is, land, vineyards, forests, and serfs already bound to the soil, or other things comprised under the category of inheritable property, except gold, silver, jewels, arms, clothing, serfs not bound to the soil, and such things as are recognized to be saleable.

But we have decided that this should not be forbidden to other free men.

12. If, moreover, women, as often happens, shall be sought in legitimate marriage by men from another kingdom, the just demands of those requesting these women shall not be denied, for they shall be allowed both to give and receive women, and thus to join peoples together. The women in question shall retain possession of their property in the kingdom which they left, although they need to live in another in order to be with their husbands.

13. Concerning the hostages who have been given as pledges and who have been sent by us to different places to be guarded, we desire that that king in whose kingdom they are kept not permit them to return to their native land without the consent of the brother from whose kingdom they were taken. In the future each brother shall mutually aid the other in receiving hostages, if one brother shall have made a reasonable request of another. Also we order the same concerning those who have been sent into exile for their crimes or who shall be sent.

14. If a strife, dispute, or controversy over the boundaries or limits of the kingdoms should arise between the parties that cannot be settled or ended by the witness of people, then we desire that, in order to settle the doubtful question, the will of God and the truth of the matter shall be sought by the judgment of the cross, and that such a contention shall never be settled by violence or judicial combat. If, indeed, any vassal from one kingdom, in the presence of his lord, shall have accused a vassal from another kingdom of infidelity against the brother of his lord, let his lord send him to the brother so that he may there prove what he has said concerning the vassal of the latter.

15. Above all, moreover, we order and command that the three brothers in person shall undertake in common the care and defense of the church of Saint Peter, just as it was done formerly by our grandfather, Charles, and by our father, king Pepin of blessed memory, and afterwards by us, so that with the aid of God they may strive to defend it against its enemies and may cause it to have its deserved rights, as far as shall be in their power and as reason shall demand. Likewise, also, concerning the other churches which shall be under their power, we command that these shall have their proper rights and honor, and the pastors and rectors of venerable places shall have power over the property which pertains to the holy places themselves in whichever of those three kingdoms the possessions of those churches shall be.

16. But if there be any infringement upon these statutes and conventions by any accident or through ignorance—and we hope this will not be the case—we command that [our sons] shall strive as quickly as possible to remedy the matter in accordance with justice, lest perchance by delay a greater evil arise.

17. Moreover, concerning our daughters—the sisters of our aforesaid sons—we order that after our departure from this life each one shall be allowed to choose the brother under whose guardianship and protection she wishes to

live. And if any one of them shall choose a monastic life, she shall be allowed to live in honor under the protection of the brother in whose kingdom she chose to live. Moreover, if any one of them is justly and reasonably sought in marriage by a worthy man, and the married state is pleasing to her, she shall not be refused by her brothers, if the intentions of the man who demands and of the woman who consents shall be honorable and reasonable.

18. Concerning our grandsons, the sons of our aforesaid sons, already born or who shall be born hereafter, we command that none of our sons, for any reason whatsoever, shall cause any one of the grandsons who has been accused before him to be put to death or mutilated or blinded or forcibly tonsured without a just trial and examination. We desire that [these grandsons] be honored by their fathers and uncles and that they be obedient to them in proper subjection, as is fitting in the case of such a [familial] relationship.

19. In the last place, it seems to us that this ought to be commanded so that any decrees or constitutions which may be profitable and useful to them, which we may wish to add in the future to these our decrees and precepts, shall be observed and obeyed by our beloved, aforesaid sons, just as we have commanded that these decrees and prescriptions [themselves] shall be obeyed and observed.

20. Moreover, all of these things, which we have so arranged and set forth in order, we have so decreed, that so long as it may please the divine majesty to preserve our life, our power shall be the same over the kingdom preserved by God and over that empire as it has been up to this time in all our royal and imperial rule and ordination and domination, and so that we may enjoy the obedience of our beloved sons and of our peoples beloved by God, with all the submission which is due to a father from his sons and to an emperor and king from his peoples. Amen.

Questions: In what ways is Charlemagne here attempting to overcome the problem of Germanic partition or, at least, its most harmful features? Who does he include? Who does he exclude? How specific is the division of lands? In what ways was it based on earlier ancestral and established regional divisions? What sorts of problems might have arisen from this document? What was to be the fate of the imperial title and of the empire itself?

23. The Diet of Aachen in 813

Charlemagne's careful division of his kingdoms proved, in the end, to be unnecessary, for he outlived all but one of his three sons: young Charles died in 811 at thirty-nine years of age and Pepin in 810 at thirty-three. If the partition of 806 favored young Charles and seemed to contain an incipient principle of primogeniture, the imperial title had still not been treated as heritable. It may have been, as F. L. Ganshof suggested, that Charlemagne considered the name of 'emperor' to be a personal honor that would die with him. Or it may be that he simply never conceived of a way in which a singular title or, indeed, a single empire could be divided between three sons. By early 812 that problem had disappeared as Charlemagne was left with but one son to succeed him. At the palace an imperial party, perhaps led by Einhard, now urged Charlemagne to share the imperial title with Louis the Pious. This event was later recalled by one of Louis's poets, the exiled Ermold the Black.

Source: trans. P.E. Dutton from Monumenta Germaniae Historica: Poetae Latini Aevi Carolini, vol. 2, ed. E. Dümmler (Berlin, 1884), p.24-26.

The aged Emperor Charles, respected by the whole world,
    Called for a council to be held at Aachen.
Seated up high on his golden throne, with his chosen counts
    Collected all around him, Charles began [to speak]
"Listen to me, my counts, you who rely upon my support,
    For I am going to tell you things we know to be true.
While there was energy in my youthful body,
    I exerted myself in war and the pursuit of power.
Not by any laziness or cowering fear on my part, I maintain,
    Did foreign enemies [ever] attack Frankish borders.
Now my blood grows sluggish and dire old age makes me slow,
    And flowing white hair falls down over a pale neck.
My war-like right hand, once famous throughout the world,
    Now shakes as my blood grows cold.
Children born to me have died and, though it is sad [to say],
    With their duties done, they [now] lie buried.
But the child who once seemed better and more pleasing to the Lord,
    Has now been granted to me forever.
Christ has not abandoned you Franks, rather he has left behind,
    From my offspring a worthy son.
That distinguished and pleasing son always obeyed my orders,
    And carried out my imperial will.
For the love of God, he restored the rights of churches;
    He made the kingdoms placed under his control better.
You have seen the many trophies which he once sent me from his
    Conquest of the Moors: the king, arms, and captured people.
O Franks, from your faithful hearts, give me your advice,
    I shall at once carry out the same."
Then Einhard, who was much loved by Charles,
    And also wise, clever, and abounding in goodness,
Fell before Charles's feet and kissed the ground where he walked.

Learned Einhard first began with the following advice:
"O emperor, celebrated on high and on earth and sea,
   You who bestow your imperial name upon your son,
There is nothing we can add to your plan,
   Nor has Christ given any human a better plan than this.
With respect I urge you to carry out, as soon as possible,
   What merciful God directed you in your heart to do.
O kind one, you have a son with a good character,
   Who, because of his merits, is able to rule your kingdoms.
All of us, both the high and the low, desire his rule,
   The church wants him, and Christ himself supports him.
After the sad disappearance of your authority he will be able
   To maintain the law with force, intelligence, and faith."
With happiness Caesar nodded in approval and prayed to Christ,
   He sent for his son to come quickly.
Good Louis was at that time happy to be ruling the kingdom
   Of Aquitaine, as I related earlier.
Why should I delay? Louis traveled at once to the palace of his father.
   In Aachen the priests, people, counts, and his father rejoiced.
Charles began to speak once again and in these words
   Spoke to his dear son and explained:
"Son, dear to God, to your father, and to conquered peoples,
   God gave you to me as a comfort.
You yourself can see how I am declining in my old age,
   For the time of my death is almost upon me.
The government of my kingdom, which God himself gave to me,
   However unworthy I am, remains my primary concern.
Neither applause nor a whim compels me, trust me,
   To speak to you so, but the love of piety.
Francia gave birth to me and Christ granted me my position,
   For Christ gave me my father's kingdoms to hold.
I held these kingdoms and regained still more,
   I was the pastor and the shield of our Christian flock.
I was the first of the Franks to take up the name of Caesar,
   I have given the name of Romulus to the Franks to retain."
He said these things and [then] placed a crown of gold and gems,
   The symbol of the empire, upon his son's head.
"My son, accept my crown, for it is Christ who [truly] bestows it,
   Take it up, my son, as the very ornament of the empire.
May the merciful one who bestowed this pinnacle of honor upon you,
   Confer upon you as well the capacity to please him."
Then the father and son happy with this outstanding public event,
   Put on, with the piety of God [in mind], a great banquet.
O that was a day of festivities not to be forgotten for many years!
   O Francia, you are [now] ruled by two emperors.
Francia rejoice openly, for golden Rome also applauds,
   And other kingdoms now gaze [enviously] upon your empire.

Questions: How was this portrayal of events designed to appeal to Louis? What is the poet's attitude towards Charlemagne? Is the depiction of Einhard as the imperial advocate of Louis the Pious believable? What would have persuaded Charlemagne to share his imperial title?

CHAPTER THREE

THE TIME OF LOUIS THE PIOUS

(814–840)

Carolingian Monks

A nineteenth-century drawing [after Vétault] of four monks in full liturgical dress as shown in the presentation miniature of the so-called Vivian Bible. This manuscript was produced about 845 at Saint Martin of Tours and survives today in the Bibliothèque Nationale in Paris (B.N. Lat. 1).

24. Lament on Charlemagne's Death

When Charlemagne died in early 814, many were deeply saddened, including those closely devoted to him at the palace and the anonymous monk of Bobbio who wrote the following lament. But Louis's supporters and disgruntled parties throughout the kingdom were enthusiastic about the arrival of a new and more just ruler. Indeed Louis began his reign as a reformer determined to undo some of the injustices and corruption that had dogged his father's final decade. Thus when Ermold had described (in doc.23) the sluggish and inactive blood of the old Charlemagne, he must have been reflecting the opinion of the new court about the flaws of the old.

Source: trans. P.E. Dutton from Monumenta Germaniae Historica: Poetae Latini Aevi Carolini, vol. 1, ed. E. Dümmler (Berlin, 1881), pp.435-436.

From [eastern] lands where the sun rises to western shores,
People are [now] crying and wailing.
Alas for miserable me.

Beyond the oceans an overpowering sadness
Grips crowds of people with great sorrow.
Alas for miserable me.

The Franks, the Romans, all Christians,
Are stung with mourning and great worry.
Alas for miserable me.

The young and old, glorious nobles
And matrons, all lament the loss of their Caesar.
Alas for miserable me.

Rivers of tears keep forever flowing,
As the the world laments the death of Charles.
Alas for miserable me.

Universal Father of all orphans,
Of pilgrims, of widows, of virgins.
Alas for miserable me.

O Christ, you who govern the heavenly host,
Grant a peaceful place to Charles in your kingdom.
Alas for miserable me.

All faithful Christians ask this of you,
The holy elders, widows, and virgins ask for it.
Alas for miserable me.

An engraved tomb of earth now covers
The resting [form of] Emperor Charles.
Alas for miserable me.

May the Holy Spirit who governs all things
Lift up his soul to that place of peaceful repose.
    Alas for miserable me.

Woe to you Rome and to the Roman people,
The great and glorious Charles is lost [to you].
    Alas for miserable me.

Woe to you fair Italy, you without equal,
And woe to all your noble cities.
    Alas for miserable me.

Francia has endured awful wounds [before],
But never has suffered such great sorrow as now,
    Alas for miserable me.

When in the earth of Aachen
It has interred the august and eloquent Charles.
    Alas for miserable me.

Night now brings me only dire dreams,
And the new day has brought no light.
    Alas for miserable me.

[O that horrible day] for all the Christians of the world,
Which handed over the respected emperor to death.
    Alas for miserable me.

O Columbanus, conclude your wailing,
And devote your prayers for him to God,
    Alas for miserable me.

That the Father of everything, the merciful Lord,
May give to Charles a most brilliant place [in heaven.]
    Alas for miserable me.

O God of all the human and heavenly host,
And Lord of the infernal regions,
    Alas for miserable me.

Take up into your holy abode with your apostles,
O Christ, kindly Charles.
    Alas for miserable me.

Questions: Does the monk's emotional state change as the poem progresses? Is the poem personal or is the lament a largely formal one?

25. Thegan's *Life of Louis*

Two biographies of Louis the Pious were written by contemporaries, one by an anonymous author popularly known now as the Astronomer because of his interest in things astronomical and the other by Thegan who was a Frankish noble and the suffragan bishop of Trier. Thegan was the Old Oligarch of Louis the Pious's world, forever furious at the rise of lower-class and servile men to positions of power and prominence.

Source: trans. J. R. Ginsburg in collaboration with D.L. Boutelle, in D.L. Boutelle, Louis the Pious and Ermoldus Nigellus: An Inquiry into the Historical Reliability of *In honorem Hludowici*, (Ph.D. diss.: University of California, Berkeley, 1970), pp.309-334; revised and printed with permission.

Our Lord Jesus Christ ruling forever! In the 813th year of his Incarnation, which is the 45th year of the reign of the glorious and orthodox Emperor Charles, that Charles who was descended from the lineage of Saint Arnulf, Christ's bishop, as we have learned through ancestral tradition and as many histories testify. When Saint Arnulf was a duke in his youth, he begat Duke Ansegis, who begat the elder Duke Pepin [II], who begat Charles Martel. The elder Duke Charles begat Duke Pepin [the Short], whom the Roman Pontiff Stephen consecrated and anointed king. The elder King Pepin [the Short] begat Charles, whom the Roman Pontiff Leo consecrated and anointed emperor on Christmas Day in the church where the most blessed body of Peter, the prince of the apostles, lies.

2. The aforesaid emperor, when he was a young man, pledged himself in marriage to a girl of a most noble Swabian family, by the name of Hildegard, who was related to Godfrey, duke of the Alemanni. Duke Godfrey begat Loching, who begat Nebi; Nebi begat Emma, who begat the most blessed Queen Hildegard. After the emperor married her, he fathered upon her three sons, of whom one was called by his father's name, Charles, the second, Pepin, who was king over Italy, the third was called Louis, who was king of Aquitaine. For a long time their father lived with them happily and instructed them usefully in the liberal arts and worldly laws.

3. But he who was the youngest had, from infancy, always been taught to fear and love God, and he would distribute whatever he had of his own to the poor in the name of the Lord. For he was the best of Charles's sons, just as from the beginning of the world the younger brother often exceeds the older in merit. Among the sons of the first parent of the human race this was first demonstrated in the case of him whom the Lord called righteous Abel in his Gospel. Abraham had two sons, but the younger turned out better than the older. Isaac had two sons, but the younger was chosen. Jesse had many sons, but the youngest, who was a shepherd, was elected and anointed as king over all Israel, governing the kingdom by God's order. From this man's seed Christ, who had once been promised, was thought worthy to be born. It would take time to list [all] such examples and parallels.

4. After Louis came of age, he betrothed himself to the daughter of the most

noble Duke Ingram, who was the nephew of Chrodengang, the blessed bishop. This maiden was called Ermengard, whom Louis made his queen with the advice and consent of Charles, and Louis had three sons by her while his father was living—one of whom was called Lothar, another Pepin, and the third, his namesake, Louis [the German].

5. Emperor Charles ruled and cared for his kingdom usefully and well. In the 42nd year of his reign [in 810], his son Pepin died at the age of 33. The following year [in 811] Charles, his firstborn son by Queen Hildegard, died. Only Louis remained to rule the kingdom.

6. When the emperor realized that the day of his death was drawing near, for he was indeed an old man, he called his son Louis to him [in 813], together with all his army, bishops, abbots, dukes, counts, and their subordinates. He held a general assembly with them at his palace at Aachen peacefully and honorably admonishing them to show fidelity to his son; asking all—from the greatest to the least—if it was pleasing to them that he give his title of emperor to his son Louis. They all responded enthusiastically that this was the advice of God in this matter. That being done, on the following Sunday Charles donned royal dress and put his crown upon his head. He walked, outfitted and adorned with distinction, just as it was fitting. He came to the church which he himself had built from its foundations and went to the altar, which had been built in a higher place than the other altars and consecrated in honor of our lord Jesus Christ. He ordered that a golden crown, another than the one which he wore on his head, be placed on the altar. For a long time they prayed, his son and himself. He spoke to his son in the presence of the whole multitude of his bishops and nobles, advising Louis especially to love and fear the omnipotent God, to preserve His precepts in all ways, and to govern and defend the churches of God from depraved men. He ordered Louis always to show unfailing mercy to his younger brothers and sisters, his nephews, and all his relatives. Then he directed Louis to honor the bishops as fathers, to love the people as sons, to compel and direct haughty and worthless men into the ways of salvation, and to be a consoler of monks and a father to the poor. [Louis was further advised] to appoint faithful and God-fearing ministers, who would hold unjust gifts in loathing. He should eject no one from his office without a specific indictment, and he should reveal himself as above reproach at all times in the presence of God and all people. After Charles had revealed these words and many others to his son before the multitude, he asked Louis if he would be obedient to his precepts. And Louis answered that he would gladly obey and preserve all the precepts that his father had ordered, with the help of God.

Then his father ordered him to pick up the crown, which was on the altar, with his own hands and to put it on his head so that Louis might remember all the precepts which his father had entrusted to him. So Louis executed his father's orders. That done, and having heard a solemn Mass, they went to the palace. The son supported his father both in going and returning, while he was with him. Not many days later Charles honored Louis with magnificent and numerous gifts and dismissed him to return to Aquitaine.

Before they separated, while embracing and kissing each other, they began to cry on account of the joy of their love. Louis went to Aquitaine, and the lord emperor held onto his title and kingdom honorably, just as he deserved.

7. After they had separated, the lord emperor began to do nothing but devote himself to prayers and almsgiving and to correcting books. In the last days before his death he had, with the help of Greeks and Syrians, excellently corrected the four Gospels of Christ, which are assigned the names of Matthew, Mark, Luke, and John.

In the following year [814], which was the 46th year of his reign, in the month of January, fever overtook the lord emperor after bathing. His weakness grew worse day by day. Eating and drinking nothing except a small amount of water for the refreshment of his body, after the seventh day he began to struggle much with himself and ordered his most familiar Bishop Hildebald to come to him to give him the sacraments of the Lord's body and blood to strengthen [him for] his death. After this, Charles struggled in infirmity that day and the following night. On the next day, as the sun was rising, knowing what was going to happen, Charles extended his right hand, with what strength he could, and made the sign of the blessed cross on his forehead and over his chest and his whole body. Finally, drawing his feet together, extending his arms and hands above his body, he closed his eyes, singing this verse gently: "Into your hands, Lord, I commend my spirit." Immediately after this, in ripe old age and full of days, he died in peace. On that very same day his body was buried in the church which he himself had built at the palace at Aachen, in the 72nd year of his life, the 7th Indiction.

8. After the death of the most glorious Emperor Charles his son Louis proceeded from Aquitaine, came to the palace at Aachen, and received all the kingdoms, which God had given his father, without any objection. It was the 814th year of the Incarnation of the Lord, and the first year of his reign. Following his father, he settled in the palace and immediately ordered with all possible haste that they show him all his father's treasure in gold, silver, precious gems, and all other goods. He gave his sisters their legal part, and whatever remained, he gave for the soul of his father. The largest part of the treasure he sent to Rome in the time of the blessed Pope Leo, and whatever remained over this, he distributed all of it to the priests and poor, wanderers, widows and orphans, keeping nothing for himself except one silver table, three-layered in form like three shields joined into one. This he kept out of love of his father, but he redeemed it with another valuable which he bequeathed on his father's behalf.

9. After this, legates came to him from all kingdoms, provinces and foreign nations. All those who were subject to his father promised to observe peace and fidelity toward Louis and offered immediate and unforced allegiance. Among those who came were the Greek legates with Amalarius, bishop of Trier, who was the legate of Charles of pious memory to the prince of Byzantium, whose name I do not remember. On their arrival, they found Louis seated on his father's throne because the Lord had ordained thus. Louis,

receiving them kindly, accepted their gifts with expressions of thanks, and held a friendly meeting with them while they were with him. Not many days later he adorned them with great honors and dismissed them to go to their own lands. He sent his own *missi* before them to prepare for them whatever they desired for their work while they were in his kingdom.

10. In the same year Louis ordered that all the charters, which had been issued during the time of his ancestors on behalf of the churches of God, be renewed, and he strengthened them with the signature of his own hand.

11. Meanwhile the legates of the Beneventans came, who entrusted to Louis's power all the lands of Benevento and promised to deliver thousands of gold pieces per year in tax. This they have done right up until today.

12. At the same time Bernard, the son of Louis's brother Pepin, came and gave himself to Louis as a prince and promised his fidelity with an oath. Lord Louis received him freely, honored him with great and noble gifts, and permitted him to return safely to Italy.

13. At the same time Louis sent legates over his whole kingdom to make inquiries and find out if any injustice had been perpetrated against anyone. If they found anyone who wanted to say this and could prove this with truthful witnesses, Louis ordered [the accuser] to come immediately into his presence with the legates. The legates, going out [into the country], found a large number of people oppressed either by the appropriation of their patrimony or the plundering of their freedom. [The abuses] were being practised by evil means by unjust ministers, counts, and subordinates. All these acts, which had been impiously done in the days of his father by the hands of evil ministers, the prince ordered suppressed. He returned patrimonies to the oppressed; he freed those unjustly pressed into servitude, and he ordered charters to be made for all and confirmed them with a signature in his own hand. This was a lengthy inquiry.

14. In the next year [815] of his reign he held his general assembly in the territory of Saxony and there he decreed many good things. Danish legates came to him requesting peace; all who were in the surrounding pagan countries came to him. Bernard came to him there, and Louis sent him back to Italy. After Louis confirmed the confines of his kingdom in these territories, he returned to his seat in the palace at Aachen and there spent the winter.

15. In the following year [816] Louis sent his army against the Slavs who lived in the east. The Franks overcame them and were victorious by the gift of God. That done, each of them returned to his own lands.

16. That same year the Roman Pope Leo died and Stephen succeeded him. He, immediately after he received the pontificate, ordered that all the Roman people promise fidelity to Louis by an oath, and sending his legates to Louis, he announced to him that he wished to see him in whatever place was pleasing. Hearing this, Louis, full of great joy, began to rejoice and immediately

ordered his *missi* to go to meet the blessed pontiff with great greetings and to prepare supplies. Lord Louis went to meet the pope after his *missi* [had departed]. Meeting him in the huge field of Rheims, each descended from his horse, and Louis prostrated himself with his whole body on the ground before the feet of the pope three times. On the third time he stood erect and greeted the pope with these words, saying: "Blessed is he who comes in the name of the Lord. God is the Lord and He enlightens us." And the pope answered: "Blessed is our Lord God, who allows our eyes to see the second King David." Embracing and kissing each other in peace they proceeded into the church. When they had prayed for a long time, the pope straightened himself and in a lofty voice, with his clergy, bestowed lavish praise on Louis.

17. Later the pope honored Louis with many large gifts, and Queen Ermengard as well, and all Louis's dignitaries and ministers. On the next Sunday, in church before solemn mass, Stephen consecrated Louis—in the presence of the clergy and all the people—and anointed him emperor. He placed on his head an extremely beautiful golden crown, ornamented with precious gems, which he had carried with him. And he called Queen Ermengard empress and put a golden crown on her head. As long as the blessed pontiff was there, they held a daily meeting concerning the needs of the holy church of God. And the lord emperor honored him with large and numerous gifts—three times and more than Louis had received from him—just as it is customary to do, [that is,] to give more than to receive. Then Louis released him to return to Rome with his legates, whom he ordered to show honest service everywhere on the journey.

18. After the pope came to Rome, not many days later he died. In a short while it was made clear by the manifestation of God in several miracles that Stephen was living as a true worshipper of God. Pope Pascal succeeded him.

19. Returning from Rheims, Louis came to his seat at the palace at Aachen. Daily he was upstanding in sacred virtues which are too numerous to list. He was of medium height, with large, clear eyes, a lucid expression, a long, straight nose, lips neither too thick nor too thin, a strong chest, broad shoulders, very strong arms—so that no one could equal him in shooting a bow or in throwing a spear—long hands, straight fingers, long and gracefully proportioned legs, long feet, and a virile voice. He was very learned in the Greek and Latin languages, but he could understand Greek better than he could speak it. He could speak Latin as well as his native tongue. He well understood the sense of all Scriptures: spiritual, moral and analogical. He rejected the national poems, which he had learned as a youth, wanting neither to read nor hear nor teach them. He was strong in his limbs, agile and energetic, slow to anger and quick to show mercy.
　　Every morning of every day he proceeded to church in order to pray: genuflecting, he touched his forehead to the ground, praying humbly for a long time, sometimes with tears. He was always adorned with all good behavior. He was so generous—as never before was heard of either in old books or in modern times—that he gave royal estates, which were his father's, grand-

father's and greatgrandfather's, to his vassals in perpetuity. And he confirmed charters which he strengthened by his own signature and the impression of his ring. He had done this for a long time.

He was moderate in food and drink and restrained in his dress. He was never resplendent in gold clothing, except on high festivals, just as his fathers were wont to do. On those days he put on nothing but a shirt and breeches, woven with gold and with a gold fringe; girdled with a gold belt and with a gleaming gold sword, [he had] gold leggings and a cloak woven with gold, wearing a golden crown on his head and holding a golden staff in his hand. Never did he raise his voice in laughter, not even when on high festivals musicians, jesters, and mimes along with flutists and zither-players, who were supplied for the delight of the people, proceeded into his presence at the table. The people laughed a great deal [on those occasions] in his presence, but he never showed his white teeth in a smile. Every day, before eating, he gave alms to the poor, and wherever he was, he had houses of hospitality with him. Moreover, in the month of August, when the deer are very fat, he spent his time hunting them until the time to hunt wild boars came.

20. He did everything prudently and cautiously, doing nothing indiscriminately, except that he entrusted more to his counselors than he should have; this was caused by the study of psalmody and his constant attention to reading and other things in which he was not a novice. Because a very evil practice had existed for a long time—namely that the highest bishops were made from the basest slaves—Louis did not prohibit it. Nevertheless, it is the greatest evil among the Christian people, as the Books of Kings testify regarding Jereboam, son of Nabad, who was a slave of King Solomon and after him held the rulership over the ten tribes of the sons of Israel. Scripture says of him: "After these words Jereboam returned not from his evil way, but on the contrary made of the lowest of the people priests of the high places; whosoever wanted [this], he consecrated him, and he became one of the priests of the high places." On account of this the house of Jereboam sinned, was destroyed, and was removed from the face of the earth.

After such men as these have seized the summit of government, they are never so mild as formerly, nor so tame, so that immediately they begin to be irascible, quarrelsome, slanderous, obstinate, injurious, and threatening to all subjects. Through this kind of activity they seek to be feared and praised by all. They strive to pull their basest relatives from the yoke of slavery and give them freedom. They instruct some of them in liberal studies; others they marry to noble women, and they compel the sons of the nobility to accept their female relatives in marriage. No one can live with them with equanimity except those alone who have such marriages with them: the rest, truly, with great sadness, moaning, and weeping, count their days. The relatives of these men, after they have learned something, deride and despise their old nobles. They are haughty, unstable, incontinent, immodest, and shameless. Little good remains in any of them. After they renounce from themselves sacred reverence to their Lord, they do not wish to understand canonical scripture—what is called the Canons of the Apostles—for there it decrees: "But if a bishop shall have impoverished parents, let him endow them as he would poor people, so that ecclesiastical property shall not perish." They do not wish to accept the book of Saint Gregory which is entitled *The Pastoral Rule*. For no one can believe how they behave except those alone who suffer this evil without any relief. Their relatives, after they have learned something—which for those giving and receiving is the greatest danger—are enticed to holy orders. And although they may be somewhat learned, nevertheless the multitude of their crimes overwhelms teaching. It generally happens that the priest in church has not dared to challenge the negligent or harmful ones with canonical justice on account of the crimes of their relatives. That sacred ministry is generally despised by most because it is performed by such men. Therefore, let the almighty God, along with kings and princes, deign henceforth to stifle and eradicate this very evil practice, so that it may no longer occur among Christian people. Amen.

21. Louis designated his son Lothar so that after his own death Lothar would receive the kingdoms that God had entrusted to Louis through Charles's hands, and so that he would have the title and empire of his father. The other sons were outraged by this.

22. In that same year [817] Bernard, the son of Pepin born of a concubine, exalting himself against his uncle through the urgings of evil men, wished to expel Louis from the kingdom. For he had impious counselors on this side and that. Hearing this, Louis proceeded from the palace at Aachen and came to the city of Chalon-[sur-Sâone] where Bernard came to meet him with his impious counselors. They presented themselves and were commended [to Louis]. The emperor celebrated Christmas there.

Returning from Chalon, Louis came to his seat at Aachen, and after Easter he held a large general assembly, and investigated all such wretched conspiracies of unfaithful men. Moreover, several from both the Franks and Lombards were found to have fallen into this sedition. All were sentenced to death, except the bishops, who were shortly afterward deposed because of their confessions. These were Anselm of Milan, Theodulf of Orléans, and Wolfold of Cremona. Louis was unwilling to exercise that judgment of death which had been made against the others, but his counselors blinded Bernard as well as his instigators—Eggideo, Reginhard, and Reginhar who was Hardrad's grandson. (Hardrad was a most unfaithful duke of Austria who had previously decided to revolt against Charles and to threaten his kingdom, and who was condemned to the same punishment as his grandson and the latter's supporters received.)

23. On the third day after the loss of his eyes Bernard died [818]. Hearing this, Louis wept with great grief for a long time and made confession in the presence of all his bishops and undertook penance by their decision for this reason: because he did not prohibit his counselors from doing that maiming. Therefore, he gave much to the poor in order to purge his soul.

24. At the same time Louis ordered his brothers Drogo, Hugh, and Theoderic to be tonsured so as to mitigate discord; and he ordered them to be instructed in liberal studies. Afterwards, he placed them honorably: he gave Drogo an episcopacy and Hugh many monasteries.

25. Then Louis proceeded to the territory of Brittany with his army, and Morman, the Breton leader, was killed, and Louis brought all that land under his sway. Returning from there, he found Queen Ermengard feverish and not many days later she died in peace.

26. In the following year [819] Louis married the daughter of his Duke Welf, who was of the most noble progeny of the Bavarians. The name of the virgin was Judith, who on her mother's side—whose name was Eigilwi—was from most noble Saxon lineage. Louis made her his queen. She was very beautiful. That same year he held his general assembly there at the royal estate of Ingelheim.

27. In the following year [820] Louis sent his army against the eastern Slavs. The leader of the Slavs was named Ljudovit. The Franks put him to flight and laid waste to that land. Returning from there, they went home.

28. The next year [821] Louis held his general assembly, and there Lothar, his firstborn son by Queen Ermengard, received the daughter [called Ermengard] of Count Hugh in marriage. Hugh was of the stock of a certain duke, Etih by name, who was cowardly above all men. For the members of his household had prophesied [dire things] to him with the result that he almost never dared to put his feet out of doors. At that time infidelity already threatened Louis. This was shown to him by the behavior of Lothar's father-in-law and many other wicked men. Returning from there, Lothar went to Worms with his wife.

29. In the following year [822] Louis held his general assembly in the palace at Attigny. From there he sent his son Lothar with his wife Ermengard to Italy. The lord emperor proceeded from Attigny to Frankfurt, where he celebrated Christmas.

30. Later [823] Louis sent his legates, Adalung, the venerable abbot and priest, and Hunfrid, who was duke of Rhaetia, to the territory of Rome on account of a certain accusation which the Roman people brought against the Roman Pope Pascal, accusing him of being the murderer of several men. The pontiff purified himself with an oath in the Lateran Palace in the presence of these legates and the Roman people as well as thirty-four bishops and five priests and deacons. After these *missi* had gone away, the pope immediately died. The Roman people did not wish to bury him in the sacred church of Saint Peter the Apostle until Pope Eugenius succeeded him and ordered them to bury Pascal's body in the place which he had built while living.

31. In the following year [824] Louis proceeded again to Brittany and laid waste to that whole land with a great blow on account of their infidelity.

32. In the next year [825] Louis was at the palace at Aachen with his army and there legates of the Bulgars came bearing gifts. Louis received them graciously and dismissed them to return to their own land.

33. In the following year [826] Louis was at the royal palace at Ingelheim and Harald of the Danes came to him there. Louis elevated him from the sacred baptismal font, and the Empress Judith elevated Harald's wife from the font. Then the lord emperor gave him a large part of Frisia and adorned him with honorable gifts and dismissed him to go with his legates in peace.

34. In the next year [827] Louis sent his army to meet the Saracens. In the following year [828] he proceeded from Ingelheim, and after his general assembly he came to Commercy.

35. In the next year [829] Louis came to Worms where he gave his son Charles (who was born of the Empress Judith) the land of Alemannia, Rhaetia, and some part of Burgundy in the presence of his sons Lothar and his namesake [Louis the German]; and they, along with their brother Pepin, were, from this time on, outraged.

36. In the next year [830] the lord emperor proceeded from the palace at Aachen and came to Compiègne where his son Pepin with his father's principal magnates—the Archchaplain Hilduin, Bishop Jesse of Amiens, Hugh and Matfrid, Abbot Helisachar, Godfrey, and many other perfidious ones—came to meet him. They wished to expel Louis from the kingdom, which was prevented by his beloved namesake [Louis]. These brazen men made many accusations against him, which it is impious to say or believe. They charged that Queen Judith had been violated by a certain Duke Bernard [of Septimania], who was of royal lineage and the godson of the lord emperor. They told all these lies. Taking Queen Judith, they forced her into monastic habit and sent her to a monastery; tonsuring her brothers, Conrad and Rudolph, they sent them to a monastery.

37. In that same year Louis proceeded to the fortified royal residence at Nijmegen, which is situated above the Waal, and many men from all over his kingdom came to him. Among them came his adversaries. But the lord emperor overcame them: he divided them and commended them. His son Lothar promised fidelity in an oath [to the effect] that he ought never to commit such acts after this. There Jesse was deposed by the just judgment of the bishops. Louis's namesake son was there, who in all his father's troubles showed himself his supporter. From there the lord emperor came to his seat at Aachen; his wife came there to meet him at the bidding of Gregory, the Roman pontiff, with the just decision of the other bishops; Louis received her with honor.

38. In the following year [831] Louis was at the palace of Thionville with his sons Lothar and Louis. There Duke Bernard came, purging himself of unchastity after no one was found who dared to impute that crime to him with arms.

39. The next year [832] after Easter it was heard that Louis's namesake, on the advice of Lothar, had determined to visit his father as an enemy. He came to the monastery of Saint Nazarius and stayed there for a short time

until his father, coming to Mainz, collected an army and pursued him. The son returning home, awaited his father's arrival and desired to defend himself. The father arrived and ordered his son to come to him. Louis received him kindly; they had a peaceful meeting and not many days later they separated with great love. The son settled at home, and the father returned to Francia.

40. When Louis came to the palace at Frankfurt, his son Lothar came to meet him there, asking his father that he be permitted to clear himself because neither through his will nor his urgings had his brother made trouble for his father. And how true this is, is known to several.

41. While the king was staying there, it was heard that his son Pepin wished to raise a sedition against him. Louis excitedly came to the city of Limoges to meet him and ordered Pepin to go to Francia with his wife and children. At first, hearing his father's order, Pepin began to go to the palace at Doué, but he returned and went to Aquitaine. Louis returned from Frankfurt and came to his seat at Aachen, but he was not there long. He left and came to the city of Worms before the sacred time of Lent.

42. After Easter [833] Louis heard that his sons again desired to come to him, and not peacefully. He gathered an army and proceeded to meet them on the great field which lies between Strasbourg and Basel, which to this day is called the Field of Lies, where the fidelity of most men was destroyed. His sons proceeded to meet him with the Roman Pope Gregory. Their father consented to none of their demands. A few days later Louis and Gregory held a meeting and after a short talk, the pope specially honored Louis with large and innumerable gifts. After each returned to his own tent, Louis sent royal gifts to the pontiff through Adalung, the venerable abbot and priest.

Then several men conspired to abandon the Emperor and to go over to his sons, especially those who had offended him before. Others followed and one night the largest part left him: leaving their tents, they went over to his sons. On the next day those who remained came to the emperor who admonished them, saying "Go to my sons. I do not wish any of you to lose your lives or limbs on account of me." And they, filled with tears, withdrew from him.

The sons had already separated his wife from him, confirming by an oath that they wanted her neither to die nor to be disabled. They immediately sent her to the city of Tortona in Italy and held her there. Not much later they captured their father and took him with them. After this, they separated: Pepin proceeded to Aquitaine, Louis to Bavaria.

43. Lothar took his father with him to the palace at Compiègne and there, along with the bishops and several others, he deposed Louis. They ordered Louis to go to a monastery and spend all the days of his life there. But he, refusing, did not agree to their wish. All the bishops were annoying to him, and especially those whom he had honored from the most servile condition as well as those who had been brought to this dignity from foreign nations.

44. Then the bishops chose a shameless and most cruel man—Ebbo, the bishop of Rheims—who was originally of servile stock, to savagely crush Louis with the lies of the others. Daily reproaching him, they said unheard-of things, they did unheard of things. They took his sword from his thigh, putting him into monastic habit in accordance with the judgment of his slaves. Then the epilogue of the prophet Jeremiah was carried out, which says: "Slaves have ruled us." Oh, what repayment you returned to him! He made you free, not noble, which is impossible. After emancipation he dressed you in purple and in the pallium [of the bishop], and you put him in a hair shirt. He led you, undeserving, to the pontifical summit; you, by false judgment, wished to expel him from the throne of his fathers. You cruel man, why did you not understand the precepts of the Lord: "There is no slave over the Lord"? Why did you scorn the apostolic precepts of him [Paul] who was taken up to the third heaven that he might learn among the angels how to rule men? He so orders, saying: "All must be subject to divine power. For there is no power except derived from the Lord." And again another says: "Fear God. Honor the king. Servants, be subject to your masters with all fear, not only to the good and modest, but also to the lustful, for that is gratitude."

You truly neither feared God nor honored the king. If one can obtain the grace of God by doing such things, he shall indeed have the wrath of God by scorning them. Cruel man, who was your advisor or teacher? Was it not he who is king over all the children of pride? He said to God, his Creator: "All these things I give to you if you, falling down, will adore me!" O Lord, Jesus Christ, where was your angel who so easily destroyed all the firstborn of the Egyptians one night; he who in the fortress in Assyria under Sennacherib, the evil king, destroyed 185,000 unfaithful men one night, as the prophet Isaiah testifies; he who struck the younger Herod, as he was giving a speech, so that he immediately began to gush forth with worms? And you, land, which sustained him at that time, why did you not open your mouth and devour him as once you did to Dathan and Abiron? You did not understand that triple law of yours which says: "Fodder, the rod and burdens for the ass; bread, discipline and word for the slave." The prophet Zachariah prophesied to you, saying: "Thou shalt not live for you have spoken lies in the name of the Lord." God disclosed your malice and preserved this kingdom and his glory. You destroyed yourself with great impiety on account of cupidity and mendacity.

May you now fall into opprobrium all the days of your life. May your dishonor increase day by day through the rashness of cupidity and falsity, just as a small number grows larger by the art of arithmetic. Cruel man, your canonical justice is still incomplete; for it is necessary that the judgment be complete for your greater dishonor. Your fathers were goat shepherds, not counselors of princes. You, with the judgment of others, deposed Jesse from the priesthood; now he is recalled again to his original position. Either then, or now, you have shown false judgment. You were the imitator of the one described by the poet of the *Aeneid* in Book Six:

...tragic Theseus sits, and the poor wretch Phlegyas
Admonishes all, crying out in the darkness in solemn voice:

"Be warned! Learn justice and not to belittle the gods!"
This one sold his land for gold and placed it under a powerful lord,
For a price he made and unmade its laws.

What can I say to you further? Unless I had an iron tongue and bronze lips,
I could not enumerate or explain all your wrongs. But if there were anyone
who wished to probe all your evils by poetry, perhaps he could overcome
the bard of Smyrna, old Homer, Mincianus, Virgil, and Ovid. For the attack
on the most pious prince, which he suffered at the hands of most evil men,
is believed to have been nothing but a test of his goodness, just as the patience
of blessed Job. But here was a vast difference between the persecutors of
each. Those who taunted holy Job are said to have been kings in the Book
of Saint Tobias, while those who struck at Louis were the legal slaves of him
and his father.

45. Afterward they led the most pious prince from Compiègne to the palace
at Aachen. Hearing this, the younger Louis returned from Bavaria, driven
to great sadness by his father's injury. Coming to the palace at Frankfurt,
he immediately sent his legates, Gozbald, abbot and priest, and the count of
the palace, Morhard, asking and demanding that more humane feeling be
shown toward his father. His brother Lothar did not receive this message
very gracefully. After these legates returned, young Louis immediately sent
others to his father, but they were not allowed to see him.

46. Afterwards Lothar left Aachen and came to Mainz, where his brother
came to meet him. There they held an uneven meeting on account of this
fact: all those, whom Lothar had with him, were his father's opponents, unjustly; those, whom the young Louis had with him, were faithful to his father
and him. Returning from there, Lothar came to Aachen and celebrated
Christmas while his father was still imprisoned.

47. After the sacred day of Epiphany [834] young Louis again sent his legates—Grimald, the venerable abbot and priest, and Gebhard, a most noble
and faithful duke—to his father. They came to Aachen and Lothar agreed
that they might see his father in the presence of his spies, of whom one was
called Bishop Otgar, the other, the faithless Righard. The legates, coming
into Louis's view, prostrated themselves humbly at his feet. Then they gave
him the greeting of his namesake son [Louis]. They did not wish to speak
secret words to him on account of the spies who were present, but by a
certain movement of signals they made him understand that his namesake
did not consent to this punishment of his father.

48. When these *missi* departed, Lothar immediately compelled his father to
go with him again to Compiègne. Louis, consenting to [the wish of] his son,
proceeded with him. Hearing this, young Louis followed them with many
allies. When he was not far away, Lothar dismissed his father and, with his
impious advisors, withdrew from him. Louis's namesake came to him; receiving him with honor and returning him again to his seat at Aachen, he
restored Louis, with God's help, to his kingdom and his palace. There, to-

gether, they celebrated Easter. Upon hearing this, Ebbo immediately took up flight; he was caught and led by force into Louis's presence. The prince ordered him into custody.

49. That same year which was the 21st of his reign, Louis offered indulgence to all who had, when compelled, abandoned him. And this was not burdensome or difficult for him who is the most pious of emperors since previously he had spared his enemies, fulfilling that evangelical precept in which it is said: "forgive, and you shall be forgiven." He prepares a large and good reward for him, who establishes this precept: "For whom the Lord loveth, He chastiseth, and scourges every son whom He receiveth." And he, who will not accept God's correction of his own will, cannot become his son.

50. But special precautions must be taken, lest it further happen that slaves be his advisors, because if they can, they build up this [position] to the highest so that they may oppress the nobles and strive to raise themselves along with their most vile relatives. This was not becoming to Louis's dignity; it seldom happened in the time of his father of sacred memory that any such men rose to honor. The greatest discipline taught him not to [allow them to] become arrogant. There is the greatest need to follow this example now. When the most gentle prince was in his trial, such men as these were making trouble for him, who had showed those undeserving men every kindness. There is no need of asking what they do to their subjects.

51. After the emperor prevailed, he sent his faithful legates into the territory of Italy to bring back his wife, who had been so often afflicted with lies. The legates went there, received her honorably and led her with joy and happiness into the presence of the prince, who was at the palace at Aachen at that time.

52. Lothar was residing in the city of Chalon, where he committed many evils there by despoiling the churches of God. He made martyrs of his father's vassals, wherever he could seize them, with the exception only of the legates. Furthermore, he ordered a nun, by the name of [Gerberga], who was the sister of Duke Bernard, to be enclosed in a wine barrel and flung into the Arar—of which the poet sings: "Either the Parthian shall drink of the Arar, or the German of the Tigris." Holding her there for a long time until he drowned her, by the advice of the impious wives of his counselors, he fulfilled the prophet's Psalm: "With the holy you will be holy, and with the perverse, perverse."

53. After this, Louis sent his legates—Marcward, the venerable abbot [of Prüm], and others of his vassals—to Lothar with exhortatory letters in which he warned him to remember omnipotent God and his orders and to turn himself away from his depraved life so that he might realize what a severe decision it was to scorn the Lord in his precepts. For God says, among other precepts: "Honor your father and your mother," and "Whosoever speaks evil of father or mother shall be killed dead." This precept was not given by the prophets or the apostles, but God himself in Scripture ordered it to be ob-

served. And how serious it is to ignore this is soon shown in the book of Deuteronomy, where it says: "If a man shall produce a contumacious and insolent son, who will not listen to the order of his father and mother, and when corrected, shall be contemptuous to obey, let them apprehend him and lead him before the elders of the city and to the gate of justice, saying to them: 'This, our son, is insolent and contumacious. Refusing to hear our warnings, he spends his time in banquets of luxury and drinking bouts.' The people of the city shall shower him with stones and he shall die so that you may eliminate evil from your midst. And let all Israel, hearing, tremble."

54. After Lothar spoke to the *missi*, he received their legation severely and harshly, promising them threats—which still have not been fulfilled, nor will they be. The *missi*, returning from him, came to Louis and told all they had heard. Louis, sighing, gathered a copious multitude and proceeded after Lothar, to where he heard he was. His sons came to meet him—Pepin from the west and his namesake [Louis] from the east—each with a great multitude in compliance with their father. And when they hastened to Orléans, where Lothar was, with his impious seducers, whom I mentioned above, he did not wish to be at peace in accordance with his father's pleas; but one night he withdrew from Louis, as if fleeing. Then, the emperor sent his legates—Badarad, the Saxon bishop, Gebhard, the most noble and faithful duke, and wise Berengar, his relative—after him. They came to Lothar; immediately the bishop ordered him, by edict of omnipotent God and all his saints, to alienate himself from the society of his impious seducers and to allow the vassals of the emperor to demonstrate whether or not it was the will of God that their discord be permanent.

After the legation of the bishop, the dukes announced to Lothar what had been ordered to them. He asked them to step outside for a short time and immediately recalled them, praying that they might give him advice about all his actions. They instructed him to come to the mercy of his father, with the other seducers, and promised peace. And Lothar promised to come with them. Returning from there, the legates came to Louis announcing what had been done.

55. After them Lothar came to where his father, the emperor, was. Louis was sitting in his tent [which was] situated very high on a great plain where all his army could see him; his faithful sons stood next to him. Lothar came and fell at his father's feet, and after him, his father-in-law, timid Hugh. Then Matfrid and all the others who were the leaders in that conspiracy, after raising themselves from the ground, confessed that they had done wrong. After this, Lothar swore fidelity to his father, [promising] that he would obey all his orders and that he would go to Italy and remain there, not leaving except on his father's orders. Then the rest swore. After this, the most pious prince gave them indulgence if they would preserve this oath. He dismissed them to have their patrimonies and all which they had, except that which he had given them with his own hands. They separated there. Lothar with his evil supporters proceeded to Italy, and Matfrid, who was the major instigator of all those evils, immediately [afterwards] died along with several others. Those who remained were seized with fever.

56. The emperor, returning from there, came to the palace at Thionville and there passed the entire winter. After Christmas, in the next year [835] he held a great popular assembly. To that place came the most vile peasant Ebbo, against whom the bishops did not dare to move firmly, fearing that he might become their betrayer. And so they urged him to admit himself that he could in no way hold the sacred ministry. He did this and thus was completely dismissed. There was a need to correct this matter completely because it is better to exercise the just decision of the holy father in regard to him, than to show false piety under the pretext of religion.

57. That same year the emperor proceeded to the territory of Lyons where his sons Pepin and his namesake [Louis], who is still the imitator of the above written sons because he is the youngest, came to meet him. There the emperor sat with his sons while legates sent to Lothar in Italy and returning, came back to Louis. From there Louis turned back and came to his seat at Aachen. Pepin returned to Aquitaine and the emperor's namesake turned back to Germany.

58. That same year the wise and faithful Duke Berengar died on a journey; the emperor and his sons mourned him for a long time. This is the 22nd year of the reign of the Lord Louis, the most pious emperor, whom He who is blessed for eternity thinks worthy to preserve and protect for a long time, while he is sojourning happily, and whom, after these discordant times, He may allow to be led to the society of all his saints. Amen. [The text concludes here in 836.]

Questions: What themes does Thegan dwell on? How does he regard Louis and his sons? What does he count as Louis's greatest strengths? Does he acknowledge any weaknesses in the emperor? Why does he refrain from criticizing the rebellious sons of Louis? How does Thegan's biography compare with Einhard's, both in terms of style and content?

26. Benedict of Aniane: His Life and Times

By the end of the eighth century, monasticism was as localized and varied as most other aspects of early medieval society. Charlemagne may have attempted to improve monastic standards, but his reform was shallow and resisted by older monasteries which had their own strong traditions and by newer monasteries which lacked inspired leadership. It fell to Louis the Pious and his advisor Benedict of Aniane to institute a wide-reaching monastic reform of Francia based on Saint Benedict's Rule. Benedict of Aniane, whose original name was Witiza, was an Aquitanian noble who abandoned the military life in order to found a monastery on his own property around 780. His rigorous adherence to and promotion of the Rule of Saint Benedict as the basic standard for all monastic life soon attracted the attention of Louis the Pious who called Benedict to court. In 816-817, in councils held in Aachen, Louis and Benedict introduced a fundamental Benedictine reform of Frankish monasticism. Prior to the eighth century, a host of formal and informal rules and customs, some from insular and some from early Christian sources, had formed the basis of monastic life. Benedict of Aniane's great accomplishment, then, was to make the Rule of Saint Benedict the normative and central document, the charter rule as it were, of medieval monasticism. His reform of Carolingian monasticism was one of the formative influences that shaped the culture and history of Louis's reign and, indeed, of Carolingian religion. The hagiography of Benedict of Aniane that follows was written, probably in the 820s, by Ardo, one of Benedict's disciples.

Source: trans. Judith R. Ginsburg with Donna L. Boutelle, from Vita Benedicti Abbatis Anianensis et Indensis auctore Ardone, ed. G. Waitz, Monumenta Germaniae Historica: Scriptores, vol. 15.1 (Hanover, 1887), pp.200-220; revised and printed with permission.

[Prologue]

Ardo, the servant of the servants of Christ, sends greetings to the fathers in the Lord and brothers serving Lord Jesus in the monastery of Inda [near Aachen]. Long ago, most beloved brothers, your letters were sent to me, filled with love for the pious memory of our father, Abbot Benedict, and lovingly containing a brief account of his death and journey to Christ. In these you suggested to me that I write a more complete account of his life for those desiring to hear it. So far, realizing that the burden exceeded my strength, I have postponed it.

Those in the past who were writing of a life venerable in its merits, famous in its virtues, had to see to it with skillful industry that they neither omitted through negligence what is useful because they were stupefied, nor added what is superfluous by attempting to introduce new material. They wrote with a flowing pen of things they had diligently inquired into and, strengthened by the report of witnesses who were present, did not trouble the ears of experienced men by smacking of the vice of rusticity. They offered words written in healthy urbanity and polished style, so that, as I have said, they caressed the ear of the opposition.

Due to my inexperience, but wishing to obey your request, I was long silent. I undertook to have it written by more learned men, thinking it would be unfair if I should touch upon the life of such a great patron with inexperienced words and remove this necessary task from more experienced men. They are able, abounding in numerous words, to elucidate what they want forcefully and they do not fear to steer the boat through the sand-banks avoiding the stench of grammatical mistakes. Endowed with eloquence as they are, they can check the tones of the opposition when they are numerous.

I was afraid that you, wishing to correct what is incorrectly composed, and exasperated at poor construction, would judge that it ought to be disregarded. This was especially my concern because I know that you sit near the doors of the sacred hall of the palace and do not thirst for a drink from turbulent streams, but rather drink waters from the never-failing stream of the purest fountain of wisdom. This reasoning occupied me for a year. Meanwhile, the brothers whom Benedict produced with the pious support of Christ began to rouse me from my idle pursuit with biting words and to compel me to revive him for them through the deeds of his religious life. (It is agreed we are absent from him only in the society of the flesh, not from the fullness of love.)

Thus finally I undertake to develop the work. The place which was originally built by him [Aniane], along with the brothers who knew the beginning of his life, gave me the daring and a pardonable plan: that which is hardly heard by others could hardly have been seen by them. Therefore, from their information, partly collected, I am prepared to set forth as accurately as I can the ingredients of the work as though to put forth some sort of nursery.

I prepared too much. I ask this with humble prayer: if anyone shall look down on this work, let him leave it alone or correct it. If others want to read and understand it, let him [who scorns it] allow them [to read it] and [let him] devote himself to the reading of the lives of earlier fathers. If he finds that it does not stray from the path of these works in accordance with its strength, let him rejoice. On the other hand, let him not refute it by judging rashly, but, by intervening with tears, let him be a more fair and calm judge. Because I have obeyed your orders, most holy brothers, I beg that you help me by praying to God, since by your prayers I may be pardoned for my choices and [the work] may be of increasing profit for posterity.

Again I ask resolutely that you read over this work with watchful study, and that you correct whatever you judge has been improperly constructed by eliminating it. And if you find anything useful in it, preserve it perfected in the secret chamber of your heart. Our silence has ended: if we reveal any discomfort it has not been brought about by your order. You, who think about having ordered us to speak, should ascribe to yourselves what we say. And since Abbot Helisachar [of Inda and Saint-Maximin of Trier, a Goth from Septimania, and, until 819, the chancellor of Louis the Pious] has remained in a mood of love for [the work] through the changing age, just as the letter sent to us, more precious than gold itself is witness, after his examination I think it should be presented to each of you, one at a time. If anyone thinks it should be hidden away, I ask for pardon for my error; but if there is anything useful, let those who gladly obey the living bustle about imitating the life of one who is absent.

No learned man, I think, doubts that this very old practice [of imitating our betters] has been followed by kings, and that the things which are done must be understood and handed down to future years. Since my mind, partaking of many diverse things is blinded by forgetfulness, I believe that the plan derives from above, so that this long forgetfulness will be abolished as time goes by. What must be preserved is entrusted to letters, by the reading of which those who desire to read such things are pleased, delighted, and grateful.

The writing will not be judged rashly by them, even if the author happens to ring with less than polished words; they will avidly exert themselves to understand it. They allowed me to read the lives of earlier men and to entrust to posterity the things which we have seen or heard in our times and which are going to be of benefit to the growth of their souls. Nor should I be condemned for smacking of an unpolished style and for the vice of rusticity. I consider it a wholesome rule that one may produce a most beautiful honeycomb with the commonest words and enclose it with contemptible twigs. Let each man use the things which, according to his judgment, he finds are going to be pleasing to his soul. Amen.

[The Life of Benedict]

1. Abbot Benedict, a man venerable in name and deed, descended from the Goths. He was born in Gothia of noble parents. Celestial piety made him famous because of the greater reputation of his virtues. His father held the county of Maguélonne [the region of Montpellier] as long as he lived, and he was most faithful toward the Franks with all his power. Brave and clever, he was aggressive toward the enemy: he laid low the Gascons in a great massacre when they had invaded the boundaries of the Frankish kingdom for the purpose of devastating it: from them no one escaped except one whom swift flight saved.

The count entrusted his son, who spent his boyhood years in the palace of the glorious King Pepin [the Short] and his queen [Bertrada], to be raised among the students there. The young Benedict was esteemed by his fellow soldiers for he was fast and useful for everything. After this period Benedict received the office of Butler. Moreover, he went on military campaigns in the time of King Pepin. After Pepin, when the most glorious King Charles began governing the kingdom [in 768], Benedict adhered to him and served him.

Meanwhile, when his divine grace became evident, he began to be influenced by celestial love to give up the world, to burn with every effort, and to despise ephemeral honor. He saw he could attain [all these] with labor but once attained he would quickly lose them. However he hid this in his heart for five years, sharing the secret with God alone, involving himself in the affairs of the world with his body, but not his mind. He tried, during this time, to see if he could obtain the height of continence by refusing sleep to his body, restraining his tongue, abstaining from food, using wine sparingly and preparing himself for future war as if he were a trained athlete.

While he remained in his worldly clothes he wondered what he should do: assume the habit of a monk, join himself to another and pasture the sheep and cattle of all for nothing, or practice the art of a cobbler in the city and bequeath what he had to the poor? During this struggle, while his mind was fluctuating, he decided to devote himself to the monastic life.

2. In the same year [773] in which Italy was made subject to the power of glorious King Charles, Benedict's brother, wishing, rashly to cross a certain river, was seized by the swelling current. Benedict, sitting on his horse and seeing the danger his brother was in, rode right into the waves so that he might render his brother free of danger as he was crossing. With his horse swimming Benedict touched his brother's hand but, although he grabbed hold of it and wished to save the dying one, he was pulled and barely escaped dying himself. At that moment Benedict promised himself, in a vow to God, that he would not from then on fight in the world.

He sought his fatherland, but he did not disclose his plans to his father. There was a certain religious man by the name of Widmar who was blind, but resplendent in the light of the heart. To Widmar Benedict revealed himself and shared his secret; he was offered a wholesome plan. When all the preparations were made Benedict started on a journey, with the idea of going to Aachen, but when he arrived at the house of Saint Seine [at Langres], he ordered his men to return to their fatherland. They indicated that they wanted to serve God in the same monastery. Benedict asked for permission to enter and this he received. He tonsured himself and assumed the habit of a true monk.

Having been made a monk, he began to afflict his body with incredible starvation for two years and six months. He was as hostile to his own flesh as to that of a bloodthirsty beast, taking only a little food, sustaining his body on bread and water, avoiding wine as if it were a foul poison. If ever his mind weakened and he wanted to sleep he would place himself on a common blanket to rest, sometimes prostrate on the bare ground, and doze, overly tired, tiring himself more by the repose itself. Often he spent the night awake in prayer, lying on pavement stiff with ice, in bare feet.

He devoted himself so totally to divine meditation that he spent as many days as possible devoted to sacred psalmody, not breaking the rule of silence. While the rest were sleeping he moistened their shoes with water and greased them and returned them, after they were washed, to their proper places. Some, who were madmen, ridiculed him as he sat quite a distance away and threw their soldiers' boots at him. He endured their remarks with a higher purpose.

He demeaned himself in his dress with so much vileness that those who do not know what he was like can hardly be persuaded of it. His tunic was dirty and old, and he changed it only after many days had passed. The supply of lice on his squalid skin increased; these fed on limbs weakened by fasting. He had cowls ragged from their old age. If ever his tunic, which had grown rather old, was torn, he stuffed the holes with various colored rags which he had found.

These habits rendered him much disfigured. He was mocked by several, and pelted and spit upon. But his mind, fixed on heaven, when the rest dressed in more refined clothes on festive days, looked for more vile clothes to wear without any fear even before the eyes of all. During this time he never indulged his body by taking a bath, but he supervised the cleanliness of the monastery as often as the opportunity arose.

For the sake of repentance, whenever divine aid was given, so much was bestowed upon him that he wept as often as he wished. He was nourished daily on tears and groaning on account of the fear of hell, singing charmingly those words of David: "For I eat ashes like bread and mingle my drink with tears." His lips were pale from hunger and his flesh exhausted with leanness. The skin stuck to his bones just as creased skin hangs from oxen.

Because he was not so much taming his delicate body (as if it were a wild animal) as mortifying it, he was compelled by the abbot to soften the demands made upon his body, though he did not give his consent.

Declaring that The Rule of Saint Benedict was laid down for beginners or those who are weak, striving to climb toward the teachings of Saint Basil and The Rule of Saint Pachomius, he searched perpetually for what was more impossible.

In order that he might be evidence of salvation for many, he burned with love for The Rule of Saint Benedict, and as if from a unique struggle he approached the field as a new athlete about to fight publicly.

Meanwhile, he began to correct the habits of others, to denounce those who were negligent, and to prevail upon beginners to begin to imitate the good and to correct the bad by reproaching them. He, in addition to these things, added that the pantry should be guarded, and he committed the Rule of the abovesaid father to memory.

In accordance with Saint Benedict's precept, he was eager to compose himself and to grant what is lawful to those seeking it without delay, to deny to those seeking what is evil, and to excuse those seeking the impossible. And since, even for a lawful wish, he would not offer much to them, he was not looked upon with equal admiration by all.

The abbot cherished him with the highest affection because he was useful in all matters, cautious in his life, anxious for the salvation of others and, concerning the ministry, unique in speaking, prompt in obedience, affable in giving advice. Divine piety bestowed upon him the gift of intelligence and the facility of spiritual eloquence among many other virtues.

3. After five years and eight months in [these spiritually] health-giving matters, the abbot of the abovesaid monastery abandoned the world. Then all [of the monks], with one spirit and with equal consent, desired that Benedict be put in charge of them. But Benedict, realizing their customs did not agree with his, roused himself and returned to the land of his fathers.

There, on his father's and his own possession, above a stream whose name is Aniane, and near the river Arar, he built a small cell with Widmar (and a few others) near the little church of Saint Saturninus. There he lived several years in great poverty, day and night imploring divine clemency with groaning and tears so that he might advance his wish to a most efficacious end.

There were in that province certain men of the greatest holiness, namely Atilio, Nebridius, and Anianus, living religiously but ignorant of a regular rule. These men, when they met Benedict, profoundly respected him. When some adversity would overcome Benedict, he [would] immediately saddle his mule and rush to Atilio, who was the closest to him. [To Atilio he brought the tale of] the first time several men of ardent mind abandoned the world and attempted to live religiously with him. These men, broken in spirit, fearing this new way of life in which they were compelled to attain an unheard of way of abstinence (in which they took bread by weight and wine by measure), returned to the path of safety as a pig returns to its dinner and a dog returns to its vomit.

The man of God, seeing their unstable faith, was troubled and wished to return to Saint-Seine. Benedict went to Atilio for advice and when he told him what he wanted, Atilio rebuked him saying that Benedict had been shown to him from heaven and that he was a light given to men. Therefore he ought to fulfill assiduously the good that he had begun; this [calamity of losing followers] was a trick of the ancient enemy who, because he was jealous, was always hostile to good deeds.

Strengthened by this advice, Benedict fearlessly approached that which he desired to accomplish with ardent spirit. Using no other's foundation, he began to construct a new monastery and made it his purpose to reveal an unfamiliar path of salvation.

4. The venerable man Benedict, with a few brothers gathered around him, (who, when they learned his opinion, had flocked to him), began, in a place that is now memorable, to flourish and to reveal the way to those who wished a pious and celestial religion and to work with his own hands.

Benedict, lest he admonish without example and be found reprobate, made it his concern to carry out first what he said ought to be pursued. For he did not abandon the work he began when frightened by helplessness. As the apostle taught, when Benedict found himself in famine and thirst, in cold and nakedness, he urged his subjects to persist with unshaken hearts, teaching them what had been revealed to the pious: that the way which leads to heaven is a narrow and difficult way and that the sufferings of this life are very worthy for future glory.

After this teaching was strengthened, his followers exhausted themselves with even greater labor. They had no possessions, no vineyards, no flocks, no horses. They had only one mule, thanks to which, when they had to travel anywhere, the faintness of the brothers was prevented. They received wine only on Sundays and feast days. On several occasions their bodies had wasted away on account of dryness. In order to alleviate the cold weather they used blankets when they stood for divine vigils. They were paupers in possessions, but rich men in merits and the more their bodies were exhausted by scarcity, the more their minds were filled with virtue. They burned with celestial love and the solace of tears alone supported them in narrow straits.

The old enemy, seeing the unconquerable unity of the brothers, strove artfully to divide them. They had one mill in which they ground the grain they possessed. A guest, instigated by evil thoughts, came to them one night. They received him as well as they could and [allowed him to sleep with his head cradled in] the mule's saddle. But the evil guest stayed awake while they were resting, and arose and departed, taking with him the saddle on which he lay and the bucket from which he had taken water, not forgetting the tools of the mill. [Thus] he repaid good with evil. On the next day, when they discovered the loss, the pupils reported it to their teacher. Benedict taught them to bear up under the ill-treatment they had received and to consider their loss a gain, asserting that they should rather grieve for the guest, who, while he strove to acquire advantage, had forsaken his faith.

5. Meanwhile, the group of his disciples began to grow little by little. The fame of his holy religion was gradually spread by the oral report of those living around him and, extending itself, reached places situated far away. As the valley in which he had first placed his monastery was very narrow, gradually Benedict began to add to the monastery outside of the valley.

With the brothers doing the work, he himself sometimes worked alongside them. He had his hands full: sometimes he was cooking food for them to eat or was occupied with writing a book while he was busy in the kitchen; often he carried wood on his shoulder along with his disciples because of the scarcity of oxen.

There was a house on the property in which they undertook to establish the monastery. This house was enlarged and consecrated in honor of Mary, the holy Mother of God. From all places men came together demanding to make themselves subject to his teaching. The work of the monastery was quickly finished; the place was enlarged and enriched with possessions. Each one gave what he had. There were no adorned walls, no red tiles or painted, paneled ceilings: Benedict ordered them to construct the buildings with rough walls and roof them with straw. Even though the number of brothers might have been increasing, he always sought what was more common and humble.

If anyone wished to confer something from his own possessions on the monastery, Benedict received it. But if anyone tried to grant slaves or maidservants to the monastery, he shrank from it and did not allow anyone at this time to be given to the monastery by deed, but ordered that they should be freed. Moreoever, he did not want silver vessels for serving the body of Christ. At first he had wooden ones, and then ones of glass, and then, finally, he rose to ones of pewter. He refused to have a chasuble of silk, and if anyone gave him one he gave it to others to use.

7. At this time there arose a most severe famine [possibly in 779]. A multitude of paupers, widows, and orphans flocked to him and crowded around the gates and roads of the monastery. Seeing them suffering with hunger and almost swallowed up by death itself, Benedict was very disturbed because he did not know how he was going to feed such a large crowd. But since nothing is lacking to those who fear God, he ordered that the grain which was sufficient for the brothers be put aside, and the rest he ordered the brothers to dole out each day.

The meat of the cattle and sheep was given, and the milk of goats helped. The poor built huts for themselves and lived in them until the new harvest. Because grain was scarce Benedict ordered that the grain which the brothers used be put aside and measured. This was done three times. There was such a great feeling of pity in the brothers' hearts that they would liberally distribute everything. Of that which each one could take for himself, he secretly gave to those being consumed by famine. Thus the brothers [themselves] barely escaped the danger of starvation. Occasionally a dead man was found with bread in his mouth.

10. But the ancient enemy was disturbed at the increased unity of the good flock and tried to strike the hearts of some of them so that he could render the good educator bereft of his flock. He drove many from the monastery

and threw many into confusion, but he could not shake the mind of one prepared for tribulation. The Devil instigated Benedict's serfs to cause destruction and ordered them to steal horses and cattle both openly and secretly. But Benedict, who placed God before all things, lost without grief what he had possessed without love. Certainly no one ever saw him disturbed because something was missing. He never sought back what was lost or searched for what had been stolen, and he offered kindness to the thief if he was caught. He even sent him away in secret so that he would not be caught.

12. And since omnipotent God has created everything, including works and miracles at the right times through his servants, I shall touch upon a few of the miracles which He has worked through this man.

At a certain time a fire invaded a house situated next to the church of the blessed virgin Mary. When the rapidly burning flames licked the dry stubble, the brothers ran to the house, which they had built with great labor, and were sad to see it being consumed rapidly by flames. With great eagerness they attempted to prevent the fire from catching the neighboring church, for the whole force of the flame was being carried in that direction. Even father Benedict came to this sight, and the brothers immediately asked him to help them with prayers. He quickly complied with the request of the brothers and prostrated himself in tears before the altar of Mary, the blessed virgin and mother of God. As he prayed, with the aid of divine mercy, the fire turned its force in the opposite direction.

16. Nor must I pass over in silence what I, myself, saw. A certain brother was appointed prior, but he fell into arrogance and was deposed. Later he fell into such evil that he practiced robbery after leaving the monastery. [He was caught, eventually,] and Benedict ordered that he, stretched underneath his horse with his feet in chains, be brought back to the monastery. The guilty man shouted and swore that he would never leave again. Benedict ordered that the culprit, because of his foolishness, be beaten with rods. And so, after that, he remained in the monastery, living justly and piously as if the malign enemy in him had been killed.

17. Now with the help of Christ let us review, in a plain reckoning, how he, at Charlemagne's order, built another monastery in the same place.

In the year 782, the fourteenth year of Charles's reign, with the help of the dukes and counts, Benedict built another large church in honor of the Lord our Savior. There were new cloisters in this church with many marble columns which were set in colonnades. Now he did not cover these buildings with straw, but with tiles. This place was enriched with so much holiness that whoever came full of faith to seek something, and did not hesitate in his own heart but rather believed, rapidly received what he had asked for. Because it shines forth with wonderful religiosity we think it important to reveal for the future [reader] something of the nature of this place.

Benedict arrived and set out with pious consideration to consecrate the church, not in the name of any saint, but, as we have already said, in the name of the deified Trinity. To make this perfectly clear, I tell you, he decided to set three altars below the main altar, so that by these the persons of the Trinity might be symbolized.

It was a marvelous arrangement, since by the three altars the three persons of the Trinity were signified, while in the [main] altar the essential unity of the Godhead was demonstrated. The altar was solid on the outside, but inside it was hollow, thus prefiguring what Moses made in the desert. On its back this altar has a small door in which on certain days chests with the relics of the fathers are placed. Let these things said about the altar suffice and let us proceed to the furniture of the church and in what order or number it was arranged.

All the utensils which were kept in that house are known to have been consecrated to the number seven. Seven candelabra were wondrously made with artistic skill. From the stem hang shafts with little balls, lilies, rods, and goblets in the shape of nuts, like those which Beseleel fashioned with wondrous art. In front of the altar hang seven wondrous and beautiful lamps, fashioned with great labor, which are said by those who know and who wish to gaze upon them to have been made with Solomon's skill. Another seven silver lamps hang from the choir like a crown which, with cups inserted in them, receive ladles. It is the custom, especially on feast days, to burn them filled with oil. When they have been lit the whole church shines at night just as it does during the day.

Finally, three altars have been consecrated in this same church: one in honor of the Archangel Michael, another in veneration of the blessed apostles Peter and Paul, and the third in honor of the dear protomartyr Stephen.

In the church of Mary, the holy Mother of God, which was established first, there were altars to Saint Martin and Saint Benedict. The altar which stands in the cemetery is distinguished by being consecrated to the honor of John the Baptist; divine oracles have testified that no one greater has arisen among those born to women.

It may be considered with how much humility and reverence this place ought to be feared, having been fortified by so many great powers. The Lord Christ is Prince of all princes, King of all kings, Lord of all lords; Holy Mary, mother of this same God, is believed to be Queen of all virgins; Michael is preferred to all of the angels; Peter and Paul are the chief apostles; Stephen, the protomartyr, holds first place in the chorus of witnesses; Martin gleams as the gem of the bishops; Benedict was father of all monks.

And so in seven altars, in seven candelabra, and in seven lamps, the sevenfold grace of the Holy Spirit is revealed.

18. Let him know, whoever desires to read or hear this life, that Benedict was the head of all the monasteries, not only those built in the area of Gothia, but also those which were built in other regions in that time and thereafter. [These monasteries were reformed] through his example and enriched from his treasury, just as it was told before in the charter.

He devoted himself to an investigation of the Rule of Saint Benedict making it his aim to understand it. He went around to the monasteries and asked more experienced men about the things of which he was ignorant. He gathered together the rules of all the saints that he could find. He ascertained a practical norm and the healthy customs of the monasteries and handed them down to his own monks to be observed. He instructed the cantors; he taught the readers. He had grammarians and men skilled in knowledge of Scripture, among whom some later became bishops. He gathered together many books, collected precious ecclesiastical vestments, large silver chalices, silver offertories, and quite eagerly acquired whatever he saw that was necessary to the work of God.

And thus he became known to all. The fame of his holiness reached royal and imperial ears. At this time he went to the glorious Emperor Charlemagne on a mission in the interests of his monastery. With pious contemplation beforehand, Benedict, in the form of a charter, gave his monastery to the king, so that his successors might not suffer inconvenience from [Benedict's] relatives after his death. From Charlemagne Benedict received a grant of immunity containing the following:

In the name of the holy and indivisible Trinity, Charles, by the grace of God, king of the Franks and the Lombards, and Patrician of the Romans.

We believe that the greatest protection of our kingdom is increased by this: if, with benevolent devotion, we grant as benefices useful places for churches, and prescribe that they be maintained with stability and with God's protection.

Therefore, let it be known to all bishops, abbots, counts, viscounts, vicars, hundredmen, judges, and all my fideles, in the present and in the future, that the venerable Benedict, abbot of a monastery which he, himself, built from its foundations, on his own property, in honor of the Lord and our Savior, Jesus Christ, and the sacred and always virgin Mary, Mother of the same God, and other saints, in the place called Aniane, in the territory of Maguélonne, below the fort of Mount Calmense, came to our clemency and surrendered the aforesaid monastery with all its property and the ornaments of the church, and additions and territory lying around it, to our hands with the fullest deliberation, and gave the holy place itself to us to rule under our defense and domination.

Therefore, in answer to his petition for eternal repayment, we have, by our donation, granted the holy place as a benefice, so that in the churches and in the territory and fields and other possessions of the monastery which he seems to possess justly at the present time, and in any places whatever which have been collected there due to divine love, and the things which even hereafter we or others wish to increase by divine piety, we admonish, order and anathematize that no count, bishop, or any other judiciary power at any time ever dare enter, or presume to make exactions for hearing causes, or demanding fines, or make demands for food and lodging, or impose tolls, or draw the men of the monastery away, either free-men or slaves, who reside on the land of the monastery, or seek revenues on unlawful pretexts, or collect any rent at all. Let the abbot himself, or his successors, or the monks of the aforesaid monastery, the present ones and the ones in the future, on account of the Name of God, under the name of immunity, and without any disorder or opposition, be able to rule, and let no man ever dare to collect any rent for any reason whatsoever. We wish this holy place to remain under our defense and domination.

Therefore, we decree and order that neither you nor your subordinates, nor your successors, nor anyone with judicial authority presume at any time to disrupt or make exactions in the churches, the territory, the fields, or the rest of the possessions of the monastery, nor any of those things which have been written above. What we have granted on behalf of the name of God and through eternal remuneration to the monastery, let it be of increasing profit always.

And when by divine calling the venerable abbot Benedict and his successors have traveled from this world to the Lord, and the holy congregation itself wishes to elect an abbot of the better sort, and one who is faithful to us in every respect, either from that monastery or from some other place, who will be able to rule the holy congregation according to the Rule of Saint Benedict, let them have the freedom to do this through our authority and through our indulgence. And wherever they wish to have him ordained, either by themselves, or by any bishops, let them have that power by our order and consent, so long as they are servants of God, who serve God there, who are chosen to obtain the mercy of God and preserve it carefully. We entrust this matter, given to us by God, on behalf of ourselves, our wife, our children, and the stability of our kingdom.

19. This the most glorious King Charles directed to the venerable man by his edict. Benedict also received from him through an imperial charter lands suitable for grazing animals and fit to be worked.

Moreover, with great honor, almost 40 pounds of silver was given as a gift by the king, and Benedict returned in peace to his own monastery as quickly as possible. As soon as he touched the land of his fathers Benedict divided the silver into parts and sent it out to each of the monasteries for the sake of benediction.

In our times, before all other men, this was his singular gift: kindness towards all and pious consideration for all the monasteries situated around him and even far away. He visited them repeatedly and imbued them with the order of his holy life. From the things which were given to him by the faithful, moreover, he sent out, in accordance with the number of inhabitants or with his ability to do so more to those who needed more, less to those who needed less. He knew what monasteries each monk belonged to and he remembered each person's name. Since he could not give [a pallium] to each, he divided [his own pallium] and sent enough cloth [to each monastery] to make crosses. To all the monasteries, those in Provence, in Gothia, and in Gascony, he was, as it were, a nurse, fostering them and helping them.

He was loved as a father by all, venerated as a lord, and revered as a teacher. [From the income of the monastery] a share was enthusiastically kept for the poor, and he did not allow the portions for the widows to be spent for other uses. He knew the names of all the nuns and widows situated around there. Ransoms were cheerfully offered for captives.

No one, I think, ever found himself without a present if Benedict had anything, and everything was done for everyone as much as possible. Therefore each man willingly gave Benedict his wealth. This [treasury] he gathered together to be spent for the benefit of the poor, the needy, widows, captives, and monks. From these men Benedict received between 4000 and 5000 *solidi* and implements for the purpose of distributing them to the needy.

It was also a great concern of his to refresh with food not only his own monks, but also those he happened to come across, and later on he nourished them with bread from heaven. Lest, through forgetfulness, they lose this healthful food, he became accustomed to impress more words upon them so that their hearts might remain firm, saying: "Be pure in body and humble in heart, since God does not accept arrogant chastity or iniquitous humility."

Indeed, upon some he was wont to impress this: "If many precepts seem to be impossible for you, preserve this little saying: 'shun evil and do good.'" This precept remained so familiar to him that, at the time of his death, when the precepts of all the fathers had been collected, he wanted to gather together one book based on that one saying. Indeed, in every hour, in nocturns, in chapter, in the refectory, he offered his followers food for living.

20. And since, while we have been trying to reveal his benevolence, many of his virtues have occurred openly, we consider it an advantage for whoever may be unfamiliar with them, or desiring to know them, that we elucidate them.

Everyone who clung to his friendship knew for certain that Benedict surpassed all in charity. He never wished to do anything for himself, but rather what he judged useful for others. If he erred he quickly corrected it. Because of his love of charity, in order that he might save many, he went around to the cells of others and revealed to them what was hidden in the holy Rule.

Especially, full of charity, he spent many days at Arles, with many bishops, abbots and monks, revealing the secrets of the canons and elucidating the Homilies of the blessed pope Gregory to the ignorant. Full of charity, he received clerics and monks from diverse places into his monastery, supported them, placed a teacher over them, and imbued them with holy thoughts. Through charity he sent gifts to those doing him harm. Nor must we labor to reveal what all have seen better and many have experienced by yielding.

21. From the rigor of his first conversion he gradually turned aside, since the work which he had taken upon himself was impossible. But the same purpose remained. He plowed with the plowmen, he was a companion of diggers, he reaped with the gatherers. And although that region was burned by the heat of the sun, and the air, like a fire coming from an oven, was hot rather than warm, Benedict, with fervor, along with his men who were burning, hardly took a cup of water before the hour of dinner. Weary from labor, burned by fire, they desired cold water rather than wine. Nor could anyone murmur against him since he was suffering the same things. This fact brought them not a little comfort, because when he realized that he was dry with thirst he treated them more humanely.

Nor did any of those working dare to sound forth with stories. While their hands were engaged in work their tongues were engaged in Psalms. Their mouths were intent on divine meditation while they were coming, going, and working.

Often we have seen him strike the hands of those who have treated him too generously with food and drink. Often we have seen a bowl placed before him for measuring and, as those who are in charge of the cellar say, while others were drinking wine, he drank water, except on the Sabbath and on Sunday. Often he took the grease from his food, and he took excessive care that not even a little particle of common cheese be found in it. He refused to eat the meat of quadrupeds from the time of his conversion until his death. If any sickness came upon him he took chicken soup. Also, for many years, beginning in his youth, he avoided the use of butter, although the things which he denied to himself he made available to others as often as he could.

He had so much anxiety if he found even a little piece of bean or some small hairs of leek or leaves of cabbage neglected, that a sentence worthy of excommunication was made against the man whose carelessness it was shown to be. If anyone offered water to him for washing and poured out more than was proper, Benedict claimed that a sin had occurred because the man had not walked a path of discretion.

He had this singular good: if anyone had his mind troubled, as soon as he approached Benedict the tumultuous throng of thoughts went away through his wholesome advice. Often, also, when one was stricken with hostile thoughts (as I have heard from a brother), he would say: "I shall go and reveal my thoughts to lord Benedict," and immediately the tumult withdrew from him. If anyone was held back by more serious offenses, he would reveal his heart to Benedict and would receive the alleviation of consolation. If he were troubled by the disease of sadness, he would soon depart in happiness after going to Benedict.

24. Meanwhile, hearing the fame of his holiness and the holy opinion of his flock, several bishops began to ask for monks [to staff the monasteries under their supervision]. One such was Leidrad, the bishop of Lyons [from 798 to 814], who wished to rebuild the monastery which is called Ile Barbe [at Lyons] and who asked for men to show him the principles of the good life. He received about 20 disciples chosen from the flock. Over these Leidrad placed a rector and sent them to live in the territory of Burgundy. There, due to the presence of Christ the Lord, there is now a large number of monks gathered together.

Theodulf, the bishop of Orléans, when he wished to build the monastery of Saint Mesmin de Micy, asked Benedict for men experienced in monastic discipline. To him Benedict gave his assent and sent 20 monks, putting a teacher over them. They, constantly vying in holy pursuits, gathered together not a small number of monks. Let me disclose what happened there, when the venerable father went to visit them. While they were awaiting his arrival, they busied themselves out of love and with all zeal insuring that there was an abundance of fish and food not only for him, but for all the brothers. A gathering of brothers happened, fishermen were involved, and markets were scoured. But such a great problem arose, because nothing was found for sale nor could the fishermen catch anything. Over this lack of things the brothers were very worried. Meanwhile the master arrived and the joyful monks received him and he being happy congratulated them in return on their successes. But the brothers hid their shame under happy faces. Then it happened that, when one of the brothers was doing some work near the Loire river, suddenly he saw a huge fish which they call a sturgeon swimming near the shore. He was not slow to jump in and catch it and carried the fish home to his brothers. Over this there was a great deal of joy, but also great wonder. All admitted that this had happened because of the virtues of that venerable man Benedict. I heard of these things, unless I am mistaken, from a faithful brother.

Alcuin was from the Angle nation and was a deacon in rank. He was also extremely wise, venerable in his sanctity, and the abbot of the monastery of Saint Martin the Confessor, who was the bishop of Tours. Alcuin was held in great honor at the court of the glorious Emperor Charlemagne; the fame of the holiness of that man of God having been heard of and experienced. He joined himself with unshakeable charity to that one, so that from the letters sent to that one a collection in one little book was made. When gifts had been given to Alcuin, he firmly asked for monks to be given to him. To whom, when the venerable father [Benedict] had at once agreed, he sent horses carrying the monks. Alcuin gathered those monks together in a monastery whose name is Cormery which he had erected. There were, I believe, 20 monks there with a master over them. Because of the good example of their conversion a great crowd of monks gathered there.

25. I do not think it is irrelevant if Benedict's miracles, which were performed by the propitious Divinity at that time, are inserted in this work.

A certain brother was sent to carry from one cell to another a holy portable altar in which relics of Saint Denis and other saints were housed. The brother departed taking some puppy dogs with him. He hurriedly boarded a ship. The cells [he had been ordered to visit] were situated between a lake and the sea. When he returned, after several days without washing his clothes, he was careless in handling the altar. As soon as he touched land he mounted a horse, taking the puppies with him. He reached for the altar intending to carry it: then divine vengeance struck him. The horse turned itself around on that same shore by wheeling in a circle; the brother was thrown to the ground. The altar, which slipped from his hands, fell unhurt. The horse immediately died, but the brother, who had fallen, proceeded home not without great faintness. He was exhausted for a long time but finally recovered his health.

The brothers who had been sent to get the relics, upon hearing what had happened, sent out another brother. This man, since he was a priest, carried a cross with him in which there was wood of the Lord's cross. He entered the lake and his little boat was carried away by a strong gale. But as soon as the cross, which he was carrying around his neck, opposed the swelling waves, the gusts ceased. As he took rest in a cell he saw, in a dream, a man of wondrous brightness who spoke thus to him: "If you had not carried the wood of my Lord with you, you would leave this place in vain when you wished to go." Thus he was warned to carry the relics on foot. But since he did not obey, when the relics had been brought to his cell he was struck with a severe infirmity. I learned these things, to be sure, from those to whom they happened.

26. In the mountains in which the brothers were accustomed to live and care for the sheep which had to be fed, they had built a small oratorium for praying. Some women came there (after the brothers had left the place)

and, disdaining the little huts of the monks [they occupied the oratorium] saying to each other: "You hold the place of the abbot because you are standing in his place." And thus they remained in the place of prayer and reclined, not rising. The little houses in which the monks stayed in the summertime were vacant. A worthy vengeance soon pursued the women. They began to be vexed with attacks of giddiness. From this grief they were not released until their husbands followed the monks descending from the mountains with their sheep. The husbands implored the monks to utter prayers for their rash wives. After the brothers had prayed the women immediately returned to health.

27. Once an epileptic came to the monastery because his parents had brought him there. He was placed in the Church of the holy Mother of God and forever virgin Mary. When the brothers uttered a prayer for him at vigils he regained his health and departed in peace.

28. ...Let it suffice to have said these things about the miracles performed in our time. With God's help let us return to the order already begun.

29. The most glorious Louis, then king of Aquitaine, now the august emperor, by divine providence, for the sake of the whole living church in Europe, when he became familiar with Benedict's way of holiness, esteemed him and willingly obeyed his counsel. Louis even put Benedict in charge of all the monasteries in his kingdom so that he might offer a healthful norm to all.

There were certain monasteries preserving canonical rules, but ignorant of the teachings of the Rule of Saint Benedict. Obeying Louis's orders, Benedict went around to each of the monasteries, not once or twice, but many times, revealing the admonitions of the Rule and reviewing it for them chapter by chapter, confirming what was known, elucidating what was not known. Thus it happened, by divine providence, that almost all the monasteries situated in Aquitaine undertook a form of the Rule of Saint Benedict.

But [the Devil], who always envies good actions, an adversary of innocence and an enemy of peace, did not judge it advantageous if Benedict adhered any longer to the friendship of the pious king [Charlemagne], not doubting that this [friendship] would bring ruin upon his own side if their love remained inseparable even at a distance. Since he lost the glory of his own nature through pride, he took care with all his might that no man would be introduced to that good which he had lost for he grieved that man could be saved through God's mercy.

It is no wonder that the ancient enemy is tormented by the goodness of the pious and is tortured by the progress of those whom he sees are invincible, since there indeed are many men who imitate the works of his malignity. For many, and indeed we should grieve over this, are inflamed by others' advantages and incited to hatred of those whose example they ought to follow. Accompanied by a procession of these men, armed with the javelins of hate, the Devil proceeds, intending to do battle wrongly against those advantageous actions considered worthy by God.

First the Devil inflamed the minds of the clerics by derogation of Benedict when the Devil incited the hearts of the soldiers of the royal court. He even subverted the minds of some of the counts. All alike, inflamed by the torch of hate, not secretly, but openly, vomiting the poisons of a destructive mind constantly with public voices, cried out that this "pilgrim for their souls [Benedict], was a wandering monk desirous of (the possession) of things and a usurper of others' gains."

Their raging madness broke out in such a great wickedness that they tried to incite the mind of the most serene emperor Charlemagne against Benedict. But the man of God, his conscience well secured, was not moved by their derogations nor frightened by their fraudulent assertions. [Benedict] went to the palace about this matter.

As he was going there several tried to prevent him saying that if he stood in the sight of the emperor he would not be seen again beyond his fatherland because the imperial wrath would be inflamed against him. Nevertheless, he proceeded fearlessly with confidence in the mercy of God, entrusting his hope to Him for love of whom he was not sluggishly struggling. If it were to be decided that he submit to the hardship of exile, Benedict determined, ever more certainly, to serve God. If he should be driven from office, so that he would not be in command, he said that he had aspired to that for a long time.

After he stood in the sight of the emperor, his piety bent Charlemagne's mind to such tranquility that when he saw him he kissed him warmly and offered him a cup with his own hands. And Benedict, whom his rivals asserted would be banished from his own soil, returned to it with great honor.

Thus, with divine mercy ordaining it, though they tried to disgrace him they actually praised him, and he, whom they were eager to render hateful through deceit, they revealed as a man who should be venerated not only by the lesser ones, but also by the greater ones.

30. Count William [of Gellone], who was more distinguished than anyone at the court of the emperor, clung to blessed Benedict with such affection of love that despising the honors of the world, he chose Benedict as his guide on the way to salvation through which it is possible to reach Christ. After he received permission to convert he surrendered to Benedict with gifts of gold and silver and all kinds of precious clothing. Nor did he allow there to be any delay in tonsuring himself on the feastday of the apostles Peter and Paul [29 June]. He put off his clothing, embroidered in gold, and assumed the habit of the worshippers of heaven, rejoicing that he was immediately admitted to the number of the worshippers of Christ.

The valley called Gellone is about four miles away from the monastery of the blessed man Benedict. There William, while still placed in the honor of the world, had ordered a cell to be built. At Gellone, after his vows, he entrusted himself to the service of Christ. And since he was born of noble [parents] he was eager to become more noble by embracing the highest poverty of Christ. He gave up the honor which he had attained by birth for Christ....

33. The most glorious King Louis gave Benedict another monastery, where, I think, he sent twenty monks, placing an abbot over them. That monastery was situated in the territory of Poitiers and dedicated to the honor of Saint

Savinus. There the monks were placed, and, as they exerted themselves in pious pursuits, not a small number of monks was joined to them.

The king conferred another monastery on him. It was situated in the territory of Bourges and there he placed about forty monks and an abbot over them. Since the monastery had to be founded from the beginning, Benedict offered help and gave books and sacred vestments. Those who flourished in the practice of sacred religion and pious conversation, revealing the norm and also preserving a unity of spirit in a chain of peace, gathered together a very large flock of monks within the herd of Christ.

35. After the death of the most serene Emperor Charles, when his son Louis, the king of Aquitaine, undertook the care of the empire, he ordered Benedict to come to the territory of the Franks. There, in the monastery of Alsath-Maurum, Benedict gathered together several followers of his life from the monastery of Aniane.

Since this place was a great distance from the palace Benedict could not be present at the proper time when he was called. Because for many reasons he was indispensable to the emperor, Louis provided a place for him not far from the palace, where Benedict could reside with a few men. So Benedict put an abbot in charge of the brothers living at Maurum and approached with several men to obey the wish of the emperor.

There was a neighboring valley which, I think, was not more than six miles from the palace, which was pleasing to the eyes of the man of God. There the emperor ordered him to build, in a wondrous work, a monastery which is called Inda, the name of the same valley, borrowed from that of a stream. The emperor was present at the dedication of the church, and he enriched it most copiously from his own fisc. He ordered an immunity in writing and commanded that thirty monks remain there to serve God. In order to furnish the number the venerable abbot ordered brothers chosen from the well-known monasteries to come and he instructed them by his own example. They were proof of salvation for others because, by the inspiration of divine grace, they left behind the pomp of the world.

From that time on the man of God began to frequent the door of the palace, bearing the once scorned commotion for the sake of the many men who had suffered inconveniences at the hands of others, and he sought imperial succor. When [the oppressed] approached him he received them cheerfully and kissed them and heard their complaints. These were written on pages [and presented] to the emperor at the appropriate time. Sometimes the most serene emperor would stroke Benedict's scarf and sleeves because Louis was accustomed to find the pages there: on account of forgetfulness Benedict used to carry the pages in such places. When Louis found them he would read them in order to know how [to redress these grievances]. The emperor willingly heard complaints of this sort and on account of this ordered Benedict to be in the palace as much as possible.

Although there were many who advised Louis on the governing of the empire, on the disposition of the provinces, and on their own usefulness, none of those afflicted with troubles and none of the monks revealed their wants to the emperor. Benedict was the advocate for the wretched and a father for the monks, a consoler of the poor and a teacher of the monks.

He offered food for life to the rich, but he impressed the discipline of the Rule upon the minds of the monks. Although he gave advice concerning the business of all, he busily intervened concerning the necessities of the monks.

36. Louis also put Benedict in charge of all the monasteries in his empire so that just as he had instructed Aquitaine and Gothia in the rule of life he might also imbue Francia with his wholesome example. There were many monasteries which had once been established according to a rule, but little by little the rigor had lessened and the regular order had almost perished.

Moreover, so that just as there was one profession for all there might also be one healthful practice for all the monasteries, Benedict, at the bidding of the emperor, met several days with the fathers of the monasteries and as many monks as possible gathered together. When all were congregated at the same time to discuss the Rule afresh, Benedict elucidated the obscure for all, explored what was doubtful, took away the old errors, and confirmed the useful practices and dispositions. After the justice of the Rule and the doubtful matters had been brought to a useful end, with the approval of all, he revealed the customs which the Rule explained less well.

Concerning this he established a capitulary and offered it to the emperor to be confirmed, so that Louis might order it to be observed by all the monasteries situated in his empire. (We direct readers who wish to study it [to the document itself].)

The emperor immediately offered his consent to Benedict and placed inspectors throughout each of the monasteries to see whether those things which had been ordered were being observed. The work was completed and made prosperous with the help of divine mercy. One established rule was observed generally by all and all the monasteries were thus brought to a form of unity as though they were imbued by one teacher in one place. A uniform standard in drink, in food, in vigils, and in all measuring was set down.

And since he established a rule to be observed throughout the other monasteries, so he instructed his own monks living at Inda with every effort so that the monks coming from diverse regions would not require to be told how to act because they would see in the habits of each, in the walk of each, and in their dress, a regular and clear form of discipline.

37. On account of the indiscreet fervor of many, the inept tepidity of others, and the blunted sense of those less capable, Benedict established a limit and a way of life, handing it down to all to be observed. He drew them back lest they seek what is superfluous, and ordered them to shake off torpor and to seek to fulfill their program.

He ordered them to fulfill many rules, but there were many which he, in his daily practice, sought to discharge. About these he kept silent, but through these the life of a monk is adorned, as if by jewels, and without them such a life may be considered lax, loose, and without order.

The venerable abbot disclosed that which ought to be observed and determined to execute it without any delay or pretense of excuse. The things which he recognized ought to be abandoned or changed he gave to his disciples after he put an end to the disagreeable situation. If a page of the

Rule did not reveal something clearly or was completely silent about it, he arranged and completed it rationally and fittingly, helped by divine aid.

38. ...He made a book, collected together from the rules of the different fathers, so that the Rule of Saint Benedict would be foremost of all. He ordered monks to read it every morning at the periodic sitting. In order that he might show those who refused to do their duty that nothing frivolous or vain was put forth by Saint Benedict, but that his own rule depended on others, he composed another book with the maxims of the rules collected together, to which he gave the name Concordia Regularum. That the doctrine of Saint Benedict might take precedence the contents were rationally added to it, following it. He put together another book of homilies of the holy doctors, which has been published for the monks, and he ordered them to read it every evening.

39. Benedict saw that many men were busy in acquiring monasteries with every effort, and that they were striving to obtain them not only by prayers but also through gifts. These men were spending the monks' stipends for their own use. Because of this practice several monasteries were bankrupt. Others were held by [lay abbots or priests] after the monks had fled.

Benedict approached the most pious emperor on account of this cause and entreated him to render clerics free from struggles of this sort and the monks free from this danger.

The most glorious emperor gave his assent and decreed in writing that all the previously mentioned monasteries in his empire in which the abbots were regular should remain stable at all times. He ordered it to be enacted and signed it with his ring, and thus he removed the cupidity of many and the fear of the monks.

There were also certain monasteries owing gifts and services. On account of this some monasteries came to such great poverty that food and clothing were lacking for the monks. When Benedict brought these affairs to Louis's attention, the most pious emperor ordered the monasteries to perform service only so far as they were able so that nothing would be lacking for those serving God; and through this they might pray to God on behalf of him, his children, and the most pious state of the whole empire. For those monasteries which had been left under the power of the canons he established separately the means by which they could live according to a rule, and he gave these to an abbot.

41. After this Benedict began to be worn down by various sicknesses and to prepare for a new struggle. His body was depleted after many years of continual vigils, constant tears, harsh fasting, labors, and meditations. But he, who had attained the height of virtue by overcoming vices, nobly struggled with infirmities, girded with the arms of patience, and received a double palm of victory from his King after overcoming his enemies. For the more strongly he was stricken with sickness, the more intently he persisted either in prayers or in reading. No one found him in leisure, no one found him sluggish in the work of God; no one found him occupied in vain and frivolous stories. For either he himself worked hard at reading or he eagerly listened

to someone else reading.

Whoever found him alone except when he was weeping? Who, when approaching him suddenly, found his cheeks dry and him not either prostrate on the ground or standing with his hands reaching to heaven? Or, lest the page of a sacred volume be wet with too many tears, how many found him resisting tears in a battle? The strength of his flesh was failing, but the exertion of his mind persisted even harder than adamant; once his rigor was begun it was almost everlasting.

He did not undertake the eating of meat from the day of his conversion. Even at his end, when he was worn out by faintness, he rarely indulged in a bath. He was accustomed to change his clothes after forty or more days. He used to order the brothers to read aloud the lives and deaths of the sacred fathers; his mind recuperated with this reading, enduring even stronger.

O good Jesus, with what sighs and tears his soul was filled as it burned, desiring to be released and to be with Christ. Nevertheless he did not refuse to endure labor if it was necessary for the brothers.

When his sickness grew stronger, he addressed the emperor familiarly and was taken from the monastery. Bidding farewell to the brothers, spending the whole night in prayers and Psalms, he completed the regular office of that day. But when he had completed the regular office of another day and wished to pay up his journey, he arrived at this conclusion: "You are just, Lord."

Singing this verse he said, "I am failing," and added, "do with your servant, Lord, according to your mercy." And thus between the words of his prayer he let out his spirit adorned with virtue....

Questions: Can historians and students of medieval culture find useful information in the story of a saint's life? Does Ardo's account seem reliable and, if so, why? What qualifications must we make when reading all hagiographies? Can we through Ardo's portrait gain an indication of Benedict's character? How did his contemporaries and monks judge him? What changes occurred in his own monastic practices? What drove Benedict to give up military life and take up a monastic life? How involved with politics was Benedict and why?

27. The *Ordinatio Imperii* of 817

The 'Ordinatio imperii' is surely the most important constitutional document of the ninth century, both for its attempt to make the imperial title heritable and for its part in fostering the events that were to trouble Louis's reign. Why in 817 Louis decided to take this step is not certain. The Royal Frankish Annals reported that early in the year the emperor had been nearly killed when a wooden arcade at Aachen had fallen on him and twenty of his companions (see doc.7.32). Just as likely an explanation is that the imperial party that had worked to elevate Louis and to promote ideals of unity within church and state now urged him to find a means of preserving the empire. Louis's document is clearly indebted to Charlemagne's 'Division of his Kingdoms' (doc.22), but here he made a principle of primogeniture the means for determining which son should be emperor and why he should have priority and predominance. But he and his counselors also attempted to promote the harmony of the brothers, so that the kingdom might be peaceful, secure against outsiders, and a single empire.

Source: trans. B. Pullan in Sources of the History of Medieval Europe from the Mid-Eighth to the Mid-Thirteenth Century (New York: Barnes & Noble, 1966), pp.38-42; reprinted with permission.

In the name of the Lord God and our Savior Jesus Christ, Louis, by the decree of divine providence, the emperor augustus.

When, in God's name, in the month of July of the year of the Lord's Incarnation 817, indiction ten, in the fourth year of our reign, we had at our palace of Aachen in the customary manner gathered together the sacred assembly and common council of our people in order to study the welfare of the church and our whole empire and were engaged upon these things, it happened all at once that by divine inspiration our loyal subjects advised us to deal with the state of the whole realm and with the question of our sons in the same way as our parents, maintaining the peace and security which God had everywhere granted us. But although this advice was given with devoted loyalty, it did not seem to us nor to men of sound judgment that, out of love or favor to our sons, the unity of the empire preserved for us by God ought to be destroyed by men, lest this should allow any scandal to arise in the holy church and lest we should offend him who holds all kingdoms in his possession. Therefore we thought it necessary that, with fasting and prayer and almsgiving, we should obtain from him the answer which we in our weakness did not presume to give. After three days of such solemn celebration, and, we believe, at the command of almighty God, it was accomplished that we and all our people together voted to elect our beloved eldest son Lothar. So, as the divine decree had pointed to him, it pleased us and all our people to crown him solemnly with the imperial diadem, and to appoint him our consort and, God willing, successor to the empire by common vote. It was generally agreed to confer upon his brothers, Pepin and our namesake Louis, the title of king, and to determine the places (those named below) in which upon our decease they shall yield royal power under their elder brother according to the articles drawn up below, which contain the arrangement we have established between them. It has pleased us to debate with all our loyal subjects these articles for the welfare of the empire, for the preservation of everlasting peace between our sons and for the protection of the whole church; and, having discussed them, to write them down and afterwards sign them with our own hands, so that with God's help they may be preserved inviolate by the common devotion of all men even as they have been enacted by their unanimous vote, to maintain everlasting peace between our sons and all the Christian people: saving in all things our imperial power over our sons and our people, and all the obedience which is shown to a father by his sons and to an emperor and king by his people.

1. We wish Pepin to have Aquitaine and Gascony and the entire mark of Toulouse, and four counties in addition to that: Carcassonne in Septimania, and Autun, Avallon, and Nevers in Burgundy.

2. Again, we wish Louis to have Bavaria and the Carinthians, Bohemians, Avars, and Slavs to the east of Bavaria, and, in addition, to have two royal manors, Lauterhofen and Ingolstadt, at his service in the district of Nordgau.

3. We wish the two brothers who bear the title of king to have power of their own to distribute all honors within their dominion, provided only that in bishoprics and abbeys the proper ecclesiastical procedure is observed and that other offices are given in an honorable and useful manner.

4. Again we wish them, once a year at a suitable time, to go to their elder brother with gifts, either together or separately as circumstances permit, in order to visit and see him and in mutual brotherly love discuss vital matters and those connected with the common welfare and everlasting peace. And if it happens that one of them is unavoidably prevented from coming at the usual suitable time, he must inform the eldest brother of this by sending him ambassadors and gifts. He must not, on a flimsy pretext, slide out of coming as soon as a suitable opportunity presents itself.

5. We wish and advise the eldest brother, when either one or both his brothers, as aforesaid, come to him with gifts, to reward them in kind and brotherly love with a still more generous gift, as greater power is by God's consent vested in him.

6. When his younger brothers make a reasonable request for aid against foreign nations, we wish and command the elder brother, as reason dictates and the situation allows, to bring them suitable help either in person or through his loyal lieutenants and armies.

7. Again, we wish them henceforth not to presume to declare war upon or make peace with foreign nations hostile to this empire preserved by God without the advice and consent of their eldest brother. But they must try to repress sudden hostile risings or unexpected invasions by themselves, as far as they are able.

8. Supposing ambassadors have been sent by foreign nations to make peace or declare war, or hand over cities or castles, or on any other important business, they shall on no account answer them or send them back without their eldest brother's knowledge. But if ambassadors are sent to him from any country and reach one of them first, he shall send them honorably with his own loyal ambassadors to his brother's presence. But they may give an answer by themselves concerning matters of less consequence, depending on the nature of the embassy. But we advise them never to fail to inform their

eldest brother how matters stand within their own territories, so that he may be found always alert and prepared to do anything that the need and profit of the kingdom shall demand.

9. We also see fit to ordain that, to avoid discord, after our decease the vassals of each brother shall hold a benefice only in the dominion of his own lord and not in that of another. But every man may honorably and securely keep his own property and inheritance, wherever it is, having regard for justice, according to his law and without being wrongfully disturbed. And every free man who has no lord shall be allowed to commend himself to any of these three brothers he shall choose.

10. But if, which God forbid, a thing which we do not desire, it happens that any of the brothers, out of that greed for earthly possessions which is the root of all evil, dismembers or oppresses churches and poor men, or uses that tyranny which is the height of cruelty, let him first (as the Lord commands) be secretly warned to amend once, twice, thrice, through loyal ambassadors. If he will yield to them, let him be summoned by one brother and in the presence of the other admonished and reprimanded in fatherly and brotherly love. And if he utterly despises this salutary admonition, let the common decision of all determine what is to be done about him; that the imperial power and the common decision of all may coerce the man who cannot be restrained from his wicked deeds by a salutary admonition.

11. The rectors of churches in Francia shall have the same power over their possessions in Aquitaine or in Italy or in other regions and provinces subject to this empire as they had in the time of our father and are recognized as having in our own.

12. The brothers may have any tribute, taxes or monies they can demand and obtain within their dominion, so that they may use them to provide for their own needs and can the better prepare gifts to be sent to their eldest brother.

13. If, after our decease, the time comes for any of the brothers to marry, we wish him to take a wife with the advice and consent of his eldest brother; and we decree that care must be taken, in order to avoid discord and take away opportunities for harm, that none of them presumes to take a wife of foreign nationality. But the vassals of all brothers, for the purpose of strengthening the ties of peace, may take wives from any country they choose.

14. If any of them dies and leaves legitimate children, his dominion shall not be divided between them, but the people shall assemble and elect the one of them whom God desires. The eldest brother shall receive him as a brother and son, and, being honored as a father, shall in every respect observe this decree in his relations with him. They shall discuss with dutiful love how to take care of the other children and treat them wisely as our parents did.

15. But if any of the brothers dies without legitimate children, his dominion shall revert to the eldest brother. And if it happens that he has children by mistresses, we advise the eldest brother to show mercy to them.

16. If it happens that any of the brothers on our death is not yet lawfully of age according to Ripuarian Law, it is our will that, until he reaches the prescribed age, the eldest brother shall take charge of and govern him and his kingdom in the same way as we have done. And when he comes of age

he shall wield his power over all things in the approved manner.

17. May the kingdom of Italy be subject to our son Lothar in everything, if God wishes him to succeed us, just as it was to our father and as it is subject to us, God willing, at the present time.

18. Also, we advise all our people in their devotion, and in their steadfast and most sincere loyalty, which is celebrated among all peoples, that, if our son who succeeds us at God's command departs this life leaving no legitimate children, they may for the safety of all, for the peace of the church and for the unity of the empire, in electing one of our children, if any survive their brother, follow the procedure we laid down for his election, so that in the appointment they may seek to fulfill, not the will of man, but the will of God.

Questions: In what ways does the 'Ordinatio imperii' differ from Charlemagne's 'Division'? Which was the bolder constitutional arrangement? Have the territorial units remained basically the same? Does the 'Ordinatio' radically alter the power structures of the Carolingian world or does it reinforce them? Who is left out of Louis's arrangement? What grievances would this document give rise to, and did Louis try to anticipate and deal with them?

28. The Vision of the Poor Woman of Laon

Obviously not everyone was happy with the 'Ordinatio Imperii'. The two younger brothers, as Thegan had noticed, were upset by their enforced inferiority (doc.25.21), and there were some royal players who had been effectively neglected. Though Charlemagne in the 'Division of his Kingdoms' (doc.22.5) had made provision for the sons of his sons to retain their fathers' kingdoms, in the 'Ordinatio' Louis entirely ignored the position of Bernard, the son of his dead brother Pepin, in Italy. Thegan was quick to point out that Bernard was the son of a concubine and, therefore, not legitimate, a fact that was of some importance to Louis and Benedict of Aniane. Almost immediately, in late 817, Bernard and his supporters plotted some resistance in Italy, but Louis acted quickly to suppress the uprising. Bernard was blinded, a punishment that would have effectively removed him from the prospect of high office. This was the first great crisis of Louis's reign and seems to have been remembered at Reichenau where Heito, a former bishop of Basel, composed a vision which is a strikingly critical indictment of Louis's action.

Source: trans. P.E. Dutton from H. Houben, "Visio cuiusdam pauperculae mulieris: Überlieferung und Herkunft eines frühmittelalterlichen Visionstextes (mit Neuedition)," *Zeitschrift für die Geschichte des Oberrheins* 124, NF 85 (1976), pp.41-42.

There was in the district of Laon a certain poor woman who was once seized by a state of ecstasy. When she returned from [her rapture], she reported many wondrous things. A certain man dressed in a monk's habit, she said, had led her to a place where she saw the peaceful repose of the saints and the punishment of wrongdoers. It is of such things that the apostle Paul writes in his letter, "Things which the eye has not seen and the ear has not heard and which have not entered into the heart of mankind."

For she saw there a certain prince of Italy [Charlemagne] placed in torment and she saw many other famous people, some in a state of punishment, some in a state of glory. She asked her guide if that [emperor] would return to eternal life in the beyond. The guide said: "He certainly should, for if the Emperor Louis, his son, fully provides for seven memorial services on his behalf, he will be released."

She also saw Pico [Count Bego], who was a friend of this king [Louis], lying on his back in agony as two black demons melted gold and poured it into his mouth, saying [as they did so]: "Because in the world you were always thirsty like this, but could never be satisfied, drink now until you are full."

She also saw Queen Ermengard placed in torment, for she had three boulders like giant teeth grasping her, one placed upon her head, another upon her chest, the third upon her back, and they were always dragging her down into the depths. I am about to tell you something remarkable, for Ermengard cried out to the poor woman and said: "Go and ask my lord emperor if he thinks it worthwhile to help me in my wretched condition. And give him a sign so that he will know that you were sent by me, which is that in the crisis of my deposition I spoke with him alone in a garden. He knows this [event] well, because up until today the same conversation was a secret to all except us."

While the woman and her guide walked on from that point, the woman's guide showed her a wall, whose upper reaches stretched up to the heavens, and beyond it was another wall, which was entirely inscribed with golden letters. She asked him what this was. "It is," he said, "the terrestrial paradise into which no one shall enter unless [his name] is found written there." And he ordered her to read. But she said: "I have not learned how to read." "I know," he said, "but nevertheless read!" The woman read and found that the name of Bernard, once king, was inscribed in letters more brilliant than any other there. But the name of King Louis was so faint and almost obliterated that it could scarcely be seen. But she said: "Why is that name so obliterated?" Her guide answered: "Before he carried out the murder of Bernard, no name had been clearer on the wall. The killing of Bernard led to the obliteration of that name. Go and take diligent care not to hide any of this from the king."

But the woman, not being brave, kept quiet. Before long the guide again admonished her, but as before she kept quiet. On a third occasion he came to her and said: "Why is it that you do not obey the word of God?" To which, she answered: "O lord, I am a poor person and I dare not reveal these things in public." To which the guide said: "You shall not enjoy the use of your eyes [again] until you have exposed these things in the presence of the king." Instantly the eyes of the woman were cast into darkness. After many days she came into the presence of the king, told him everything, and received back her sight.

Questions: Why would a Carolingian writer choose a vision text as the best vehicle for political protest? Why is the visionary a poor woman? Why might Ermengard have been a special target of criticism?

29. Louis's Public Penance in 822

In 821 Benedict of Aniane, who had supplied the moral backbone for Louis the Pious's early reign, died. It is probably not coincidental that the very next year at Attigny the emperor performed public penance for his misdeeds and welcomed a new set of advisors to court. It may be, however, that this act of confession and penance was not humiliating, but rather praiseworthy and concilatory, since it recalled a similar action by the Emperor Theodosius before Saint Ambrose. The account below is the entire entry for the year 822 in the so-called Royal Frankish Annals. These annals were written at the palace by some individual such as Hilduin of Saint Denis who would have seen some of the events himself, collected oral reports of others, and consulted some records kept at the palace. By February or March of 823, he would have written up this entry.

Source: trans. P.E. Dutton from Annales Regni Francorum..., ed. G.H. Pertz and F. Kurze in Monumenta Germaniae Historica: Scriptores Rerum Germanicarum in Usum Scholarum, vol. 6 (Hanover, 1895), pp.157-159.

In the region of the Thuringians, in a certain place near a river, a slab of earth fifty feet in length, fourteen feet in width, and a foot and a half in depth was cut off the land and lifted up without human hands. It was found some twenty-five feet distant from the place where it started. Similarly in the eastern part of Saxony, which lies near the border of the Sorabians, in a certain rugged area near a lake which is called Arendsee, the earth swelled up into a mound. Without any human intervention it rose up in one night into the shape of a rampart that stretched one league in length.

Duke Winigis of Spoleto, now exhausted by his old age and having given up on secular life, gave himself up to monastic life, but not long afterwards, overcome by the weakness of his body, he died. Suppo, the count of the city of Brescia, took his place.

After receiving the advice of his bishops and nobles, the lord emperor was reconciled with those brothers whom he had ordered, against their will, to be tonsured. And so because of this deed and others—that is, what was done against Bernard, the son of his brother Pepin, and what was done against Abbot Adalhard and his brother Wala—he made a public confession and performed penance. He carried this out in the presence of all of his people at the assembly which he held in August 822 at Attigny. At this gathering he took the trouble to correct with the greatest care whatever things of this sort he and his father had done.

An army was sent from Italy into Pannonia to complete the war against Ljudovit. At the approach of the army, Ljudovit fled from the forsaken city of Sisak to the Serbs, who are said to hold a great part of Dalmatia. Having killed one of their dukes, the one who had welcomed him, Ljudovit assumed power in his city. Nevertheless, after sending his legates to the army of the emperor, he promised that he himself wanted to come into the presence of [Louis.]

Meanwhile the Saxons built, at the command of the emperor, a castle across the Elbe in a place called Delbende and, having driven off the Slavs from that place, placed a body of Saxon warriors there as a defense against

Slav invasions.

The counts of the Spanish march passed over the River Segre into Spain. There they ravaged the countryside, set fire to many villages, and seized considerable booty, before returning. In the same fashion, after the fall equinox a campaign was waged by the counts of the Breton march in the territory of a certain Breton Wihomarc, who was then a rebel. The counts destroyed everything with sword and fire.

With the assembly at Attigny over, the lord emperor went to the Ardennes to hunt. He sent his son Lothar to Italy and arranged for his relative, the monk Wala, and Wala's brother, the Abbot Adalhard, and Gering, the master of the doorkeepers, to go with him. Lothar was to rely on their advice in both domestic business and in matters pertaining to the interests of the kingdom. He ordered Pepin to go to Aquitaine, but first made him accept as his wife the daughter of Count Theotbert of Madrie. After the wedding was celebrated Pepin departed for his western lands. After the autumn hunt was finished, Louis crossed the Rhine to winter in a place that is called Frankfurt.

There, having called for a general assembly, with the nobles whom he ordered to gather there he examined the issues that pertained to the well-being of the eastern parts of his kingdom. At this gathering he listened to all the legations of the eastern Slavs, that is, the Obodrites, Sorbs, Wilzi, Bohemians, Moravians, Praedenecenti, and the Avars living in Pannonia, and received gifts from them. At the same assembly there were legations from the Northmen—from the side of Harald as well from the side of the sons of Godefrid. After all these legations were heard and dismissed, Louis wintered there at Frankfurt. As he had commanded, new buildings had been constructed for this purpose.

Questions: Why would Louis seek pardon for the sins that both he and his father had committed? What old wrongs were corrected? What actions followed from this penance? How does the annalist organize his reports of different events in the empire? Why does he include unusual natural phenomena in his entry?

30. The Polyptyque of Saint-Germain-des-Prés

Charlemagne's interest in rational estate management certainly spread to the church-men of the realm. A number of polyptyques or inventories of church properties were compiled in the ninth century, the most impressive of these being the lengthy one made of the resources of Saint-Germain-des-Prés. Abbot Irmino may have ordered this inventory in the early years of Louis the Pious's reign. The territory held by the monastery was approximately 2210 square kilometers, though much of the area would have been heavily forested. Over 2000 households holding more than 10,000 individuals are listed in the inventory. Though there is much disagreement about the meaning of individual terms and the reliability of parts of the inventory, the polyptyque is, nevertheless, a rich source of information about the social history of Carolingian Europe. Two separate short entries are translated below and after each readers will find a chart with which they can begin to break down some of the demographic data contained in the polyptyque.

Source: trans. P.E. Dutton from Polyptyque de l'Abbaye de Saint-Germain-des-Prés, ed. A. Longnon, vol. 2 (Paris, 1886-1895), pp.158-161, 256-257.

11. Brief Concerning Neuillay

Neuillay was situated in a heavily wooded part of northern France with no vineyards and hence its economy was geared towards pasturing pigs and preventing pigs from eating cultivated wheat. There were six-and-a-half farm units [mansi] at Neuillay and sixteen hearths. The slaves, who were actually serfs of a lower standing, owed more service to the lord than the lidi and coloni; those were social and legal conditions intermediate between the slaves and the free. These distinctions of legal status may have been growing less significant even at the time this inventory was made. Other terms can be given rough values: 1 bunuarium = 3.4 acres; 1 arpent = .2 acres; 1 perch = 412.5 square yards; 1 modium of dry or liquid measure = 64 liters; 1 league = 2.25 miles or 3.6 kms.

At Neuillay there is a manse [farm unit] that belongs to the lord; it has an abundance of other buildings. It has there ten small fields containing 40 bunuaria in land, which can be sown with 200 modia of oats; nine arpents of meadow-land from which 10 loads of hay can be collected. There is a forest there, which is, according to estimation, 3 leagues in length, 1 league in width, in which 800 pigs can be fattened.

1.   Electeus a slave and his wife, a colona by the name of Landina, who are dependents of Saint Germain, live at Neuillay. He holds half a farm that has 6 bunuaria of arable land, a half arpent of meadow. He plows four perches of winter wheat and thirteen of spring wheat. He spreads manure on the lord's fields, and does nothing else nor owes anything, because of the service that they provide.
2.   Abrahil a slave and his wife a lida by the name of Berthidlis, are dependents of Saint Germain. These are their children: Abram, Avremarus, Bertrada. And Ceslinus a lidus and his wife a lida by the name of Leutberga. These are their children: Leutgardis, Ingohildis. And Godalbertus a lidus.

These are their [his] children: Gedalcaus, Celsovildis, Bladovildis. These three [families] live in Neuillay. They hold a farm having 15 bunuaria of arable land and 4 arpents of meadow. They do service in Anjou and in the month of May at Paris. For the army tax they pay 2 sheep, 9 hens, 30 eggs, 100 planks and as many shingles, 12 staves, 6 hoops, and 12 torches; and they take 2 loads of wood to Sûtré. They enclose 4 perches with stakes in the lord's court, 4 perches with hedge in the meadow, and as much as necessary at harvest time. They plow 8 perches with winter wheat, 26 perches with spring wheat. As well as their labor and service, they spread manure on the lord's fields. Each of them pays 4 denarii on his head.

3. Gislevertus a slave and his wife a lida by the name of Gotberga. These are their children: Ragno, Gausbertus, Gaujoinus, Gautlindis. And Sinopus a slave and his wife a slave Frolaica. These are their children: Siclandus, Frothardus, Marellus, Adaluildis, Frotlidis. And Ansegudis a slave. These are their [her] children: Ingalbertus, Frotbertus, Frotlaicus, Frotberga. These three [families] live in Neuillay. They hold 1 farm having 26 bunuaria of arable land and 8 arpents of meadow. They pay like the above.

4. Maurifius a lidus and his wife a colona by the name of Ermengardis. Ermengildis is their son. And Gaudulfus a lidus and his wife a lida by the name of Celsa. Gaudildis is their son. These two [families] live in Neuillay. They hold 1 farm having 28 bunuaria of arable land and 4 arpents of meadow. They pay like the above.

5. Ragenardus a slave and his wife a colona by the name of Dagena. Ragenaus is their son. And Gausboldus a slave and his wife a lida by the name of Faregildis. These 2 [families] live in Neuillay. They hold 1 farm having 11 bunuaria of arable land and 4 arpents of meadow. They make [payment] like the above.

6. Feremundus a slave and his wife a colona by the name of Creada. And Feroardus a slave and his wife a lida by the name of Adalgardis. Illegardis is their daughter. And Faroneus a slave. And Adalgrimus a slave. These four [families] live in Neuillay. They hold 1 farm having 8 bunuaria of arable land and 4 arpents of meadow. They make [payment] like the above.

7. Gautmarus a slave and his wife a lida by the name of Sigalsis. These are their children: Siclevoldus, Sicleardus. That one lives in Neuillay. He holds a quarter of a farm having 1 and a half bunuaria of arable land and 1 arpent of meadow. He pays a quarter of what a whole farm pays.

8. Hildeboldus a slave and his wife a lida by the name of Bertenildis. These are their children: Aldedramnus, Adalbertus, Hildegaudus, Trutgaudus, Bernardus, Bertramnus, Hildoinus, Haldedrudis, Martinga. And Haldemarus a slave and his wife a colona by the name of Motberga. These are their children: Martinus, Siclehildis, Bernegildis. These two [families] live in Neuillay. They hold half a farm having 6 bunuaria of arable land and a half arpent of meadow. They return half of what is owed by a whole farm.

9. Bertlinus a lidus and his wife a colona by the name of Lantsida. These are their children: Creatus, Martinus, Lantbertus. He lives in Neuillay. He holds a quarter of a farm having 3 bunuaria of arable land and 2 arpents of meadow. He does service. He ought to pay a quarter of what a whole farm pays, but to look after this debt he takes care of the pigs.

10. In Neuillay there are 6 and a half inhabited farms; another half a farm

is uninhabited. There are 16 hearths [families]. For the army tax they pay 12 sheep; in head tax 5 *solidi* and 4 *denarii*; 48 chickens, 160 eggs, 600 planks and as many shingles, 54 staves and as many hoops, 72 torches. They take 2 cart-loads to the wine harvest, and 2 and a half in May, and half an ox.
11. These are the slaves: Electeus, Gislevertus, Sinopus, Ragenardus, Gausboldus, Feremundus, Gedalbertus, Faroardus, Abrahil, Faroinus, Adalgrimus, Gautmarus, Hildevoldus. They pay with torches and by carrying.
12. These are the lidi: Maurifius, Gaudulfus, Bertlinus, Ceslinus, Gedalbertus.
13. These are the female slaves: Frotlina, Ansegundis, Alda, Framberta. They keep the chickens and make cloth, if wool is supplied to them.
14. These are the female lidae: Berthildis, Leutberga, Gotberga, Celsa, Faregildis, Sigalsis, Bertenildis. They pay 4 *denarii* in tax.
15. Ragenardus holds 1 bunuarium from the lord's property. Gislevertus holds, apart from his farm, 2 fruitful fields.

Demographic Data Broken Down by Farm and Family Size

Farm	Adults						Children			Family
	SLAVE		LIDUS/A		COLONUS/A					Size
	m.	f.	m.	f.	m.	f.	m.	f.	no.	no.
1a.										
2a.										
b.										
c.										
3a.										
b.										
c.										
4a.										
b.										
5a.										
b.										
6a.										
b.										
c.										
d.										
7a.										
8a.										
b.										
9a.										

Totals:

Average family size:
Average number of children in each:
Average number of children if 6c. and 6d. are removed:
Percentage of boys to girls:
Number of presently childless couples:

Number of widowers:
Number of widows:
Number of bachelors:
Percentage of the population composed of children:
Number of marriages between people of different status:
Number of marriages between people of the same status:

18. Brief Concerning Coudray-sur-Seine

Coudray had a very different rural economy from that of Neuillay, for here the cultivation of grapes dominated. Hence payments on these eleven-and-a-half free (that is, not servile) farms or manses were different and more concentrated on wine and not at all upon pigs.

1.   In Coudray there are 11 and a half free farms that pay each year 5 and a half oxen for the army tax, 33 chickens, 165 eggs.
2.   There is in Coudary a farm belonging to the lord having 60 bunuaria of arable land in which 175 modia of wheat can be sown; 14 arpents of vineyards in which 230 measures of wine can be collected; 10 arpents of meadow in which 40 loads of hay can be collected; 25 bunuaria of woods.
3.   Gerbertus a colonus and his wife a colona by the name of Adalgundis are dependents of Saint-Germain.   They have living with them 2 children with these names: Bismodus, Gerberga.   He holds 1 free farm having 11 bunuaria of arable land and 2 arpents of vineyards.   He pays to the army tax a half an ox, 2 measures of wine in pannage; and he plows 7 perches. In payment he makes 1 arpent of wine; 3 chickens, 15 eggs.   Manual labor, wood-cutting, cartage services, handiwork, as much as is required.   Payment for wood due: 1 foot.
4.   Teutgrimus a colonus and his wife a colona by the name of Ingberta are dependents of Saint-Germain.   Teutberga is their daughter.   He holds 1 free farm having 6 bunuaria of arable land and 1 arpent of vineyards.   He pays as above.
5.   Hiltbertus a colonus of Saint-Germain and his wife a slave hold a free farm having 12 bunuaria of arable land and [2] arpents of vineyards.   He pays as above.
6.   Amalgis a colonus and his wife a free woman by the name of Ardelindis are dependents of Saint-Germain.   Odilelmus a colonus and his wife a slave by the name of Ermengardis are dependents of Saint-Germain.   They have living with them 2 children with these names: Leudricus, Gisloina.   These two [families] hold 1 free farm having 2 bunuaria of arable land and 2 arpents of vineyards.   This farm pays the same as above.
7.   Sicharius a colonus of Saint-Germain and his wife a free woman by the name of Solisma.   Sicharia is their daughter.   Ermbradus, [a dependent] of Saint-Germain, and his wife [a dependent] of Saint-Germain, have living with them 5 children by these names: Hildebertus, Godalbertus, Madalgarius, Ermbrada, Elia.   These two [families] hold 1 free farm having 11 and a half bunuaria of arable land and 2 arpents of vineyards.   This farm pays the same

as above.

8. Sicboldus a colonus of Saint-Germain and his wife a free woman by the name of Ercamberta. Agebertus a colonus of Saint-Germain. These two [families] hold 1 free farm having 11 bunuaria of arable land and 2 arpents of vineyards. This farm pays the same as above.

9. Godebertus a lidus. Mattheus a colonus of Saint-Germain and his wife a colona by the name of Cristiana. These two [families] hold 1 free farm having 7 bunuaria of arable land, 1 arpent of vineyard, and 3 parts of an arpent.

10. Ermenulfus a colonus of Saint-Germain. Ingulfus a colonus of Saint-Germain. These two hold 1 free farm having 7 bunuaria of arable land and 2 and a half arpents of vineyards. This farm pays the same as above.

11. Airbertus a colonus of Saint-Germain. Adalradus a colonus and his wife a colona by the name of Frotlindis are dependents of Saint-Germain. These two [families] hold 1 free farm having 10 bunuaria of arable land and 2 arpents of vineyards. This farm pays [the same as above.]

12. Edimius a colonus and his wife a colona by the name of Electa are dependents of Saint-Germain. Frothardus a colonus of Saint-Germain has his mother with him. These two [families] hold 1 free farm having 5 bunuaria of arable land and 1 and a half arpents of vineyards. This farm pays [the same as above.]

13. Ermenoldus a colonus and his wife a colona by the name of Walda are dependents of Saint-Germain. They have living with them 2 children with these names: Sicrada, Sigenildis. Teutgarnus a colonus and his wife a colona by the name of Ermentrudis are dependents of Saint-Germain. Melismus is their son. These two [families] have 1 free farm having 11 bunuaria of arable land and 1 arpent of vineyard, and 2 parts of an arpent.

14. Airoardus a colonus of Saint-Germain holds half a farm having 5 bunuaria of arable land and 1 arpent of vineyard. He makes other payments as if that of half a farm.

Demographic Data Broken Down by Farm and Family Size

| Farm | Adults | | | | | | Children | | Family Size |
| | SLAVE | | LIDUS/A | | COLONUS/A* | | | | |
	m.	f.	m.	f.	m.	f.	m.	f.	no.	no.
3a.										
4a.										
5a.										
6a.										
b.										
7a.										
b.										
8a.										
b.										
9a.										
b.										
10a.										
b.										
11a.										
b.										
12a.										
b.										
13a.										
b.										
14a.										

Totals:
*Note: free and dependent persons in this column or make separate columns.

Average family size:
Average number of children in each:
Percentage of boys to girls:
Number of presently childless couples:
Number of widowers:
Number of widows:
Number of bachelors:
Percentage of the population composed of children:
Number of marriages between people of different status:
Number of marriages between people of the same status:

Questions: Can we assume that all the inhabitants of a manor are listed? Who might be left out? What information collected in the polyptyque can be quantified and what cannot? Compare and contrast the economies of the two different communities. Are there discernible patterns in the names that these people gave to their children?

31. Agobard of Lyons
and the Popular Belief in Weather Magic

Louis the Pious's reforming spirit was soon taken up by the clerics of his realm. One day in 815 or 816, Agobard, the suffragan bishop of Lyons, came upon a crowd that was about to stone to death some people accused of stealing crops by means of weather magic. Not long afterwards, the bishop composed a treatise against this popular superstition, in part to impress his fellow reformers, for it is unlikely that it had any effect on his parishioners. Both the incidents he reports here concern the rural economy, that is, the success of grain crops and cattle farming. In a world with no insurance against crop failures, devastating storms, or epizootics, the lot of the Carolingian farmer was precarious and full of gnawing anxiety.

Source: trans. P.E. Dutton from Agobard of Lyons, De grandine et tonitruis, ed. L. Van Acker in Agobardi Lugdunensis Opera Omnia, in Corpus Christianorum: Continuatio Mediaevalis, vol. 52 (Turnhout: Brepols, 1981), pp.3-15.

1. In these regions almost everyone—nobles and common people, city folk and country folk, the old and young—believe that hail and thunder can be caused by the will of humans. For as soon as they have heard thunder or seen lightning, they say: "The wind has been raised." When asked why it is [called] a raised wind, some with shame, their consciences troubling them a little, others boldly, as is the way of the ignorant, answer that the wind was raised by the incantations of people who are called storm-makers [*tempestarii*]. Hence it is called a raised wind.

Whether that is true, as is popularly believed, should be verified by the authority of Holy Scripture. If, however, it is false, as we believe without doubt, it ought to be emphasized just how great the crime is of him who attributes to humans the work of God....

2. We have seen and heard of many overcome by such great madness and deranged by such great foolishness that they believe and claim that there is a certain region called Magonia [Magic Land] from which ships travel in the clouds. These ships, [so they believe], carry crops that were knocked down by hail and perished in storms back to that same region. Those cloud-sailors [are thought to] give a fee to the storm-makers and to take back grain and other crops. So blinded are some by this great and foolish belief that they believe that these things can [actually] be done.

We [once] saw many people gathered together in a crowd who were showing off four captives, three men and a woman, as though they had fallen out of some such ships. These people had been held for some time in chains. But at last, as I said, they were exhibited to that crowd of people in our presence as [criminals] fit to be stoned to death. Nevertheless the truth did come out. After much argument, those who exhibited those captives were, as the Prophet says, "confused, just as the thief is confused when apprehended."

3. Because this error, which in this area possesses the minds of almost everyone, ought to be judged by reason, let us offer up the witness of Scrip-

ture through which the matter can be judged. After inspecting those witnesses, it will not be us, but truth itself that will overcome that stupid error and everyone who recognizes the truth will denounce the instruments of error and say with the Apostle: "No lie is of the truth." What is not from the truth is especially not from God, and because it is not from God, he hears not its words....

7. If therefore the almighty God through the power of his arm whips the wicked with new waters, hail, and rains and whose hand it is impossible to flee, then those people are entirely ignorant of God who believe that humans can do these things. For if people can send hail, then they can make it rain anywhere, for no one ever sees hail without rain. They could also protect themselves from their enemies, not only by the theft of crops, but also by taking away a life. For when it happens that the enemies of the storm-makers are in a road or a field, they could kill them, they could send an entire hail-storm down upon them in one mass and bury them. Some claim that they themselves know some storm-makers who can make a diffuse pattern of hail that is falling throughout a region fall instead in a heap upon a river or a useless forest or upon a tub under which the storm-maker himself is hiding.

Often we have heard it said by many, that they knew that such things were certainly done in [specific] places, but we have never yet heard anyone claim that they themselves had seen these things. Once it was reported to me that someone said that he himself had seen such things. With great interest I myself set out to see him, and I did. But when I was speaking with him and encouraging him, with many prayers and entreaties, to say whether he had seen such things, I [nevertheless] pressed him with divine threats not to say anything unless it were true. Then he declared that what he said was indeed true and he named the person, the time, and place, but nevertheless confessed that he himself had not been present at that time....

11. ...Terrified by the sound of thunder and by flashes of lightning, the faithful, although sinners, call for the intercession of the holy prophet, but not our half-faithful people who, as soon as they hear thunder or feel a light puff of wind, say that "The wind has been raised," and then issue a curse: "Let that cursing tongue be parched. May the tongue that makes [this storm] now be cut off." Tell me, I beg you, whom do you curse, a just person or a sinner? For a sinner cannot, as you often say out of your own infidelity, raise up the wind, because he has no power, nor can he command evil angels....

13. Also in our times we sometimes see that, with the crops and grapes harvested, farmers cannot sow [the next crop] on account of the dryness of the land. Why do you not ask your storm-makers to send their raised winds to wet the land so that you might sow them then? But because you do not do that, nor did you ever see or hear of anyone doing it, listen to what the Lord himself, the creator of all things, the ruler, governor, arranger, and provider says to his blessed servant Job about things of this sort....

14. Look at the great works of God, the existence of which the blessed Job

himself was not able to admire fully and loftily. If the Lord has a treasure-trove of hail that He alone sees, and which even the blessed Job never saw, where do the storm-makers discover what the blessed Job never found? Neither can we find it nor could anyone guess where it is. The Lord inquires of his faithful servant if he knows who gave a path to the most violent rains and a passage to the resounding thunder. Those against whom this is directed show themselves to be puny men, devoid of holiness, justice, and wisdom, lacking in faith and truth, hateful even to their neighbors. [Yet] they say that it is by the storm-makers that violent winds, crashing thunder, and raised winds are made....

15. This stupidity is not the least part of this unfaithfulness, for it has now grown into such a great evil, that in many places there are wretched people who say indeed that they do not know how to send storms, but nevertheless know how to defend the inhabitants of a place against storms. They have determined how much of a crop they should be given and call this a regular tribute [canonicum]. There are many people who never freely give tithes to priests, nor give alms to widows, orphans, and other poor people. Though the importance of alms-giving is preached to them, is repeatedly read out, and encouraged, they still do not give any. They pay the canonicum, however, voluntarily to their defenders, by whom they believe they are protected from storms. And all of this is accomplished without any preaching, any admonishment, any exhortation, except the seduction of the Devil....

16. A few years ago [that is, in 810] a certain foolish story spread. Since at that time cattle were dying off, people said that Duke Grimoald of Benevento had sent people with a dust which they were to spread on the fields, mountains, meadows, and wells and that it was because of the dust they spread that the cattle died. He did this [they say] because he was an enemy of our most Christian Emperor Charles. For this reason we heard and saw that many people were captured and some were killed. Most of them, with plaques attached, were cast into the river and drowned. And, what is truly remarkable, those captured gave testimony against themselves, admitting that they had such dust and had spread it. For so the Devil, by the secret and just judgment of God, having received power over them, was able to succeed over them that they gave false witness against themselves and died. Neither learning, nor torture, nor death itself deterred them from daring to give false witness against themselves. This story was so widely believed that there were very few to whom it seemed absurd. They did not rationally consider how such dust could be made, how it could kill only cattle and not other animals, how it could be carried and spread over such a vast territory by humans. Nor did they consider whether there were enough Beneventan men and women, old and young, to go out from their region in wheeled carts loaded down with dust. Such is the great foolishness that oppresses the wretched world....

Questions: How receptive would the people of Agobard's diocese have been to the bishop's attempt to reform their popular beliefs? For whom would he have composed such a piece? What advantages did the belief in weather magic give to farmers in the Carolingian world? How, in the story of Grimoald's poisoners, had political issues become public and popular? What was the function of rumor in the Carolingian world?

32. Of Bread and Provisions in the Statutes of Adalhard of Corbie

Adalhard was, of course, the cousin of Charlemagne and an important political figure. In the very year of Louis's public penance and his recall to public favor, Adalhard drew up a set of regulations on how the large monastery of Corbie, over which he was abbot, was to be run.

To understand the Carolingian economy one must appreciate the importance of cereal crops in it. Dairy products and pigs fattened in local woods had a supplementary role to play in the daily diet, but bread was the main food. Adalhard's provisions would seem to suggest that monks and others ate about three-and-a-half to four-and-a-half pounds of bread per day. Monasteries were also magnets attracting the poor of the Carolingian world, in part because they had regularized the charitable dispensation of food. But in a world with a subsistence economy and hunger always a very real threat, this must have made monks feel somewhat besieged by beggars. Adalhard and Corbie also reflect a drive towards economic rationality that also figured so prominently in Benedictine monasticism, for to feed 350 monks every day was a major economic enterprise. The Carolingians were also economic and technological innovators; water-mills, for instance, could now be found on every Carolingian river and served lords and monasteries. Corbie alone seems to have been in control of 15 mills.

Source: trans. P.E. Dutton from L. Levillain, "Les Statuts d'Adalhard," Le Moyen Age, 2nd series, 4 (1900), pp.354-359.

4. We have decided to give daily to the hospice of the poor: 45 loaves of bread made of wheat and rye weighing 3 1/2 pounds; 5 loaves made of wheat or spelt such as the household serfs receive. That makes 50 loaves altogether.

Let those loaves be divided up in this way: the twelve poor who spend the night there should each receive his own loaf and in the morning a half a loaf for the day's travel. The two hostellers who serve there should each have one loaf from the above number of loaves. The five loaves made of wheat ought to be divided among the traveling clerics who are led into the refectory before their day's travel and the sick who are looked after in the hospice. We commit the distribution of the bread to the will of the hosteller, so that if a great number of poor should come—either more or less needy, as for instance some being weak from starvation or being little children—that one should decide what needs to be done. Because if sometimes it should happen that fewer poor people come, the hosteller and his master, the senior gate-keeper should keep in mind in every way that less should be dispensed than the number written above on account of the lesser number of those coming, so that when again more come what is left over can be dispensed.

To the other poor people coming and going on the same day, it is usual to give a quarter of a loaf or, as we have said, according to what the hosteller shall determine to be required by the greater or lesser number of poor or out of necessity. Other food should be bestowed according to custom.

Concerning drink: a half measure of beer is to be allotted daily, that is 8 sextaria from which 4 sextaria are to be divided among those 12 poor described above, so that each should receive 2 cups. From the other 4 sextaria, 1 cup is to be given to each of the clerics whose feet are washed by the monks; and 1 cup to the servant Willeran. The part that remains is left to the disposition of the hosteller who should distribute it either to the sick or to other poor people.

Concerning wine, however, that shall be at the disposition of the prior. The senior gate-keeper ought, according to resources, to look after the needs of the sick in food and drink in those things which are lacking to the hosteller for the work of the sick. If pilgrims from a great distance away should happen to visit and they exceed the number written above, the gate-keeper should provide for them what is necessary, so that what is set aside for daily needs not be threatened.

5. We even add to the bread of the poor other foods besides the 30 measures of cheese or lard and 30 measures of beans which are given: a fifth part of the tithe which the gate-keeper receives in eels or new cheese from the cellarer, which it is usual for 10 shepherds to give or from that which is given in tithes by our manors. Likewise also we add an entire fifth of the tithe of cattle, that is, in calves, in sheep, or in all that are given in flocks to the gate-keeper, even in horses.

As well we have decided to give to the same gate-keeper a fifth of whatever silver should come to the gate-keeper through the hands of the senior gate-keeper. Concerning which silver we want the following distribution to be made: that daily not less than 4 *denarii* should be given away. And if the number will have been less from that fifth part than can suffice to make this daily distribution, the abbot, if he so wishes, should supply it from somewhere else. And if it will have grown beyond that, he shall not draw away more. Let the gate-keeper provide wood for the poor according to custom, or other things which are not written down here, such as: cloth for the beds, [chamber] pots, and whatever other things [are needed]. All these things as written down above should be given from those things which come to the gate [of the monastery], on account of that supplement of silver as described above. Besides that, let the hosteller receive old clothes or shoes from the chamberlain to give to the poor according to custom.

Therefore we beg that all upon whom there is the duty of giving, either in donation or distribution, in this monastery should direct their attention to the will of God, rather than to the example of our parsimony, since each of us is about to deliver up a reckoning on his own behalf.

6. [Concerning] the calculation or amount of grain or bread—in what way, from where, and how much—that ought to come to the monastery each year, or how the provisioner of the bread ought to distribute it.

We desire that each year 750 baskets of well dried and cleaned spelt should arrive here, each basket having 12 modia [or measures], well packed and scraped, according to that new modium which the Emperor [Louis] established. And let that grain come from those manors which the emperor has specially placed in our care, if necessary from all; but if not [from all], from those which the emperor resolved upon with the abbot.

Thus we have set down such a number in order that on each day of the year (of which there are 365) [the monastery] should have 2 baskets which altogether makes 730 baskets. We decided to add 20 baskets so that the amount should exceed rather than fall short [of what is necessary]. And although grain is known to produce flour sometimes of better quality, sometimes of worse, sometimes fuller, sometimes poorer, we nevertheless, judging conservatively, hope that from those 2 baskets 10 modia [of flour] can always be made. Thus 30 individual modia should make 300 loaves of bread.

We are sure that at any time we will number not less than 300 [monks], and sometimes more, either in the monastery itself or arriving at the monastery. Since we should not number more than 350 [monks], we nevertheless, because there are sometimes fewer, sometimes more than 400, wish to so set down [that number as the base]. And if at any time there should be 400 [of us], we wish to establish that in those times when there are less than 400, there should grow a surplus which can be given out when there are more [of us]. Nevertheless seldom does it happen that there are more of us, since most often it happens that there are many less than 400. Let us add therefore from that which comes daily from the mills 4 modia and that makes 120 loaves. Put all that together and there are 420 loaves [daily]. Thus, look, we have not only [enough] for the 400 who are rarely [here], but even daily for 20 [more] who are very seldom here, but we [do this] because we want all our resources, which ought to be dispensed by our helpers, to be more than enough in order that there always be a surplus rather than a shortage.

To that which comes from the mills we still add 1 modium and that makes [altogether] 450 loaves daily from 15 mills. The number collected, therefore, through all the days for an entire year is 5475 modia. Let us add 25 to those from the mills and make it 5500, from which 3650 should be of spelt. The remaining 1850 ought to come from the mills, because there, just as we said above, we wish to have a surplus rather than a shortage. Thus in the first place we decided to add 20 baskets and [then we added] over and above the daily bread for the 400 dependents [another] 25 modia. Since nevertheless, as we said above, our number is more often less than 400 or certainly [not far] beyond 400, and because at the mill itself cattle, pigs, diverse kinds of birds, dogs, and occasionally horses ought to be kept, we add besides from those mills 150 modia and that makes 2000 modia in total that ought to come from the mills.

Meanwhile these things are so said and recorded until such time as we are able to decide whether it is necessary to add or subtract anything. Nevertheless we advise and urge the provisioner of the bread that whatever can be known by means of measuring and counting the days, weeks, and months of the year, he should with all diligence not neglect to know, just as when a period of change comes he should report back to us how he would proceed in managing [the distributions of] the present year.

So that he might know this more efficiently, he should first separate off those dependents who are always to have and to be given equal amounts, the number of whom is always equal, unless perhaps sometimes it is less, for it never happens that it is more. Then he should carefully calculate the [amount of the] bread of the monks when they eat once and when twice in a day, and he should always set out separately that which is reckoned for the work of them. And he should consider how much [they need] in those times when they eat only once a day and how much when they eat twice. And he should weigh out how much [is needed] per week in both times, whether in the times of great or little demand. And we think that he should be able to discover how much bread or measure to pass out for their work.

Among that group ought to be counted all who receive the bread of the monks, with the exception of the guests who do not receive this daily. Let him be sure, however, lest he make too great [a count] concerning the bread of the monks, that he be equally firm about the excess of the remaining, because if he should make this [change in the distribution] in a period when he investigates that amount, the bread itself ought to be removed and another set down for it, because as we said, we eat sometimes twice a day, sometimes once, and now there are more of us, now fewer and we can never precisely determine how many monks there will be. If the [provisioner] can himself find a better way of investigating this, he should do so with God's help.

Likewise [the same is true] concerning our manorial serfs. Likewise also the number of those who come to our gates is never certain, [but] if with the same idea, as we said above, the provisioner began to estimate by days, weeks, and months, when it is that he gives a little, when a modest amount, when the most, we think even with all that [information] that it is [still] not possible to discover exactly how he should manage [the distribution] through an entire year. But from those knocking [at the gate], from students, from the remaining clerics or lay people whether they be ours or outsiders, it can easily be found out in what way he can help them. We even recommend that he not neglect to consider the following: that bread is not given according to one measure to each one, but more is given to some, less to others. And for this reason it is necessary for the provisioner to think about the sizes of the loaves of bread, how many loaves can be made from one modium [of flour] of greater, modest, and smaller [size]. And we hope, once this is done, that all these things will be clearly evident to him. It was only by beginning [such an investigation] that I was able here to examine the question of what amount of grain should come henceforth to the monastery [on an annual basis]. Under these divisions which we can make we hope to be able to discover this clearly: that is, the first division is into our servants and poor workers who always ought to receive equal amounts, second into the monks, the third into the manorial serfs, the fourth into guests, the fifth into those knocking [at our gate] and students, the sixth into individual dependents [monks] here and there; from which [divisions], nevertheless, as we said, we can not determine the amount which each ought equally to have.

7. Concerning mills and malthouses we wish the rule to be as follows:

First a farm with six bunuaria [of land] should be given to each miller, because we want him to be able carry out what is asked of him and to mill all the grain brought to him. He should possess oxen and the necessary tools with which he can work and support himself and his entire family. He should have pigs, geese, and chickens to keep, a mill to construct, and all the building supplies needed to repair that mill, a dam to set straight, mill-stones to acquire, and everything that is necessary for constructing and maintaining a mill he should have and do. For this reason we do not wish any other service from him: not any service with cart or horse, no manual labor, plowing, or sowing, no harvest work or gathering of hay, no preparation of cereals or hops to be used in brewing, no wood-cutting [duties]. He should do nothing else of manorial work for his lord, but should be fully devoted to the interests of himself and his mill. He should, however, from his own resources feed pigs, geese, and chickens which he ought to fatten from [the chaff or leftovers of] his mill; he should give us eggs. He should devote himself to tending to those things alone which, as we have said, need to be done in the interests of the [operation of the] mill and its production.

Since for our work, as we said above, 2000 modia ought to come from the mills to the monastery, we did not say this in order to separate off that other grain from the granary, but [the provisioner] himself should investigate whether in this year it is necessary to add or subtract according to the number of dependent monks and the on-going work at the monastery in that year, for there are wine-harvests, garden work, haying, and other similar work [to be] done by the monks. By this amount [of milled wheat] the monastery ought to survive the year.

We also want [the provisioner] in the presence of the millers to make an estimate of the value of the new modium against the old ones, since those modia, however many there are, should be made from them with proper equivalency. According to these [new] modia of whatever size agreed upon by them, they should, henceforth, pay their tax either in wheat or in cereals for brewing.

We want, moreover, each of those millers to have a complete mill with 6 wheels. If a miller does not wish to have 6, but half of that full mill, which is one with 3 wheels, he should not have more than half the land which belongs to that farm, that is 3 bunuaria, and his co-worker should have the other 3. And between those two they should return a full milling and perform the full service that pertains to that mill in work, on the dam, on the bridge, or in other things as assigned to each miller.

Questions: What was the character of the daily monastic diet? How efficient would Corbie's economy have been if Adalhard's rules were strictly followed? What problems were likely to arise in instituting and managing this rule-bound institutional economy? What economic advantages were granted to the miller? If a wheat crop failed how vulnerable was Corbie to severe shortages? What steps could be taken to overcome such a shortage?

33. A Royal Judgment of Pepin in 828

*A monastery such as Corbie had thousands of serfs, just as Saint-Germain-des-Prés
had and recorded in its polyptyque. These farmers might dispute taxes and service
dues with their monastic lords, but their only real hope was to take the dispute to
the king's court or placitum where the king and twenty-four of his faithful followers
would hear the complaint and the response of the defendant, and then render a
judgment. The 'descriptio' referred to here was a polyptyque, so that finally the case
turned on written evidence.*

Source: trans. J.L. Nelson, "Dispute Settlement in Carolingian West Francia," in The Settlement
of Disputes in Early Medieval Europe, ed. W. Davies and P. Fouracre (Cambridge: Cambridge
University Press, 1986), p.49; reprinted with permission.

Pepin by the grace of God king of Aquitaine. When we in God's name, on
a Tuesday in our palace at the villa of Chasseneuil in the county of Poitou
near the River Clain, were sitting to hear the cases of many persons and to
determine just judgments, there came certain men, named Aganbert, Agan-
fred, Frotfar, and Martin, they as well as their fellows (*pares*) being coloni of
Saint-Paul from the villa of Antoigné belonging to the monastery of Cormery
and its abbot Jacob. There they brought a complaint against that abbot and
his advocate, named Agenus, on the grounds that the abbot and his officers
had demanded and exacted from them more in rent and renders than they
ought to pay and hand over, and more than their predecessors for a long
time before then had paid and handed over, and that they [the abbot and
his officers] were not keeping for them such law as their predecessors had
had.

Agenus the advocate and Magenar the provost of the monastery were there
present, and made a statement rebutting that claim, as follows: neither the
abbot nor they themselves had exacted, or ordered to be exacted, any dues
or renders other than their predecessors had paid to the monastery's representatives for thirty years. They forthwith presented an estate survey (*descriptio*) to be read out, wherein was detailed how, in the time of Alcuin's abbacy,
the coloni of that villa who were there present, and also their fellows, had
declared on oath what they owed in renders, and what was still to pay, for
each manse on that estate. The survey was dated to the thirty-fourth year
of King Charles's reign.

The coloni there present were then asked if they had declared [the statements in] that survey and actually paid the renders stated in the survey for
a period of years, and if that survey had been true and good, or did they
wish to say anything against it or object to it, or not? They said and acknowledged that the survey was true and good, and they were quite unable to
deny that they had paid that render for a period of years, or that they themselves, or their predecessors, had declared [the statements in] that survey.

Therefore we, together with our faithful men, namely Count Haimo [and
twenty-three named men ending with John, count of the palace] and many
others, have seen fit to judge that, since those coloni themselves gave the
acknowledgment as stated above that the survey was as they had declared it,
and as it was written down in the document there before them, and that

they had paid the said renders for a period of years, so also must they pay and hand over the same each and every year to the representatives of that house of God.

Therefore we order that, since we have seen the case thus heard and concluded, the above Agenus the advocate and Maginar [*sic*] the provost should on behalf of that house of God receive a record of it, showing that it has been done in this way and at this time.

I Deotimus, deputizing for John count of the palace, have recognized and subscribed.

Given on 9 June in the fifteenth year of the reign of our lord Louis the serene emperor. Nectarius wrote out and subscribed it.

Questions: What disadvantages did farmers face in appealing to the king's justice? What role did written records play in determining land rights and dues?

34. Einhard and His Holy Relics: The *Translatio*

It may strike the reader as strange that the man who had written the coolly classical and definitive biography of Charlemagne could a few short years later write an impassioned account of the relic trade and his active promotion of it. If Suetonius had been the model for the former, Augustine's 'City of God' may have been the model for the latter. Since northern Europe had been the site of few martyrdoms, saints' bones had to be obtained from cemeteries in the south. Carolingian churchmen wanted saintly patrons and, therefore, relics in order to dedicate newly constructed churches. As well the Carolingian peoples did not generally go on long distance pilgrimages because of the insecurities and expense of travel. Instead, their churches were structurally designed to create within a single building an internal pilgrimage that led from relic to relic, from chapel to chapel. By the late 820s Einhard was looking not only for a saintly tool that would allow him to hoard prestige and prominence, but also for a saintly advisor on politics, a protector for the kingdom. All of these advantages he found in the relics of Marcellinus and Peter. What the reader can also see in this book are some of the debilitating illnesses that beset the Carolingian population, the mobility of people as they moved from town to town in search of cures, and some precious moments of revealing social process.

Source: trans. B. Wendell, The History of the Translation of the Blessed Martyrs of Christ Marcellinus and Peter: the English Version (Cambridge: Harvard University Press, 1926); here the complete translation is printed, but in a form that was substantially revised against the Latin edition of G. Waitz, in Monumenta Germaniae Historica: Scriptores, vol. 15.1 (Hannover, 1888), pp.239-264.

The Translation and Miracles of the Saints Marcellinus and Peter

[Preface]

To true worshippers and lovers of the true God and of our Lord Jesus Christ and of his saints, Einhard, a sinner.

Those who have committed to letters and to memory the lives and deeds of the just, and of men who obey divine commands, seem to me to have wished little else than by such examples to encourage others to correct bad habits and to join in praising the omnipotence of God. And they have done this not only because they were free from malice but because they abounded in charity, which desires the good of all. Now since their worthy purpose is so very clearly only to bring about the ends which I have mentioned, I see no reason why they should not be imitated by many. And since I am sure that the pages which I have written, as well as I could, about the translation of the bodies of the blessed martyrs of Christ, Marcellinus and Peter, and about the signs and wonders that God wanted to be made manifest through them for the good of those believing, were composed with the same wish and purpose, I have decided to revise them and to offer them to those readers who love God. For I not only think that this work should not seem empty and purposeless to any of the faithful, but I also venture to believe that I shall have worked fruitfully and usefully, if I shall have succeeded in stirring any reader to the praise of the Creator.

[Book 1]

1. When still at court and busy with daily business, I used often to think in many different ways about the rest that I some day hoped to enjoy. Then I came across a secret place, far removed from the vulgar crowd and, by the generosity of Louis, the prince whom I then served, I obtained possession of it. This place is in the German forest, lying midway between the Neckar and Main rivers, and in our times is called Odenwald by the inhabitants and their neighbors. When, according to my powers and means, I had built there not only houses and other buildings for permanent dwelling, but also a church suitably designed for the celebration of the divine service, I began to wonder in the name and honor of what saint or martyr it should be dedicated. And when I had spent a great deal of time in this state of doubt, it happened that a certain deacon of the Roman church by the name of Deusdona, who desired to request the help of the king in some problem of his own, came to court. When after he had stayed there for some time and the business on which he had come was settled and he was arranging to return to Rome, he was, as a visitor, invited by me one day, out of politeness, to come and share a frugal dinner with me. There, while talking a good deal at table, we happened in our conversation to reach a point where mention was made of the translation of the blessed Sebastian [Hilduin of Saint-Denis had acquired the relics of Sebastian in 826], and of the many neglected tombs of the martyrs in Rome. Then, our conversation turned to the dedication of my new church and I began to ask him how I could obtain some piece of the true relics of the saints who lie buried in Rome. At this he at first hesitated a little, and answered that he did not know how this could be managed. Then when he perceived that I was eager and anxious about the matter, he promised that he would answer my question on another day.

After that evening, when he was invited by me again, he took from the folds of his garment a written note and requested that I read it when I was alone, and that I would be so good as to tell him whether I liked what was written there. I took the note and, as he requested, I read it in secret. The contents were as follows: he had at home many relics of the saints, and he was willing to give them to me, if I could help him get back to Rome. He knew that I had two mules. If I would give him one of these, and send with him a reliable man of my own, who could receive the relics from him and bring them back to me, he would send them to me immediately. The general tone of his request pleased me, and I made up my mind to test the value of his uncertain promise without delay; so, having given him the animal he asked for, and added money for his journey, I ordered my notary, whose name is Ratleig, who had himself made a vow to visit Rome for the purpose of prayer, to accompany him. So setting out from Aachen—for at that time the emperor was there with his court—they came to Soissons and there they talked with Hilduin, the abbot of the monastery of Saint-Médard. The deacon [Deusdona] had promised the abbot that he would arrange for him to secure possession of the body of the holy martyr Tiburtius. Excited by these promises, the abbot sent along with them a certain priest, a crafty man by the name of Lehun, with orders to bring back the body of this martyr when he had received it from the deacon. Thus the journey began as they made their way toward Rome as fast as they could.

2. Now it happened, after they had reached Italy, that the servant of my notary, whose name was Reginbald, was overcome by a tertian fever [malaria], and this led, because of its repeated attacks, to a serious delay in their journey, for when he was gripped by intense fever they could not travel. There were few of them and they did not wish to be separated from each other. At this time, when the trip had been much slowed by the inconvenience and they were trying to accelerate their pace as much as they could, three days before they came to the city, there appeared in a vision to him who was sick with the fever a man in the dress of a deacon who asked him why his master was hurrying to Rome. And when he told him all he knew about the promises the deacon had made to send me relics of the saints and those made to the Abbot Hilduin, he said: "This will not come to pass as you suppose, but very differently, yet the final outcome of the mission for which you came shall be fulfilled. That deacon who asked you to come to Rome will do little or nothing of what he promised you. Therefore I want you to follow me and carefully remember the things that I am about to show and relate to you."

Then taking him, as it seemed to him, by the hand, he made him climb with him to the summit of a very high mountain. And when they stood there together: "Turn," he said, "to the east, and observe the country lying before your eyes." When he did so, and observed the country spoken of, he saw buildings of vast size, built close together like some great city, and asked by his companion if he knew what it was he replied that he did not know. Then his companion said: "It is Rome that you see." And he presently added: "Direct your eyes to the remote parts of the city, and see if any church appears to you in those regions." After he said that, he saw one church clearly, "Go and tell Ratleig," said his companion, "for in the church that you have just seen lies hidden the thing that he should carry back to his master: and so let him get to work, so that he might lay his hands on it as quickly as possible and carry it back to his master." And when he said that none of those who had come with him would put any faith in what he said about things such as these, his companion answered and said: "You know that those traveling with you are troubled because for many days you have suffered from a tertian fever that has not yet abated." And he said: "It is as you say." "Therefore," said his companion, "I want this to be a sign to you, and to those to whom you shall relate the words I have spoken to you, for from this hour you shall be so cured, by the loving kindness of God, from the fever by which until now you have been detained, that it will not affect you at all for the rest of this journey." Awakened by these words, he made haste to report to Ratleig everything that he seemed to have seen and heard. When Ratleig reported these things to the priest who was traveling with him, it seemed to both of them that the proof of the dream would be whether the promise of health came true. For on that very day, following the nature of the disease from which he had been suffering, a fever should have attacked the one who had seen the [visionary] dream. And that it was not a vain fancy but rather a true revelation was clear, for neither on that day nor on any of those that followed did he experience in his body any trace of the fever that he had been suffering. So it came to pass both that they believed in the vision and no longer had faith in the promises of Deusdona, the deacon.

3. When they arrived in Rome, they took up residence near the church of the blessed Apostle Peter, which is called Ad Vincula, in the house of the deacon with whom they had come, and they remained with him for some days, awaiting the fulfilment of his promises. But he, who was quite unable to make good on his promises, excused himself for not doing so by various strategies of delay. At last, when they spoke to him about it, they asked him why he wanted to mock them so. At the same time they requested that he not hold them up any longer by deceiving them, thus preventing with vain hopes their return home. When he had heard them out, and perceived that he could no longer cheat them with trickery of this sort, he first informed my notary that he could not have the relics promised to me, because his brother, to whom on his departure from Rome he had entrusted both his house and all he possessed, had gone to Benevento on business and he had no idea when he would return. Since he had given him those relics for safe-keeping, along with his other moveable property, he could not find them anywhere in the house; therefore, he was [not] able to see what he should do, because for his part there was nothing sure to hope for. After he had said this to my notary, who complained of being deceived and tricked by him, he talked in I know not what empty and misleading terms with the priest of Hilduin, who had cherished the same hopes, and so got rid of him. But the next day, when he saw them in low spirits, he urged them to come with him to the cemeteries of the saints; for it seemed to him that they might find something there that would satisfy their wishes, and that there was no need for them to go home empty-handed. But, although this proposal pleased them and they wished to set about what he had urged them to do as soon as they could, he put off the business, in his usual way, and by this delay cast their minds, which for a little while had been more cheerful, into such despair that, giving up on him altogether, they decided, although their

business was completely unfinished, to return home.

4. But my notary, remembering the dream that his servant had had, began to urge his companions to go, without their host, to the cemeteries which he had promised to show them. So, having found a guide who regularly conducted travelers to those holy places, they first came to the church of the blessed martyr Tiburtius, on the Via Labicana, three miles away from the city, and examined the tomb of the martyr as carefully as they possibly could; and discussed with the greatest secrecy whether it could be opened so that no one would notice the fact. Then they descended into the crypt connected to this church, in which the bodies of the blessed martyrs of Christ, Marcellinus and Peter, were buried. Having examined the nature of this monument also, they went home, thinking that they could hide what they had been up to from their host. But it turned out otherwise than they expected. For, although they did not know how, knowledge of what they had done quickly reached him. Worried that they might achieve their desires without him, he made up his mind to figure out their intention as quickly as possible. And since he had a full and detailed knowledge of those holy places, he politely told them that they should all go there together, and, if God should deign to favor their wishes, they should make a common decision to do whatever seemed best to them.

They agreed to his plan, and by common consent fixed on a time for setting out. Then, after fasting for three days, they went by night, unnoticed by any of the inhabitants of Rome, to the place I have mentioned. Once in the church of Saint Tiburtius, they first attempted to open the altar under which his holy body was believed to lie. But the strenuous nature of the work they began was little to their liking, for the monument, built of very hard marble, easily resisted the inexpert hands of those who were trying to open it. So leaving the burial place of that martyr, they went down into the tomb of the blessed Marcellinus and Peter, and there, having invoked our Lord Jesus Christ and having prayed to the holy martyrs, they managed to raise from its place the stone with which the top of the tomb was covered. When they had taken this off, they saw the most holy body of Saint Marcellinus set in the upper part of the tomb and close to his head a marble tablet with an inscription on it which gave them clear proof of just which martyr's limbs lay in that place. So, as was proper, they lifted up the body with the greatest reverence, and, having wrapped it in a clean fine linen, they handed it over to the deacon to carry and to keep for them. Then they put the stone back into place, lest some trace of the body's removal should remain visible. Then they returned to their dwelling place in the city. But the deacon declared that in the house where he lived, near the church of the blessed Apostle Peter which is called Ad Vincula, he would and could safely guard the body of the most blessed martyr of which he had taken charge. So he gave it to a monk by the name of Luniso to guard. Thinking that this would satisfy my notary he began to urge him, now that he had obtained the body of the blessed Marcellinus, to return to his own country.

5. But Ratleig was thinking and turning over in his mind a very different scheme. For, as he afterwards told me, it seemed to him by no means ac-

ceptable that he should go home with the body of the blessed Marcellinus alone, for it would be a great shame if the body of the blessed martyr Peter, who had been his fellow in suffering, and for five hundred years or more had lain with him in the same tomb, should be left there when [Marcellinus] was departing. And this idea having caught hold in his mind, he so struggled with it as it dawned on him and tormented him that neither food nor the approach of sleep would seem enjoyable or good to him until the bodies of the martyrs, who had been joined together in suffering and in the tomb, were joined together on that journey which he was about to make. But in what way this [reunification of the relics] could be achieved, he did not know, for he knew that he could not find a Roman to give him help in this matter, nor was there anyone to whom he would dare reveal his secret plans. Laboring under this anxiety, he happened to meet a foreign monk by the name of Basil who two years before had traveled from Constantinople to Rome. He lived on the Palatine hill with four disciples in a house with other Greeks, who were of the same religious persuasion as he was. He went to him and explained the nature of his troubles. Then, encouraged by his advice and trusting in his prayers, he discovered such strength in his own heart that he determined to attempt the deed as soon as he could, despite the danger to himself. He sent for his companion, the priest of Hilduin, and first proposed to him that they should once again go secretly, as they had done before, to the church of the blessed Tiburtius, and try again to open the tomb in which the body of the martyr was believed to be buried.

This plan pleased [both of them] and, in the company of their servants, they set out secretly at night, their host having no idea where they were going. When they had come to the church, and prayed for success before its doors, they entered the church. They split up; the priest with one group went to hunt for the body of the blessed Tiburtius in his church and Ratleig with the others descended into the crypt connected to the church to [search for] the body of the blessed Peter. Having opened the tomb without any difficulty, he took out the sacred limbs of the holy martyr, with no opposition, and put them, once they were in his possession, into a silken bag, which he had made ready to hold them. Meanwhile, the priest who was searching for the body of the blessed Tiburtius, having spent a great deal of time in useless work and seeing that he could make no progress, gave up on his efforts, and joined Ratleig in the crypt, and began to ask him what he should do. Ratleig answered that he thought that the relics of Saint Tiburtius were [already] found, and then explained what he meant. A little while before the priest had arrived in the crypt, he had found in the same tomb in which the bodies of the saints Marcellinus and Peter lay, a hole, round in form and dug three feet deep and one foot wide, and placed inside it was a substantial quantity of fine dust. It seemed to both of them that this dust might have been left by the body of the blessed Tiburtius if his bones had been removed from there. So that it might be harder to find, this dust might have been placed just between the blessed Marcellinus and Peter in the same tomb. [Thus] they agreed that the priest should take the dust and carry it away with him as the relics of the blessed Tiburtius. Having thus considered and disposed of this business, they returned to their lodgings with the things that they had found.

6. After this, Ratleig spoke to his host and requested the return of the holy ashes of the blessed Marcellinus that he had entrusted to his safe-keeping. Since he now wished to return to his own country, he did not want to suffer any unnecessary delay. [Deusdona] not only restored at once what was asked for, but also presented [Ratleig with] a substantial quantity of saints' relics, tied up in a bundle, which was to be carried to me. When asked what their names were, he answered that he would tell me himself when he came to see me. He advised, however, that these relics should be treated with the same respect as that shown to the other holy martyrs, because they had acquired as much merit in the sight of God as the blessed Marcellinus and Peter and that I would realize this as soon as I knew their names. Ratleig took the gift that was offered, and, as he was advised, placed the bundle with the bodies of the holy martyrs. Having consulted with his host, he arranged that the holy and much-desired treasure, placed and sealed up in caskets, should be carried as far as Pavia by the host's brother Luniso, of whom we made mention before, and also by Hilduin's priest who had come with him. As for Ratleig, he remained with his host in Rome, watching and listening for seven successive days, to see if anything about the removal of the bodies of the saints came to the notice of the Romans. When he heard no stranger talking about this deed and when he judged that this business was still unknown, he set out after those whom he had sent ahead, taking his host along with him. They found them waiting for them in [the region of] Ticino, in the church of the blessed John the Baptist, which is commonly called Domnanae, and which was at the time, through a benefice of the kings [Louis and Lothar], in my possession. They decided that they too would stop there for a few days, both to refresh the beasts on which they were riding and to prepare themselves for the longer journey ahead.

7. At the time of this delay, a story arose that ambassadors of the holy Roman church, sent by the pope to the emperor, would soon arrive there. Thus, worried that, if they were found there when they arrived, some inconvenience for themselves or even an obstacle might arise, they decided that some of their party should hurry to depart before the embassy arrived. The rest, however, would stay there and, after the matter over which they were anxious had been carefully investigated and the embassy had proceeded on its way, they would make haste to follow their friends, whom they had sent on ahead. So when they had thus settled things among themselves, Deusdona and Hilduin's priest left before the ambassadors from Rome arrived, and made what haste they could for Soissons, where Hilduin was believed to be. But Ratleig, with the true treasure which he carried with him, remained at Pavia to wait until the ambassadors of the Apostolic See had come and gone, so that when they had crossed the Alps he might make his own journey more safely. Still he feared that Hilduin's priest, who had gone with Deusdona and who had full and complete knowledge of all that had been done and arranged between them, and who seemed so cunning and slimy, might attempt to place some obstacle along the route by which he had planned to travel. So he made up his mind that he had best go another way. He first sent on to me the servant of our steward Ascolf with letters in which he informed me both of his own return and that he was bringing the treasure

which with divine assistance he had discovered. Then, after determining the resting places made ready for the Romans and believing that they must have now passed the Alps, he left Pavia and in six days came to Saint-Maurice [a distance of approximately 240 kms or 150 miles]. There, having procured what seemed necessary, he placed those holy bodies, enclosed in their casket, upon a bier and from that point on he carried them publicly and openly, with the help of the people who flocked to meet him.

8. When he had passed the place which is called the Head of Lake [that is, Villeneuve in Switzerland] he found a fork in the road by which the ways leading to Francia are divided in two. Taking the path to the right he came, through the territory of the Germans, to Soleure, a town in Burgundy. There he met the people whom, after the news of his return had reached me, I had sent from Maastricht to meet him. When the letters from my notary were brought to me by my steward's servant [Reginbald], of whom I spoke before, I was at the monastery of Saint Bavon on the river Scheldt. Informed by reading these letters of the advent of the saints, I ordered one of my household to go from Saint-Bavon to Maastricht, there to collect a company of priests and other clergy, as well as laymen, and then to hurry to meet the approaching saints at the very first place he could find them. Thus, with no delay, he and his party, in a few days, met up with those who were transporting the saints at the place I mentioned above. They joined together and were accompanied from that point on by an ever increasing crowd of chanting people. Soon they came, with the great rejoicing of all, to the city of Argentoratus, which is now called Strasbourg. From there they sailed down the Rhine until they came to a place called Portus where they disembarked on the east bank of the river, and, after a journey of five days and with a great crowd of people rejoicing in praise of God, they came to the place called Michelstadt. That place lies in that German forest which today is called Odenwald, and is about six leagues distant from the river Main. When they found there the church newly built by me, but not yet dedicated, they bore the holy ashes into it, and there set them down, as if they were to remain there forever.

9. When this news was brought to me, I hurried there as fast as I could. Three days after my arrival, at the end of the evening service, a servant of Ratleig, acting on his orders, remained alone in the empty church and with closed doors sat next to those holy bodies in a small chapel, as though guarding them. Suddenly he was overcome by sleep and saw, as it were, two doves come flying in through the right window of the apse and land on the top of the bier above the bodies of the saints. One of the doves was all white, the other dappled with the colors white and gray. When they had walked up and down on top of the bier for a good while and had made again and again the cooing sound made by doves, as if they were talking, they flew out through the same window, and were to be seen no more. Immediately afterwards a voice was heard above the servant's head: "Go," the voice said, "and tell Ratleig to inform his master that those holy martyrs are unwilling to have their bodies rest in this place, for they have chosen another place to which they want to be taken at once." The speaker of this message could not be

seen by him, but when the sound ceased he awoke, and roused from sleep he told Ratleig when he came back to the church what he had seen. The next day, as soon as he could come to me, Ratleig reported to me what his servant had told him. Now, although I did not dare to spurn the sacred secret of this vision, I nevertheless decided that it must be confirmed in some more definite fashion. In the meantime I had the holy ashes removed from the linen packages wrapped with cords in which they had traveled, and had them sewn up in new cushions made of silk. When I examined them and noticed that the relics of the blessed Marcellinus were smaller in quantity than those of Saint Peter, I thought that [perhaps Saint Marcellinus] had been smaller in stature and in the dimensions of his body than the holy Peter. That this was not the case was later made clear by the dicovery of a theft; where, when, by whom, and how this theft was accomplished and uncovered I shall tell you at the proper time. For the time being the sequence of the story as I have begun to tell it must be structured and held to without any diversion.

10. Now after I had examined that great and marvelous treasure, more precious than any gold, the casket in which it was contained began to displease me a great deal, because of the poorness of the material out of which it was made. Desiring to improve it, I directed one of the sacristans, one day when the evening service was over, to find out for me the dimensions of the casket as measured in rods. To do this he lit a candle and lifted up the hanging clothes with which the casket was covered; then he noticed that the casket was, in a wondrous way, dripping all over with a bloody liquid. Alarmed by the strangeness of the thing, he took the trouble to inform me at once of what he had seen. Then I went there with the priests who were present and, full of wonder, saw for myself that astonishing miracle. For as columns, slabs, and marble statues are accustomed to sweat and drip when rain is coming on, so that casket with its most sacred bodies was found to be wet with fresh blood and sprinkled all over with it. The unusual, indeed unheard of, nature of the miracle alarmed us. Thus, after speaking of the matter, we decided to spend three days fasting and praying, so that we might be worthy to know by divine revelation what that great and ineffable sign meant and what it urged us to do. When the three days' fast was over and evening was already growing late, that liquid composed of frightening blood began suddenly to dry up. In a wondrous fashion the liquid that had dripped for seven successive days without stopping, as if it were an incessant stream, dried up so quickly in a few hours that when the bell called us to the night service, for it was Sunday and we celebrated before dawn, and we went into the church, no trace of the blood could still be found on the casket. But the linen cloths that hung about the casket had been so sprinkled with fluid that they were stained with spots like blood-stains. I ordered them to be preserved. To this day considerable evidence of that great, unheard-of prodigy remains on those linens. It is agreed that the fluid had a somewhat salty taste similar to the quality of tears, that it was thin like water, but that it possessed the color of true blood.

11. In the quiet of that same night, two youths were seen standing beside

him by one of our servants by the name of Roland, and, as he himself bore witness, they urged him to tell me many things concerning the need to translate the bodies of the saints. They showed him where and how this should be done, and, with terrifying threats they demanded that I should be told without delay. As soon as he could see me, he carefully told me everything that he had been commanded to tell. When I had learned of these things, I began to fill with anxiety and to turn over in my mind what I ought to do: whether fasting and prayers should again be observed, and God once more appealed to for the resolution of our questions or whether some devout and faultless servant of God should be sought, to whom we could make plain the worry in our hearts and the degree of our perplexity, and from whom we might request that, by his prayers, he should discover for us a clear direction from God concerning this matter. But where and when could such a servant of Christ's household be found by us, particularly in those parts? For although certain monasteries had been established not far from the place where we were, nevertheless, by reason of the rude customs common in the region, there were few men or, perhaps, none about whom anything of this sort or even the slightest rumor was reported. Meantime, while I was so troubled and was praying for the assistance of the holy martyrs, and eagerly requesting all who were there with us to do the same, it happened that for several days no night passed in which it was not revealed in dreams to one, two, or even three of our companions that those bodies of the saints must be translated from that place to another. At last, as he himself acknowledges, there appeared in a vision to a priest by the name of Hiltfrid, who was among those gathered there, a certain man in priestly garment, remarkable for the venerable whiteness of his hair, and clothed in white, who accosted him with words like these: "Why," he said, "is Einhard so hard of heart and so obstinate that he will not put faith in so many revelations, and thinks that these many divinely inspired counsels, which have been sent him, may be despised? Go and tell him that what the blessed martyrs desire to be done with their bodies cannot remain undone. Since until this moment he has put off satisfying their wish in this matter, let him now, if he does not wish the merit of this deed to pass to another, make haste to obey their command and carry their bodies to the place which they have chosen."

12. After these warnings and others of various sorts had been brought to me, it seemed to me that the new translation of the holy ashes must not be postponed any longer. And so, having sought advice, we decided that we should hasten to accomplish the thing as fast as it could be done. Thus, at dawn one day, after the morning service was finished, after making ready quickly but with the greatest of care everything that seemed necessary for this convoy, we took up that holy and priceless treasure, amid very great grief and lamentation from those who were to remain in that place, and starting on our way we began to carry it, accompanied by a multitude of the poor who in those days had flocked there from all sides for the purpose of receiving alms. The people who lived around that place knew nothing about our plans and purpose. The sky was heavy with dark clouds, which would soon turn into heavy rain if a divine power did not prevent it, for all night long it had rained so hard without stopping that it had seemed hardly possible

to begin our journey next day. But that doubt of ours, which came from the weakness of our faith, was resolved, by the grace which is on high through the merits of his saints, very differently from what we had expected, for we found that the way by which we were traveling had been transformed into quite another state than the one we had anticipated. We found little mud and discovered that the streams, which are apt to rise in heavy and continuous rain as had fallen that night, were hardly swollen at all. When leaving the forest, we came close to the nearest villages and were met on our way by multitudes giving praise to God. They accompanied us for a distance of about eight leagues, devoutly helping us to carry our holy burden and singing God's praise they diligently joined their voices with ours.

13. But when we saw that we could not arrive that day at our destination, we turned aside at a village called Ostheim, which could be seen from the road. Just as evening was falling we bore those holy bodies into the church of Saint Martin which is found in that village, and, leaving there most of our company to keep watch over the relics, I myself, with a few others, hurried towards the place to which we were destined. Throughout the night, I made ready all those things that custom demands for the reception of the bodies of saints.

But to the church where we left the sacred treasure of those remains came a nun by the name of Ruodlang who was shaken with palsy. She belonged to the convent of Machesbach [Mosbach], which is distant from that church by the space of one league, and had been brought there in a cart by friends and neighbors. She had passed the whole night among the people gathered there to watch and pray beside the bier of the saints, and she recovered the strength in all her limbs. On her own feet, with no one supporting or assisting her at all, she walked back the next day to the place from which she had come.

14. But we, stirring at daybreak, went out to meet our companions who were coming, having with us a numberless throng of our neighbors, who excited by the news of the approach of the saints had gathered before our doors even at the first gleam of dawn, so that they might journey with us to meet the saints. We came upon them at the place where the brook Gernsprinz empties into the river Main [near Aschaffenburg]. Thence, traveling together and singing in unison the praise of the mercy of our Lord Jesus Christ, we bore those holy remnants of the most blessed martyrs, amid the great joy and exultation of all who could be there, to Upper Mulinheim, for so that place is called in modern times. But, because of the great throng of people who had gone before us and who had filled up the town, we could neither make our way to the church nor carry the bier into it. And so in a field near by, on rising ground, we set up an altar under the open sky. After setting the bier down beside the altar, we celebrated the solemn offices of the Mass. When these were finished and the multitude had gone back to their work, we bore those most holy bodies into the church as demanded by the blessed martyrs, and there, having placed the bier before the altar, we carefully celebrated the Mass once again. While the celebration was going on there, a boy of about fifteen years, by the name of Daniel, from the

Portian region, who had come there with other poor people to beg and who was so bent over that unless he lay down on his back he could not see the sky, approached the bier. All of a sudden, as if struck by a blow, he fell down. After he laid there for a long time, like one sleeping, all his limbs were straightened, and regaining the strength of his muscles he got up before our eyes and was sound. These things came to pass on the sixteenth day before the Kalends of February [17 January], and the light of that day was so great and so clear that it equaled the splendor of the sun in summer and the calmness of the air was so gentle and sweet that it seemed with soft sunshine to surpass the season of spring.

15. The next day we placed the holy bodies of the blessed martyrs, enclosed in a new shrine, in the apse of the church, and, as is the custom in Francia, we erected over it a wooden frame and covered it with cloths of fine linen and silk for the sake of beauty. Nearby we set up an altar. Beside the altar, one on each side, we placed the two standards of our Lord's Passion which had been carried before the bier on our journey. We took pains, within the limits imposed by the poorness of our means, to make that place fitting and suitable for the celebration of divine services and we appointed clergy who would keep wakeful watch there night and day, and carefully and continually sing the praises of the Lord. When these had been called to their posts, not only by my mandate but by a royal diploma that had been sent to us along the way, I was summoned to the palace and, with the Lord making my journey a successful one, I returned in a spirit of great exultation.

[Book Two]

1. Only a few days after I had come to court, having risen early as is the custom of court officials, I went to the palace first thing in the morning. There I found Hilduin, of whom I made mention in the former book, sitting by the door of the royal bedchamber awaiting the appearance of the emperor. Having greeted him as is customary, I asked him to rise and to come over to a certain window from which there is a view of the lower parts of the palace. Leaning against it side by side, we talked a great deal about the translation of the holy martyrs Marcellinus and Peter and about that wondrous miracle which was revealed in the flow of blood with which, as I have recorded, that casket sweated for seven days. When we came to that part of our conversation in which mention was made of the garments which were found with the bodies, and I said that the robe of the blessed Marcellinus was of wondrously fine texture, he answered, like one who knew the object as well as I did, that what I said about the robes was true. Astonished and perplexed by this, I proceeded to ask him how this knowledge of garments that he had never seen could have reached him. Staring at me, he kept silent for a little while, and then said "It is better, I think, for you to hear from me what, if I do not speak, you will soon learn from others. I should inform you fully about a matter which any other informer would not tell you about as fully, nor indeed can, for it is so provided by nature that no one can speak the whole truth about a thing he knows not by experience but by the accounts of others. I trust so greatly in your character that I believe you

will deal justly with me when, by my story, you know the whole truth about what has happened."

And when I had answered him in a few words [to the effect] that I would not deal with him otherwise than was appropriate, he said: "The priest, who on my orders went to Rome for the purpose of bringing me the relics of the blessed Tiburtius, found that he could not accomplish the goal for which he had come. After your notary received the relics of the holy martyrs about which we have been talking and had decided to return home, he formed a plan that he should remain in Rome a little longer, while the priest himself along with Luniso, the brother of Deusdona, and with the men, who were to carry those holy ashes, should go on before him as far as Pavia, and should there await his arrival with Deusdona. The plan pleased them both, and leaving the two of them at Rome, the priest, with Luniso and the servants who bore the relics, set our for Pavia. When they arrived there, the caskets containing the holy ashes were placed in your church behind the altar, and in that church were guarded by clergy and laity with constant vigilance. But one night, when the priest himself along with others was on watch in the church, it happened, as he maintains, that, around the middle of the night, sleep gradually stole over every single person who was gathered there to guard [the relics], except the priest. Then he fell to pondering and it seemed to him that without some great cause it could not have come to pass that so sudden a slumber should overcome so many men. And so, deciding that he ought to avail himself of the opportunity placed before him, he rose up, and with a lighted candle made his way silently to the caskets. Then, burning the cords of the seals by putting the flame of the candle close to them, he quickly opened the caskets without a key and took a small portion of each body. Then he fastened the seals together again, as if they had been unbroken, with the ends of the burnt cords. When no one saw what he had done, he went back to his own seat. Afterwards, when he had returned to me, he gave me the relics of the saints thus obtained by theft, and at first declared that they were not the relics of Saint Marcellinus or Saint Peter, but of Saint Tiburtius. Then, out of some fear unknown to me, he told me in secret from which saints the relics had come, and fully explained to me by what means he had got hold of them. We have placed these relics in Saint-Médard's in a place where honor is formally shown to them and where they are worshipped with great reverence by all who come there, but whether it is right for us to have them is for you to decide."

When I heard these words, I remembered what I had heard from a certain man with whom I had spent some time during my recent journey to the palace. In conversing with me, he said, among other things: "Have you not heard the rumor about the holy martyrs Marcellinus and Peter which is floating about in these parts?" And when I answered that I knew nothing of it, he said, "Those who come from Saint Sebastian [at Saint-Médard] tell us that a certain priest of the Abbot Hilduin, who made the journey to Rome with your notary, when they were on their way back and had in a certain place lodgings in common, and all your men were heavy with drink and sleep, and completely ignorant of what was going on, opened the caskets in which the bodies of the saints were enclosed, and took them out, and going his way carried them to Hilduin, and that they are now at Saint-Médard's. Apparently little of the holy dust remained in the caskets that were brought to you by your notary." Remembering these words, and comparing them with those which were spoken to me by Hilduin, I was gravely disturbed, especially because I had not as yet found the way to destroy that abominable rumor spread abroad by the wiles of the Devil or to remove it from the hearts of the deceived masses. Nevertheless I judged it best that I should request Hilduin to return to me the very thing which, after that voluntary admission, he could not deny had been taken from my caskets, carried to him, and received by him. This I took care to do as soon as I possibly could, and although he was a little harder and slower than I might have wished in coming to an agreement, he was nevertheless overcome by the earnestness of my prayers, and yielded to my insistence, though a little while before he had declared that, particularly in this matter, he would yield to the demands of no one.

2. Meanwhile, having sent letters to Ratleig and Luniso—for they were in the place where I deposited the bodies of the martyrs [Upper Mulinheim]—I carefully informed them about what kind of rumor concerning the martyrs was spreading through most of Gaul, admonishing them to consider whether they could recall or remember any such moment on their journey, or anything like what Hilduin claimed concerning his priest's actions. Coming to me at once at the palace, they related a story that was very different from the one that Hilduin told. For first they declared everything which that priest had told Hilduin to be false, for after they left Rome no opportunity had been given either to that priest or to anyone else to commit a crime of that sort. Yet at the same time it was clear that this very thing had happened to the holy ashes of the martyrs, but at Rome in the house of Deusdona through the greed of Luniso and the cunning of Hilduin's priest, at that time when the body of the blessed Marcellinus, removed from its tomb, was hidden in the house of Deusdona. This they declared was the nature of the theft. That priest of Hilduin, disappointed in the hope he had of obtaining the body of Saint Tiburtius, undertook, in order not to return completely empty-handed to his lord, to obtain by deceit what he could not come by honestly. So approaching Luniso, for he knew him to be poor and, therefore covetous, and offering him four gold and five silver coins, he seduced him into committing this bit of treachery. Accepting the proffered money, he opened the chest in which the body of the blessed Marcellinus had been placed and locked up by Deusdona, and gave that good-for-nothing scoundrel full power to take from it what he chose, as he had hoped would be the case. In that robbery he was not moderate, for he took away as much of the holy ashes of the blessed martyr as could be contained in a vessel holding a pint. That the deed was done in this way, Luniso himself, who had plotted it with the priest, admitted, throwing himself at my feet, crying and sobbing. When the truth of the matter was discovered, I ordered Ratleig and Luniso to go back to the place from which they had come.

3. After I had talked with Hilduin and an agreement had been reached between us about when the holy relics should be returned to me, I ordered two clerics of our household, namely Hiltfrid and Filimar, one a priest, the

other a subdeacon, to go to venerable Soissons for the purpose of receiving the relics. By means of those two I sent to the place from which those same relics were to be carried away, for the sake of blessing, one hundred gold coins. When they came on Palm Sunday to the monastery of Saint-Médard, they stayed there for three days and once they had received that incomparable treasure for which they had been sent, they returned, accompanied by two monks from that same monastery, with all the speed they could manage to the palace. Nevertheless they delivered the relics not to me, but to Hilduin. Having received them, he placed them in his private chapel, to be kept there until, after the many engagements of Easter were over, he would have spare time in which to show me what was to be returned before he returned it. When a week or more after holy Easter had passed and the king had left the palace to go hunting, Hilduin, according to what had been agreed upon between us, took those relics from his oratory where they had been kept safe and carried them into the church of the Holy Mother of God [Charlemagne's chapel at Aachen] and there placed them on the altar. Then he caused me to be fetched to receive them. Opening up the box in which the relics were contained, he showed it to me, that I might see what it was that he was giving back to me and what it was that I was receiving.

Then, lifting that same box from the altar he placed it in my hands, and having offered up suitable prayer, he took it upon himself to lead the choir and ordered those of the clergy who were skilled in psalmody to chant an anthem befitting the praise of the martyrs. And so singing he followed us, bearing off that priceless treasure, as far as the doors of the church. From there, in slow procession with crosses and candles, we made our way, praising the mercy of God, to an oratory that had been built with crude hands in our house, and into it—for no other place was to be found there—we bore the holy relics.

4. But in that procession of ours, which I have said we made from the church to our oratory, something miraculous happened, which I think I should not neglect to mention. For when we were coming out of the church, and singing praise to our Lord God with loud voice, such a great and sweet scent filled all that part of the city of Aachen that looks westward from the church that almost all the inhabitants of that part of the city, and all those at the same time who for any reason or business found themselves in that part of the city, were so divinely moved by the fragrance that, putting down all the work they had in hand, they all made haste, running as fast as they could, first to the church, and then, as it were following the scent, to our oratory into which they had heard that those relics had been carried. So within our gates there was an immense crowd of people, at once professing joy and wonder. Though many of those who had gathered together did not know what was happening, nevertheless with gladness and exceeding joy they offered up praise together to the mercy of almighty God.

5. But, after with spreading fame, it was proclaimed far and wide that the relics of the holy martyr Marcellinus had been brought to that place, there gathered together, not only from the city of Aachen itself and neighboring or adjacent towns, but also from places and villages much further away, such

a constant and huge crowd that, except for evenings and at night, there was no easy access for us to that oratory to celebrate divine service. The infirm were brought from all over, and those who suffered from various disorders were set down by their kinsfolk and friends beside the walls of the oratory. You could see there almost every kind of bodily affliction in both sexes and in all ages being cured, by the virtue which comes from Christ the Lord and by the merit of the most blessed martyr. Sight was given to the blind, gait to the lame, hearing to the deaf, speech to the dumb; even paralytics and those deprived of all strength in their bodies were brought there by the hands of others, and, made sound, they returned home on their own feet.

6. When word of these events was carried by Hilduin to the ears of the king [Louis the Pious], he first resolved that on returning to the palace he would without delay visit our oratory, where these things were wrought, and there do reverence to the martyr. But advised by Hilduin not to do so, he ordered that the relics should be carried to the larger church, and when they were taken there he paid reverence to them with humble prayer, and after the solemnities of the Mass had been celebrated he made an offering to the blessed martyrs, Marcellinus and Peter, of a certain manor, situated near the river Ahr, named Ludovesdorf, having fifteen farms and nine arpents of vineyards. And the queen [Judith] made an offering of her girdle, made of gold and jewels, and weighing three pounds. When these things were done, the relics were carried back again to their proper resting place, that is into our oratory, and there they stayed for forty days or more, until the emperor left the palace to go hunting in the forest, as is his yearly custom. When this was done, we too, after making ready whatever seemed necessary for our journey, set out with those same relics from the town of Aachen.

7. Now at the very moment when we were starting out a certain old woman, very well known at the palace, of about eighty years of age and laboring under a contraction of the sinews, was cured within our very sight. As we later learned from her own statement, she had been burdened with this disease for fifty years and had performed the business of walking by crawling about like a quadruped on her hands and knees.

8. So having begun our journey, aided by the merits of the saints, we came with the help of the Lord, on the sixteenth day to the village of Mulinheim, where when we set out for court we had left the holy ashes of the blessed martyrs. On that journey how much joy and how much happiness was brought by the coming of those relics to the people gathered along our way I cannot pass over in silence, and yet no account can fully do justice to it. Yet I must try to tell it, lest a thing that very greatly praises God, should seem, as if by laziness, to be swallowed up in silence. First, indeed, my mind moves me to tell you what we ourselves saw when we went out from the palace, in the presence of many. There is a stream called the Wurm [which flows into the Ruhr], lying about two thousand paces from the palace of Aachen, with a bridge across it. We stopped there for a time, so that the multitude which had followed us to that point from the palace and now desired to go back might have a place to pray. And there a certain man

from among those who were praying came close to the relics with another, and, looking his companion in the face, said, "For the love and honor of this saint, I free you from the debt which you know you owe me." For he owed him, as the man himself admitted, half a pound of silver. Again, another man, leading to the relics a fellow whom he had taken by the hand, said "You killed my father and, therefore, we have been having a blood-feud, but now, for the love and honor of God and of this saint, with all hatred put aside, I wish to join and pledge faith to you that from this time forth there shall forever be friendship between us. Let this saint be the witness of this love agreed upon by you and me, and let him work vengeance upon any who shall attempt to break this peace."

9. At this point the crowd that had started out from the palace with us, after worshipping and kissing the holy relics, with many tears which from excess of rejoicing they could not keep back, returned home. And with another great company which met us there, singing Kyrie eleison without interruption, we proceeded on our way to a place where we were joined in a similar manner by others rushing towards us. Then the second great crowd, like the first, having made a prayer, returned again to their daily duties. In this manner, day after day, we were accompanied from the break of dawn until dusk by crowds of people singing praises to Christ the Lord, and so made our way from the palace of Aachen to the village of Mulinheim, the Lord guarding the success of our journey. And there upon the altar, behind which the casket containing the holy ashes of the martyrs had been placed, we set down those relics in a jeweled box.

10. There they stayed in place until the month of November, when, getting ready to go back to the palace, we were warned by a vision that we should not leave that place before we had rejoined the relics once again to the body from which they had been stolen. How it was revealed that this ought to be done should not be passed over in silence, because not only in a dream, as is usual, but also by certain signs and warnings it was made clear to those charged with the duty of keeping watch that the blessed martyrs were entirely determined in this matter that their commands should be obeyed exactly.

11. There was a cleric by the name of Landolf who was appointed to keep watch in the church. It was also his job to strike the bell and he had his bed near the eastern door of the church. When, after the custom of vigils and matins, he had risen in his usual manner and had struck the bell, and the service being finished before daybreak, he wanted to go back to sleep, he prostrated himself for the purpose of supplication before the holy ashes of the martyrs. There, as he claims, when he began to repeat the fiftieth Psalm, he heard close to him on the pavement, as it were, the sound of the feet of a man walking back and forth. Stricken with no small fear, he raised himself a little on his knees and began to look about in every direction, because he suspected that one of the poor, with the doors of the church shut, was skulking about in some corner. But when he saw that no one else but he was within the walls of the church, he readied himself again for prayer and started to recite the Psalm he had begun before. But, before he could

finish a single verse, the jeweled box, containing the holy relics of the blessed
Marcellinus, which had been placed on the altar made such a loud ringing
noise that you would have thought it had been smashed open, as if by the
blow of a hammer. Two doors of the church also, that is the western and
the southern, as if some one were shaking and pounding them, made the
same sound.

Frightened and greatly perplexed by these things, for he had no idea what
he ought to do, he rose from the altar and threw himself in great fear on
his bed. Soon overcome with sleep, he saw a man, with a face he had never
seen, standing by his side, who addressed him with words like these: "Is it
true," he asked, "that Einhard so wishes to rush back to the palace that before
he goes he will not rejoin the relics of Saint Marcellinus which he has brought
here, in the place from which they were removed?" And when he answered
that he knew nothing of this matter, that one said: "Arise at first light and
tell Einhard by order of the martyrs not to dare to go from here or to start
off in any direction until he has restored those relics to their proper place."
He sat up wide awake, and was careful to impart to me, as soon as he could,
that which he had been ordered to tell me. And I, thinking that in business
of this kind nothing should be done carelessly, and indeed judging that what
was commanded should be carried out without any delay, gave orders on
that very day to make ready what seemed necessary for that purpose. On
the next day, with the most anxious care, I delicately joined those relics once
again to the body from which they had been separated. For which the blessed
martyrs were thankful, as can be seen by the plain witness of the miracle
that followed. For the next night, while we were sitting in the church for
the solemn office of matins, a certain old man, deprived of the use of his
legs, came to prayer, painfully crawling on his hands and knees. In the
presence of us all, by the strength of God and the merits of the most blessed
martyrs, he was so perfectly cured at the very hour when he came in, that
when he walked he no longer needed the use of a crutch. He also declared
that he had been deaf for five successive years, and that together with the
use of his feet hearing had been restored to him. And so, when all these
things had come to pass, I set out, as I said above I wished to do, for court,
there to pass the winter pondering many things in my mind.

[Book Three]

[Preface]

I am about to write something about the cures and miracles which the most
blessed martyrs of Christ, Marcellinus and Peter, brought about in various
places after their most holy bodies had been carried from Rome into Francia.
Rather [I should say] that it is through their blessed merits and loving prayers
that the king of martyrs himself, our Lord Jesus Christ, deigned to perform
[these acts]. I have deemed it necessary in this short preface to mention
that most of the things I have decided to write down were brought to my
attention by the reports of others. In these reports I, nevertheless, have
faith, since I was persuaded firmly by the things which I myself have seen
and knew to have occurred in my presence. Thus without any trace of worry,

I have been able to believe those things to be true which were reported by those who maintain that they had witnessed these things, even though I might, up until then, have had little or no [personal] knowledge of the persons from whom I heard these things. Of all these [miracles and cures] it seems to me that the first I should set down are those that occurred in that place [Mulinheim]—to which those same most blessed martyrs directed that their holy ashes should be translated—and which were seen by me personally. Next I should set down those things that were done in the palace of Aachen under the very eyes of the court. Then, I believe, I ought to record those things that were done in various places to which, at the request of religious people and by my help, the holy relics of those saints were transported. Thus, by following this order of narration, nothing should be omitted of all the signs and miracles that managed to come to the attention of my feeble powers. Now that the preface is complete, let us set forth the miracles themselves that must be related.

1. After the holy bodies of the most blessed martyrs, as has already been set forth in the previous books, by their own bidding and our compliance, had been carried to the great joy of the faithful to the place in which they now rest, and when the solemnities of the Mass had been celebrated in the open air, they were lifted up by the hands of priests. At that time there was not an insignificant number [of priests] gathered together there and they set the bier on which the [relics] were carried down near the altar. Another service was just beginning when, suddenly a certain young man, who was afflicted with a breakdown of his kidneys and, therefore, was bent over and hobbling on crutches, broke forth from the midst of the crowd of people who were standing about and, wanting to bow down in worship, fell over upon his knees, but in a marvelous way, for it was as if someone had pulled him away or, rather, dragged him back, so that he fell face up and for a very long time lay like someone asleep. Then, as though awakening, he lifted himself up into a sitting posture and, next, a little while later, stood up with no one helping him. Standing on his feet in the midst of the crowd pouring around him, he gave thanks along with others for his restored health and he joined in the praises of the mercy of God. He indicated to us, in answer to our questions, that he had come to Mulinheim with other poor people and pilgrims from the Portian country and that his name was Daniel.

2. At almost the same hour and, indeed, at almost the same moment, if I might say so, at which [Daniel] within the church and before the altar had, by the power of Christ and the intercession of the martyrs, recovered his health, an old woman who was paralyzed and deprived of the use of almost all her limbs was lying outside the doors of the church. She called upon the martyrs to help her and then her insides, or so it seemed to all who were standing about watching, began to shake as though she were about to vomit. Then, she did begin to vomit, throwing up a great quantity of phlegm and bile. After this, she sipped a small amount of cold water and asked to be lifted up from the spot where she was lying. Hobbling with a crutch she went into the church, and when she had worshipped the martyrs she recovered the strength in her limbs and returned to her home on foot.

3. In the meantime a man by the name of Willibert, who had a house not far from the church in which the bodies of the blessed martyrs now rest, approached the bier, among others who gathered to pay reverence to the saints, and offered up a gift of forty silver coins. When he was asked by us who he was and what he wished to achieve with the offering of this gift, he answered that a few days before he had been overcome by a very great weakness and that he had sunk to such an extreme point that, despaired of by all who had seen him, he had been urged, for the good of his soul, to give away all his property immediately, and so he had done. With all the bequests arranged now and the holy places to which they should be given, one of his servants lamented loudly that they had managed matters wrongly and negligently because none of his property had been given to the saints who had recently arrived from Rome. Then he had asked those standing nearby if they knew of any possession left to him that could be sent to the martyrs. Now at that time they were in Michelstadt and it had not yet been made clear to them by any signs that they ought to leave that place. Then someone answered him, saying that from all his goods only one pig remained and that it had not been decided to whom it should be given. He rejoiced and gave orders that it should be sold and that after his death the value of it should be sent to supply candles for the martyrs. As soon as he had uttered these words, he claims, he felt so sudden a relief from his malady that straightway, all his pain vanished and he wanted to eat. After eating, he recovered his strength so quickly that the next day he was able with great ease to go about all the business and work which the nature of his business demanded. After this the pig was sold and he gave the money, according to his vow, to the blessed martyrs.

4. The remaining wonders and miracles that God brought about through them for the good of men, I have decided to describe as they occur to my memory, although the order in which they are related is, I think, of no importance. For in telling of them, the chief thing to consider is what happened and why, rather than when.

Now when the relics of the blessed martyrs had been placed with solemn rites in that same church, where according to the custom of our established religion the holy offices of the Mass are daily celebrated, it happened one day, when the divine service was in progress and we had taken our place in the upper parts of the church, that looking down at the people gathered together below [we saw] a certain half-naked cleric, who had come with others to the service. He was standing in the midst of the crowd when, all of a sudden, he fell down so heavily that for a long time he lay on the pavement like one dead. When some of those around him tried to lift him up into a standing position, for he was having difficulty breathing, such a great flood of blood poured from his mouth and nostrils that the whole front part of his body—from his chest and stomach right down to the clothes covering his groin—was covered with the outflowing [blood]. When they brought water to refresh him, he recovered his strength and could speak clearly. Later when he was questioned by us, he declared that from infancy up to that moment he had been unable to hear anything or to speak. His land, he said, was Britain and he himself was one of the Angles. In order to visit with his mother, who was undertaking a pilgrimage to Rome, he had started on this journey with other pilgrims who wished to travel together to Rome. [Hence] he had come to that place, but when his companions carried on he remained behind. The day on which he was made healthy was the seventh after he had reached the place. When we asked him his name, he answered that he was completely ignorant of his name, because from the time when he became deaf he had never heard his name.

5. A few days later, when as usual we were gathered together in the church for the evening service, a deaf and dumb girl, whom her father and her brother had taken from the district of Bourges to many places with saints in search of a cure, was at last brought to that place and made to stand with others in that same church. Suddenly, as if overcome by madness, she slammed together as hard as she could the tablets by whose noise she used to seek alms and then she fell down raving in front of the people gathered there. Then running to the left-hand wall of the church and leaping up three feet or more as if she was about to climb it, she fell down on her back. When she had lain there a little while, more like someone dead than someone sleeping, and was covered all over by the blood that flowed without stopping from her mouth and nostrils, she was lifted up by the bystanders and carried into the middle of the church. When she had lain there as well for a little while, she sat up as if awakened from a deep sleep. Then, stretching out her hands to those who were standing beside her, she begged them with what movements of the head were in her power to lift her to her feet. Once she had been lifted up, she was led to the altar. When she saw Ratleig there, standing with the other clergymen near the altar and looking at her, she at once burst forth with these words: "You are Ratleig," she said. "You are known by this name and you are the servant of these saints." When he asked her how she knew this or who had told her his name, she said: "The saints themselves, who rest here, came to me when I lay as if I were asleep and put their fingers into my ears and said to me: 'When you have been lifted up and make your way to the altar, know that the young clergyman whom you will see standing before you looking at you is called Ratleig. He is our servant, for he brought our bodies to this place.'" And truly it was so, for he was the very man, as I recorded in the first book, whom I had sent to Rome to receive the relics of the saints from a certain deacon and to carry them to me. Thus this girl, in this way and in our presence, was freed from the spirit of evil and was restored to full bodily health by the power of the most blessed martyrs. Her father and brother, who had brought her there, declared that she had been deaf and dumb since birth.

6. Now though I myself did not see the miracle which I am about to relate, I am able to believe the account of those who told it to me no less than if I had seen the miracle with my own eyes. Thus, without hesitation or any doubt, I have decided to decribe it not as if I had heard of it, but as if I myself had actually seen it.

Certain merchants from the city of Mainz, who were in the habit of purchasing grain in the upper parts of Germany and transporting it to their city by the river Main, carried to the church of the blessed martyrs a blind man, an Aquitanian by the name of Aubrey, whom they had taken aboard their boat, at his own request, for the sake of earning the favor of God. He disembarked [at Mulinheim] and was received as a guest in the house of the guardian of the church, where he stayed for seven days or more. Besides being blind, which seemed natural to him since he lacked eyes, he suffered from a dreadful and unsightly infirmity of his whole body. Such a great trembling in all his limbs shook him so violently that he was entirely incapable of passing food to his mouth with his own hands. One day, while he was lying fast asleep in the morning at the house where he was staying, he saw in his sleep a certain man come up to him and urge him to rise without hesitation and hurry to the church. He said that the time had arrived when, through the power of the saints, he should be freed from that pitiable suffering. Awakened and led into the church, he sat down on a stone in front of the gate. At that moment within the church, a divine service was going on, as is the custom, and when those prayers were finished that precede the sacred reading of the Gospel, the Gospel was read out. Hardly had two verses been read, when, all of a sudden, as if struck by a blow, that trembling man cried out very loudly: "Help me, Saint Marcellinus!" Although everyone in the church was greatly disturbed by the noise, most, because of their respect for the reading of the Gospel, stayed where they were, but many ran over to see the cause of this clamor. As they later declared, they found [Aubrey] in the place where he had been sitting, now lying stretched out flat on his back, while blood poured from his nostrils down over his chin and chest. When he was lifted up by them and had revived after sipping some cold water, he told them that it had seemed to him, when he had cried out, that someone had struck him with a blow to the head, and so he had begged for the help of the blessed martyr. But it seems that this blow was good for him, because from that very moment no more sign of the unsightly trembling could be seen in his body. After that he stayed for almost two years in that place, and, as he himself declared, there was no night in those two years on which he did not see in his dreams those martyrs who had made him whole. He heard from them many things that he was commanded to tell others. We now see that many of those things are coming true, which he foretold would come to pass.

7. A few days later we saw another man afflicted with a similar disorder who was cured in the same church by the merits of those same saints in a similar way. For one night, when we were sitting in the church to celebrate the matins service and to hear the readings of the divine law, a man entered in the dress of a cleric. He was hobbling on a crutch and his limbs shook so much that he could hardly govern his tottering footsteps. While leaning against the wall to pray, he cried out in a loud voice and then fell flat on his face. After a little time had passed, he rose up cured of the disorder that had gripped him. When we asked him if, while he was recovering his health, he had seen anything besides what we all were able to see, he said that a little before he had come into the church he went to pray at the old church, which lay a short distance away to the west of the new church, where the martyrs were then resting. Since it was locked up, he had prayed at the doors. Then, when he had stood up and had started to go to the [new]

church, he saw a certain cleric with venerable white hair, robed in a white stole, going before him to the place where he himself wished to go. He followed, as he himself asserts, to the entrance of the church. When they both arrived there, he who had been in front stood aside, pressing himself against the left-hand door post, as if he wanted the one he had previously been in front of to enter first and he ordered him to do so with a nod of his head when the man hesitated to enter. When he had entered and bowed down in prayer, [the white-haired cleric] stood behind his back and, with his fist, struck him on the back of the neck and knocked him down. Then he vanished immediately. No one else except the one who was cured was able to see him.

8. At about the same time, having risen in the night, we went to the church and found before the [inner] doors of the church a boy who was lying in the narthex and was so pitiably curled up that his knees touched his chin. He asked one of those who followed us to carry him into the church. Moved by pity, [that man] lifted him up and set him down in the church, near the chancel. All of a sudden, that boy was overcome by sleep and slept where he lay. He did not fully awake until, by the intercession of the saints, he was completely cured of that pitiable contraction [of his limbs]. Awaking on his own, he rose up from the place where he had been carried in the arms of another and made his way to the altar, so that he might give thanks to God. When daylight came and we could speak with him, he declared three times before the bell of the church sounded that he had been accosted by a certain cleric, who was not known to him, and urged to let nothing prevent him from coming to church at the time of the matins service. That he had done, and then, as we saw, he had been completely cured while asleep in the church. He looked as if he were about fifteen years old.

9. Likewise we saw another cured in the same place in a similar way at about the same time, not a boy as the other was, but a very old and feeble man struck down with a similar disease. We found him one night when we came to the door of the church, at the very threshold, to celebrate the matins service. Hobbling on his knees, he supported himself on two crutches, and thus by his slow pace delayed our entrance. When we were standing behind his back and were brought to a stop by the slowness of his pace, a fragrance of the sweetest smell came forth from the church and filled our nostrils, surpassing by its presence any mixture of spices and thymes ever skilfully put together. He entered at last, and in our presence lay down close to the chancel, as if he were about to go to sleep. We also entered and took our places, and together with the others chanted, in the usual way, the Psalms which were being said. But when the first reading began, we heard that same old man groan and cry out like someone in trouble. A little later we saw him rise to a sitting position, and then, having taken up the crutches with which he used to walk, he stood up on his feet. That was all we saw, but he declared that it had seemed to him as he lay there that two men had grabbed hold of him, one by his shoulders and arms, the other by his knees and feet. It seemed that by their pulling they had stretched out the tendons that had contracted. Besides the tightened tendons, he asserted that he had

been bothered by deafness, but when he had lifted himself up into a sitting position it was as if his head had been struck very hard by a fist. At the same time he had heard the voice of someone commanding him to hear henceforth. The old man, cured in this way, declared that he came from the district of Aargau in Switzerland and that he was of German stock.

10. Another man, also afflicted with a similar tightening of his tendons, said that he came from the city of Liége, where the remains of Saint Lambert rest. One Sunday night, after the matins service was finished and we had returned from church, a priest was celebrating in proper manner the sacrament of the Host of Salvation for the benefit of those who had come from afar and were in a hurry to return to their daily duties. That man fell down on the pavement in the presence of all who had gathered there and lay there for a little while as if he were fast asleep. Then, as if he had been awakened from sleep, he stood up without any help. Then someone standing nearby picked up the crutches which he had been accustomed to use. When he fell, they had slipped from his hands and lay a little way off. The bystander held them out to him, but he refused them, saying: "May I never touch those things again!" So, cured in this manner, he went back on foot to the land from which he had made his way, more crawling than walking, to the threshold of the martyrs.

11. Not long afterwards, in the month of November, in keeping with my habit of spending the winter at the palace, I made ready to travel to court. Having started out on the journey, I had crossed the Rhine and had stopped to rest at the royal manor called Sinzig. After dinner there, which had occupied some portion of the evening, I was withdrawing with my servants to the privacy of the bedroom where I was to sleep when, suddenly, the servant who was accustomed to providing me with a drink entered in a rush as though he had some news to report. Looking at him, I asked, "What do you want to tell me? I can see that you have something, I know not what, you want to bring to my attention." Then he said, "Two marvels have just happened in my presence, which I have come to describe to you." When I ordered him to tell me whatever he wanted, he said, "A little while ago, when you got up from supper and entered this chamber, I went down with my fellow-servants to the cellar which is under the room where you ate. There we had begun to serve beer to the servants who came for it, when a boy sent by one of our fellow-servants came in with a flagon in his hand which he loudly demanded us to fill up for him. When it was filled, he also requested a little bit of that beer for himself to drink. It was given to him in a can which by chance stood empty on the barrel which contained the beer. When he put the can to his lips to drink, the boy cried out in great astonishment that it was wine, not beer. When the one who had filled up the flagon and had drawn the draught from the same tap, began to accuse him of lying, the boy said 'Take it and taste it, and then you will know that I have spoken not some lie, but the truth.' He took it and tasted it, and declared that to him the flavor was more like wine than beer. Then a third and a fourth, and the rest who were present there, testing and marveling one by one, drank up all that was in the can. Many who tasted it out of the

can bore witness that it had the taste of unmixed wine, not of beer.

"In the meantime, while they stood thunderstruck in amazement and admiration at the wonder of this sign, it happened that a candle, whose light they were using there and which was fastened to the wall near the barrel, fell down on the wet pavement, though no one touched it. It was so quenched that not even the smallest spark of flame remained burning in it. One of them, snatching it up, ran for the door, for he was worried by the dreadfulness of the dark. Before he got out, though he was on the very threshold, he cried: 'Holy martyrs Marcellinus and Peter help us!' At that appeal, the candle, which he held in his hand, began burning."

When I heard these things I presently, as was fitting, praised and gave thanks to almighty God, who always and everywhere glorifies his saints, and who wanted with such a show of their powers to make their servants happy, [that is,] we who then had brought the holy relics of them with us. But, when the story was finished, I ordered the one who had brought me the news to go back to his abode. Then, when I had laid back down to sleep, I began to think over many things and to wonder what that changing of beer into wine, that is of the worse drink into the better, might mean or signify and why a miracle of this sort had happened there in a royal residence and not in the place where the most holy bodies of the blessed martyrs, who through the power of Christ had worked their wonders, lay buried. Although by long and careful pondering I could come to no sure answer to this question, I nevertheless felt sure, and shall always feel confident, that the holy power on high, through which these miracles and others of this kind are believed to be worked, never allows anything to happen or to be done without good reason among the creatures whom I do not doubt belong to his providence and government.

12. So, having started on my journey, as I said above, I proceeded to court. For at that time the Emperor Louis, who was staying at the palace in Aachen, had given orders that an assembly of lords should take place at mid-winter. Among others, I too was commanded to be present, and so, forced to be away from proximity to the blessed martyrs, I experienced a less than joyful stay at the palace. Now after exactly a month had passed since my arrival, I sent a member of my household, a man by the name of Elleanhard, and ordered him to hurry with as much speed as he could to the door of the blessed martyrs. Once he had visited the brothers whom, when setting out, I had placed there to celebrate the divine service, and had carefully inquired into everything that had happened there, he was to return to us at once. When he arrived there, he stayed for three days. But, on the fourth, when he was making ready to return to us, that blind man by the name of Aubrey, of whom I spoke above, detained him as he was about to set out. He said that he should not begin his journey until he had seen a wonder that would make me exceedingly happy when I was told of it. He also added that the most blessed martyrs had appeared to him while he was asleep the night before and had given him orders to seek out a poor man, by the name of Gisalbert, who was pressed down by a large hump on his back and, thus, was bent over and leaned on short crutches. When he was found he was supposed to bring him, at the time of matins service, to the chamber which is

above the narthex of the church and close to the relics that rest there. Thus, by the merits and power of the saints whose relics those were, he might be freed from the deformity of his hump and from the inconvenience of being bent over. [Elleanhard] yielded to the request and put off until the next day the journey on which he had been ready to set out. The blind man, searching for the poor man he had been ordered to seek out, found him and, as he had been ordered, placed him in the upper part of the church near the relics at the time of the matins service. Now those relics, a fact we did not yet know, were those of the blessed martyr Marius and his wife and sons, that is Martha, Audifax, and Abacuc. For they also had been brought to us together with the bodies of Saint Marcellinus and Saint Peter and in the same chest. He who had brought them did not know whose relics they were, for he [Deusdona] who had sent them to me had promised that he would come to me and tell me with his own lips the names of the saints whose relics these were, which came to pass later. But the poor man who had been set down beside them by the blind man, when the second lesson of the night service was being read out as usual, uttered a loud cry, striking fear into those who heard him. When some of the clergy along with the one who had been ordered to watch there ran to him, they found him face down and stretched out before the altar, and the pavement which was beneath his mouth was wet with a great deal of blood. Lifting him up and refreshing him with the water they brought there, they led him down into the lower parts of the church so that all might give thanks, for he was now cured and stood erect. Nor was there any trace left of that curvature like a camel's hump. When this miracle occurred in this manner, he whom I had sent there returned to me as fast as he possibly could and, when he told me what he had seen, he filled me with great joy and exultation.

13. Not long afterwards Ratleig, who, as we described in the former books, brought the holy ashes of the martyrs from Rome, arrived, having been ordered, as he said, to bring me a little book containing many chapters. The reason for it he said was this: the blind man of whom we have been speaking had advised him on the authority of the martyrs to write down and carry those headings to me and he said that I should take them and offer them to the emperor for him to read. I took the little book from him and read it, and when it was corrected and written down anew, I offered it, as he had ordered, to the emperor. The emperor took it and read it, but of the things that this little book ordered or advised him to do he took the trouble to fulfill very few. Now what those headings contained, or what they recommended to be done or what was left undone by him, would be better set out in another place than this. Nevertheless I think that the manner in which it was revealed and ordered that the little book ought to be made and to be given to the king not only should not be passed over, but should be written down as openly and as clearly as it can be.

Ratleig said that it had happened in this way. "A few days ago when we gathered together in church as is our custom to celebrate the night service, that blind man whom you know came to me, begging me to step aside with him into a more secret place. I did as he wished, and with him entered the cell where I usually sleep. He spoke first, saying 'Tonight, a little before we were awakened by the ringing of the bells, there appeared to me in a vision a man with venerable white hair who was clothed in a white garment and held in his hand a golden wand. He spoke to me with these words: "Make sure, Aubrey," he said, "that you fully understand everything that I am about to say to you and hold it fast in your memory, so that you can repeat it clearly to others who will write it down. For I want these things to be written down and shown by your master to the Emperor Louis who is to read them. For it is extremely necessary not only for these things to be known, but also acted upon by that prince into whose kingdom these martyrs have come by the command of God."

'Thereupon [the figure in white] began to dictate in order a dozen or more chapters and he urged me to relate and explain them one by one to you and to four others whom I shall name for you. After this you should make a little book of these things and take it to your master who now resides in the palace, and you should ask him, on the authority of the martyrs, to present it as soon as he possibly can to the emperor. After that, [the figure in white] added, "Do you know who I am, who urges you to do these things?" Without hesitation I answered that he was Saint Marcellinus. But he said to me: "It is not as you think, for I am the archangel Gabriel and I have assumed the shape and form of Marcellinus because the Lord God has placed me in charge of everything that concerns those martyrs, and I have come now to tell you what I want you to write down, because it is the will of God that those things shall be brought on their authority, without the imposition of any delay, to the knowledge of the king. Go, as I have commanded you, at the first light of dawn after the matins service is over, and tell what you have heard to those to whom I have ordered you to tell it." Then I said, "There is no one who will believe that an angel has spoken to me, or has ordered me to carry this news." [Gabriel] answered and said: "That is not so, for I shall give you a sign to demonstrate in their presence: and when they have seen it they will have no doubts about the things that you tell them on my orders. So therefore I want you to ask Ratleig to set down before you two new unlit candles. Take one in your right hand and the other in your left and go stand before the altar. When you have finished narrating everything that I commanded you to tell, inform your listeners that by this sign—that is, if the candles in your hands catch fire while they watch, but without anyone bringing visible fire—they should believe these things, which you told them, to be true and ordered by an angel of God."'

When all this had happened, that little book was written out and brought to me and I presented it to the king. He, for his part, received the book and read it throughout. It seemed proper to me to mention this little book among the other miracles [of the saints], for on the occasion when it was ordered that marvelous and unprecedented lighting of the candles happened [just as] the angel foretold. The angel himself lit those candles in the name of the merits of the blessed martyrs.

14. At almost the same time, when Ratleig returned to the church of the martyrs, another little book was brought to us from there. It contained the words and arguments of a certain demon who called himself Wiggo. These words were uttered by him in the presence of many witnesses before the

altar, near where the holy ashes of the martyrs rest, in answer to the questions of a priest who had performed an exorcism over the one who was possessed. It is said to have happened in the following way.

There is a manor in the country of Niedgau called Höchst, which belongs to the monastery of Saint Nazaire. From there a girl about sixteen years old, who was possessed by that wandering spirit, was brought by her parents to the church of the martyrs. When she came before the tomb containing their holy bodies and the priest had read over her head the words of exorcism, according to the custom, then the priest began to question the demon as to how and when he had entered into her. The demon answered the priest not in German which was the only language the girl knew, but in Latin. When the priest was struck with wonder and asked how she knew Latin, when the girl's parents, who were present there, were completely ignorant of Latin, the demon answered, saying: "You have never seen my parents." Then the priest said, "Who are you and where did you come from, if these are not your parents?" The demon, speaking through the lips of the girl, said: "I am an officer and a disciple of Satan, and for a very long time I was the gate-keeper of hell, but for the last few years I have, with eleven confederates, ravaged the kingdom of the Franks. We destroyed and utterly ruined grain, grapes, and all the other crops that spring from the earth for the use of humans. We killed herds [of cattle] with murrain. We let loose plague and pestilence among humans, and all the troubles and the evils that they have now suffered from for a long time, as they so deserved, we did and they bore." When the priest asked him why a power of this sort had been granted to him, he said, "On account of the wickedness of this people, and of the manifold sins of those who rule over them. For they love profit and not justice, they fear humans more than God, they oppress the poor, they will not listen to widows and orphans crying out to them for help, and they do justice only to those who pay. Aside from these sins, there are many and almost countless others which are daily committed both by the people themselves and by their rulers: perjury, drunkenness, adultery, murder, theft, and rapine are forbidden by no one and, once committed, are punished by no one. The more powerful people are devoted to base profits and abuse the higher place given to them so that they might rule their inferiors and give themselves up to pride and vainglory. They exercise their hatred and malice not against distant peoples, but against their neighbors and those with whom they are allied. Friends have no faith in friends, brothers hate brothers, and fathers do not love their sons. There are few who faithfully and devoutly pay tithes, fewer still who give alms; and this because they consider lost to themselves whatever they are commanded to give to God or to the poor. They do not fear to have unfair measures and false weights, though it is against God's command. They try to get the better of each other by fraud; they are not ashamed to bear false witness; they do not respect Sundays and Feast Days, but then, just as on other days, they work as their own interests dictate. Because of these things and many more which God has either commanded people to do or not to do, and because this people by disobeying his commands is guilty of disobedience, we have been allowed—no, we have been ordered—to do those things that I named above, one by one, so that the people might atone for their lack of faith. For those people are unbelievers and liars since they do not care to keep the promises they made in baptism." All these things the demon said in Latin through the lips of the German girl.

When the priest began to command that he come out of her, [Wiggo] said, "I will exit, not because you commanded it, but because of the power of the saints who will not allow me to stay in her any longer." Having said this, he threw the girl down on the pavement and made her lie there for a little while, face down, as if she were asleep. But a little while later, after [Wiggo] had gone, the girl, as if waking from sleep, rose up, because of the power of Christ and the merits of the blessed martyrs, cured. All who were there saw her and marveled that after the demon had left her she could not speak Latin. Thus it is clear that not she, but the demon had spoken [Latin] through her. Alas what grief! To what a pitiful depth have our times fallen when not good men but evil spirits are our teachers and the inciters of vice and those who encourage crime [now] remind us of the need for reform.

15. At almost the same time a nun by the name of Marctrude, from the region of Wetterau, had been so stricken for ten years with a dreadful case of paralysis, that thoughout that time she could hardly use any part of her body for human functions. Her relatives, despairing of her recovery, had carried her to every holy place to which they could take her. Nevertheless when she was brought by them to the church of the martyrs, and at the time of the night service by the chancel, through the merits and mediation of those saints she was given back without delay the health she longed for, and so fully and perfectly did the strength return to all her limbs that she who had been carried there on a litter returned home on foot. But when she began to return home, on the journey itself she was seized again by the same disorder from which she had been happy to be freed. Thus, repenting her return, she begged to be taken back to the threshold of the martyrs. Hardly had she been brought back when at once she received again the cure which she had lost by departing. Hence she made a vow that she would never again willingly depart from [the place] where honor was paid to the bodies of the saints, and she built herself a little cell, so that she might dwell not far from the church. From that time forward, she remained there and piously devoted herself to the service of the martyrs.

16. It is also well known that another woman, not much later, was freed by the same blessed martyrs from a very troubling disorder. This fact is known to have been accomplished as follows. In the region of Niedgau there is an estate called Oberursel which lies about six leagues from the church of the martyrs. At this place a certain woman awoke from sleep early [one morning] and sat up in her bed. Like those rousing themselves from sleep, to shake off drowsiness she stretched herself by extending her arms and by yawning. But she opened her mouth a little wider than she should have and the joints of her jaw near the ears slipped out of place. Her open mouth was now fixed in a permanent yawn, for she was unable to shut her mouth and, looking more like a mask than a human being, she paid the price for that unwise yawn. When she brought this matter to the attention of the poor women who lived on the same estate, they came running over and tried to help

alleviate her suffering with herbs and silly incantations. But their vain and superstitious confidence had no effect. Indeed whatever these unskilled hands did to help or to cure the sufferer instead bothered her and hurt her. Thereupon a brother of that woman's husband came over and gave the sound advice that she should be taken without delay to the church of the martyrs. He said that she would be cured there, if she was ever to be cured anywhere. So they began to lead her there, mounted on a packhorse. But when they came close to the church, they made her get down off the packhorse and walk on her own feet. When she had come to the spot where the bell-tower of the church could be seen, those who were leading her urged her to lift up her eyes and look at it. As she looked up and saw [the tower], all of a sudden she recovered her health. Everyone with her fell down on the earth there and gave thanks for the mercy of God in what words of praise they knew, and getting up they hurried into the church. After they had worshipped the most holy martyrs and made offerings according to their means, they went back, with great rejoicing, to their own business. I saw that woman and talked to her, and learned of the things that were done for her from her own lips.

17. Now I want to tell [you] what I myself saw on the birthday of the blessed martyrs. A certain deaf and dumb boy, who had come there three years before, and who had been made the porter in the house of the guardian of the church, was sitting, when the feast day was past and the vespers service was over, close to the door. Suddenly he got up and went into the church, and, at the right side of the altar, he fell down upon his face. When the sacristan, who was placing a candelabrum with candles before the altar, found him lying there, he took the trouble to tell me at once. I and those who were with me went quickly to the church and found him lying there just as the sacristan had reported. When we urged him to rise, he could not be stirred, for he was like one overcome by a heavy sleep. But a little while later he sat up, as if awaking, and seeing us standing about him he stood up, and to those who were near him he spoke in Latin. Now there are certain members of our household who say that, about six months before, when that same boy was asleep one night in the house of one of our men, he spoke two words in his sleep, and at that moment recovered his hearing, which up until that time he had lacked as much as speech. They concluded this from the fact that after he had awakened from that sleep he was careful to do everything that anyone ordered him to do. But what seems most remarkable in this wonder is that he then understood not only those who spoke Latin, but the vernacular as well; yet when he was cured he discoursed not in [German], but in Latin [alone]. He said that he had seen the blessed martyrs and had heard from them many things which he was supposed to tell others. But when he did not relate these things at once, but put them off to be told on some other day, they were so forgotten by him that he could remember nothing of what he had heard. Since he did not know his own name, I ordered him, because of the prosperous effect of the miracle, to be called Prosper. And he is alive now, and holds the same office he held before in the household of the guardian of the church.

18. Now the day before Prosper recovered his speech (that is, on the eve of the feastday of the saints), a certain youth, who was also deaf and dumb, entered the church. While, with gestures of supplication he was imploring the help of the saints, he too by the aid of God was cured of both his afflictions. Like the other, [Prosper], he too had never heard his name, so I called him Gottschalk. After the power of speech was granted to him through the merits of the saints, he spoke not like Prosper, but in the manner of his people in a barbarous tongue [German].

19. Now when necessity forced me, according to custom, to travel to the king's court, in the month of December on the Kalends [1 December], if I recall correctly, I left the house of the martyrs and reached next day the town which in modern times is called Wiesbaden and there spent an evening. In order to pass more easily through the forest which lies all around that place, we arose earlier than usual, and sent our servants ahead of us with the baggage. After they had left the town in which we delayed and had started on their way, such a darkness of black night surrounded them that they could not tell which way to turn. Besides it was very cold, and the earth, covered with frost, would not show them the path. As the tops of the hills through which they needed to travel were covered with clouds, they could not see how far off or how near they were. In addition to this, a heavy fog fell on the valleys which, filling their sight with its thickness, impeded them when they could have proceeded on their journey. When they saw that they were impeded by so many obstacles and could not tell what to do, they dismounted from their horses and tried to find by groping the road which they could not see. But when this helped them little, they mounted their horses again, deciding that they had better run the risk of losing their way, of which they were very afraid, than make a long delay. So proceeding in the dark a little way further they came to a cross which had been set up in memory of the blessed Marcellinus on the road by which they were to travel. Now the reason why that cross was placed there was that, when I was returning two years before from the palace, and was bearing the relics of the blessed Marcellinus, which had then been given back to me, the inhabitants of the town in which we had just passed the night, had met us at that point. In memory of this fact, they had set up [the cross], in reverence to the blessed martyr as if it were an inscription or a monument. When these servants, more by straying than by finding their way, had arrived from there, they formed a plan to wait there for their companions who were following. Lest they should lose their way, they called to them by the sound of a horn. When they were all assembled together, they called on the blessed martyrs to bring them aid and, lifting up their voices on high, they three times chanted the Kyrie eleison.

When this had happened, a great flash of light shone over them, shimmering forth from the heavens for so long that it matched the clarity of daylight. That lightning gave them so much help in continuing their journey, that the fog lifted and the darkness broke and they were able to proceed on their way without getting lost throughout the night, though they were traveling through woods and hills dark with forests. With the first flash, too, came such warmth along with the light that they said they felt as if it were the heat of a burning fire. By that flash of light not only the fog but also the frost, which till then had covered the hills and the entire forest, was so burned off that when the third flash came hardly any trace of the bitter cold remained. We were told these things by those who had seen and experienced them on the evening of the same day, after we came to our lodging-place. Putting faith in their words, we gave praise to the mercy of almighty God by giving thanks because through the merits of his saints he had deigned to help and comfort us in our time of need.

20. Although all the works which we have known to be done for the help of mortals through the merits of the blessed martyrs are great and should be attributed to divine power, the strength of almighty God is nevertheless so openly and clearly evident in the miracle which I have decided to commit to writing that no room for doubt is left but that whatever He wills to do for every one of his creatures He can most easily bring to pass.

In the region of Niedgau there is a village called Suntilinga, in which a certain priest by the name of Waltbert held a church. Afflicted in his mind, to the great sorrow of his people, he was brought to the church of the martyrs. Three of those with him were his brothers, one a priest and two laymen; the fourth, a close relative, was a monk of the monastery of Hornbach, in which the priest himself had been raised from an early age. When I asked them if any drug had been measured out for him by some physician, they said, "As soon as we understood that he was afflicted with this disorder, we took him to the monastery in which he was brought up. When the physicians there had done many things for him according to the skill of their art and could not drive the sickness out of him, our friends advised us to bring him to the mercy of these saints, for we believe that they can save him, since we have heard that many others have been cured here." After this they were received in the lodging-house and spent four days with us, taking him daily to the church and making him lie down before the holy ashes of the martyrs. But on the fifth day his brother the priest and the monk who had come with him, requested that I keep him there with his two brothers, the laymen, until they could come back again, for they said that they would return again in three days. I did as they asked and entrusted him to our priest Hiltfrid. When he had been received by the priest and taken to the cell in which he lodged himself, around the evening of the same day the madness by which he was gripped came on more violently and, snatching up a knife that chance happened to place before his raging mind, he tried to kill one of his brothers, who was keeping watch over him. But his brother escaped death by fleeing and told our men, who were near by, about the insanity of [his brother]. Then the priest, to whom I had entrusted the care of that man, proposed and persuaded me that I should allow him to be bound. So tied down with iron chains, he was put to bed and, with the doors locked, he was left alone in his cell. His brothers lay before the door and watched with great care as if he were determined to break out. The chains with which he was bound were of such a kind that while he was in them he could not turn to the right or to the left, nor lie any other way except flat on his back.

So he went to sleep and, as he himself declared, did not wake up until the middle of the night. But he woke up when the roosters began to crow and found that he was not only free of his chains, but also of the affliction of madness with which he had been troubled. At once with his entire mind he turned to the praise of God with Psalms and hymns and he sang them with such overflowing thankfulness, even if he was alone, and so clearly that he awoke everyone who was sleeping near his cell. Then getting up, he went to the door and asked his brothers, who were lying there, to let him out that he might satisfy the demands of nature. But they thought that this was a trick by the madman and did not dare to consent. They sent for their host, who had locked him up there, and begged permission to speak with him. After he had spoken with him and, by the reasonableness of his answers, understood him to be of sound mind, he opened the door and let him out. Receiving him back, he asked him what had become of the chains with which he had been bound. He answered "The chain with which you bound me is safe, and if you wish to know where it is, look for it and you will find it." Lighting a candle, they found the chain lying in front of the bed in which they had made him rest, and it was arranged in the same manner and tied with the same knots as it had been when they had fastened him with it to that bed and left him alone in the cell. Who could have done this, except the one who made all things from nothing and who can do with the things he has ordained wonders which can neither be understood by reason nor explained by the speech of humans? For who can either imagine in thought or describe in words how that priest was freed from those chains, for it is clear to us that no one without help could free himself from knots of that sort if he was bound with them as that priest was when he was shut up alone in that cell? Those who brought him there, after they returned and found him cured and in full possession of his mind and memory, went back with him, rejoicing and giving praise to God, to their home. I did not learn from the reports of others that this event happened in this way, but, by the will of God, I myself knew it, for I was still present. Thus I write about it with confidence, because, as they say, it happened that I came to learn of it by visible truth. But inasmuch as all the things which I have decided to write down about the power of the martyrs cannot be finished in this present [book], let this book end here, so that what remains may be better taken up in another [book].

[Book Four]

[Preface] In relating the signs and powers that I have proposed that I would write down in this book, it seems to me that those should be placed first which, as they happened at the palace, came to be known not only by the people, but by the prince himself and his chief men, and, so to speak, by all the court. Also at that time there were no other relics [at the palace] than those of the blessed Marcellinus and Peter in our little oratory, where these same miracles occurred, so that any cures or wonders known to have happened there belong to and should be attributed to them. The most blessed martyrs have also, as we shall see in what follows, worked their many powers and miracles in the resting places of other saints, [so that] it might reasonably seem as if they [Marcellinus and Peter] were working alongside the saints in whose churches they came to rest. That is an understandable opinion, since those who are believed to have equal merit before God, are thought, and not absurdly [so], to work in common when performing miracles. But that this is not the whole story is proven by the fact, which is clearly evident, that no wonders were worked in those places before the relics of the blessed martyrs were transported there. But now, as we have promised, let us set forth the miracles which occurred in the palace.

1. There was a young man among the chamberlains of the king, a Greek by the name of Drogo, who was gripped by fever. For some months he was troubled by a drawn-out and debilitating state of health, either because of the negligence of his companions or because of the ignorance of his physicians. After Abbot Hilduin had returned the relics of the blessed Marcellinus to me, as is described in the second book, Drogo was advised in his dreams to go to our oratory and to light a candle bought for four *denarii* there, and to call on Saint Marcellinus, whose head was declared to be there, to give him help. He was assured that if he did this, he would soon be delivered from the affliction which he had long suffered. He believed the one admonishing him so and did what he was told to do as soon as he possibly could. Immediately he was made healthy again and, recovering the strength of his limbs, he walked home on his own feet.

2. There was also in the same place another young man by the name of Gerlach from the city of Rheims, among those who had been commanded to come from that city to construct the buildings of the palace. About half a year before, in the street where he lived, he was seized by such a powerful and immense tightening of his tendons that his feet touched his buttocks and his knees touched his chin. His friends and neighbors, carrying him in their arms, bore him into the aforesaid oratory. Since they could not set him down in any other way, they laid him down upon his face, and they asked with great devotion for the holy martyr to restore his health. The day was Sunday and the hour of the day when he was brought there was the third, and he lay there until the ninth hour. When the service of that hour was completed by the clergy, behold there came from the shrine which contained the holy relics of the blessed martyr so pervasive a fragrance of the sweetest, yet unusual scent, that it filled the whole little cell of the oratory. In marvel at it all who were there presently rose up, and peered at one another with curious looks, to see if they had all sensed the same thing. Suddenly they saw [Gerlach] who was lying nearby. It seemed as if he was being pulled by hands grasping him and that his limbs, which had contracted during his illness, were being straightened. Understanding that divine power was at work, they lifted up the man and set him down before the altar. When he was set down there they begged, with much wailing, for divine help and, in the sight of all, [Gerlach], who had been carried into the oratory by the hands of others, was made so straight that he went out from the oratory on his own feet. Nevertheless he is even still known to bear in his body a trace of the suffering which he underwent, for he has ever after so limped with his left shin and foot that he has needed a crutch to govern his pace. Why he was not fully cured, let anyone say what they wish. As for me, I can only surmise that it was necessary for his inner health that some trace of his

outward trouble should remain with him.

3. There is an old city, distant from the town of Aachen by the space of eight leagues, called Jülich. From that territory a certain girl, afflicted with a similar malady and in a similar way, was brought by her mother and others of her family to the oratory. Because of the crowd of people who were by chance gathered at that time to hear the solemn offices of the Mass, they could not carry her in and so laid her down outside the east window of the oratory, waiting for the opportunity, once the crowd of people had dispersed, to bear her more easily into the oratory. But in the middle of the service, when the Gospel had been read out and the offering of the host of our salvation was finished, they saw that she was seized with spasms and that a sweat had broken out over her whole body. She seemed to fall into a sleep. Concluding, with reason, from these signs that the power of God was present, they lifted her up and set her down on a square slab of stone which lay nearby. There, in the presence of all who had hurriedly come together in order to see this miracle, she completely recovered, with the help of God and in the space of an hour, health in all her limbs.

Among the other spectators there were some Jews, one of whom was named David. After the fulfilment of this sign, he came running quickly to the window of the cell in which I was staying, and calling to me told me of the miracle which he had seen, giving thanks to God who through his martyrs had taken the trouble to work such great miracles for the good of humans.

4. There was in the same town a certain blind man of advanced age, who, as he himself declared, had been stricken with sudden blindness three years earlier and was in the habit of begging alms along with other poor people by going from door to door. While he was asleep in his little hut he saw in his sleep a certain man standing by his side, who said that if he wanted to see [again] he should go to our oratory, for there was a doctor there who could restore light [that is, sight] to one asking for it. He refused, for the the light that he offered was accursed. "What use do I now have," he said, "for sight, when I lost it so long ago? It is not decent for one who sees to beg, I am old and feeble and cannot work." Then the one who was speaking to him answered: "Go without delay, for whether you want to or not you will recover your sight." He obeyed the command and made his way to the oratory, where he passed the night. When nothing happened all night long he returned to his hut. There the one who had appeared to him before in his sleep appeared again, and just as he had urged him before, commanded him to go to the oratory. He did as he was ordered, but even then nothing happened. Reminded a third time he came again, and when he knelt before the altar to pray he recovered his sight. While this man was still blind, I often used to see him in the midst of the other poor and sick begging at our house. Thus I have sought for no other proof of the return of his sight, because I have trusted the proof of my own direct awareness [of the case].

5. Now when the rumor of these events and many others of the powerful works [of the saints] were spreading throughout the towns and regions near Aachen, a woman from the land of the Ripuarians, who had already been

blind for a long time, both wanted to recover her sight and believed she could, and so she asked to be taken to the oratory. When she came there, she remained in fasting and prayer for three days and nights. But when, despite being there, she perceived no indication of the cure she desired, she was taken back home. After a few days had passed, having again fostered the realistic hope of recovering her sight, she asked to be led back to the holy relics. She was led back by a single servant, for those who had led her there earlier judged her hope vain and empty and did not want to go [back] again. When [the blind woman and her servant] came to the cemetery of the palace of Aachen, which is situated on the hill overlooking the city on the eastern side, at that very point to which he had led and guided her, she recovered her longed-for sight. It was as if divine grace had come there to meet her. Then, full of wonder and astonishment, she ordered the servant who had guided her to follow her: "Up until now," she said, "I followed along where you led me, but now I do not need your guidance, because I see the way we must go. With the help of God, I see the part of town in which the holy relics rest, to which I have longed to come. Be alert and careful that when we are within the city you take me straight to the oratory of the martyrs." When she had said that, he guided her to the oratory, and there she gave thanks, and she told us of the miracle wrought for her, and so, restored to sight and rejoicing, she returned to her own people.

6. Eschweiler is a royal manor four leagues away from the palace of Aachen. There a certain man was stuck at home and was in great difficulty because of a lingering problem with his bowels. His family so despaired of his condition that it seemed as if he could be cured by no means except cautery. A physician was called for this purpose and a day was appointed for this profitless burning. Meanwhile it was revealed in sleep to a certain woman, who lived in the same place, that he should not resort to a remedy of this kind as a cure, because it would do the patient no good, he could hardly bear the pain of it, and it was entirely unnecessary. On the other hand, if he wished to be made whole, he should go to the palace at Aachen and ask for our oratory. He should have himself carried into it and should not leave it before three days were up. In this way he should recover his health entirely. When he was told this, he summoned his friends and family, and begged them for his sake to fulfill the commands contained in the revelation. They soon placed him on a pack-horse and led him to the oratory. Placing him in it, as had been ordered, they went away, proposing to return after the three days were up. Left there for three days and nights, and praying to the Lord for the recovery of his health, he was so completely cured that he declared nothing of that pain, from which he had so long suffered, remained in his bowels. When, as they had promised, his friends came back for him and found him as healthy as they had hoped he would be, he returned home not on the back of a beast, as he had arrived, but with the use of his own feet and to the great happiness and joy of all of them.

7. There is another royal estate in the Meuse region, which lies about eight leagues from Aachen, and the inhabitants call it Gangelt. There a woman had a daughter of some eight years of age who was so weakened by the

dreadful disease of paralysis that for a long time she could hardly move any one of her limbs for their normal functions. When the mother heard reports of the miracles, she conceived in her pious heart the hope of recovering her daughter's health. At once she took the trouble to carry her in her own arms to the oratory. When she arrived there in the morning at breakfast time and found none of the clergy on hand (for shortly before they had dispersed in order to eat), she nevertheless entered and set her daughter down on the pavement. Lighting a small wax candle, which she had brought as an offering, she placed it on the same piece of pavement in front of the girl and bowed herself down with the greatest reverence to pray before the holy ashes. When that was done, without any delay, the girl who, without her mother's knowledge, had recovered through divine grace the health and strength of all her limbs, stood up. She lifted up the candle which lay beside her and stood behind her [mother] who was bent over. When [the mother's] prayer was done, she lifted her head up from the pavement, but saw neither the candle nor her daughter in the place where she had left them. She stood up and, turning around, saw her daughter standing close beside her holding the candle. When she saw that there was no one there to whom she could report the wonder that had been brought about—for besides the poor who lay there in order to beg, there was no one but herself and her daughter within the walls of the oratory when the miracle happened—she went home on foot with her daughter now safe and well. She fulfilled her vows with an act of thanksgiving.

How I learned of this miracle I shall briefly describe. Gerward, the librarian of the palace, to whom the care of the works and buildings of the palace had been committed by the king, was coming back from Nijmegen on his way to the palace of Aachen. When he stopped one night at that royal estate [Gangelt], he asked his host if he had lately heard any news from the palace. He answered, saying: "Nothing just now is so much talked about among the courtiers as the signs and powers that are being worked in the house of Einhard by certain saints whose relics he is said to keep in the oratory of his house. To the worship of [these saints] all our neighbors daily rush and whoever is brought there ill is cured." [Then] he began to tell him about the daughter of that woman and how a few days before she had been cured. Then Gerward said, "Go and bring that woman to me so that she might herself speak to me, because I want to hear her." The woman came and clearly set forth everything, just as it had happened. Gerward, when he came to the king next day, told him what he had learned of the miracle from the account of that woman. When, following custom, I entered [the king's presence] and stood before him, he told both me and others standing nearby what Gerward had reported to him of this miracle, marveling and giving praise to divine mercy and power. So it came about that the sign that had happened in our house without our knowledge was in this way made known to us.

8. It should be sufficient that [we] have related these accounts of the miracles of the blessed martyrs that occurred at the palace in the present work. Now we must come to those wonders that were accomplished in places to which, at the request of religious men and due to my generosity, the relics of those

same martyrs came and in which even up until the present they are [still] worshipped with great devotion. The first one I gave them to was George, a priest and head of the monastery of Saint Salvius the Martyr, which is in the region of Famars in the city of Valenciennes. He sent them to that monastery from the palace at Aachen by means of a certain deacon. When the deacon in the company of only one companion came to the region of Hesbaye to the royal domain called Visé and dismounted in a field near the town for the purpose of resting his beasts, all at once one of the inhabitants of that place, who was bent over with a hump and whose jaw was also swelled up (for, as he himself said, he had long suffered from great trouble with his teeth), came storming into the same field, with an iron pitchfork on his shoulder, and asked angrily why those animals were grazing in his field. Then the deacon, who was carrying the relics of the martyrs and who was making ready to hang them on the top of a pole which he had set up for that purpose in the same place, said "It is better for you to kneel down before the relics of these saints, which I hold here in my hands, and to pray to God that through the merits of these same saints He might think it worthwhile to free you from the pain which you suffer. For the swelling which is to be seen on your face is the proof that there is a great pain in your mouth." At once the man cast aside the pitchfork which he held in his hand and threw himself down on his face before the relics. As the deacon advised, he made a prayer to God for his health. Not much later, he got up from his prayer so cured that the swelling was gone from his face, the pain in his teeth had disappeared, and so had the hump with which his back had been burdened. Then, running as quickly as he could into the village, he called on all his relatives and neighbors to praise God and give thanks to Christ the Lord. So there came together in the field a great multitude of people, and a crowd gathered from all the regions around that place, to give thanks for him who had been made whole. Everyone begged the deacon to spend the night there and he could not deny them, for they were prepared, unless he consented, to hold him there against his will. Then they kept watch all night long and the whole region echoed with the praise of God. But next day, when the deacon began to start on his way, the entire crowd of people gathered together accompanied him on his departure with great reverence. Nor would they either stop or turn back until they were met by others whom the report of this miracle had excited, who came out to meet them.

9. In this way the holy relics of the martyrs, by reason of this miracle, were taken up by the peoples of those parts and were carried by the guidance of the Lord to the church of Saint Salvius, to which George had sent them. This miracle, it should be stated, was related to me by George himself. About the other [miracles], which are now to be described, I received from him a little book whose order (and sequence) runs as follows:

10. In the fourteenth year, by the blessing of Christ, of the empire of Louis Augustus [that is, 828], when to confirm the faith of the Christian people, as in the beginning of the lately born church, the Lord deigned to show signs and wonders in the very palace of the king, George the priest sought and received from Einhard the abbot, in the palace of Aachen, relics of the blessed

martyrs of Christ, Marcellinus and Peter, whose bodies he had received from Rome, carried by the hands of his own men. Placing them in a casket, which he had suitably adorned with gold and jewels, he sent them in the hands of his deacon, Theothard by name, to the church of Saint Salvius the Martyr, which at that time he held in benefice from the king. When that deacon came to the royal town called Visé, there ran up in front of him a hunch-backed man, so troubled and tormented by aching teeth that for fifteen whole days he had been unable to swallow food, but only water. When, urged by the deacon to kneel down and pray before the relics which he was bearing, he had reverently and imploringly called on the Lord Christ to have mercy upon him, through the intercession of the holy Marcellinus and Peter all discomfort was driven from his body and he rose up from prayer cured. This miracle happened on the thirteenth day before the Kalends of July [19 June]. (That was more fully narrated by me above, because I took the trouble to compose that according to the [oral] report of George.)

On the third day the deacon came with the relics to Valenciennes and, as he had been ordered, he carried them reverently and honorably into the church of Saint Salvius. Then a young man named Dominic, from the royal domain which is called Les Estinnes came; he had already been so troubled for a whole year by the disorder which the Greeks call a spasm that he could hardly keep his right hand still. Rather it kept moving round and round as if he were turning a hand-mill. The moment that the saints entered, he was so cured by the merits of the blessed martyrs that later on no trace of that horrible shaking was evident.

On the fourth day, that is on the feast of the blessed John the Baptist [24 June], a certain old woman by the name of Gerrada, who declared that she had been blind for a year, called on the blessed martyrs while the solemnities of the Mass were being celebrated. Through the merits of the saints and in the presence of all who had gathered there, she recovered the light that she had sought through faith.

Likewise, on the feast of Saint Salvius, which falls on the sixth day before the Kalends of July [26 June], a deaf and dumb man, amid the solemnities of the Mass, was deemed worthy to receive, through the request of the martyrs, both hearing and speech. On the same day a certain old woman from the region of Laon by the name of Rodeltrude, who for three years had not seen the light of the sky, recovered her sight while the same Mass was being celebrated.

On the fifth day before the Kalends of July [27 June], while the divine service was in progress, a boy of about seven years of age by the name of Donitian, who had been blind from birth, was given light through the merits of the blessed martyrs.

On the eve of the festival of the blessed apostles Peter and Paul, that is on the fourth day before the Kalends of July [28 June], a little girl by the name of Theotbalda being, it was thought, about nine years of age, and who had seen nothing for three years, gathered with a multitude of people at the hour of the holy office. Helped by the merits of the martyrs, she recovered her lost sight through the mercy of God. On the same day a man by the name of Dado, from the village of Petit-Pont, who had been bent over for six years and could not lift himself toward the sky and, therefore, walked bowed forward with short crutches under his armpits for the purpose of holding him up, at the same hour and in the same place, by the mercy of God and by the merits of the blessed martyrs, was made straight and whole.

On the fourth day before the Nones of July [4 July], a widow by the name of Adalrada, whose eyes had been deprived of light for four years, having heard reports of the miracles conceived, with no false faith, the hope of getting back her sight. Taking a staff in her hand, she started off alone without a guide for Valenciennes. When she drew near the town, it seemed to her that with her right eye she saw as it were a single ray of sunshine and, from that point on, she prayed with a pure heart for the pity of God that through the intercession of his saints he would allow her to see the church of Saint Salvius. Immediately she was heard and, through the mercy of the Lord, obtained without delay what she had desired. On the same day also another woman from the country of Noyon by the name of Hruoitla, who had been blind for five years, recovered, amid the solemnities of the Mass and by the gift of the Lord Christ through the merits of his saints, the light which she had lost.

On the Octave of the Apostles, that is on the day before the Nones of July [6 July], a certain man by the name of Gunthard, from the same area, struck down as it were by paralysis, was led by his relatives to the church of Saint Salvius. They said that he had now suffered from this illness for a year and that the left part of his body was so weak that he could neither lift his hand to his mouth nor wash himself, nor put on his shoes. But, by the mercy of God and the merits of the saints, at the time of the morning service, while it was being celebrated, he was cured. Likewise another man by the name of Hildebon, coming from the monastery that is called Saint-Martin-aux-Jumeaux, who had been blind from childhood and through all his life had not seen the light of the sky, while the Mass was being celebrated on that same day in the same church, recovered through the same saints and by the mercy and help of the same Lord, his sight and was found worthy to see clearly all the things that he had never seen before.

On the day of the Nones of July [7 July], a little girl by the name of Reginlindis, who seemed to be not more than seven years old, and who had been blind for three years, took her place with others in the church to hear the divine service. By the intercession of the merits of the saints, sight was restored to her in the presence of the whole multitude.

On the fourth day before the Ides of July [12 July], a blind woman by the name of Alagia, who for almost two years had lacked sight, amid the holy solemnities of the Mass, with the beseeching prayers of the saints, was given light again by our Lord Jesus Christ. On the same day a very old blind man from the village of Gheule by the name of Ermenward, who had been able to see nothing for fourteen years, came into the church for the evening service and called on the blessed martyrs, and immediately, his blindness disappearing, he recovered, by the help of the Lord, his long-desired sight.

On the seventh day before the Kalends of August [26 July], a certain girl who was possessed by an unclean spirit was brought into the church while the office of the holy Mass was being celebrated. There, through the power of Christ and the merits of the blessed martyrs, the evil spirit fled away and she recovered the soundness of her mind and the health of her body.

11. These are the miracles and wonders that our Lord Jesus Christ deigned to work, through the merits of his holy martyrs Marcellinus and Peter in the city of Valenciennes for the good of the human race. These the priest George took the trouble to send to us in the form of a small book and we thought that they should be inserted into this work of ours. This George is a Venetian, who traveled from his own country to our emperor and, in the palace of Aachen, set up with wondrous skill an organ which in Greek is called hydraulic.

Another little book was sent me from the monastery of Saint-Bavon, which is situated near the river Scheldt in the place called Ghent, where that stream is joined with the Lys, by the brothers who there serve God. At their request I sent relics of the martyrs of Christ to their monastery. In that little book these things are found in the following order:

12. In 828, relics of the holy martyrs of Christ, Marcellinus and Peter, came to the monastery of Saint Bavon, on the fifth day before the Nones of July, the sixth day of the week, which is written VI [3-5 July]. Now three days later, that is the next Sunday, which was the third day before the Nones of July, a blind girl by the name of Hartlinda from the village called Vosselare, who had, according to her father and mother, lacked the use of her eyes for eight years, when she was led before the altar on which the holy relics of the martyrs were placed, in the presence of all who were there, by the mercy of the Lord, recovered her sight.

Eight days later, that is on the fourth day before the Ides of July [12 July], another girl also blind, by the name of Helrada, was brought there from the village called Machelen. Her parents reported of her that on the eighth day after she was baptized she was stricken with a sudden blindness. But she too presently, in the presence of the holy ashes of the martyrs, recovered, the Lord giving back to her the light she had lost so long ago.

Three days later, which was the day before the Ides of July [14 July], a girl, all bent over, by the name of Bildrada, came from the village of De Bouret, which belongs to the monastery of Saint Vaast. When, before the aforesaid relics of the saints, she had humbly asked the Lord Christ for the restoration of her health, in the presence of all who were there she stood up erect and was deemed worthy to recover her entire bodily health in a moment of time.

Later, on the twelfth day before the Kalends of August [21 July], a woman by the name of Eddela, a serf of Saint-Amand, from a village called Baesrode, who for many years was said to have lacked sight, happily praying there, recovered her sight. On the same day a serf of Saint-Bavon by the name Eberald, from the village of Mullen, who also had been blind for many years, was, in the full sight of everyone who was present there, cured. On the same day two widows also, who had been blind for many years, were there given light: one was named Blidwara, from the village of Eessene, while the other, called Ricberta, is said to have been from the village of Wormhoudt.

Twenty-five days later, that is, on the feast of the Assumption of Saint Mary [15 August], a woman by the name of Anganhilda, from the village of Ghoy, in the presence of the holy relics of the martyrs, with everybody looking on and marveling at what had happened, was so bent over that she could hardly stand up to look at the heavens.

The next day, that is, on the seventeenth day before the Kalends of September [16 August], in the same church and witnessed by the same people, she was made straight and restored to her former state. It was as if she had never been bowed down to earth by any trouble in her body.

Later, on the twenty-second day of the month of September, that is on the tenth [day] before the Kalends of October [22 September], a man named Liodold, from the region of Toxandrien, from the village which is named Heppen, was by reason of the weakness in his left leg and foot forced to hold himself up, when walking, on two crutches. There, within view of everyone, he was so perfectly cured that thereafter in walking about he had not the slightest need of crutches.

Now on the fourth day after the accomplishment of this miracle, that is on the seventh before the Kalends of October [25 September], a young man named Hunwald, who was deaf and dumb and also had a twisted left hand, and came from the village called Chièvres, came before the holy relics of the martyrs. There he prayed humbly and was made so whole that it was as if he had never been either deaf or dumb or in any way afflicted by the contraction of the muscles in his hand.

On the following day, that is on the sixth before the Kalends of October [26 September], a woman by the name of Engilgarda, who for many years had been afflicted with the serious problem of paralysis, in the same church, through the merits of the blessed martyrs, was cured in the presence of everyone. She was a serf belonging to the bishopric of Tournai, from the village which is named Warcoing.

Next day, that is the fifth before the Kalends of October [27 September], another woman, this one called Ramburga, from the village of Bettingen, who was very feeble because of a similar sort of trouble in the lower part of her body, recovered, in the sight of all who were there, in the presence of the same relics of the saints, the full strength of her limbs. By the will of God she was made free in a moment of time from the sickness under which she was said to have suffered for ten years. On the same day a blind man named Germar, from the village of Schaltheim, which is situated on the seacoast of Frisia near the mouth of the river Scheldt, when he had prayed there for the mercy of God on the loss which he suffered and when he had called on the blessed martyrs, he was found worthy to receive with joy the long-denied light.

On the fourth day after this miracle came to pass, by the will of the Lord, that is on the second day before the Kalends of October [30 September], a female serf from Saint-Bavon, by the name of Gundrada, from the village of Audeghem, who for almost three years had not seen the sun, when she bowed herself in prayer before the altar recovered, by the generosity of the Lord Jesus because of the merits of his saints, the light which she had lost.

13. A third little book was sent to me by the monks of the monastery of Saint Servais the Confessor, which is situated on the bank of the river Meuse, in the city which is today called Maastricht. It is about eight leagues in distance from the palace of Aachen and is much frequented by a multitude of inhabitants and especially by merchants. The text of this book, if I re-

member it well, seemed to be put together in this way:

14. The advent of the holy martyrs of Christ, Marcellinus and Peter, to the city of Maastricht, took place on the day before the Nones of June [4 June]. For on that day a vast multitude of people proceeded out from the city to meet them, having assembled to receive them. They praised and blessed God for his limitless and unspeakable mercy in that He cared enough to visit through such mighty patrons a people that believed and had faith in Him. When, with these praises and spiritual rejoicings, they came to the church of Saint Servais, and when there, amid the great thankfulness of all, the solemnities of the Mass had been celebrated, and all had returned to their work, the casket in which the holy ashes had been brought, was placed to the right of the altar in the chancel. That entire day was one of great happiness and rejoicing for the people who lived in that city.

When, in order to celebrate the evening service, I entered that same church, among the other people gathered there was a boy by the name of Berngisus, whom his friends had brought there from the region of Condrieu a few days before, for he had been blind from birth. All of a sudden, in the presence of all of them, he fell down on the pavement, and lay there a good while as if heavy with sleep. After a time, he opened his eyes and looked upon, by means of the gift of the Lord Christ because of the merits of his saints, the light that he had never seen before.

Five days later, that is on the sixth day before the Ides of June [8 June], a man with the surname Hildimar, who was deaf and dumb, received, by the power of Christ and in the presence of those same holy relics of the saints, both hearing and speech, as well. On the same day also a girl of the household of Saint-Lambert [of Liége] by the name of Adallinda, who was not only deaf and dumb, but also blind and curled up in such a wretched way, because of a shortening of the muscles throughout her body, that her knees touched her breast, was placed by her relatives beside the holy relics of the martyrs. There, in the presence of all who were gathered together, she quickly and marvelously recovered, by the grace of God, both sight and hearing, her speech and the straightness and strength of all her limbs.

The next day, that is on the fifth before the Ides of June [9 June], when a royal serf [or slave] by the name of Berohad, from the village of Crecy, whose body on the right side had become through the contraction of his muscles weak and useless, was brought before the relics of the saints. He presently stood up, and without any delay was restored to the health which he longed for. Similarly a girl from the town of Maastricht itself, by the name of Theothild, whose right hand was snarled and twisted by a similar trouble to such an extent that it was useless for any purpose, was in a similar way cured on the same day before the same relics of the saints. When these events were seen, the people collected in the church began, by reason of their great and exultant happiness, to lift up their voices on high, singing praises to the Lord in hymns and litanies. All of a sudden a certain deaf boy came forward and stood in the midst of the crowd of people like one stunned and thunderstruck. When he came before the altar of the holy Savior, which is placed in the middle of the church, blood gushed forth from his nostrils and he was granted that power of hearing which he had long lacked.

The next day, that is on the fourth before the Ides of June [10 June], it seemed to us that the litter which held the holy ashes of the martyrs ought to be raised up higher, so that it might be somewhat above the altar on which it was placed and so more easily seen by those approaching it. While we were doing this, and while so doing were singing litanies in praise of God, a certain girl of the household of Saint-Servais, whose feet from birth had been twisted by shortened muscles and whose hands had been rendered useless by lengthened muscles, and who was dumb as well, was brought by her family into the church and placed beside the litter. Suddenly she was restored to health, so that at the same hour she acquired the power of speaking, of walking, and of using her hands fully for all her needs.

Now a certain woman of the city of Maastricht itself had a blind maid-servant by the name of Adalgarda. She brought her into the church and committed her to the holy martyrs Marcellinus and Peter, that through their intercession, she might be found worthy to recover her sight, and there she left her. After the vespers service was over, she was standing in that same church when, all of a sudden, as though struck by someone, she fell down on the pavement. After writhing there for a time, at last, to the great astonishment and wonder of the bystanders, she rose up and could see clearly. This happened on the Ides of June [13 June], at eventide, just when the shades of night were beginning to fall.

A man from the province of Burgundy, the area of Geneva, by the name of Theotgar, was suffering from the disorder which physicians call by the Greek word 'spasm', but which in Latin may be called 'trembling' because of the constant movement of the limbs. He came into the church and took his place in the midst of the crowd of people who were gathered together, as is usual on a Sunday [that is, 14 June 828], to hear the solemnities of the Mass. When, after the Gospel had been read, they were reciting the symbol of Christian belief, all of a sudden he fell down shaking on the ground. While the divine service went on, he lay there almost without movement and more like one dead than one alive. When the holy service was over, a great deal of blood gushed forth from his nostrils and, to the great wonder of the people who were looking on, he stood cured and no longer trembled. This miracle happened on the eighteenth day before the Kalends of July, that being a Sunday, as is set down above.

But on the fourth day of the week, that is on the fifteenth before the Kalends of July [17 June], a boy by the name of Folchard, from the monastery which is called Meldert, who was deformed by a pitiable shortening of the muscles in his legs and feet, was cured in the same place and in the sight of everyone.

On the eleventh day before the Kalends of July [21 June], a certain man came to the church and entered along with others. His right hand and arm kept moving round and round in an astonishing manner, as if he were grinding a hand-mill and must do so without stopping. He said that this agitation had come upon him because he had used a mill one Sunday, which is forbidden by the commandment. Now for a whole year he had paid this penalty. When he approached the holy relics of the martyrs, and there, full of faith, invoked them, suddenly that mill-like motion was put to peaceful rest. This man said that he came from the monastery of the Irish which is called Fosse, and that he was named Dothius.

On the eve of [the feast-day of] Saint John the Baptist, which is the ninth day before the Kalends of July [23 June], a certain man [belonging to] Maastricht came to the church of Saint Servais. He said that he was from the city of Tournai. He declared that he had been deaf and dumb from childhood and had been taken by his relatives to Saint Sebastian [the relics in Soissons] where he began both to hear and to speak, but imperfectly, for his words were hardly intelligible. Nor, when others spoke to him, could he hide his [continuing] hardness of hearing. When he came there to the morning service, he threw himself down before the holy relics and fell fast asleep. Not much later, as if wakened by someone shaking him, he asked the bystanders who had struck him a blow in the mouth. When they all answered that no one had done so, he stood up and was cured and at once heard and spoke perfectly without any impediment. On the same day, while the holy solemnities of the Mass were being celebrated, a woman by the name of Madallinda brought two wax candles, for the purpose of making light in the church. One of these she gave with her right hand to the sacristan for him to light, but the other she kept in her left hand as though it were to be lighted later by the other candle. But in a wondrous way, when the sacristan ignited the one given to him, the other, the one remaining in the woman's hand, was kindled before the eyes of all by a divine power.

A monastery of nuns, called Eike, is located on the river Meuse. There a woman consecrated to God, by the name of Saliga, lay suffering; her whole body except her right arm was afflicted with the dreadful disease of paralysis. To her, in the still of the night, a certain man from the number of her neighbors seemed to stand beside her and to address her in words like these: "What are you doing?" he seemed to say. When she answered that she was only resting in her own bed, he said, "Have you heard anything about the saints who have come to Saint-Servais in Maastricht?" When she told him that she had heard nothing about them, he said: "Arise and go there as quickly as you can, for there you will recover strength in all your limbs." But since, on waking, she did not bother to do so, she was again advised on the following night, by the same man and in like manner, to set out for Maastricht. Again, as before, she ignored the voice of warning and its command, and put off her start. But on the third night she saw the same man come up beside her and ask with a certain severity why she spurned his advice. He struck her in the side with the staff which he then seemed to hold in his hand and ordered her to set out at once for Maastricht. Daring not to disobey the command of the third vision, she called together her neighbors and friends who transported her to Maastricht. They set her down in the church of Saint Servais, near the holy ashes of the martyrs. After she had waited there for the return of her promised health, at last on the fifth day after she had come there, to the great wonder of all, she was deemed worthy to recover full and complete physical health.

15. There remain two splendid miracles that I not only believe should not be forgotten, but would, if written down, make the most suitable end of my fourth volume, which is now at hand. Although these wonders appear to

have been worked by the blessed martyrs Marcellinus and Peter in common with other saints, for one of them occurred on the coming of the relics of Saints Protius and Hyacinth, and close beside these relics themselves, and the other certainly had to do with the relics of Saint Hermes, on his birthday, nevertheless it seems that they ought to be assigned especially to them [Marcellinus and Peter], since these miracles happened in that church in which the most holy bodies of those saints were resting. The trustworthiness of these accounts rests with those of us who were present and who were allowed by God to see them. With no preamble, let us come directly to the miracles themselves which are to be narrated.

16. Pope Gregory [IV], who succeeded Eugenius [II] and Valentine in the office of the papacy, desired to enlarge the church of Saint Mark the Evangelist, in which he had been priest and to build a monastery close to it. So he searched the cemeteries and the churches built at a greater distance from the city to see if he could find there the bodies of holy martyrs. When he found them, he took the trouble to transport them to the church which he was generously rebuilding. Now it happened that, by chance, when the tomb of the most blessed Hermes was about to be opened and his holy body to be taken out from there, one of our household, who in that same year had gone to Rome for the purpose of prayer in the manner of the penitent, joined together with other pilgrims and gathered in the church of the martyr. When he had carefully examined the proceedings that were going on, he with good cause conceived, with a simple heart, the hope of acquiring the relics of the martyr. Visiting Deusdona, the deacon so frequently mentioned in the first book, he implored him with all his might to obtain even a small portion of those relics from the guardians of the place and to give it to him so that it might be brought to me. [Deusdona] at once accepted his request and promised that he would act without delay. Having given a fee to the guardians, he received relics not only of Saint Hermes, but also of Saints Protius and Hyacinth, whose bodies had been placed in the same church. He troubled to send these relics by means of a member of his household whose surname was Sabbatinus along with our own man, the one who had persuaded him to do what he had done. What he himself was able to obtain of the body of the blessed Hermes, he brought to us personally as a gift of great price. When we were told of the advent among us of the relics of Saints Protius and Hyacinth, we went out in procession to meet them and we took them up, as was fitting, in an honorable way, and carrying them into the church with hymns and prayers we set them down, together with the bier on which they had come, beside the bodies of the blessed Marcellinus and Peter.

The next day, a certain woman from a neighboring manor, which is called Baldradestadt, who was possessed by a demon, entered the church with other people. There the evil spirit began to rage and threw her down flat on the ground, and made his malice evident by proclaiming it in the presence of all. When he was asked by the priest that exorcised her who he was and where he had come from, and when and why he had entered into her, he answered each question, and declared that he was not only a demon, but the most evil of all living things. When the priest asked him the reason for such a great wickedness, he confessed that an evil will had been allotted to him. When again he was asked if he had ever been in heaven, he confessed that he had been in heaven, but had been expelled from there because of his pride. Asked by the same one whether he had seen Christ the Lord, he said that he had been seen by Him in hell, at the time when, for the salvation of the human race, He had deigned to die and had descended there. But when it came to the point where he asked him if he knew the names of the martyrs whose relics had been brought to that church the day before, he said, "Their names are very well known to me, for when they suffered I was standing close beside them, and I was tortured with boundless envy by their eternal glory. Even here I suffer from their opposition, for they torture me with torment beyond belief and they are forcing me unwillingly to leave this vessel in which I have long been hiding." The priest said unto him, "When you come out where will you go?" He said, "I shall take the worst of roads, and shall seek distant and deserted places." After this, when he had told the priest who had ordered him to do so both the time and the manner of his entering into her, he turned himself to the woman and said: "Before I come out of you, unhappy woman, I will shake and break your bones and I will leave you weak; [these are signs] that I have been in you." When she, as though conscious of her infirmity, began with a humble and submissive voice to implore the aid of the saints, he presently, foaming and howling violently through her mouth, commanded her as she tried to speak to hold her tongue. It was amzing for us who were there to see how that foul spirit spoke through the mouth of that little woman in a manner so different from her own, for she uttered so pure a man's voice and then again a woman's that there seemed to be not one person there but two, bitterly disputing and lashing one another in turn with abuse. In truth there were two voices quarreling with each other according to their different wills. The one was the demon's who wanted to strike the body he inhabited, the other was the woman's, who longed to be freed from the enemy by whom she was being held. This diversity of wills could clearly and openly enough be understood from the unlikeness of their voices and the great difference in the words which they hurled at each other. Now when, according to custom, the office of the heavenly mystery was over and the time came for us to leave the church and to look after our physical needs, we ordered the woman to be kept there with the guardians until we could return, having faith that through the virtue of Christ and the merits of his martyrs, the treacherous possessor of her would soon come forth. Our hope did not deceive us, for when, after eating, we came back to church, we found that the demon had been expelled and that she was safe and sound, in possession of all her wits, and lifting up her voice in the praise of God. Now it is clear that this wonder occurred on the coming of the relics of the blessed martyrs of Christ, Protius and Hyacinth, in the manner we have set forth. But that miracle which is ascribed to Saint Hermes, and in what manner it came about will be made clear in the narrative that follows.

17. Cologne, established on the Rhine, is the metropolitan city in the territory of the Ripuarians. In it there was a certain woman so weakened by a chronic stretching of the muscles from the loins downward that she was denied the

ability to walk other than in a sitting posture with her feet stretched out in front, pushing herself with hands placed on the ground and in this manner propelling herself forward. After hearing of the miracles and wonders that the Lord had worked through his holy martyrs Marcellinus and Peter for the cure of the sick and the weak, she was seized with a great desire to visit their church. Since she could not travel any other way comfortably, she was conveyed on the boat of merchants who were going there for the feast of those saints. She arrived there on the day of their nativity and stayed there a good while in the hope of recovering her health, but when she perceived that the cure was delayed, she decided to go on to Mainz. In all truth the cure was just delayed, not denied, for it would be brought about not elsewhere but here, and not then but at a later time. The feast of Saint Alban [22 June], the martyr, was drawing near and there is in Mainz both a church and a very celebrated monastery [in his name]. When she came there and asked the Lord, while she stood beside the shrine of the martyr, for the restoration of her health, she saw in her sleep a certain young cleric come close to her, holding in his hand some new shoes. He ordered her to take them and put them on her feet, which she did. Then he commanded that, with these on her feet, she should go back to the place from which she had come and there await the coming of the physician who would, without doubt, cure her. When she awakened, she put faith in that vision and returned to the healing threshold of the holy martyrs with all the speed she could muster. She remained with the other poor in that place for two months, awaiting the fulfillment of what the vision had promised.

Now, while this was happening, sometime in the middle of August, the deacon Deusdona (of whom we made frequent mention in the first book of this work) brought us from Rome a great present, a single joint of the finger of the blessed martyr Hermes. Receiving it, we enclosed it in a little box and placed it in the upper part of the church, above the door by which they enter from the west. But the woman who, as I have said, came there because of the divine advice of her vision, and after two whole months found that none of the promised help had arrived, began to think that she had been deceived by a vain dream and that she should return to her own country. She made a deal with the traders who would transport her and she would embark upon their boat to return to her own country on the next Sunday, which was the fifth day before the Kalends of September and also the day when the anniversary of Saint Hermes was to be solemnly celebrated [28 August]. Now when the night had fallen that was to precede the day fixed for her departure, and I, according to my custom when the night service is finished, left to go to bed, and all the others were exiting from the church, that woman, wanting to go in, sat herself down on the threshold. There, in the presence of all, overcome by a certain faintness, she held her tongue for a little while. Then, after a good deal of blood had run out from all her toenails, she returned to herself and held out her hand to those about her. Lifted to her feet she began to walk to the tomb of the martyrs. When she came there, she threw herself down in prayer before the altar and there lay for so long that the hymn which the rejoicing and happy multitude were devoutly singing to the praise of God was finished. When it came to an end she rose up cured, but she no longer wished to return home to her country.

Now that miracle is rightly to be credited to the blessed Hermes, on whose feast day and beneath whose relics it was wrought. But nevertheless the most holy martyrs Marcellinus and Peter may have had their part to play in the work, which came to pass in their church. The woman who was cured always called on them throughout the whole length of her pilgrimage to help her.

18. These then are some of the numberless miracles of the saints either seen by me or reported to me by the truthful accounts of the faithful that we have decided to commit to letters and memory. I do not doubt that they will be pleasant reading for lovers of Christ and worshippers of his martyrs, for nothing seems beyond their power, if the doing of it pleases almighty God. But I hope that unbelievers and those that belittle the glory of the saints may be induced not to read them at all, for I do not doubt that they would be unappealing to them, lest, offended by the crudity of my style, they might not be able to avoid blasphemy and jealousy, and so make clear that they hate God and their neighbors whom they are commanded to love.

Questions: Why did Einhard write this book? How could someone who had received stolen goods (the relics) be so dismayed by another's theft of them? Why does Hilduin delay the return of the relics? Was Deusdona a relics salesman or a helpful Italian churchman? Did Einhard actually receive the relics of any saint? Did Hilduin receive the body of Tiburtius? How does the possession of the relics enhance Einhard's prestige at the palace? What does Einhard's book tell us about the poor, travel and mobility, and the economy in the Carolingian world? What were the most common infirmities that people tried to cure in the presence of the saints' bones? How did Einhard and Hilduin imagine the relics to work? What part does the politics of 828-830 play in Einhard's story?

35. Claudius of Turin's Complaint

Einhard's account of the powers of his saints was so spirited and argumentative because there were not only skeptics, but learned critics of the cult of the saints. Claudius of Turin would seem to have been one of those. Claudius was a Spaniard who had first begun to work for Louis the Pious when Louis was king of Aquitaine. Later he could be found at Aachen in the palace school where he continued to comment on the Bible. By about 816, Louis named him bishop of Turin in Italy and he proved to be an energetic prelate. About 824 Theodemir, the abbot of Psalmody near Nîmes, charged at court that Claudius spoke against the reverence of images and the true cross, against papal authority, pilgrimages of penance to Rome, and the power of the saints. The Irish scholar Dungal claimed that Claudius had removed the reading of the saints' names from the litany and deemed the celebration of saints' feast-days a useless and vain practice. A small portion of Claudius's formal reply to Abbot Theodemir follows.

Source: trans. A. Cabaniss, in Early Medieval Theology, ed. G.E. McCracken and A. Cabaniss, in The Library of Christian Classics, vol. 9 (Philadelphia, Westminster Press, 1957), pp.241-248; reprinted with permission.

Your letter of chatter and dullness, together with the essay subjoined to it, I have received from the hands of the bumpkin who brought it to me. You declare that you have been troubled because a rumor about me has spread from Italy throughout all the regions of Gaul even to the frontiers of Spain, as though I were announcing a new sect in opposition to the standard of catholic faith—an intolerable lie. It is not surprising, however, that they have spoken against me, those notorious members of the Devil who proclaimed our head himself [Christ] to be a diabolical seducer. It is not I who teach a sect, I who really hold the unity and preach the truth. On the contrary, as much as I have been able, I have suppressed, crushed, fought, and assaulted sects, schisms, superstitions, and heresies, and, as much as I am still able, I do not cease to do battle against them, relying wholeheartedly on the help of God. For which reason, of course, it came to pass that as soon as I was constrained to assume the burden of pastoral duty and to come to Italy to the city of Turin, sent there by our pious prince Louis, the son of the Lord's holy catholic church, I found all the churches filled, in defiance of the precept of truth, with those sluttish abominations—images. Since everyone was worshipping them, I undertook singlehanded to destroy them. Everyone thereupon opened his mouth to curse me, and had not God come to my aid, they would no doubt have swallowed me alive.

Since it is clearly enjoined that no representation should be made of anything in heaven, on earth, or under the earth, the commandment is to be understood, not only of likenesses of other gods, but also of heavenly creatures, and of those things which human conceit contrives in honor of the creator. To adore is to praise, revere, ask, entreat, implore, invoke, offer prayer. But to worship is to direct respect, be submissive, celebrate, venerate, love, esteem highly.

Those against whom we have undertaken to defend God's church say, "We do not suppose that there is anything divine in the image which we adore.

We adore it only to honor him whose likeness it is." To whom we reply that if those who have abandoned the cult of demons now venerate the images of saints, they have not deserted their idols but have merely changed the name. For if you portray or depict on a wall representations of Peter and Paul, of Jupiter, Saturn, or Mercury, the latter representations are not gods and the former are not apostles, and neither the latter nor the former are men, although the word is used for that purpose. Nonetheless the selfsame error always persists both then and now. Surely if men may be venerated, it is the living rather than the dead who should be so esteemed, that is, where God's likeness is present, not where there is the likeness of cattle or (even worse) of stone or wood, all of which lack life, feeling, and reason. But if the works of God's hands must not be adored and worshipped, one should ponder carefully how much less are the works of men's hands to be adored and worshipped or held in honor of those whose likenesses they are. For if the image which one adores is not God, then in vain should it be venerated for honor of the saints who in vain arrogate to themselves divine dignities.

Above all, therefore, it should be perceived that not only he who worships visible figures and images, but also he who worships any creature, heavenly or earthly, spiritual or corporeal, in place of God's name, and who looks for the salvation of his soul from them (that salvation which is the prerogative of God alone), that it is he of whom the apostle speaks, "They worshipped and served the creature rather than the Creator."

Why do you humiliate yourselves and bow down to false images? Why do you bend your body like a captive before foolish likenesses and earthly structures? God made you upright, and although other animals face downward toward the earth, there is for you an upward posture and a countenance erect to heaven and to God. Look thither, lift your eyes thither, seek God in the heights, so that you can avoid those things which are below. Exalt your wavering heart to heavenly heights.

Why do you hurl yourself into the pit of death along with the insensate image which you worship? Why do you fall into the Devil's ruin through it and with it? Preserve the eminence which is yours by faith, continue to be what you were made by God.

But those adherents of false religion and superstition declare, "It is to recall our Savior that we worship, venerate, and adore a cross painted in his honor, bearing his likeness." To them nothing seems good in our Savior except what also seemed good to the unrighteous, namely, the reproach of suffering and the mockery of death. They believe of him what even impious men, whether Jews or pagans, also believe who doubt that he rose again. They have not learned to think anything of him except that they believe and hold him in their heart as tortured and dead and always twisted in agony. They neither heed nor understand what the apostle says: "Even though we once regarded Christ according to the flesh, we now regard him thus no longer."

Against them we must reply that if they wish to adore all wood fashioned in the shape of a cross because Christ hung on a cross, then it is fitting for them to adore many other things which Christ did in the flesh. He hung on the cross scarcely six hours, but he was in the Virgin's womb nine lunar months and more than eleven days, a total of two hundred and seventy-six solar days, that is, nine months and more than six days. Let virgin girls therefore be adored, because a Virgin gave birth to Christ. Let mangers be adored, because as soon as he was born he was laid in a manger. Let old rags be adored, because immediately after he was born he was wrapped in old rags. Let boats be adored, because he often sailed in boats, taught the throngs from a small boat, slept in a boat, from a boat commanded the winds, and to the right of a fishing boat ordered them to cast the net when that great prophetic draught of fish was made. Let asses be adored, because he came to Jerusalem sitting on an ass. Let lambs be adored, because it was written of him, "Behold, the Lamb of God, who takes away the sins of the world." (But those infamous devotees of perverse doctrines prefer to eat the living lambs and adore only the ones painted on the wall!)

Still further, let lions be adored, because it was written of him, "The Lion of the tribe of Judah, the Root of David, has conquered." Let stones be adored, because when He was taken down from the cross he was placed in a rock-hewn sepulcher, and because the apostle says of him, "The Rock was Christ." Yet Christ was called a rock, lamb, and lion tropologically, not literally; in signification, not in substance. Let thorns of bramble-bushes be adored, because a crown of thorns was pressed upon his head at the time of his Passion. Let reeds be adored, because with blows from them his head was struck by the soldiers. Finally, let lances be adored, because one of the soldiers at the cross with a lance opened his side, whence flowed blood and water, the sacraments by which the church is formed.

All those things, of course, are facetious and should be lamented rather than recorded. But against fools we are compelled to propose foolish things, and against stony hearts to hurl, not verbal arrows and sentiments, but stony blows. "Return to judgment, you liars," you who have departed from the truth, who love vanity, and who have become vain; you who crucify the Son of God anew and hold him up for display and thereby cause the souls of wretched ones in disordered masses to become partners of demons. Estranging them through the impious sacrilege of idols, you cause them to be cast away by their own creator and thrown into eternal damnation.

God commanded one thing; they do otherwise. God commanded them to bear the cross, not to adore it; they wish to adore what they are spiritually or corporally unwilling to bear. Yet thus to worship God is to depart from him, for he said, "He who wishes to come after me, let him deny himself and take up his cross and follow me." Unless one forsake himself, he does not approach the One who is above him; nor is he able to apprehend what is beyond himself if he does not know how to sacrifice what he is.

If you say that I forbid men to go to Rome for the sake of penance, you lie. I neither approve nor disapprove that journey, since I know that it does not injure, nor benefit, nor profit, nor harm anyone. If you believe that to go to Rome is to do penance, I ask you why you have lost so many souls in so much time, souls whom you have restrained in your monastery, or whom for the sake of penance you have received into your monastery and have not sent to Rome, but whom you have rather made to serve you. You say that you have a band of one hundred and forty monks who came to you for the sake of penance, surrendering themselves to the monastery. You have not permitted one of them to go to Rome. If these things are so (as you say,

"To go to Rome is to do penance"), what will you do about this statement of the Lord: "Whoever causes one of these little ones who believe in me to stumble, it is expedient for him that a millstone be hung around his neck and that he be drowned in the deep, rather than cause one of these little ones who believe in me to stumble"? There is no greater scandal than to hinder a man from taking the road by which he can come to eternal joy.

We know, indeed, that the Evangelist's account of the Lord Savior's words are not understood, where he says to the blessed apostle Peter "You are Peter, and on this rock I will build my church, and I will give you the keys of the kingdom of heaven." Because of these words of the Lord, the ignorant race of men, all spiritual understanding having been disregarded, wishes to go to Rome to secure eternal life. He who understands the keys of the kingdom in the manner stated above does not require the intercession of blessed Peter in a particular location, for if we consider carefully the proper meaning of the Lord's words, we find that he did not say to him, "Whatever you shall loose in heaven shall be loosed on earth and whatever you shall bind in heaven shall be bound on earth." One must know hereby that that ministry has been granted to bishops of the church just so long as they are pilgrims here in this mortal body. But when they have paid the debt of death, others who succeed in their place gain the same judicial authority, as it is written, "Instead of your fathers, sons are born to you; you will appoint them princes over all the earth."

Return, O you blind, to the true light that enlightens every man who comes into this world, because the light shines in darkness, and the darkness does not envelop it. By not looking at that light you are in the darkness. You walk in darkness and you do not know whither you are going, because the darkness has blinded your eyes.

Hear this also and be wise, you fools among the people, you who were formerly stupid, who seek the apostle's intercession by going to Rome; hear what the same oft-mentioned most blessed Augustine utters against you. In *On the Trinity*, book eight, he says, among other things, "Come with me and let us consider why we should love the apostle. Is it because of the human form, which we hold to be quite ordinary, that we believe him to have been a man? By no means. Besides, does not he whom we love still live although that man no longer exists? His soul is indeed separated from the body, but we believe that even now there still lives what we love in him."

Whoever is faithful ought to believe in God when he makes a promise, and by how much the more when he makes an oath. Why is it necessary to say, "O that Noah, Daniel, and Job were present here." Even if there were so much holiness, so much righteousness, so much merit, they, as great as they were, will not absolve son or daughter. He therefore says these things that no one may rely on the merit or intercession of the saints, for one cannot be saved unless he possess the same faith, righteousness, and truth which they possessed and by which they were pleasing to God.

Your fifth objection against me is that the apostolic lord was displeased with me (you state that I displease you as well). You said this of Paschal [I], bishop of the Roman church, who has departed from the present life [in 824]. An apostolic man is one who is guardian of the apostle or who exercises the office of an apostle. Surely that one should not be called an apostolic man who merely sits on an apostle's throne but the one who fulfills the apostolic function. Of those who hold the place but do not fulfill the function, the Lord once said, "The scribes and Pharisees sit on Moses's seat; so keep and perform whatever things they tell you. But be unwilling to act according to their works, for they talk but they do not practice."

Questions: What popular religious trends does Claudius object to? Could his skepticism have overcome the Carolingian cult of the saints? What might he have said to Charlemagne who apparently wore a talisman, now in Rheims, with a piece of the true cross or the Virgin's hair set inside?

36. The Penitential of Halitgar

Ebbo, the archbishop of Rheims, complained that current penitential practices were confusing in the late 820s. He asked Halitgar, the bishop of Cambrai, who was an expert on penitential practices, to produce a new penitential. Halitgar died before he could fulfill the request, but he left behind among his writings five books on penance, to which he added what he called a Roman Penitential. This penitential would seem to be a complex compilation of materials drawn by the bishop himself from Insular and earlier Frankish sources.

Source: trans. J.T. McNeil and H.M. Gamer, Medieval Handbooks of Penance (New York: Columbia University Press, 1938), pp.297-314; reprinted with permission.

[Preface]

Here begins the sixth [book]. We have also added to this work of our selection another, a Roman penitential, which we have taken from a book repository of the Roman Church, although we do not know by whom it was produced. We have determined that it should be joined to the foregoing decisions of the canons for this reason, that if perchance those decisions presented seem to anyone superfluous, or if he is entirely unable to find there what he requires respecting the offenses of individuals, he may perhaps find explained, in this final summary, at least the misdeeds of all.

[Prologue]

How Bishops or Presbyters Ought to Receive Penitents

As often as Christians come to penance, we assign fasts; and we ourselves ought to unite with them in fasting for one or two weeks, or as long as we are able; that there be not said to us that which was said to the priest of the Jews by our Lord and Savior: "woe unto you scribes, who oppress men, and lay upon their shoulders heavy loads, but you yourselves do not touch these burdens with one of your fingers." For no one can raise up one who is falling beneath a weight unless he bends himself that he may reach out to him his hand; and no physician can treat the wound of the sick, unless he comes in contact with their foulness. So also no priest or pontiff can treat the wounds of sinners or take away the sins from their souls, except by intense solicitude and the prayer of tears. Therefore it is needful for us, beloved brethren, to be solicitous on behalf of sinners, since we are "members one of another" and "if one member suffers anything, all the members suffer with it." And therefore, if we see anyone fallen in sin, let us also make haste to call him to penance by our teaching. And as often as you give advice to a sinner, give him likewise at once a penance and tell him to what extent he ought to fast and expiate his sins; lest perchance you forget how much it behooves him to fast for his sins and it become necessary for you to inquire of him regarding his sins a second time. But the man will perhaps hesitate to confess his sins a second time, and be judged yet more severely. For not all clerics who come upon this document ought to appropriate it to themselves or to read it; only those to whom it is needful, that is, the presbyters. For just as they who are not bishops and presbyters (those on whom the keys of the kingdom of heaven have been bestowed) ought not to offer the sacrifice, so also others ought not to take to themselves these decisions. But if the need arises, and there is no presbyter at hand, a deacon may admit the penitent to holy communion. Therefore as we said above, the bishop or presbyters ought to humble themselves and pray with moaning and tears of sadness, not only for their own faults, but also for those of all Christians, so that they may be able to say with the Blessed Paul: "Who is weak and I am not weak; who is scandalized and I am not on fire." When therefore, anyone comes to a priest to confess his sins, the priest shall advise him to wait a little, while he enters into his chamber to pray. But if he has not a chamber, still the priest shall say in his heart this prayer:

Let Us Pray

Lord God Almighty, be Thou propitious unto me a sinner, that I may be able worthily to give thanks unto Thee, who through Thy mercy hast made me, though unworthy, a minister, by the sacerdotal office, and appointed me, though slight and lowly, an intermediary to pray and intercede before our Lord Jesus Christ for sinners and for those returning to penance. And therefore our Governor and Lord, who will have all men to be saved and to come to the knowledge of the truth, who desirest not the death of the sinner but that he should be converted and live, accept my prayer, which I pour forth before the face of Thy Clemency, for Thy menservants and maidservants who have come to penance. Through our Lord Jesus Christ.

Moreover, he who on coming to penance sees the priest sad and weeping for his evil deeds, being himself the more moved by the fear of God, will be the more grieved and abhor his sins. And any man who is approaching for penance, if you see him in a state of ardent and constant penitence, receive him forthwith. Him who is able to keep a fast which is imposed upon him, do not forbid, but allow him to do it. For they are rather to be praised who make haste quickly to discharge the obligation due, since fasting is an obligation. And so give commandment to those who do penance, since if one fasts and completes what is commanded him by the priest, he will be cleansed from his sins. But if he turns back a second time to his former habit or sin, he is like a dog that returns to his own vomit. Therefore, every penitent ought not only to perform the fast that is commanded him by the priest but also, after he has completed those things that were commanded him, he ought, as long as he is commanded, to fast either on Wednesdays or on Fridays. If he does those things which the priest has enjoined upon him, his sins shall be remitted; if, however, he afterwards fasts of his own volition, he shall obtain to himself mercy and the kingdom of heaven. Therefore, he who fasts a whole week for his sins shall eat on Saturday and on the Lord's day and drink whatever is agreeable to him. Nevertheless, let him guard himself against excess and drunkenness, since luxury is born of drunkenness. Therefore the Blessed Paul forbids it, saying: "Be not drunk with wine, wherein is luxury," not that there is luxury in wine, but in drunkenness. Here ends the Prologue.

[Direction to Confessors]

If anyone perchance is not able to fast and has the means to redeem himself, if he is rich, for seven weeks [penance] he shall give twenty *solidi*. But if he is very poor, he shall give three *solidi*. Now let no one be startled because we have commanded to give twenty *solidi* or a smaller amount; since if he is rich it is easier for him to give twenty *solidi* than for a poor man to give three *solidi*. But let everyone give attention to the cause to which he is under obligation to give, whether it is to be spent for the redemption of captives, or upon the sacred altar, or for poor Christians. And know this, my brethren, that when men or women slaves come to you seeking penance, you are not to be hard on them nor to compel them to fast as much as the rich, since men or women slaves are not in their own power; therefore lay upon them a moderate penance.

Here begins the form for the administration of Penance.

In the first place the priest says, Psalm 37, "Rebuke me not O Lord in thy indignation." And after this he says, "Let us pray," and Psalm 102, "Bless the Lord O my soul" as far as "shall be renewed." And again he says: "Let us pray," and Psalm 50, "Have mercy," as far as "Blot out my iniquities." After these he says, Psalm 63, "O God, by thy name," and he says, "Let us pray," and says, Psalm 51, "Why dost thou glory," as far as "the just shall see and fear." And he says, "Let us pray:"

O God of whose favor none is without need, remember, O Lord, this Thy servant who is laid bare in the weakness of a transient and earthly body. We seek that Thou give pardon to the confessant, spare the suppliant, and that we who according to our own merit are to blame may be saved by thy compassion through our Lord Jesus Christ.

Another Prayer

O God, beneath Whose eyes every heart trembles and all consciences are

afraid, be favorable to the complaints of all and heal the wounds of everyone, that just as none of us is free from guilt, so none may be a stranger
to pardon, through our Lord Jesus Christ.

A Prayer

O God of infinite mercy and immeasurable truth, deal graciously with our
iniquities and heal all the languors of our souls, that laying hold of the
remission which springs from Thy compassion, we may ever rejoice in Thy
blessing. Through our Lord Jesus Christ.

A Prayer

I beseech, O Lord, the majesty of Thy kindness and mercy that Thou wilt
deign to accord pardon to this Thy servant as he confesses his sins and
evil deeds, and remit the guilt of his past offenses—Thou who did'st carry
back the lost sheep upon Thy shoulders and did'st harken with approval
to the prayers of the publican when he confessed. Wilt Thou also, O
Lord, deal graciously with this Thy servant; be Thou favorable to his
prayers, that he may abide in the grace of confession, that his weeping
and supplication may quickly obtain Thy enduring mercy, and, readmitted
to the holy altars and sacraments, may he again be made a partaker in
the hope of eternal life and heavenly glory. Through our Lord Jesus
Christ.

Prayers of the Imposition of Hands

Holy Lord, Father Omnipotent, Eternal God, Who through Thy son Jesus
Christ our Lord hast deigned to heal our wounds, Thee we Thy lowly
priests as suppliants ask and entreat that Thou wilt deign to incline the
ear of Thy mercy and remit every offense and forgive all the sins of this
Thy servant and give unto him pardon in exchange for his afflictions, joy
for sorrow, life for death. He has fallen from the celestial height, and
trusting in Thy mercy, may he be found worthy to persevere by Thy rewards unto good peace and unto the heavenly places unto life eternal.
Through our Lord Jesus Christ.

Here begins the Reconciliation of the Penitent on Holy Thursday. First he
says Psalm 50 with the antiphon "Cor Mundum."

A Prayer

Most gracious God, the Author of the human race and its most merciful
Corrector, Who even in the reconciliation of the fallen willest that I, who
first of all need Thy mercy, should serve in the workings of Thy grace
through the priestly ministry, as the merit of the suppliant vanisheth may
the mercy of the Redeemer become the more marvelous. Through our
Lord Jesus Christ.

Another Prayer

Almighty, everlasting God, in Thy compassion relieve this Thy confessing servant of his sins, that the accusation of conscience may hurt him no more unto punishment than the grace of Thy love [may admit him] to pardon. Through our Lord Jesus Christ.

Another Prayer

Almighty and merciful God, Who has set the pardon of sins in prompt confession, succor the fallen, have mercy upon those who have confessed, that what is bound by the chain of things accused, the greatness of Thy love may release.

A Prayer over the Sick

O God, Who gavest to Thy servant Hezekiah an extension of life of fifteen years, so also may Thy greatness raise up Thy servant from the bed of sickness unto health. Through our Lord Jesus Christ.

[Prescriptions of Penance]

Of Homicide

1. If any bishop or other ordained person commits homicide. If any cleric commits homicide, he shall do penance for ten years, three of these on bread and water.
2. If [the offender is] a layman, he shall do penance for three years, one of these on bread and water; a subdeacon, six years; a deacon, seven; a presbyter, ten; a bishop, twelve.
3. If anyone consents to an act of homicide that is to be committed, he shall do penance for seven years, three of these on bread and water.
4. If any layman intentionally commits homicide he shall do penance for seven years, three of these on bread and water.
5. If anyone overlays an infant, he shall do penance for three years, one of these on bread and water. A cleric also shall observe the same rule.

Of Fornication

6. If anyone commits fornication as [did] the Sodomites, he shall do penance for ten years, three of these on bread and water.
7. If any cleric commits adultery, that is, if he begets a child with the wife or the betrothed of another, he shall do penance for seven years; however, if he does not beget a child and the act does not come to the notice of men, if he is a cleric he shall do penance for three years, one of these on bread and water; if a deacon or a monk, he shall do penance for seven years, three of these on bread and water; a bishop, twelve years, five on bread and water.
8. If after his conversion or advancement any cleric of superior rank who has a wife has relations with her again, let him know that he has committed

adultery; therefore, that he shall do penance as stated above.

9. If anyone commits fornication with a nun or one who is vowed to God, let him be aware that he has committed adultery. He shall do penance in accordance with the foregoing decision, each according to his order.

10. If anyone commits fornication by himself or with a beast of burden or with any quadruped, he shall do penance for three years; if [he has] clerical rank or a monastic vow, he shall do penance for seven years.

11. If any cleric lusts after a woman and is not able to commit the act because the woman will not comply, he shall do penance for half a year on bread and water and for a whole year abstain from wine and meat.

12. If after he has vowed himself to God any cleric returns to a secular habit, as a dog to his vomit, or takes a wife, he shall do penance for six years, three of these on bread and water, and thereafter not be joined in marriage. But if he refuses, a holy synod or the Apostolic See shall separate them from the communion of the Catholics. Likewise also, if a woman commits a like crime after she has vowed herself to God, she shall be subject to an equal penalty.

13. If any layman commits fornication as the Sodomites did, he shall do penance for seven years.

14. If anyone begets a child of the wife of another, that is, commits adultery and violates his neighbor's bed, he shall do penance for three years and abstain from juicy foods and from his own wife, giving in addition to the husband the price of his wife's violated honor.

15. If anyone wished to commit adultery and cannot, that is, is not accepted, he shall do penance for forty days.

16. If anyone commits fornication with women, that is, with widows and girls, if with a widow, he shall do penance for a year; if with a girl, he shall do penance for two years.

17. If any unstained youth is joined to a virgin, if the parents are willing, she shall become his wife; nevertheless they shall do penance for one year and [then] become man and wife.

18. If anyone commits fornication with a beast he shall do penance for one year. If he has not a wife, he shall do penance for half a year.

19. If anyone violates a virgin or a widow, he shall do penance for three years.

20. If any man who is betrothed defiles the sister of his betrothed and clings to her as if she were his own, yet marries the former, that is, his betrothed, but she who has suffered defilement commits suicide—all who have consented to the deed shall be sentenced to ten years on bread and water, according to the provisions of the canons.

21. If anyone of the women who have committed fornication slays those who are born or attempts to commit abortion, the original regulation forbids communion to the end of life. What is actually laid down they may mitigate somewhat in practice. We determine that they shall do penance for a period of ten years, according to rank, as the regulations state.

Of Perjury

22. If any cleric commits perjury, he shall do penance for seven years, three

of these on bread and water.

23. A layman, three years; a subdeacon, six; a deacon, seven; a presbyter, ten; a bishop, twelve.

24. If compelled by any necessity, anyone unknowingly commits perjury, he shall do penance for three years, one year on bread and water, and shall render a life for himself, that is, he shall release a man or woman slave from servitude and give alms liberally.

25. If anyone commits perjury through cupidity, he shall sell all his goods and give to the poor and be shaven and enter a monastery, and there he shall serve faithfully until death.

Of Theft

26. If any cleric is guilty of a capital theft, that is, if he steals an animal or breaks into a house, or robs a somewhat well-protected place, he shall do penance for seven years.

27. A layman shall do penance for five years; a subdeacon, for six; a deacon, for seven; a presbyter, for ten; a bishop, for twelve.

28. If anyone in minor orders commits theft once or twice, he shall make restitution to his neighbor and do penance for a year on bread and water; and if he is not able to make restitution he shall do penance for three years.

29. If anyone violates a tomb, he shall do penance for seven years, three years on bread and water.

30. If any layman commits theft he shall restore to his neighbor what he has stolen [and] do penance for the three forty-day periods on bread and water; if he is not able to make restitution, he shall do penance for one year, and the three forty-day periods on bread and water, and [he shall give] alms to the poor from the product of his labor, and at the decision of the priest he shall be joined to the altar.

Of Magic

31. If one by his magic causes the death of anyone, he shall do penance for seven years, three years on bread and water.

32. If anyone acts as a magician for the sake of love but does not cause anybody's death, if he is a layman he shall do penance for half a year; if a cleric, he shall do penance for a year on bread and water; if a deacon, for three years, one year on bread and water; if a priest, for five years, two years on bread and water. But if by this means anyone deceives a woman with respect to the birth of a child, each one shall add to the above six forty-day periods, lest he be accused of homicide.

33. If anyone is a conjurer-up of storms, he shall do penance for seven years, three years on bread and water.

Of Sacrilege

34. If anyone commits sacrilege (that is, those who are called augurs, who pay respect to omens), if he has taken auguries or [does it] by any evil device, he shall do penance for three years on bread and water.

35. If anyone is a soothsayer (those whom they call diviners) and makes divinations of any kind, since this is a demonic thing he shall do penance for five years, three years on bread and water.

36. If on the Kalends of January, anyone does as many do, calling it "in a stag," or goes about in [the guise of] a calf, he shall do penance for three years.

37. If anyone has the oracles which against reason they call "Sortes Sanctorum," or any other "sortes," or with evil device draws lots from anything else, or practices divination he shall do penance for three years, one year on bread and water.

38. If anyone makes, or releases from, a vow beside trees or springs or by a lattice, or anywhere except in a church, he shall do penance for three years on bread and water, since this is sacrilege or a demonic thing. Whoever eats or drinks in such a place, shall do penance for one year on bread and water.

39. If anyone is a wizard, that is, if he takes away the mind of a man by the invocation of demons, he shall do penance for five years, one year on bread and water.

40. If anyone makes amulets, which is a detestable thing, he shall do penance for three years, one year on bread and water.

41. It is ordered that persons who both eat of a feast in the abominable places of the pagans and carry food back [to their homes] and eat it subject themselves to a penance of two years, and so undertake what they must carry out; and [it is ordered] to try the spirit after each oblation and to examine the life of everyone.

42. If anyone eats or drinks beside a [pagan] sacred place, if it is through ignorance, he shall thereupon promise that he will never repeat it, and he shall do penance for forty days on bread and water. But if he does this through contempt, that is, after the priest has warned him that it is sacrilege, he has communicated at the table of demons; if he did this only through the vice of gluttony, he shall do penance for the three forty-day periods on bread and water. If he did this really for the worship of demons and in honor of an image, he shall do penance for three years.

43. If anyone has sacrificed under compulsion [in demon worship] a second or third time, he shall be in subjection for three years, and for two years he shall partake of the communion without the oblation; in the third year he shall be received to full [communion].

44. If anyone eats blood or a dead body or what has been offered to idols and was not under necessity of doing this, he shall fast for twelve weeks.

Of Various Topics

45. If anyone intentionally cuts off any of his own members, he shall do penance for three years, one year on bread and water.

46. If anyone intentionally brings about abortion, he shall do penance for three years, one year on bread and water.

47. If anyone exacts usury from anybody, he shall do penance for three years, one year on bread and water.

48. If by power or by any device anyone in evil fashion breaks into or carries off another's goods, he shall do penance as in the above provision and give

liberal alms.

49. If by any device anyone brings a slave or any man into captivity or conveys him away, he shall do penance as stated above.

50. If anyone intentionally burns the courtyard or house of anybody, he shall do penance as stated above.

51. If anyone strikes another through anger and sheds blood or incapacitates him, he shall first pay him compensation and secure a physician. If he is a layman [he shall do penance] for forty days; a cleric, two forty-day periods; a deacon, six months; a presbyter, one year.

52. If anyone engages in hunting, if he is a cleric he shall do penance for one year; a deacon shall do penance for two years; a presbyter, for three years.

53. If anyone belonging to the ministry of the holy church is dishonest in respect to any task or neglects it, he shall do penance for seven years, three years on bread and water.

54. If anyone sins with animals after he is thirty years of age, he shall undergo [a penance of] fifteen years and shall [then] deserve the communion. But let the nature of his life be inquired into, whether it deserves somewhat more lenient treatment. If he continually persists in sinning, he shall have longer penance. But if those who are of the above-mentioned age and have wives commit this offense they shall undergo [a penance of] twenty-five years in such a way that after five years they shall deserve the communion with the oblation. But if some who have wives and are more than fifty years old commit this sin, they shall deserve the viaticum [only] at the end of life.

Of Drunkenness

55. One who is drunk then with wine or beer violates the contrary command of the Savior and his Apostles, but if he has a vow of holiness, he shall expiate his guilt for forty days on bread and water; a layman, indeed, shall do penance for seven days.

56. A bishop who commits fornication shall be degraded and do penance for sixteen years.

57. A presbyter or a deacon who commits natural fornication, if he has been elevated before taking the monastic vow, shall do penance for three years, shall ask pardon every hour, and shall perform a special fast every week except during the days between Easter and Pentecost.

Of Petty Cases

58. If by accident anyone in neglect lets the host drop and leaves it for wild beasts and it is devoured by some animal, he shall do penance for forty days. But if not [by accident], he shall do penance for one year.

59. If he communicates it in ignorance to those excommunicated from the Church, he shall do penance for forty days.

60. If through negligence the host falls to the ground, there shall be a special fast.

61. We ought to offer [the sacrament] for good rulers; on no account for evil rulers.

62. Presbyters are, indeed, not forbidden to offer for their bishops.

63. He who provides guidance to the barbarians shall do penance for three years.

64. They who despoil monasteries, falsely saying that they are redeeming captives, shall do penance for three years and shall give to the poor all the things which they have taken off.

65. He who eats the flesh of animals whose [manner of] death he does not know, shall do penance for the third part of a year.

66. We set forth the statutes of our fathers before us; boys conversing by themselves and violating the regulations of the seniors shall be corrected with three special fasts.

67. Those who kiss simply, seven special fasts. Lascivious kissing without pollution, eight special fasts. But with pollution or embrace, they shall be corrected with fifteen special fasts.

Of Disorders Connected with the Sacrifice

68. If anyone does not well guard the host, and if a mouse eats it, he shall do penance for forty days. But he who loses his chrismal [the pyx] or the host alone in any place whatever so that it cannot be found, shall do penance for the three forty-day periods or for a year.

69. Anyone who spills the chalice upon the altar when the linens are being removed, shall do penance for seven days.

70. If the host falls into the straw, [the person responsible] shall do penance for seven days.

71. He who vomits the host after loading his stomach to excess shall do penance for forty days; if he casts it into the fire, twenty days.

72. A deacon who forgets to offer the oblation, and fails to provide linen until they offer it, shall do penance in like manner.

73. If those little animals are found in flour or in any dry food or in honey or in milk, that which is about their bodies is to be thrown out.

74. He who treats the host with carelessness so that it is consumed by worms and comes to nothing shall do penance for the three forty-day periods. If it was found entire with a worm in it, it shall be burnt, and then its ashes [shall be] concealed under the altar, and he who has been neglectful shall do penance for forty days.

75. If the host falls to the ground from the hand of the officiant, and if any of it is found, every bit of what is found shall be burnt in the place in which it fell, and its ashes [shall be] concealed beneath the altar, and the priest shall do penance for half a year. And if it is found, it shall be purified as above, and he shall do penance for forty days. If it only slipped to the altar, he shall perform a special fast.

76. If through negligence anything drips from the chalice to the ground, it shall be licked up with the tongue, the board shall be scraped, and [the scrapings] shall be burnt with fire; and he shall do penance for forty days. If the chalice drips on the altar, the minster shall suck it up, and the linen which came in contact with the drip shall be washed [three?] times, and he shall do penance for three days.

77. If the priest stammers over the Sunday prayer, which is called 'the per-

ilous,' once, forty Psalms; a second time, one hundred strokes.

78. If one has taken his father's or brother's widow, such a person cannot be judged unless they have previously been separated from each other.

Of Homicide

79. If anyone slays a man in public expedition without cause, he shall do penance for twenty-one weeks; but if he slays anyone accidentally in defense of himself or his parents or his household, he shall not be under accusation. If he wishes to fast, it is for him to decide, since he did the thing under compulsion.

80. If he commits homicide in time of peace and not in a tumult, by force, or because of enmity in order to take [the victim's] property, he shall do penance for twenty-eight weeks and restore to his wife or children the property of him whom he has slain.

Of Sick Penitents

81. But if anyone comes to penance, and if sickness ensues, and if he is not able to fulfill that which has been commanded him by the priest, he shall be received to holy communion, and if it is God's will to restore him to health, he shall fast afterwards.

82. If anyone fails to do penance and perchance falls into sickness and seeks to take communion, he shall not be forbidden; but give him the holy communion and command him that if it please God in his mercy and if he escapes from this sickness, he shall thereafter confess everything and then do penance.

Of Those Who Die Excommunicate

83. But if anyone had already confessed has died excommunicate and death seized him without warning, whether in the road or in his house, if there is a relative of his let the relative offer something on his behalf at the holy altar, or for the redemption of captives, or for the commemoration of his soul.

Of Incestuous Persons

84. If anyone takes in marriage his wife's daughter, he cannot be judged unless they have first been separated. After they are separated, you shall sentence each of them for fourteen weeks, and they shall never come together again. But if they want to marry, either the man or the woman, they are free to do so, but he shall not marry her whom he sent away.

85. In the case of one who takes in marriage a close relative or his step-mother or the widow of his uncle, and of one who takes his father's wife or his wife's sister—the decision is grave: [such an offender] shall be canonically condemned.

Of Things Offered to Idols

86. If while he is an infant anyone through ignorance tastes of those things which were offered to idols or of a dead body or of anything abominable, let that person fast for three weeks.

87. On account of fornication, moreover, many men do not know the number of the women with whom they have committed fornication: these shall fast for fifty weeks.

88. But if he ate without knowing it was offered to idols or a dead thing, pardon shall be given him, since he did this unaware, nevertheless, he shall fast three weeks.

Of Theft Committed through Necessity

89. If through necessity anyone steals articles of food or a garment or a beast on account of hunger or nakedness, pardon shall be given him. He shall fast for four weeks. If he makes restitution, you shall not compel him to fast.

90. If anyone steals a horse or an ox or an ass or a cow or supplies of food or sheep which feed his whole household, he shall fast as stated above.

Of Adultery

91. If any woman misleads her mother's husband, she cannot be judged until she gives him up. When they are separated she shall fast fourteen weeks.

92. If anyone who has a lawful wife puts her away and marries another, she whom he marries is not his. He shall not eat or drink, nor shall he be at all in conversation with her whom he has wrongly taken or with her parents. Moreover, if the parents consent to it, they shall be excommunicated.

If a woman seduces the husband of another woman, she shall be excommunicated from the Christians.

93. If anyone of the Christians sees a Christian walking about, or one of his own relatives wandering, and sells him, he is not worthy to have a resting place among Christians, until he redeems him. But if he is not able to find the place where he is, he shall give the price which he received for him and shall redeem another from servitude and fast for twenty-eight weeks.

Of the Penance for Those Thrice Married

94. If any man's wife is dead, he has the right to take another, likewise, also, in the case of a woman. If he takes a third wife, he shall fast for three weeks; if he takes a fourth or a fifth, he shall fast for twenty-one weeks.

Of Him Who Lacerates Himself

95. If anyone cuts off his hair or lacerates his face with a sword or with his nails after the death of a parent, he shall fast for four weeks, and after he has fasted he shall then take communion.

96. If any pregnant woman wishes to fast, she has the right to do so.

97. A quack [herbalist], man or woman, slayers of children, when they come to the end of life, if they seek penance with mourning and the shedding of tears—if he desists, receive him: he shall fast for thirty weeks.

Of Things Strangled

98. If any dog or fox or hawk dies for any cause, whether he is killed by a cudgel or by a stone or by an arrow which has no iron, these are all "things strangled." They are not to be eaten, and he who eats of them shall fast for six weeks.

99. If anyone strikes with an arrow a stag or another animal, and if it is found after three days, and if perchance a wolf, a bear, a dog, or a fox has tasted of it, no one shall eat it; and he who does eat of it shall fast for four weeks.

100. If a hen dies in a well, the well is to be emptied. If one drinks knowingly of it, he shall fast for a week.

101. If any mouse or hen or anything falls into wine or water, no one shall drink of this. If it falls into oil or honey, the oil shall be used in a lamp; the honey, in medicine or in something else needful.

102. If a fish has died in the fishpond, it shall not be eaten; he who eats of it shall fast for four days.

103. If a pig or a hen has eaten of the body of a man, it shall not be eaten nor be used for breeding purposes, but it shall be killed and given to the dogs. If a wolf tears an animal, and if it dies, no one shall eat it. And if it lives and a man afterwards kills it, it may be eaten.

Of Polluted Animals

104. If a man has sinned with a goat or with a sheep or with any animal, no one shall eat its flesh or milk, but it shall be killed and given to the dogs.

105. If anyone wishes to give alms for his soul of wealth which was the product of booty, if he has already done penance, he has the right to give it. Here endeth.

Questions: Since 'a period of penance on bread and water' is added to the basic penance, what does penance primarily consist of? If a man murdered someone, would the specified penance suffice to make amends for the act? What sexual practices are condemned here by the Roman penitential? What differential rates of penance apply to people according to their positions in society?

37. Saint-Riquier (Centula): Its Precious Goods

Saint-Riquier or Centula was a wealthy monastery that had received, especially in Charlemagne's time, generous patronage. The piece below is taken from an inventory of goods drawn up in 831 and preserved in Hariulf's twelfth-century history of the monastery.

Source: trans. C. Davis-Weyer, Early Medieval Art, 300-1150, in Sources & Documents in the History of Art, ed. H.W. Janson (Englewood Cliffs, New Jersey: Prentice-Hall, 1971), pp.95-96; reprinted with permission.

The principal churches are three in number. The main church is dedicated to the Savior and to Saint Richarius, the second to the Virgin, the third to Saint Benedict. In the main church are three altars, the altar to the Savior, the altar of Saint Richarius, the altar of the Virgin. They are made out of marble, gold, silver, gems, and various kinds of stones. Over the three altars stand three canopies of gold and silver, and from them hang the three crowns, one for each, made of gold and costly stones with little golden crosses and other ornaments. In the same church are three lecterns, made of marble, silver and gold. Thirty reliquaries, made of gold, silver and ivory, five large crosses and eight smaller ones, twenty-one altar knobs, three of which are gold and the others of silver. Also seven knobs which belong to standards made of silver and gold. Fifteen large candlesticks of metal with gold and silver work, seven smaller ones. Seven circular chandeliers of silver, seven of gilded copper, six silver lamps, six lamps of gilded copper. Thirteen hanging vessels of silver, two shell-shaped pendants of silver, three large ones of bronze and three small ones. Eight censers of gilded silver and one of copper. A silver fan. Sidings around the head end of the shrine of Saint Richarius, and two small doors made of silver, gold, and precious stones, six small doors made of gold and silver around the foot of his shrine, and six others which are similar. Before the altar of the saint stand six large copper columns with gold and silver work, carrying a beam also made of copper with gold and silver work. There are three other smaller beams around the altar, made of copper with gold and silver work. They carry seventeen arches made of gold and silver work. Underneath these arches stand seven bronze images of beasts, birds, and men....One gospel book, written in gold and its silver box set with jewels and gems. Two other boxes for Gospel books, of silver and gold, and a folding chair made of silver, belonging to them. Four golden chalices, two large silver chalices, and thirteen small ones. Two golden patens, four large silver patens, and thirteen smaller ones, one brazen paten, four golden offertory vessels or chalices, sixty silver ones, and a large one of ivory with gold and silver work. One large silver bowl, four small silver bowls, one brass bowl, four knives(?) of silver, two silver pitchers with handbowls. One silver drinking vessel. One silver bucket, two of copper and metal, one with silver work. One silver can, one lead can. One ivory tablet set in gold and silver, two large ivory tablets, two small ones, one cypress tablet with silver work. Two silver keys, one brazen and gilded. One golden staff, fitted with silver and crystal. One crook and crystal.

Questions: How did monasteries and churches manage to acquire and retain such a range of precious goods in a world dominated by subsistence agriculture and little trade? Where did the precious metals come from to make these artifacts? What religious significance did these precious objects have?

38. The Emperor Louis's Palace at Ingelheim

If Aachen had been Charlemagne's chief palace in the latter part of his reign, Ingelheim came to serve the same function for Louis the Pious. The poet Ermold must have visited it about 825, though he described it from memory years later while in exile, and he saw the elaborate scheme of frescoes in the church and royal hall.

Source: trans. C. Davis-Weyer, Early Medieval Art, 300-1150, in Sources & Documents in the History of Art, ed. H.W. Janson (Englewood Cliffs, New Jersey: Prentice-Hall, 1971), pp.84-88; reprinted with permission.

This palace [Ingelheim] lies on the fast-flowing Rhine
Where rich fields and orchards abound.
Here stands the large palace, with a hundred columns,
With many different entrances, a multitude of quarters,
Thousands of gates and entrances, innumerable chambers
Built by the skill of masters and craftsmen.
Temples dedicated to the Lord rise there, joined with metal,
With brazen gates and golden doors.
There God's great deeds and man's illustrious generations
Can be reread in splendid paintings.
The left recalls how in the beginning,
Placed there, as I believe, by the Lord, men inhabit you, O paradise!
And how the perfidious snake tempts Eve of the innocent heart,
How she tempts Adam, how he touches the fruit,
How, when the Lord comes by they cover themselves with fig leaves,
How, because of their sin, they then labored on the soil.
Out of envy over the first offering a brother murdered a brother
Not with a sword but with his own wretched hands.
After that the painting traces innumerable events,
According to the order and manner of the Old Testament account:
How deservedly the Flood came over the whole world,
How it rose higher and finally swept away all living creatures,
How the Lord in his mercy saved a few in the Ark,
Also what the raven did, and your deed, O dove!
Thereupon the history of Abraham and his progeny are depicted,
And the deeds of Joseph and his brothers and of the Pharaoh.
How Moses frees the people from Egyptian servitude,
How Egypt perishes and Israel wanders
And the Law, given by the Lord, written on twin tablets,
Water from rock, quail falling down for nourishment,
And the long promised foreign land which was given
As soon as Joshua appeared, a leader for his people.

And then the large crowd of prophets and kings
Is depicted, whose equally famous deeds shine brightly,
And the works of David and the deeds of powerful Solomon,
The temples built by divine effort,
Then the captains of the people, who and how many,
And the most exalted priests and princes.
The other side commemorates the earthly deeds of Christ
Which he offered after his Father sent him down to earth,
And how first the angel descends to tell Mary,
And how Mary answers, "Behold the handmaid of the Lord,"
How Christ is born, announced long before by holy Prophets,
How the Lord is bundled in diapers,
How the shepherds receive the divine commands of the Thunderer,
And then how the Magi were worthy to behold God,
How Herod rages, fearing Christ might succeed him,
And has killed the children who he thought deserved death,
How Joseph fled into Egypt and brought the child back,
How the child grew and obeyed his parents,
How he, who came to save all those long condemned with his own
        blood,
Desired to be baptized,
How Christ fasted like a human,
How he confounded the Tempter with his wisdom,
How he then through the world taught of his Father's gentle yoke,
And mercifully gave back to the sick their former occupations,
How he even restored dead corpses to life,
And how he disarmed demons and drove them far away,
How, betrayed by one of his disciples and by the wild and savage
        people
God himself chose to die like a man,
How, rising, he appeared to his disciples,
And how he, for all to see, rose to the heavens and reigns over the
        world.
These are the things with which the art of painting
And the artist's subtle hand have filled the church.
The royal palace as well gleams with painting and sculpture,
And celebrates the great and spirited deeds of man.
The exploits of Cyrus are recounted and also the many savage
Battles which were waged during the time of Ninus.
Here you may see how the fury of a king [Cyrus] raged against a river
And how he finally avenged the death of his favorite horse.
Next to this is the wretched man triumphantly invading
A country ruled by a woman;
For this his head was thrown into a winebag filled with blood.
Neither are Phalaris's horrible deeds concealed,
How he with cruel art murdered miserable people,
How Pyrillus the famous goldsmith and caster of bronze
Joins him and how the wretch sacrilegiously,
Quickly, and with too much skill, made a brazen bull for Phalaris,

So that the merciless one may destroy the tender limbs of human
    bodies in it,
But quickly the tyrant enclosed him in the bull's belly,
And the artifact brought death to its own artifex.
One sees how Romulus and Remus laid the foundation of Rome,
How the former with his own impious hands killed his brother,
How Hannibal was always involved in evil warfare,
Depicting him with one eye, for he had lost one,
And how Alexander claimed the world through war,
How the power of Rome grew and reached the sky.
On the other side of the building we can admire the deeds of our
    forefathers,
Who were much closer to the pious faith.
To the acts of the Caesars of splendid Rome
The equally admirable deeds of the Franks are added:
How Constantine out of love forsakes Rome
And builds himself Constantinople;
The fortunate Theodosius is depicted there
And his celebrated deeds and acts:
Here Charles the First [Martel] the Frisians' conqueror is depicted,
And his tremendous deeds in arms;
Here one sees you, Pepin [the Short], as you restore law to the
    Aquitanians,
Uniting them after your victory to your kingdom;
And the wise Charles shows his gracious face,
And bears rightfully on his crowned head the diadem;
Here stands a Saxon warband, daring him to battle;
He fights them, masters them, and draws them under his law.

*Questions: Do the two fresco schemes complement each other and in what ways? How
has the official painter connected Carolingian rulers to world history? Did he choose
the most important or memorable accomplishments of each ruler to celebrate?*

39. The Astronomer's Account of the Rebellions

*In 830 and 833 Louis the Pious's sons, Lothar, Pepin of Aquitaine, and Louis the
German, rebelled. The Astronomer, the other biographer of Louis, provides us with
a sympathetic portrayal of the emperor as a wronged father.*

Source: trans. A. Cabaniss, Son of Charlemagne: A Contemporary Life of Louis the Pious (Syracuse,
New York: Syracuse University Press, 1961), pp.89-103; reprinted with permission.

44.1. Later [in March and early April 830], during the Lenten season, while
the emperor was traveling through the places lying close to the sea, the chiefs
of the evil faction, not willing to delay any longer, displayed the sore which
had been hidden for a while. First, the great nobles contrived among themselves a league, then attached the lesser ones to them. Part of them was
always desirous of change after the manner of greedy dogs and birds which

look for another's defeat to add to their satiety. Relying therefore upon the number and consent of many, they approached the emperor's son Pepin, alleging his being slighted, Bernard's arrogance, and the despising of others, and claiming indeed (what is wicked to relate) that Bernard [of Septimania] was an incestuous polluter of Pepin's father's bed. They insinuated furthermore that his father was baffled by certain delusions to such a degree that he was in no way able to avenge these things nor indeed even to perceive them. It was therefore necessary, they said, that a good son suffer his father's shame with indignation and that he restore his father to reason and honor. Not only would a reputation for virtue pursue the one doing this, they asserted, but also an extension of his earthly realm—by this remark dissembling their guilt. The young man, therefore, enticed by these incentives, proceeded with them and with many of their troops to Verberie by way of the city of Orléans, since Odo had been removed from that place and Matfrid had been reinstated. But when the emperor learned with absolute certainty about the deadly armed conspiracy against himself, his wife, and Bernard, he allowed Bernard to protect himself by flight. He requested his wife, however, to remain in Laon and to settle in the monastery of Saint Mary; but he himself hastened to Compiègne.

44.2. Those who came to Verberie with Pepin (Warinus and Lantbert having been dispatched along with as many others as possible) caused Queen Judith to be brought before them from the city and basilica of the monastery. Threatening death by torture, they compelled her to promise that, if ample opportunity were given her to speak to the emperor, she would persuade him to devote himself to a monastery, laying aside his arms and having his hair shorn, and that she herself would also do similarly, placing the veil upon her head. The more eagerly they desired this procedure, the more easily they put credence in her acquiescence. Sending some of their men with her, they brought her to the emperor. When he had given her permission to speak more privately, he allowed her to take the veil in order to escape death, but he demanded time to deliberate his tonsure. Since he always lived kindly toward others, the emperor was depressed by their unjust hatred which was so great that they loathed the very existence of him by whose favor they were alive and without whose favor they would have been justly and lawfully deprived of life. When the queen returned to them, they restrained themselves from other injuries indeed, but yielding to the shouting of the public, they had her carried away into exile and thrust into the monastery of Saint Radegunda.

45.1. Later, about the month of May, the emperor's son Lothar came from Italy and found him at Compiègne. As he was approaching, the entire faction hostile to the emperor joined itself to him. He seemed to impute nothing dishonorable to his father at that time, yet he approved what had been done. Lastly, contrary to the emperor's pledge, Bernard's brother Heribert was sentenced to the loss of his eyes and his first cousin Odo was disarmed and sent away into exile, as if they were accomplices and promoters of those things which were shouted against Bernard and the queen. Continuing there for a while, the emperor in name only passed the summer. But when autumn was drawing near, those who were of contrary opinions to the emperor wished for a general gathering to be held somewhere in Frankland. The emperor secretly resisted, distrusting the Franks and entrusting himself to the Germans. The emperor's sentiment therefore prevailed that the people come together at Nijmegen. Fearing that the multitude of opponents would overwhelm the paucity of his faithful ones, he gave order that each person coming to the diet employ a single retainer only. He enjoined Count Lambert to have care of the frontiers reckoned to him and directed Abbot Helisachar to exercise justice there. At length therefore the assembly gathered at Nijmegen. All Germany flocked thither to serve as aid to the emperor. Wishing still further to break the power of his adversaries, the emperor accused Abbot Hilduin, asking why he approached in a hostile manner although he had been ordered to come alone. The latter, unable to answer satisfactorily, was forthwith commanded to leave the place and spend the winter with only a few men in a campaign tent near Paderborn. Abbot Wala was commanded to retire to the monastery of Corbie and there show himself as one bound by the Rule.

45.2. When they who had gathered to oppose the emperor observed that their forces were being depleted, they surrendered to abject haplessness. Throughout a whole night, assembling and meeting at the quarters of the emperor's son Lothar, they urged him either to go to war or to withdraw somewhere away from the emperor's influence. They spent the entire night in this deliberation. In the morning the emperor ordered his son not to confide in the common enemy, but to come to him as son to father. Heeding these words, in spite of those around him trying to dissuade him, he approached his father. He was not assailed with harsh rebuke, but was chided with moderate leniency. When Lothar entered the recesses of the royal residence, the crowd, splitting in two by instigation of the Devil, began to rage. The fury would have mounted to bloodshed on both sides if imperial wisdom had not been on the watch. For while they were in an uproar and were almost ready to rush into a mad passion, the emperor appeared before them all with his son. Immediately the animal-like excitement abated. When the emperor's address had been heard, the entire popular disorder subsided. The emperor thereupon gave command that all leaders of the wicked conspiracy be kept under individual guard. When they were later brought to judgment, the emperor permitted none of them to be slain, although all the magistrates of the law and emperor's sons had decreed by legal decision that they suffer the death penalty as persons guilty of *lèse-majesté*. But employing, as it seemed to many, a milder procedure than was fitting (although kindness and mercy were his custom), he commanded the laymen to be tonsured at suitable places and the clerics to be detained in similarly appropriate monasteries.

46.1. When these things had been accomplished, the emperor repaired to Aachen for the winter. Throughout the season he kept with him his son Lothar. In the meanwhile he sent to Aquitaine and recalled his wife and her brothers, Conrad and Rudolf, who had been tonsured a long time ago. Yet not until she had purged herself of the charges in the manner prescribed did he again accept her with the honor due a wife. After that was done, on the Purification of Saint Mary [2 February 831] he granted life to all those sentenced to death. He then allowed Lothar to go to Italy, Pepin to Aquitaine, and Louis to Bavaria; but he himself kept the Lenten season and the solemnity of Easter at Aachen. When the Paschal observances therefore had been completed, the emperor set out to Ingelheim. Finally, not unmindful of his accustomed mercy, which, as Job says of himself, grew up with him from the beginning and seems to have emerged with him from his mother's womb, summoning those whom he had dispersed throughout various localities as their offenses required, he reinstated them in their own properties. To those who had been tonsured he granted leave to remain thus or to return to their former condition as they wished. Then, after having dispatched his son Lothar to Italy, the emperor crossed through the Vosges into the district of Remiremont and there indulged in fishing and hunting as long as it was agreeable to him.

46.2. Later in the season of autumn he enjoined his people generally to gather in Thionville. At that place three legates of the Saracens (two of whom were Saracens, one a Christian) came from regions beyond the sea bearing noble gifts from their fatherland, different kinds of perfumes and garments. When peace had been sought and secured, they were sent back. Bernard was also present, who in the aforesaid manner had saved himself by flight and had lived a long while in banishment along the frontiers of Spain. He therefore approached the emperor to seek a means of purging himself in the manner usual among the Franks, namely, to challenge the person hurling the accusation and to wipe out the charge by force of arms. But since the accuser did not present himself when summoned, the purgation was executed by oaths, weapons not being necessary. The emperor had ordered his son Pepin to appear at this diet, but the latter withheld himself from the assembly, although he did come after the diet. The emperor, thereupon wishing to chastise him for disobedience and churlishness, required him to remain with him and indeed held him at Aachen until the Lord's Nativity. Pepin, however, taking it amiss to be detained against his will, resorted to flight and without his father's knowledge departed to Aquitaine. The emperor continued to remain in winter quarters at Aachen as he had begun.

47.1. When the rigor of winter had been safely endured and the approach of spring [832] was at hand, it was announced to the emperor that several movements were stirring in Bavaria. To repress them he left hurriedly, came to Augsburg, quelled the insurrections, returned without delay, and ordered a public assembly to be held in Orléans. Thither he ordered Pepin, who reluctantly came forward. Reflecting that the advice of certain evil men had corrupted his son's mind as much by threats as by promises, and fearing Bernard especially, whose counsel Pepin was at that time said to be following (for Bernard was lingering in Aquitaine), the emperor crossed the Loire and came with his retinue to Jouac le Palais in the territory of Limoges. There the case of both having been aired, Bernard was deprived of his honors since he was suspected of disloyalty, although the challenger would not come to the assembly. But Pepin, for the correction of his vicious manners, he ordered to be brought under private guard to Trier. Although he was conducted thither and treated very kindly, he was stealthily released at night by his own men among the guards, and until the emperor's return from Aquitaine he roved about wherever he could and would.

47.2. At that time the emperor decreed a particular division of the realm between his sons Lothar and Charles, which as a promise succumbed not a whit to extraordinary hindrances which must be related. It appeared that the emperor might withdraw from Aquitaine at a suitable time, but after a short period he convoked the people on Martinmas and sought without success in some manner to recall his fleeing son Pepin. But while the latter was eluding him, a very harsh, rigorous winter settled in. At first came torrential floods, then icy bitterness freezing the wet earth, making it so perilous that even with expert horses it would be a remarkable person who would resort to such a mode of travel. The army, therefore, becoming disheartened by an effort so great and so inconvenient, suffered repeated and dangerously unexpected attacks by the Aquitanians. The emperor decided to go to the villa called Rets and there to cross the Loire river to spend the winter in Frankland. And so he did, although less honorably than befitted him.

48.1. The Devil, long hostile to the human race and to peace, was in no wise tricked by the emperor's success, but was stirring up the sons through the cunning of his accomplices, persuading them that their father wished to destroy them wantonly, not reflecting that he who was very mild to foreigners could be inhuman to his own. But, since "evil communications corrupt good manners," and a gentle drop of water striking very often is wont to bore through the hardest stone, it finally came to pass that they caused the emperor's sons to form a common league and muster as large an army as they could. They invoked Pope Gregory under the pretext that he alone ought and could reconcile sons to father. Afterwards, however, the truth became obvious. Later in the month of May [833] the emperor came to Worms with a strong force and there debated for a long time what should be done. Through designated emissaries, Bishop Bernard and others, he urged his sons to return to him. It was asked respecting the pope of the Roman see why, if he were present after the manner of his predecessors, he contrived such great delays so as not to meet the emperor. A rumor spread abroad and confirmed what was true about the others, but it alleged that the Roman pope was present to ensnare the emperor and the bishops in the toils of excommunication if there were any disobedience to his will and that of the emperor's sons. But that audacious presumption was insufficient to steal away the emperor's bishops who declared that they would in no wise yield to his judgment. For if the pope had come to excommunicate, he would have gone away himself excommunicated, since the authority of the ancient canons held otherwise.

48.2. At length the assembly was held on the festival of John, Christ's holy forerunner [24 June 833], at the place which—from what happened there—has been branded with a name of perpetual infamy, the "Field of Lies." For those who had sworn fealty to the emperor lied, and the name of the place where that occurred has remained ever since a witness of the faithlessness. When they stood, however, with ranks arrayed not far from each other and the rush to arms was imminent, it was announced to the emperor that the Roman pope was approaching. The emperor, in battle formation, received him as he came, although less fittingly than was appropriate, charging that he who had come in such an unaccustomed manner would have prepared a similar reception for him. But the pope, escorted into the field tent, pressed the emperor with oaths that he had undertaken so great a journey for no reasons other than the report that the emperor was struggling against his sons in unyielding discord and the pope's desire to sow peace between both parties. The emperor's position was then stated and the pope remained with him several days before being sent back to the sons to contrive a mutual peace. Partly distracted by bribes, partly seduced by promises, partly frightened by threats, almost all the people were surging like a torrent to the sons and their followers. The pope's efforts were in vain. With as many troops brought thither and wrested from the emperor, the defection became stronger day by day, so that on the feast of Saint Paul [29 June] the populace, fawning upon his sons, was threatening to launch an attack on the emperor. Not able to resist those forces, the emperor ordered his sons not to expose themselves to popular pillaging. They in turn commanded him to abandon camp and come to them, asserting that they would eagerly go out to meet him. And so they did, but the emperor warned his sons, as they leaped from their horses to meet him, to remember their promise concerning himself, his son [Charles], and his wife, and to preserve unimpaired the things which they had formerly promised. Embracing them as they replied suitably, he proceeded to their camp. As he was going, his wife was led away and directed to the tents of Louis [the German]. But Lothar escorted the emperor along with Charles, then still a boy, to his own tents, and made them remain with a few men in a pavilion prepared for the purpose.

48.3. After these events the people were bound by oaths and the empire was partitioned among the brothers by a threefold division. Received by King Louis, his father's wife was again banished, this time to Italy, to the city of Tortona. Observing such things, Pope Gregory returned with heavy grief to Rome. Pepin went back to Aquitaine and Louis to Bavaria. Then Lothar, taking along his father, who rode behind in a private capacity with appointed deputies, came to the villa of Marlenheim where he lingered as long as he could. Arranging such matters as appeared and satisfying the people, but appointing an assembly at Compiègne, he crossed the Vosges by way of Maurmünster and came to Mediomatricus (which is Metz by another name). He moved up to Verdun and entered the city of Soissons. There he ordered his father to be held under strict surveillance in the monastery of Saint Médard and Charles committed to Prüm, but not tonsured. Lothar hunted eagerly until in the season of autumn, that is, on the Kalends of October, he went to Compiègne, as had been decreed, leading his father with him.

49.1. While he was there an embassy from the emperor of Constantinople, Mark, the archbishop of Ephesus and first swordsman of the emperor, accredited to his father, met him [Lothar], offered the gifts designated for him, but withheld those sent to his father. Although dispatched to his father, Lothar received the legate as though coming to him, listened to him, then dismissed him to carry back an account of this almost incredible tragedy. At the same assembly, although many were suspected of loyalty to the father and of rebellion against the son, some tempered their asseverations with simple words, but others with oaths. Yet such mercy and such a change of things, with the authors released, inspired every one. Wherefore the conspirators of the unheard-of crime, fearing that if things were reversed the consequences might not be tolerable, used an ingenious argument (so it seemed) with some of the bishops, namely, that in addition to that for which the emperor had already done penance, an irrevocable public penance, with arms laid aside, should again be decreed to satisfy the church. But not even the civil laws bring punishment twice upon one fault committed only once and our law may not hold God to judge twice on the very same issue. A few disputed the decision, many assented, but the majority, as usual in such affairs, agreed verbally so as not to offend the magnates. Thus adjudged, although absent, unheard, not confessing, not tried, they compel the emperor, before the body of Saint Médard the Confessor and Saint Sebastian the Martyr, to lay aside his weapons and place them on the altar. Then, clothed in dark colored vesture, they thrust him under keep with a large guard.

49.2. This business completed by Martinmas, the people were granted leave to go back to their own lands, full of sadness for such deeds. Lothar, leading his father along, returned to winter at Aachen. All during the winter the people of Frankland and of Burgundy, of Aquitaine and of Germany, assembled in throngs to express indignation at the emperor's misfortune. Count Eggebard and Constable William indeed organized against Frankland an association for the purpose of reinstating the emperor. Abbot Hugo was dispatched from Germany to Aquitaine by Louis and by those who had fled thither, by Bishop Drogo and the rest, to arouse the interest of Pepin. Bernard and Warinus were inflaming the people in Burgundy with persuasive addresses, were enticing them with promises, were binding them with oaths, and were uniting them into one will.

50.1. The winter passed and spring [834] presented its rosy face. Lothar—his father having been taken through the Haspengau countryside—set out and came to the city of Paris where he had commanded all his faithful to meet him. Against him advanced Count Eggebard and other nobles of that country with a great band collected to fight for the emperor's liberation. Matters would have reached that eventuality if the most pious emperor, on guard against the peril of the many as well as of his own, had not by command and adjuration prevented them from this undertaking. The assembly was finally held in the monastery of Saint Denis the Martyr.

51.1. But Pepin, departing from Aquitaine with a great host and coming up to the Seine, halted there since demolished bridges and sunken boats prevented a crossing. Then Counts Warinus and Bernard, with a great many allies assembled from the regions of Burgundy, came up to the Marne. There, partly delayed by the severity and unreasonableness of the wind, partly checked to muster their allies, they settled for several days in the villa of Boneuil and those estates which lie around. The holy season of Lent was at hand. In the first week, on the fifth feria, legates (Abbot Atrebaldus and Count Gautselm) were sent by them to the emperor's son Lothar, demanding that the emperor be released from the bonds of confinement and handed over to them. If Lothar would heed their demand, they would place themselves at his disposal for the sake of the dignity and honor which he formerly had from his father. If otherwise, they would seek him out, at their own peril if need be, and with God as judge they would attack those resisting in this matter. To the ultimatum Lothar replied reasonably that no one suffered more in his father's calamity or rejoiced more in his father's good fortune than he did; that the blame of priority imputed to him should not be so attributed since they too had deserted and betrayed the emperor; and that the mark of prison confinement was not unlawfully imprinted upon his father since it was in accordance with an episcopal judgment. Sent forward, therefore, with this explanation, the legates returned to those who had commissioned them.

51.2. Counts Guerinus and Odo, and Abbots Fulco and Hugo, were ordered to come to consider with him [Lothar] how their demand could be fulfilled. The emperor's son Lothar also gave order that emissaries be dispatched tomorrow to learn the time of the approach of the aforesaid men, so that he could meet them on the agreed day to treat concerning the case. But the plan was changed. Leaving his father at Saint-Denis, he and those induced by his favor repaired to Burgundy, to Vienne, where he chose to pitch camp. The ones who had remained with the emperor urged him to resume the imperial badges of honor, for although he was put away from communion with the church in the manner aforesaid, yet was he in no wise content with that hasty decision. On the morrow, being Sunday [1 March 834], he sought to be reconciled by the ministry of the bishops in the church of Saint Denis, and he agreed to be girded with arms by the hands of the prelates. In this matter the joy of the people increased so greatly that even the weather, which seemed to suffer with him as he endured injury, now rejoiced with him as he was relieved. For up to that time the force of the tempests and violence of rains had beat so heavily that waters had flooded beyond wont and winds had rendered the channels of rivers impassable. But at his absolution the elements seem to have conspired, so that soon the raging winds became gentle and the face of the sky reverted to its ancient and long impeded serenity.

52.1. The emperor undertook a journey from that place, but did not seek to pursue his departing son, although many were pressing him to do so. From that place therefore he went to Nanteuil and thereafter to the royal villa of Quierzy where remaining a while he awaited his son Pepin and the ones who were tarrying beyond the Marne. He waited also for those who had taken refuge beyond the Rhine with his son Louis and for that son Louis himself who was on his way to him. While he was there in the mid-season of Lent (when even the joyfulness of the day itself smiled and the ecclesiastical *cantilena* of the Office [Introit] encouraged, saying: "Rejoice, Jerusalem, and all you who love her, make holy day"), a great multitude of his faithful ones met him with mutual rejoicing. Receiving them kindly and thanking them for the integrity of their fealty, the emperor dismissed his son Pepin to Aquitaine with joy; the others he allowed to return rejoicing to their own lands. He came, however, to Aachen, where he received Judith Augusta, Rathaldus the bishop and Boniface and Pepin bringing her back from Italy. Thereafter he kept his son Charles with him for a long time. With accustomed devotion he observed the solemnity of Easter. After the celebration he busied himself with hunting in the Ardennes forest. When the holy feast of Pentecost had passed, he gave attention to hunting and fishing in the regions of Remiremont.

Questions: How does the Asronomer account for the first rebellion of the sons? Does he acknowledge any fault on the part of Louis? What were the fates of Judith, Charles, and Bernard in the rebellions? What were the lies of the 'Field of Lies'? What role did the pope play in the second rebellion? How did power seem to shift as the rebellions unfolded? Could Louis have been set back on his throne on either occasion without the assistance of a son and some loyal magnates? Was the net effect of the two rebellions to increase the power of the nobles and to decrease royal power and dignity?

40. Paschasius Radbertus's Defense of Wala

Paschasius Radbertus was a monk at Corbie during the abbacies of the two brothers Adalhard and Wala. Later in the 850s after he had himself been the abbot of the monastery, Paschasius wrote the extraordinary second book of his Life of Wala. It is one of the oddest pieces of medieval hagiography, since it takes the form of a dialogue between monks of Corbie who spend much of their time defending the political reputation of Wala, who had been a principal player in the political machinations of both rebellions. Paschasius makes frequent allusion to the plays of Terence in his work and his interlocutors give pseudonyms to the famous people they discuss. Wala himself is called Arsenius, an early Christian monk.

Source: trans. A. Cabaniss, Charlemagne's Cousins: Contemporary Lives of Adalard and Wala (Syracuse, New York: Syracuse University Press, 1967), pp.160-164, 191-196; reprinted with permission.

8.1. *Adeodatus*: Alas, dreadful it is that such monstrous, such horrible damage have grown up in the realm, although sins added to sins through partisanships have required it. When we seek why it was that Arsenius [Wala] should again have thrust himself into such sharp and such pernicious kinds of danger, perhaps he could not foresee what end they might have whom he wished to meet. We beg you to clarify.

8.2. *Paschasius*: It is true, brother, that he saw the ills which daily arose without number and without measure. But he could not foreknow the future. As much as he could, Arsenius wished to meet and resist them for loyalty to realm and king, for devotion to country and people, for the religion of churches and safety of the citizens. All these were dearer to him than his own life. But since such matters had not been checked and repressed initially, since faults were compelling, they had superior power with impunity toward the mischief of everyone. There was no one already strong and wise enough to prevent. When he recovered from his infirmity, the same one began to hear from all sides infamous and obscene, shameful and foul reports, not of ordinary kind as had never been heard in this our age. Because of this, his heart, so fond of religion, was soon disturbed.

8.3. The palace became a theater [in 829], formerly of honor, in which such great recurring illusions of soothsayers were welling up as were believed not to exist in the whole world. He could not restrain himself from tears of grief and love when these matters were reported to him day and night by good men, most eminent and most truthful. The more Arsenius loved Christ's church and emperor with his people and offspring, the more he was afflicted with grief. Chiefs of the palace of both orders were coming and declaring all such things to be true or rather worse than popularly reported. He thereupon decided to come and try by his reproof, persuasion, and counsel to help, so that the scourge might be averted before it disturbed and overturned everything. Thus he did what he could. He spoke with the emperor and leaders concerning what he had heard. He forewarned what he felt in those matters that were happening.

8.4. The seditious monster himself [Bernard of Septimania] he even addressed, with every expression of loyalty and friendship, since the latter's father and he had been close friends. For once upon a time Arsenius had taken as his wife the latter's sister, daughter of a most noble and high-minded man. From the cradle he had, like a father, displayed a holy disposition, care, and solicitude toward him in all respects, more even than if he were his father. But when he saw that he was already blind and mad in mind and that he was already rushing headlong, he said whatever he could. But Naso [that is, Bernard] would not listen, for he was already abandoned in morals and drunk with venom of desire. When Arsenius realized that he was making no progress, he returned without result to his monastery, grieving and mourning over what he had observed. After a brief lapse of time, the rulers and chiefs of the palace, banished and deposed, soon followed him, weeping and bemoaning.

8.5. By one shameless person all laws of the empire were violated and the best men driven away. Everywhere the strongest and most eminent men were crushed, not by the strength of that debaucher, but by guile and fraud of the worst deception. Each one reported things worse than the worst. From hither and yon all were converging upon Arsenius and were begging counsel from him as if from a fountain of wisdom. Moaning and bewailing, that one was peering upward toward God with all his mind, if perchance God might send aid in such perils. One by one he exhorted each of them first to stand fast and wait for God's judgment and then to return to the palace to watch, to understand, and to persuade the better qualities of salvation. Let them strive with whatever pressure they could to prevent such great disturbances. But the highest ones were driven away, outstanding ones were hurled down. Wanton ones were assembled, the vainest were honored, and scoundrels were introduced.

8.6. When such facts had been ascertained, they related to Arsenius evils of the age which have scarcely ever been heard of before, how in so glorious an empire everything had thus been suddenly and completely altered. The palace had become a brothel where adultery is queen and an adulterer reigns. Crimes are heaped up, all unmentionable kinds of soothsaying and sorcery are demanded, such as I never believed to have still remained in the world. Of all evils nothing has been omitted, and everything is gossiped about by everyone. Nonetheless, the sober and wary man was moved only to tears until a plot was disclosed and indeed strengthened by the very ones who were fully aware of such perverse plans. The tyrant sought by some means secretly to slay the emperor so it would appear that he died of his own infirmity. Thereafter his sons and the best princes of the realm were to be murdered by whatever guile he could plan. These matters were reported by the most sober and truthful men and there could be no doubt about them.

8.7. Severly dejected and grieving, Arsenius kept sending suitable and approved persons of holy religion to be in the palace surreptitiously among those who were in any way in those plans. They were to remain for as long a time as needful to investigate carefully what might be the true situation. As soon as anything was said, although supposedly in secret, they were able to discover just when and how the tyrant decided what to attempt. Thereupon they reported as a matter of certainty that those who were aware of the plan had ordered such crimes. Together with the supreme consuls and certain holy bishops, as well with supreme officials of the palace, he began immediately to ask what he should by virtue of faith in Christ do to avert what was designed to overthrow the whole empire. With one voice, with weeping and wailing, all the servants of God who were present, the great and the greatest, declared insistently that he would not be faithful to God and His holy church if he could aid in such dangers but refused to do so.

8.8. With many urging and with the plan disclosed, he and the choicest and the most outstanding men reached a great decision for the sake of faith in Christ, the condition of the empire, peace of the churches, love of king and realm, the safety of the sons. He was inflamed by God's zeal that the adversary's deceit might not prevail, that the dignity of the country might be preserved, that safety might continue for its citizens. Devoted to the freedom of all, Arsenius exposed his own safety for the sake of justice and fealty. If he had sought to be favorable to the priests, he would have been more pleasing to everyone and more esteemed by all. But since he was strong of mind, eminent in holiness, invested with justice, established in faith, grounded in charity, clothed with weapons of virtue, he chose rather to die than to uphold such villainy and such cruel crime which would be for ruin, destruction, and eternal damnation to all, if they should consent. He therefore undertook nothing rashly of himself, so that he could come to the aid of the most Christian princes, the prelates of the churches, and all the people, and to free all from such harsh peril of death, for one death menaced all good men.

8.9. *Adeodatus*: One thing only we ought to lament, but harsher events have happened to compel us to include them in our lamentation. They are so much more bitter and cruel than we originally proposed to bewail. It is therefore fitting to subsume them all under one lament. Arsenius should not be grieved for so much as that the tragic events should be deplored so that God's wrath may be averted from us. Nonetheless, what we thus grieve should be entrusted to tears, lest this person of ours be embroiled in the crimes of adversaries. Although there may be opportunity for pleading, we cannot reply to each what is spoken for each. Let us therefore beg the grace of piety rather than hurl censorious accusations. Let us offer the sorrow of our hearts rather than undertake the part of our noble friend for his defense. If then we shall have done anything more sharply or freely than we ought or than they themselves might wish, we beg that they may be unaware of so much inexperience and intemperance as they think should be conceded to pious sorrow or justice.

8.10. There can be no profounder sorrow than this of ours, in which so great a father now suddenly removed is lamented. He who was worthy of much love is still daily persecuted, is still torn to shreds by powerful evil infamies and hatred. In him and with him we savagely deplore at one and the same destruction of the country, upheaval of the churches, misfortunes of the poor, overthrow of wealth, invasions of barbarians, slaughter of multitudes, wars of over-weening ones, snares of all, and (most horrible) destruction of souls. When Arsenius was spurned, when he was not heeded, all these ills happened. I beg therefore, do not falter, even though pursued by threats and provoked by defamation. Let not anyone say that such things should not be heaped up nor unfolded in lamentation. Let him know that nothing is more appropriate, especially when such ills are increasing, when truth is attacked by hatred, when justice is vanquished. So it was that Jeremiah the prophet, after chidings, persecutions, and incitements, turned to lamentation and wept bitterly over what had happened because of transgressions.

18.1. *Paschasius*: As you have often read, the legates returned without success [June 833], without honor, without the fruit of his great effort. Yet during the night following the day on which he withdrew, the hand of the Lord was laid upon all the people with God's just judgment. The minds of all were changed and everyone was smitten and terror-struck by the fear of God. Without persuasion or urging by anyone (so far as I could ascertain), they abandoned the emperor on that night [on the Field of Lies]. Others from the least to the greatest approached Honorius [that is, Lothar] and joined his camp. In the morning all their tents appeared pitched about him, so that each might exclaim on the part of the sons and pontiff, "Manu", which is to say, "What is it?" To all who were unaware it was miraculous. On the day before they were so strong and constant, confident in multitude, in promises of all, in the advice of pontiffs and senators, in the authority of the father, in multiplied oaths. Yet they were so utterly changeable and vacillating that without deliberation and determination by anyone they had left Caesar alone with Justina [that is, Judith]. In the course of a night they had flown completely around, like chickens under wing, to the son against whom they had resolutely come out. When they had pitched camp, only one people appeared in the morning.

18.2. In the very early morning twilight, therefore, we came to the aforesaid pontiff to relate the miracle that had happened. Behold, one of the Romans in the midst exclaimed and began to sing, "The right hand of the Lord has shown strength," and the rest following. It was thereupon adjudged by the same holy man and by all who had gathered about that a distinguished and glorious empire had fallen from the hand of the father so that Emperor Honorius [Lothar] might take it up and receive it, since he was the heir and since he had also been made a partner by his father and the people. If he should not accept it, all with one mind said that they would choose one who would bring them aid and defense. When this had been discussed, Honorius agreed and by some kind of decision accepted the sole government of the entire empire, inducing his father to his side. When I had observed the situation, I interrupted Arsenius and said, "Such a fortuitous matter seems a great evil to me, that without serious counsel and careful arrangement so great an empire should be suddenly and completely changed. Moreover, he who was made a partner in good faith might soon formally demand for himself the entire monarchy by overthrowing his father."

18.3. He replied, "It was ours to come here to labor with good will for all and give counsel of peace for all, to calm the internal war which was impending. But now, as there is no one who listens to us, so there is not one who gives attention to what we have taught. As you have read, everyone fears, desires, rejoices, or grieves. They fear what had happened, lest what was done be again formally demanded. They desire, while there is time, more speedily to reach what he had or acquire what he never had. They rejoice and exult eagerly about honors for themselves, for everyone seeks his own and very few seek what belongs to God and to utility. The remainder grieve, who fear to lose, since it was by their daring counsel that the august Caesar did such things against his sons."

19.1 *Adeodatus*: So far as I understand, they were also birds of prey rather than consuls. They believed in nothing but strengthening their own honors. Each one sought to grasp as much as he could for himself. Since the empire had slipped from the father's hand, they ought to have been eager to discuss with the pontiff, Honorius, and his brothers why it had fallen. Then they should have at once corrected, strengthened, established a condition whereby it might thereafter remain united and unshattered. It would have been becoming for the foremost and noblest ones to watch with prudence and advice that the commonwealth and the ruinous state of the whole empire should not again perish through discord. For there is usually no other end of discord among eminent and powerful men except complete annihilation or complete dominance of the victor. Only so come unity of the realm and restoration of peace and harmony. But that one was not reasonably confirmed on the throne, nor has the victor obtained the mastery with God, for his father fell by God's judgment, not by the victor's.

19.2. Full peace was not restored as long as each sought only his own. The kingdom was therefore, again undone by the son's hand, and it sank lower. Since neither of them walked before God sincerely, it still today [in the 850s] lies weakened and divided. There also remained a concealed hatred among the brothers and a wound deeply implanted in their hearts and seared in the minds of the greatest men. For them the commonwealth stretches and slips from worse to worse. Opportunities are sought and each one bides his time. The authority of kings, which was suitable and profitable for government, has fallen and unanimity is shattered and rent asunder. Judgment and right have perished. The franchises of men are multiplied, but enervated in power they make no progress. Scarcely a man is found who will set himself forward for safety of the fatherland or offer himself to dangers for its citizens. According to the statement of Truth [that is, Scripture], a kingdom divided is daily desolated and corrupted. Where there is no pilot, the people rush headlong into ruin.

19.3. Here and there individual ones have deserted God as governor, when with lying heart they inquired into the differences. So it was on a certain day that the chiefs and consuls of the palace entered secretly and watchfully. They divided the whole empire among themselves with the imperial son, giving no attention to the prerogatives of parents, the equalities of the magnates, the innumerable number of nobles, even the formerly meritorious faithful, nor still more grievously to the dignity of churches and to heartfelt reverence for God. Arsenius arrived when this had already been accomplished. Confounded when they learned of his presence, they brought to him the plan of distribution, inquiring if there was anything displeasing. Very shrewdly he replied, "The whole matter has been well arranged, except that you have left to God nothing that is his right, nor have you arranged anything that might please good people." But when he had presented his position, he began to be more sorrowful because no one heeded him. He was indeed overwhelmed by the greed and blindness of men.

19.4. It came to pass, therefore, that moment by moment the royal power, already tottering, was falling into ruin rather than being bolstered. Crimes were increasing, discord was again inflamed; quarrels were aroused; plots were nourished. The imperial father was reanimated by the urging of many to consider himself obliged to seek restoration to the throne of empire. Here and there seditions were incited and differences augmented, so much so that there is no house, no city, no town, no countryside, no province where discord does not still reign. On the other hand, greater perils increased until the august father should be restored on the seat of the realm and the son expelled.

20.1. *Paschasius*: He was not expelled as you assert nor did he act unwisely as you complain; for with the august father at his side, he maintained and preserved the kingdom and empire which had fallen. In the deprivation of power and in the sentence of the prelates who induced him to penance, he allowed nothing therein but what the entire senate and people compelled. All these matters our Arsenius moderated by God's grace lest either party should act more cruelly against the other than nature permits or more detestably for such a great crisis. But when the devouring flame of discord raged more and more, the imperial father refused voluntarily to soften and acquiesce. That he might not be guilty of parricide, the imperial son, of his own accord, did acquiesce and left his father again on the throne of empire. He sought indulgence that he might depart a free man, together with all his followers, because the wrath of God had boiled over, had poured hither and yon over all the people. According to Job, on all sides abound the tents of robbers who daringly enough provoke God with their own defiled deeds. Arsenius was already making less progress with his plans. Everywhere floodgates of desire were opened and greed was inflamed.

20.2. He therefore chose a momentary lull in activities to depart from their midst. Although God had given all things into their hands, no one sought God from the heart, with whom are wisdom and fortitude, counsel and understanding. It is clear that none may build up him whom the Almighty himself would destroy; none may loose him whom He would lock up. And so, because He was in turn destroying those whom He had raised up and was raising up again those whom He had locked up, Arsenius preferred to depart, a free man, rather than to remain among them as a servant of sin. Already astonished that no courage or ability existed in men, he deemed rightly that it would appear as wisdom rather than foolishness, for according to the scriptural testimony he knew both the deceiver and the deceived.

20.3. When he had witnessed many guiles and frauds fighting each other here and there, he caused the son to defer to the father and to withdraw with his army unharmed. He also caused the father and those of his party to remain in the empire so that all might understand that He alone was the all-powerful King who brings councillors to a foolish end and judges to dullness. He also loosens the baldrics of kings and girds their reins with rope, as we have seen truly happen to this one. But since neither party had wholly sought God worthily, they were changed in turn in alternate successes and the people were scourged. So all may understand that He is God who renders priests inglorious and supplants magnates. Otherwise, except by their own faults, would there be such great harassment and confusion of all. The lips of truthful ones had been changed and the teaching of old men taken away. Arsenius alone was not powerful against all except only what he did that the turn of events should not deteriorate further. Many here and there were urging just such, since strife and scorn had been poured out upon princes. But alas, what then stood in the way to prevent civil war from arising among them, we afterward saw done.

20.4. Nonetheless our Arsenius preferred to die rather than to agree to or to be present at any such condition. He therefore persuaded the son to withdraw with all his men; and similarly, the father to resume power over the empire so badly treated. For God, who changes the hearts of "the princes of earth and deceives them to walk vainly in pathless ways," had hardened His heart. To His judgment Arsenius entrusted everything lest something more infamous befall them. For with faults on every side, it was sad to realize what Job said, "They will coax as if in darkness and not in light. He will cause them to wander like drunk men. For he alone is, whose thought no one can turn aside. But by his just judgment he will cause whatever he has wished." Doubtless these things which had happened, which were daily becoming worse and increasing, were judgments.

20.5. Although it was late, he foresaw that which here and there in the present is discerned as already completed. So he chose rather to take flight than to remain with any of them. I was witness that the father wished very earnestly to retain him with him with all honor and highest office, if he would take an oath of fealty from his men. Then the imperial son sought to take him with him. But listening to neither of them, no, resisting them courageously, he departed from both. Entering Italy, on winged step, he betook himself to the monastery of Saint Columbanus [Bobbio]. At the urging of the brother, he undertook to rule it so that it would not be invaded by plunderers as all others had been. As long as he lived there, he ruled it nobly and peacefully.

Questions: Why did Paschasius compose this hagiography? What role did powerful churchmen like Wala play in political events, specifically in the rebellions? In the rebellion of 830, what were the charges made against Bernard of Septimania? Why had he become such a lightning rod? Was Paschasius an eye-witness to some of the events of 833? How is Paschasius's view of the two rebellions different from that of the Astronomer? How politicized was the Carolingian church?

41. The Letters of Einhard

Letter-writing was a common means of communication by the learned and official classes of the Carolingian empire. The collection of Einhard's letters translated below comes from the last fifteen years of his life. The letters may, indeed, have been preserved as examples of how to write business correspondence, which would explain why so many names are dropped and replaced with N. (which may sometimes simply stand for 'nomen' or name). Portions of the textual tradition are also defective; these lacunae are indicated by ... .

Though generally associated with Charlemagne and his court, Einhard may have been an even more important and respected figure at Louis the Pious's court. It was from Louis and not Charlemagne that Einhard received his land holdings. In his letters one sees Einhard acting in many roles: as royal servant, lord, husband, lay-abbot, property holder, go-between, friend, and intellectual. The social dimension of these letters as well as their reflection of Einhard's perilous political position in the period between 830 and 834 are particularly interesting.

Source: trans. H. Preble in Papers of the American Society of Church History, 2nd series, vol. 1 (New York: G.P. Putnam's Sons, 1913), pp.111-158; revised.

1. To Ansgisus, the abbot of Saint-Wandrille (circa 823-825).

Einhard himself had been the lay-abbot of Saint-Wandrille between 816 and 823.

To my dearly beloved brother in Christ, the revered Ansgisus, everlasting salvation in the Lord.

I beg your dearly beloved self to deign not to be annoyed but rather to regard it with kindness and good nature that in view of the needs of a man once a vassal of ours, now a vassal of my lord Lothar, I appeal to you to suffer him to hold upon any terms that please you a benefice which I gave him, until such time as I shall be able, with the Lord's help, to give him some compensation from another benefice through the generosity of my lords. You will find me all the more ready and eager to serve your wishes and profit if you deign to comply with my request in this matter. I hope you will ever flourish in the Lord.

2. To Bernharius, the bishop of Worms (circa 825)

To the holy and deservedly venerated lord, Bishop [Bernharius], Einhard wishes everlasting salvation in the Lord.

Though it saddens me very much to hear that you are in such a painful condition of body, beloved lord, yet I find no small consolation in the fact that I feel assured that this pain has profit for you and looks to the purging of the soul. For I believe that divine mercy is permitting you to suffer so long with this bodily disease that it may receive you perfected when departing from this body. As to offering prayers for you, let me tell your dear self that to the utmost strength and ability that God deigns to grant me, I will strive through those whom I think worthy to be heard, just as I see that you also have confidence in feeble me. Although we must never despair of recovering bodily health since God is able to do whatever He wants with his creatures, yet it is better for everyone of us to make himself ready for what is certain than for an uncertainty to neglect what is necessary in a sort of hope for something better. I hope you will always prosper in the Lord.

3. Bernharius, the bishop of Worms, Responds to Einhard (826).

The rest of Einhard's correspondence is one-sided, as the collection preserves his letters, but not any from his correspondents, though in the letter below and once in Lupus of Ferrières's correspondence we see both ends of an exchange with Einhard.

To my dear friend Einhard, Bernharius, now in my last hours, yet faithful to you and yours while breath remains, as God is my witness.

To your affection, my beloved friend, I commend my soul when it has gone from its sin-bound body, that you may deign to have it admitted to association with you and your faithful ones, to the end that the poor soul, aided by earnest and holy prayers, and the petitions of pious monks, may be privileged to receive some place of refreshing rest.

With this brief preface, then, because of the great and excessive straits of the flesh of the spirit, I beg you, my beloved friend, by the love of God and your friendship for my unworthy self, to devote the utmost care to the churches entrusted to little me, that after my demise ravening wolves may not invade the holy place and scatter the lowly flock, but rather a guide may be given to them who knows how to love or fear God, and to help in mercy those put under him.

Our most faithful monks and yours at the monastery of N. have chosen Folquicus to preside over them, the one among them who is closest to me. He is young in years, indeed, but old, I think, in character. You know his pedigree well, a son of N., brother of N., and related to many nobles. They have sent him to Worms, and commended him in person while I am still alive, during the visit he has deigned to pay me. Compelled by prayers, he promised emphatically and agreed with many tears to me or my relatives, in the presence of Count N. and my lord N., that if God so willed they should choose him to take my place. Therefore remember sweet friend, that this is not to be postponed, but strive with all your power to have it done.

I am sending along a pallium which I beg you to order given to the brothers at Saint-Servais [Einhard's monastery at Maastricht], as a remembrance of me. I have ordered that my mule be given to your charity. Let my beloved sister [in Christ] Emma [Einhard's wife] help in these things. I commend my soul to thee. My distress does not allow me to say more, but again I commend my soul to your prayers.

4. To Amalharius, a priest of Metz (828-829).

To Amalharius, most revered servant of Christ, Einhard a sinner.

I do not know who anticipated the arrival of the boy, who brought me your letter, and caused word to be sent to you that you should come to the emperor the day after Palm Sunday. But after I received your letter, and asked the emperor about the matters you wished, he directed me to write to you to celebrate the holy day of Easter at home, and to order the remainder of your retinue to come after you in such fashion that when they had come to you at court, and your orders had been received, and the scheme of your mission had been imparted to you, you could start upon your journey without delay. I hope you will ever flourish in the Lord.

5. To his Monastic Deputy in Maastricht (circa 828).

Abbot Einhard to our Deputy [or Vidame] and faithful man, greeting in the name of Christ.

Be it known to you that we wish you to send some men to Aachen to repair and restore our buildings, and to see to it that the things which we need to have there, that is flour, cereals for brewing, wine, cheese, and so forth, reach there at the proper time, as is usual. Furthermore we wish you to send to Lanaeken the oxen that are to be slaughtered and have them slaughtered there. One of these we wish you to have given to Hruotlouge, and the entrails and offal that cannot be kept for our use we wish you to give to the household servants in the same place. With the Lord's help we wish to reach the palace around the time of the mass of Saint Martin [11 November], if we are still alive. Therefore we wish you to make all these things known to those who serve our church, and to direct them to do in our name and at our expense just as we direct you to do. Farewell.

6. To Geboin, the count palatine (prior to 830).

Glorious Count Palatine. Einhard sends greeting in the Lord.

I ask your beloved self to deign to hear this man of my country, David by name, who wishes to lay his troubles before you, and if you find his case a good one, procure him the opportunity to appeal to our lord the emperor. For he is a vassal of my lord Lothar, and therefore not only because of my request but also out of regard and affection for his lord, you ought to help him. I hope I may have the good fortune to see you soon safe and sound.

7. To Hruotbert (prior to 830).

To the grand, honored, and illustrious Hruotbert, glorious count, eternal salvation in the Lord.

I ask your kind self to deign to send me word what your pleasure is as to what ought to be done in regard to the case of my man Alafrid—whether it is to be dismissed altogether, or whether he should still hope to come to his just deserts through your assistance. For I have informed my lord the emperor of the whole case as it has been investigated by you through the testimony of truthful persons along with the counts palatine, Adalhard and Geboin, and he answered me that he was astonished that the case had not already been brought to an end. Therefore I pray your beloved self to deign to send me word now what my man [Alafrid] ought to do about his case. I hope you will always flourish in the Lord.

8. To Count Poppo (prior to 830).

To the grand, honored, and illustrious Poppo, glorious count, Einhard wishes everlasting salvation in the Lord.

I have been told that you have asked that I inform you upon three points. It is indeed difficult for me to do so in regard to one of them, that is, whether a woman, whom you know better than I do, can without fault be taken in marriage by you. For as far as the dispensation which you received at Aachen is concerned, I want no other compensation than your friendship. As to Jupille [near Liège], I am ready to do according to what was agreed upon between us when we spoke together upon the subject, and therefore I cannot give you any further information now by letter. I hope you will always flourish in the Lord.

9. To his Monastic Deputy at Fritzlar (828-830).

Einhard in Christ's name to his Deputy, N.

I am very much astonished that all the things which I entrusted to you to do have been left as they have been left. For I hear that of the grain which you were to send to Mulinheim to make meal or flour, you have sent none, nor anything else except thirty pigs, and those not fine ones but mediocre, as well as three modia of vegetables; of the rest nothing.
And not only this but also throughout this whole winter I have seen nothing either of you or of anyone sent by you who could give me any report about those parts. If I am to derive no greater benefit from Fritzlar than you have brought me, I do not know why I should bother to hold that benefice. Now, therefore, if you care anything about my favor, I ask you to make a vigorous effort to correct your negligence, and inform me speedily what I have a right to expect from you.

10. To Emperor Louis (829-830).

Although I confidently believe that my most pious lord is ever mindful of his patron saints, Christ's blessed martyrs, Marcellinus and Peter, who by God's secret decree left Rome, and came to France to exalt and protect your kingdom, and for some reason deigned to accept hospitality from me, a sinner, yet a great necessity lies upon me to remind you frequently of the things that pertain to their honor, lest perchance I incur danger and detriment to my soul if I am less attentive than I should be to their admonitions. For, although they are most merciful, having even spared their slayer, yet I fear to offend their king, our Lord Jesus Christ, for love of whom they did not hesitate to die, if he should find me lazy in bringing forth the honors that are appropriate to their service.

Accordingly, most pious lord, I humbly admonish your excellency, and beg you to deign to remember that [contractual] exchange of place in which the reverend bodies of the martyrs rest which was made with Bishop Otgar, and to make the place definitively theirs, for the conveyance of which you handed over something of your own property to Saint-Martin.

Likewise I presume to remind your merciful self of my prayers in which, at the time when I was enfeebled and in fear of the approach of death, I suggested to you that you should deign to give to your same most gentle patron saints something from your benefices for the support of those who are to serve God at the resting place of the most sacred bodies of the holy martyrs, according to the hope you gave me then by your most kind promises, for I ought not to be deceived in my desire, and not only for this reason but because you ought to visit your mercy upon those whom I have reared for your service, and assist them with these benefices. I trust most confidently that in this you must win the favor of God and his saints, if you deign to cause me to accomplish my wishes in this matter.

I likewise ask you to deign to reflect and consider what reward awaits you with God, and how your fame will grow in this world if through you and in your time the place of the rest of the holy martyrs shall be so equipped and increased and adorned with both buildings and the other things essential that even its construction shall be attributed to your name, and your memory and that of the martyrs shall be celebrated together in the mouths of all nations forever.

And finally I ask and earnestly beg your great clemency to deign to look with loving pity upon miserable and sinful me now in my old age and great infirmity, and to cause me to be freed and exempted form secular cares, and to allow me in peace and tranquility to live beside the tombs of Christ's blessed martyrs, who are your patron saints also, under your protection and in obedience to these same saints and in the service of God and our Lord Jesus Christ, so that that inevitable and final day, which is apt to come upon the age at which I have now arrived, may find me not busied with vain and transitory cares but rather free to pray and read, and devoting my thoughts to meditation upon the divine law.

11. To the Emperor Lothar (829-830).

Einhard had been one of the advocates of Lothar's imperial position, but by 829 he knew of the building tension between Louis and Lothar. This letter, if it is Einhard's work, must reflect his disappointment over the threatened collapse of familial and imperial unity.

My lord, the pious emperor, live forever! How much care and anxiety my humble self feels for your imperial majesty I cannot easily express in words. For I have ever loved you as I have loved my most pious lord, your father, and I have wished for the safety of both alike ever since, with the approval of all his people, he made you the associate of his name in the kingdom, and commanded little me to devote my care to you and be your constant mentor, in molding your character and encouraging the pursuit of what was right and profitable. And although you have found my labors in these matters less profitable than they ought to have been, yet my faithful intention has not failed, and does not fail now, so that it will not suffer me to be silent, but rather forces me to admonish you in regard to your salvation, and briefly to set forth the things in which you ought to guard against danger to yourself.

Your imperial majesty should know that it has come to the notice of my humble self that certain persons, seeking their own advantage rather than yours, are working upon your gentle disposition and trying to persuade you to neglect your father's advice, and abandon the obedience due him, by leaving the post committed to your keeping and management by your most pious father, and coming to him against his will and desires and without his orders, and remaining with him although that is not pleasing to him. What can be imagined to be more wrong-headed and unseemly? See what the character of such effort to persuade you is, and how much evil it contains. For in the first place, as it seems to my humble self, it encourages you to hold of small account God's command which bids that honor be shown to parents, and to count as nothing the length of days which is promised as the reward for keeping that commandment; furthermore, to cast aside obedience, and take upon yourself disobedience instead, and to rise in contumacious arrogance against him towards whom you ought to have shown yourself humbly submissive; more than this, to drive away affection through contemptuous disobedience, and to allow a want of harmony, which never ought to find even mention between you, to grow to such an extent that hate is arising between those between whom there should be love. This ought most vigorously to be guarded against. For I think your wisdom is well aware what an abomination before God a son is who is contumacious and disobedient to his parents, since, as you can read in Deuteronomy, God commanded through Moses that such a one be stoned by all the people. Therefore I have thought that your pious self ought to be admonished to use the wisdom given you by God and guard against danger to yourself, and not think that this divine utterance can be scorned by anyone whatever, written though it be in the old law [the Old Testament]. For it is one of many which, as our elders and teachers, the holy fathers, have held, are to be observed in present times as well as past, in Christian times as well as Jewish. I love you, God knows, and therefore I admonish you thus faithfully, and you ought to consider not the worthlessness of the person who admonishes but the soundness of the advice. I hope...[the manuscript breaks off at this point].

12. The Emperor Louis to the People of Merida in Spain (830).

Einhard occasionally acted as a secretary for his royal patrons; here he is the writer of a letter for the emperor.

In the name of the Lord God and of our Savior, Jesus Christ, [Louis], by ordinance of divine providence august emperor, to all the nobles and all the people of Merida, greetings in the Lord.

We have heard of your tribulation and of the various woes you are suf-

fering from the cruelty of King Abdiraman, who through excessive greed for
your property which he has tried to take from you has often visited you with
violence and oppression; as also we find his father Abolaz did, who by unjust
extortions forced you to pay him sums which you did not owe, and thereby
made of friends enemies and of obedient vassals insubordinate and disobedient ones. For he plotted to take away your freedom also, and to burden
and humble you with unjust taxes and tribute. But, as we have heard, you
have always valiantly resisted like brave men the wrongs put upon you by
wicked kings, and have bravely withstood their cruelty and greed. This we
have learned from many reports you are also now doing.

Therefore we have been pleased to address this letter to you, and to comfort you, and urge you to continue as you have begun in defending your
freedom against a bitterly cruel king, and to scorn, as you have done hitherto,
any submission to his fierceness and fury. And since this same king is most
certainly as much our adversary and enemy as he is yours, let us fight with
common purpose against his ferocity.

For we desire with the help of almighty God to send our army this coming
summer to our border to encamp there ready and waiting until you send
word that it ought to advance, if so it seems good to you, that we should
direct this same army, with a view to helping you against our common enemies who are dwelling on our borders, to the end that if Abdiraman or his
army wishes to march against you, they may be prevented by our army from
being able to march against you in support of him and his army.

For we will say to you that if you are willing to turn away from him and
to turn to us, we will allow you to enjoy your ancient freedom fully and
without any diminution, and we will permit you to be exempt from tax or
tribute and will not order you to observe any other law than that under which
you desire to live, nor do we desire to treat you in any other way than to
regard you honorably as friends and allies in the defense of our realm. We
hope that you will always flourish in the Lord.

13. To the Empress Judith (830).

*This illness of Einhard may have conveniently coincided with the overthrow of Louis
by his sons and their supporters beginning in March and April 830.*

May my most pious lady deign to learn that I, your servant, have been afflicted
with such bodily ills since I came away from Aachen that I could hardly get
from Maastricht to Valenciennes [a distance of 110 miles or 176 kms.] in ten
days. There so violent a pain in my kidneys and also in the spleen attacked
me that I could not accomplish even one mile on horseback in a whole day.

Therefore I beseech that your pious self will allow me by your grace to
go by water to Saint-[Bavon], and to rest there until almighty God shall deign
to give me the strength to make the journey. For as soon as I can ride, I
will hurry to you or to my lord the emperor as it shall please you that I do.
Now I humbly pray that your pious self will deign to excuse me to my most
merciful lord, when you come to him, for my not having come to you. God
is my witness that I write you no untruth in regard to my health, and not
only that but also there are certain other ills much more serious which I am

suffering, about which I cannot speak except to an intimate friend.

Yet know this, that you cannot acquire a greater reward at this time before God than if you bring it about that I be permitted to hasten as soon as I am well enough to the service of Christ's holy martyrs. For I can get there by water in fifteen days from Saint-[Bavon].

14. To a Friend (April 830).

If my feebleness of body did not prevent, I should not be sending this letter but rather coming myself to be with you in these events that are taking place with you. Now being in great distress I beg your kind self to deign to intercede for me with our most pious lord and emperor. For the queen [Judith] ordered me when she went away from Aachen, and I could not go with her, to come after her to Compiègne. Obeying her commands I hardly got as far as Valenciennes with great difficulty in ten days. Thence, because I was not strong enough to ride, I went by water to Saint-[Bavon]. For an excessive looseness of the bowels and a pain in the kidneys so followed each other alternately in me that there was not a day after I started from Aachen that I did not suffer from one or the other trouble. There are likewise other ills which came from that sickness with which I was laid up last year, namely, a constant numbness of the right thigh and an almost unendurable pain in the spleen. Afflicted with these sufferings I am passing a very sad life with almost nothing cheerful in it, especially because I am afraid that I shall die in a place other than I should wish and engaged in other occupations than serving Christ's holy martyrs.

Therefore I adjure and beseech you by Christ's blessed martyrs Marcellinus and Peter to deign to intercede for my humble self with the most pious emperor, so that he may not be angry with me because I did not come to meet him as did those who could. I should surely have come if I had been able, and I shall come as soon as I am able, and whether absent or present I shall remain ever faithful to him. I pray your kind self, therefore, to deign to inform me by letter as speedily as you can about what has taken place and what is taking place around you. I hope you will always flourish in the Lord.

Everything that is now happening in this realm was predicted two years ago by the revelations of Christ's martyrs [see Aubrey's dreams and the exorcism in doc.34 above].

15. To the Emperor Louis (April 830).

To a great lord, an ordinary servant.

[I hope] my most pious lord remembers how you gave me permission to betake myself to the service of Christ's blessed martyrs when my lady [Judith] came to you. This I desired to do, but my lady ordered me to come to Compiègne, and in obedience to her orders I started to go after her to Compiègne as soon as I could arrange my horses. On setting out I was seized with a pain in the spleen and also the kidneys, and was so ill that I hardly reached Valenciennes from Maastricht in ten days. Seeing there that

I could not ride and having found a boat, I came on the next day to Saint-[Bavon] by water, and now lying here in great pain and distress I beg and beseech your pious self to give me permission to proceed to the place in which the sacred bodies of your pious patron saints rest. For I can get there from Saint-Bavon in fifteen days by water. You can win a great reward for yourself before God, if you allow me to go to the service of his saints, if indeed I shall be able to reach there alive. I believe that these holy martyrs must intercede for you before God if you will set their service before [my] service to yourself. For in no other place in your realm can I do greater good than there if you will help me in the matter.

16. To a Bishop (May 830).

To the holy and deservedly revered lord, the most reverend Bishop N., Einhard, a sinner.

I cease not to give the heartiest thanks I can to God almighty and our Lord Jesus Christ, since I have learned that my glorious and God-preserved and ever-to-be-preserved lord, the Emperor Lothar, has come safe and sound from Italy, and you, my very dear friend, with him, and I hope and pray that he will speedily allow me to come where I may enjoy your bodily presence. Yet meanwhile I commend my humble self to your Christian love and through you to his piety, and beg that you will not allow yourselves to entertain any sinister suspicion of my humble self because of anybody's suggestions. I call God and the holy martyrs Marcellinus and Peter to witness that I cannot find words to express the love and devotion that I am conscious of feeling towards you. And therefore I ask with confidence that when I come I may find you disposed to me as I feel sure that I have deserved of you. I hope your holiness will ever flourish in Christ, and not forget my feeble self.

17. To a Certain E. (mid-830).

To the holy and deservedly revered lord, E., Einhard wishes eternal salvation.

Although there are very many things about which I should like to know, yet there are two about which my desire for information is strongest just now. One is, where and when this general assembly [which was held at Nijmegen in October] is to be held; the other, whether my lord Lothar is to return to Italy, or to remain with his father. Let your kind self not object to informing me on these two points, for I need to know them more than the other things that are going on around you. For on them depends what I ought to do, if the divine mercy shall deign to look with favor upon me and enable me to be of any use. I hope soon to see you in flourishing condition, best beloved of my friends.

18. To Count G. (830).

To his beloved brother G[eboin?], a glorious count and magnate, Einhard wishes everlasting salvation in the Lord.

I have ever felt your kindly affection for me, but never more than now, when you have obtained for me permission to proceed to the service of the saints Marcellinus and Peter, who on account of this deed will be sure to intercede with God. Therefore I thank your kind self as heartily as I know how, and earnestly beg that in accordance with your kind custom you will deign ever to speak for me both with my lord the emperor and with his sons, especially my lord Emperor Lothar, in whose pious devotion I have great confidence, unworthy as I am.

For the rest, I ask you to be good enough to reward the painter N., your devoted servant, and help him, and deign to intercede for him with my lord the emperor, if you see a favorable opportunity to do so, that he may not through anyone's hostility lose the benefice which he won by serving his lord's will. It is not necessary for me to name to you those whom he fears in this matter, for they are as well known to you as to me. I only ask you to deign to help him as far as you can. I hope you may always flourish in the Lord.

19. To a Noble Friend (830?).

To his beloved and faithful friend, N., a glorious noble, Einhard wishes eternal salvation in the Lord.

Because I have such well founded confidence in you that I can in no way hesitate to run for help to your kindness in all of my own emergencies and those of my friends, I am now sending you with this letter my fellow countrymen and friends, Aristeus and Theothous, begging that you will deign to receive them in your usual friendly way, and in their needs which they will impart to you to help them with my lord, the Emperor Lothar, and his most pious father, so that they shall have the same great confidence in you that I have. I hope you may always flourish, best and dearest of friends.

20. The Emperor Louis to Count G. (832, before December).

Louis, by the ordination of divine providence august emperor to Count G. in the name of the Lord God and our Savior Jesus Christ.

Be it known to you that we wish you, when this letter of ours reaches you, to prepare immediately without any delay to go to meet our *missus*, H., at our city of Heilbronn on the eighteenth of December, that is a week before Christmas, and what he shall enjoin upon you in our name to do along with our other faithful counts and vassals, to do it zealously and conduct yourself therein according to the confidence we have in your faithfulness. Fare you well.

21. The Emperor Louis to his Vassal H. (November 832).

To his faithful H., in the name of the Emperor Louis, by the ordination of divine providence august emperor, to our faithful H., in the name of the Lord God and our Savior Jesus Christ.

Be it known to you that we wish you to bid that one of your sons, our vassals, who you know can best do it, be ready, when Count R., and our *missus* H. desire to send us any word by him, to proceed without delay or lack of speed to Tours; there he will find, the Lord willing, either ourself or our beloved spouse. See that you show no negligence therein if you desire to hold our favor. I hope you will always flourish in the Lord.

22. The Emperor Louis to his Vassal T. (the end of 832).

Louis, by the ordination of divine providence august emperor, to our faithful T., in the name of the Lord God and our Savior Jesus Christ.

Be it known to you that we wish you to prepare yourself, whenever Count Hr[uotber]t and our *missus* H. desire to send us any word by you, to be able to proceed with that message to Tours without delay or any lack of speed; there you will find, God willing, either ourself or our beloved spouse. See that you show no negligence therein if you desire to hold our favor.

23. To the Imperial *Missus* A. (end of 832)

To his beloved brother and friend, Lord *Missus* A., Einhard wishes everlasting salvation in the Lord.

I thought it was well known to you that our men whom we have in those parts were according to the ordinance and command of our lord the emperor on coast-guard duty not only at the time when he went to Tribur, but also when he kept on to Orléans. And therefore it does not seem to me just that men should have to pay the heerban [the fine for not appearing when summoned] who were nowhere except where the emperor himself had commanded. And therefore I pray your beloved self to grant us a postponement until our lord the emperor comes, and we will remind him of his command, and then he can give such orders as please him. I hope you will always flourish in the Lord.

24. To Egilolf and Hunbert (late 832).

To the beloved brethren in Christ and devoted servants of Christ, Egilolf and Hunbert, eternal salvation in the Lord.

I know that you are aware that Bishop Wolfgar of blessed memory bestowed at my request a benefice of three manses and twelve serfs from the domain of Saint-Kilian [in Würzburg], in the district of Durbargau, in a place called Megentheim, upon our man Gerbert. But in as much as he could remain in the enjoyment thereof only so long as the bishop still lived in the body, I pray your kind selves to allow the said Gerbert to hold that benefice, as he has done, until a bishop shall have been ordained in that see and it shall have been agreed between him and me what should be done in regard to the benefice in the future. I hope that you will always flourish in the Lord.

25. To King Louis [the German] (after 30 June 833).

[I pray the clemency] of my lord and most glorious king, that you will not be angry with me because I neither ... nor afterwards came into your presence. For I did this out of no lack of respect for you nor out of laziness, but because I was ill and suffering from fever, as I am still doing. And I hardly succeeded in coming into the presence of my lord Lothar, your brother, and, having received permission from him, to return to the holy martyrs, when he also was allowed to depart from you two.

And my returning home was for no other reason than that though a division of the kingdom had been made among you such as was made, I did not know it. For the report had come that the part of the eastern districts of Francia in which I am sojourning and have a small benefice was to belong to the kingdom of my lord Lothar. Hence I earnestly beg your clemency to permit me to hold and enjoy the benefice until I receive permission from my lord Lothar to come to you and put myself into your hands—if I shall succeed in attaining this. For it is my purpose to come faithfully and devotedly into your service, if God shall deign to grant me life and health.

26. To a Priest and to a Deputy (before October 833).

In the name of Christ, Einhard, the abbot, to N., a priest, and N., a Deputy, our trusty men, greeting in the Lord.

Be it known that we desire you to cause presents to be prepared according to custom, for the service of my lord Lothar and of his spouse, Ermengard, as is usual for a man to make for the service of his lord. And when Lothar returns from Orville to Compiègne, we desire that they be presented there, and afterwards we desire that you send us word about how they were received by him or by her. Farewell.

27. To a Certain U. (late 833).

Einhard to his U. everlasting salvation.

Frumold, son of Count N., whose sister N. he has as his wife, has a rather small benefice in Burgundy, in the Geneva region, where his father was count, but he is suffering from infirmity rather than old age, being troubled with a chronic case of severe gout, and is afraid that he will lose the benefices unless you kindly come to his aid, because in consequence of the infirmity that weighs upon him he cannot appear at court. He therefore prays that in this emergency you will deign to ask our lord, the emperor, to permit him to hold the benefice which the emperor's grandfather granted him, and his father permitted him to hold, until such time as, having recovered his strength, he can appear before him and commend himself in the regular way. Your feeble, old comrade wishes you all prosperity, best beloved of comrades.

28. To a Count (late 833).

To the grand, honored, and illustrious N., glorious count, Einhard wishes everlasting salvation in the Lord.

N., an imperial vassal, brother of Count N.'s wife, wished to appear before our lord the emperor, but being weighed down by gout and old age was unable to do so in consequence of his infirmity. As soon as he is able, he will come to render service to him. Meanwhile he asks that he be allowed to hold the benefice which our lord the Emperor Charles gave him in Burgundy, in the Geneva district, until such time as he can appear before the emperor and put himself in his hands. To me also it seems proper and expedient that what he desires be done, because he is a good and discreet man and of good repute among his neighbors, and you will do well if you deign to help him in this matter. I hope you will ever flourish in the Lord.

29. To a Certain Count (late 833).

To the grand, honored, and illustrious N., the glorious count, Einhard wishes eternal salvation in the Lord.

I ask your kind self to deign to help this young man, N., with our lord the emperor, that he and his brother may not lose a benefice which they hold. For they have fifteen manses in the Tournai district and five beyond the Rhine [the former district was in Lothar's kingdom, the latter in Louis the German's]. He wishes to serve our lord the emperor with the benefice which is in the Tournai country, and to have his brother put himself in N.'s hands with the benefice beyond the Rhine, yet so that they shall hold the entire benefice in common. But the brother does not want to agree to this unless commanded by our lord the emperor. For unless this is done, they will lose the benefice beyond the Rhine. Therefore he prays your good self to deign to ask our lord the emperor to order his brother to do so, and he is ready to sign such a compact as pleases our lord the emperor that he means to hold his benefice always in common with his brother. I hope you will always flourish in the Lord.

30. To a Bishop (late 833?).

To the holy and deservedly revered lord, most reverend N., Einhard, a sinner.

This priest, N., by name, has asked me very urgently to intercede with you for him, in the hope that you will deign to deal mercifully towards him. He is, as he declares, in a situation of great poverty, especially now when the little benefice that he held in Bavaria has been taken away from him and given to another. Thus he does not know what he is to do now or how to serve his overlord, unless through your intercession my lord Lothar will deign to give him some sort of indemnification to support him. I hope you will always flourish in the Lord, not forgetting me, but deigning to commend my humble self to the most pious emperor.

31. To a Priest (late 833?).

To the holy and deservedly venerated lord, N., priest of the most high God, Einhard, a sinner.

We were very glad to have your relative and trusty man Eburo come to us, and although he was to stay for some time with us, he is in a hurry to return to you. Still we have not wished to let him go without a letter from us, lest if he return empty-handed he may be thought not to have come to us at all. In regard to the matters, however, about which he thought he would have something definite to take to you, I cannot send you anything definite or give you any indication through him because the changes that have recently taken place in this realm have thrown us into such a state of confusion that we do not in the least know what we ought to do, except, according to the words of Jehoshaphat, to turn our eyes unto the Lord, and, in Philo's words, to pray for divine help since human fails. But Eburo, the bearer of these presents, though he is your own very dear relative, we venture to commend to your acceptance. For we trust in God that, though it were impossible now, we shall have the right at some other, more favorable time to send him back to you in glad and cheerful spirits with the help of the divine mercy. We hope that the divine grace will always and everywhere keep your holiness in good health, and that you will not forget us.

32. To an Abbot (late 833?).

To the holy and deservedly revered N., most reverend Abbot N., [Einhard], a sinner.

I have learned from what my friends say that N. (I do not know whether I ought to call him an abbot or bishop, but you know perfectly well who he is) has the habit of asking your sound and most wise advice in matters having to do with his interests. Therefore it has seemed well to beg your holiness to deign to speak to the said man on behalf of his nephew Eburo now sojourning with me, and ask him not to deceive him in the hope he gave him, but rather to continue the kindness to him which he promised him. And that was to deign to help him in his straitened circumstances from his own resources, in order that he may not, in consequence of lack of money and need of essential things, experience the necessity of giving up the place in which he himself put him. And this will certainly happen unless he takes measures beforehand to prevent it happening. This provision can easily be made if he is willing to abide by the promises by which he drove him to do as he wished. I hope your holiness, remembering my humble self, will always flourish in Christ the Lord.

33. To Louis the German (early 834?).

My lord, your most pious father, ordered N. from the monastery of N. to aid and cooperate with us in the building of the basilica of Christ's blessed martyrs Marcellinus and Peter, your patron saints. But it seems to me that they are not likely to do anything about that work unless an order from your merciful majesty comes to them ordering them again to help us in this work according to the directions of my lord, your father. Therefore, in order to make known to you the reason for this work, I have taken pains to send to your high majesty this letter of supplication from my humble self, by which I would ask and humbly petition that for the love and honor of Christ's martyrs, your patron saints, you will deign to give attention to the building of their basilica, that this thing may be accomplished through your help, and that you will give us for the aforesaid bishop your sacred command by a letter from your glorious and authoritative hand which they shall not dare to disregard. Thus will your reward increase with God and the blessed martyrs will intercede for you, that your kingdom may ever be increased and strengthened, and stand safe and protected from the plots and hostile attacks of evil spirits and malicious men. I hope and pray that my lord the king may flourish and live forever.

34. To King Louis [the German] (833-834).

I want to appeal to your pious self on behalf of an intimate friend of mine, N., to wit, your faithful subject, that you may deign to receive him, and when he has commended himself to your protection give him some consolation from the benefices which are known to be open and free here in our neighborhood. For he is a noble, and faithful, and well trained for good service in any kind of duty that may be entrusted to him. For he served your grandfather and your father faithfully and energetically, and is ready to do the same by you if God wills to grant him life and health. He is fairly ill now, and therefore cannot come to your pious self in person, but will come as soon as he is able. Accordingly I pray your pious self to permit me to know what I may promise him from your goodness, that he may live in good hope until he can come to you in person.

35. To a Certain F. (autumn 834).

Einhard to F. everlasting salvation.

I do not ask you to write me anything about the state of things at court, because there is nothing pleasant to hear about what is going on there. About you and my other friends, if with the exception of yourself any remain, I am very anxious to know where you are and what is happening with you. Therefore I have taken pains to send this letter to your good self that I may thus remind you to write to me how things are with you, that is, how you are and where and when there is a possibility of our seeing each other, if we are still alive. For I have often longed to see you and talk with you, but never more ardently than now, because I have never felt a greater need of conferring about, and discussing with a friend, the regulation of my life, and that I would do with no one more gladly than with you, for in none have I greater confidence.

I am sending a letter by this boy to Abbot N., and I will ask you to see that he is escorted there by one of your people if he can go on, or if by chance he cannot go farther because the beasts are tired out as is apt to be the case, I beg that you will receive from him the letter I am sending to Folco [the abbot of Saint-Wandrille], and will send it to him by somebody, and beg him to answer me, and send back to you the answer he may be pleased to make. And will you please see that the answer comes to me as soon as you find a suitable bearer? I hope that you ever flourish in Christ, best beloved of my friends, and remember me.

36. To an Abbot (autumn 834).

To the very reverend Abbot N., worthy of the deepest veneration, Einhard, a sinner.

As I remember my request so I fancy you have not forgotten your promise, although many different obstacles afterwards arose, which might well not only have left that conversation of ours in abeyance for the time being but even have consigned it to lasting oblivion. I mean the conversation in which, being both on duty at the court, we spoke of the roof of the basilica of Christ's blessed martyrs Marcellinus and Peter, which I am now striving to construct, albeit with great difficulty, and it was agreed between us to buy lead for the price of fifty pounds. Now, although the work in the basilica has not yet reached the point that necessity compels me to remind you of the roofing, yet in view of the uncertain bounds of mortal life it always seems best to hasten to complete with the Lord's help the good work we have begun. Accordingly I beg your kind self to deign to inform me by letter about the purchase of this same lead, that I may know whether any beginning has been made yet, and, if none has yet been made, in what way the business is to be begun and with the Lord's help completed. Therefore I ask your very kind self not to object to informing me about this matter by letter. I hope you will always flourish in the Lord, and remember me.

37. Einhard's Wife, Emma, to Blidthrut (828-836).

To her dearly beloved sister Blidthrut, your friend and well wisher Emma wishes eternal salvation in the Lord.

A serf of yours from Mosbach, Wenilo by name, has taken a certain free woman to himself in marriage, and now, in fear of your anger and that of his lord Albuin, has sought refuge at the shrine of the saints Marcellinus and Peter. I beg your charitable heart to deign to intercede with Albuin in my name for the man so that he may, with his favor and yours keep the woman he has taken to wife. I hope you will ever flourish.

38. Emma to N. (before 836).

To her revered and beloved lord and son, N., Emma your faithful [grand-mother?] wishes eternal salvation in the Lord.

After your trusty messenger N. came to us, and gave me your letter, I gladly strove to do whatever I could recognize as expedient in it. It is for you to consider and weigh well how the things you are arranging to do among yourselves shall be found to be not only expedient but also right on both sides, and to see that there shall be no just reason to find fault with those who for the sake of the advantage of many...to do.... This, as I see it, can only come about if everything is done at its proper time, because as you know very well, only those things, according to Solomon, have good results that are properly done at the right time. I hope, my dear son, you will ever prosper in Christ.

39. To Gozbert [the abbot of Saint-Gall] (816-836).

To the revered Abbot Gozbert, devout servant of Christ, Einhard, a sinner.

I pray that your holiness will deign to take notice as to the case of this man, Bebo by name, that I gave him a benefice attached to the monastery of Saint-Cloud, because he served me to my satisfaction. And after I had commended him to my lord Lothar, I obtained from my lord the emperor the grant to him of that benefice for all the days of his life. Therefore I ask and beg of your dearly beloved self that you will not suffer any obstacle to be put in his way as to this benefice until, the Lord willing, I shall have an opportunity to confer with you. I am writing to you about this because I know of the wicked desires and boundless greed of certain people who have no regard for the injury done to their neighbors in cases where they have the power to satisfy their own most grasping greed. I hope you will always flourish in the Lord.

39a. To Lupus of Ferrières on the Death of Emma in 836.

Einhard to his Lupus, greeting.

All my interest and all my solicitude in regard to affairs of my own or my friends have been taken away and wholly dissipated by the profound grief I have experienced over the death not long ago of my faithful wife, my most dear sister [in Christ] and companion. And it seems impossible that it should end, for my memory clings so tenaciously to the thought of such deaths that it cannot be wholly torn from it. More than this, the grief itself is constantly added to and the wound received is aggravated by the fact that my prayers have not been of any use and the hopes that I had placed in the merits and intercession of the martyrs have completely disappointed my expectations. Thus it comes about that the consolatory words of friends, which are apt to heal the melancholy of others, cause my heart's sore to become raw again and freshly open, when they urge me to bear with calmness the blows of fortune which they do not themselves feel, and when they think that I ought to rejoice in a thing in which they are unable to point out a single trace of joy or gladness. For what mortal who has his wits and a sound mind does not bewail his lot and judge himself unhappy and most miserable when plunged into affliction he finds Him, whom he had believed would listen to his prayers, alienated and inexorable? Do not these things seem to you such as might call forth sighs and tears from a puny little man, drive him to groans and lamentations, even plunge him into the depths of despair? And verily they would have done so unless, supported by the help of divine pity, I had suddenly turned to the inquiry of what in cases of disasters of this sort our elders and betters had decided should be held to and observed. There were at hand excellent teachers, by no means to be despised but in every way to be listened to and followed, the glorious martyr Cyprian, to wit, and those most illustrious expounders of Holy Writ, Augustine and Jerome. Encouraged by their views and salutary argumentation, I tried to raise up my heart weighed down with heavy woe, and began to think over sedulously what I ought to feel in regard to the death of my dear partner whose mortality rather than her life I saw was ended. I even tried to see whether I could not make myself accomplish in myself by reasoning that which length of time is wont to bring about, namely, that the wound which a sudden accident had inflicted upon my heart through an unexpected death should begin to form a cicatrix and to heal through the application of self-consolation. But the extent of the hurt resists skilled treatment, and though the things offered by those teachers for the mitigation of deep grief are most salutary, like remedies tried by physicians at once most skilful and most gentle, the wound which is still bleeding is not yet ripe for healing.

You will perhaps wonder at this and say that pain born of an occasion of this kind ought not to have been so lasting, as if it were in the power of the sufferer when that should end, the beginning of which he did not have in his power and did not foresee. Yet the extent or duration of pain and sorrow seems capable of measurement by the amount of the losses which have befallen one, and when I feel these so terribly every day in every act, in every occupation, in the whole management of my home and household, in ordering and arranging all the things that have to do with sacred or secular duties, how can it be that the wound which has brought all these great troubles upon me should not rather, when thus frequently touched, reopen and break forth anew than heal or be made whole? For I think and do not fear that this idea will deceive me, that the pain and anxiety which have come upon me from the death of my dear partner will abide with me forever until that period of time which God has willed to bestow upon me for this poor temporal life shall reach its due ending and be finished. Yet I find this profitable rather than harmful to me thus far, since it checks and holds back as by bridle or reins my mind that would hasten to joy and well-being, and recalls to the remembrance of death the heart that the repose and forgetfulness of old age had lured to hope and love of length of days. I see that I have not much time left to live, though how much it is destined to be is wholly unknown to me, but this I know most certainly, that both a new-born child may shortly die and an old man cannot live long. And accordingly I hold that it will be far more expedient and blessed to pass that brief uncertain time in grief than in joy. Because if according to the Lord's words blessed and happy are they that mourn and grieve, on the other hand they shall be unhappy and wretched who do not fear to pass the end of their days in constant and continuous joy.

I thank you and am grateful to your affection that you have deigned to comfort me with your letter, for you could not have given a greater or surer proof of your love towards me than by holding out the hand of exhortation to me as I lie in distress and by bidding me to rise whom you could not fail to know over-whelmed in heart and crushed down with sorrow. Farewell, most dear and beloved son.

40. To the Emperor Louis the Pious (after June 837).

The ancients almost all judged that the appearance of new and unusual stars indicated that things sinister and sad rather than pleasant and prosperous were to come upon poor mortals. Only the writings of the Holy Gospel bear witness to the apparition of a new star that was propitious, and we are told that the wise men of the Chaldeans saw it, and inferring from its tremendous brilliancy that the eternal king had just been born, offered with reverence gifts befitting such high majesty.

But that star which recently appeared is reported by all who say that they saw it to have been harsh and gloomy of aspect and to have flashed in a threatening manner. This, I think, forms a presage in keeping with our just deserts, and indicates the coming of the disaster which we deserve. For what difference does it make whether threatening wrath is foretold to the human race by a man or an angel or a star? The essential thing is to understand that the apparition of the star was not casual but was a warning to mortals to strive to avoid the danger to come by penitence and appeals to the mercy of the Lord. As seen in the prophecy of Jonah, the overthrow of the city, which had been foretold by him, was postponed by the divine mercy because men turned to the remedy of repentance, and God acted towards the people as He promised through Jeremiah to do when He commanded him to go down to the house of the potter, and to hear his words there beside the artisan as he worked. This we trust that He will also do towards us if, like those men of old, we neglect not to repent with all our hearts.

And O that the disaster which a Norman fleet is said to have brought recently upon parts of this realm might have atoned for the sins indicated by this terrible star! But I fear that what was signified by so deadly a portent is to be visited by a heavier punishment, although those upon whom such a mighty tempest from the ocean fell so furiously would seem to have suffered a harsh and heavy enough vengeance on themselves and all theirs.

May my most pious lord, the emperor, flourish and live happily in all things!

41. To a Count (839?)

To the grand and honored and illustrious man, glorious Count N., Einhard wishes eternal salvation in the Lord.

My lord the emperor commanded through Dagolf the hunter that Count N. should cause all the counts who are in Austrasia to come together into one place, that is, Hatto and Poppo and Gebehard, and their comrades, to consider what must be done if anything new came up about the regions of Bavaria. Then it seemed well to them that both you and Atto should attend the same assembly. Therefore they ask you to consider, and send them word in what sort of place you think their meeting can best be held. For N. thinks this might be desirable.

42. To Abbot Hrabanus [Maurus] (822-840).

To the revered servant of Christ, the reverend Abbot Hrabanus, Einhard, a sinner.

A vassal of yours, Gundhart by name, has asked me to intercede for him with your holiness, that he may be allowed to absent himself from the muster which is to take place at this time, and may stay at home without offense to you, nay, with your approval. He asserts that he is driven to this staying at home by strong necessity in as much as he is involved in a quarrel and does not dare to attend this muster with his enemies and men who are plotting against his life, especially with that count under whose command the muster is to be held, who, he says, is a most bitter enemy to him. Therefore he asks that he may not be pushed into such danger by an authoritative order of yours. He will attend to making provision to pacify the collector of the heerban if he comes and summons him, and will do it without putting you to any trouble. I should not appeal to you in this case if I had not assured myself of the man's difficulties and dangers. I hope that you will always flourish.

43. To Otgar, the archbishop of Mainz (826-840).

To his holy and deservedly revered lord, the reverend Archbishop Otgar, Einhard, a sinner.

This brother, Werdric by name, is of the congregation of Saint-Boniface [that is, the monastery of Fulda] and is staying with us by permission of his abbot, because he is related to me. I now send him to you, that you may order him to be ordained deacon if you see that this can be done canonically because of the reason that is contained in the letter his abbot recently addressed to me when I asked him about the case. I send you by this same monk that letter itself to read, and you will immediately see from it, I think, whether the consecration can be performed now or should be put off until another time. I hope and pray that the heavenly grace will always and everywhere guard your holiness in devoted service to itself, most holy and reverend father.

44. To Otgar, the archbishop of Mainz (826-840).

To his holy and deservedly revered lord, the reverend Archbishop Otgar.

A certain priest, Hruodrad by name, has come to me saying that he belongs to your tributary town of Mayen and had received permission from your suffragan bishop and the other brethren to go to Rome and that in the month of March, but afterwards, when he had reached Mainz, he could not find people with whom he could carry out that journey. Therefore he betook himself to a certain man of our region, Hildebert by name, to stay with him until he should find people going to Rome. These he says he has now found, and he has asked me to secure your permission for his carrying out the journey. For he wishes, as he declares, to carry out the journey as speedily as possible and return to his own dwelling-place. Therefore I pray your holiness to deign to bestow upon him the permission which he seeks, and not to let it prejudice his case that he has tarried so long on the way, because many obstacles arose in his path and he did against his will what he could not help doing. I hope your holiness will remember my feeble self and will always flourish in Christ, most holy and reverend father.

45. To Hetti, the archbishop of Trier (828-840).

To his holy and deservedly revered lord, the reverend Archbishop Hetti, Einhard, a sinner.

Having learned from the letter of your holiness what you wish, I have attended to doing it without delay, namely sending to you the relics that you wrote to say you wanted to have for the dedication of your new basilica. And I have done it gladly, having such confidence in you that I am sure that the honor which we ought to have shown to their whole bodies, had not sloth and negligence stood in the way of the honor due, will be shown to whatever bit of sacred ashes of the blessed martyrs comes to you.

In regard, however, to the matter you wished to learn from me, I am quite unable to give you information, for almost nothing is apt to come to my knowledge from there, nor am I much interested in the knowledge of these things, from which I derive little pleasure and no profit. I hope your holiness will remember my feeble self, and will always flourish in the Lord, most holy and reverend father.

46. To Count Hatto (828-840).

To my beloved friend Hatto, the glorious count, Einhard wishes eternal salvation in the Lord.

A vassal of yours, Hunno by name, has come to the shrine of the saints Marcellinus and Peter asking pardon for having joined himself in marriage, without your permission, to a fellow serf belonging to you. Therefore, I beg your kind self to let him attain indulgence in this matter if you find this fault worthy of pardon. I hope you will always flourish in the Lord.

47. To Count Poppo (828-840).

To the grand, honored, and illustrious man, the glorious Count Poppo, Einhard sends greeting in the Lord.

Two poor men have taken refuge at the shrines of Christ's blessed martyrs, Marcellinus and Peter, admitting that they are guilty and have been convicted of stealing big game in a nobleman's woods. A part of the fine they have paid and part they still have to pay, but, as they declare, they have not the means of paying because of their poverty. Accordingly I pray your kindness to deign, so far as possible, to spare them for love of Christ's martyrs with whom they have sought refuge, that they may not be utterly ruined for a transgression of this sort, but may feel that it has profited them in your eyes to have sought refuge at the tombs of the holy martyrs. I hope that you may ever flourish in the Lord.

48. To his Deputy, Marchrad (828-840).

To our beloved friend Marchrad, glorious Deputy, Einhard wishes eternal salvation in the Lord.

Two serfs of Saint-Martin's [of Mainz], from Hedabach, Williramnus and Otbert by name, have fled to the shrine of Christ's blessed martyrs, Marcellinus and Peter, because their brother had killed a companion of his, and they ask that they be allowed to pay the proper wergild for their brother, and that he be exempted from punishment of his life and limb. Accordingly I ask your beloved self to deign to spare him as far as possible, for the love of God and his saints at whose shrine the brothers have sought refuge. I hope you will ever flourish in the Lord.

49. To an Archbishop (828-840).

To the holy and deservedly venerated reverend lord, N., Einhard, a sinner.

A serf of Saint-Mary's, N. by name, who belongs in the jurisdiction of your holiness, has come to the shrine of Christ's blessed martyrs, Marcellinus and Peter, asking indulgence because of a crime he has committed in killing a companion as the result of a quarrel which arose between them. Accordingly I pray your holiness to deign to spare him out of reverence for these martyrs at whose shrine he has sought refuge, and, remitting punishment in limb and by scourging, to allow him by a payment of money to compound and repair the wrong which he has done in evil intent. I hope your holiness will always flourish in Christ, most holy and reverend Father.

50. To a Count (828-840).

To the grand and honored, and illustrious man, N., the glorious count, Einhard wishes everlasting salvation in the Lord.

Trusting greatly in your friendship ... I do not hesitate to ask about the rights of the blessed martyrs of Christ, Marcellinus and Peter, which are in our monastery, and also about certain slaves ... which our advocate, N., sought for in person with you and hopes he can get if he has your help. Accordingly I beg your kind self to deign to aid him not only in this matter but also in other things, to the end that you may through this win over those martyrs of Christ as your champions and intercessors with God.

51. To a Count and Judge (828-840).

To his beloved brothers in Christ and friends, Count N. and Judge N., the glorious *missi* of our lord the emperor, Einhard sends greeting in the Lord.

Our men who come to us from those parts are in the habit of telling us of your goodwill and kindness towards us, in that you save our men and spare them in every situation in which you can spare them, as well in the heerban as in other matters coming under your commissionership. Hence we would show you great gratitude as we should, and we pray God and his saints that not only here in this present life but also in the future life the recompense of the fitting reward of your deeds be granted to you. We also promise that you may confidently hold our humble selves always ready to do your will. Farewell.

52. To the Monk Gerward (830-840).

Gerward was the palace librarian of Louis the Pious.

To his beloved brother Gerward, Einhard wishes everlasting salvation in the Lord.

I am uncertain whether I ought to think that you did not understand my letter or that you did not care about my danger, but I am more readily led to believe that in consequence of some preoccupation you did not read and understand with enough care what I wrote than to think that your affection lacked interest in the danger threatening me.

For you urge me, nay, advise me, to give up guarding the martyrs, which I have been ordered to do unceasingly on the spot, and make for the court, since a week's absence is reported as likely to turn out to my disadvantage. But this cannot be averted, not only as far as sojourning at court is concerned, but even as to the journey necessary to reach the court, especially by me who both because of the difficulties of the way and my feeble bodily health have seldom been able to get from Aachen to the shrines of the martyrs in less than a week. But now I ask and urgently pray that you read again and understand what I wrote to you, and disdain not to write back to me, as I some time ago asked in my letter, what you may think best as to that revelation and the orders by which I am bound. There will be no lack of messengers if you wish to send what you write to my Deputy, Bonottus. I hope that you will always flourish in the Lord, most dear and loving brother and lord.

53. To the Monks of Seligenstadt (834-840).

In the name of the most high God. [Einhard], a sinner, to the beloved monks abiding in the monastery of Christ's blessed martyrs, Marcellinus and Peter, everlasting salvation in the Lord.

Be it known to your fraternity that with the help of the Lord I am safe and sound, and desire to read and know the same about you. And I admonish your fraternity to see to it diligently that you remember me as you have promised before the holy martyrs, my patron saints, whom you have the duty of serving daily, that the Lord in loving kindness may grant me to find you safe through their intercession ... I exhort you, therefore, with fatherly solicitude, beloved brethren, to be mindful of your promise, and ever solicitously to take care to commend yourselves to the Lord and his saints, that the ancient enemy [Satan] may not be able to snare you or by any cleverness lead you astray. Constantly intent upon the praise of God and ... and obedience, attending the churches of God, and helping each other ... , bearing one another's burdens, shall you be able to more easily win the eternal kingdom here ... through the favor of Christ and his holy martyrs. With these ... are, I speak according to the Apostle, priests of Christ, with all honor and diligence ... an example to the younger monks ... days that shall come in kindness ... one another ... and gladly persist to the joys of Easter, by divine grace ... study to keep your ... as I have given them to you. And devote yourselves to showing all obedience to your vows and all diligence, that your honor may be unsullied in the future, and the profit of your souls show vast increase from day to day by the Lord's help. May your holy fraternity prosper and flourish ... my loving brethren.

And let this my letter be solemnly read before all the monks, and its dictates obeyed.

54. To Bishop James (before 840).

To the most revered Bishop James, reverend in Christ, Einhard, a sinner.

This cleric, Otmar by name, has brought me a letter from your holiness in which you ask me to give this same cleric permission to abide with you, though he was born and brought up in this region, and after considering the character of the case I have decided to comply with your request in such a fashion that this same cleric shall have permission to abide with you as you ask, along with his brothers and mother, but shall pay his dues each year at Saint-Servais [of Maastricht], as has been appointed by our brethren. And the matter of the ordination of this same cleric shall be in your hands to do whatever you think best about it. For you are conversant with his morals and speech, and know whether he is fit to take some holy order upon himself. I hope your holiness will keep me in remembrance and always flourish in Christ.

55. To the Priest Liuthard and the Deputy Erembert (before 840).

In the name of Christ. Abbot Einhard to his faithful priest Liuthard and his Deputy Erembert, greetings in the Lord.

Be it known to you that we have enjoined upon Willibald our faithful priest, as we believe, to receive our dues from our vassals both at Saint-Bavon and at the monastery of Blandin [near Ghent]. Therefore we send him to you because we wish you to aid him in receiving the same dues both fully and in good money; and when he has received them, we wish you to aid him in the opportunity to bring them to us. I hope you will ever flourish in the Lord.

56. To a Deputy (before 840).

In the name of Christ, Einhard, the abbot, to N., greetings in the Lord.

I notify you that we need wax for our service, and cannot procure any in these regions because there has been but a small production of honey these last two years in this country. Therefore I wish you to consider and arrange with N. to have, if it is possible, a donkey load come with our vassals who are returning to us from those parts after the feast of Saint Bavon. Fare you well and pray for us.

57. To his Disciple Vussin (before 840).

To my dear son Vussin, greeting in the Lord.

For I fear and am very much afraid, my son, that having left the fold you may not be able to help forgetting yourself and me. For immature youth, unless restrained by the bridle of discipline, finds it hard to keep to the way of righteousness. Therefore, my child, study to emulate the upright, and offend in no way him whom I have always been urging you to follow. Mindful of your profession, lay hold upon learning his commands and all that he approves to whom you have committed your whole self. Taught by this and trained in the practice of it, you will lack none of the benefits of life's knowledge. As I have said to you in conversation, cultivate eagerness to learn, and leave nothing untouched that you can acquire of the grand branches of knowledge from the brilliant and copious ability of the speaker. Above all, remember to emulate the uprightness in which he excels, for language and rhetoric and the other branches of liberal knowledge are vain things and harmful to the servants of God, unless by divine grace they are seen to be the basis of good character. For "knowledge puffs up, but charity edifies." I would rather see you dead than puffed up and teeming with sins. For the Savior directed us to learn not the miracles he did but gentleness and humbleness of heart. Why continue? You have often heard me say these things and others of the sort. May you some day delight in those things by which through God's help purity of heart and body is attained.

I send you, therefore, such obscure words and names from the books of Vitruvius [on ancient architecture] as happened to occur to me for the moment, that you may seek a knowledge of them from the same place. And I believe that the greater part of them can be made clear to you through the little box which Master E. made with ivory pillars after the fashion of ancient works. And with regard to what Vitruvius calls perspective look up what Virgil calls a stage-setting in the third book of the Georgics. He says:

[How] it is pleasant [to lead the solemn procession]
To the shrines, and see the slain bullocks,

Or how the stage-setting shifts as the side scenes are turned,
And how the Britons woven into it raise the crimson curtain.

Farewell.

58. To a Monk and Good Friend (before 840).

To his beloved brother and very dear friend N., Einhard wishes eternal salvation in the Lord.

Count N. has asked me to beg you to allow him to keep those pigs that you sent to his territory to feed until they become fatter and healthier and he can buy them for the Lord's service at a fair price. For, knowing of our friendship, he thought I could obtain this from you, and I, confident in your affection, ask that you will not disdain to comply with his wish in this matter. I hope you will ever prosper in the Lord.

59. To a Monk (before 840).

Einhard to his beloved brother N., greeting in the Lord.

I wish you would order Egmunel in my name to make me sixty square tiles measuring two feet on each side and four inches thick, and two hundred smaller ones measuring ten inches each way and three inches thick. I send you word by this man about the sorrel seed which I wish you would have sown in a wide place. It is wont to grow into a large crop. Farewell.

60. To a Vassal (before 840).

In the name of Christ. Einhard, the abbot, greeting to our faithful man.

You know that according to my ability I have taken pains to comply with your wish in causing your daughter to be returned to you. Therefore I ask you for the honor and love of Saint-N. and of me to agree with me in this, that, if I get that man made free, you will allow him to receive this same daughter of yours in marriage, because it seems to me better that she be united again to that man if he is made free than that she be rejected by all men. Farewell.

61. To R. (before 840).

Einhard to his dear son R., eternal salvation in the Lord.

The man you sent to me came on the twenty-third of August, and since you wrote that you had no doubt of his fidelity I have not hesitated to entrust to him everything that I wanted to have reach you. For I judge it better to trust to a faithful man than to paper, for if a paper or parchment slips from the bearer, everything secret that it contains is disclosed, but a trusty messenger will not betray his trust even under torture. All, therefore, that I should have wished to say to you if you were present, I have indicated in an intimate way to your faithful man, whom I have found devoted to you and faithful in all things, especially because he neither concealed nor evaded anything of what you charged him to say. I hope you are well.

62. To a Vassal (before 840).

In the name of Christ. Einhard, a humble abbot, to one faithful and beloved, eternal salvation in Christ.

I doubt not that you remember how you committed yourself and yours to me, and since your own will decreed that it be so, it is my duty in turn, whenever opportunity arises, to give you and yours worthy support in every way so far as I know how and have the ability. Be it known, therefore, to your beloved self that that vassal of ours and your daughter desire with the Lord's favor and your consent to obtain each other as man and wife. Therefore I have determined to send to you messengers to inform you that it seems suitable to the mother and brother and all the relatives, if it is your pleasure, that it be done. Moreover I not only wish that it be confirmed, but if you give me authority to carry it through, I desire in honorable fashion as quickly as may be, to provide worthily both in the matter of benefices and of other things. Moreover this same vassal will give the dowry and is increasing the gifts, and the only thing left is that you should either come yourself without delay to conclude the matter now or give me permission to conclude it. For we know what with God's favor we can do at the present moment, but what a day may bring forth we know not. Hence it is written, let not your hand nor your foot be idle, but do with all your might what your hand finds to do. Saying no more on this, therefore, I will ask you to hasten to inform me about this matter by letter through this messenger ... Fare you well ... [in] Christ.

63. To a Bishop (before 840).

To the holy and deservedly revered lord, N., priest of the most high God, Einhard, a sinner.

This vassal, Agantheo by name, is my relative, and has been for some time in my service, but in as much as he now desires to pass his days under your dominion, my humble self is pleased that he has chosen to be in a place of such friendly relations to me, and I have therefore determined to give him this letter of recommendation, that through my intervention he may have easier access to your holiness and may find a home with you because I declare him to be related to me. I beg you, therefore, to deign to receive him, and take him into your service. I think you will not find him an unprofitable servitor. I hope you will ever prosper in the Lord.

64. To a Bishop (before 840).

Einhard to the deservedly revered lord N.

Because of a scarcity of ministers of the altar, necessity forces me to petition your holiness to deign to ordain this cleric, N. by name, as a deacon. For not only in age but also in learning he is suitable for this. Therefore I send him to your kind presence, that we may receive him back consecrated by you in the aforesaid rank. I hope you will always flourish in the Lord.

65. To an Unnamed Person (before 840).

To his beloved and revered brother in Christ, N., Einhard wishes everlasting salvation in the Lord.

... of my man N .... are ready ... your pigs. For thus I have been told, and in as much as this same N. has long served me devotedly and faithfully, I ask your dear self, so far as it can be done, to deign to spare him in the matter of that composition for which he is in debt to you by law; that I may find him useful for my service and you may justly find me ever more ready and eager to do your bidding. I hope you will always prosper.

66. Blessings for a Monarch (before 840).

Einhard may have composed this royal acclamation for Louis the Pious's full return to imperial power on 2 February 835, the feast of the Purification of the Blessed Virgin, at Thionville.

A lowly person presumes to offer to the loving kindness of a splendid lord some pieces of prayer. These are so many chants and other prayers to follow the Purification of the Blessed Virgin. So may the King immortal give you safety in the present life, and cause you to rejoice with his saints in glory celestial forever!

The hand that through the loving kindness of God reigns over life forever raised up the Key-bearer that he might not be drowned in the sea.

Questions: How were letters sent in the ninth century? In what ways did Einhard use letters to manage his properties? As a royal functionary, what was Einhard's role in the years between 830 and 834? How were benefices changing hands and how did this involve Einhard? Do we have in letter 39a an indication of Einhard's deep love and affection for Emma? Is there a change in his attitude towards his saints between 828 and 836? What are the material and social conditions of Einhard's world as seen through his letters?

Holy Women

A nineteenth-century drawing [after Vétault] of Saint Paula and her followers, books and scrolls in hand, as they receive instruction from Saint Jerome (who is not shown). The original scene was painted by a Turonian artist in 845 in the Vivian Bible. The flowing garments and headdress may be the typical dress of Carolingian noble women, since we see the same worn by Charles the Bald's queen in the Bible of San Paolo Fuori le Mura.

42. Rudolf of Fulda, *The Life of Saint Leoba*

Einhard may have imported into Francia the bones of foreign saints, but other Carolingian writers looked closer to home for native saints. The early Carolingian and Merovingian periods now received at the hands of Carolingian writers their own hagiographic histories. Hincmar of Rheims, for instance, documented the career of Saint Remi, while Lupus of Ferrières composed accounts of the lives of Saint Maximin and Saint Wigbert, and Walahfrid Strabo wrote a Life of Saint Gallus. Rudolf, who wrote this Life of Saint Leoba about 835, was a disciple of Hrabanus Maurus. Leoba had been the abbess of Bischofsheim near Mainz and died in 779. Rudolf's account is interesting not only for the information it gives us about a female saint and her public and political importance, but also for his attitude towards the reliability of information about recent history.

Source: trans. C.H. Talbot, in The Anglo-Saxon Missionaries in Germany: Being the Lives of SS. Willibrord, Boniface, Sturm, Leoba and Lebuin, together with the Hodoeporicon of St. Willibald and a Selection from the Correspondence of St. Boniface (New York: Sheed and Ward, 1954), pp.205-226; reprinted with permission.

The small book which I have written about the life and virtues of the holy and revered virgin Leoba has been dedicated to you, O Hadamout, virgin of

Christ, in order that you may have something to read with pleasure and imitate with profit. Thus by the help of Christ's grace you may eventually enjoy the blissful reward of him whose spouse you now are. Most earnestly do I beg you and all the nuns who unceasingly invoke the name of the Lord to pray for me, so that I, Rudolf, a monk of Fulda and a wretched sinner, in spite of my unworthiness to share the fellowship of the elect of God, may through the merits of those who are pleasing to Him receive pardon of my sins and escape the penalties due to them.

[Prologue]

Before I begin to write the life of the blessed and venerable virgin Leoba, I invoke her spouse, Christ, our Lord and Savior, who gave her the courage to overcome the powers of evil, to inspire me with eloquence sufficient to describe her outstanding merits. I have been unable to discover all the facts of her life. I shall therefore recount the few that I have learned from the writings of others, venerable men who heard them from four of her disciples, Agatha, Thecla, Nana, and Eoloba. Each one copied them down according to his ability and left them as a memorial to posterity.

One of these, a holy priest and monk named Mago, who died about five years ago, was on friendly terms with these women and during his frequent visits to them used to speak with them about things profitable to the soul. In this way he was able to learn a great deal about her life. He was careful to make short notes of everything he heard, but, unfortunately, what he left was almost unintelligible, because, whilst he was trying to be brief and succinct, he expressed things in such a way as to leave the facts open to misunderstanding and provide no basis for certainty. This happened, in my opinion, because in his eagerness to take down every detail before it escaped his memory he wrote the facts down in a kind of shorthand and hoped that during his leisure he could put them in order and make the book more easy for readers to understand. The reason why he left everything in such disorder, jotted down on odd pieces of parchment, was that he died quite suddenly and had no time to carry out his purpose.

Therefore it is not from presumption but in obedience to the command of my venerable father and master, Abbot Hrabanus, that I have tried to collect together all the scattered notes and papers left by the men I have mentioned. The sequence of events, which I have attempted to reconstruct for those who are interested in knowing them, is based on the information found in their notes and on evidence I have gathered from others by word of mouth. For there are several religious men still living who can vouch for the facts mentioned in the documents, since they heard them from their predecessors, and who can add some others worthy of remembrance. These latter appeared to me suitable for inclusion in the book and therefore I have combined them with material from the written notes. You will see, then, that I have not only recognized and completed the work set on foot by others but have written something on my own account. For it seems to me that there should be no doubt in the minds of the faithful about the veracity of the statements made in this book, since they are shown to be true both by the blameless character of those who relate them and by the miracles which are frequently performed at the shrine of the saint.

But before I begin the narration of her remarkable life and virtues, it may not be out of place if I mention a few of the many things I have heard about her spiritual mistress and mothers, who first introduced her to the spiritual life and fostered in her a desire for heaven. In this way the reader who is made aware of the qualities of this great woman may give credence to the achievements of the disciple more easily the more clearly he sees that she learned the elements of the spiritual life from so noble a mistress.

In the island of Britain, which is inhabited by the English nation, there is a place called Wimbourne, an ancient name which may be translated "Wine-stream". It received this name from the clearness and sweetness of the water there, which was better than any other in that land. In olden times the kings of that nation had built two monasteries in the place, one for men, the other for women, both surrounded by strong and lofty walls and provided with all the necessities that prudence could devise. From the beginning of the foundation the rule firmly laid down for both was that no entrance should be allowed to a person of the other sex. No woman was permitted to go into the men's community, nor was any man allowed into the women's, except in the case of priests who had to celebrate Mass in their churches; even so, immediately after the function was ended the priest had to withdraw. Any woman who wished to renounce the world and enter the cloister did so on the understanding that she would never leave it. She could only come out if there was a reasonable cause and some great advantage accrued to the monastery. Furthermore, when it was necessary to conduct the business of the monastery and to send for something outside, the superior of the community spoke through a window and only from there did she make decisions and arrange what was needed.

It was over this monastery, in succession to several other abbesses and spiritual mistresses, that a holy virgin named Tetta was placed in authority, a woman of noble family (for she was a sister of the king), but more noble in her conduct and good qualities. Over both the monasteries she ruled with consummate prudence and discretion. She gave instruction by deed rather than by words, and whenever she said that a certain course of action was harmful to the salvation of souls she showed by her own conduct that it was to be shunned. She maintained discipline with such circumspection (and the discipline there was much stricter than anywhere else) that she would never allow her nuns to approach clerics. She was so anxious that the nuns, in whose company she always remained, should be cut off from the company of men that she denied entrance into the community not merely to laymen and clerics but even to bishops. There are many instances of the virtues of this woman which the virgin Leoba, her disciple, used to recall with pleasure when she told her reminiscences. Of these I will mention but two examples, so that from these the rest may be conjectured.

In that convent there was a certain nun who, because of her zeal for discipline and strict observance, in which she surpassed the other, was often appointed prioress and frequently made one of the mistresses. But as she was too incautious and indiscreet in enforcing discipline over those under her care, she aroused their resentment, particularly among the younger members of the community. Though she could easily have mollified them and met their criticisms, she hardened her heart against taking such a course of action and went so far in her inflexibility that even at the end of her life she would not trouble to soften their hearts by asking their pardon. So in this stubborn frame of mind she died and was buried; and when the earth had been heaped over her, as the custom is, a tomb was raised over her grave. But this did not appease the feelings of the young nuns who hated her, and as soon as they saw the place where she was buried they reviled her cruelty and even climbed on to her tomb, as if to stamp upon her corpse, uttering bitter curses over her dead body to assuage their outraged feelings. Now when this came to the ears of the venerable abbess of the community she reprehended the young nuns for their presumption and vigorously corrected them. She went to the grave and noticed that in some extraordinary way the earth which had been heaped over the corpse had subsided and lay about six inches below the surface of the surrounding ground. This sight struck her with great fear. She understood from the subsidence of the ground how the dead woman had been punished, and judged the severity of God's sentence upon her from the sinking of the grave. She therefore called all the sisters together and began to reproach them for their cruelty and hardness of heart. She upbraided them for failing to forgive the wrongs they had suffered and for harboring ill feelings on account of the momentary bitterness caused by harsh discipline. She told them that one of the fundamental principles of Christian perfection is to be peaceable with those who dislike peace, whereas they, far from loving their enemies as God had commanded, not only hated their sister whilst she was alive but even pursued her with their curses now that she was dead. She counseled them to lay aside their resentment, to accept the ill-treatment they had received, and to show without delay their forgiveness: if they wished their own sins to be forgiven by God they should forgive others from the bottom their hearts. She begged them to forget any wrongs inflicted by the dead woman before her death and to join with her in prayer that God, in His mercy, would absolve her from her sins. When they had all agreed to follow her advice, she ordered them to fast for three days and to give themselves earnestly to watching, prayer, and the recitation of Psalms for the repose of her soul.

At the end of the fast on the third day she went with all the nuns into the church, singing litanies and invoking the Lord and His saints; and after she had prostrated herself before the altar she prayed for the soul of the deceased sister. And as she persevered in prayer, the hole in the grave, which previously had appeared to be empty, suddenly began to fill in and the ground rose, so that the moment she got up from her knees the grave became level with the surface of the ground. By this it was made clear that when the grave returned to its normal state the soul of the deceased sister, through the prayers of Tetta, had been absolved by divine power.

On another occasion it happened that when the sister who looked after the chapel went to close the door of the church before going to bed after Compline she lost all the keys in the darkness. There were very many of them belonging to various things locked away in the treasury of the church, some of silver, others of bronze or iron, all fastened together with a metal clasp. When she rose at the sound of the bell for Matins and could not find the keys for opening the doors of the church, she lit a candle and carefully searched all the places in which there was any hope of finding them; and as if one search was not enough, she went over the same ground again and again looking for them. When she had done this several times without success, she went to the abbess, who as usual had anticipated the hour for the night office and was deep in prayer, whilst the others were still at rest. Trembling with fear, the nun threw herself at the feet of the abbess and humbly confessed the negligence of which she was guilty. As soon as the abbess heard it she felt convinced that it was the work of the Devil, and, calling the sisters together, she recited Matins and Lauds in another building. When this was ended, they all gave themselves to prayer. At once the wickedness of the old enemy was brought to light, for, whilst they were still at prayer, a little dead fox was suddenly seen at the doors of the chapel holding the keys in his mouth, so that what had been given up as lost was found. Then the venerable mother took the keys and ordered the doors to be opened; and going into the church accompanied by the nuns, who at that time were about fifty in number, she gave thanks to God in hymns and praise for mercifully hearing His servants who had trusted in Him and for putting the wicked spirit to confusion. For he who had said "I will set my throne higher than God's stars" was transformed for his pride into a beast, and he who would not humbly submit to God was unmasked as a fox through the prayers of the nuns and made to look foolish.

Let these instances of the virtues of the venerable mother Tetta suffice. We will now pursue our purpose of describing the life of her spiritual daughter, Leoba the virgin.

[The Life of Saint Leoba]

As we have already said, her parents were English, of noble family and full of zeal for religion and the observance of God's commandments. Her father was called Dynno, her mother Aebba. But as they were barren, they remained together for a long time without children. After many years had passed and the onset of old age had deprived them of all hope of offspring, her mother had a dream in which she saw herself bearing in her bosom a church bell, which on being drawn out with her hand rang merrily. When she woke up she called her old nurse to her and told her what she had dreamt. The nurse said to her: "We shall yet see a daughter from your womb and it is your duty to consecrate her straightway to God. And as Anna offered Samuel to serve God all the days of his life in the temple, so you must offer her, when she has been taught the Scripture from her infancy, to serve Him in holy virginity as long as she shall live." Shortly after the woman had made this vow she conceived and bore a daughter, whom she called Thrutgeba, surnamed Leoba because she was beloved, for this is what Leoba means. And when the child had grown up her mother consecrated her and handed her over to Mother Tetta to be taught the sacred sciences. And because the nurse had foretold that she should have such happiness, she gave her her freedom.

The girl, therefore, grew up and was taught with such care by the abbess and all the nuns that she had no interests other than the monastery and the pursuit of sacred knowledge. She took no pleasure in aimless jests and wasted no time on girlish romances, but, fired by the love of Christ, fixed her mind always on reading or hearing the Word of God. Whatever she heard or read she committed to memory, and put all that she learned into practice. She exercised such moderation in her use of food and drink that she eschewed dainty dishes and the allurements of sumptuous fare, and was satisfied with whatever was placed before her. She prayed continually, knowing that in the Epistles the faithful are counseled to pray without ceasing. When she was not praying she worked with her hands at whatever was commanded her, for she had learned that he who will not work should not eat. However, she spent more time in reading and listening to Sacred Scripture than she gave to manual labor. She took great care not to forget what she had heard or read, observing the commandments of the Lord and putting into practice what she remembered of them. In this way she so arranged her conduct that she was loved by all the sisters. She learned from all and obeyed them all, and by imitating the good qualities of each one she modeled herself on the continence of one, the cheerfulness of another, copying here a sister's mildness, there a sister's patience. One she tried to equal in attention to prayer, another in devotion to reading. Above all, she was intent on practicing charity, without which, as she knew, all other virtues are void. When she had succeeded in fixing her attention on heavenly things by these and other practices in the pursuit of virtue she had a dream in which one night she saw a purple thread issuing from her mouth. It seemed to her that when she took hold of it with her hand and tried to draw it out there was no end to it; and as if it were coming from her very bowels, it extended little by little until it was of enormous length. When her hand was full of thread and it still issued from her mouth she rolled it round and round and made a ball of it. The labor of doing this was so tiresome that eventually, through sheer fatigue, she woke from her sleep and began to wonder what the meaning of the dream might be. She understood quite clearly that there was some reason for the dream, and it seemed that there was some mystery hidden in it. Now there was in the same monastery an aged nun who was known to possess the spirit of prophecy, because other things that she had foretold had always been fulfilled. As Leoba was diffident about revealing the dream to her, she told it to one of her disciples just as it had occurred and asked her to go to the old nun and describe it to her as a personal experience and learn from her the meaning of it. When the sister had repeated the details of the dream as if it had happened to her, the nun, who could foresee the future, angrily replied: "This is indeed a true vision and presages that good will come. But why do you lie to me in saying that such things happened to you? These matters are no concern of yours: they apply to the beloved chosen by God." In giving this name, she referred to the virgin Leoba. "These things," she went on, "were revealed to the person whose holiness and wisdom make her a worthy recipient, because by her teaching and good example she will confer benefits on many people. The thread which came from her bowels and issued from her mouth, signifies the wise counsels that she will speak from the heart. The fact that it filled her hand means that she will carry out in her actions whatever she expresses in her words. Furthermore, the ball which she made by rolling it round and round signifies the mystery of the divine teaching, which is set in motion by

the words and deeds of those who give instruction and which turns earth-
wards through active works and heavenwards through contemplation, at one
time swinging downwards through compassion for one's neighbor, again
swinging upwards through the love of God. By these signs God shows that
your mistress will profit many by her words and example, and the effect of
them will be felt in other lands afar off whither she will go." That this
interpretation of the dream was true later events were to prove.

At the time when the blessed virgin Leoba was pursuing her quest for
perfection in the monastery the holy martyr Boniface was being ordained by
Gregory, Bishop of Rome and successor to Constantine, in the Apostolic See.
His mission was to preach the Word of God to the people in Germany.
When Boniface found that the people were ready to receive the faith and
that, though the harvest was great, the laborers who worked with him were
few, he sent messengers and letters to England, his native land, summoning
from different ranks of the clergy many who were learned in the divine law
and fitted both by the character and good works to preach the Word of God.
With their assistance he zealously carried out the mission with which he was
charged, and by sound doctrine and miracles converted a large part of Germany to the faith. As the days went by, multitudes of people were instructed
in the mysteries of the faith and the Gospel was preached not only in the
churches but also in the towns and villages. Thus the Catholics were strengthened in their belief by constant exhortation, the wicked submitted to correction, and the heathen, enlightened by the Gospel, flocked to receive the grace
of baptism. When the blessed man saw that the church of God was increasing
and that the desire of perfection was firmly rooted he established two means
by which religious progress should be ensured. He began to build monasteries, so that the people would be attracted to the church not only by the
beauty of its religion but also by the communities of monks and nuns. And
as he wished the observance in both cases to be kept according to the Holy
Rule, he endeavored to obtain suitable superiors for both houses. For this
purpose he sent his disciple Sturm, a man of noble family and sterling character, to Monte Cassino, so that he could study the regular discipline, the
observance and the monastic customs which had been established there by
Saint Benedict. As the future superior, he wished him to become a novice
and in this way learn in humble submission how to rule over others. Likewise, he sent messengers with letters to the abbess Tetta, of whom we have
already spoken, asking her to send Leoba to accompany him on this journey
and to take part in this embassy: for Leoba's reputation for learning and
holiness had spread far and wide and her praise was on everyone's lips. The
abbess Tetta was exceedingly displeased at her departure, but because she
could not gainsay the dispositions of divine providence she agreed to his
request and sent Leoba to the blessed man. Thus it was that the interpretation of the dream which she had previously received was fulfilled. When
she came, the man of God received her with the deepest reverence, holding
her in great affection, not so much because she was related to him on his
mother's side as because he knew that by her holiness and wisdom she would
confer many benefits by her word and example.

In furtherance of his aims he appointed persons in authority over the
monasteries and established the observance of the Rule: he placed Sturm as

abbot over the monks and Leoba as abbess over the nuns. He gave her the monastery at the place called Bischofsheim, where there was a large community of nuns. These were trained according to her principles in the discipline of monastic life and made such progress in her teaching that many of them afterwards became superiors of others, so that there was hardly a convent of nuns in that part which had not one of her disciples as abbess. She was a woman of great virtue and was so strongly attached to the way of life she had vowed that she never gave thought to her native country or her relatives. She expended all her energies on the work she had undertaken in order to appear blameless before God and to become a pattern of perfection to those who obeyed her in word and action. She was ever on her guard not to teach others what she did not carry out herself. In her conduct there was no arrogance or pride; she was no distinguisher of persons, but showed herself affable and kindly to all. In appearance she was angelic, in word pleasant, clear in mind, great in prudence, Catholic in faith, most patient in hope, universal in her charity. But though she was always cheerful, she never broke out into laughter through excessive hilarity. No one ever heard a bad word from her lips; the sun never went down upon her anger. In the matter of food and drink she always showed the utmost understanding for others but was most sparing in her own use of them. She had a small cup from which she used to drink and which, because of the meager quantity it would hold, was called by the sisters "the Beloved's little one." So great was her zeal for reading that she discontinued it only for prayer or for the refreshment of her body with food or sleep: the Scriptures were never out of her hands. For, since she had been trained from infancy in the rudiments of grammar and the study of the other liberal arts, she tried by constant reflection to attain a perfect knowledge of divine things so that through the combination of her reading with her quick intelligence, by natural gifts and hard work, she became extremely learned. She read with attention all the books of the Old and New Testaments and learned by heart all the commandments of God. To these she added by way of completion the writings of the church Fathers, the decrees of the councils, and the whole of ecclesiastical law. She observed great moderation in all her acts and arrangements and always kept the practical end in view, so that she would never have to repent of her actions through having been guided by impulse. She was deeply aware of the necessity for concentration of mind in prayer and study, and for this reason took care not to go to excess either in watching or in other spiritual exercises. Throughout the summer both she and all the sisters under her rule went to rest after the midday meal, and she would never give permission to any of them to stay up late, for she said that lack of sleep dulled the mind, especially for study. When she lay down to rest, whether at night or in the afternoon, she used to have the Sacred Scriptures read out at her bedside, a duty which the younger nuns carried out in turn without grumbling. It seems difficult to believe, but even when she seemed to be asleep they could not skip over any word or syllable whilst they were reading without her immediately correcting them. Those on whom this duty fell used afterwards to confess that often when they saw her becoming drowsy they made a mistake on purpose to see if she noticed it, but they were never able to escape undetected. Yet it is not surprising that she could not be deceived even in her sleep, since He who keeps watch over Israel and neither slumbers nor sleeps possessed her heart, and she was able to say with the spouse in the Song of Songs: "I sleep, but my heart watcheth."

She preserved the virtue of humility with such care that, though she had been appointed to govern others because of her holiness and wisdom, she believed in her heart that she was the least of all. This she showed both in her speech and behavior. She was extremely hospitable. She kept open hours for all without exception, and even when she was fasting gave banquets and washed the feet of the guests with her own hands, at once the guardian and the minister of the practice instituted by our Lord.

Whilst the virgin of Christ was acting in this way and attracting to herself everyone's affection, the Devil, who is the foe of all Christians, viewed with impatience her own great virtue and the progress made by her disciples. He therefore attacked them constantly with evil thoughts and temptations of the flesh, trying to turn some of them aside from the path they had chosen. But when he saw that all his efforts were brought to naught by their prayers, fasting, and chaste lives, the wily tempter turned his attention to other means, hoping at least to destroy their good reputation, even if he could not break down their integrity by his foul suggestions.

There was a certain poor little crippled girl, who sat near the gate of the monastery begging alms. Every day she received her food from the abbess's table, her clothing from the nuns, and all other necessities from them; these were given to her from divine charity. It happened that after some time, deceived by the suggestions of the Devil, she committed fornication, and when her appearance made it impossible for her to conceal that she had conceived a child she covered up her guilt by pretending to be ill. When her time came, she wrapped the child in swaddling clothes and cast it at night into a pool by the river which flowed through that place. In this way she added crime to crime, for she not only followed fleshly sin by murder, but also combined murder with the poisoning of the water. When day dawned, another woman came to draw water and, seeing the corpse of the child, was struck with horror. Burning with womanly rage, she filled the whole village with her uncontrollable cries and reproached the holy nuns with these indignant words: "Oh, what a chaste community! How admirable is the life of nuns, who beneath their veils give birth to children and exercise at one and the same time the function of mothers and priests, baptizing those to whom they have given birth. For, fellow-citizens, you have drawn off this water to make a pool, not merely for the purpose of grinding corn, but unwittingly for a new and unheard-of kind of baptism. Now go and ask those women, whom you compliment by calling them virgins, to remove this corpse from the river and make it fit for us to use again. Look for the one who is missing from the monastery and then you will find out who is responsible for this crime." At these words all the crowd was set in uproar and everybody, of whatever age or sex, ran in one great mass to see what had happened. As soon as they saw the corpse they denounced the crime and reviled the nuns. When the abbess heard the uproar and learned what was afoot she called the nuns together, told them the reason, and discovered that no one was absent except Agatha, who a few days before had been summoned to her parents' house on urgent business: but she had gone with full permission. A messenger was sent to her without delay to recall her to the monastery, as Leoba could not endure the accusation of so great a crime to hang over them. When Agatha returned and heard of the deed that was charged against her she fell on her knees and gazed up to heaven, crying: "Almighty God, who knowest all things before they come to pass, from whom nothing is hid and who hast delivered Susanna from false accusations when she trusted in Thee, show Thy mercy to this community gathered together in Thy name and let it not be besmirched by filthy rumors on account of my sins; but do Thou deign to unmask and make known for the praise and glory of Thy name the person who has committed this misdeed."

On hearing this, the venerable superior, being assured of her innocence, ordered them all to go to the chapel and to stand with their arms extended in the form of a cross until each one of them had sung through the whole psalter, then three times each day, at Tierce, Sext and Nones, to go round the monastic buildings in procession with the crucifix at their head, calling upon God to free them, in His mercy, from this accusation. When they had done this and they were going into the church at Nones, having completed two rounds, the blessed Leoba went straight to the altar and, standing before the cross, which was being prepared for the third procession, stretched out her hands towards heaven, and with tears and groans prayed, saying: "O Lord Jesus Christ, king of virgins, lover of chastity, unconquerable God, manifest thy power and deliver us from this charge, because the reproaches of those who reproached thee have fallen upon us." Immediately after she had said this, that wretched little woman, the dupe and the tool of the Devil, seemed to be surrounded by flames, and, calling out the name of the abbess, confessed to the crime she had committed. Then a great shout rose to heaven: the vast crowd was astounded at the miracle, the nuns began to weep with joy, and all of them with one voice gave expression to the merits of Leoba and of Christ our Savior.

So it came about that the reputation of the nuns, which the Devil had tried to ruin by his sinister rumor, was greatly enhanced, and praise was showered on them in every place. But that wretched woman did not deserve to escape scot-free and for the rest of her life she remained in the power of the Devil. Even before this God had performed many miracles through Leoba, but they had been kept secret. This one was her first in Germany, and, because it was done in public, it came to the ears of everyone.

On another occasion, when she sat down as usual to give spiritual instruction to her disciples, a fire broke out in a part of the village. As the houses have roofs of wood and thatch, they were soon consumed by the flames, and the conflagration spread with increasing rapidity towards the monastery, so that it threatened to destroy not only the buildings but also the men and beasts. Then could be heard the mingled shouts of the terrified villagers as they ran in a mob to the abbess and begged her to avert the danger which threatened them. Unruffled and with great self-control, she calmed their fears and, without being influenced by their trust in her, ordered them to take a bucket and bring some water from the upper part of the stream that flowed by the monastery. As soon as they had brought it, she took some salt which had been blessed by Saint Boniface and which she always kept by her, and sprinkled it in the water. Then she said: "Go and pour back this water into the river and then let all the people draw water lower down the stream and throw it on the fires." After they had done this the violence of the conflagration died down and the fire was extinguished just as if a flood had fallen from the skies. So the buildings were saved. At this miracle the whole crowd stood amazed and broke out into the praise of God, who through the faith and prayers of his handmaid had delivered them so extraordinarily from a terrible danger.

I think it should be counted amongst her virtues also that one day, when a wild storm arose and the whole sky was obscured by such dark clouds that day seemed turned into night, terrible lightning and falling thunderbolts stuck terror into the stoutest hearts and everyone was shaking with fear. At first the people drove their flocks into the houses for shelter so that they should not perish; then, when the danger increased and threatened them all with death, they took refuge with their wives and children in the church, despairing of their lives. They locked all the doors and waited there trembling, thinking that the last judgment was at hand. In this state of panic they filled the air with the din of their mingled cries. Then the holy virgin went out to them and urged them all to have patience. She promised them that no harm would come to them; and after exhorting them to join with her in prayer, she fell prostrate at the foot of the altar. In the meantime the storm raged, the roofs of the houses were torn off by the violence of the wind, the ground shook with the repeated shocks of the thunderbolts, and the thick darkness, intensified by the incessant flicker of lightning which flashed through the windows, redoubled their terror. Then the mob, unable to endure the suspense any longer, rushed to the altar to rouse her from prayer and seek her protection. Thecla, her kinswoman, spoke to her first, saying: "Beloved, all the hopes of these people lie in you: you are their only support. Arise, then, and pray to the Mother of God, your mistress, for us, that by her intercession we may be delivered from this fearful storm." At these words Leoba rose up from prayer and, as if she had been challenged to a contest, flung off the cloak which she was wearing and boldly opened the doors of the church. Standing on the threshold, she made a sign of the cross, opposing to the fury of the storm the name of the High God. Then she stretched out her hands towards heaven and three times invoked the mercy of Christ, praying that through the intercession of Holy Mary, the Virgin, He would quickly come to the help of his people. Suddenly God came to their aid. The sound of thunder died away, the winds changed direction and dispersed the heavy clouds, the darkness rolled back and the sun shone, bringing calm and peace. Thus did divine power make manifest the merits of his handmaid. Unexpected peace came to his people and fear was banished.

There was also another of her deeds which everyone agrees was outstanding and memorable, and which I think it would be wrong to pass over in silence. One of the sisters of the monastery named Williswind, of excellent character and edifying conduct, was attacked by a grave illness; she suffered from what the doctors call hemorrhoids, and through loss of blood from her privy parts was racked by severe pains of the bowel. As the ailment continued and increased from day to day in severity, her strength ebbed away until she could neither turn over on her side nor get out of bed and walk without leaning on someone else. When she was no longer able to remain in the common dormitory of the monastery because of the stench, her parents who lived close by asked and obtained permission for her to be taken on a litter to their house across the Tuberaha. Not long afterwards, as the sickness gained hold, she rapidly drew near her end. As the lower part of her body had lost all sense of feeling and she was barely able to breathe, the abbess was asked by her parents not to come and visit the sick nun but to pray to God for her happy decease. When Leoba came, she approached the bed, now surrounded by a weeping throng of neighbors, and ordered the covering to be removed, for the patient was already enveloped in a linen cloth, as corpses usually are. When it was taken away she placed her hand on her breast and said: "Cease your weeping, for her soul is still in her." Then she sent to the monastery and ordered them to bring the little spoon which she usually used at table; and when it was brought to her she blessed milk and poured it drop by drop down the throat of the sick nun. At its touch, her throat and vitals recovered; she moved her tongue to speak and began to look round. Next day she had made such progress that she was able to take food, and before the end of the week she walked on her own feet to the monastery, whence she had previously been carried on a litter. She lived for several years afterwards and remained in the service of God until the days of Louis [the Pious], king of the Franks, always strong and healthy, even after the death of Leoba.

The people's faith was stimulated by such tokens of holiness, and as religious feeling increased so did contempt of the world. Many nobles and influential men gave their daughters to God to live in the monastery in perpetual chastity; many widows also forsook their homes, made vows of chastity and took the veil in the cloister. To all of these the holy virgin pointed out both by word and example how to reach the heights of perfection.

In the meantime, blessed Boniface, the archbishop, was preparing to go to Frisia, having decided to preach the Gospel to this people riddled with superstition and unbelief. He summoned his disciple Lull to his presence (who was afterwards to succeed him as bishop) and entrusted everything to his care, particularly impressing on him a solicitude for the faithful, zeal for preaching the Gospel, and the preservation of the churches, which he had built in various places. Above all, he ordered him to complete the building of the monastery of Fulda which he had begun to construct in the wilderness of Bochonia, a work undertaken on the authority of Pope Zacharias and with the support of Carloman [Pepin the Short's brother], the king of Austrasia. This he did because the monks who lived there were poor and had no revenues and were forced to live on the produce of their own manual labour. He commanded him also to remove his body thither after his death. After giving these and other instructions, he summoned Leoba to him and exhorted her not to abandon the country of her adoption and not to grow weary of the life she had undertaken, but rather to extend the scope of the good work she had begun. He said that no consideration should be paid to her weakness and that she must not count the long years that lay ahead of her; she must not count the spiritual life to be hard nor the end difficult to attain, for the years of this life are short compared to eternity, and the sufferings of this world are as nothing in comparison with the glory that will be made manifest in the saints. He commended her to Lull and to the senior monks of the monastery who were present, admonishing them to care for her with reverence and respect and reaffirming his wish that after his death her bones should be placed next to his in the tomb, so that they who had served God during their lifetime with equal sincerity and zeal should await together the day of resurrection.

After these words he gave her his cowl and begged and pleaded with her not to leave her adopted land. And so, when all necessary preparations had been made for the journey, he set out for Frisia, where he won over a multitude of people to the faith of Christ and ended his labors with a glorious martyrdom. His remains were transported to Fulda and there, according to his previous wishes he was laid to rest with worthy token of respect. The blessed virgin, however, persevered unwaveringly in the work of God. She had no desire to gain earthly possessions but only those of heaven, and she spent all her energies on fulfilling her vows. Her wonderful reputation spread abroad and the fragrance of her holiness and wisdom drew to her the affections of all. She was held in veneration by all who knew her, even by kings. Pepin [the Short], king of the Franks, and his sons Charles [Charlemagne] and Carloman treated her with profound respect, particularly Charles, who, after the death of this father and brother, with whom he had shared the throne for some years, took over the reins of government [in 768]. He was a man of truly Christian life, worthy of the power he wielded and by far the bravest and wisest king that the Franks had produced. His love for the Catholic faith was so sincere that, though he governed all, he treated the servants and handmaids of God with touching humility. Many times he summoned the holy virgin to his court, received her with every mark of respect and loaded her with gifts suitable to their station. Queen Hildegard also revered her with a chaste affection and loved her as her own soul. She would have liked her to remain continually at her side so that she might progress in the spiritual life and profit by her words and example. But Leoba detested the life at court like poison. The princes loved her, the nobles received her, the bishops welcomed her with joy. And because of her wide knowledge of the Scriptures and her prudence in counsel they often discussed spiritual matters and ecclesiastical discipline with her. But her deepest concern was the work she had set on foot. She visited the various convents of nuns and, like a mistress of novices, stimulated them to vie with one another in reaching perfection.

Sometimes she came to the monastery of Fulda to say her prayers, a privilege never granted to any woman either before or since, because from the day that monks began to dwell there entrance was always forbidden to women. Permission was only granted to her, for the simple reason that the holy martyr Saint Boniface had commended her to the seniors of the monastery and because he had ordered her remains to be buried there. The following regulations, however, were observed when she came there. Her disciples and companions were left behind in a nearby cell and she entered the monastery always in daylight, with one nun older than the rest; and after she had finished her prayers and held a conversation with the monks, she returned towards nightfall to her disciples whom she had left behind in the cell. When she was an old woman and became decrepit through age she put all the convents under her care on a sound footing and then, on Bishop

Lull's advice, went to a place called Scoranesheim, four miles south of Mainz. There she took up residence with some of her nuns and served God night and day in fasting and prayer.

In the meantime, whilst King Charles was staying in the palace at Aachen, Queen Hildegard sent a message to her begging her to come and visit her, if it were not too difficult, because she longed to see her before she passed from this life. And although Leoba was not at all pleased, she agreed to go for the sake of their long-standing friendship. Accordingly she went and was received by the queen with her usual warm welcome. But as soon as Leoba heard the reason for the invitation she asked permission to return home. And when the queen importuned her to stay a few days longer she refused; but, embracing her friend rather more affectionately than usual, she kissed her on the mouth, the forehead, and the eyes and took leave of her with these words: "Farewell for evermore, my dearly beloved lady and sister; farewell most precious half of my soul. May Christ our creator and redeemer grant that we shall meet again without shame on the day of judgment. Never more on this earth shall we enjoy each other's presence."

So she returned to the convent, and after a few days she was stricken down by sickness and was confined to her bed. When she saw that her ailment was growing worse and that the hour of her death was near she sent for a saintly English priest named Torhthat, who had always been at her side and ministered to her with respect and love, and received from him the viaticum of the body and blood of Christ. Then she put off this earthly garment and gave back her soul joyfully to her Creator, clean and undefiled as she had received it from Him. She died in the month of September, the fourth of the Kalends of October. Her body, followed by a long cortege of noble persons, was carried by the monks of Fulda to their monastery with every mark of respect. Thus the seniors there remembered what Saint Boniface had said, namely, that it was his last wish that her remains should be placed next to his bones. But because they were afraid to open the tomb of the blessed martyr, they discussed the matter and decided to bury her on the north side of the altar which the martyr Saint Boniface had himself erected and consecrated in honor of our Savior and the twelve Apostles.

After some years, when the church had grown too small and was being prepared by its rectors for a future consecration, Abbot Eigil, with permission of Archbishop Heistulf, transferred her bones and placed them in the west porch near the shrine of Saint Ignatius the martyr, where, encased in a tomb, they rest glorious with miracles. For many who have approached her tomb full of faith have many times received divine favors. Some of these which occur to me at the moment I will set down plainly and truthfully for my readers.

A certain man had his arms so tightly bound by iron rings that the iron was almost covered by the bare flesh that grew up around it on either side. One of these had already come off one arm and had left a deep scar that was plain to see. This man came to the church and went round the shrines of the saints, praying at each altar. When he reached the tomb of the holy virgin Leoba and began to pray some hidden force expanded the iron ring and, breaking the clamps, cast it from his arm, leaving it all bloody. With joy and gladness he gave thanks to God, because by the merits of the blessed nun he, who until that moment had been bound in fetters on account of his sins, was released.

There was another man from Spain, who for his sins was so afflicted that he twitched most horribly in all his limbs. According to his own account he contracted this infirmity through bathing in the river Ebro. And because he could not bear his deformity to be seen by his fellow-citizens he wandered about from shrine to shrine, wherever he had a mind to go. After travelling the length of western Francia and Italy, he came to Germany. When he had visited several monasteries to pray there, he came to Fulda, where he was received into the pilgrim's hospice. He stayed three days there, going into the church and praying that God would be appeased and restore him to his former state of health. When he entered the chapel on the third day and had gone from altar to altar praying, he automatically came to the shrine of the holy virgin. He ended his prayer there and then went down to the western crypt above which the body of the holy martyr Boniface lies at rest. Prostrate in prayers, he lay like one asleep, but not twitching as he usually did when he slept. A saintly monk and priest name Firmandus, who used to sit there because he had an infirmity which prevented him from standing, noticed this and was struck with astonishment. He ordered those who wished to lift him not to touch him, but rather to wait to see what would happen. Suddenly the man got up and, because he was cured, he did not twitch. On being questioned by the priest, who, as an Italian, understood his language, he said that he had had an ecstasy in which he was a venerable old man, vested in a bishop's stole, accompanied by a young woman in a nun's habit, who had taken him by the hand, lifted him up and presented him to the bishop for his blessing. When the bishop had made the sign of the cross on his breast an inky-black bird like a raven had flown out of his bosom and through the hood of his tunic; as soon as it alighted on the ground it changed into a hen and then transformed itself into the shape of a very ugly and horrible little man, who emerged from the crypt by the steps of the north entrance. No Christian man can doubt that he was restored to health through the prayers of the holy virgin and the merits of the blessed martyr. The two, though they do not share a tomb, yet lie in one place and never fail to look on those who seek their intercession with the same kindliness now that they are in glory as they did when they lived on earth and showed pity and compassion on the wretched.

Many other marvels did God perform through the prayers of the holy virgin, but I will not mention them lest by prolonging my story I inflict tedium on the reader. But I recall these two, because several of the brethren who are still alive have borne witness in words that are not lightly to be disregarded that they saw them. I also was present when they occurred. I write this, then, for the praise and glory of the name of our Lord Jesus Christ, who glorifies those who glorify him and who grants to those who serve him not only the kingdom of heaven but also in this world nobility and honor. To whom be glory with the Father and the Holy Spirit for ever and ever, Amen.

Questions: For whose edification would such a hagiography have been written? Are there discernible differences between the daily lives and practices of nuns and monks?

To what extent was even Leoba a part of the politics of her day? What were Leoba's great virtues according to the hagiographer and what ideals and examples did he wish to promote? How did the people living near her convent regard Leoba? Why would Rudolf have written the Life of Leoba around 835?

43. The Final Days and Death of Louis the Pious

The last years of Louis the Pious remained unsettled and he died in 840 after a campaign against his rebellious son Louis the German. The following is the Astronomer's account.

Source: trans. A. Cabaniss, Son of Charlemagne: A Contemporary Life of Louis the Pious (Syracuse, New York: Syracuse University Press, 1961), pp.120-125; reprinted with permission.

62.2. With very great fatigue and with the aforesaid ailments assailing his health [old age and difficulty in breathing], he came to Aachen as the most holy Paschal solemnity [28 March 840] drew near and there observed it with accustomed devotion. He then hastened to complete the business undertaken. Crossing the Rhine, he penetrated Thuringia by forced march, where he learned that Louis [the German] was lingering. Since Louis's conscience would not suffer him to delay there longer seeing that his father was already at hand, he despaired of the effort and trusted to flight for safety. Obtaining passage he returned to his lands through the country of the Slavs. In the meanwhile the emperor ordered a general assembly to be gathered in the city of the Vangiones which is now called Worms. And since the affairs of Louis were thus in abeyance, his son Charles was returned with his mother to Aquitaine. The emperor sent his son Lothar to Italy, requiring him to take part in the assembly to deliberate with him and others about this matter.

62.3 At that time, on the third day of the Major Litany [5 May 840], a failure of the sun occurred in a preternatural manner. For at the sun's withdrawal, darkness prevailed to such an extent that nothing seemed to differ from true night. The fixed order of stars was perceived as though none of the heavenly bodies suffered from the vigor of sunlight. The moon, which had appeared over against the sun, moved little by little eastward, first restoring light to the sun on the western part like a horned crescent, according to its own fashion when the first or second phase is observed, and thus by growth the entire wheel of the sun again received its full beauty. Although this prodigy is attributable to nature, it was brought to completion with lamentable result. For it presaged that the great light of mortals which shone for all, a lampstand placed in God's house above (I refer to the emperor of most pious memory), would be very swiftly taken from human affairs and that the world would be left in darkness of tribulation at his departure.

62.4 He soon thereafter began to waste away with nausea and to receive food and drink with vomiting stomach, to be oppressed with wracking sighs, to shake with choking rattles, and thus to fail in strength. For when nature is deserted by its mainstays it is obvious that it is exhausted and vanquished.

Perceiving this he ordered summer campaign tents to be set for him on an island near the city of Mainz, where abandoned by his powers he committed himself to his bed.

63.1. Who may unfold the emperor's apprehension for the condition of the church or his grief for its agitation? Who is there to recount the flood of tears which he shed for the hastening of divine mercy? For he grieved not that he was to depart, but what he knew would come to pass, saying that he was wretched whose last days would close with such woes. There came to comfort him venerable prelates and many other servants of God, among whom were Hetti, revered bishop of Trier; Otgar, archbishop of Mainz; and Drogo, brother of the lord emperor, bishop of Metz, and archchaplain of the sacred palace. As near to him as the emperor knew that Drogo was, so much the more intimately he entrusted himself and all his possessions to Drogo. Through the same Drogo the emperor performed the duty of confession, "the sacrifice of a troubled spirit and a humbled heart," which God does not despise. Throughout the forty days the emperor's only food was the Lord's Body, as he praised the justice of God, saying: "Just art Thou, O Lord, since in the past I have not spent the season of Lent in fasting, I am now compelled to keep the same fast to thee."

63.2. He ordered that his venerable brother Drogo cause the ministers of his chamber to come before him and that he bid the household properties, the royal equipment to be described one by one, that is, crowns, arms, vessels, books, and clerical garments. The emperor gave instruction to Drogo, as seemed proper, what should be distributed to churches, to the poor, and lastly to his sons Lothar and Charles [Pepin had died in December 838 and Louis was in revolt]. He assigned to Lothar indeed a crown, and a sword encrusted with gold and gems, to be held on condition that he keep faith with Charles and Judith and that Lothar accord to Charles, and maintain, the full portion of the realm which, God and the nobles of the palace being witness, the emperor had bestowed upon Charles at the same time with Lothar and in his presence. When these matters had been duly accomplished, he gave thanks to God because he knew that nothing now remained his own.

63.3. During this transaction the venerable prelate Drogo and the other bishops were offering thanks to God that they should be edified by seeing him, whom the choir of virtues had always attended, now pursuing them steadfastly to the end like the tail of an animal and rendering all of his life "a sacrifice utterly acceptable to God." Yet their joy was darkened by his last will and testament. For fearing that he might choose to remain unreconciled to his son Louis, they knew that a wound often cut open or burned by cautery might generate a harsher pain for the one sustaining it. Relying nevertheless upon the unconquered patience which he always exercised, they kept playing gently on his mind through his brother Drogo, whose words the emperor was unwilling to spurn. At first he did display bitterness of mind. Considering for a while he tried, with what little breath was left, to speak of how many great inconveniences he had suffered from Louis and of what Louis should deserve for doing such things against nature and God's precept. "But," he said, "since he cannot come to me to make satisfaction, I now perform the satisfaction which is mine, with you and God in witness. I forgive him everything wherein he has sinned against me. It will be your duty to advise him that, if I have forgiven him things so often done wrongly, he may not forget that he was the one who led his father's grey hairs to death with sorrow and in such matters despised the precepts and warnings of God our common Father."

64.1. When these things had been done and said (it was on the evening of the sabbath), he ordered that the nocturnal vigils be celebrated before him and that his breast be fortified by the sign of the holy cross. As long as he was able, he repeatedly with his own hand sealed his forehead and breast with that sign. But when he became weary he asked with a nod that it be done by the hands of his brother Drogo. He remained therefore all that night stripped of bodily strength, possessed only of a rational mind. On the morrow, which was Sunday [20 June 840], he commanded the mystery of the altar to be made ready and the solemnities of Mass to be celebrated by Drogo. He also ordered that Holy Communion be given him by Drogo's hands according to custom, and that after this a little shallow of tepid drink be offered him. Sipping this he prayed his brother and those standing about to give attention to care of their bodies, that as long as he lingered so long should they be refreshed.

64.2. The moment of his departure being imminent, joining thumb with fingers (he had been accustomed to do this when he was summoning his brother with a nod), he called for his brother. Drogo approached with the other priests. The emperor, commending himself with what words he could and with nods, asked to be blessed and requested those things to be done which are wont to be done at the departure of a soul. As they did that, so many have related to me, he turned his eyes to the left side, as if offended, and with as much strength as he could muster he exclaimed twice, "Hutz! Hutz!" (which signified, "Avaunt!"). It is obvious that he saw a malign spirit whose fellowship he, living or dying, did not want to share. But with eyes lifted heavenward, the more threateningly he gazed hither, the more joyfully he strained thither, so that he seemed to differ not a whit from one laughing. In such a manner therefore he obtained the end of the present life and went away to rest happily, so we believe, because, as it has been said truthfully by a truth-speaking teacher: "He cannot die badly who has lived well."

64.3. He departed on the twelfth day before the Kalends of July in the sixty-fourth year of his life. He presided over Aquitaine throughout thirty-seven years, but he was emperor twenty-seven. His soul having withdrawn, Drogo, his brother and bishop of Metz, with the other bishops, abbots, counts, royal vassals, and a great throng of clergy and people took up the emperor's remains and caused them to be transferred with high honor to Metz and interred in a noble manner in the basilica of Saint Arnulf, where his mother was also buried.

Questions: What were Louis's final concerns? Did he leave the matter of his succession undetermined or had it long been clear that the brothers would have to fight for their pieces of the kingdom?

CHAPTER FOUR

THE TIME OF THE CIVIL WAR

(840–843)

Warriors

A nineteenth-century drawing [after Woltmann and Woermann] of the host of Joab, one of David's generals, as it marches upon a city of unbelievers. The ninth-century manuscript from which the drawing was made is the Golden Psalter of Saint-Gall and survives there today as Codex 22. Though the figures and story may be from the Old Testament, the dress and arms are typically Carolingian. The warriors wear chain mail, carry ninth-century spears, and rest their feet in stirrups. Even the fire-breathing dragon banner borne in front of the warriors was not unknown.

44. Nithard's History

Nithard was the son of Angilbert of Saint-Riquier and Charlemagne's daughter Bertha. As he tells us, he was asked by the young Charles the Bald in 841 to compose an account of Charles's time. The period between 840 and 842 was a particularly difficult time for Charles and his half-brother Louis the German as their brother Lothar actively campaigned for territorial and constitutional supremacy over his brothers. Lothar still hoped to achieve the imperial predominance promised to him in the 'Ordinatio imperii', but long since undermined by his father. Nithard's history is the most interesting and elegant history written in the ninth century, not only because Nithard was a participant in these turbulent events, but also because of Nithard's own changing attitude towards his world. Janet Nelson has argued that while the first three books were written for the king, the last was written by a disenchanted Nithard as a private history. What the reader should look for in Nithard's history is the distance between the historian's ideals and the actual events he sketches. For on the one side stand notions of fraternal concord, ideas about what constitutes a perfectly peaceful society, and the characterization of civil war as a trial by ordeal, while, on the other, stand desperate alliances, oaths such as the famous Oaths of Strasbourg, and the bloody battle of Fontenoy with its late-comers, non-combatants, and traitors.

Source: trans. B.W. Scholz with B. Rogers, in Carolingian Chronicles: Royal Frankish Annals and Nithard's Histories (Ann Arbor: The University of Michigan Press, 1970), pp.129-174; reprinted with permission.

[Book 1: 814-840]

When you [Charles the Bald] had innocently suffered your brother's persecutions for almost two years, as you, my lord, know best, you ordered me, before we entered the city of Châlons, to write the history of your time. This assignment, I confess, would have been pleasant and welcome if the press of events had allowed me time to do it justice. But if you find this work less ample or less polished than it should be, considering the importance of the events, you and your people owe me all the more forbearance since you know that as I wrote I was caught up in the same turmoil as you were.

I was inclined, it is true, to pass over events that occurred in the time of your pious father, but the real cause of your conflicts will become clearer to the reader if I begin by touching upon some matters known to have taken place in his time. Besides, it also seems highly inadvisable to omit altogether the venerable memory of your grandfather [Charlemagne], and therefore my story shall begin with him.

1. When Emperor Charles of blessed memory, rightfully called the Great by all nations, died at a ripe old age, about the third hour of the day, he left the whole of Europe flourishing. For in his time he was a man who so much excelled all others in wisdom and virtue that to everyone on earth he appeared both terrible and worthy of love and admiration. Thus, he made his whole reign in every way glorious and salutary, as was apparent to everyone. But above all I believe he will be admired for the tempered severity with

which he subdued the fierce and iron hearts of the Franks and barbarians. Not even Roman might had been able to tame these people, but they dared do nothing in Charles's empire except what was in harmony with the public welfare. He ruled happily as king for thirty-two years and held the helm of the empire with no less success for fourteen years.

2. Louis was the heir of all this excellence. He was the youngest of Charles's legitimate sons and succeeded to the throne after the death of the others. As soon as he had certain news of his father's death, he came straightway from Aquitaine to Aachen. No one objected when he asserted his authority over the nobles arriving on the scene but reserved judgment on those whose loyalty seemed doubtful. At the beginning of his rule as emperor he ordered the immense treasures left by his father to be divided into three parts, one part he spent on the funeral, the other two parts he divided between himself and those of his sisters who were born in lawful wedlock. He also ordered his sisters to remove themselves instantly from the palace to their monasteries. His brothers Drogo, Hugo, and Theoderic, who were still very young, he made companions of his table and ordered to be brought up in his palace. To his nephew Bernard, Pepin's son, he granted the kingdom of Italy. Since Bernard defected from Louis a little later, he was taken prisoner and deprived of his sight as well as his life by Bertmund, governor of the province of Lyons. From that time on Louis feared that his younger brothers might later stir up the people and behave like Bernard. He therefore had them appear before his general assembly, tonsured them, and put them under free custody into monasteries.

When this had been taken care of, he made his sons enter legal marriages and divided the whole empire among them so that Pepin was to have Aquitaine, Louis Bavaria, and Lothar, after his father's death, the whole empire. He also permitted Lothar to hold the title of emperor with him. In the meantime Queen Ermengard, their mother, died, and a short time later Emperor Louis married Judith, who gave birth to Charles [in 823].

3. After Charles's birth, Louis did not know what to do for him since he had already divided the whole empire among his other sons. When the distressed father begged their help on Charles's behalf, Lothar finally gave his assent and swore that his father should give to Charles whatever part of the kingdom he wished. He assured Louis by oath that in the future he would be Charles's protector and defender against all enemies. But after being incited by Hugo, whose daughter Lothar had married, Matfrid, and others, he later regretted what he had done and tried to undo it. This behavior did not in the least escape his father and Judith. So from then on Lothar secretly sought to destroy what his father had arranged. To help him counter Lothar's plot the father employed a man named Bernard, who was duke of Septimania. He appointed Bernard his chamberlain, entrusted Charles to him, and made him the second man in the empire. Bernard recklessly abused the imperial power which he was supposed to strengthen and undermined it entirely.

At that time Alemannia was handed over to Charles by decree. Lothar, as if he had at last found a good reason to complain, called upon his brothers and the whole people to restore authority and order in the empire [the revolt of 830]. They all suddenly converged on Louis at Compiègne, made the queen take the veil, tonsured her brothers, Conrad and Rudolf, and sent them to Aquitaine to be held by Pepin. Bernard took to his heels and escaped to Septimania. His brother Herbert was captured, blinded, and imprisoned in Italy. When Lothar had taken over the government, he held his father and Charles in free custody. He ordered monks to keep Charles company; they were to get him used to the monastic life and urge him to take it up himself.

But the state of the empire grew worse from day to day, since all were driven by greed and sought only their own advantage. On account of this the monks we have mentioned above, as well as other men who deplored what had happened, began to question Louis to see if he were willing to reconstruct the government and stand behind it if the kingdom were restored to him. Above all he was to promote religious worship, by which all order is protected and preserved. Since he readily accepted this, his restoration was quickly agreed upon. Louis chose Guntbald, a monk, and secretly sent him to his sons Pepin and Louis. Guntbald went ostensibly on religious business, but he promised that Louis would increase the kingdom of both Pepin and Louis if they would assist the men who wanted him back on the throne. The promise of more land made them only too eager to comply. An assembly was convoked, the queen and her brothers were returned to Louis, and the whole people submitted again to his rule. Then those who had been on Lothar's side were taken before the general assembly and either condemned to death or, if their lives were spared, sent into exile by Lothar himself. Lothar also had to be content with Italy alone and was permitted to go there only on the condition that in the future he would not attempt anything in the kingdom against his father's will.

When matters rested at this and there seemed to be a moment's respite, the monk Guntbald, whom we mentioned above, immediately wanted to be second in the empire because he had done so much for Louis's restoration. But Bernard, who had formerly held this position, as I said before, tried eagerly to regain it. Also Pepin and Louis, although their kingdoms had been enlarged as promised, nevertheless both tried hard to be first in the empire after their father. But those who were in charge of the government at that time resisted their desires.

4. At the same time Aquitaine was taken from Pepin and given to Charles, and the nobility which was on King Louis's side did homage to Charles. This event infuriated the malcontents whom I mentioned. They let it be known that the government was poorly run and incited the people to demand fair rule [in the revolt of 833]. They freed Wala, Helisachar, Matfrid, and the others who had been sent into exile and urged Lothar to seize power. Under the same pretext and by continual petitions, they also won over to their side Gregory, pontiff of the supreme Roman See, so that his authority would help them do what they planned.

The emperor with all his forces confronted the three kings, his sons, with their immense army, and Pope Gregory with his entire Roman entourage. They all gathered in Alsace and set up camps at Mount Siegwald. By promising various favors the sons prevailed upon the people to defect from their father. After most of his men had fled Louis was eventually captured. His wife was taken from him and sent into exile to Lombardy, and Charles was held with his father under close guard.

Pope Gregory, filled with regret over his journey, returned to Rome later than he had planned. Lothar had seized the empire again, but what he had so unjustly and easily won, he justly lost again even more easily, the second time around. Pepin and Louis saw that Lothar intended to seize the whole empire and make them his inferiors, and they resented his schemes. Hugo, Lambert, and Matfrid also disagreed as to which of them should be second in the empire after Lothar. They began to quarrel, and, since each of them looked out for his own, they entirely neglected the government. When the people saw that, they were distressed. Shame and regret filled the sons for having twice deprived their father of his dignity, and the people for having twice deserted the emperor. Therefore, they all now agreed on his restoration and headed for Saint-Denis, where Lothar was then holding his father and Charles.

Seeing that this flare-up was more than he could deal with, Lothar took up arms before the others had assembled, released his father and Charles, and hurried by forced marches to Vienne. When the emperor was returned to them, a large number of men present were ready to use force in support of the father against the son. They flocked with the bishops and the whole clergy into the basilica of Saint Denis, offered praise to God in all piety, placed crown and arms upon their king, and then assembled to deliberate on the remaining matters.

Louis refrained from pursuing Lothar, but sent envoys after him who were to order him to leave promptly across the Alps. When Pepin came to him, Louis received him graciously, thanked him for what he had done toward his restoration, and allowed him to return to Aquitaine as Pepin requested. There was a gathering of the emperor's vassals who used to run the government and had fled. With these men he marched quickly to Aachen to spend the winter there. Finally, his son Louis came to him. The emperor received him joyfully and told him to stay with him for his protection.

When in the meantime those who guarded Judith in Italy heard that Lothar had fled and Louis ruled the empire, they seized Judith and escaped. They arrived safely at Aachen and delivered her as a welcome present to the emperor. But she was not admitted to the royal bed until she had established her innocence of the offenses with which she had been charged. In the absence of an accuser she did so by an oath taken with her kinsmen before the people.

5. At this time Matfrid, Lambert, and the others of Lothar's party were in the Breton March. Wido and all the men between the Seine and Loire were dispatched to drive them out. They assembled in a large force. The small number of Lothar's men put them at a great disadvantage, but at least they moved as one man. Wido's large army made him and his men secure but quarrelsome and disorganized. No wonder they fled when it came to battle. Wido was slain as well as Odo, Vivian, Fulbert, and an uncounted number of the people. The victors hastily informed Lothar of this, urging him to come to their assistance with an army as fast as he could. Lothar gladly

complied and came with a large force to Chalon, laid siege to the city, and stormed it for three days. After he had finally captured the place, he burned the city and its churches. He ordered Gerberga [Bernard of Septimania's sister] to be drowned in the Saône like a witch and Gozhelm and Senila to be beheaded. But he granted Warin his life, forcing him to swear he would support Lothar in the future with all his might.

Lothar and his men were in high spirits because of their two successful battles and hoped for an easy conquest of the whole empire. They marched to the city of Orléans to deliberate on unsettled business. Upon hearing this the emperor assembled a strong army in Francia. With the aid of Louis and all his men on the far side of the Rhine, he set out to take revenge for the great crime committed by his son against the empire. Hoping that he might cause the Franks to defect as before, Lothar decided on a direct confrontation. So the two forces met and pitched camp by a river near the village of Chouzy. But the Franks were sorry that they had deserted their emperor twice, and considered it shameful to commit the same act again. They spurned any attempt to make them defect. Lothar saw that this was no time for either flight or fight and finally gave up the struggle. First it was agreed that within a stipulated number of days he would cross the Alps and in the future not dare to enter the territory of Francia or make a move without his father's consent. Lothar and his men swore that they would keep these promises.

6. When these matters had been settled, the father ruled the empire with his former advisers. He realized that as long as he lived the people would not desert him, as had been their habit before. He convoked an assembly at Aachen in winter and gave Charles a part of the kingdom bounded in the following way: from the sea along the borders of Saxony as far as the borders of the Ripuarians, all of Frisia; in the lands of the Ripuarians the counties of Moilla, Haettra, Hammolant, and Maasgau; the whole land between the Meuse and Seine as far as Burgundy with the county of Verdun, and in Burgundy the counties of Toul, Ornois, Blois, Blasois, Perthois, the two counties of Bar; the counties of Brienne, Troyes, Auxerre, Sens, Gatinais, Melun, Etampes, Chartres, and Paris; and then along the Seine as far as the ocean and along the coast as far as Frisia all bishoprics, abbeys, counties, royal estates, and everything within the above boundaries and all that went with them, wherever it was located and was known to belong to the emperor. He gave this to his son Charles with all divine and paternal authority and implored the mercy of almighty God that it remain in his hands.

Hilduin, abbot of the church of Saint Denis, and Gerard, count of the city of Paris, and all others living within this territory came together and took an oath of fealty to Charles. When Lothar and Louis heard of this they were very much annoyed and arranged a conference. During their meeting they saw that there was no adequate excuse for being angry about anything that had happened. They shrewdly concealed that they intended to do anything against their father's will and broke up. This meeting raised a storm, but it subsided quickly. The emperor then came to Quierzy about the middle of September [838] and easily suppressed another revolt. He conferred arms and crown upon Charles as well as a part of the kingdom between the Seine and Loire. He also reconciled Pepin and Charles, at least to all appearances; then he graciously permitted Pepin to return to Aquitaine and sent Charles into the part of the kingdom he had given him. On Charles's arrival all inhabitants of those lands came to commend themselves to him and swear fealty.

It was then announced that Louis had revolted against his father and intended to seize the entire part of the kingdom on the far side of the Rhine. When his father heard what he was doing, he came to Mainz, where he convoked an assembly, crossed the Rhine with his army, and forced Louis to flee into Bavaria [in 839]. Then he returned jubilantly to Aachen, since by God's will he had victory wherever he turned. Louis was getting old and his mind was beginning to falter because of his many troubles. Queen Judith and those nobles who were working for Charles, as Louis wished them to, feared that the hatred of the brothers would pursue them until death if the emperor died without settling his affairs. For this reason they thought it wise for Louis to secure the support of one of his sons and that at least this son and Charles could work together and resist the malcontents if the others were unwilling to preserve harmony after their father's death.

Since the matter was urgent, they discussed it day and night until they came to the unanimous decision that an alliance be made with Lothar if he proved trustworthy. For Lothar, as I said earlier, had sworn at one time before father, mother, and Charles that the emperor should give Charles whichever part of the kingdom he wished. Lothar promised that he would agree to the decision and protect Charles against all enemies as long as he lived. This oath encouraged Charles's partisans to choose emissaries and send them to Lothar in Italy. They promised that all his crimes against Louis would be forgiven and the whole kingdom except Bavaria divided between himself and Charles, if he would enforce his father's will regarding Charles from now on. Since this arrangement seemed acceptable to Lothar and his men, both parties swore to their good intentions and pledged to carry them out.

7. Accordingly they all came to Worms where an assembly had been convoked [on 30 May 839]. At this assembly Lothar humbly fell at his father's feet in the presence of all and said: "I know, Lord Father, that I have sinned before God and you. I don't ask for your kingdom but for your forgiveness and that I may be worthy of your grace." Louis behaved like a pious and mild father. He forgave the petitioner for what he had done and granted him his grace, if he would never again injure Charles or the kingdom against his father's will. Louis kindly raised and kissed him and thanked God for the lost son with whom he had been reconciled. Then they went to dine together, postponing until the next day talks on the other matters which they had sworn they would discuss. On the next day they began their conference. As he wished to carry out what his emissaries had sworn, the father said: "Look, my son, as I promised, the whole kingdom is lying before you; divide it as you please. If you divide it, Charles shall have the choice of the parts. But if we divide it, the choice will be yours."

For three days Lothar tried to divide the empire but was not at all able to do so. He then sent Joseph and Richard to his father asking that Louis and his men should divide the kingdom and he be granted the choice of the parts. They assured the king's party by the oath they had already sworn that the only reason Lothar would not divide the kingdom was his ignorance of the land. Therefore, the father with his men divided the whole kingdom, except Bavaria, as equally as possible. Lothar and his men chose the part east of the Meuse and received it immediately. He agreed that the western part should be conferred on Charles and announced with his father before the whole people that they wished things to be settled in this way. Then the father reconciled the brothers as best he could, fervently imploring them to love each other. He also begged them with many exhortations to protect one another, professing that nothing in the world meant more to him.

When all this was settled, the father graciously and peaceably sent Lothar to Italy, enriched by the grace of his forbearance and the gift of the kingdom. He reminded Lothar how often he had broken the oaths he had so frequently sworn to his father, and how often Louis had forgiven him his offenses. He warned Lothar, entreating him fervently not to break those agreements which they had recently made and which he had confirmed as his will before all the people.

8. At the same time the father received the news that Pepin had died. There were some who waited to see what Louis would order to be done about his grandsons' share in the kingdom. But others seized Pepin's eldest son, also named Pepin, and set up an unlawful regime. On this account the emperor settled his business with Lothar as reported and then went with Charles and his mother by way of Chalon to Clermont. There he graciously received those who waited for him. Since he had once given Aquitaine to Charles, he advised and even commanded the Aquitanians to do homage to his son. They all did homage and swore fealty to him. After this the emperor sought for ways to curb the usurpers.

At this very time Louis, as usual, came out of Bavaria and invaded Allemania, accompanied by a number of Thuringians and Saxons whom he had stirred up. This event called the emperor from Aquitaine, and he left Charles with his mother at Poitiers, celebrated holy Easter at Aachen, and then continued his march to Thuringia. After his son Louis had been driven back the emperor forced him to buy his way through the land of the Slavs and to flee to Bavaria. When this conflict was settled the emperor convoked an assembly at the city of Worms, for July 1, to which he summoned his son Lothar from Italy to talk about Louis with himself and other trusted men.

When things had come to this pass, with Lothar in Italy, Louis on the far side of the Rhine, and Charles in Aquitaine, Emperor Louis, their father, died on an island near Mainz on June 20. His brother Drogo, bishop and archchaplain, buried him with due honors at Saint-Arnulf's in his city of Metz in the presence of bishops, abbots, and counts. Louis lived for sixty-four years, ruled Aquitaine for thirty-seven years, and held the imperial title for twenty-seven years and six months.

[Book 2: June 840-June 841]

I have laid bare the roots of your conflicts as far as time and talent permitted.

Now every reader who wants to know why Lothar resolved to pursue you and your brother after your father's death may judge for himself, connect the threads, and see whether Lothar acted lawfully. I shall now try to show, as far as memory and talent serve me, how vigorously he carried out his plans. But I ask you to consider the difficulties which arose for my humble self from this trouble and entreat you to overlook any omissions in this work of mine.

1. When Lothar heard of his father's death, he immediately sent emissaries everywhere, especially all over Francia. They proclaimed that he was coming into the empire which had once been given to him. He promised that he wished to grant everyone the benefices which his father had given and that he would make them even bigger. He gave orders also that oaths of fealty should be exacted from those who were still uncommitted. In addition, he ordered that all should join him as fast as they could; those who were unwilling to appear he threatened with death. He himself advanced slowly since he wanted to find out how the wind was blowing before he crossed the Alps.

Presently, men from everywhere joined him, driven by either greed or fear. When Lothar saw that, his prospects and power made him bold, and he began to scheme about how he might best seize the whole empire. He decided to send an army against Louis first, since this would not take him out of his way, and to devote himself with all his might to the destruction of Louis's forces. In the meantime he was shrewd enough to send emissaries to Charles in Aquitaine, informing Charles that he was friendly toward him, as their father had demanded and as was proper for one to feel toward a godchild. But he begged him to spare their nephew, Pepin's son, until he had spoken to him. Having settled this, he turned to the city of Worms.

At that time Louis had left part of his army as a garrison in Worms and had gone to meet the Saxons who were in revolt. But after a small skirmish Lothar put the defenders to flight and, crossing the Rhine with his entire army, headed for Frankfurt. Here they suddenly came upon each other, Lothar approaching from one side and Louis from the other. After peace had been arranged for the night, they pitched their camps, not exactly in brotherly love, Lothar right at the place where they had met and Louis at the point where the Main flows into the Rhine. Since Louis's opposition was vigorous and his brother was not sure that he could make him give in without a fight, Lothar thought it might be easier to get the better of Charles first. He therefore put off battle with the understanding that he would meet Louis again at the same place on November 11. Unless an agreement could be negotiated beforehand, they would settle by force what each of them was going to get. And so, giving up his initial schemes, Lothar set out to subdue Charles.

2. At this time Charles had come to Bourges to the assembly which Pepin was going to attend, as his men had sworn. When Charles had learned what he could from everybody, he selected as ambassadors Nithard and Adalgar and dispatched them as speedily as possible to Lothar, enjoining and entreating him to remember the oaths they had sworn each other and to preserve what their father had arranged berween them. He also reminded him that

he, Charles, was his brother and godson. Lothar should have what belonged to him, but should also permit Charles to have without a fight what his father had granted him with Lothar's consent. Charles pledged, if Lothar should do this, that he was willing to be loyal and subject to him, as it is proper to behave toward one's first-born brother. Besides, Charles promised that he would wholeheartedly forgive whatever Lothar had done to him up to that time. He implored him to stop stirring up his people and disturbing the kingdom committed to him by God, and sent word to Lothar that peace and harmony should rule everywhere. This peace he and his people considered most desirable and were willing to preserve. If Lothar did not believe this, Charles promised to give him whatever assurances he wanted.

Lothar pretended to receive this message kindly, but permitted the emissaries to return with greetings only and the reply that he would answer fully through his own envoys. Moreover, he deprived Charles's emissaries of the benefices which his father had given them because they did not want to break their fealty and join him. In this way he unwittingly betrayed his designs against his brother. Meanwhile, all men living between the Meuse and the Seine sent to Charles, asked him to get there before the land was taken over by Lothar, and promised to wait for his arrival. Charles quickly set out with only a few men and marched from Aquitaine to Quierzy [in August 840]. There he received graciously those who had come from the Charbonnière and the land on this side of it. Beyond the Charbonnière, however, Herefrid, Gislebert, Bovo, and the others duped by Odulf disregarded their sworn fealty and defected.

3. At the same time a messenger coming from Aquitaine announced that Pepin and his partisans wanted to attack Charles's mother. Charles left the Franks at Quierzy by themselves, but ordered them to move his way if his brother should attempt to subdue them before his return. In addition, he dispatched Hugo, Adalhard, Gerard, and Hegilo to Lothar. Repeating everything that he had said before, he entreated Lothar again for God's sake not to subvert Charles's men and further to whittle away at the kingdom which God and his father had given to Charles with Lothar's consent. After making this appeal to Lothar he rushed into Aquitaine, fell upon Pepin and his men, and put them to flight.

Meanwhile, Lothar was returning from the confrontation with Louis and being joined by every man on this side of the Charbonnière [in October 840]. He thought it best to cross the Meuse and advance as far as the Seine. On his way there Hilduin, abbot of Saint-Denis, and Gerard, count of the city of Paris, came and met him. They had broken their fealty and defected from Charles. When Pepin, son of Bernard, king of the Lombards, and others saw this treachery, like slaves they also chose to break their word and disregard their oaths rather than give up their holdings for a little while. That is why these men broke faith, followed the example of those we mentioned already, and submitted to Lothar. Then Lothar became bold and crossed the Seine, sending ahead, as he always did, to the inhabitants between the Seine and the Loire men who were to make them defect by threats and promises. He himself followed slowly, as usual, heading for the city of Chartres. When he learned that Theoderic and Eric were on the way with the rest who had decided to join him, he resolved to proceed as far as the Loire, putting his confidence in his great numbers. Charles returned from the pursuit in which he had dispersed Pepin and his followers, and since he had no place where he could safely leave his mother, they both hastily departed for Francia.

4. In the meantime Charles heard of all these defections and that Lothar was determined to hound him to the death with an immense army, while Pepin on one side and the Bretons on the other had raised arms against him. So he and his men sat down to think about all these troubles. They easily found a simple solution. Since they had nothing left but their lives and their bodies, they chose to die nobly rather than betray and abandon their king.

They headed in Lothar's direction, and both sides thus approached the city of Orléans. They pitched camps at a distance of barely six Gallic miles from each other, and both parties dispatched emissaries. Charles only asked for peace and justice, but Lothar tried to think of a way he could deceive and get the better of Charles without a fight. This scheme came to nothing because of strong resistance on the other side. Then Lothar hoped that his own forces would continue to grow from day to day, and he thought he might be able to conquer his brother more easily when Charles's following had further dwindled.

But he was disappointed in the hope and refrained from battle. The condition of the truce was that Charles should be granted Aquitaine, Septimania, Provence, and ten counties between the Loire and the Seine, with the stipulation that he should be satisfied with them and remain there for the time being until they met again at Attigny on May 8. Lothar promised that he was indeed willing to talk over and settle the interests of both parties by mutual consent. The leaders of Charles's party also realized that the problems at hand were more than they could handle. They feared, if it came to a battle, that they might be hard put to save the king in view of their small numbers, and all of them set great store by his talents. So they consented to the stipulations if only Lothar from now on would be as loyal a friend to Charles as a brother should be, permit him to hold peacefully the lands he had allotted to him, and in the meantime also refrain from hostilities against Louis. Otherwise they should be absolved from the oath they had sworn.

By this device they both rescued their king from danger and soon freed themselves from an oath. For those who had sworn this had not yet left the house when Lothar tried to seduce some of them from Charles and by the next day in fact he received a few defectors. He immediately sent them into the lands which he had assigned to his brother, to stir up trouble so that they would not submit to Charles. Then he moved on in order to receive homage from those coming to him out of Provence and tried to think of ways to overcome Louis by force or deception.

5. In the meantime Charles came to the city of Orléans and gave a warm welcome to Theobald and Warin who had come to him from Burgundy with some other men. Then he turned toward Nevers to meet Bernard [of Septimania], whom he had ordered to come there. But Bernard put off his appearance before Charles as usual, claiming he had sworn to Pepin and his

men that neither of them should enter into an agreement with anybody without the other's consent. So he declared that he would go to Pepin. If he could prevail upon his men to come with him, he said this would suit him well; but if not, then he promised to take back his oath, to return to Charles within fifteen days, and to submit to his rule.

For this reason Charles came again to Bourges to meet Bernard [in January 841]. When Bernard arrived and proved to have done nothing at all, Charles was greatly annoyed about the tricks this man had played first on his father and now on him. Fearful that he might not be able to catch him in any other way, Charles decided to make a surprise attack upon him. But Bernard saw it coming at the last minute, took to flight, and barely escaped. Charles managed to kill some of Bernard's people and left others behind wounded and half dead. Some who were not injured he captured and treated as prisoners of war. Their entire baggage he allowed to be plundered.

At this Bernard grew humble and a little later approached Charles as a contrite petitioner, declaring that he had always been true to him. He also said that recently he had wished to be loyal, had it been possible, and, in spite of the outrage done to him, was going to be unswervingly faithful in the future. And if anyone called him a liar, he promised to refute the charge by force of arms. Charles believed this and accepted Bernard as a friend, proving his good will by bestowing presents on him and his favor as well. He also told him to coax Pepin and his followers to submit to Charles as he had promised.

When this affair was settled, he turned to the city of Le Mans to win Lambert, Eric, and the others to his side. He received them with great kindness and then at once sent to Nominoë, duke of the Bretons, in order to find out whether or not he was willing to submit to his authority. The duke followed the advice of the majority, sent presents to Charles, and promised under oath to keep faith in the future.

When this business was out of the way and the time for the assembly to meet at Attigny [on 8 May 841] was approaching, Charles wondered what he and his men would have to do to act prudently and yet not violate their good faith. He therefore called together his confidential advisers, described how matters stood, which was already known to everybody, and then asked them how they believed he and his men could best extricate themselves from their predicament. He declared that he wished wholeheartedly to serve the public welfare and would not hesitate to die for it if that should be necessary.

At these words everybody's courage seemed to rise. They recalled the snares which in the days of his father Lothar had tried to set for the emperor and Charles and after their father's death, with the same relentlessness, against his brothers. Everyone remembered especially the oaths which Lothar had recently broken. They declared that they wished Charles could readily obtain full justice from Lothar, but had no reason to believe he could. Therefore, they all considered it advisable that Charles should not fail to come to the announced assembly if at all possible. Should Lothar be willing to put the public welfare ahead of his own, as he had promised, this would please everybody, and they would welcome him. But if not, then Charles should rely on the justice of his case and thus on the help of God and of his vassals and not fail to claim with all his might whatever part of the kingdom his father had given him with the consent of the vassals on both sides.

6. Thus, Charles ordered all his partisans in Aquitaine to follow him and his mother. Those from Burgundy and the land between the Loire and the Seine who wished to be under his authority were also to come along. But he himself with all present set out on the aforementioned march [in March 841], although it seemed difficult. Reaching the Seine, he found Guntbold, Warnar, Arnulf, Gerard, and all counts, abbots, and bishops from the Charbonnière and this side of it. They had apparently been left there by Lothar to prevent Charles from crossing the river if he should do so without Lothar's permission. Besides, the river had flooded so that it could not be forded and those who guarded it had either smashed all the boats to bits or sunk them. Gerard had also destroyed every bridge he found. So crossing the river was not an easy matter and gave no end of trouble to those who wanted to get to the other side.

While their minds were busy with plans for dealing with all these difficulties, they learned that merchant ships had been driven from the mouth of the Seine by a violent tide and had drifted ashore near Rouen. When he arrived on the scene Charles filled twenty-eight of the boats with armed men. He got on board himself and sent messengers to announce that he was on his way and that he forgave everyone who wished to be forgiven for what he had done. To those who did not seek his pardon he announced that they should let him have the kingdom given to him by God and go live somewhere else. They would not agree to this, but when they saw the fleet approaching and recognized both Charles and the cross on which they had taken their oath, they immediately left the riverbank and took to flight.

Charles was unable to pursue them because the horses delayed his crossing. He now [in April 841] headed for Saint-Denis to praise God and pray there. When he arrived, Charles found out that those whom he had put to flight had united with Arnulf, Gerard, and the rest and planned to surprise Theobald, Warin, Otbert, and the others who were on their way to Charles under orders from him. So Charles continued to Saint-Germain[-des-Prés near Paris] to offer his prayers there. After traveling all night long, at dawn he safely met Warin with his companions where the Loing flows into the Seine. He continued the march with them and reached the city of Sens.

From here he set out at night and made his way through the forest of Othe, hoping that his enemies were in this forest, as had been reported to him, for he had decided to attack them wherever and however he could. And he would have done it, too, if those who were in fear of their lives had not learned that death was waiting at their doorstep. This news frightened them terribly and everyone fled wherever he could. Charles could not pursue them because his companions and horses were tired out, so he devoted Maundy Thursday [14 April] to rest and on the next day proceeded to the city of Troyes.

7. While Charles was thus heavily engaged, Lothar, as I said before, bent his whole mind to subjugating Louis by deceit or force, or, preferably, destroying him altogether. In this enterprise he included Bishop Otgar of Mainz and Count Adalbert of Metz, who were just the men for the job, since both of

them had a mortal hatred of Louis. Adalbert had by then recovered from the disease which had incapacitated him for almost a year, so he could now take part in the fratricide. His counsel was considered so valuable in those days that nobody wanted to dispute a word of it. At his suggestion Lothar assembled a countless multitude from every side and set off across the Rhine. As usual, he sent messengers ahead to try to seduce the fickle populace by threats and promises. Louis's followers feared that they might not be able to resist such an immense army. Some of them defected, going over to Lothar, and some fled, leaving Louis behind in very great difficulty. Since there was no help in sight anywhere, Louis departed with the few men he had and retreated to Bavaria.

After this defeat, Lothar believed Louis was finished. So he left Duke Adalbert, whom we mentioned earlier as count, behind to obtain the people's oath of fealty, and at all costs to prevent Louis from going to Charles. But Lothar himself prepared to march against Charles after finding out that he had crossed the Seine. On his way to Aachen to celebrate Easter, Lothar quickly sent scouts ahead since he wanted to know exactly where Charles was and with whom.

8. Something really strange and remarkable happened to Charles on this holy eve of Easter. Neither he nor anyone else in his entourage had anything with him but their arms, horses, and the shirts on their backs. But when Charles stepped from his bath and was going to put on the same clothes he had taken off, suddenly messengers from Aquitaine were standing outside with his crown and all his royal and liturgical attire.

Who could fail to be amazed that a few men, strangers almost, had been able to carry so many talents of gold and a countless number of gems over so many stretches of land and remain unharmed while pillage threatened everywhere. What is most surprising, I believe, is that they were able to arrive at the proper place and on the proper day and hour, although not even Charles himself knew where he and his people were supposed to be. It even seemed that this could only have happened by divine favor and divine will. Charles's companions were filled with amazement and everybody was inspired with high hopes for salvation. Then Charles and his whole entourage jubilantly turned to the celebration of the feast.

When it was over he kindly received Lothar's envoys and made them dine with him. He ordered them to return the next day, promising to send his own emissaries to take care of the matter which his brother had submitted to him. Lothar's embassy wanted to know why Charles had crossed the boundaries which Lothar had set for him without permission. But since the deed was done, he ordered Charles to remain there, at least for the time being, where Lothar's emissaries found him, until he was instructed whether he should come to the meeting place agreed on beforehand or to another which suited Lothar better.

Through his own emissaries Charles answered that he had gone beyond the stipulated boundaries because Lothar had gone back on all the good things which he had promised and sworn by oath. In violation of his sworn oath Lothar had stirred up several of Charles's men and put them under his own rule; he had deprived others of their lives, and, furthermore, as much as he could, he had stirred up the lands which he should have made subject to Charles. But worst of all, he had made war on his brother and forced him to seek the help of the pagans. Despite Lothar's breaches of faith, Charles declared he would come to the meeting which they had mutually arranged. If Lothar wished to look for ways to assure the common good as he had promised, this would please Charles. But if not, then Charles would wholeheartedly obey the counsels of his vassals and do the will of God for the kingdom which had been given to him by God and his father with the consent of his people.

After making all this clear to Lothar, Charles set out on his march and arrived at Attigny [on 7 May 841] one day earlier than had been agreed on. But Lothar deliberately failed to appear. Instead, he sent one messenger after another with various complaints and took precautions lest Charles should suddenly attack him.

9. In the meantime envoys had come from Louis who announced that he would help Charles if only he knew how. Charles answered that help was just what he needed, thanked him for his good will, and immediately sent back the same emissaries so that they could get things moving right away. For four days and more he waited there for Lothar's arrival, but Lothar never came. Then Charles convoked an assembly and deliberated how he might act more prudently toward Lothar in the future.

Some said he should go and meet his mother since she was on her way with the Aquitanians. But the majority either advised him to march against Lothar or declared that he should at least decide on a place to wait for Lothar's arrival. They felt he should do this because if he changed his itinerary everyone would say he had run away. Such talk would only embolden Lothar and his followers. Besides, those men who had been afraid to join either party so far would pin their hopes on Lothar and flock to him everywhere. This is exactly what happened when, in spite of much objection, Charles was won over to the former view.

So he went to the city of Châlons. When he had received his mother and the men of Aquitaine there, the report suddenly arrived that Louis had fought a battle against Adalbert, duke of the Austrasians, and defeated him; that he had crossed the Rhine and was coming as fast as possible to help Charles. This news spread rapidly through the whole camp, and Charles's overjoyed followers all thought they should set out to meet Louis.

When Lothar heard what was going on, he announced to his assembled men that Charles had taken flight and that he wished to pursue him as quickly as possible. By this stroke he both raised the spirits of his faithful followers and encouraged lukewarm ones to come over to his side, turning them into more solid supporters. Charles pitched camp in an inaccessible place surrounded by swamps and water, and only then learned he was being followed by Lothar. Immediately, he set out to meet him, so that there would be nothing in the way of an open battle if that was what Lothar had in mind. On hearing this Lothar set up camp and gave his worn-out horses two days of rest. Lothar and Charles kept jockeying their positions, frequently exchanging emissaries, but without being able to settle anything. All this time Louis and Charles were coming closer and closer to each other and finally they met. At their meeting they discussed and deplored the unrestrained violence with which Lothar had treated them and their men, intending to deliberate the next day on what might best be done in the future.

They met at dawn and held a council at which they complained a great deal about their calamity. When both had finished the story of their sufferings at Lothar's hands, they decided unanimously to select noble, wise, and well-meaning men from the holy order of bishops and the laity. They would send Lothar word by these men of what their father had arranged between them and what they had suffered from him after their father's death. Moreover, they would implore Lothar to remember almighty God and to grant peace to his brothers and to the entire church of God. He was to concede to each what rightly belonged to him according to the expressed will of father and brother. They also were to offer Lothar whatever they had in their entire army except horses and arms, so that he would yield to their rightful demands. If he would heed these warnings and requests, they would be pleased. But if not, Charles and Louis declared, they could most certainly hope for divine help, as long as they looked only for a fair settlement and made this offer to their brother in all humility. This plan seemed reasonable. Indeed it was so, and they immediately carried it out.

10. But Lothar considered the offer useless and rejected it. He sent word by his own envoys that he wanted nothing but a battle, and he immediately set out to meet Pepin, who was on his way to Lothar from Aquitaine. Louis and his men quickly learned of this and were deeply worried, for they were very worn out by the length of their march as well as by battles, many troubles, and, above all, the lack of horses. Despite their condition they feared that they might leave an unworthy memory to their descendants if a brother failed to give aid to his brother. To avoid this disgrace they preferred to submit to every misery and even, if necessary, to death rather than lose their reputation for invincibility. This greatness of soul enabled them to overcome their sadness and to cheer each other up, and they joyfully set out in great haste to reach Lothar as soon as possible.

Near the city of Auxerre both armies met each other unexpectedly [on 21 June 841]. Lothar immediately moved a short distance out of his camp, with his armed men, fearing that his brothers might plan to attack him at any minute. Since his brothers realized what he was up to, they left some men behind to make camp, and, taking along others who were armed, immediately marched against Lothar. They exchanged emissaries and arranged a truce for the night. The camps were at a distance of about three Gallic miles from each other. A small swamp and a forest lay between them, which made it hard to get back and forth.

At daybreak [22 June] Louis and Charles sent word to Lothar that they were very unhappy with his rejection of peace and insistence on battle. But since he wanted it that way, that was the way it would be. If there had to be a battle, though, there should at least be no treachery. They first ought to invoke God with fasting and prayers. Then, they promised to give Lothar a place to cross the swamp if he wanted to face them on their side of it. They wanted nothing to prevent the confrontation of the armies and to fight without any deceitful tricks. They ordered their emissaries to swear their good faith if Lothar accepted the proposal, and if not, they asked him to permit them to cross over to his side and their emissaries would swear to that. As usual, Lothar promised to answer by his own envoys. But when the emissaries had returned, Lothar immediately set out, heading for Fontenoy to set up camp there. The brothers rushed after Lothar on the same day, passed him, and set up their camp near the village of Thury. On the next day [23 June] the armies, ready for battle, moved out for some distance from their camps.

Louis and Charles sent word ahead to Lothar, telling him to remember that they were brothers, to leave the church of God and the whole Christian people in peace, to concede to his brothers the lands given to them by their father with Lothar's consent, and to keep the lands his father had left him, not because he deserved them, but out of mercy alone. They offered him as a present whatever could be found in their whole army with the exception of arms and horses. If that did not please him, they would each grant him a portion of the kingdom, one as far as the Charbonnière, the other as far as the Rhine. If he were to reject this, they would divide all of Francia into equal parts, and whichever part he wished should be under his rule.

To this Lothar answered, as usual, that he would communicate by his own envoys whatever was acceptable to him. He promptly sent Drogo, Hugo, and Hegibert, informing Louis and Charles that they had never made such proposals to him before and that he wanted time to consider them. The fact of the matter was that Lothar was manufacturing delays because Pepin had not yet arrived. But he had Ricuin, Hirmenald, and Frederic swear that he requested this armistice only because he wanted to seek the common good of both his brothers and the whole people, as justice among brothers and Christian people demanded.

Louis and Charles believed this oath. When both sides had sworn peace, for this day and the next, and to the second hour of the third, which fell on June 25, they returned to the camp to celebrate Saint John's Mass on the next day. Lothar secured Pepin's support on that very day and then sent word to his brothers that they should consider how he might discharge the august office of emperor, since they knew that this title had been solemnly conferred on him; furthermore, that he was happy to look after the interests of them both. Lothar's emissaries were asked whether Lothar was willing to accept the proposals submitted by Louis and Charles or whether he had given them a definitive declaration of his own. But the emissaries answered they had not been told what to say about that.

Any hope for justice and peace from Lothar seemed to have vanished. So Charles and Louis told him, if he could think of nothing better, he should either accept one of their proposals or know that they would put the issue in the hands of God on the next day, June 25, as I said before, at the second hour, a course of action which Lothar had forced on them against their will. Lothar arrogantly rejected their proposal, as he always did, answering them that they would see what he was going to do. While I was writing this at the Loire near Saint-Cloud, an eclipse of the sun occurred in Scorpio in the first hour of 18 October [841], a Tuesday.

After breaking off these negotiations Louis and Charles rose at dawn, occupied the peak of a mountain near Lothar's camp with about one-third of their army, and waited for Lothar's arrival and the striking of the second hour [seven o'clock in the morning], as their men had sworn. When both had come, they fought a violent battle on the brook of the Burgundians. Louis and Lothar were engaged in heavy fighting in a place called Brittas; there Lothar was overcome and fled. The troops which Charles confronted at the place commonly called Fagit immediately took flight. But the part of [Lothar's] army which attacked Adalhard and the others at Solemnat, to whom I gave vigorous assistance with God's help, fought bitterly. There the fight was a draw, but in the end all of Lothar's party fled.

With the end of the first battle that Lothar fought this book may end.

[Book 3: June 841-March 842]

Although I am ashamed to hear of anything bad in my people, it especially pains me when I have to report it. Therefore, I was inclined, without deliberately ignoring my orders, to consider my work complete with the longed-for end of the second book. But I have agreed to add a third book of the events in which I myself took part, lest some misguided man dare to record them inaccurately.

1. After the battle had been vigorously fought to the end, as I said before, Louis and Charles deliberated on the battlefield what should be done about their scattered opponents. Some were filled with rage and advised pursuing the enemy, but some, especially the kings themselves, took mercy on their brother and the people. As always, Charles and Louis wished piously that their opponents would turn away from evil greed and with God's grace join them and be of one mind in true justice, now that they had been smitten with God's judgment in this defeat. They suggested things be left to the mercy of almighty God. Since everyone agreed to this they ceased fighting and plundering and returned to camp about the middle of the day to talk over what they ought to do next.

The booty and the slaughter were immense and truly astonishing, but the mercy of the kings and of the entire people was equally remarkable. For several reasons they decided to celebrate Sunday [26 June] in the same place. After Mass on Sunday they buried friends and enemies alike, the faithful and the faithless, and with equal sincerity comforted as best they could those felled by blows and only half-alive. They also sent messengers after the foes who had fled the scene and offered them pardon of all offenses if they wished to return in good faith.

After that the kings and their followers in their grief over their brother and the Christian people began to ask the bishops what they should do in this situation. So all the bishops, acting as one man, came together to hold council. A public assembly found that Louis and Charles had fought for justice and equity alone, as God's judgment had made clear. For this reason every one of them, he who commanded as well as he who obeyed, was to consider himself in this conflict an instrument of God, free from responsibility. But whoever knew that he had either counseled or committed anything on this campaign from wrath or hatred or vainglory or any passion, was to confess secretly his secret sin and be judged according to the measure of his guilt. To honor and praise God's display of justice, a three-day fast was arranged and celebrated gladly and solemnly. This was done for the remission of the sins of their deceased brothers (for they knew they were not faultless and had committed many sins, willingly and unwillingly), so that with God's help they might be freed from them; and, finally, so that the Lord, who up to that moment had been their succor and protector in a just cause, would forever remain so.

2. When this was taken care of, Louis decided to march to the Rhine. Charles, on the other hand, for various reasons, but mainly to attempt to overcome Pepin, thought it best to move into Aquitaine. Bernard, duke of Septimania, although no further from the place of the above battle than about three leagues, had not helped either party. But as soon as he learned that Charles had won a victory, he sent his son William to the king with orders to do homage to Charles if the latter were willing to give him the benefices which William held in Burgundy. Bernard also boasted that he was willing and able to make Pepin and his people submit to Charles by the most advantageous of treaties. Charles received this embassy kindly and did as Bernard asked, reminding him that he should make good his promise to win over Pepin and his people.

Since everywhere troubles seemed to have vanished and all had high hopes, Louis proceeded with his men to the Rhine. Charles and his mother headed for the Loire. But the public welfare was unduly neglected. Once separated, everyone carelessly wandered off wherever he felt like going. When Pepin heard of this, he put off the alliance with Charles in which he had been interested a moment earlier. Bernard, it is true, came to Charles, but did not agree to do homage. But some men deserted Pepin and the only advantage Charles got from the whole campaign was the homage of these defectors.

In the meantime Adalhard and the others whom Charles had sent to the Franks to learn if they [the defectors] were willing to return to him, came to Quierzy, where the Franks had asked him to send envoys. They found only a few men there, however. These men said they would not hesitate to join Charles on the spot if he were present; since he was not, they claimed not to know if he were even alive. For Lothar's partisans had spread the rumor that Charles died in battle and that Louis was wounded and had fled. It was, therefore, not advisable, they said, in such uncertain circumstances, to make a treaty with anybody. But Guntbold and the rest who had joined forces made moves to attack Charles's emissaries and would actually have done so if they had dared. For this reason Adalhard and the others sent to Charles, asking him to try to come and help them as fast as he could and to see if he could find out whether the Franks were really willing to join him, as they maintained. The emissaries themselves, however, went to the city of Paris to wait for Charles's arrival.

As soon as Charles received their news, he at once set out for this region. When he reached the Seine, he met Adalhard with the others at Epône. Charles was worried about the impending conference which he had arranged with his brother at Langres for September 1. But he still thought it best to reach Langres by a fast march through Beauvais, Compiègne, Soissons, and further on, by Rheims and Châlons. His aim was to keep the appointment with his brother and yet to give any Frank who wished to do so the chance to join his side. But the Franks looked with contempt at the small number of his followers, as the Aquitanians had done, and under various pretexts postponed submission to him for the time being.

Seeing their reaction, Charles quickened his march. When he reached the city of Soissons, the monks of Saint-Médard came out to meet him and begged him to translate the bodies of the the the saints Médard, Sebastian, Gregory, Tiburtius, Peter and Marcellinus, Maria, Martha, Audifax and Abacuc, Honesimus, Maresma, and Leocadia into the basilica where they now rest and which had then been partly constructed. He agreed to that, remained at Soissons, and, as they had requested, translated the bodies of the saints on his own shoulders with all due veneration. By a solemn charter he added the village of Berny to the estates of this church.

After taking care of this, he proceeded to Rheims. When he got there he was informed that Louis was unable to come to the meeting they had arranged at Langres because Lothar threatened his kingdom with a hostile force. Also his uncle Hugo and Gislebert, count of the Maasgau, sent word that they would join Charles with other men if he should enter their territory.

3. So [in early September 841] Charles marched toward Saint-Quentin both to help his brother and to receive these men if they really wanted to join him. There he met Hugo, who had let Charles know he was coming. From Saint-Quentin, Charles headed for the area of Maastricht. As soon as Lothar heard what Charles was up to, he broke off his pursuit of Louis, which he had only just decided on anyway. Lothar then set out from Worms to the assembly which had been convoked at Thionville, and thought about how he might attack Charles.

When Charles heard of this at Wasseiges, he sent Hugo and Adalhard to coax Gislebert and the others over to his side. He also sent Rabano to Louis, letting him know that Charles had come to help him; that Lothar, on hearing this, had stopped pursuing Louis and was going to attack Charles with all his troops. Charles begged and pleaded with Louis to do all he could to help him at once, as he had in the past. He also sent the venerable Bishop Emmon to Lothar with the standard orders to beg Lothar in all humility to remember that Charles was his brother and godson; to remember what their father had arranged between them, which Lothar and his men had sworn to preserve, and also to remember that only recently divine judgment had made it clear which side God was on. If he would rather forget these things, he should at least not persecute the holy church of God any more, have mercy on the poor, the widows, and the orphans, and stop attacking the kingdom given to Charles by his father with Lothar's consent. Above all, Lothar should not compel Christian people to face each other again in a mutual slaughter. After making his position clear to Lothar, Charles went to the city of Paris to wait for the arrival of his brother Louis and his other vassals whom he had summoned.

When Lothar heard what Charles was doing, he headed for the same city, because he had with him a considerable force of Saxons, Austrasians, and

Alemanni. With every confidence in their support he came to Saint-Denis. He found there about twenty ships; in addition, as usual in September, the Seine was shallow and easy to ford. In view of this Lothar and his men boasted that it was a simple matter for them to come across and pretended that they were eager to do just that.

So Charles ordered some men to guard Paris and Meulan, and others to take up positions wherever he knew there were fords or ferries. He himself pitched camp [in October 841] in a central position, across from Saint-Denis near Saint-Cloud so he could if necessary prevent Lothar from crossing or help his men if Lothar should plan to attack them anywhere. To make it easy to learn where help was needed, he arranged signs and guards at critical points, as is usually done on the coast. Besides, strange to tell, while the sky was clear and, as far as we knew, no rain had then fallen for two months, the Seine suddenly began to rise and of its own accord made all the fords impassable.

When this was the way things turned out, and Lothar saw that he was prevented from crossing anywhere, he sent word to Charles that he was ready to make peace with him if Charles would give up his sworn alliance with his brother Louis. Lothar said he would withdraw from the alliance with Pepin, which had also been confirmed by oaths. Charles should have the land west of the Seine except Aquitaine and Septimania and they should be united in eternal peace. The truth was that Lothar believed this ruse might make it easier for him to trick them both and seize the whole empire.

But Charles answered him that he was unwilling to break the treaty which he had made with his brother out of necessity. Furthermore, he added, it seemed not a bit fair to him that he should surrender to Lothar the kingdom from the Meuse to the Seine which his father had given him, especially, since so many of the nobility in these areas now supported him. It was quite improper that these nobles should be deceived about his loyalty to them. Since winter was not far off, Charles proposed that each, if he so desired, should keep the benefices which their father had given them. But in the spring, unless they had reached an agreement by old arrangements or new ones, they all should meet, either with a few men or their entire following, and decide by force of arms what each could rightfully claim. Lothar rejected this proposal as usual and turned from Saint-Denis to Sens to meet Pepin, who was coming to him from Aquitaine. Charles, on the other hand, looked for ways to unite with Louis to gain support.

4. In the meantime [in October 841] Charles was informed that his sister Hildegard [the daughter of Ermengard and, therefore, Charles's half-sister] had taken one of his men, Adalgar, prisoner and was holding him in captivity with her in the city of Laon. This inspired Charles to select men who were right for the task and, though it was late in the day, to rush at once to Laon. The city was about thirty leagues away. He rode all night, in spite of the severe cold, and about the third hour of the day [ten o'clock] his sister and the inhabitants of Laon suddenly learned that Charles was there with a tremendous force and the entire city about to be surrounded by armed men. Terrified by this news and realizing that they could not hope to escape or defend the walls, they sought a truce for the night, surrendered Adalgar on

the spot, and promised meekly to hand over the city without a fight the next day.

While these negotiations were going on, the soldiers, gravely annoyed with the delay of their business and angered because of the exhausting struggles of the night before, began to converge on the town to destroy it. No doubt the place would have been immediately given over to flames and plunder had not Charles himself, moved by compassion for the churches of God as well as for his sister and the Christian people, made great efforts to calm the soldiers down with threats and flattery. After persuading them to give up, he granted his sister's request and withdrew from her city to Samoussy. On the next day Hildegard indeed did homage to him, as she had vowed, and restored the city unharmed and without a fight to his power. Charles received his sister kindly, forgiving her everything she had formerly done against him. He spoke to her with many tender words and graciously promised her all the kindness a brother owes his sister if in the future she would be willing to side with him. Then he let her go wherever she wished. He imposed his rule on the city and having settled these affairs returned to his men, whom he had left near Paris.

After receiving Pepin at Sens Lothar was undecided about what to do. Charles had taken part of his army across the Seine and sent it [in November 841] into the forest which is commonly called La Perche. Since Lothar feared that they might interfere with him or his men, he decided to attack them first. By doing so he hoped he could destroy them with ease, frighten the rest into submission, and above all bring Nominoë, duke of the Bretons, under his control. But Lothar tried to carry out these designs in vain, for every one of them was frustrated. Charles's whole army escaped safely from him, nor did he attract any of Charles's followers to his side; and Nominoë arrogantly rejected everything that Lothar suggested to him. This was how things stood when Lothar suddenly received news that Louis and Charles, each with an immense army, were seeking to join forces. Seeing himself surrounded by troubles on all sides, Lothar began to withdraw from Tours, after a long and useless diversion, and eventually arrived tired and with worn-out troops in Francia. Pepin now regretted that he had joined Lothar and withdrew to Aquitaine.

Meanwhile, when Charles heard that Bishop Otgar of Mainz and others were keeping his brother Louis from crossing the Rhine, he quickly went into Alsace by way of Toul [in February 842], entering at Saverne. At news of this Otgar and those with him relinquished the bank of the Rhine and retreated, while everybody fled swiftly wherever he could.

5. Thus, on the fourteenth of February Louis and Charles met in the city which at one time was called Argentaria but is now commonly called Strasbourg. There they swore the oaths which are recorded below; Louis in the Romance language and Charles in the German. Before the oath one addressed the assembled people in German and the other in Romance. Louis, being the elder spoke first, in this manner:

"You know how often after our father's death Lothar has assaulted my brother and me and has tried to wipe us out. Since neither brotherhood, nor Christian faith, nor any other argument could make for peace with justice among us, we were compelled in the end to submit the matter to the judgment of almighty God, prepared to be content with what God decided was due to each of us. In this contest, as you know, we had the victory by the mercy of God. Lothar was defeated and fled with his men wherever he could escape. But afterwards, moved by brotherly love and compassion for our Christian people, we did not want to pursue and annihilate our opponents. As before, we asked them only that in the future justice be done to each.

"Yet after all this, Lothar is still not content with the divine judgment and does not stop persecuting my brother and me with armed might. Moreover, he is also ruining our people by fire, plunder, and slaughter. Therefore, we have come together here, driven by dire necessity. And since we believe you doubt that our brotherly love is strong and that our loyalty will last, we have both decided to swear an oath before your eyes.

"We are not doing this out of wicked greed but, if God gives us peace with your help, to safeguard the general welfare. Should I dare, however, which God forbid, to violate the oath that I am going to swear to my brother, I release each of you from his obedience and the oath he has sworn to me."

When Charles had spoken the same words in the Romance language, Louis as the elder first swore to uphold the following in the future:

Pro Deo amur et pro christian poblo et nostro commun salvament, d'ist di in avant, in quant Deus savir et podir me dunat, si salvarai eo cist meon fradre Karlo et in aiudha et in cadhuna cosa, si cum om per dreit son fradra salvar dift, in o quid il mi altresi fazet et ab Ludher nul plaid nunquam prindrai, qui, meon vol, cist meon fradre Karle in damno sit.	For the love of God and for our Christian people's salvation and our own, from this day on, as far as God grants knowledge and power to me, I shall treat my brother with regard to aid and everything else as a man should rightfully treat his brother, on condition that he do the same to me. And I shall not enter into any dealings with Lothar which might with my consent injure this my brother Charles.

When Louis had concluded, Charles swore in the German language by the same words as follows:

In Godes minna ind in thes christianes folches ind unser bedhero gehaltnissi, fon thesemo dage frammordes, so fram so mir Got geuuizci indi mahd furgibit, so haldih thesan minan bruodher, soso man mit rehtu sinan bruher scal, in thiu thaz er mig so sama duo, indi mit Ludheren	For the love of God and for the Christian people's and our salvation, from this day on, as far as God grants me knowledge and power, I shall treat my brother as a man rightfully should treat his brother, on condition that he do the same to me; and I shall not enter into anything with Lothar that might

in nohheiniu thing ne gegango,   with my consent injure [Louis].
the, minan uuillon, imo ce
scadhen uuerdhen.

The oath, however, which the followers of the two brothers swore, each in
their own language, went like this in Romance:

Si Lodhuuigs sagrament que son	If Louis keeps the oath which he
fradre Karlo jurat conservat	swore to his brother Charles, and
et Karlus, meos sendra, de suo	my Lord Charles does not keep it
part non l'ostanit, si returnar	on his part, and if I am unable
non l'int pois, ne io ne neuls	to restrain him, I shall not give
cui eo returnar int pois, in	him any aid against Louis nor
nulla aiudha contra Lodhuuuig	will anyone whom I can keep from
nun li iu er.	doing so.

In the German language it went like this:

Oba Karl then eid then er	If Charles keeps the oath which
sinemo bruodher Ludhuuuige	he swore to his brother Louis,
gesuor geleistit, indi	and my Lord Louis breaks the oath
Ludhuuuig, min herro, then er	he swore to him, and if I am
imo gesuor forbrihchit, ob ih	unable to restrain him, I shall
inan es iruuenden ne mag, noh	not give him any aid against
ih noh thero nohhein, then ih	Charles nor will anyone whom I
es irruuenden mag, uuidhar	can keep from doing so.
Karle imo ce follusti ne	
uuirdhit.	

When this was done, Louis went down the Rhine by way of Speyer to Worms,
whereas Charles took the route by Wissembourg along the Vosges.

The summer during which the aforementioned battle was fought was extremely cold, and all produce of the field was gathered very late. But fall
and winter took their natural course. On the very day on which Louis and
Charles and the nobles of the people concluded their treaty a great deal of
snow fell, followed by a severe cold spell. A comet appeared in the months
of December, January, and February until the time of the conference at Strasbourg, ascended through Pisces at the center, and disappeared after the end
of this meeting between the constellation which is called Lyra by some and
Andromeda by others and the darker Arcturus. After these brief comments
on the progress of the seasons and of a star let us return to the course of
our history.

When they arrived at Worms, they selected emissaries and immediately
sent them to Lothar and into Saxony. They decided to wait between Worms
and Mainz for their arrival and that of Carloman [the son of Louis the Ger-
man].

6. Here it may not be out of place, since it is a joyous matter and one
deserving mention, to say something about the character of these kings and

the harmony which prevailed between them.

They were both of medium height, handsome and graceful, and expert in every kind of exercise. Both were bold and generous as well as prudent and well spoken. But every noble quality mentioned was surpassed by the sacred and venerable peace among the brothers. Almost all their meals they took together, and anything of value they possessed they gave each other in great kindness. They ate and slept in the same house. They dealt with public as well as private matters in the same spirit. Neither demanded anything but what he considered useful and agreeable to the other.

For exercise they arranged frequent games in the following way. People would get together in a place suitable for a show and with the whole crowd standing on either side, Saxons, Gascons, Austrasians, and Bretons in teams of equal numbers first rushed forth from both sides and raced at full speed against each other as if they were going to attack. Then one side would turn back, pretending that they wished to escape from their pursuers to their companions under the protection of their shields. But then they would turn round again and try to pursue those from whom they had been fleeing until finally both kings and all the young men with immense clamor rushed forward, swinging their lances and spurring on their horses, pursuing by turns whoever took flight. It was a show worth seeing because of its excellent execution and discipline; not one in such a large crowd and among such different peoples dared to hurt or abuse another, as often happens even when the opponents are few and familiar to each other.

7. While this was going on, Carloman joined his father at Mainz with an immense army of Bavarians and Alemanni. Bardo, who had been sent to Saxony, also came there and reported that the Saxons had rejected Lothar's demands and were happy to do whatever Louis and Charles told them. Lothar had been foolish enough to ignore the envoys that had been sent to him. This exasperated Louis and Charles as well as the entire army and they decided to move against him.

So they started after Lothar on March 17, Charles by the difficult route across the Vosges, Louis both on land and on the Rhine by way of Bingen, and Carloman by way of Einrichi, and they arrived at Koblenz about the sixth hour of the next day [one o'clock in the afternoon]. First they went to Saint-Castor's for prayer and heard Mass; then the kings in full armor boarded ship and quickly crossed the Moselle. Seeing this, Bishop Otgar of Mainz, Count Hatto, Heriold, and everyone Lothar had left there to prevent Louis and Charles from crossing, were seized by fear, relinquished the riverbank, and took to flight. When Lothar at Sinzig learned that his brothers had crossed the Moselle, he fled at once from his kingdom and capital and did not stop until he had reached the bank of the Rhône, accompanied only by the few men who had decided to follow him and leaving everything else behind.

Where Lothar ended his second battle, the third book may end.

[Book 4: March 842-March 843]

Not only would I like to rest from the labor of this history, as I said already, but my mind, filled as it is with all sorts of complaints, tries sorrowfully and unceasingly to withdraw from all public life. But since fortune has tied me first to one event and then to another and unhappily whirls me in violent storms, I cannot imagine how I may enter my haven. In the meantime, though, when I find some leisure, is there any harm in trying, as I have been instructed, to commemorate the deeds of our princes and nobles by writing them down? So I shall take up the fourth book of this history and, if I cannot be useful to posterity in other ways, I will at least by this effort disperse the haze of error about these matters for those who come after us.

1. As soon as Louis and Charles were sure Lothar had left his kingdom, they headed for the palace at Aachen, which at that time was the capital of Francia, and on the day after their arrival considered what might best be done about their brother's abandoned people and kingdom. It seemed to them that first they should submit the matter to bishops and priests, of whom a large number were present. By their counsel, as though by divine command, it would be discovered how these troubles got started in the first place. Since this seemed good advice and rightly so, the matter was put into their hands.

These men examined Lothar's deeds from the very beginning; how he had driven his father from the kingdom; how often by his greed he had caused Christian people to break their oaths; how often he himself had broken his promises to his father and brothers; how often he had tried after the death of their father to disinherit and destroy his brothers; how much murder, adultery, destruction by fire, and crime of every sort the entire church had suffered because of his most execrable greed. In addition, they charged that he did not have the knowledge to govern the commonwealth nor could they find a trace of good will in his conduct of the government. In view of this Lothar deserved that the just judgment of almighty God drove him first from the battlefield and then from his own kingdom.

So it was their unanimous opinion that divine vengeance had cast him out because of his wanton negligence and delivered the kingdom into the hands of his brothers as the better men so that they would rule it in justice. But they did not give the brothers permission to receive it until they had asked them in public whether they intended to rule the kingdom along the same lines as their exiled brother had, or in accordance with the will of God. When Louis and Charles answered that they were willing to govern and rule themselves and their people according to His will, as much as God granted them knowledge and power, the bishops and priests declared: "We ask, admonish, and order you on divine authority to take over this kingdom and to rule it in accordance with the will of God."

Then each of the brothers chose twelve men for this task, of whom I was one; and what seemed to these twelve a fair partition of the kingdom between the brothers satisfied them both. In this division, fertility or equal size of the lands was not considered so much as the fact that they were adjacent and fitted into the territory already held by one or the other of the brothers. Louis received all of Frisia and other lands...but Charles...[the manuscript is defective here].

2. After this had come to pass each brother received homage from the people

who were now under his rule as well as an oath that from now on they would be loyal to him. Charles crossed the Meuse to order the affairs of his kingdom, but Louis went to Cologne on account of the Saxons.

Since I consider the affairs of the Saxons to be very important, I believe that they should not be omitted. Emperor Charles, deservedly called the Great by all peoples, converted the Saxons by much effort, as is known to everyone in Europe. He won them over from the vain adoration of idols to the true Christian religion of God. From the beginning the Saxons have often proved themselves by many examples to be both noble and extremely warlike. This whole tribe is divided into three classes. There are those among them who are called *edhilingi* in their language; those who are called *frilingi*, and those who are called *lazzi*; this is in the Latin language nobles, freemen, and serfs. In the conflict between Lothar and his brothers the nobility among the Saxons was divided into two factions, one following Lothar, the other Louis.

Since this was how matters stood, and Lothar saw that after his brother's victory the people who had been with him wished to defect, he was compelled by various needs to turn for help anywhere he could get it. So he distributed public property for private use; he gave freedom to some and promised it to others after victory; he also sent into Saxony to the immense number of *frilingi* and *lazzi*, promising them, if they should side with him, that he would let them have the same law in the future which their ancestors had observed when they were still worshipping idols. Since they desired this law above all, they adopted a new name, "Stellinga," rallied to a large host, almost drove their lords from the kingdom, and each lived as their ancestors had done according to the law of his choice. But Lothar had also called in the Norsemen to help him, had put some Christians under their lordship, and permitted them to plunder others.

Louis thus feared that the Norsemen and Slavs might unite with the Saxons who called themselves Stellinga, because they are neighbors, and that they might invade the kingdom to revenge themselves and root out the Christian religion in the area. It was especially for this reason, as we noted above, that he went to...[a gap in the manuscript] and at the same time did all he could to avert other hazards to his kingdom lest this most horrible disaster befall the holy church of God. When he had seen to this matter they went to Verdun, Louis by Thionville and Charles by Rheims, to consult on what should be done next.

3. At the same time the Norsemen laid waste Quentovic, then crossed the sea from there and ravaged Hamwig and Northunnwig [in Britain], too. But Lothar, when he had withdrawn as far as the bank of the Rhine, took up residence there and made use of the shipping on this river. By doing so he drew as many men as he could from all sides for his support. Still, he dispatched an envoy to his brothers, informing them that he was willing, if only he knew how, to send his magnates to them to negotiate about peace.

He received the answer that he should send anyone he wished and that he could easily find out where to come. They themselves, however, continued their march by Chalon to Troyes. When they had come as far as Mellecey, Joseph, Eberhard, Egbert, and others of Lothar's party came to them and declared that Lothar knew he had wronged God and his brothers and that he did not wish the conflict between them and the Christian people to last any longer. If they wished, they might add a little to the third part of the kingdom because of the imperial title which their father had granted to him and because of the dignity of the empire which their grandfather had added to the kingdom of the Franks. But if they did not wish to do that, they should only concede to him the third part of the whole kingdom with the exception of Lombardy, Bavaria, and Aquitaine. Each of them should rule his part of the kingdom with God's help as best he could. Each should enjoy the other's help and good will. To their subjects they should mutually grant peace and justice, and with God's will there should be eternal peace among them.

When Louis and Charles heard this and when it pleased them and their entire people, they met in council with their magnates and considered with grateful hearts what they should do about Lothar's proposals. They declared that this accord was what they had desired right from the very beginning of their quarrel and, although it could not be worked out because of the violations that were committed in the meantime, that they had often proposed it to Lothar. They thanked almighty God, whose help finally let them see their brother, through God's grace, ask for that peace and harmony which he had always rejected.

But they submitted the matter as usual to bishops and priests; for no matter where divine authority decided to steer these affairs, they wanted to be ready with joyous hearts for its command. Since everyone thought it best that there should be peace among the brothers, Louis and Charles gave their consent, called for emissaries, and granted Lothar's request. When they had spent more than four days on the partition of the kingdom, they finally decided to offer him as the third part of the kingdom the land between the Rhine and Meuse as far as the source of the Meuse, and from there to the source of the Saône, and then along the Saône as far as its junction with the Rhône, and from there along the Rhône as far as the Tyrrhenian Sea all bishoprics, abbacies, counties, and royal estates on this side of the Alps with the exception of...[another short lacuna in the manuscript]. If he should refuse that, then they should determine by force of arms what belonged to each.

Although this division seemed to some more generous than it should be, it was submitted to Lothar by Conrad, Cobbo, Adalhard, and others. Louis and Charles themselves meanwhile decided to remain at Mellecey until their envoys returned, waiting for Lothar's response.

But when the emissaries came to Lothar, they found him as usual a little less ready for compromise. He said that he was not satisfied with what his brothers had proposed to him as it was not an equal share. He also complained about the fate of his followers, since in the share which had just been offered to him he would not have enough to compensate them for what they had lost. I do not know how they were tricked into doing this, but the emissaries therefore increased Lothar's share beyond the stipulated part, as far as the Charbonnière. Furthermore, if he should accept this within a period of time agreeable to them, they swore that his brothers under oath would then divide the whole kingdom with the exception of Lombardy,

Bavaria, and Aquitaine as fairly as possible into three parts, that he would have the choice of the part he wanted, that they would grant him his share for the rest of his life on condition that he did the same to them, and that they would swear to execute this proposal if he wanted them to prove their good faith. Lothar swore that this was what he wanted and that he would carry out his part of the bargain on condition that his brothers did what their emissaries had just sworn to him.

4. Thus, about the middle of June [842], on a Thursday, Lothar, Louis, and Charles, each with an equal number of their nobles, met near the city of Mâcon on the island called Ansilla and swore each other this oath, namely, that from that day on and in the future they would keep the peace among each other and that in the assembly which their vassals had arranged they would under oath divide the entire kingdom, except Lombardy, Bavaria, and Aquitaine, into three parts as equally as possible, that Lothar should have the choice of the parts of the kingdom, and that each should help his brother all the days of his life to preserve the part which each received on condition that each brother acted toward his brothers in the same way. After settling this business and exchanging words of peace, they departed in peace and returned to their camps to talk over other matters the next day.

Although it was hard to do, they finally reached an agreement that until the assembly to be held on October 1, each should remain peacefully in the part of his choice. Louis then went to Saxony and Charles to Aquitaine to settle their affairs. But Lothar, it seemed, was already sure about the choice of the parts of the kingdom. He went hunting in the Ardennes Mountains and deprived of their benefices all the nobles in his territory who had been obliged to defect from him when he left his kingdom.

Louis, however, distinguished himself by putting down, not without rightful bloodshed, the rebels in Saxony who, as I said before, called themselves Stellinga. Charles, on the other hand, made Pepin flee to Aquitaine. Since Pepin hid there, Charles could do nothing else that deserves to be recorded. But to keep an eye on this land he left behind a certain Duke Warin and others who seemed to be loyal to him. Moreover, Egfrid, count of Toulouse, ambushed some of Pepin's companions who had been sent to murder him and slew others. Charles set out for the assembly which he had convoked with his brother Louis at Worms.

When he arrived at Metz on September 30, he found that Lothar had come to Thionville before the announced assembly met and was living there in defiance of their agreement. To those of Louis's and Charles's party who were to stay at Metz for the division of the kingdom it did not seem quite safe to divide the kingdom at Metz while their lords were at Worms and Lothar at Thionville. The distance from Worms to Metz is, after all, about seventy leagues while from Thionville to Metz it is only about eight leagues. They also remembered that Lothar had often been all too easily inclined and too prompt to deceive his brothers. For this reason they did not dare to put their lives in his hands without any security.

So Charles, who was concerned about their safety, sent to Lothar and told him to give hostages, if he wished Charles's and Louis's emissaries to stay at Metz with Lothar's. Charles wanted to be sure of their safety since Lothar

had come to Thionville and was staying there against his word. Otherwise
he should send his emissaries to them at Worms and they would give him
whomever he wished as hostages. Another proposal was that they should all
stay at an equal distance from Metz. But if he did not want this either, their
emissaries should meet at a centrally located place of his choice; for Charles
said that he would not risk the safety of so many noble men. Eighty men
distinguished by their high nobility had been selected from the whole people,
and if one did not take precautions against their ruin, he declared, an immense injury could be inflicted on him and his brother.

Then finally they agreed, in fairness to both sides, that their emissaries,
one hundred and twenty in all, should meet without hostages at Koblenz and
there divide the kingdom as equally as possible.

5. They met there on the nineteenth of October, and to avoid the outbreak
among their followers of any strife for any reason those men who had come
from Louis and Charles pitched camp on the eastern bank of the Rhine and
those who had come from Lothar stayed on the western bank. And every
day they went to Saint-Castor's to confer together. When the emissaries of
Louis and Charles took up the division of the kingdom, it was asked with
many complaints whether anyone of them was thoroughly familiar with the
whole empire. When nobody was found, the question was raised why their
emissaries had not in the meantime traveled around the empire trying to
make a survey. The emissaries of Charles and Louis replied that Lothar did
not want them to do that, and then Lothar's emissaries said it was impossible
for one who did not know the whole story to divide anything equally. In
the end it was asked, since they were to divide the kingdom under oath as
equally and fairly as they knew how, whether they were able to swear to that
sincerely, knowing that nobody could do it without proper knowledge. This,
too, was submitted to the decision of the bishops.

When the bishops from both sides met in the basilica of Saint Castor,
those of Lothar's party declared that he who sinned in taking the oath could
atone for it, and that it was better for them to sin and atone, than for the
church of God to suffer further from rapine, murder, arson, and adultery.
Those of Louis's and Charles's party, on the other hand, asked why they
should sin against God since it was not necessary. They said that it was
better to make peace among themselves, and at the same time send messengers throughout the entire empire to survey it. Only then, they argued, was
it possible to swear that they were dividing safely and fairly something of
which they had certain knowledge. In this way, they assured Lothar's party,
it was also possible to avoid perjury and other crimes, unless blind cupidity
stood in the way. They testified that by making this proposal they wanted
to avoid violating their oaths or giving anyone else an excuse to do so. In
total disagreement they all went back to their people, whence they had come.

Then [in October 842] everyone met again in the same building and
Lothar's partisans declared that they were ready for their oath and to divide
the empire as had been sworn. Louis's and Charles's followers said that they
were ready, too, but only if it were possible for them. In the end, since
neither side dared to agree to the wishes of the other side without the approval of their lords, they arranged for a peace among themselves until they

would be able to know which of these proposals their lords were willing to accept. It seemed that this could be accomplished by the fifth of November. They departed after confirming a truce until this date.

On this day a violent earthquake struck most of Gaul. On the same day the worthy Angilbert was translated to Centulum [Saint-Riquier], and his body, without the help of spices, was found to be incorrupt twenty-nine years after his death. This man was a descendant of a family not unknown in those days. Madhelgaud, Richard, and he came from the same stock, and Charles the Great deservedly held them in high esteem. With Bertha, a daughter of the same great king, Angilbert begot my brother Hartnid and me, Nithard. At Centulum Angilbert constructed a magnificent building in honor of almighty God and Saint Richard and ruled magnificently the monastic family committed to him. Here he ended his life happily and was laid to rest in peace.

Having touched briefly on my own background I want to return to the proper course of my history.

6. When all the envoys, as I said before, returned to their kings and reported to them what had happened [in November 842], the brothers agreed that there should be peace among them until the twentieth day after Saint John's Mass [14 July 843]. They did so partly because the nobles having once tasted danger did not want any more fighting. To arrange peace the leading men of the people from both sides met at Thionville. They swore that in the meantime the kings would keep the peace among themselves, that they would not fail to divide the kingdom as equally as possible at this assembly, and that Lothar, as had been sworn, should have the choice among the parts. Then each departed wherever he wanted to go. Lothar headed for Aachen to spend the winter there, Louis went to Bavaria, and Charles came to Quierzy to take a wife.

At the same time the Moors, on whom Sigenulf, brother of Sigihard, had called for help, invaded Benevento. At the same time too the Stellinga in Saxony rebelled again against their lords. But when it came to battle they were put down in a great bloodbath. And so they, who had dared to rise without lawful power, perished by it.

Charles, as I said before, took a wife, Ermentrude, daughter of Odo and Ingeltrude, who was a niece of Adalhard. Charles's father in his time had loved this Adalhard so much that he did anything in his whole empire that Adalhard wanted. Adalhard cared little for the public good and tried to please everyone. Again and again he advised Charles's father to distribute liberties and public property for private use and, since he knew how to manage it so that everyone got what he asked for, he ruined the kingdom altogether. This is how he was easily able at this time to coax the people to do whatever he wanted. It was for this reason above all that Charles married Ermentrude, because he believed that with Adalhard's help he could win over a large part of the people to himself.

After the wedding had taken place on December 14 [842], he celebrated Christmas at Saint-Quentin. At Valenciennes he decided which of his vassals would remain to defend the land between the Meuse and the Seine. He and his wife headed for Aquitaine in the winter of the year of our Lord 843.

This winter, however, was excessively cold and long, full of diseases, and rather harmful to agriculture, livestock, and bees.

From this history, everyone may gather how mad it is to neglect the common good and to follow only private and selfish desires, since both sins insult the creator so much, in fact, that He turns even the elements against the madness of the sinner. I shall easily prove this by examples still known to almost everyone. In the times of Charles the Great of good memory, who died almost thirty years ago, peace and concord ruled everywhere because our people were treading the one proper way, the way of the common welfare, and thus the way of God. But now since each goes his separate way, dissension and struggle abound. Once there was abundance and happiness everywhere, now everywhere there is want and sadness. Once even the elements smiled on everything and now they threaten, as Scripture which was left to us as the gift of God, testifies: "And the world will wage war against the mad."

About this time, on March 20 [843], there occurred an eclipse of the moon. Besides, a great deal of snow fell in the same night and the just judgment of God, as I said before, filled every heart with sorrow. I mention this because rapine and wrongs of every sort were rampant on all sides, and now the unseasonable weather killed the last hope of any good to come.

Questions: Why does Nithard begin and end his history with Charlemagne? What is the general tone of Nithard's history and does it shift from book to book? Does the fact that Nithard was a layman and a soldier determine the style and emphases of his history? In what terms does Nithard characterize the two rebellions against Louis the Pious? How does Nithard regard the Battle of Fontenoy? Is Lothar the villain of Nithard's history? Is Charles the hero? Why did Louis and Charles swear as they did, in the language of the other's subjects, at Strasbourg? What made the division of lands by the brothers so complex? What does Nithard consider to be the principal problems rampant in his day?

45. Engelbert at the Battle of Fontenoy

The otherwise unknown author of this lament, Engelbert (or Angilbert), reveals how deeply the Battle of Fontenoy on 25 June 841 shook contemporaries. Like Lucan in his Civil War, the poet's point is to destroy any glorious reputation for this fratricidal battle, to wrap the fields of Fontenoy in Frankish blood. Yet the poet remains a partisan of Lothar and cannot put away his own royal interests. Moreover, the reader might like to compare God's place as the arbiter of the outcome of the battle here and in Nithard's account.

Source: trans. P.E. Dutton from Monumenta Germaniae Historica: Poetae Latini Aevi Carolini, vol. 2, ed. E. Dümmler (Berlin, 1884), pp.138-139.

1. When dawn with morning light divided off the foul night,
    That was not the Sabbath day, but Saturn's mixing-bowl.
    An ungodly demon delights over the brothers' broken peace.

2. War screams aloud as here and there dire fighting breaks out,
   A brother readies death for his brother, an uncle for his nephew;
   Sons refuse to give to fathers what they deserve.

3. No slaughter was ever worse on any field of war;
   The law of the Christians was shattered by this shedding of blood,
   Whence the company of hell and the mouth of its three-headed dog
   rejoice.

4. The powerful right hand of God [Christ] guarded Lothar,
   And that victor fought bravely alongside his army:
   If others had fought the same way, there would soon have been
   general peace.

5. But look, even as Judas betrayed the Savior,
   So your dukes betrayed you, my king, in the conflict;
   Be on your guard, lest you be cheated like the lamb following the wolf.

6. The common people call the place, both the spring and the village,
   Fontenoy,
   Where that massacre and bloody downfall of the Franks [took place]:
   The fields tremble, the woods tremble, the very swamp trembles.

7. Let no dew, no gentle showers, no pouring rain moisten the grass
   On which brave men, skilled warriors, fell;
   Fathers and mothers, sisters and brothers, friends all weep for them.

8. I, Engelbert, fighting alongside the others, saw
   This crime unfold, which I have described in verse;
   I alone of many from the first line of the army remained.

9. I looked down into the deeps of the valley and along the peak of a
   ridge,
   Where brave King Lothar was battling against his enemies,
   Who were fleeing to the open side of a brook.

10. On the sides of both Charles and Louis,
    The fields are white with the shrouds of the dead,
    Just as the fields become white with birds in autumn.

11. This battle is not worthy of praise, not fit to be sung.
    Let the east, south, west, and north
    Mourn them who unluckily fell to their deaths there.

12. Let not that accursed day be counted in the calendar of the year,
    Rather let it be erased from all memory,
    May the sun's rays never fall there, may no dawn ever come to [end its
    endless] twilight.

13. That night, that bitter night, that too awful night,
    On which brave men, skilled warriors, fell;
    Fathers and mothers, sisters and brothers, friends all weep for them.

14. O what grief and wailing! The dead lie there naked,
    While vultures, crows, and wolves savagely devour their flesh:
    They shake since they lack graves and their corpses lie there to no end.

15. I shall not more fully describe the wailing and howling:
    Let each hold back his sadness as well as he can,
    Let us pray to the Lord for their souls.

Questions: For whom was this poem written and for what purpose? What role does God play in the Battle of Fontenoy as seen through Engelbert's poem? Who does Engelbert blame? What images does the poet use?

46. The Treaty of Verdun, 843

Nithard had stopped short of the treaty of Verdun in his history and, indeed, no copy of the treaty survives. Yet the treaty and its date have often been used to mark the starting point of various national histories and no textbook of western civilization is without its simple drawing of the tripartition of Europe. After students have examined the drawing and the accounts of the treaty from the Annals of Saint-Bertin and Fulda, they might like to consider why each king kept the regions where they were already established and why Lothar's imperial pretensions determined the final form of the middle kingdom.

Source: trans. P.E. Dutton from Annales de Saint-Bertin, ed. F. Grat, J. Vielliard, S. Clémencet (Paris: Klincksieck, 1964), pp.44-45; from Annales Fuldenses siue Annales Regni Francorum Orientalis, ed. G.H. Pertz and F. Kurze in Monumenta Germaniae Historica: Scriptores Rerum Germanicarm in Usum Scholarum (Hanover, 1891), p.34.

[Annals of Saint-Bertin]

843

Charles went to meet his brothers as agreed upon and they came together at Verdun. There the lots were distributed: Louis taking everything beyond the Rhine [on the east side]; on this side [the west side] of the Rhine, he took the cities and regions of Speyer, Worms, and Mainz. Lothar received the lands lying between the Rhine and the Scheldt River where it runs to the sea, and also Cambrai, Hainault, Lomme, and Castricium, and those counties on this side [the west] of the Meuse which are contiguous, until the Saône flows into the Rhône and until the Rhône flows into the sea. The same holds for all the counties lying on either side of the [Rhône]. Except for these lands he obtained only Arras and that was from the kindness of his brother Charles. They conceded the rest to Charles as far as Spain. After oaths were sworn, at last each departed to his own part.

[Annals of Fulda]

843

The kingdom [of Francia] having been sketched out by the magnates and having been divided into three, the three kings, coming together in the month of August at Verdun, a city in Gaul, divided the kingdom among themselves. Louis received the eastern part, Charles held the western, [and] Lothar, who was the eldest, chose the middle portion among them. And peace having been agreed upon between them and confirmed with an oath, each returned to arrange and protect the lands of his kingdom. Charles, marching to Aquitaine as if to a part that belonged to his kingdom by law, was hostile towards his nephew Pepin and harassed him with many invasions, but his army frequently suffered great loss [there].

Two Maps of the Treaty of Verdun, 843

Facing Page: Top: from C. Oman, The Dark Ages, 476-918, 5th ed. (London: Rivingtons, 1905), p.410. Bottom: from J.H. Robinson, An Introduction to the History of Western Europe, I: The Background of Modern History, 2nd ed. (Boston: Ginn and Company, 1924), p.119.

Questions: How are these two maps different? What would account for the differences? In making the division what did the negotiators use as borders? What difficulties did the dividers of the kingdom face? What was the principle upon which the division was made? Is the division a rational one? Could it be enduring, or was it meant to be?

PARTITION TREATY
OF
VERDUN
843.

Boundaries of Kingdoms ▬▬▬
Boundaries of Districts -----

Hamburg

Saxony
KINGDOM

Thu-
ringia

Frisia

Austrasia

Aachen

Franconia
Mainz

OF

Regensburg

Tributary Sclavonic Tribes

Neustria
Paris

KINGDOM

Suabia

Bavaria

LEWIS

OF
Aquitaine

Bordeaux

CHARLES

Burgundy

Lyons

Provence

Pavia

Lombardy

LOTHAR

Spanish March

Barcelona

ROME

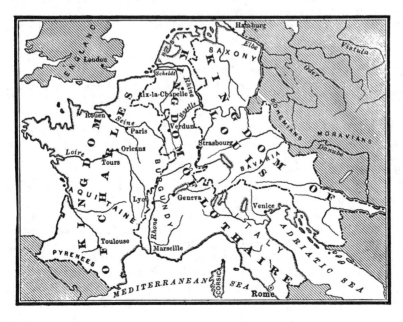

London

Hamburg

Elbe

Vistula

SAXONY

Scheldt

Aix-la-Chapelle

Rhine

KINGDOM

BOHEMIANS

Oder

Rouen

Seine

Moselle

Paris

Verdun

Strasbourg

MORAVIANS

Loire

Orleans

Danube

Tours

BURGUNDY

BAVARIA

KINGDOM

AQUITAINE

Lyon

Geneva

Venice

Rhone

OF

ITALY

Toulouse

OF LOTHAIRE

ADRIATIC SEA

PYRENEES

Marseille

KINGDOM OF CHARLES

MEDITERRANEAN SEA

CORSICA

Rome

47. Dhuoda's Advice to Her Son

Dhuoda was the wife of Bernard of Septimania, the chamberlain of Louis the Pious who had been accused in 830 of committing adultery with the Empress Judith and, hated by Louis's sons, was driven from court. In 841 Dhuoda, who had been at work protecting her husband's interests in the Spanish March, learned that her son, William, had, in effect, been handed over to Charles the Bald as a hostage to secure Bernard's good conduct. She wrote her Manual in order to counsel him, as only a mother could, she said, about how to survive and prosper in a difficult world. Her rich and complex treatise served in part as a way for Dhuoda to reconstitute her embattled and separated family. She also wanted to establish a circle of prayer that would bind up her family, living and dead, and win her a place in heaven. But, if Dhuoda lived much beyond 843 when she sent the Manual to William, she must have suffered even greater grief, for her husband was shortly afterwards murdered by Charles the Bald and William himself was executed in 850 when he was but twenty-four years old.

Source: trans. P.E. Dutton from Dhuoda, Manuel pour mon fils, ed. P. Riché, Sources Chrétiennes, vol. 225 (Paris: Editions du Cerf, 1975), pp.84-86, 338-358.

[Preface to the Manual]

With our lord Louis [the Pious] once happily flourishing in the empire, with Christ's favor, in his eleventh year, on the third Kalends of July [29 June 824], at the palace of Aachen in a wedding ceremony, I became the legal wife of my lord and your father Bernard [of Septimania]. Again in the thirteenth year of [Louis's] reign, on the third Kalends of December [29 November 826], with God's help, as I believe, your birth, my most beloved first born son, into this world through me took place.

With the troubles and calamities of this world growing worse by the day and with many ups and downs and disruptions in the kingdom, the emperor went the way of all [mortals]. Just short of the twenty-eighth year of his reign [which began in 813 while Charlemagne was still alive], [Louis], somewhat prematurely, reached the end of his life. The year following his death, your brother was born on the eleventh Kalends of April [22 March 841]. He was the second child born to me [you being the first], with God's mercy, in the city of Uzès. In fact Bernard, the lord and father of both of you, ordered Elefantus, the bishop of Uzès, to take that little one, before he had been baptized, and to bring him into his presence in Aquitaine where he was staying with his retainers.

But since I have been parted from you for a long time and am living, on the orders of my lord, in this city where I now rejoice in [Bernard's] struggles, I have taken the trouble, because of my love for both of you, to have this little book (its size is in keeping with my intelligence) copied and sent to you. Although I am beset by many difficulties, nevertheless let this one thing happen according to the will of God, if he so wishes, that I might look upon your face once. Indeed I would wish for this, if the power [to do so] was given to me by God, but because salvation is far away from me as a sinner, I [can only] wish for it, and in this wishing my determination grows weaker.

I have heard that your father, Bernard, has commended you into the hands of the lord, King Charles [the Bald]. I urge you to do your dignified duty in this business to the best of your will. All the same, as the Scriptures say, "Seek the kingdom of God in all things and other things will then be given," those things which are necessary for you to enjoy your soul and body.

[Book 10]

1. Concerning Your Times

1. You have finished now four times four years.
   If my second child were to reach the same age,
   I would copy out another little book for his person.

2. And if you were to reach the age of 36,
   And if I were to see you again,
   I would with more words urge upon you even stronger things.

3. But because the time of my end hastens towards me,
   And sickness everywhere wears my body out,
   I have rushed to put together this book for the use of you and your
      brother.

4. Knowing that I shall not live another twenty years.
   I urge you to savor this book as though it were a pleasant drink
   And honey-laced food meant for your lips.

5. For the date when I married your father
   And the date when you were born occurred on the
   [Same Kalends] of [different] months, as I told you above.

6. Know that, from the first verse of this little book,
   Until its last syllable,
   Everything has been designed for the purpose of your salvation.

7. That you may more easily follow what is written there,
   Read the acrostic verses.

8. The little verses written above and below, and everything else,
   I myself have composed [or dictated] for the benefit of your soul and
      body,
   And I do not cease even now urging you to read them and keep them
      close to your heart.

2. On the Verses Made from the Letters of Your Name

In the original Latin the first letter of the first word of each of the first seventeen stanzas can be put together to spell out VERSI AD VVILHELMUM: Verses for William.

1. That you might be strong and thrive, O best of sons,
   Do not be reluctant to read the words I have composed and
   Sent to you and may you effortlessly discover things
       That please you.

2. The word of God is alive; look for it
   Diligently and learn its sacred teaching,
   For then your mind will be stuffed with
       Great joy forever.

3. May the immense and powerful King, being radiant and kind,
   Care to cultivate your mind in all things,
   Young man, and to guard and defend you
       Every minute of every day.

4. Be humble in mind and chaste in body,
   Be ready to give proper service,
   Show yourself constantly kind to all people,
       Both the great and the not so great.

5. Above all, fear and love the Lord God
   With your full heart and soul and expend all your strength,
   Next fear and love your father
       In all things.

6. Do not regret continually serving
   The glorious offspring [Charles the Bald] of [that] race,
   With its line of ancestors, for he shines
       With the great.

7. Esteem magnates and respect those of high rank at court;
   Be humble with the low;
   Associate yourself with the well intentioned; be sure not to
       Submit to the proud and the imprudent.

8. Always honor the true ministers
   Of the sacred rites, the worthy bishops;
   Always commend yourself simply and with outstretched hands
       To the custodians of the altars.

9. Frequently give assistance to widows and orphans,
   Give food and drink to pilgrims;
   Offer hospitality; stretch out your hands
       With apparel for the naked.

10. Be a strong and fair judge in legal disputes;
    Never take a bribe;
    Never oppress anyone, for the great Giver
        Will repay you.

11. Be generous with gifts, but always vigilant and modest,
    Make a sincere effort to get along with everyone,
    Rejoice in humble things, for the image of this will
        Stay with you.

12. There is One who weighs up everything,
    A bestower who grants to each according to merit,
    Assigning for [good] words and works the greatest of gifts:
        The constellations of the heavenly stars.

13. Thus, my noble son, you should take care
    And seek constantly to obtain
    The great advantages [of heaven], and spurn
        The fires of pitch-black wood.

14. Although, at sixteen, you are in the very flower
    Of your youth, your delicate limbs
    Age [along with you] step by step
        As you proceed through life.

15. I long to see your face,
    But the prospect seems distant to me.
    Even if the power should be given to me,
        Yet still I do not deserve this.

16. Would that you might live for Him who shaped you,
    May you enter into, with gentle spirit, a fitting association
    With his servants; may you with joy rise up again when your
        Life is done.

17. My mind surely turns to thoughts of death,
    But still I want you to read carefully the pages of this book,
    As I have written them [for you], and keep them constantly
        Foremost in your mind.

18. These verses, with the help of God, are now done
    As you finish your sixteen years
    At the start of December, on the Feast of Saint Andrew [30 November],
        And the Advent of the Word.

3. A Postscript Concerning Your Public Life

The words of this little book are complete, which, as I was able, I have composed [or dictated] with happy heart and commanded to be copied out that they might be useful to you in your development.

For I want and advise that when, with the help of God, you have come to the appropriate time, you will establish your [own] household advantageously according to the proper grades of rank and, as is written about a certain man, "like the most tender little woodworm," do everything in your public life faithfully and in due course.

I do not know whether I shall survive until I can see you, and I am uncertain if I deserve to and am uncertain over my health, and I am shaken amid the turbulence of my feeble struggle. Although this is the way things stand for me, yet everything remains possible for the Almighty. It is not within human power to do everything, but rather people achieve only as much as God decides to grant. According to Scripture, "It is not of him that wills nor of him that runs, but of God who shows mercy." Because of this, and trusting in God's mercy, I say nothing other than: "As it shall be the will of God in heaven, so let it be done." Amen.

4. Returning to Myself, I Mourn

Out of the profound depths of my love and my longing for your handsome face, I have almost forgotten myself but, even with the doors closed, I desire now to enter again into my own heart. But, because I am not worthy to be counted among the number listed before, nevertheless I ask you, with your considerable affection for me, and others not to stop praying for the remedy of my soul.

It is not hidden to you how, with constant illnesses and other troubles—just like the words of the one who said, "In perils from my own nation, in perils from the Gentiles, etc."—I have endured all these and similar things with my fragile body and in keeping with my limited worth. In fact, with God's help and by the grace of your father Bernard, I have surely escaped from all these perils, but my mind returns reflectively to those moments of liberation. I have, in the past, frequently been negligent in praising God. When I should have been praying at the seven [canonical] hours, I was instead seven times as slothful at those seven hours. For this reason, with all humility and all my power, I beg for the pleasing prospect of praying continually for the mercy of the Lord on behalf of my offenses and sins and that He may think me worthy to lift up, [however] damaged and weighed down, to heaven.

While you see that I am [still] alive in this world, alertly attempt in your heart to exert yourself so that, not only through vigils and prayers, but also by giving charity to the poor, I might deserve, when [finally] seized from my body and from the chains of my sinning, to be received kindly in every way by our kind Judge.

Constant prayer by you and others is needed by me now. It will be more, much more needed, after my death, which I believe will come very quickly. From an immense fear of what the future has in store for me, my mind is searching about everywhere. I am unsure from my merits just how I can be freed in the end. Why? Since I have sinned in thought and speech. Speech itself, if idle, leads to wicked business. Still, although things stand like this, I shall never despair of the mercy of God, not now, not ever. For me to achieve salvation at some point, I leave no other, my noble son, who might work as hard on my behalf as you. Many others too will work on my behalf because of you.

For the sake of my lord and master, Bernard, so that my service on his behalf in the [Spanish] March and in other places might not be useless, and so that he might not abandon you and me as is the practice of some men,

I am aware that I have fallen deeply into debt. From great need, I have often received into my hands loans not only from Christians, but also from Jews. I have paid back as much as I could, and I shall continue to do so as far as I can, but if, after my death, something remains outstanding, I ask and beg that you diligently find out who my creditors are. Once they are located, you should pay them everything owed not only from my own resources, if anything remains, but also from the resources you possess now and from those that you will, with God's grace, legitimately obtain in the future.

What more should I say? I have reminded you repeatedly about how you should act towards your little brother. I ask this as well, that if he should reach the right age, he too should take the trouble to pray for me. I urge you both, as if you were standing together now, to take the trouble to offer frequently on my behalf the libations of sacrifices and the offerings of the Host.

In this way when my Redeemer will have ordered me to leave this world, he will care to prepare a place of peaceful repose for me. If this happens because of the worthy prayers of you and other people, then the one whom we call God might receive me into heaven with the saints.

Here the Manual finishes. Amen. Thanks be to God.

5. The Names of the Dead

You will find here, briefly listed, the names of some people I omitted earlier. They are: William [of Gellone, the father of Bernard], Cunigund [the wife of William], Gerberga [the daughter of William who was drowned in the Saône by Lothar in 834], Witburgis [the second wife of William], Theoderic [a son of William], Gozhelm [a son of William who was decapitated by Lothar in 834], Guarnarius [possibly the father of Dhuoda], Rothlindis [possibly the mother of Dhuoda].

There are other relatives from this line still living, with God's help, for it falls entirely to the One who created them to recall them. What should you do on their behalf, my son, except say with the Psalmist: "We that live bless the Lord from this time now and forever."

Likewise, if any member of your family dies, that too belongs to the power of God to order. I ask that if you survive your uncle, lord Aribert [another son of William], you order his name to be inscribed with the names above and that you [also] pray for him.

6. About the Epitaph I Ask You to Inscribe on My Tomb

When I too have completed my time, order my name to be copied down with the names of the other dead. What I want, and what I long for with all my energy as if it were taking place at this very moment, is that you order these little verses to be carved on the stone face of the tomb that will cover my body in that place where I am to be buried. In this way, those who see the epitaph on my tomb may be inclined to pour out worthy prayers to God on my behalf, however unworthy I am.

But you readers of this Manual, whoever you are, think about the words that follow below and speak to God now on my behalf, as if I were already shut up in my tomb, so that I might gain salvation.

Read here, O reader, the little verses of my epitaph!
Into the Hands of God.

Shaped of earth, the body of Dhuoda
Lies buried in this mound.
  Powerful King, receive her.

This earth around her took back to the lower regions
The insignificant mud of her body:
  Benign King, grant indulgence to her.

The earthen shadows of the tomb, wet with her wound,
Are all that is left her.
  You, O King, forgive her sins.

Whether you be a man or woman, young or old,
As you walk back and forth here, I ask you to say this:
  Holy God, dissolve her chains.

Locked in the tomb of a great wound
She ended her earthly life.
  You, O King, forgive her her sins.

Lest that foul snake snatch away her soul,
Pray and say these words:
  O Forgiving God, give her relief.

Let no one pass this place without reading this.
I beg everyone to pray, saying this:
  Sweet God, give her rest.

Order, O kind one, that she receive
Everlasting light in the company of the saints.
  May she receive the Lord's Amen after her demise.

Alpha and Omega.

Questions: Can a modern reader understand the psychological makeup and emotions of Dhuoda? If not, is there any point in reading the Manual which seems driven by Dhuoda's desire to speak from the heart to her absent son? How distraught over William's enforced service to Charles the Bald is Dhuoda? Why would she write such a book? What ideals does she wish to recommend to William? Is she at all critical of Bernard? What does she want for herself?

48. Walahfrid Strabo's Little Garden

Walahfrid rose to prominence at Louis the Pious's court as a client of Judith and the tutor of young Charles the Bald. When the revolts of 830 and 833 occurred, his life was severely disrupted. In 838 he was made the abbot of the great monastery of Reichenau, but in 840 he was driven from his post by Louis the German as the king sought control of eastern Francia. Though Walahfrid sought assistance from the Emperor Lothar, Louis eventually restored the monk to his office in 842. It is probably from these years of disruption that Walahfrid's little book on his herb garden at Reichenau comes, for Walahfrid's pastoralism in the Hortulus may be almost as political as Virgil's was in the Georgics. Walahfrid drowned in the river Loire in the summer of 849 while on royal business for Louis.

Source: trans. R.S. Lambert, in Hortulus or the Little Garden: A Ninth-Century Poem by Walafrid Strabo (Wembley Hill, Middlesex: The Stanton Press, 1923).

How To Make A Garden

Though a life of retreat offers various joys,
None I think will compare with the time one employs
In the study of herbs, or in striving to gain
Some practical knowledge of nature's domain.
Get a garden! What kind you may get matters not,
Though the soil be light, friable, sandy and hot,
Or alternately heavy and rich with stiff clay;
Let it lie on a hill, or a slope gently away
To the level, or sink in an overgrown dell,
Don't despair, it will serve to grow vegetables well!
Provided no sloth takes the edge off your zeal,
And you never permit yourself scornful to feel
Of the infinite pains a true gardener must take,

The Difficulties of Gardening

Last winter—that symbol of age and decay,
That consumer of all the whole year stores away—
Was driven by spring to take refuge and hide
In the uttermost corner of earth's other side.
While his conqueror—crown and chief pride of the year,
Bade languishing nature recover her cheer,
And quickly removed every vestige and trace
Of the glutton, and put on all things a new face.
As the weather grew milder and fine days occurred,
And flowers and herbs by the west wind were stirred,
The soft tips of their shoots, so long lost to our sight,
In the bosom of earth to escape the frost's bite,
Began to reach out. Verdure clothed every tree;
Rough grass covered the mountain, and fine sward the lea.
Then the little court-yard that adjoins my front door

And eastward extends its diminutive floor,
Became covered with nettles, that spread and grew high,
And reared up their venomous stings to the sky.

Nettle

What was I to do? Their roots formed a thick mat
Just like what the plow-boys so cleverly plait
For their stables, of osiers twined in a knot
To protect horses' hooves from the damp and the rot.
Well, away with delay! Armed with mattock and rake,
I attack the caked earth. From each dull clot I break
The wild nettles, expose many worms to the day
And scatter the molehills that get in my way.
Next I leave the whole plot to be baked, like a bun,
By the breath of the south-wind and heat of the sun.
Only, lest the soil slip and drift out of its place,
With four pieces of timber I edge the whole space,
And then heap the bed up on a gentle incline.
Next, I rake till the surface is powdered and fine;
And lastly, to make its fertility sure,
I impose a thick mulch of well-rooted manure.
And now—a few vegetable seeds let us sow,
And watch how the older perennials grow!

Perseverance and Its Reward

The little crop soon by occasional rains
Is sprinkled. At night the moon kindly sustains
Each seedling with dew. But if drought should prevail,
I must boldly step into the breach with a pail.
For fear lest the thirsty plants wilt in the sun,
To and fro with full buckets of water I run.
But it must not be poured in a casual spurt,
Or the seeds will get scattered, the stems suffer hurt.
No—using the palm of my hand as a sieve,
The pure water in drops I must carefully give.
And now, before long, my whole garden is seen
Transfigured, and clothed in a robe of soft green.
What though there's a corner all rainless and dry
Where the roof of my dwelling shuts out the blue sky,
So that nothing will grow? For the opposite side
In perpetual shadow rejoices to hide,
And the wall is so high that the fiery heat
Of the sun never falls on the ground at its feet.
Thus there's scarcely a seed I entrust to the earth
Without excellent hope it will come safe to birth.
Even plants that appear to be stunted by drought
Can be lifted, and safely transplanted about.

Moved to happier quarters they soon grow apace,
And in time with fresh seed-pods replenish their race.
But now I must sharpen my wits and my speech,
And try to describe by its name and to teach
The virtues of every plant that I grew,
That the least may have honor, where honor is due.

Sage

To Sage must be given the pride of first place,
Sweet-scented, a flavor for drink, full of grace.
For so many an ailment it offers relief,
It deserves to rejoice in an evergreen leaf.
But its bane is itself. When the flower-pods seed,
The offspring grow up full of malice and greed,
And quickly, unless they are rooted away,
Consume their own parents and make them decay.

Rue

Next somber-green Rue in the shady bed lies,
With leaves fresh in colour, but puny in size.
It flowers on short umbelliferous shoots
That admit sun and air to the stem and the roots.
Foul odors and humors disperse at its touch,
And its power to cure all diseases is such
That even from poisons unknown it protects,
And the noxious drug from the system ejects.

Southern Wood

Next the shrub Southern-wood should be noted with care,
With its plentiful foliage sharp, like fine hair.
Pluck a few of the sweet-smelling herbs with their sticks;
In medicinal draughts they are useful to mix.
It reduces a fever, expels cruel darts,
And whenever a weapon has pierced several parts,
Any unobserved bleeding it stops and relieves,
In short, it has virtues as many as leaves!

Pumpkin

In like manner the Pumpkin, though feeble when small,
Bears huge shady leaves and aspires to grow tall.
It casts out long tentacles far on all sides,
And, just as the ivy insensibly glides
Up the stem of an elm, and entwines the whole tree,
In its arms, till the bark disappears in a sea
Of evergreen leaves from the base to the top:

Or just as a vine which is offered a prop
Makes haste with its clusters to cover the whole
And speedily climbs the full height of its pole—
There the ruddy grape hangs on the arm of its friend
On its broad lower leaves, whilst the tendrils extend
Ever upward, dividing the leaves at the crest—
So my lowly-born Pumpkin with love is possessed
For the alder I give him to teach him to rise,
And round it in circles his tentacles' ties.
No hurricane wind could unloose such a grasp,
For at every fresh joint he puts forth a new clasp;
And since into twain every tendril divides,
The prop is encircled from opposite sides.
Just as thread on a spindle is wound by a girl
In many a spiral and regular whorl,
So each twig of the alder is bound by a chain
Which enables the Pumpkin new foothold to gain.
More cleverly still, by the aid of this prop,
He can climb a steep shed and fly over its top.
Moreover, what fruit! Who can fail to acclaim
Its nobly-proportioned, symmetrical frame,
As smooth as if turned on a lathe? With what grace
From its slender long stem it hangs down in its place!
And then, from that delicate neck there swells out
What a body, prodigious, vast, wanton and stout,
All belly, all paunch? In whose cavernous heart
Swell infinite seeds, each imprisoned apart,
But bearing the promise of harvests-to-be.
Nay, more; if you patiently wait you will see,
(Should the fruit be yet soft, with its juice fresh within,
Ere the autumn has drained it and toughened the skin)
What a wonderful meal it will offer when fried;
For the slices lap up the hot fat, and provide
The daintiest dish that the table can show.
Again, if it be left in the open to grow
And cut when the sun has matured the hard rind,
Your Pumpkin will serve as a jug, you will find.
Throw away the inside and keep only the peel,
And polish it smooth on a lathe or a wheel.
In its belly a generous pint you can store,
Or, if the long neck be included, much more.
And if it be caulked with a resinous glue,
It will long keep your wine uncorrupted and true.

Melon

The same little plot where the Pumpkin is found
Rejoicing in marshy and low-lying ground,
Its fellow and kinsman will certainly suit,

That sprawls in the dust, and bears globular fruit.
It commonly grows on some bare patch of earth,
And brings a fine crop of rich Melons to birth.
When the heat of the summer has tinged them with gold,
They are ripe for the gatherer's basket to hold.
Some are rounded and smooth; some have bellies that jut
In a long, oval curve, like an egg or a nut.
Like a drip of that paste ladies use for their skin
Which, before it with water is mixed and made thin,
Must be kneaded by hand, till 'tis soft to the touch:
As the fingers squeeze hard, and it yields to their clutch,
It finds a small crevice, and thence oozes out
And bulges and swells in a fat, heavy gout;
While the slippery core at it nethermost tip
Adjusts it proportions to how the hands grip.
When a Melon is stabbed by a knife to the heart,
Great rivers of juice through the aperture start
Mixed with marrow and pulp; through the hole in the side
You may shake it all out. 'T is the spoil and chief pride
Of the garden, a choice and delectable feast
That will tickle your palate, yet not in the least
Set your teeth upon edge. Down it slips like a dream,
And refreshes your soul with its icy-cool stream.

Wormwood

Next wormwood produces its sharp-tasting fruits,
Which it bears, like the mother of herbs, on tough shoots;
But unlike is the hue of its leaf, and the smell
Of its branches; its taste is more bitter, as well.
For expelling a fever or quenching a thirst
Undoubtedly Wormwood of herbs is the first.
If your temples turn giddy or suffer from ache,
A decoction of Wormwood is what you should make.
Boil a handful of leaves, and then strain off the juice,
And refresh the whole head with a thorough good sluice.
Then, when you have made the scalp clean, sweet and fair,
Plait the leaves in a fillet to tie up your hair.
Soon the fillet will shrink and the hair be held tight,
And the herb's many virtues be brought to the light.

Horehound

Now shall I tell of the use and the power
Of redoubtable Horehound? Bitter and sour
To the palate it is, though the odor is sweet.
A draught of this herb should be taken to meet
Sudden pains in the heart. Heated up it is best,
And drunk after dinner, your food to digest.

Again, if your step-mother bears you ill-will
And mixes a poisonous aconite pill
In your food, and rejoices to see you look sad
As you swallow the drug and begin to feel bad,
Never worry—but drink off a cup of this herb.
Your step-mother's evil designs it will curb.

Fennel

Next to Fennel we must not omit to give praise
Whose sturdy stems many a spreading branch raise;
For equally sweet is its flavor and smell.
It is good for weak eyes, I have heard many tell,
And should you have boils in the stomach, the seed,
If taken in goat's milk, will answer your need.
(This medicine has an additional use,
The bowels, if sluggish or stubborn, to loose)
And if from the root you prepare a rich soup,
Mixed with wine, it will keep off the asthma and croup.

Cornflag [Gladiola]

Nor must you be forgotten, sweet lily, whose name
From the Latin for 'sword' in its origin came.
As the summer begins, in my garden I mark
Your deep, ruddy blossoms, whose hue is as dark
As the violet, or as that ill-fated flower
Which bloomed long ago in Apollo's high bower
The day that his favorite died, and received
The name Hyacinth from the god, as he grieved;
And still to this day on its petals we read
The syllable 'Ai', and recall the sad deed.
First, we pound in a mortar a piece of your root;
Next the shreds that remain with strong wine we dilute.
This makes a decoction that serves to allay
All disease of the bladder, and drives pain away.
Then it renders the work of the laundry more light,
For with it our clothes are made clean, stiff and white.

Lovage

Among herbs that have odor I must not forget
In my dear little garden strong Lovage to set.
But alas! both its scent and its sap are unkind.
They are bad for the eyes, and will make a man blind.
Still, when mixing your herbs in a poison to heal,
Add a few seeds of Lovage—their praise it will steal!

Chervil

O Erato, thou who hast wrought into song
So many great wars, such an infinite throng
Of heroical deeds, do not scorn my desire,
But this my poor vegetable-epic inspire!
Though the stem of the Chervil be straggly and weak,
And its seed mean and paltry, not easy to seek
In the thick of the leaves, it is green all the year
And freely bestows of its comfort and cheer
On the poor. In addition, a taste of it serves
To prevent apoplexy and serve throbbing nerves.
If ever the gripes on your belly should seize,
A poultice of Chervil will soon give it ease.
Mix in a few Poppy-leaves fresh from the field,
And add Penny-royal—and then you'll get healed.

Lily

Now how can my verses, so meager and trite,
Do justice to Lilies, all dazzling and white?
Whose purity shines like the virginal snows,
Whose odor like frankincense tickles the nose.
No Parian marble that hue can excel,
No Spikenard oil overpower that smell.
Suppose that some treacherous serpent should bite,
And its poison, acquired by inherited spite,
Should inject in the wound, so that cruel death dart
Unseen through the devious veins to the heart;
Take a pestle, and beat up a Lily quite fine,
And drink the juice—mixed with Falernian wine!
The rest of the leaves that are bruised you may place
On a pimple or spot that disfigures your face:
Then the strength of the poultice will be understood.
(For a paralyzed limb it is equally good).

Poppy

The Poppy, I fancy, recalls to our mind
How the goddess Demeter, unable to find
Persephone stolen, was stricken with grief
And anxious to gain for her thoughts some relief.
And so a decoction of Poppy she drank,
And immediately into oblivion sank.
The same remedy serves, if you're ever distrest
By a nasty, black carbuncle inside your chest.
The belching of wind it will quickly allay,
And take the foul taste in your mouth right away.
The Poppy lifts up a huge head full of seed

To the sky, on a neck that's as thin as a reed.
Like the African apple, beneath a broad skin
A rich cargo of grain it keeps hidden within.
And the name of the Poppy is said to be due
To the 'pop' of the seeds in your mouth as you chew.

Clary

A shady herb next in the border I spy
Called Clary, which lifts up its foliage high
On a powerful stem. It is rarely employed,
And the doctors, I find, almost seem to avoid
The use of it. Still, it makes excellent beer,
Which kindles the heart with its savory cheer.

Costmary

Next Costmary hides, not the meanest or last
Of the herbs that I grow. When the bowels are fast,
A bit of its root, if made into stew,
Your belly will purge, and its health will renew.

Mint

One herb in my garden I grow without stint—
I like an abundance of good, common Mint.
What a number of separate species and kinds
Of different color and power one finds!
According to singers, one sort will dispel
All harshness, and make the voice clear as a bell.
For continual rasping soon dries up the throat;
Drink some peppermint—that will enliven your note!
Another delectable species provides
With its foliage plenty of shade on all sides:
Like the elder, it puts out a fresh set of shoots
From its branches, the higher they grow from the roots.
The scent of this kind is distinct, and the taste
Especially bitter—but why do I waste
My time in a detailed attempt to describe
The uses and names of the whole minty tribe?
To do so, I might just as well ascertain
The number of fish in the Indian Main,
Or how many sparks can old Vulcan espy
From his furnace at Etna soar up to the sky!

Penny-royal

Space prevents me describing more thoroughly, too,
The herb Penny-royal and all it can do.

Its value in India is reckoned as dear
As a peck of black Indian pepper is here.
Who can doubt of its power our ills to allay,
When a people so rich as the Indians pay
Any price to obtain it, and readily bring
To us ivory, gold, every wonderful thing?
Praise be to wisdom and power of God,
Who to every country that man ever trod
Has given some one and peculiar kind
Of wealth! What is rare and not easy to find
Over here, is as common elsewhere upon earth
As the things that we hold in lowliest worth.
And those in their turn that at home we despise,
Are considered abroad a magnificent prize.
Thus each part of the world on another depends,
And trade to the universe unity lends.
If stewed, Penny-royal, my friend, is of use
As a draught or a poultice, the bowels to loose.
As these evident, well-proven facts I relate,
Common-sense will permit me from hearsay to state
That a sprig of this herb placed between the two ears
Is a certain protection against any fears
Of a sun-stroke, supposing your head to be exposed
There now, if Thalia had not interposed
With an order to take in my sails and make port,
The full tale of its virtues I here would report!

Parsley

Though Parsley is little esteemed nowadays
In our gardens, and only its flavor gets praise,
Still it has its own virtues and helps us at need.
If you swallow a powder prepared from the seed,
A stricture it readily serves to dispel.
If a bit of leaf you can manage as well,
This guarantees perfect digestion at meals.
Suppose now, 'His Majesty' bilious feels—
Mix vinegar, Parsley and water in one;
Then the belly recovers, the gripes are soon done.

Betony

Over mountain and forest, through meadow and dale,
No lack of this herb will be found to prevail.
It is common enough, though exceedingly prized,
And it not only grows, but is naturalized
In my garden. For Betony boldly I claim
That it really deserves its exceptional fame.
Indeed, if I try to add even a word

To this popular verdict—the task is absurd.
For whatever I say of its power to bless
Cannot make it more famous, and might make it less!
Now whether you pluck it and cook it while green,
Or dry it for use when foul winter is seen;
And whether you like it to drink thick and strong,
Or prefer to refine it (the labor is long):
This herb will respond to your every desire.
Indeed, there are people who so much admire
Its numerous properties, that they assert
That from every possible internal hurt
The body by Betony's aid can be freed.
In accordance with this, day by day they proceed
To toss off a dose of the powerful herb.
Again, if a wound in the head should disturb
Your peace and contentment, and threaten to rot,
Clap a poultice of Betony-leaves on the spot.
Then watch how the strength of the herb is revealed,
As the sore disappears and the wound is soon healed.

Agrimony

The whole country too in this herb is arrayed,
But it commonest shows in the forest's deep shade,
Where its regular growth makes it easily known.
It has various virtues. Supposing you groan
With the direst of pains in your belly, just take
A dose of it powdered—away goes the ache!
Again, in a wound if a fragment of steel
Gets imbedded, try this way of making it heal.
Take a leaf, and well bruise it, and place it with care
Where the mouth of the wound is exposed to the air.
If you rub a few drops of sour vinegar round,
The trouble will pass and the place be made sound.

Ambrosia

Nearby is a herb that most people would name
Ambrosia. Whether 't is really the same
As the plant that we can find in the writers of old
I very much doubt. Still, the doctors, I'm told,
Advise that their patients, when heavily bled,
On Ambrosia-tea should be nourished and fed.

Catmint

Of the many perennial flowers that sprout
In my garden, by no means the last to come out
Is Catmint. With leaves like a nettle's it grows,

But oh! from the tip what aroma it throws.
No wonder its virtues were praised in the past;
And nowadays, even, it is not the last
Or the the meanest of herbs. If you mix up its juice
With some essence of roses, you have for your use
A magnificent salve, by whose means it is proved
All manner of scars can be wholly removed.
Unsightly disfigurements speedily yield,
And the skin its old color recovers when healed.
Though your head when a festering fissure be sore,
This ointment will make the hair grow as before.

Radish

At the end of the border the Radish is found,
With its broad cap of leaves and root deep in the ground.
A piece of this hot-flavoured root bitten off
And chewed, will expel the most shattering cough;
And a similar cure, as a rule, will proceed
From taking a powder prepared from the seed.

Rose

Now were I not spent with the length of my song
And afraid with new matter its course to prolong,
For the lovely wild Rose a rich crown I would mould
Of Arabian pearls and of Lydian gold.
Though of Tyrian purple we cannot make boast
From the marches of France unto Germany's coast,
Still, year after year in our hedges there grows
With profusion of yellow and crimson, the Rose.
The flower of flowers men call it, and well,
For it passes all others in beauty and smell.
From its petals a marvelous oil one distils
Which is useful for no one knows how many ills.
Now the Lily in fame with the Rose can compare,
For its odor still further extends in the air;
But if once the white petals be broken or bruised,
You will marvel to see how the scent is diffused
And suddenly wafted away into nought.
So the flower of chastity, strong in the thought
Of the blessing of God, shines in beauty of form
And, if never defiled by some passionate storm
Of worldly affection or bodily love,
Exudes a sweet scent other scents far above:
But if anything mars its original grace,
The sweet odor departs, a foul stench takes its place.

These two famous flowers should call to our mind
The two greatest gifts of the Church to mankind.
In the blood of her martyrs she plucks a red Rose,
And in sign of her faith a white Lily she shows.
O virginal mother! O store of ripe seed!
Inviolate maid, wed to heaven indeed,
Dove of purity, bride, heaven's queen, faithful friend,
O pluck Roses in war, but when wars have an end,
Pluck Lilies for joy! For of thee comes the heir,
The scion of Jesse, the scepter to bear;
Only sower and raiser of man's ancient seed,
Who sanctified Lilies in word and in deed,
Who by His death gave to the Roses their hue,
Who gave peace on earth, and alas! left wars too,
Who the virtues of Roses and Lilies combined,
And eternal rewards will for both of them find.

Dedication to the Abbot of Weissenburg

Dear Father Grimaldus, this trivial gift
Your very obedient servant makes shift
To send you, in hopes it will serve to reveal
The profound veneration that I, Strabo, feel
For your powerful learning and excellent wit.
When under the hedge of your garden you sit
In a bower of leaves by your apple-tree made
Reinforced with a peach's inferior shade,
Whilst the boys of your school (happy center of light)
Amuse themselves gathering up in your sight
The most silvery fruit with the softest of bloom,
And try in the palms of their hands to make room
For the curve of some great swelling apple to hide;
Then, dear Father, this poem a text will provide
For your lessons. And as you peruse it, I pray,
Emphasize what is good, cut the bad clean away!
Now in righteousness ever God make you abound,
That with life everlasting your soul may be crowned.
In this may the will of the Father and Son
And the life-giving Spirit appear, and be done!
Or seek a short cut—the one fatal mistake!
And provided you have no objection to soil
And harden your hands with good open-air toil,
And are willing to push a full dung-barrow out
On the parched earth, and there spread its contents about.
The advice given here is not copy-book rule,
Picked up second-hand, read in books, learned at school,
But the fruit of hard labor and personal test
To which I have sacrificed pleasure and rest.

Questions: Is Walahfrid's little garden a peaceful place, untroubled by the events of the outside world? Does he grow anything to eat in his herb garden? Are all the things that he grows useful and medicinal? What kinds of imagery does he employ? What roles do myth and religion play in the poem?

CHAPTER FIVE

THE TIME OF THE THREE KINGS AND THEIR SONS

(844–877)

Charles the Bald

An eighteenth-century drawing [after Montfaucon] of Charles the Bald as shown in the Psalter of Charles the Bald (Paris, Bibliothèque Nationale, Lat. 1152). In his right hand he carries a short scepter; nestled in his left is a globe. The right hand of God, that is, Christ, is crowning Charles. The verse above says, "When Charles, crowned with great honor, sits [on his throne], He is like Josiah and equal to Theodosius."

49. The Annals of Xanten for the Years 844 to 862

Heinz Löwe has argued that the entries in the so-called Annals of Xanten until 860 were written by Gerward, once the librarian of Louis the Pious and an aquaintance of Einhard. The annals of the last years in this sequence were later revised by an annalist located at Cologne. Thus the Annals of Xanten leave the reader with a strangely distorted record of these years. The death of the Emperor Lothar in 855, for instance, has been dropped because Lothar's fate may have mattered less to a Cologne annalist who was committed to Louis the German and his eastern Frankish interests. The reader might like to look for other changes of regional and royal perspective as the Cologne reviser edited the annals between 852 and 859 and then began to write his own entries.

Source: trans. J.H. Robinson, revised by F.A. Ogg, in F.A. Ogg, A Source Book of Mediaeval History: Documents Illustrative of European Life and Institutions from the German Invasions to the Renaissance (New York: American Book Company, 1908), pp.158-163; revised and added to here.

844. Pope Gregory departed from this world and Pope Sergius followed in his place. Count Bernard [of Septimania] was killed by Charles. Pepin, king of Aquitaine, together with his son and [William] the son of Bernard, routed the army of Charles, and there fell Abbot Hugo [of Saint-Quentin; he was an illegitimate son of Charlemagne]. At the same time King Louis [the German] advanced with his army against the Obodrites [Slavs], one of whose kings, Gestimulus by name, was killed; the rest came to Louis and pledged him their fidelity, which, however, they broke as soon as he was gone. Thereafter Lothar, Louis, and Charles came together to hold a council in Diedenhofen [near Yütz], and after a conference they went their several ways in peace.

845. Twice in the region of Worms there were earthquakes; the first on the night following Palm Sunday [23 March], the second on the holy night of Christ's Resurrection [29 March]. In the same year unbelievers [Northmen] invaded Christian lands at many points, but more than twelve thousand of them were killed by the Frisians. Another group attacked Gaul; more than six hundred of them perished there. Yet, due to his apathy, Charles [the Bald] gave them thousands of pounds of gold and silver so that they would leave Gaul, and that they did. Nevertheless the monasteries of many saints were destroyed and many Christians were led into captivity.

After these events, King Louis once more led a great army against the Obodrites. When the unbelievers learned of this they sent ambassadors, as well as gifts and hostages, to Saxony, and sued for peace. When Louis had granted peace, he returned home from Saxony. Thereafter the thieves were afflicted by a terrible pestilence, during which the chief criminal among them, a man by the name of Ragnar Lodbrok, who had robbed Christians and holy places, was struck down by the hand of God. Then they took counsel and threw lots to determine from which of their gods they should seek safety. But the lots did not fall out happily, and on the advice of one of their Christian prisoners that they should cast their lot before the God of the

Christians, they did so, and the lot fell happily. Then their king, Rorik, together with all his unbelieving people, refrained from meat and mead for fourteen days. When the plague stopped, they returned all their Christian prisoners to their own land.

846. As usual, the Northmen plundered eastern and western Frisia and set fire to the town of Dordrecht, with two other villages, before the eyes of Lothar, who was then in the castle of Nijmegen, but could not punish the crime. The Northmen, with their boats filled with immense booty, including both men and goods, returned to their own land.

In the same year Louis proceeded from Saxony against the Obodrites beyond the Elbe. He personally led his army against the Bohemians, whom we call Czechs, but it was very dangerous. Charles advanced against the Bretons, but achieved nothing. At this same time, as no one can mention or hear without great sadness, the mother of all churches, the basilica of the apostle Peter, was seized and plundered by the Moors or Saracens, who already occupied the area of Benevento. The Saracens slaughtered all the Christians whom they found outside Rome [and] those inside or outside this church. They also captured religious men and women. They pulled down the altar of the blessed Peter and many others, and their crimes from day to day brought sorrow to Christians. Pope Sergius died this year.

847. After the death of Sergius little news of the apostolic see came to our ears. Hrabanus [Maurus], the master and abbot of Fulda, was solemnly chosen archbishop and successor to Bishop Otgar, who had died. Here and there the Northmen attacked Christians and engaged in a battle with the counts Sigir and Liuthar. They continued up the Rhine as far as Dordrecht, and nine miles further to Meinerswijk, where they turned back, having taken their booty.

848. On 4 February, towards evening, lightning flashed and thunder was heard, and the unbelievers, as was their custom, inflicted injury on Christians. In the same year King Louis held an assembly of his people near Mainz. At this synod of bishops a heresy by certain monks concerning the predestination of almighty God was exposed. Once convicted, these monks in the presence of all were beaten and sent back to Gaul whence they had come. Thanks to God, the condition of the church remained unharmed.

849. With King Louis ill, his army proceeded from Bavaria against the Bohemians, but many of [his soldiers] were killed and the remainder returned, greatly humiliated, into their own land. The unbelievers from the North as usual wreaked havoc on Christendom and grew stronger daily, but it is painful to say more of this matter.

850. On 1 January, on the octave of the Lord, towards evening, a great deal of thunder was heard and a mighty flash of lightning was seen. An excess of water harmed the human race during this winter. In the following summer a raging heat burned the earth. Leo, pope of the Apostolic See, an extraordinary man, built a fortification around the church of Saint Peter, the apostle.

The Moors, however, attacked the coastal towns of Italy here and there. The Northman Rorik [the Dane], brother of the younger Heriold, who earlier fled in dishonor from Lothar, again took Dordrecht and committed much treachery against Christians. In the same year a great period of peace existed between the two brothers—the Emperor Lothar and King Louis—and they spent many days together in the Osning [mountains near Westphalia] hunting. Many were astonished [by that peace]. And in peace they parted from each other.

851. The bodies of certain saints were sent from Rome to Saxony: Alexander, one of the seven brothers, and those of Romanus and Emerentiana. In the same year [on 20 March] the most noble Empress Ermengard, wife of the Emperor Lothar, died. The Northmen inflicted a great deal of harm in Frisia and around the Rhine. A huge army of them gathered on the Elbe in opposition to the Saxons and some Saxon towns were besieged, others were burned down. They greatly disturbed Christians. A meeting of our kings took place [near Meersen] on the Meuse.

852. The swords of the pagans [Northmen] were red hot [this year]. There was excessive heat and a famine followed. The fodder for the animals was insufficient, but pasturage for pigs was plentiful.

853. There was a great famine in Saxony, so that many were forced to survive on horse meat. The Northmen, as well as the many foul things they commit everywhere against Christians, burned the church of Saint Martin, bishop of Tours, the place where his body rests [on 8 November 853].

[854] In the spring Louis, the eastern king, sent his son of the same name to Aquitaine to obtain possession of the kingdom of his nephew Pepin [II].

[855] The Northmen chose a king [Rorik II] with the same name as the preceding one and related to him, and the Danes, with renewed strength, attacked Christians from the sea.

[856] A great plague of swelling tumors raged among the population and consumed them with awful festering sores so that their limbs fell off even before they died [possibly ergotism which is caused by eating spoiled rye wheat].

[857] Louis, the eastern king, held an assembly of his people in the territory of Worms.

[858] On 1 January, as the matins Mass was being celebrated, one earthquake struck Worms and three more struck Mainz before daybreak.

[859] On 5 February thunder was heard. The king returned from Gaul. The whole kingdom had been corrupted and nothing was improved.

[860] The holy bishop Liutbert piously supplied the monastery called Freck-

enhorst with many relics of the saints, namely those of the martyrs Boniface and Maximus and of the confessors Eonius and Antony, and he added a portion of the manger of the Lord and of his grave and likewise something of the dust of the Lord's feet as He ascended to heaven. In this year the winter was long and the above-mentioned kings again had a secret meeting on the island near Koblenz, and they exhausted [supplies] around there.

Lothar [II], the king of the Ripuarian Franks, abandoned without just cause his legitimate wife, the sister of the cleric Hubert [the abbot of Saint-Maurice]. In the same year that brother [Hubert, living in Charles the Bald's kingdom] received her in his own lands. King [Lothar II] publicly took up with his concubine [Waldrada], for whose love he abandoned his wife.

[861] Louis [the German] set up the impious count Hugh, which seemed a great shame to almost everyone. For now the disputes of our kings and the destruction of the pagans throughout our lands is too disagreeable to relate.

[862] King Louis held an assembly first at Worms and after that at Mainz, and there Lothar [II] came to him. [They] planned to raise an army to send against the Slavs [Obodrites] which, afterwards, they did. But it achieved nothing. In the same year the winter was very severe and changeable, with much rain, so that the winter was almost entirely without frost, as was experienced at the church of Saint Victor [in Xanten].

Questions: How important do the annalists think the invasions are? What are the main interests of the annalists? How can one tell that there has been a change of annalists or a revision of the text between 852 and 860? Are the Annals of Xanten very informative?

50. Gottschalk and the Predestination Controversy

Civil war and invasions were not the only source of disunity in the years after Louis the Pious's death, for a major theological dispute broke out. Gottschalk, who propounded an Augustinian doctrine of double predestination, is one of the most intriguing of all Carolingian personalities. His father, a Saxon noble, gave Gottschalk as a boy to the monastery of Fulda as an oblate, a pious gift on behalf of his own soul. At Fulda and Reichenau, Gottschalk not only received a superior education, but made friends such as Walahfrid Strabo and Lupus of Ferrières. But he was unhappy and in 829, when he was about twenty-five, he petitioned a council to free him from his monastic bonds since his father had forced him as a child to take them up. Hrabanus Maurus opposed the action. Gottschalk moved to the monastery of Orbais, became a priest, and in the period between 835 and 845 he undertook a pilgrimage to Italy and parts further east. It was then that he apparently began to immerse himself in the anti-Pelagian treatises of Augustine and to teach a doctrine of double predestination.

1. His Song of Exile

This rhythmical lament, in its shorter form, is one of the most haunting and famous of ninth-century poems. Whether it refers to the loneliness of his monastic days, his move from Fulda to Reichenau, or his years at Orbais is not clear, but like everything else touched by Gottschalk the poem has a highly personal and emotionally charged quality.

Source: trans. P.E. Dutton, from Monumenta Germaniae Historica: Poetae Latini Aevi Carolini, vol. 3, ed. L. Traube (Berlin, 1896), pp.731-732.

O my little friend, why would you ask me,
Why would you demand, my tiny son,
   That I sing a sweet song,
   When I am an exile, far from home
   On this distant sea?
O why do you order me to sing?

My miserable boy, it would be better for me,
To cry, O my little friend,
   Better to wail than sing
   Such a song as you order me to sing,
   My dear love.
O why do you order me to sing?

You had better know, tiny one,
That you should, little brother,
   With your kind heart pity me
   And, with your humble mind,
   Lament along with me.
O why do you order me to sing?

You realize, my little student,
You realize, my little companion,
   Just how long I have been here in exile
   Just how long I have suffered here,
   Just how many days and how many nights.
O why do you order me to sing?

You realize that the little people
Known as Israel,
   Were once commanded
   To sing in Babylon
   Far away from the borders of Judea.
O why do you order me to sing?

Not even they could sing,
Nor should they, therefore, have to sing
   A sweet song
   Before the people
   Of a strange land.
O why do you order me to sing?

But because, my distinguished friend,
You continue to demand it,
  I shall sing to the Father and to the Son
  And to the Holy Spirit,
  That proceeds from both.
  Of my own accord I now sing.

You are blessed, O Lord,
Father, Son, and Holy Spirit,
  Triune God, One God,
  Highest God, kind God,
  Fair God.
  Of my own will I now sing.

For a little while [longer] I, an exile,
Am set on this [distant] sea, my Lord.
  It has been almost two years already,
  But it is time now
  To take pity on me.
  Most humbly I ask for your mercy.

In the meantime, with my little boy and I
Set down in this place,
  I shall sing to you, kindest King,
  A sweet song,
  With my lips, with my heart,
  Every day and every night.

2. Hrabanus Maurus's Characterization of Gottschalk's Doctrine

As early as 840, Hrabanus Maurus had heard from Noting, the bishop of Verona, that Gottschalk was teaching predestinarian doctrines in Italy. The abbot of Fulda began his campaign against his former monk almost immediately, as he attempted to have Gottschalk driven out of northern Italy. In part, he did this by grossly simplifying and misrepresenting the monk's doctrines.

Source: trans. P.E. Dutton, from Ad Notingum episcopum Veronensem de praescientia ac praedestinatione Dei, ed. in J.P. Migne, Patrologia Latina, vol. 112, cols. 1540C7-1541A11.

In the first place, he [Gottschalk] dares to say that his creator, who is the greatest good, is malevolent and he has decided that his work perishes in vain and without reason.

In the second place, he tries to assert that the Truth itself, which promises in Holy Scripture rewards to those who believe and strive actively to attain eternal life, deceives, and he predicts the punishment of death for sinners and [even] those who are penitent.

In the third place, he proclaims that the just judge, who will judge the living and dead fairly, is unjust, since he maintains that the Lord does not return rewards to those who do good things nor torments to those who do evil.

In the fourth place, he does not in his error fear to teach that the Redeemer of the world shed his blood in vain and that [the Lord] cannot come to the assistance of those believing and resting hope in him because of the inevitableness of predestination.

In the fifth place, [he maintains] that our Savior does not fill up from the human condition the number of good angels which the Devil reduced when he fell through his pride.

In the sixth place, he prefers the Devil more in his teaching, since he passed over to the power of the Devil's punishment those to whom divine grace had decided to extend eternal salvation.

In the seventh place, he is hostile to most of the human race, since he said that it cannot be rescued from the Fall of our first parent[s, Adam and Eve], from the condition of our own sins, and from the power of enemies by faith in Christ and the sacrament of baptism. Instead, bound by the harmful predestination of the maker, the human race is sinking into hell.

And so all these things having been demonstrated, [Gottschalk] is proved to be his own worst enemy, since not only does he ready the fires of hell for himself in this way, but even in this, that by seducing others through the doctrine of his error away from the way of truth he makes them the companions of his own damnation. For which reason [Gottschalk] himself will surely suffer a fitting punishment in the eternal fires [of hell].

3. Gottschalk's Own Simple Statement

Gottschalk's theology was, of course, more sophisticated and Augustinian than his opponents were ever prepared to admit. In 848, before a council at Mainz and Hrabanus Maurus, its new archbishop, Gottschalk made a simple statement of his belief in double predestination that was preserved by Hincmar of Rheims.

Source: trans. P.E. Dutton, from Hincmar, De praedestinatione Dei et libero arbitrio posterior dissertatio, ed. in J.P. Migne, Patrologia Latina, vol. 125, cols. 89D8-90A7.

I, Gottschalk, believe and confess, publicly declare and bear witness that, from God the Father through God the Son, in God the Holy Spirit, and I affirm and maintain before God and his saints, that predestination is double, either of the elect to heaven or of the reprobate to death. Just as an unchangeable God unchangeably predestined, even before the creation of the world, all his elect by his free grace to eternal life, so the same unchangeable God by his just judgment unchangeably predestined all the reprobates, who on Judgment Day will be damned fully and deservedly on account of their evil merits, to everlasting death.

4. Gottschalk's Return to Gaul

After the council at Metz in 848 had condemned Gottschalk as a heretic, he was sent to Hincmar, the archbishop of Rheims, his rightful ecclesiastical superior. The annalist of the Annals of Saint-Bertin at this time was Prudentius of Troyes, who was somewhat sympathetic to Gottschalk's teaching, but so hostile is the entry that it seems likely that Hincmar of Rheims later revised this portion of the annal for 849.

Source: trans. P.E. Dutton, from Annales de Saint-Bertin, ed. F. Grat, J. Vielliard, and S. Clémencet (Paris: Klincksieck, 1964), pp.56-57.

Gottschalk, a man of Gaul, a monk and priest of the monastery of Orbais of the parish of Soissons, was bloated with his knowledge and given to certain superstitions. He went to Italy in the name of religion, but was then shamefully banished. He next sought out Dalmatia, Pannonia, and Noricum, and taught there with pernicious speech and writing certain things—especially under the name of predestination—opposed to our salvation. In the presence of King Louis the German he was discovered and convicted by a council of bishops. Finally he was forced to return to the metropolitan city of his diocese, Rheims, over which that venerable man Hincmar presides. To the extent that he deserved to be punished for his lack of faith, he received it there. That most strenuous defender of the Christian faith, King Charles [the Bald] called together a council of the holy bishops of that diocese and commanded Gottschalk to be presented before them. [Gottschalk] was led in, was publicly whipped, and was forced to cast into flames his books with their many assertions.

If Hrabanus and Hincmar thought that imprisoning Gottschalk at Orbais would put a stop to the predestination controversy he had started, they were woefully wrong. Within the next fifteen years, Eriugena, Prudentius, Hincmar himself, Lupus of Ferrières, Florus and the church of Lyons, and Ratramnus would all write long treatises on predestination.

Questions: What conditions contributed to the continuation of this controversy? Why did Hrabanus and Hincmar react so strongly to Gottschalk and his teaching? What factors—theological, social, and political—might explain the rise of the predestination controversy in the ninth century?

The Emperor Lothar I

A nineteenth-century drawing [after Woltmann and Woermann] of Lothar as copied from the striking portrait of him found in the Lothar Gospels made at Saint-Martin of Tours about 850.   The manuscript today is Paris, Bibliothèque Nationale, Lat. 266.   Lothar holds in his right hand a long scepter and behind him stand two noble retainers with arms.

51. The Epitaphs of Ermengard and Lothar

Though Lothar had failed to dominate his younger brothers and Francia, as the 'Ordinatio imperii' had once suggested he would, he remained emperor and began to share the title with his son Louis II of Italy in 850. Indeed, the poets, if anything, increased the imperial dimensions of Lothar's fame, even as the reality decreased. The Empress Ermengard died in 851 after thirty years of marriage to Lothar. In September 855 the emperor himself, now sixty years old and sick, retired to the monastery of Prüm where he was tonsured and became a monk. There he also divided up his lands between his three living sons, Louis II, Lothar II, and Charles of Provence. He died within a week.

1. Hrabanus Maurus, The Epitaph of Ermengard

Source: trans. P.E. Dutton, from Monumenta Germaniae Historica: Poetae Latini Aevi Carolini, vol. 2, ed. E. Dümmler (Berlin, 1884), pp.239-240.

Let whoever approaches this temple with proper piety,
  Know who is buried in this tomb.
A woman, one who was an empress and noble by birth, lies here,
  Ermengard was the name given to her.
She ordered from the outset the construction of this royal place,
  For the praise of Christ and as a resting place for herself.
For this pious woman received the relics of saints from Rome,
  She brought them here and deposited them.
Through their merits she should gain the joys of [eternal] life,
  And with prayers she should receive indulgence for her sins.
Living chastely, she spurned earthly pleasures,
  Gave to the poor, and was quick to do good.
She lived nobly and left to others the example of her goodness,
  Readying [all the while] joyful rewards for herself.
This woman lived through her juvenile years,
  And had just begun her mature years, when she died.
Leaving behind earthly kingdoms, she entered the heavens,
  Where Christ and the saints hold the true joys.
I ask this of you, my reader, commend her to God properly,
  With constant prayer, so that Christ might receive her.
Let her live happily in joy with Christ,
  Always blessed in the midst of the angelic choir.
I Hrabanus composed these verses, for I was saddened
  By her death, but rejoice over her peaceful repose.

The Empress Ermengard died in 851 in the fourteenth Indiction, the thirteenth Kalends of April [20 March] on the day before the Sabbath at the sixth hour and she found peaceful rest.

2. Lament for Lothar

Source: trans. P.E. Dutton, from Monumenta Germaniae Historica: Poetae Latini Aevi Carolini, vol. 4, ed. K. Strecker (Berlin, 1896), pp.1074-1075.

O Caesar, you were once as great as the world is immense,
But now you are closed up within this confining tomb.
From your example let everyone know that they too will fall,
For the [achievement of] glory can never defeat death.

Once the glorious empire bloomed,
But now with its Caesar dead it droops.
Glory will have no other form than this:
To be buried with you when you die.

O how great is the grief with which sad Rome,
Shining Rome with its priests, is suddenly beset?
Rome wounded already by the death of [Pope] Leo [IV, on 17 July]
Now, O Augustus, is further unnerved by your death.

Laws enacted by the fathers of old
Which over time had worn thin,
[Lothar] reformed them as they were
And worked to reestablish them in Roman suits.

You, O Caesar, strove for distant lands and kingdoms,
Which no one else could direct,
Honoring Romans with the powerful arch [of your protection],
You strove for civil peace.

What land does not mourn your death, O Caesar,
What land did not fear you while you were alive?
But the land that feared you while you were alive,
Now mourns, O Caesar, your death.

For you were so gentle to the conquered,
So firm towards untamed peoples.
That those who rightly feared you do not mourn,
While those who rightly mourn did not fear you.

Mourn your name, O Rome, which is now darkened,
And mourn the extinction of your two lamps [Lothar and Leo],
Smash your arches and offer up a triumph
Of your own to your enemies.

Questions: What, according to the poet, were Lothar's principal accomplishments? In what terms–formal or familiar, as patron or friend–does Hrabanus describe Ermengard?

52. Sedulius Scottus, *On Christian Rulers*

Sedulius Scottus was an Irishman who seems to have arrived in Liège in the 840s.
He wrote poems there for his ecclesiastical patron Bishop Hartgar and sent others to
Lothar and Ermengard. Of special importance is this book, which he wrote around
855, for Lothar II or Charles the Bald. It is what contemporaries thought of as a
Mirror for the Prince, a special literature designed to form the character of young
princes by showing them examples of good and bad rulers from the past. Those
familiar with Machiavelli's The Prince can compare and contrast the character and
usefulness of the advice in the two works.

Source: trans. E.G. Doyle, in Sedulius Scottus, On Christian Rulers and the Poems, Medieval &
Renaissance Texts & Studies, vol. 17 (Binghamton: State University of New York at Binghamton,
1983), pp.51-61; reprinted with permission.

[Preface]

Every profession that is prominent in the triple world
Should be guided by art, for art's gifts are many.
With art the Creator of all made the lands, seas, stars, and heavens
And with art he rules the entire beautiful universe.
The wisdom of the heavenly Thunderer has set man through
Lofty arts over all the creatures of the earth.
Art controls the war-chariot and steers ships on course
And is necessary for a triumphant military campaign.
And so, the state needs art's assistance so that
It may prosper with a just ruler and a happy people.
On this account, I, traversing the flowery meadows of divine
Books, have gathered garlands for you, illustrious king,
To adorn the diadem of your supreme mind and
To glorify scepters ruling in accord with Christ's will.
With my thumb fragrant with balsam I have gathered
Baskets of the healing herbs of divine dogma.
Drink the waters of Israel's clear fountains
To satisfy the thirsty palate with a most sweet liquid!
For these are the glory of kings and garlands for glittering scepters:
The tenets of the Lord, the examples of the ancients,
And the deeds, famous over the world, of renowned princes.
By these arts may your kingdom thrive and triumph,
And be prosperously governed for a great many years
Until you ascend to the heavenly court,
Where the perpetual glory of just rulers prevails.

[The End of the Preface]

With you the beginning and the end, O Christ the King;
May you, O God, be the alpha and omega of your servant's work.

[On Christian Rulers]

1. Why it is necessary for the pious ruler, endowed with royal power, to dedicate above all else worthy honors to God and to his holy churches.

As soon as a Christian ruler has received the royal scepter and the government of the kingdom, it is fitting that he first return acts of thanksgiving and suitable honors to God and to the holy church. In fact, from the very beginning the state is most gloriously consecrated when royal solicitude and sacred devotion are aroused with both holy fear and love of the heavenly King and when care is taken for the glorious benefit of the church by prudent counsel, so that he whom royal purple and other symbols of royal authority adorn externally will also be adorned internally by praiseworthy vows to God and to his holy church. For indeed, a king is notably raised to the summit of temporal rule when he devotes himself with pious zeal to the almighty King's glory and honor. And so, let the pious ruler fervently strive to obey the will and holy commands of the supreme master of all things by whose divine will and ordination he does not doubt himself to have risen to the summit of authority. This is affirmed by the apostle who says: "There is no authority unless it be from God; moreover, all the authorities which exist have been established by God." Therefore, so much as an upright ruler acknowledges that he has been called by God, to the same degree he is vigilant with dutiful care that he regularly determines and examines all things before God and men according to the scales of justice. For, what are the rulers of the Christian people unless ministers of the Almighty? Moreover, he is a faithful and proper servant who has done with sincere devotion whatever his lord and master has commanded to him. Accordingly, the most upright and glorious princes rejoice more that they are appointed to be ministers and servants of the most High than lords or kings of men. For this reason blessed David, an illustrious king and prophet, often called himself the servant of the Lord. Also, renowned Solomon, David's son, calling upon the Almighty, said, among other things: "Consider your servant's prayer and his entreaties, O Lord, my God; hear the hymn and prayer which your servant utters before you this day, so that your eyes both day and night may watch over this temple about which you said: 'There will be my name!'" The emperor Constantine the Great of celebrated memory, who believed and fulfilled the mystery of the saving cross and the Catholic faith, did not claim credit for himself when by his joyous rule religion vigorously flourished. Rather, he gave thanks that almighty God had deigned to make him the useful servant of his will. Lo, that most distinguished emperor rejoiced more to have been a servant of God than to have possessed an earthly empire. Thus Constantine, because he had been the servant of divine will, extended a peaceful reign from the sea of Britain to the lands of the East. And because Constantine had subjected himself to the Almighty, with power and faith he won all the hostile wars which were waged under him. He constructed and enriched Christ's churches with splendid treasures. As a result, divine favor granted him triumphant victories, for, without doubt, the more pious rulers subject themselves humbly to the King of kings, the more they ascend on high to the summit of glorious distinction.

Who, moreover, may not marvel at how many honors Solomon returned to the Lord after he had received the scepter of kingship with God's backing; how with the most prudent devotion he constructed and marvelously adorned the Lord's temple; and finally, how many conciliatory sacrifices he offered to God? In the end, Solomon received the fruits of his devotion and prayer, just as the Lord, appearing to him said: "I have heard the prayer and entreaty which you offered before me. I have consecrated the temple you built so that I may confer my name there forever, and my eyes and my heart will remain there always. As for you, if you walk before me just as your father walked in simplicity of heart and in justice and if you do everything I have commanded to you and preserve my laws and judgments, I will establish the throne of your sovereignty over Israel forever just as I promised your father, David, saying: 'No one of your line will be removed from the throne of Israel!'" And so, if King Solomon deserved to attain such a glorious reward in return for sacred devotion and for constructing the Lord's earthly temple, how precious a mark of glory will a ruler possess if beloved by God he constantly adorns the holy Church, which is the spiritual tabernacle of the living God? Let us now conclude with the delightfulness of verse what we have briefly related in prose.

He who bears a flourishing kingdom's noble scepter should
First offer vows and prayers to the heavenly Throne.
All kingdoms, peace, and the life and prosperity
Of distinguished leaders depend upon God's sacred will.
For royal honor and kingship's radiant diadem consist of
Sacred fear of the heavenly Throne and love of God.
Just as milk-white lilies adorn a flowery field,
And as the rose blushes in its scarlet countenance,
So a just ruler blooms with a flowering of virtues
And begets sacred fruits in the summit of his mind.
Both glorious purple and the glittering scepter of
His father David adorned King Solomon;
But prudent zeal of heart inwardly adorned
That youthful king more in glorifying God.
Let your state glow like the morning star,
And in newly rising accomplish illustrious vows.

2. How an orthodox ruler should first govern himself.

He who has ascended to the summit of royal dignity by the grace of God should remember that he whom divine will has ordained to rule others should first rule himself. *Rex* is from the verb *regere*, to rule. A man may know that he is rightly addressed by the title of king if he does not fail to rule himself with reason. Hence, let an orthodox king strive with utmost effort so that he who desires to command his subjects well and determines to correct others' errors may not himself commit the evils he strictly reproves in others and may endeavor to practice before all the virtues which he enjoins upon them. Moreover, a just ruler commendably rules himself in six ways: first of all, when he restrains with severity the illicit designs of the will; second, when he considers useful counsels pertaining both to his own benefit and to that of his people; third, when he avoids issuing idle, useless or noxious trifles of inane speech; fourth, when he savors with his mind's palate, more than honey and the honeycomb, both the prudence and words of glorious princes as well as the words of divine scripture; fifth, when he is fearful of committing any dishonor of a pernicious deed; and sixth, when he notably performs lofty deeds whether praiseworthy or of glorious spirit so that he who shines inwardly before the Lord with a devout will may also shine publicly before the people in word and action.

It is fitting for a ruler to observe a threefold rule, namely fear, order, and love. Unless he is equally feared and loved, his rule will in no way stand firm. A ruler, therefore, should attend to good offices and kindness that he may be loved, and should seek to be feared by justly avenging, not offenses against himself, but offenses against the law of God. It behooves such a ruler to be humble in his own eyes, just as it is written: "They have appointed you ruler. Do not permit yourself to be elevated, but, rather, be among them like one of themselves." To be rightly called ruler, he must rule justly not only over men, but also over the passions of his body and mind, just as a certain wise man once said: "Whoever acts properly will be king; whoever acts improperly will not." Let the ruler be most prudent in counsel, at one time in conversation, as reason demands, awesome, but more frequently affable by the grace of sweetness. Let him be a conqueror of sensuality, a victor over pride and savage ferocity, a friend of good men, an enemy of tyrants, and an enemy of criminals and their crimes. Let him be most prudent in war, most steadfast in peace, and most trustworthy in faithful promises. Let him place the divine ahead of the human, deterring his subjects from evil and urging them to good; rewarding with abundance and absolving with compassion; and making good men out of evil ones and excellent men out of good ones.

A ruler should be holy and of benefit to the state; praiseworthy in kindness; notable for every goodness and distinguished in piety, fortitude, morality, and justice; and a man most honorable and worthy of an imperial throne, always keeping the fear of God before his eyes and weighing his judgment according to the just decree of the Almighty who grants salvation to kings and performs whatever he wishes in heaven and on earth and towards every creature. For, He is the lord of all things, and before him everything in heaven, on earth, and in the infernal regions bends its knee. And in his hand rests all power in heaven and on earth, since he is the King of kings and the hope for glory of all who rule justly and piously.

He who rules the passions of his will and subdues the
Dissolute lures of the flesh is rightly called a king.
Although a king hold a glorious place in marks of honor,
Who by his strength overcomes a tawny lion,
Yet it is more praiseworthy to subdue insolent pride,
And to tame anger as if it were a ferocious beast.
That ruler is called great who has crushed fierce enemies
And as a victor, crowned in laurel, brings back gleaming trophies;
But there is greater glory for a ruler decked with heavenly

Arms who is able to conquer invisible enemies.
The power to bridle the mind through art is greater
Than possessing the might of the triple world;
For a just king's heart shines like the temple of the Lord,
And it is the throne of God, the heavenly Judge.
The abode gleams more precious than yellow gold
And delights in possessing its beacon of justice.

3. The art and diligence by which a transitory kingdom can remain stable.

Wise men have judged the transitory kingdom of this world to be like the turning of a revolving wheel. For just as the turning of a wheel that at one moment presses down what it holds at the top and at another raises up what it holds at the bottom, so the glory of an earthly kingdom sustains sudden rises and sudden falls and, therefore, contains not real but imaginary and fleeting honors. Only that kingdom is real which endures forever. Now the earthly kingdom, because it is transitory and fleeting, never reveals the truth but only some slight semblance of the truth and of the eternal kingdom. In fact, just as a rainbow, which adorns the vault of heaven with dazzling colors, quickly disappears, so, to be sure, the honor of worldly fame, however much adorned for the moment, is sooner fleeting away.

With what art, therefore, with what action, and with how much vigilance can this transitory kingdom be held to some form of stability? Can an earthly kingdom be kept stable, perhaps, either by violent force of arms or by the tranquil harmony of peace? On the contrary, in the arms and rumblings of war there is great instability. What is more uncertain and more unstable than military campaigns, where there is no sure outcome to the wearisome combat and no victory assured, where often more illustrious men are overthrown by lesser ones, and where equal misfortunes sometimes befall both sides, who both expect victory but in the end enjoy nothing but calamitous miseries? Who can explain how many evils occur under the false name of peace, when even that peace believed constant and firm among good men is sometimes transformed by the perverse counsels of the wicked into destructive tumults of discord, and whence great instability appears in a transitory peace!

What else remains, therefore, except that a king's heart and complete confidence should be fixed not in the force of arms and men nor in the deception of transitory peace, but rather, in the mercy of the Almighty who knows how to uphold the kingdom he granted in both adversity and prosperity? And so, the prince's heart and constant devotion in governing his office should not withdraw from that Lord who has conferred upon him such great favor and a glorious ministry. For if the most high Ruler should see a prince unfaithful, whom He has ordained his faithful servant, He might angrily pluck from that prince the office which He has conferred upon him. For if an earthly king can rescind his authority from any unfaithful man and bestow it on another whom he knows to be more faithful, how much more can the divine Ruler of all men, whom the clouds of no man's treachery can deceive, withdraw his favors from false men and bestow them on others known to be proper servants of his will? Thus the impious King Saul of

Israel was deprived of his kingdom and his life because he did not stand before the Lord as a faithful minister; however, the Almighty found David a man truly chosen after his own heart, and so He raised David to the summit of royal power because He chose him in the foreknowledge that he would be a faithful minister. A prudent ruler, therefore, should strive to keep his heart steadfast in the grace of the most High if he wants the transitory kingdom entrusted to him to maintain some appearance of stability. And, since the Lord is just and merciful, and must be adhered to with a devout heart, a ruler should display manifold works of mercy that he might obtain a great and glorious reward. Let him both cherish and maintain justice, and let him scorn unjust and evil deeds among his subjects and correct them with a zeal which is praiseworthy and in accord with wisdom. So long as a ruler is steadfast in divine precepts, his kingdom becomes more and more stable in this world and is led with divine help to the eternal joys of stability.

As a turning wheel swiftly revolves and
Presses in cycle its highest points downward,
Which it rotates in fickleness on
　　Its axle,

So the powers of the earth, throughout the triple world,
Are unable to maintain the lofty summit of glory
When it has fallen away, though they have come to
　　Cherish golden scepters.

The splendid glory of the kingdom of Israel's
Illustrious people had been raised on high
So long as it preserved the sacred and mystical
　　Powers of the law;

Whence it prevailed in the triumphs of the
Lord and overcame fierce enemies,
While the Thunderer's kindness glorified
　　His people.

Alas! The sacred holy land of father Abraham was
Laid low by innumerable catastrophes whenever
Its people scorned to bend their necks to
　　The Creator.

But the sole remedy of such a people was at once
To entreat the most High with prayers,
For he alone has the power to uphold kingdoms
　　With perpetual will.

Princes of this world, joyfully offer the incense
Of prayer to our almighty Lord and magnify him
Before whom the supernal princes of
　　Heaven tremble.

4. Royal authority should not be embellished so much with power and bold strength as with wisdom and pious discipline.

All royal power, which has been divinely established for the benefit of the state, should be embellished not so much with vain powers and earthly might as with wisdom and the veneration of God. For, if the eminence of the king is adorned by religion and wisdom, then, without a doubt, the people will be governed by the art of prudent counsel, enemies will be cast down by a merciful Lord and both the provinces and the kingdom will be preserved. Indeed, God intended this to be the nature of man, that he should desire and seek after two things, namely religion and wisdom. Moreover, devout wisdom is the most salutary virtue, the light of pious souls, a heavenly gift and a joy which will last forever. Whoever, therefore, wants to rule gloriously, to govern the people wisely, and to be mighty in counsels should seek wisdom from the Lord who gives abundantly and ungrudgingly to all. And let him strive for such wisdom with zealous effort and love so that this saying: "Blessed is the man who finds wisdom, and who abounds in understanding," as well as other things which are enumerated among the praises of wisdom may distinguish him. For that blessed ruler truly merits praise who is illumined with the splendor of wisdom which is the source of counsels, the font of sacred religion, the crown of princes and the mother of virtues, and compared to it all the glitter of precious gems is deemed worthless. Wisdom is most prudent in counsels, remarkable in eloquence, magnificent in deeds, strong in adversity, moderate in prosperity, and perspicacious in judgments. It adorns those who love it with heavenly grace and makes them shine like the heavenly firmament, as it is written: "Just men will shine like the stars, and wise men like the heavenly firmament."

Wisdom exalted Solomon above all the kings of the earth, for he cherished it from his youth and became a lover of its beauty. Hence, as it is written in the Book of Kings, the Lord appeared to Solomon in a dream one night and said: "Ask something of me and I will give it to you." When Solomon, though just a boy, requested a discerning heart that he might judge the Lord's people and distinguish between good and evil, he received this response from God: "Since you have asked for the word, and since you have not asked for a long life for yourself or riches or the lives of your enemies, but for the wisdom for a discerning judgment, here and now I have done what you asked. I have given you a heart so wise and shrewd that there has never been anyone like you up till now, and after you there will come no one to equal you. I have also granted you what you did not ask for, namely wealth and glory, so that not one of all the kings of former days can compare with you. And I will give you long life, if you follow my way and keep my laws and commandments, just as your father, David, followed them." O how ineffable is the bountifulness of divine grace! For, if divine grace is sought with a just heart and a pious intention, it gives more than what is asked. Lo, King Solomon asked for neither gold, nor silver, nor any other earthly treasures but rather for the riches of wisdom; moreover, he who had rightly requested a single gift received double, for he was not only enriched with wisdom, but was exalted by the illustrious glory of kingship. Hence, an excellent example is given to the kings of the earth: if they wish to reign long and prosperously in this world, let them ask with a pious heart for spiritual rather than carnal gifts. It befits a prince worthy of God's love, therefore, to have the will to learn and the desire of heavenly things; thus, he truly sets his heart in God's hand and will peacefully rule his kingdom by God's grace and throughout a multitude of years.

A ruler who wishes to be an upright judge,
Who rejoices in the scale and balance of justice,
And who is eager to pierce falsehoods with a spear
 Of glorious truth,

Should call upon the Father of Light, who created the
Fiery sun and moon, and the glittering cosmos,
That he might shine in thoughts radiant with
 Wisdom's light.

Let him study the prayers of impartial Solomon,
Which flew suddenly through the heavens and
Penetrated the golden palace of the
 Lord of Hosts.

Did not Solomon, enlightened with understanding,
Acquire a skillful judgment, whereby he wisely
Governed upon the royal summit of the
 Hebrew people?

Of what worth is all the glitter of yellow gold,
And of what value are the purples of
Crimson adornment, honors and Scythian gems and
 A diadem,

If sharpness of mind, neglected, becomes dull
So that it cannot perceive the true light by
Which it may discriminate between good, evil, justice,
 Right and wrong?

Hence, the glory of a ruler is to love you,
O Christ, the world of the Father and Sage Light,
For you reign supreme over the earth and the
 Heavenly kingdoms.

In your right hand abides blessed peace
And in your left abundant treasures.
You are the Prince of Glory who crowns the humble
 And overthrows the rich.

5. The duty of pious guidance which a ruler ought to fulfill with regard to his wife, his children, and his household.

A pious and wise king performs the office of ruling in three ways: as we have shown above, he should first rule himself with reasonable and meritorious discipline; second, his wife, his children, and his household; and third, the people entrusted to him. Hence, a just prince must not only rule himself, while he rejects evils and chooses and firmly upholds what is good, but he must also direct others more closely related to him, namely, his wife, his children, and his household with prudent care and familial affection. And by accomplishing this, a prince attains a double palm of glory in that when he himself is just and holy, he makes others related to him just and holy too, in accordance with the Psalmist who said: "You will be pure with the pure and blameless with the man who is blameless." For it does not suffice to possess personal honor, unless it is embellished with the propriety of a chaste and modest wife, and with the propriety of children, friends, and servants, as David said: "He who walks in immaculate ways served me." Just as a lily of the field is enhanced in beauty by the manifold beauty of other plants and of violets and just as the moon shines more pleasingly in the glow of the surrounding stars, so, truly, a just and wise king is greatly adorned by the fellowship of other good men.

A ruler, therefore, should perspicaciously endeavor to have a wife who is not only noble, beautiful, and wealthy, but also chaste, prudent, and compliant in holy virtues. For, so much as a wife is closer (to man) in law, to that extent she becomes either noxious with the poison of wickedness or pleasing with the sweetness of morals. To be sure, a foolish wife is the ruin of a household, the exhaustion of wealth, the fullness of crimes, and the abode of all evils and vices, who ornaments her exterior mien with diverse observances, but knows not how to adorn the interior beauty of her soul. Whomever she loves today, she hates tomorrow, just as a certain man once said: "A wife unfaithful to her husband is the shipwreck of all things." However, a chaste and prudent wife, diligently attending to useful matters with a humble demeanor and cheerful speech, peacefully manages her children and family; and, on behalf of her husband's welfare, if necessary, she sets her life against death and defends his wealth with an honorable reputation. Whoever was her friend yesterday is her friend today. In effect, she becomes the increase of wealth, the support of the household, the delight of her husband, the glory of the family, and the union of all virtues. Indeed, it is proper for such a one not only to be bound and subservient to her husband with a chaste bond, but also to reflect always an image of holiness and pious behavior, and to be an inventress of prudent counsels. Just as by the persuasion of an evil wife pernicious dangers are begotten, so by the counsel of a prudent wife many benefits are produced that are pleasing to the Almighty, whence the apostle said: "The unbelieving husband will be saved by a believing wife."

Not only unbelieving but also pious and orthodox princes often ponder and give heed to the marvelous prudence in their wives, not reflecting on their fragile sex, but, rather, plucking the fruit of their good counsels. Hence, it is said about Placilla, the venerable wife of the glorious emperor Theodosius, that through her the prince, though he himself was upright, just, and wise, enjoyed another useful opportunity by which he might triumph from good works. His wife, having instructed herself completely beforehand, often admonished the prince concerning divine laws. She was not puffed up by the dignities of royal power but was inflamed by divine love. In fact, the abundance of blessings she received increased her love for her benefactor; and indeed, she came unexpectedly to high station. She took the greatest care of the crippled and lame, but not by using slaves or other servants; rather, she acted through herself, coming to their dwellings and offering to each what he needed. In this way visiting the hospitals of the churches, she ministered to the sick with her own hand, cleaning their pots, tasting broth, offering spoonfuls, breaking bread, serving food, washing cups, and doing all the other things which are customarily performed by slaves and servants. To those who tried to restrain her from such things she would say: "It is the office of our emperor to distribute gold; but I offer this service on behalf of that Emperor who has conferred upon me so many blessings." Moreover, to her husband she would often say: "You should always remember, my husband, what you once were and what you are now. If you always remember these things, you will never be ungrateful to your benefactor, but will lawfully rule the empire you have received and will appease the author of all these things." And, with such words, she presented to her husband some useful profit and abundant virtue.

A pious and wise king rules himself, his family and
   His subject with threefold direction.
A wife virtuous in morals stands forth as the glory of the king
   Like a fruitful vine.
Nobility in threefold virtue should beautify her with the
   Roses of a chaste heart;
For if milk-white necks glisten with lovely elegance,
   Chastity should glisten even more.
As Christ united the Church to him with a chaste love,
   So a wife should cleave to her husband;
In her heart gentle simplicity like the beauty of a dove
   Should always abound.
Piety, prudence and sacred authority should adorn her,
   Just as gracious Esther shone.
A king and queen should cherish the bonds of peace;
   In both there should be agreement and concord.
Hateful discord must not separate the pair whom the divine
   Law of peace has joined together,
Discipline should rule their glorious offshoots
   So that seemly branches may flourish.
A withered young branch never thrives on a vigorous tree.
   A good cultivator provides for this:
If a ruler and his queen are to rule the people justly,
   Let them first rule their own family.
Let them decorate the heavens with descendants created as if from
   The noble stock of Abraham.

Questions: What are Sedulius's sources and what is his purpose? Does he deal with the real problems that faced rulers? Could it be that Sedulius and other churchmen assumed that rulers like Charles the Bald knew all too well how to rule in the real world, but needed to be reminded of the ideals of Christian rule? In the fifth chapter, why does Sedulius lay such emphasis upon the ruler's selection of an appropriate wife, but spends almost no time on how to raise obedient children, though disobedient sons had been a problem for rulers like Louis the Pious? Why would Sedulius try to alert a young king to the dangers of war?

53. Lothar II's Divorce

Whatever arguments Sedulius made to King Lothar II about the proper governance of his household were in vain. In 855 Lothar married a noble woman by the name of Theutberga, despite the fact that he had for a long time lived with, and seems to have loved, a woman named Waldrada. Moreover, Waldrada had given birth to Lothar's illegitimate son, Hugh, while Theutberga remained without child. Thus, Lothar began to plot to divorce his barren wife, but conditions had changed in the century since Charlemagne had summarily divorced his Lombard bride. To complicate matters further for Lothar, his uncles Louis the German and Charles the Bald had their eyes on Lotharingia and, therefore, wanted to preserve Lothar's barren marriage, since if their nephew died without a legitimate heir they could legitimately divide up his kingdom between them.

1. Adventius of Metz's Defense

Adventius became bishop of Metz in 855 and was a high advisor and ambassador of Lothar II. Therefore, it fell naturally upon him, as upon other high ecclesiastics of Lothar's realm, to defend his king's divorce. But Adventius is below also defending his own innocence, since he claims to have not been a witness to some of the early events. He is also vague about what constitutes a legal marriage, since Waldrada's union with Lothar II was of the older Germanic type called Friedelehe and not formally recognized by the church.

Source: trans. P.E. Dutton, from the Libellus de Waldrada, ed. E. Dümmler, in Monumenta Germaniae Historica: Epistolae, vol. 6 (Berlin, 1902-1925), pp.215-217.

August Lothar [I] of holy memory was elected emperor by the people of the realm of the Romans. He governed at the summit of the kingdom of the Franks and, among his other considered actions, he gave, in the name of the divine faith, a noble virgin named Waldrada to his son, the lord Lothar [II], so that he might have and hold her in the faith of God as his own into the future. And that this joining might appear to be just, [Lothar I] handed over 100 manses in the grant of the marriage gift to the glorious boy, who was not yet independent [that is, of age], although he was the future heir to his father, but he remained [at that time] under tutors and governors, just as the apostle [Paul] says about such things: "the heir as long as he is a child does not differ from a servant, though he be lord of all, but is under tutors and governors until the time appointed by the father." For as long as the aforementioned emperor held supremacy over the kingdom of the Franks, the aforementioned boy adhered to the girl given to him by his father's grant. That [association] was not brought about in secret, because the truth has no secrets, but was brought about within the public view of the bishops and magnates, as his teachers and his uncle Leutfrid [the brother of the Empress Ermengard] acknowledge. When the lord Lothar, the emperor, died, at the time when he was being mourned, the lordless Hubert [abbot of Saint-Maurice], with his associates, brought his sister Theutberga forward to the lord King Lothar, that most distinguished boy, and [Hubert] fraudulently united her with him, threatening that there would be a danger to the state of the king's kingdom if he did not listen to his counsel. The king gave in, although he did not wish to, as he himself acknowledges.

The rumor of the worst vile practices followed Theutberga and she was reputed to be guilty of incestuous intercourse with her brother Hubert. An account of her confession was brought forward, was freely read out by her, she was condemned by the judgment of the councillors, and was saved by the mercy of the bishops. She took flight. The most pious lord, King Lothar, sent information about this event to Rome through distinguished men and ordered them to disclose its circumstances. The most holy Pope Nicholas having learned of it sent his confidential agents, Radoald, the bishop of Porto, and John, the bishop of Cervia, into Francia and he decided to hold a general council in the city of Metz. There the most glorious King Lothar with the entire gathering of his primates, nobles, and councillors was present and sat in the holy synod. There he revealed the reasons for his action to the legates of the Roman church: how his father of most excellent memory, lord Lothar, the perpetual Augustus, handed over to him in the faith of God and with his own hands the noble virgin [Waldrada] and he related other things, which we listed above. But because Theutberga publicly confessed to her fault in this crime in the council which took place in the city of Metz, all the nobles of the entire kingdom of the Franks approved [the divorce]. A prudence that is as much temporal as spiritual shines in them, whose fathers, grandfathers, and ancestors ruled the empire with the experience of the council of the Romans. I have admired that family which, in the time of the august Emperor Louis [the Pious] and the most magnificent Lothar, was always adorned with the title of the consulship. The entire population has approved the special prerogative (not at all to be dismissed) of the guidance of that family, especially since the condemnation of crimes has not been brought against it, but rather the noble character of its goodness has been exalted in praise. For which reason, because many people indiscriminately imagine things concerning these [events] and supply various kinds of interpretations, I have decided to treat and examine these things and shall take the trouble to explain them out of respect for the faithful. When the most pious emperor gave that girl marked by the nobility of her body to his son Lothar, I was not yet bound down by the weight of the episcopal office nor was I present at these events. When Theutberga was escorted in and a second marriage was brought about, I was almost entirely in the dark, except for some rumors. These things having run their course, I was sought out by the clergy and elected by the people, I was canonically consecrated bishop [in 855], and I understood things to stand like this: [our] most Christian emperor in the faith of Christ and in his own [good] faith gave the virgin [Waldrada] to his son. The faith of God does not provide a prostitute, but repudiates such, saying: "Thou shall not commit adultery." And the Psalmist says: "thou hast destroyed all them that go a whoring from thee." Paul, who was girded with the faith of God, claimed this, saying: "For this ye know, that no whoremonger, nor unclean person, nor covetous man, who is an idolater, hath any inheritance in the kingdom of Christ and of God." That man carrying the stigma of Jesus on his body, that is the standard of the faith, does not abide adulterers, but strikes them with the blade of his holy utterance, saying: "Nor will adulterers inherit the kingdom of God." The Lord, who is faithful and gives holy and faithful things to David, and who did not take away from the orthodox Emperor Lothar the power to marry his son to any girl he had chosen, says in the Gospel: "Whoever shall put away his wife and marry another, commits adultery." Whence, hearing these things piously and devoutly, let them obey and serve the ancient canons, because the limits set by the fathers [of the church] should never be crossed. For the holy canons declare that a woman given by a father's gift is free of blame. The emperor, who was devoted to cherishing the divine, did not allow his son, King Lothar, to engage in the foul crime of fornication. [Rather] the declaration of Lothar [II] and all the nobles concerning the union with Waldrada exists, because his father in the faith of God gave her to him.

But concerning Theutberga, because she has confessed and proved the evil of her crime concerning that shocking intercourse [sodomy] with her impudent brother, likewise they protest entirely. She was not frightened by us with the least terrifying things, nor comforted by sweet persuasions. The Lord himself, however, according to the apostle, says: "If it be possible, as much as lies within you, live peaceably with all people." Hearing the voices of noble advisors, just as earlier and up to this time we have remarked, and because the advice of the nobles was heard and approved, we thought in this way in all our endorsements and interpretations [of events] that if Theutberga confessed to the aforesaid crime, she was unworthy of belonging to the royal family. And if Waldrada was, in the faith of God and by the gift of the father, joined to the king, I did not dare to blaspheme against the faith of God, lest the Scripture pierce me violently with a lance of words, saying: "Do not suffer blasphemers to live." The Apostle gives license for "every person to be fully persuaded in his own mind."

2. Gunther's Furious Protest

Adventius may have worded his defense so carefully because he already knew of the difficulties of the archbishops, Gunther of Cologne and Theutgaud of Trier, who had gone to Rome in late 863 to present Lothar's case to Pope Nicholas. They had, to their considerable shock, heard Nicholas overthrow the results of the council of Metz and depose them. Hincmar of Rheims, one of the great opponents of Lothar's presumptive divorce, reported in the Annals of Saint-Bertin for 864 the violent turn the case had taken.

Source: trans. P.E. Dutton, from Annales de Saint-Bertin, ed F. Grat, J. Vielliard, S. Clémencet (Paris: Klincksieck, 1964), pp.105-112, 116.

864...With Gunther inciting him, Louis, called the emperor of Italy, was angry, though it brought him injury, because the papacy had reduced, as we set out above, to a lower rank the representatives of his brother Lothar who were sent to Rome by means of his own solemn promise and intervention. He proceeded to Rome with his wife [the Empress Engelberga] and in the company of those same representatives, Theutgaud and Gunther. It was his intention for the bishops to be restored by the Roman pope or, if this did not happen, to apply force in some violent way. When the pope learned of this [plan], he called for a period of fasting and prayer by himself and the Romans so that with the support of the apostles God might fill the emperor with a good thought and reverence towards holy religion and the authority of the papacy. The emperor arrived in Rome and was living near the basilica of Saint Peter. When the Roman clergy and people, who were observing the fast with crosses and prayers, went to the basilica of Saint Peter and had begun to mount the steps before the basilica of Saint Peter, they were pushed down to the bottom by the emperor's men and [there] they were beaten with many blows. Their crosses and standards were destroyed and those able to get away fled. In this tumult, a remarkable and venerable cross made most handsomely by Helen [the mother of Constantine] of holy reputation, in which she had set [a piece of] the wood of the true cross and which she gave to Saint-Peter in greatest reward, was broken to bits and cast into the mud. From the mud, it is reported, some people from England collected up the bits and gave them back to their keepers. The pope was at the Lateran Palace when he learned of these disgraceful events. Later he discovered from a certain messenger that he himself was to be seized and so in secret he boarded a boat and took himself across the Tiber to the church of Saint Peter, where for two days and two nights he remained without food and drink. In the meantime, the man by whose boldness the venerable cross had been broken to bits died and the emperor was laid low with a fever, for which reason he sent his wife [Engelberga] to the pope. On her promise of safe passage, the pope visited the emperor and, after a frank discussion—as is proper between them—the pope went back to the Lateran Palace. Then the emperor commanded Gunther and Theutgaud, still reduced in rank, as they were when they came with him, to return to Francia.

Then Gunther conveyed these diabolical chapters previously unheard of through his brother, the cleric Hilduin, and his men to the pope. He sent these chapters with this preface to the bishops of Lothar's kingdom after returning to Rome with the help of Louis, as set out above. [Gunther] instructed [Hilduin] that if the pope did not want to accept those chapters, he should set them on the body [that is, the tomb] of Saint Peter.

"Gunther and Theutgaud send greetings in the Lord to their holy and venerable brothers and bishops.

We humbly ask you dearest brothers to give us at once the comfort of your prayers, we who constantly pray for you. Do not be troubled or frightened by those sinister rumors about us that may have reached your ears. We are confident of the forgiving mercy of our Lord, since the traps of enemies will not dominate over our kingdom or over us, nor will our adversaries rejoice over us. For although the lord Nicholas, who is called pope and who counts himself an apostle among the apostles and who thinks of himself as the emperor of the whole world, had desired to condemn us because of the impulse and wish of those to whom he is partial and in conspiracy with, nevertheless he has found resisters all down the line, and with the assistance of Christ, to his insanity. Whatever he did then was regretted a great deal shortly afterwards.

We have sent you the following chapters in which you can understand the nature of our complaint against the pope. Having left Rome and traveled far away, we were again called back to Rome. As we commence this return [to Rome], we have composed these [chapters] for you, so that you might not be amazed by our ongoing absence. Seek out our lord king [Lothar II] frequently yourselves, and also through your agents and letters. Reassure him and secure for him whatever friends and supporters you can. Always entreat with admonitions King Louis [the German] and diligently explore with him the common good, since our peace exists in the concord between those [two] kings. Be of firm mind and peaceful heart, O nobles and brothers, since with God's help we hope to draw your attention to things to which, without error, you can turn your minds, with the Lord's spirit teaching you, and learn what you should do and how you should do it. Be sure to take the trouble to advise the king in everything, so that he not act on the various suggestions [made to him] until he himself understands the [underlying] causes of things. Moreover, dearest brothers, it is crucial for us and praiseworthy to preserve in unbroken fashion the faith we promised to our king in the presence of God and men. May almighty God think it worthy to maintain you in his holy service.

1. Hear us, lord Pope Nicholas. Fathers and brothers, our diocesan bishops, sent us to you and we came of our own free will, namely to speak with your magisterial power about those things which we judged together [in the council of Metz], according as it seemed to us and was known to those considering and approving the authorities and reasons which we set out in writing, so that your wisdom, having considered everything, might show to us what it perceives and wants [to do about this matter]. And if your holiness discovers something better, we humbly urge you to inform us and teach us about it, for we with our fellows are ready to admit whatever you, with firm lessons, introduce as more correct and more likely.

2. But we have been waiting for your answer for three weeks and you have provided us with nothing definite and no doctrine. One day in public you said that we seemed to be pardonable and innocent according to the claims of our little book.

3. At last, suspecting no animosity, we were called and led into your presence. The gates there were locked [behind us] and a conspiracy like that of a thief was hatched. A crowd of clerics and laymen mixed together was collected and you undertook to crush us violently among so many people. Without a synodal or canonical examination, with no one accusing us or bearing witness against us, with no separation of the discussion into parts or any demonstrative exploration of authorities, without a confession coming from our lips, with our other metropolitan and diocesan bishops and our fellow brothers being absent, entirely beyond the agreement of all people, you wanted with

your own will alone and with tyrannical anger to condemn us.

4. In no manner did we accept your accursed opinion which is foreign to paternal kindness, outside fraternal charity, and unjustly pronounced against us and unreasonably against canonical law. Instead we, with the entire body of our brothers, denounce and reject it as if it were a curse pronounced in vain. We wish, in fact, not to receive you into our communion and company, since you prefer to associate with those who are condemned and anathematized for abandoning and condemning our holy religion. Raising yourself up arrogantly, you spurn the communion and brotherly company of the entire church and, by the puffing up of pride, you make yourself unworthy and all alone.

5. Thus by the rashness of your frivolous nature you have pronounced the destructuion of anathema on yourself by your own judgment, proclaiming: "Let him be anathematized who does not follow papal orders." You must have recognized that you have often violated divine laws and sacred canons as well, making them useless as often as you could and not wanting to follow in the footsteps of your forerunners, the preceding bishops of Rome.

6. Thus now that we have experienced your fraudulent and crafty ways, we have not been provoked by the libel, as it were, against us, but we were livid over your iniquity. We were not concerned with the character of our worthlessness, but have in mind the entirety of our order to which you are attempting to apply force.

7. Let us briefly repeat the main point of our particular representation. Divine and canonical law openly establishes and even the respected laws of the world stipulate that it is not permitted for anyone to give a noble virgin to any man, particularly if that girl never wished to agree to an illegal union. Because [Waldrada] was joined to her man [Lothar II] with the permission of parents, with faith, and with conjugal emotions and love, let her be considered not a concubine, but fully his wife."

The pope, however, did not want to accept these chapters. Hilduin roused to arms with Gunther's men entered the church of Saint Peter without proper respect. As his brother Gunther had commanded what he was to do if the pope would not receive the chapters, [Hilduin] wanted to cast those diabolical writings upon the body of Saint Peter. Forbidden to enter by the keepers of the place, Hilduin and [Gunther's] men began to strike those men with sticks until one of them died there. Then Hilduin cast that writing· upon Saint-Peter's body and both he and those with him, with swords drawn to protect themselves, exited from the church. With the sorry deed done, they returned to Gunther.

After a few days, the emperor departed from Rome where many robberies had been committed by his company, where houses had been ruined, nuns and other women raped, people killed, and churches violated. The emperor came to Ravenna and there observed Easter Sunday in such a way as God and the apostles deserved. On 30 March Gunther came to Cologne and presumed to celebrate the Mass and to confer the sacred unction, as one would expect from a godless man. But Theutgaud respectfully abstained from his [former] office, just as he had been ordered. Then with other bishops stirring up trouble around Lothar, [the king] took away the bishopric from Gunther and gave it to his adviser Hugh, the son of Conrad (King Charles's uncle) and his aunt. Hugh was a cleric with his tonsure, but with an ordination only as a subdeacon. In his habits, however, and in his life he was out of step with even those of a faithful layman. When this happened, Gunther was stirred up and, bearing off whatever remained in the church treasury of Cologne, he again returned to Rome. He would now, because of the papal command, reveal all the fictions of Lothar and himself about Theutberga and Waldrada. But the bishops of Lothar's kingdom sent little books of penitence and canonical declarations to the pope, since they had wandered greatly from the truth of the Gospels, from apostolic authority, and from the holy rules in the case of Theutberga and Waldrada. But Lothar sent Bishop Ratold of Strasbourg with writings filled with the usual falsehoods about his excuse and his willing correction. [Lothar] traveled through Gondreville and Remiremont to join up with his brother at Orbe....

Hubert, the married cleric and abbot of the monastery of Saint Martin, who possessed the monastery of Saint Maurice and other holdings of Louis, the emperor of Italy, against his will, was slain by his men. Theutberga, his sister, overthrown by Lothar, came into the care of Charles [the Bald] who gave her the monastery of Avenay....

Despite Lothar II's apparent attempt to placate the pope and return to Theutberga, he continued to strive to reunite with Waldrada. When he died in 869, he was still married to Theutberga and still without a legal heir.

Questions: Why would Pope Nicholas have taken such a hard line against an attempted divorce by a Carolingian king, when not a word of complaint had come from the papacy when Charlemagne divorced Desiderata? Why did Adventius survive this controversy, while Gunther fell? Is Hincmar's report in the Annals of Saint-Bertin a fair one?

54. Otfrid of Weissenburg on Old High German

Charlemagne may have been interested in the German language, as Einhard noted, but it was in Louis the German's kingdom that the Frankish interest in Old High German deepened and expanded. A number of German works, including the apocalyptic poem the Muspilli, can be associated with Louis's reign, but the grandest of these is the Evangelienbuch of Otfrid of Weissenburg who once studied at Fulda under Hrabanus Maurus. Otfrid dedicated his book on the life of Christ to Louis the German and some other patrons. Around 863, he asked Liutbert, the new archbishop of Mainz, to approve the book, perhaps before he sent it to the king. Not only are Otfrid's reflections on the differences between Latin and German fascinating, but he helps us to remember that though Carolingian writers communicate so aptly in Latin, they were all thinking much of the time in their own native languages of Old High German or Old French.

Source: trans. F.P. Magoun, Jr., "Otfrid's Ad Liutbertum," PMLA 58 (1943), pp.872-889; reprinted with permission.

In transmitting [it] to your most excellent judgment that you may approve the style of the present book [the *Liber Evangeliorum*], I have first of all taken pains to explain to you at the outset the reason for which I have ventured to compose it, lest, should it prove worthless, the mind of any of the faithful might try to impute [this] to the presumption of my unworthy person.

When formerly the noise of [worldly] futilities smote on the ears of certain men exceedingly well-tried [in God's service] and the offensive song of laymen disturbed their holy way of life, [I was] asked by certain [monastic] brethren worthy of consideration and especially [moved] by the words of a certain reverend lady, Judith by name, who urged [me] very often that I should compose for them in German [that is, in Frankish] a selection of the Gospels, so that a little of the text of this poem might neutralize the trivial merriment of worldly voices and [that], engrossed in the sweet charm of the Gospels in [their] own language, they might be able to avoid the noise of futile things.

Also adding to [their] petition the complaint that the bards of the pagans, such as Virgil, Lucan, Ovid and very many others, [had] adorned the deeds of their [people] in their native [Latin] tongue—from the sayings of whose works we know the world now to be in a state of uncertainty—they [my petitioners] praised the actions of men exceedingly well-tried [in God's service], likewise of our [Christian] faith, [namely], of Juvencus, Arator, Prudentius and many others, who in their own [Latin] tongue fittingly adorned the sayings and miracles of Christ. They [my petitioners] said that we [Franks], indeed, though instructed in the same faith and the same grace, were sluggardly in setting forth the very brilliant splendor of the divine words in our own language.

Since, because of Christian love for those who urgently spurred me on, I was unable to refuse this [petition], I have acted not as one skilled [in poetical composition] but rather as one impelled by the prayer of [monastic] brethren. Supported, indeed, by the aid of their prayers, I have written down a selection from the Gospels, composed [by me] in Frankish, now and then interspersing allegorical and tropological words, so that he who shudders at the difficulty of a foreign language in them [Latin writings] may here [in the *Liber Evangeliorum*] in his own language become familiar with the most holy words and, understanding in his own language the Law of God, may, therefore, guard well against straying from it by even a little through his own [erroneous] thinking.

And so in the first and last parts of this book I have written [this], proceeding as a mediator among the four Evangelists, and I have, as far as I have been able, composed almost completely [and] in sequence among these only what this one or another of [the] others wrote.

In the middle, lest perchance readers should suffer severely from an excess of words, I, though already exceedingly weary—for this [middle part] I composed last of all—on account, however, of the above-mentioned urgency [of my petitioners], reluctantly omitted both many of Christ's parables and miracles and [much of] his teaching, and I no longer tried, as I set out [to do], to compose it in [pericope] sequence but according as they [that is, the Gospel episodes] occurred to my poor memory.

And, indeed, I have divided this work into five books. Of these the first commemorates the Nativity of Christ; it ends with the baptism and the teaching of John [the Baptist]. The second, since his disciples have already been called together, reports how He made himself known to the world by certain miracles and by his renowned teaching. The third relates somewhat of the fame of the miracles and of his teaching [addressed] to the Jews. The fourth, indeed, tells how He, nearing his passion, voluntarily suffered death for us. The fifth commemorates his resurrection, afterwards his conversation with the disciples, the ascension, and the day of judgment.

Although the books of the Gospels are four, these [here], as I have said, I have divided into five because their [that is, the Gospel's] holy, four-square [numerical] evenness adorns the [numerical] oddness of our five senses, and [through this] all things superfluous in us, not only in the way of deeds but also of thoughts, turn toward the exaltation of heavenly things. Whatever sin we commit in the [five senses of] sight, smell, touch, taste and hearing, this same sinfulness we purge in the recollection of the text of these [four Gospels]: Let unprofitable sight become dark [in the face of harmful impressions], [our sight] illuminated by the Gospel words! Let sinful hearing not be noxious to our hearts! Let smell and taste free themselves from sin and unite in the sweetness of Christ! and let the innermost parts of the heart hold by memory these [Gospel] selections written in German!

For just as this rude [Frankish] language is unpolished and unruly and unused to being restrained by the regulating curb of the art of grammar, so, too, in many [Frankish] words it is difficult to spell either on account of the piling up of letters [that is, consonant-combinations] or on account of a sound foreign [to Latin].

For sometimes it [Frankish] calls for in its sound, as I think, three [consecutive] u's [that is, uuu], the first two consonantal, as it seems to me; the third with the vocalic sound remaining.

Sometimes, indeed, I have been unable [despite their inappropriateness] to avoid [in writing] the vowel-sounds [that is, the letters] a or e or i or u; here the Greek y seemed to me [preferable] to be written. And even to this letter [that is, y] this [Frankish] language is sometimes ill adapted, often in a certain [reduced vowel-]sound attaching itself to no character [of the alphabet] except with difficulty.

Contrary to [or extending beyond] the usage of Latin this [Frankish] language often uses k and z, which the [Latin] grammarians say are among the superfluous letters; but sometimes on account, I think, of the hissing of the teeth z's are used in this [Frankish] language; k's however, on account of the back sound-quality [in certain words].

It [Frankish] also very often, though not invariably, tolerates the [grammatical] figure of metaplasm [that is, elision by metrical licence] which scholars of the art of grammar call 'synaloepha'—and unless readers pay attention to this, the words of a phrase sounded rather inelegant—[these same scholars] sometimes keeping the [elided] letters in writing [Frankish], sometimes, indeed, omitting [them] according to the custom of the Hebrew language, by whom [that is, the Hebrews], as some say, it is customary entirely to drop and pass over these [vocalic] letters in a manner of 'elision within the lines.'

Not that the run [that is, metrical flow] of this text [the *Liber evangeliorum*] is restricted by metrical overexactness, yet it regularly calls for the [grammatical] 'scheme' of end-rhyme. For words at the end [of an off-verse] require a sound-quality suitable and fitting and similar to the preceding [rhyme-word of the on-verse].

And because of this [figure of metaplasm] it [Frankish] very often tolerates synaloephic elision, not only between vowels but even between other letters; and unless this is effected, a protraction of the letters [that should be elided] quite often results in a sound unsuitable to the utterance of the words [rhyme]. This [elision] we find, if we pay proper attention, we effect very often in our ordinary speech.

The poetic diction of this [Frankish] language requires, indeed, both that a soft [or meretricious] and slippery elision [by synaloepha] be avoided by the reader, and that end-rhyme, that is, a like ending of words, be observed by the poets.

Sometimes, indeed, here the thought must be kept open [for example, by proper punctuation] through two or three or even four [long] lines in the text, so that what the text means may be made clear to readers.

Here quite often i and o are found written in conjunction—and similarly the other vowels [that is, a,e,u] in conjunction with the former [i]—sometimes remaining in sound as separate vowels, sometimes joined, the former [i] passing [in such cases] over to the phonetic value of the consonants [that is, a consonant].

Whereas in Latin two negatives affirm, indeed, the words of a sentence, according to the usage of this [Frankish] language they almost invariably negate. And though I might sometimes have been able to avoid this [double negation], nevertheless on account of everyday usage I have taken pains to write as customary speech has showed itself [to be].

The nature, indeed, of this [Frankish] language permitted me to preserve neither the number nor the genders [of Latin]. Sometimes, indeed, I have rendered a masculine of the Latin language by a feminine in this [Frankish] and in like manner I have perforce mixed other genders. I have varied a plural number with a singular and a singular with a plural and thus quite often have perforce fallen into a barbarism and a solecism.

I might put down from this book [the *Liber evangeliorum*] examples in German of all these faults noted above, except that I would avoid the derision of readers; for, when the unpolished words of a rustic language [such as Frankish] are sown in the smooth ground of Latin, they give occasion for loud laughter to readers. This [Frankish] language is, indeed, regarded as rustic because it has at no time been polished up by the natives either by writing or by any [grammatical] art.

Indeed, they [Franks] do not, as do many other peoples, commit the stories of their predecessors to [written] record nor do they adorn [in literary style] the deeds or the life of these [same] out of appreciation for [their] distinction. But if on rare occasions it does happen [that Franks write of such matters], by preference they set forth [the narrative] in the language of other peoples, that is, of the Romans or the Greeks. They guard against [grammatical] crudity in other [languages], yet are not ashamed of a crude blunder in their own. In other [languages] they are shocked to transgress [grammatical] art by even a little letter, yet their native [Frankish] language produces a fault in almost every single word.

A remarkable thing [it is], however, that great men, constant in good judgment, distinguished for careful attention, supported by nimbleness [of wit], broad in wisdom, famed for sanctity, should carry over all these [virtues] into the glory of a foreign language and not have the habit of composition in their native language.

It is, however, fitting that in whatever manner, either in [grammatically] corrupt or in the language of [grammatically] perfect art, the human race should praise the Author of all things, who gave them the plectrum [that is, an instrument] of the tongue to sound among themselves the word of his praise; Who seeks in us not the adulation of polished words but a devout mood of meditation and the accumulation of works by pious toil, not empty lip-service.

This book, therefore, I have taken care to transmit to your [that is, Liutbert's] wise judgment for approval. And because my humble self was educated, [though] all too little, by Hrabanus [of Fulda] of revered memory, formerly worthy bishop of your see [of Mainz], I have taken care to commend [this book] to the dignity of your episcopal office and to the wisdom in you equal [to this dignity]. If it please the eyes of your holiness and should [your holiness] not judge that it should be rejected, may your [episcopal] authority grant that it may be used at will by all the faithful. But if, indeed, it does not seem at all fitting and [seems rather to be] on a plane with my carelessness, may that same reverend and holy authority [of yours] reject [it]. Indeed, my humble little self urges that the matter of either [course of] action [that is, episcopal approbation or disapprobation] be determined by your opinion.

May the supreme Trinity and the perfect Unity of all things deign for a long time to keep you unimpaired in usefulness and remaining in an upright [way of] life. Amen.

Questions: Why did Otfrid write the Evangelienbuch? Was there an existing audience of people who could read German or was his work to be read out? How does Einhard's claim that there was a collection of Germanic poems written down fit with

*Otfrid's claim that the Germans were not in the habit of writing such things down?
How difficult did Otfrid find the task of translating (or adapting) from Latin into
German?*

55. The Vision of Charlemagne

*This vision was written at Mainz, perhaps as late as 870. It too may have been
composed for Louis the German and, thus, the presence of the Old High German
words in it is another indication of the cultural mix at work in Louis's kingdom.
The reader might like to consider what arguments can be mounted against this text
coming from the time of Charlemagne and Einhard.*

Source: trans. P.E. Dutton, from the Visio Caroli Magni, ed. P. Jaffé, in Bibliotheca rerum germanicarum, vol. 4 (Berlin: 1868), pp.701-704.

Charles, once the emperor of the Franks and of diverse peoples, was in the
habit, wherever he spent the night either at home or on campaign, of having
lamps and [wax] tablets placed close by his side. Whatever he saw in his
dreams worth remembering, he took the trouble to write down, lest he forget
it.

One night, when he had readied himself for bed and had given himself
up to sleep, he saw a person approach who was bearing an unsheathed sword
in his hand. Although apprehensive, he asked him who he was and where
he had come from. In response, he heard him say: "Receive this sword given
to you by God as a gift. And read the writing set out on it and remember
it, since that [inscription] will be fulfilled in the stated times." When he had
taken the sword and had carefully inspected it, he found that there was writing inscribed in four places on the sword. In the first place near the handle
of the sword was written RAHT; in the second place, RADOLEIBA; in the third,
NASG; and in the fourth, near the point of the sword, ENTI. Awaking, [Char-
lemagne] ordered a light and the tablets to be brought to him and he wrote
down those same words in their exact form.

In the morning, at the canonical hour according to his custom of worship
and after his prayers were finished, he related to all his magnates who were
present the dream that he had seen. He asked them to supply him with an
interpretation [of the dream]. All were quiet save one, by the name of Einhard, who was said to be wiser than the others. He said: "O lord emperor,
the one who presented you with the sword will [surely] reveal to you, despite
our silence, the interpretation of the writing inscribed on it."

Then the emperor said: "If you wish to hear the significance of the writing,
as it seems to me and according to the strength of my meager ability, I shall
suggest it. The sword, which was transmitted to us by God, can be understood as the power fittingly transferred to us by God, since it was by the aid
of violence and with arms that we subjected many enemies to our power.
And because at the present our enemies are quieter than they were in the
times of our ancestors, there is an abundance of material success. That is
what the first word on the sword signifies: RAHT, that is, an abundance of
all things. The word inscribed in the second place, RADOLEIBA, I think will

be fulfilled in the time of my sons when I have passed from this world, namely that there will no longer be such a great abundance of material goods and certain peoples, now subdued, will break away. Thus RADOLEIBA signifies that failure will quickly come in everything. When, however, those sons have died and their sons have begun, after them, to govern, NASG will exist, which was inscribed in the third place. For the sake of filthy lucre, [those grandsons] will increase tolls and they will oppress travelers and pilgrims. Having no sense of modesty, they will collect riches with great disorder and dishonor. They will take away, with many words or with few, even the ecclesiastical properties given by me and our ancestors to clerics and monks in the service of God and they will give them as benefices to their supporters. That is what NASG signifies. But what was written on the point of the sword, ENTI, that is the end, can be understood in two ways. Either it signifies the end of the world [itself] or the end of our line, that is, that no one from our family will rule over the Franks."

The dreamer himself interpreted these things so. Abbot Einhard was in the habit of relating things to the monk Hrabanus and to many others, and likewise Hrabanus was in the same habit of repeating these things to many, of whom I, who set this down in writing, am one.

Some of these things came true in earlier times, some in modern times. For after the death of Charles, with the Emperor Louis ruling, the Bretons and many of the Slav peoples broke away and the kingdom was afflicted in many places by a lack of goods. After Louis's death, his sons Lothar, Pepin, and Louis [the German] began to extend NASG for themselves throughout the neglected kingdom. For Pepin robbed so many monasteries in Aquitaine and removed ecclesiastical properties and the instruments of clerics and monks that it would take a long time to describe. Lothar too is supposed to have done the same in Italy. Concerning which there exists a letter from the time of his son which was sent from all the bishops of the Roman church to Louis, the king of Germany, who was seeking to learn through Bishop Witgarius in what way the holy Roman church might obtain peace. Hitherto this letter was stored in the archives of Saint-Martin's [of Mainz]. In this letter, among other things, it was said to Louis: "The holy Roman church and its patron and people are generally wounded, ripped apart, reviled, humiliated, and annihilated."

Questions: Why could Charlemagne not have had such a dream? If it is not what it pretends to be, for what reason would it have been written? Why was a sword chosen as the object to bear the message?

56. Letters of Lupus of Ferrières

Lupus was, perhaps, the greatest humanist of the ninth century. He was especially interested in collecting rare manuscripts of ancient authors. If we want to know why the Latin classics survived, it was surely because of humanists like Lupus who searched out, made copies of, and emended the works of Cicero and others. But Lupus was also very involved in the events of his time as an official of Charles the Bald and abbot in the years between 841 and 863.

Source: trans. G.W. Regenos, The Letters of Lupus of Ferrières (The Hague: Martinus Nijhoff, 1966); reprinted with permission.

1. On Language and Learning

To his very dear brother Altuin [a monk of Saint-Alban close to Mainz], best wishes from Lupus [in 837].

The letter from your holiness reached me on April 29 and it clearly indicated your affection for me, which is certainly no different from that which I have enjoyed and cherish deeply. Indeed, since we lived abroad for quite a long time so harmoniously, pleasantly, and I might perhaps add, profitably, how could a love strengthened by such long association together be weakened?

Now in respect to that illness of mine concerning which you have heard, be assured that it brought me no harm but the greatest good, for God's grace which is present in all things and is everlasting surrounded me, and I suffered nothing worse than mere anxiety. It is true that an abscess developed in my right groin and merely threatened to be fatal, but it produced such an abundance of prayers wherever the report of my illness spread that I make bold to suggest that this was brought about by divine favor.

When I returned from the other side of the Rhine and discovered the condition of our monastery I decided to obey those to whom I was subjected and, by the favor of God's mercy, I am enjoying a complete rest and spending my spare time in the pleasant and profitable pursuit of reading. So you can see that I am planning no trips. If you therefore think it necessary to have a conference with me you should wait until late summer because of the present lack of pasture. At that time you can spend many days with us without any worry so far as the horses are concerned.

In the meantime I shall answer as briefly as I can the questions which you raised, at least those concerning which I think that I have acquired some knowledge.

I should never hesitate to say that a common syllable is formed from a mute and a liquid only in the case of those which are short by nature, first because nature generally takes precedence over position, and secondly, because the pronunciation of words such as the following prompts me to think so: *peccator* yields the feminine *peccatrix; amator, amatrix; venator, venatrix,* and there are many similar cases concerning which no one has ever doubted that the accent should fall on the penult. For if we should follow position, we would pronounce the feminine nouns with the accent on the antepenult, but who would not think it absurd, nay even barbaric? Finally, I find no evidence anywhere in the poets that syllables long by nature are ever shortened, although I have devoted much time and study to this question. It seems to me therefore, and to certain scholars who have considered these matters with me, and they are the best in the field, that *salubris*, *aratrum*, and similar words, should be without any question pronounced with the accent on the penult.

As for *bibliotheca*, we are shown how it should be pronounced by this verse from Martial:

> Quem mea non totum bibliotheca capit.

In the moral verses attributed to Alcuin, *statera* has the following position:

> Non tibi sit modius duplex nec statera duplex.

That *blasphemus* is a Greek word no one will question, unless he be one who pays little attention to the fact that it is spelled with *ph*. It was therefore a certain Greek who assured me that the Greeks pronounce *blasphemus* with a short penult, and our own Einhard has construed it in the very same way. Aurelius Prudentius, however, whose reputation is very great, has placed the word as follows: *Divisor blaspheme Dei*. Hence the belief has spread far and wide that *blasphemus* and *blasphemo* have their accent on the penult.

As for *nundinae*, I have found it with a long penult in a poem by Theodulf [of Orléans]. Whether he did this on his own authority or that of his teachers, responsibility for it must rest with him.

We render *loquela* and *querela* with a single *l* after the orthography of Caper. We would have no hesitation, however, in rendering *medela* the same as *suadela* if the difference in type did not interfere with the similarity in conjugation, and if the almost complete harmony of examples, which we must not ignore, did not oppose. Let us therefore remain neutral and not rashly change our usage until, if what I have said is not enough, something more convincing may be found by ourselves or by some other diligent scholars.

The *sistrum* is a musical instrument which Isis, as you have written, was represented as carrying in her hand to indicate thereby the rise and the fall of the Nile. For this reason, Virgil, to show that Cleopatra has assumed its fancied power, says with his usual perception: *patrio vocat agmina sistro*.

We render *fialae* with a short penult for the reason that those objects which we call *fialae* are made of glass, which is called in Greek *hialis*. Now you have *hialin* in Virgil:

> Carpebant hialin saturo fucato colore.

Likewise in Martial:

> Quid tibi cum fiala ligulam committere posses.

Concerning comets which have been seen there is more to fear, it seems, than to explain. And since the Holy Scriptures never mention them, we can believe or rather fear what the gentiles have learned by experience when they appeared. They have reported that comets portend pestilence, famine, and war. Hence the poet of Mantua [Virgil], in speaking of other portents at the time of Caesar's death and as the civil wars were drawing near, says: "Nor did terrible comets ever blaze forth so frequently." Josephus also mentions that a sword-shaped star hung over the city of Jerusalem for a whole year before the city was destroyed. But that we may find some hope of meeting a kindlier fate, Pompeius Trogus relates in the following passage that the future greatness of king Mithridates was predicted by a comet: "For in the year of his birth as well as in the first year of his reign a comet shone so brightly for a period of seventy days at both times that the whole sky seemed to be aglow. It traversed a quarter of the heavens, and its brilliant rays exceeded the light of the sun; and during its rising and setting four hours were spent." Moreover, this last April shortly after midnight I saw with my own eyes a rather faint star lying under the constellation of Leo, and its beam of light stretched to Spica in the constellation of Virgo. I watched this star for many days, examining it closely, but later I did not see the beam of light. Finally the star itself passed from view.

Since my return many have been eager to get that book which you requested but it must not be loaned to them. I have therefore about decided to take it away somewhere so that it not get lost. Perhaps you will get it from me when you come. Although I saw that it could be entrusted to this cleric because he is faithful to you, I am surprised, however, that you failed to observe that it could not be safely done because he is traveling on foot.

Finally, I am sorry that you have not kept me informed fully concerning our bishop, for his welfare concerns me more than anyone else's. Besides, I am almost offended because you have not written to tell me about the activities of our friend Probus, that is to say, whether he is pursuing a regular course of studies in the liberal arts in the woodlands of Germany, as he used to express it in all seriousness, or whether, as I am more inclined to think, he is compiling or has at least begun to compile his anthology and admitting into the company of the elect Cicero and Virgil and all the rest who, in his opinion, are the most excellent authors, so that the Lord may not have shed his blood in vain nor spent his time in hell to no avail, if the prophecy is true: "O death, I will be thy plagues; O grave I will be thy destruction."

Good health to you, my dearest friend, and kindly continue your love for me. Extend my humble greeting to your prior and congregation, and beg them to be so good as to beseech the Lord in my behalf and of my father and mother.

2. A Letter from July 844 to Marcward, the abbot of Prüm, on the Aquitanian Campaign.

After my escape from almost certain death while on the Aquitanian campaign [with Charles the Bald] and my release from the discomforts of imprisonment, having been saved from these perils by the abounding grace of God, in whom I put my complete trust, and through the kindness of his saints, and in particular a certain Turpio [the count of Angoulême], I returned to the monastery in good health on July 5. On arrival, I was informed by my brothers, Hatto and Ratharius [monks of Fulda], and by the reading of your letters, what I actually knew already, that you were terribly worried about my misfortune. And now I can just see how extremely happy you must be in knowing that I, whom you mourned as either imprisoned or dead, am now in the monastery safe and sound.

I too and all the brothers are filled with the greatest joy because of your successful return, and we render profound thanks to our Lord God, not only for having restored your Excellency to us, but also for providing protection to the two saints [Chrysanthus and Daria, whose relics were tranferred from Rome to Prüm in 844] by your labors. Indeed we prayed to God daily for your safe return and constantly prayed also for the translation of the saints, being easily persuaded that you would be successful because of your loving devotion to God. In fact we are all praising God for having given us more than we dared to ask for.

There is left one further step to complete our joy and that is for you to favor us with your presence. We shall insist that your letter promised us this although it did not actually say so. But if you do come, you will not only oblige your humble srvants very much, but you will also gain something yourself. You will surely bring us comfort and the desire to lead good lives, and you will become acquainted with the brothers who have taken the places of those who have died since your departure, and if such be possible, you will win their deeper devotion.

I further request that you send an industrious monk to Saint-Boniface [the monastery of Fulda] as your agent to ask Hatto the abbot to send you the *Lives of the Caesars* by Suetonius Tranquillus to be copied. It has been divided by the monks into two small manuscripts. Will you please either bring this work to me in person or if, in penance for my sins, I am presently denied that good fortune, will you have it sent by a most reliable messenger. The manuscript is certainly nowhere to be found in this vicinity, and we trust that we shall receive the benefit of your kindness in this matter too.

I wish to send your Holiness, for instruction in the German language, the son of Guago, a nephew of mine and a relative of yours, and with him two other fine young men, so that some day, if God wills, they may render useful service to our monastery. These three would be satisfied with only two teachers. Do not neglect to let us know as soon as you can whether you are willing to fulfill this request.

We had a very light yield of wine last year. We have an abundance of other things at the present time, and, through the abounding grace of God, we are enjoying a little peace, except that some seculars who would like to overrun our monastery are making trouble for us. You must therefore discharge your debt of love and pray earnestly that God will work in the hearts of the princes to accomplish that which is best for us.

3. On Recent Troubles and Warfare

Lupus sends [in November 845] heartiest greetings to the distinguished and highly respected Bishop Wenilo [the archbishop of Sens].

When I was setting out on a journey to the king [Charles the Bald] and had sent ahead men to inquire what he wished me to do, he had instructed me to meet him on the feast day of Saint Martin at the monastery of that illustrious confessor, but since official duties had called him elsewhere, I again sent messengers to him, and was pleased to obtain with the help of friends his permission to return. Now the reason why our lord the king did not reach Saint-Martin according to his plan was because, as reported by our messenger, the Bretons were having an outbreak of civil strife worse than usual and had summoned our king to Brittany so that the faction opposed to Nominoë might safely defect to him.

Concerning Pepin [II, king of Aquitaine] of whom you inquired, dear father, nothing definite was said at the palace. Only a vague rumor was going around that those who had recently deserted him were about to become reconciled to him.

Some men did indeed arrive from Aquitania and reported that the Normans had recently carried out a raid between Bordeaux and Saintes, and that our men, the Christian forces, had engaged them in an infantry battle, and all except those who were able to save themselves by flight perished miserably. They testified under oath that Seguin, the duke of Gascony, had also been arrested and put to death. This proves how true our Lord's saying is: "Every kingdom divided against itself is brought to desolation," and it shows what fruit is reserved for those who embrace a policy of dissension.

We hope that you are well.

4. On a Runaway Monk

Lupus sends greetings in the Lord [in November 846] to Ratbert [the abbot of Corbie] who deserves every good gift.

Having carefully chosen the proper time, and with the support of our Vulfegisus [a monk of Ferrières], I reminded the king [Charles the Bald] concerning Ivo: that since he had not come back to the monastery and was undoubtedly repeating what he had the habit of doing, you were asking that he not receive the protection of the king's power, lest it be with danger to himself and others if he should ever try to return. Certainly it would be unworthy of his sovereignty to allow wicked men to enter the monastery, if they were not repentant, and far worse to grant them protection from punishment.

The king, with his accustomed graciousness, after a few other remarks, replied that he would henceforth officially deny this monk the benefit of his authority, which he still held in contempt, and he said that it seemed best to him, that the man, lest he come to ruin, be held in suitable custody before his readmission to the fellowship of the monastery. As for ourselves, however, although he offered what we could scarcely have hoped to receive at all, and we appreciated it, as was proper, we strongly insisted that you do not disregard the precept of the rule nor wish to go beyond it.

I have not wished to make extravagant claims concerning your generosity until I find out whether the shipment of fish which is supposed to be on its way exceeds my feeble powers of description, not only because of the size, but also, as I imagine, the superb quality.

5. Establishing Connections

Lupus sends greeting in the Lord [between 840 and 846] to the very reverend metropolitan Orsmar [the archbishop of Tours].

Ever since I have learned about your reputation, as told me by my brother who is a very devoted friend of yours, I have been extremely eager to enjoy by experience what I have had a delightful foretaste of, thanks to him, and I am most grateful to your Holiness because you have not been too proud to vie with me in acts of kindness in receiving this brother of mine and courteously giving him your official support, and in extending, moreover, to your humble servant a most cordial invitation to share your friendship. You will easily understand whether or not I speak with sincerity of heart if ever by God's grace I shall find an opportunity to offer proof.

Since we have now learned how much to expect from you, we urge you, in the meantime, to obtain the *Commentaries* of Boethius on the *Topica* of Cicero which Amulric has in the library of Saint-Martin in a papyrus manuscript, or, as others seem to say more correctly, on paper, and that you send it to us with this courier whom we sent to you for this purpose. If anyone should inquire to whom this manuscript is to be loaned, we advise you not to mention our names, but tell him that you wish to send it to certain relatives of yours who are very eager to have it. Now if we are privileged to receive that volume by your help, we shall take very good care of it, and we shall return it at an opportune time.

Please let us know about the state of your health and your good fortune, which pleases us very much, and grant also that we shall not have written to you in vain.

6. To an Unknown Friend About an Enemy (November or December 846.)

Since you have an abundance of good reasons for taking action, do not hesitate, you and those whom you consider loyal, to overturn the schemes of a traitor who takes advantage of my kindness with unparalleled impudence by remaining in our monastery and ceases not to hurt the one who takes care of him. Clad in dishonor and imbued with jealousy of which he cannot rid himself, he is trying to drive me out. And since he is failing to win his coveted victory, he takes an insane delight in spreading abroad evil reports like one who restlessly attempts to take away from others that which he knows he will never get for himself. But why should you not restrain in every way this person with invincible and irrefutable arguments, for, according to the Holy Scriptures, the spirit of God detests him because he confuses the laws of God with the laws of man and sows discord among those who have become his brothers by nature or by religion?

By no means allow yourself to be torn away from our place by evil-doers, for, by the help of God, what you fear will not happen and what you desire will quickly come to pass, and we shall thus be free for study. Of this I am now fully convinced.

At times our Demosthenes [Lupus himself] does not even have a head of cabbage to eat, and sometimes only black bread. But he bears it patiently.

Having no hope of securing wine, he has been forced to develop a taste for beer which he must buy; and in the following respect he even surpasses Cicero, for what Cicero experienced while asleep, he experiences while awake. He is therefore not gaining strength in his lungs, nor does he take pains to improve the quality of his voice. He is giving less attention to the practice of rhetoric and is concerned rather with the business of keeping himself alive.

We certainly believe, however, that the author of all good things will bring our poverty as well as yours to an end by his abounding riches.

7. To the Same Friend (November or December 846.)

There is nothing for you to fear, for our enemies, both domestic and foreign, though most harmful to themselves, will not harm me because God who has commanded and permitted me to put my trust in him will deign to protect his humble servant. We must therefore laugh at every effort of those who are torn by unremitting jealousy and writhing in unbounded covetousness.

8. To the Same Friend (846-847.)

Considering the persistence of the struggle and granting my determination to win, will you, a wise judge of our needs, see that the generous amount of grain which I left with you serves our needs. For if you will apply yourself diligently to the planting of the crops and the feeding of the animals, and to genuine hospitality, my particular concern, I have no doubt that there will be enough left to provide a comfortable living.

9. On His Incompetence as a Soldier

To his very special friend, Bishop Pardulus [of Laon], Lupus extends greetings in the Lord [in June 849].

I was not officially summoned by our lord the king [Charles]. That is why I did not come to the meeting. I have had this very letter sent to you, so that if I happen to be mentioned, you can show that I remained behind with good reason. Furthermore, since you have admitted me into the circle of your friends, I ask that now as well as in the future, whenever God grants you the opportunity, you will endeavor to keep me safe by your intercession. As you know, I have not learned how to strike an enemy nor parry a blow, nor indeed to execute all the other duties of the infantry and cavalry, but our king does not need soldiers alone. If a campaign is started, I beg that you, and, if necessary, Hincmar [of Rheims], tell him to respect my position and assign me duties which will not be utterly inconsistent with it, since he has little regard for my studies. If you sincerely love me, you can manage this in such a way that I shall not only cause no offense, but even win some favor. Thus have I already found and proved your wisdom.

So, when you have time and the opportunity, assist me and everyone you can, I beg, being assured that God will, on the one hand, give you a just reward and that we, on the other hand, will keep fresh the memory of your deeds of kindness.

Send me back a letter which will please me, and kindly remember me always. Best wishes.

10. On These Dangerous Times

To Hilduin [the abbot of Saint-Martin of Tours and archchaplain of Charles the Bald], master of ecclesiastics, a man of great reputation, position, and restraint, Lupus extends good wishes [in June 854] for success both now and in the days to come.

It is not surprising that your Highness supposed we could safely guard your treasure, especially because the location of our monastery has been unknown to you. For, if you had been acquainted with it, you certainly would not have sent us the treasure to be kept for long, no, not even for a mere three days. Although this place of ours seems difficult of access to marauders—no longer is any place, no matter how far away or hard to reach, distant to them (a deserving reward for our sinful ways), nevertheless, the rapacity of thieves is actually encouraged by the weakness of our monastery and a lack of men capable of resisting them. Moreover, protected by the forest, they are able to rush out unopposed by defenses or a force of men, and then returning into the adjoining forest, to scatter out so as to get safely away with the money and to leave their pursuers behind in a futile search. Your own men have recently discovered that this is so, and Ivo who has been with us here for a long time can bear witness to it.

Give us, therefore, the benefit of that wisdom for which you are so deservedly praised, that our fears may be allayed and your own best interests promoted. Provide that this risk, which could be costly, be shifted elsewhere so that, if what we fear should happen, you will not be tortured when it is too late by regrets nor we, on the other hand, receive blame which is not deserved.

I hope that your Eminence is well and happy.

11. On the Liberal Arts

To his very dear Aeneas [the bishop of Paris], Lupus extends wishes for everlasting salvation [at some point between 856 and 862].

Our king has a very deep interest in education, just as you have, and I have expressed to him, among other things, my strong desire to reestablish the liberal arts by cultivating the study of them again and by teaching others, if it meets with the favor of God, the author of all good things, and if he himself who is soon to enjoy leisure will kindly allow me to have a share in this rewarding enterprise. This proposal of mine he greeted with apparent delight and an expression of cordiality, and he promised to lend his support that I might be able to carry it out. I thought that you should know about this immediately, so that, when the time comes, you will not be lacking in words to urge him on to the accomplishment of this very important project.

Upon my return to the monastery, I received the sad news that your Hildegarius, my niece's husband, had died. Speaking on behalf of myself and the members of his family on both sides, who claim that I have much influence with you, I address this letter to your Holiness and beg that you will kindly befriend his son, for whom the father himself appealed to you for assistance. I especially urge that you very carefully select a tutor for him, equal to you in moral character and one who will insist on military obedience. If I shall accomplish this, the widow and other relatives of the deceased will eagerly accord you all due respect and veneration, and God, recognizing all your other good deeds as well, will admit you into the company of those to whom he makes this promise: "Blessed are the merciful, for they shall obtain mercy."

I hope that you are well and happy.

12. On The Royal Itinerary

To his dear friend Wulfadus [abbot of Saint-Médard and later the archbishop of Bourges], Lupus extends all good wishes [at some time between 856 and 862].

The report has spread that the king's plan of arrival has been changed. Will you therefore explain to me by a personal letter why he has made this change, when he will finally come, and where he will be staying in the meantime, so that with God's help I can then decide what I must do. I make this request because messages relayed by couriers are not reliable for they are often noticeably marred by falsehoods.

Best wishes.

Questions: How did Lupus go about acquiring books? How insecure did he think the countryside around Ferrières was? What was his attitude towards service to the king?

57. The Wandering Monks of Saint-Philibert (863)
Ermentarius

As Lupus knew, the countryside of northern Europe was dangerous in the second half of the ninth century. Life was even more precarious for monks who happened to live along rivers, since the Northmen targeted rich and vulnerable monasteries. The monks of Saint-Philibert on the island of Noirmoutier on the Loire near Nantes began to suffer repeated raids in the 830s. In 836 they abandoned their monastery and later translated the relics of their saint to a more secure home. They traveled some 300 miles before settling near Tournus. Ermentarius, a monk of Saint-Philibert, wrote the account below in 863, but drew on older reports of the great wandering. His account is not without historical insight, since he and his fellows recognized that the Northmen opportunistically struck a divided and disorganized Francia in the years after the civil war.

Source: trans. D. Herlihy, *The History of Feudalism* (New York: Harper & Row, 1970), pp.8–13; reprinted with permission.

[From the First Book of Miracles]

We wish to describe the miracles which the most mighty and gracious God deigned to display when the body of the most blessed Philibert was taken from the ocean island known as Herius [Noirmoutier] to the place which used to be called Deé [Saint-Philibert de Grandlieu]. We want also to describe those deeds of heaven done in the same place, which we were present to see, or which we know to have been truthfully reported by the faithful. First, with all my strength I pray to the most powerful and gracious Lord, that He who deigned to display so many miracles by the merits of his confessor should grant also to me the eloquence to describe them.

But before I broach these things, I thought it valuable to explain the reason why [the saint] had to be taken from that place which he loved more than anywhere else and which also had seen him deliver his soul to God and his body to the earth. Although this may be well known to almost everyone alive, nevertheless, for the benefit of those to come, I shall state that in this affair the difficulty was the sudden and unforeseen attacks of the Northmen. When these men so often converged on the island's port and, being a fierce people, savagely devastated it, the inhabitants followed the example of their leader and sought help in flight rather than in waiting for their own extermination. The inhabitants moved back and forth in accord with the seasons. For in the summer, when the weather favored navigation, they sought the monastery of Deé, which had been built for this purpose, and only during the winter did they return to the island of Noirmoutier. Even as the monks and their dependents who inhabited the island were struggling in so desperate a situation, dangers began to multiply, and for reason of the frequent raids of the Northmen, the people of the island began not only to be terrorized but to suffer the loss of their possessions and to be afflicted by extreme tribulations. But in truth this is what they feared most: that the faithless men would dig up the grave of the blessed Philibert and scatter whatever they found in it hither and yon, or rather throw it into the sea. This was known to have happened in the region of Brittany to the remains of certain

434

holy men; this we were told by those who had seen it and had fled before the most oppressive rule of these men. Peace, however, will usually follow persecution; for the Lord does not abandon those who place their hopes in Him, as He says to his disciples: "Behold I am with you all days, even to the consummation of the world." Still, we must spend some time in explaining for what purpose and when the island was deprived of so great a patron and abandoned by the entire community of monks. Do not, however, wonder that I should have said that peace follows persecution. For in our mind no little peace was obtained when the most holy body was removed to a place where his servants, secure from barbarian attack, were allowed day and night to worship the Lord.

It was the year of the incarnation of the Lord and Redeemer Jesus Christ, 836, the fourteenth indiction, the twenty-third year in which the glorious emperor Louis [the Pious] was happily reigning under the protection of divine mercy, and his son Lothar ruled in Italy, Pepin in Aquitaine, and Louis [the German] in Norica. The venerable abbot Hilbodus was governing, with the favor of the Lord, the flock of the confessor of Christ, Philibert, according to the rule of Saint Benedict. At his command I, the most miserable of all his monks—not only in deeds, but also in words—assumed the task of telling these things. The frequent and unfortunate attacks of the Northmen, as has been said, were in no wise abating, and Abbot Hilbodus had built a castle _In_ on the island for protection against the faithless people. Together with the _836..._ council of his brothers, he came to King Pepin [I, of Aquitaine] and asked his highness what he intended to do about this problem. Then the glorious king and the great men of the realm—a general assembly of the kingdom was then being held—deliberated concerning the problem with gracious concern and found themselves unable to help through mounting a vigorous assault. Because of the extremely dangerous tides, the island was not always readily accessible to our forces, while all knew that it was quite accessible to the Northmen whenever the sea was peaceful. The king and the great men chose what they believed to be the more advantageous policy. With the agreement of the most serene King Pepin, almost all the bishops of the province of Aquitaine, and the abbots, counts, and other faithful men who were present, and many others besides who had learned about the situation, unanimously _the_ advised that the body of the blessed Philibert ought to be taken from the island and no longer allowed to remain there. This decision was taken in _consensus_ the year of the Incarnation of our Lord Jesus Christ as was written above [836]. But enough! Now we shall turn our pen to describing his miracles...

[From the Second Book of Miracles]

In the preceding book I wrote, although less worthily than I should have, concerning the miracles of blessed Philibert. Insofar as I had the time, I set forth the signs of his powers and described his splendid wonders. I had promised that I would in the following book recount those miracles omitted, or which divine power might further grant. Alas, I am forced to describe not miracles but the distressing troubles of nearly all the kingdom of the west. In order that my tale possess a logical order, I must explain the delays in time. This account was written for Hilduin [the abbot of Saint-Denis], who died some time back [that is, in 842] and, as I had promised, for whoever might be interested in them. During the year of the Incarnation of Christ the Redeemer of all men, 836, a little peace smiled forth under the reign of Louis [the Pious], and amid the boundless joy of the people, as has been described, the body of the confessor was moved with solemn and universal honor, veneration, and glory. Not long thereafter, that is, four years later, the emperor died [that is, in 840]. After a similar extent of time had passed, 67 ships of the Northmen suddenly attacked the valley of the Loire and captured the city of Nantes [in 843]. They put to the sword the bishop and his clergy together with a large multitude of the people; those who escaped death were delivered into slavery. The successor of Emperor Louis was Charles [the Bald], who had been raised in the royal palace. The brothers mentioned above—Lothar and Louis [the German], for Pepin had died before his father—each possessed his own kingdom. But since concise language is to be sought in such matters (for I did not begin this work to record deeds which were better left in silence, or better lamented, but to describe the miracles of the holy confessor), there first arose strife among the brothers, and finally among the chief persons of the realm. The younger brothers, Louis and Charles, rebelled against their older brother, Lothar. Wars, horrible as an intestinal disease, were heaped on wars. A sad and miserable victory fell to the younger brothers.

But their strife gave encouragement to the foreigners. Justice was abandoned, and evil advanced. No guards were mounted on the ocean beaches. Wars against foreign enemies ceased, and internal wars raged on. The number of ships grew larger, and the Northmen were beyond counting. Everywhere there were massacres of Christians, raids, devastations, and burnings. For as long as the world shall last, this will remain evident by the manifest signs. Whatever cities the Northmen attacked, they captured without resistance: Bordeaux, Périgueux, Saintes, Limoges, Angoulême, and Toulouse; then Agners, Tours, and Orléans were destroyed. The remains of numerous saints were carried off. What the Lord warns through the prophet came close to fulfillment: "From the north shall an evil break forth upon all the inhabitants of the land." We also fled to a place which is call Cunauld, in the territory of Anjou, on the banks of the Loire, which the glorious King Charles had given us for the sake of refuge, because of the imminent peril, before Angers was taken. The body of the blessed Philibert still remained in the monastery which is called Deé, although the place had been burned by the Northmen. For it was not permitted that the banks of the Herbauge River should have been deprived of so great a patron, as long as some few of the monks were able to remain there.

Then, a few years later, an almost immeasurable fleet of Norse ships sailed up the Seine River. The evil done in those regions was no less than that perpetrated elsewhere. The Northmen [in 856-857] attacked the city of Rouen and devastated and burned it. They then captured Paris, Beauvais, and Meaux, and they also leveled the castle of Melun. Chartres was also taken. They struck into the cities of Evreux, Bayeux, and other neighboring towns. Almost no place, and no monastery, remained unscathed. Everyone gave himself over to flight; rare was the man who said: "Stay, stay, resist, fight for the fatherland, for children and relatives." Thus, losing heart and feuding among themselves, they purchased by tribute what they should have defended with arms, and the kingdom of the Christians succumbed.

The Northmen attacked Spain; they entered the Rhône River, and they devastated Italy. While everywhere so many domestic and foreign wars were raging, the year of the Incarnation of Christ 857 passed. As long as there had been in us some hope of returning to our own possessions (which, however, proved to be fruitless), the body of the blessed Philibert, as has been said, was left in his own soil. With evils surrounding us, we had not been able to obtain a definite place of security. But since a refuge was nowhere to be found, we did not permit the most holy body to be carried with us hither and yon. Now, it was more truly smuggled away from the grasp of the Northmen than carried with festive praises, and it was taken to the place we have mentioned, which is called Cunauld. This was done in such a way that, when necessity required, it might be moved elsewhere. The year of the Lord's Incarnation was 862 when the body was carried from Cunauld to Messay. It will later be evident how many miracles were shown forth in that place through his glorious merits. But first we shall describe those wonders which we omitted at the end of the preceding book. For just as the persecution of the pagans has not ceased, neither does time know how to stay its course; since the days menace me with their quick passing, already the hour and the circumstances require that I declare the miracles....

Questions: Does it worry Ermentarius that Saint Philibert did not trouble to protect his monastery from the attacks of the Northmen? How much help were the kings that the monks appealed to for protection? Who does Ermentarius blame? How did the monks of Saint-Philibert adapt to life under the threat of seasonal Norse attack?

58. A Judicial Dispute in the Loire Valley

Despite the incursions of the Northmen, the possession of productive property remained all-important in Carolingian society. The case below turned on whether the priest Isaiah had indeed given a piece of property to his nephew Nortbert or had sold it to Agintrude. Though Agintrude at the time of the dispute held the property, she and Nortbert were forced to supply written proofs and witnesses to their claims. The way in which the case unfolded is worth examining.

Source: trans. J.L. Nelson, "Dispute Settlement in Carolingian West Francia," in The Settlement of Disputes in Early Medieval Europe, ed. W. Davies and P. Fouracre (Cambridge: Cambridge University Press, 1986), pp.56-57; reprinted with permission.

This notice has been lawfully validated, telling how and in whose presence in AD 857...while through the whole area of jurisdiction (*dictio*) of the most distinguished abbot Hilduin [of Saint-Martin] and at his order and command his *missi* were striving to do justice, a certain priest of the church of Saint Hispanus in that area of jurisdiction, a man called Nortbert, came into the presence of Saraman, provost of the community of Saint-Martin, and of other noble men of that same lordship (*potestas*) on 10 June and made complaint as follows: a property of the church of Saint Hispanus, which was listed along with other estates in the document of that church, and which had been under his control (*potestas*) since the death of his uncle Isaiah who had bought that property, and which he had for a long time possessed lawfully on behalf of that church on the villa of Malebuxis, had been unjustly taken away from Saint-Hispanus's control through the action of Autbert and his sister Agintrude and her husband Amalgar.

Then Saraman the provost ordered that those persons who were in possession of that property should show their title deeds (*auctoritates*) at the appointed assembly in his presence. These title deeds they then brought before his sight and that of other noble men at Tours. But they could not settle the issue because of the absence of the neighbors to whom the case was known. It was therefore decided there that the case should be settled by judgment of the neighbors and of other *boni homines* at that villa to which the disputed property belonged.

A little while later, on 30 July, Saraman the provost above-named, with other clergy of the flock of Saint-Martin, and other good men, came to the villa of Briusgalus to which the above-mentioned property belonged. There, on the orders of his lord, he was to settle and deal with various cases. And they sat in the forecourt of the church for the convenience of the assembly of important persons. The time came for discussing this dispute. Then it was adjudged there by many noble men and by the *coloni* whose names are put in below, that Nortbert the priest should appoint his advocate, and the above-named persons [in possession of the property] should present their title deeds.

Soon one of them, Autbert, by God's inspiration it seemed, openly confessed that their title deeds were false. And to avoid having to go to hell because of this, he refused to persist in his obstinacy, and he threw the title deeds down on the altar of Saint-Hispanus. Then the above-mentioned Amalgar, acting on behalf of his wife Agintrude, accused Autbert of unjustly disputing [the validity of] his wife's title deeds.

All those who were there sitting, or standing by, were amazed at this. They discussed the matter for a long time. [They decided that] Autbert should show his documents publicly. This he did. But he was the first to testify that [both of them], that is, the one which he presented as being in the name of Isaiah, and the one which had been drawn up deceitfully at Tours, were found publicly, when read out, to be false. The reason was that those whose names were attached [to the first document], that is Notfred and Geroin, gave witness on oath that they had in no way confirmed it any time, nor had it ever been corroborated. Moreover, the scribe of that document was also present, and he there admitted openly that he had written that document but had not corroborated it. So too nearly all the *coloni* gave witness that they had not seen it being corroborated, nor were the names written down there those of *coloni* of that villa of which the disputed property formed part, but they were from another villa which was not that of the *coloni* whose names were recorded.

Thereupon, by the judgment of all present, Amalgar held the charters in his hand and was asked formally by those there sitting whether he could produce witnesses from that lordship, who would declare on oath that those documents were true. He straightway admitted openly that he could not.

Then the woman Agintrude protested: [she said] that it was through fear of the priest [Nortbert] that they were unable to find witnesses for this matter, and she named certain *coloni* who, she said, were knowledgeable about this case.

Then the provost ordered relics to be brought forward, and he named the following *coloni* [nine names follow] and he caused many others to swear, by God and by their Christianity and their good faith and the relics of the saints there present, [to say] whether that document, namely the title of sale in favor of Agintrude's side, had been lawfully and rightly corroborated; whether she had lawful tenure; and whether that property ought to belong by right to the priest Nortbert, representing Saint-Hispanus, rather than to Agintrude. To these questions, each and every one called to witness straightway testified on oath in the same way: that that title of sale had not been corroborated rightly, but fraudulently, and so could not confer rightful tenure; likewise that that document which they had obtained under false pretences at Tours was useless and of no effect; and that that property rightfully belonged to Saint-Hispanus's side rather than to Agintrude's side.

Then Amalgar admitted openly that he had been unable to supply witnesses there [at Tours] or thereafter, and that therefore those documents which he held were of no effect.

Then, by judgment of all there present, the provost Saraman asked Otbert, the advocate of Nortbert the priest, if he could prove false the documents which Amalgar still held in his hand. He replied immediately that he could prove them utterly false. Then, by the right above established and with the witnesses above noted, he made [the documents] utterly false by piercing them there in Amalgar's hands and thus tearing them through, as it had been adjudged and decided in his favor by all.

That property is at the villa called Malebuxis. The late Isaiah the priest bought it from Amalbert after paying his price, and it is described with its boundaries in the title of sale.

Thus, now that that property had rightly been returned to Saint-Hispanus's side by the judgment of all there sitting or standing by, and vindicated by their counsel, Nortbert the priest thought that he should receive this *notitia* of the outcome, so that ... it should be clear in future how rightly and reasonably the case had been tried and settled by many noble men, some of whom are noted here.

I Saraman the provost have subscribed. I Autbert the priest have subscribed. I Azaneus the deacon have subscribed. I Gislemar the acolyte have subscribed. I Gislar the subdeacon have subscribed. Sign (+) of Nautfred the judge. Sign (+) of Gervin. S. + [three names]. S. + Restodonus. S. [two names].

Questions: Was Agintrude's claim to the land false or did she simply lack the legal documents to prove her claim? If property disputes turned on the legality and quality of documents, who was advantaged and who disadvantaged? What was the nature of this legal process, who participated, how long did a case take before a decision was reached, and who made that reckoning?

59. A Charter of Immunity from Charles the Bald

David Herlihy once said that the church held more property by the end of the ninth century than it would ever again hold in the Middle Ages. If this was true, it was in part because churchmen had made themselves so central to Carolingian society and so necessary to government and the royal family.

Source: trans. D. Herlihy, The History of Feudalism (New York: Harper & Row, 1970), pp.126-128; reprinted with permission.

[11 September 859]

In the name of the holy and undivided Trinity, Charles by the grace of God king. When in the love of divine worship we favor the just and reasonable petitions of the servants of God, we do not doubt that we become strengthened by heavenly grace. Therefore, be it known to all the faithful, present and to come, of the holy church of God, that Hugo, our very dear abbot of the monastery of Saint-Germain of Auxerre, and our kinsman brought to our attention an authoritative charter of immunity of our lord father Louis, the most serene augustus, in which is related how in the tradition of his ancestors he received the said monastery, for the love of almighty God and the peace of the brothers residing there, under the fullest protection and defense of immunity. The said Abbot Hugo and the monks of the same monastery have requested the favor of a confirmation, asking that we, in the tradition of our father, receive the same monastery with the congregation there serving God, and with all possessions justly appertaining to the said monastery, under our defense and the protection of immunity. Their request, for divine love and the peace of the said monks, we have willingly accepted and we hold under the fullest defense that congregation with all possessions justly and reasonably belonging to the same monastery, so that under our protection they may quietly live, as is contained in the command of our lord father. No bishop of this diocese or any other episcopal minister may presume to exercise there any lordship [*dominium*] nor remove anything from the possessions of the same monastery or turn it to his use or diminish it or take it away. And no public judge or any official with judicial authority or any of our faithful should dare enter in our days or in days to come upon the possessions now subject to or later to be subject to the same monastery in order to hear cases or to collect fodder or tribute, or the house tax or hospitality payments, or to take guarantors or constrain the men of the same monastery, whether free or unfree, living upon the land of the said monastery. But it should be allowed to the said abbot and his successors to possess the property of the said monastery in peaceful order under the defense of immunity. Whatever the royal treasury may demand from the lands we give wholly to the same monastery, so that it may be of profit and assistance for all time to the monks serving God there in performing their office. Similarly also, they showed to our serenity the authoritative charter of our lord father, in which was related how the same most pious augustus conceded to the same monastery the entire toll from the merchants of the monks or from their men who served the same house of God, or from that which men bear on their backs, whether they come on their estates or upon their lands within or without and transact business. The entire toll through the same authoritative charter he conceded to the same monastery. We have willingly acceded to their request, and through this charter we order and command that the same monks or their merchants or their men who are known to serve the said house of God, as the command of our lord father states, should not be forced to pay any toll in the towns or in the markets or in the villages or estates or ports or gates or within the monastery or in the estates or territories or other places subject to them. And in order that this charter of our authority and immunity may be the firmer and be the better preserved in times to come, we have ordered it to be sealed below with the impression of our ring.

Done on the third of the Ides of September, the seventh indiction, the twentieth year of Charles, most glorious king. Done at Mardun in the monastery. In the name of God, happily. Amen.

Questions: How much protection and security (and against what) would this charter of immunity have given to Saint-Germain of Auxerre? Why was it given?

60. Saint Remi's Protection of People and Property

Saints such as Remi, who is sometimes called Remigius after his Latin name, were not thought to cure diseases only, but also to defend people and property against violent men. Hincmar of Rheims finished writing his lengthy account of Remi's life and miracles in 878, but he had spent most of his archiepiscopate enshrining the cult of Remi at Rheims and in Francia. He conceived of the saint as an active punisher of all those who would tamper with the property of his church, for in the ninth century most church property was thought to have been the gift of, or a gift to, the saints. Thus the real owners of the property were long-dead saints, who were quick to anger when thieves and noble bullies infringed upon their lands.

Source: trans. D. Herlihy, The History of Feudalism (New York: Harper & Row, 1970), pp.122-124; reprinted with permission.

In our age a peasant of the village of the episcopate of Rheims which is called Plumbea-fontana lived next to the royal estate which is named Rozoy-[sur-Serre], but he was not able to use his land peacefully either for harvest or for grazing because of the harassment of the residents on the royal estates. He frequently sought justice from the royal officials, but he was not able to obtain it. Then he took for himself some beneficial counsel. He cooked loaves and meat and he placed beer into jars, as much as he was able. All these things he placed into a container which is called in the vernacular a *benna*, and he placed it upon a cart. Hitching up his oxen, he hurried with a candle in his hand to the basilica of Saint Remi. When he arrived, he pleasantly surprised the poor with the bread, meat, and beer; he placed a candle at the sepulcher of the saint and beseeched him for help against the men of the royal estate who were harassing him. He also gathered the dust from the floor of the church, as much as he was able, tied it in a cloth, and placed it in the same container. He placed a shroud above it, as is usually put upon the corpse of a dead person. With his cart he returned home. Persons he met on the way inquired what he was bringing in the cart, and he responded that he was bringing Saint Remi. They all wondered at his words and deed, and thought that he had lost his mind. However, arriving with the cart in his field, he found there herdsmen from the estate of Rozoy feeding animals of different kinds. He called on Saint Remi to help him against his oppressors. The bulls and cows began with the loudest bellows to attack one another with their horns, and the he-goats to attack the she-goats with their horns, the pigs to fight with the pigs, the rams with the ewes, and the herdsmen dealt each other blows with sticks and arms. As the riot grew greater, both the screaming herdsmen and the animals according to their type began to flee toward Rozoy with the loudest noise and racket, as if a huge multitude of pursuers were beating them with sticks. The men of the royal estate, when they saw and heard these things, were struck with a great terror and believed that they had no more than an hour to live. Thus reprehended for their arrogance, they abandoned the harassment of this poor man of Saint-Remi, and thereafter the poor man held his belongings in peace and without disturbance. And since he lived near the Serre River in a muddy place, he put up with a great bother in his dwelling from snakes. Taking the dust, which he had brought with him from the floor of the church of Saint Remi, he sprinkled it throughout his house, and thereafter a snake did not appear in those places, where the dust had been scattered. By the evidence of the miracles, we can accept as certainly proved that if, firm in the faith, we ask from the heart for the help of Saint Remi, we shall be freed from the attacks of the angels of Satan, who as a serpent deceived the mother of the human race in addressing her; and by the merit and intercession of Saint Remi we shall be freed from the wicked deeds of bad men.

Truly [Saint Remi], this holy follower of the Lord, did not punish all things, so that his patience might be revealed, nor did he forgive all things, so that his providence might be shown. Although he does not in our times take vengeance so frequently against wicked men, nevertheless he has not desisted completely from the punishment of the presumptuous. Recently, a certain man named Blitgarius purchased from Bernardus, the custodian [of the church], a certain farm from the endowment of the church in the village of Thenailles. From it he drove out with blows the servants of Saint Remi, and they called upon Saint Remi to help them. This same Blitgarius answered them in derision, "Now let us see how Saint Remi shall help you. You see how he comes to your assistance." And in the midst of these words he groaned with the loudest groan and swelled up to unbelievable proportions. Thus, all of a sudden, he gasped and was dead.

Having heard these things, with the fear of divine retribution in us, we should carefully avoid blasphemy against God and his saints, taking care, lest we treat cruelly the servant of the church.... Although in our times miracles worked through His servant may not be so many or so venerable, still we may be certain that the continuing help of his intercessions will not be withdrawn from his city or from us his citizens, as we read of Jeremiah, "This is a lover of his brethren and of the people of Israel: this is he that prayeth much for the people and for all the holy city of Jerusalem."

Questions: Why were saints concerned with property issues? How did they deal with those who tampered with property? Why would Hincmar have emphasized this side of Remi's power and who was supposed to take note of it?

61. The Coronation of Charles the Bald as King of Lotharingia

Lothar II died on 8 August 869 in Italy where he had gone once again to see if he could arrange his divorce from Theutberga and the legitimization of his marriage to Waldrada. Within a month, Charles the Bald was in Lotharingia at Metz and on 9 September he was crowned the king of his nephew's kingdom. The bishops led by Hincmar of Rheims enacted the symbolically rich and ceremonious liturgical 'ordo' found below.

Source: trans. D. Herlihy, The History of Feudalism (New York: Harper & Row, 1970), pp.128-131; reprinted with permission.

[Blessings said over king Charles before Mass
at the altar of Saint-Stephen in Metz]

Adventius bishop of Metz: "O God, you who care for your people with indulgence and rule them with love, give to this your servant the spirit of wisdom, to whom you have given the exercise of discipline, so that devoted to you with all his heart he may remain always suitable for the government of the kingdom and, preserving in good works, he may with your guidance attain the eternal kingdom. Through the Lord, etc."

Hatto of Verdun: "Give, we beseech you, O Lord, to this your servant the gift of your grace, so that with your help, following your commandments, he may receive the consolation of present and future life. Through the Lord, etc."

Arnuld of Toul: "Have favor, we beseech you, O Lord, upon our days under the governance of this your servant, so that with your help both our own security and Christian devotion may be well administered. Through the Lord, etc."

Franco of Tongern: "Grant, we beseech you, Lord, to this your servant health of mind and body, so that adhering to good works he may always be worthy to be defended by your power. Through the Lord, etc."

Hincmar of Laon: "May this your servant, O Lord, receive your blessing, so that safe in body and mind he may always show to you a fitting submission and may always find the favors of your mercy. Through the Lord, etc."

Odo of Beauvais: "Preserve, we beseech you, O Lord, this your servant, and purify him mercifully with the abundance of your blessing, so that he may always abound with your knowledge and gifts."

The blessing of Archbishop Hincmar: "May the almighty Lord stretch forth the right hand of his blessing, and may He pour over you the gift of his mercy; may He surround you by a happy wall in the custody of his perfection, through the interceding merits of holy Mary and all the saints. Amen.

May He forgive you all the evil which you have committed, and grant to you grace and mercy which you humbly ask from Him; may He free you from all adversities and from all the snares of visible and invisible enemies. Amen.

May He place his good angels, always and everywhere, to go before you, to accompany you, and to follow you, for your protection; may He by his power free you from sin or the sword or the risk of all perils. Amen.

May He turn your enemies toward the kindness of peace and love, and make you gracious and lovable to those who hate you.

May He visit with saving confusion those persistent in persecuting you. May an eternal sanctification flower above you. Amen."

[At the following words, "May the Lord crown you," Hincmar the archbishop anointed him with chrism on his right ear and on his forehead, as far as the left ear, and on his head.]

"May the Lord crown you with the crown of glory in his mercy and compassion, and may He anoint you in the rule of the kingdom by the oil of the grace of his Holy Spirit, with which He anointed priests, kings, prophets, and martyrs, who through faith conquered kingdoms and worked justice and attained his promises. May you too by the grace of God be rendered worthy of those same promises, until you may enjoy their companionship in the heavenly kingdom. Amen.

May He always make you victorious and triumphant over visible and invisible enemies. May He pour continuously into your heart the fear and equally the love of his holy name. And, granting you peace in your days, may He lead you with the palm of victory to the eternal kingdom. Amen.

May He, who wished to set you as king over his people, grant that you be happy in this present world and the partaker of eternal happiness. Amen.

May He allow you happily to govern by his dispensation and your administration for a long time the clergy and people, whom with his aid He wished to be subject to your authority. May they, therefore, be obedient to the divine commands, avoid all opposition, rejoice in all good things, and be subject to your office in faithful love. May they enjoy in this present world the tranquility of peace, and merit to possess with you the inheritance of the eternal citizens. Amen. May He deign to grant this."

[At the words, "May the Lord crown you," the bishops set the crown on his head.]

"May the Lord crown you with the crown of glory and justice, so that with right faith and the abundant fruit of good words you may attain the crown of the eternal kingdom, through his generosity, to whom belongs the kingdom and the power for ever and ever."

[At the words, "May the Lord give you the will," they give him the palm and scepter.]

May the Lord give you the will and the power to do as He commands, so that going forward in the rule of the kingdom according to his will together with the palm of continuing victory you may attain the palm of eternal glory, by the grace of our Lord Jesus Christ, who lives..."

[Prayers at Mass:] "Grant, almighty God, that the venerable celebration of the feast of your blessed martyr Gorgonius may increase in us devotion and salvation. Through the Lord...

We beseech, almighty God, that your servant, who in your mercy has received the reins of the kingdom, may receive from You also increase of virtue, by which suitably adorned, he may graciously avoid monstrous vices and reach You, who are the way, the truth, and the life, who lives and reigns with God."

[At the offertory:] "Behold, O Lord, the gifts of your people offered at the feast of your saints, so that the profession of your truth may profit us for salvation. Through the Lord...

Make holy, we beseech You, O Lord, these gifts we have offered, so that they may become for us the body and blood of your only begotten Son, and may benefit our King Charles in obtaining salvation of soul and body through your generosity. Through the same..."

[After communion:] "May the communion received of your mysteries, O Lord, save us and confirm us in the light of your truth. Through the Lord...

May this saving communion, O Lord, protect your servant from all adversities, so that he may obtain the tranquility of ecclesiastical peace and after the course of these days he may attain the everlasting inheritance. Through the Lord...."

Questions: Did the bishops think they were making a king? What gave them the right, and why would Charles the Bald have accepted this form of coronation? What symbols were employed in the ceremony and what order did the ceremony follow?

62. Eriugena's *Periphyseon*: the Beginning and End

Eriugena, who is often called John Scottus Eriugena, was an Irishman like Sedulius Scottus. He seems to have come to the continent in the 840s. By 850 he was teaching at the palace school of Charles the Bald. It was there that Hincmar of Rheims and Pardulus of Laon commissioned him to respond to Gottschalk's doctrine of double predestination. But by about 862, Eriugena had begun to translate from Greek into Latin the Neoplatonic theological works of the Pseudo-Dionysius, Gregory of Nyssa, and Maximus the Confessor. With the stimulus of these difficult authors, Eriugena conceived of his sweeping philosophy of all-embracing Nature. His masterpiece, the 'Periphyseon' (About Nature), was to be the boldest synthesis of Christian thought since Augustine's 'City of God'. It takes the form of a dialogue between a Master or Nutritor and his Disciple or Alumnus.

Source: trans. I.P. Sheldon-Williams, revised by J.J. O'Meara, in Eriugena, Periphyseon (The Division of Nature), (Montreal: Bellarmin, 1987), pp.25-30, 710-715; reprinted with permission.

[The Start of Book 1]

Nutritor: As I frequently ponder and, so far as my talents allow, ever more carefully investigate the fact that the first and fundamental division of all things which either can be grasped by the mind or lie beyond its grasp is into those that are and those that are not, there comes to mind as a general term for them all what in Greek is called Φύσις and in Latin Natura. Or do you think otherwise?

Alumnus: No, I agree. For I too, when I enter upon the path of reasoning, find that this is so.

N: Nature, then, is the general name, as we said, for all things, for those that are and those that are not.

A: It is. For nothing at all can come into our thought that would not fall under this term.

N: Then since we agree to use this term for the genus, I should like you to suggest a method for its division by differentiations into species; or, if you wish, I shall first attempt a division, and your part will be to offer sound criticism.

A: Pray begin. For I am impatient to hear from you a true account of this matter.

N: It is my opinion that the division of Nature by means of four differences results in four species, [being divided] first into that which creates and is not created, secondly into that which is created and also creates, thirdly into that which is created and does not create, while the fourth neither creates nor is created. But within these four there are two pairs of opposites. For the third is the opposite of the first, the fourth of the second; but the fourth is classed among the impossibles, for it is of its essence that it cannot be. Does such a division seem right to you or not?

A: Right, certainly. But please go over it again so as to elucidate more fully the opposition[s] within these four forms.

N: I am sure you see the opposition of the third species to the first—for the first creates and is not created; it therefore has as its contrary that which is created and does not create—and of the second to the fourth, for the second both is created and creates; it therefore has as its contrary in all respects the fourth, which neither creates nor is created.

A: I see [that] clearly. But I am much perplexed by the fourth species which you have introduced. For about the other three I should not presume to raise any question at all, because, as I think, the first is understood to be the Cause of all things that are and that are not, who is God; the second to be the primordial cause; and the third those things that become manifest through coming into being in times and places. For this reason a more detailed discussion which shall take each species individually is required, as I think.

N: You are right to think so. But in what order we should pursue our path of reasoning, that is to say, which of the species of Nature we should take first, I leave it to you to decide.

A: It seems to me beyond question that before the others we should say of the first species whatever the light of minds has granted us to utter.

N: Let it be so. But first I think a few words should be said about the first and fundamental division—as we called it—of all things into the things that are and the things that are not.

A: It would be correct and wise to do so. For I see no other beginning from which reasoning ought to start, and this not only because this difference is the first of all, but because both in appearance and in fact it is more obscure than the others.

N: This basic difference, then, which separates all things requires for itself five modes of interpretation:

1. Of these modes the first seems to be that by means of which reason convinces us that all things which fall within the perception of bodily sense or [within the grasp of] intelligence are truly and reasonably said to be, but that those which because of the excellence of their nature elude not only all sense but also all intellect and reason rightly seem not to be—which are correctly understood only of God and matter and of the reasons and essences of all the things that are created by Him. And rightly so: for as Dionysius the Areopagite says, He is the Essence of all things who alone truly is. "For", says he, "the being of all things is the Divinity who is above being." Gregory the Theologian too proves by many arguments that no substance or essence of any creature, whether visible or invisible, can be comprehended by the intellect or by reason as to what it is. For just as God as He is in himself beyond every creature when considered in the innermost depths of the creature which was made by him and which exists in him; while whatsoever in every creature is either perceived by the bodily sense or contemplated by the intellect is merely some accident to each creature's essence which, as has been said, by itself is incomprehensible, but which, either by quality or by quantity or by form or by matter or by some difference or by place or by time, is known not as to what it is but as to that it is.

That, then, is the first and fundamental mode of division of those things of which it is said that they are and those [of which it is said] that they are not. For what somehow appears to be [a mode of division] based upon privations of substances and accidents should certainly not be admitted, in my opinion. For how can that which absolutely is not, and cannot be, and which does not surpass the intellect because of the preeminence of its existence, be included in the division of things, unless perhaps someone should say that the absences and privations of things that exist are themselves not altogether nothing, but are implied by some strange natural virtue of those things of which they are the privations and absences and opposition, so as to have some kind of existence?

2. Let then the second mode of being and not being be that which is seen in the order and differences of created natures, which, beginning from the intellectual power, which is the highest and is constituted nearest to God, descends to the furthermost [degree] of the rational and irrational creature, or, to speak more plainly, from the most exalted angel to the furthermost element of the rational and irrational soul, I mean the nutritive and growth

giving life-principle, which is the least part of the soul in the general acceptance of the term because it nourishes the body and makes it grow. Here, by a wonderful mode of understanding, each order, including the last at the lower end which is that of bodies and in which the whole division comes to an end, can be said to be and not to be. For an affirmation concerning the lower [order] is a negation concerning the higher, and so too a negation concerning the lower [order] is an affirmation concerning the higher and similarly an affirmation concerning the higher [order] is a negation concerning the lower, while a negation concerning the higher [order] will be an affirmation concerning the lower. Thus, the affirmation of "man" (I mean, man while still in his mortal state) is the negation of "angel," while the negation of "man" is the affirmation of "angel" and vice versa. For if man is a rational, mortal, risible animal, then an angel is certainly neither a rational animal nor mortal nor risible: likewise, if an angel is an essential intellectual motion about God and the causes of things, then man is certainly not an essential intellectual motion about God and the causes of things. And the same rule is found to apply in all the celestial essences until one reaches the highest order of all. This, however, terminates in the highest negation upward; for its negation confirms the existence of no higher creature. Now, there are three orders which they call "of equal rank": the first of these are the Cherubim, Seraphim, and Thrones; the second, the Virtues, Powers, and Dominations; the third, the Principalities, Archangels, and Angels. Downwards, on the other hand, the last [order] merely denies or confirms the one above it, because it has nothing below it which it might either take away or establish since it is preceded by all the orders higher than itself but precedes none that is lower than itself.

It is also on these grounds that every order of rational or intellectual creatures is said to be and not to be: it is in so far as it is known by the orders above it and by itself; but it is not in so far as it does not permit itself to be comprehended by the orders that are below it.

3. The third mode can suitably be seen in those things of which the visible plenitude of this world is made up, and in their causes in the most secret folds of nature, which precede them. For whatsoever of these causes through generation is known as to matter and form, as to times and places, is by a certain human convention said to be, while whatsoever is still held in those folds of nature and is not manifest as to form or matter, place or time, and the other accidents, by the same convention referred to is said not to be. Clear examples of this mode are provided over a wide range [of experience], and especially in human nature. Thus, since God in that first and one man whom He made in his image established all men at the same time, yet did not bring them all at the same time into this visible world, but brings the nature which He considers all at one time into visible essence at certain times and places according to a certain sequence which He himself knows: those who already are becoming, or have become visibly manifest in the world are said to be, while those who are as yet hidden, though destined to be, are said not to be. Between the first and third [mode] there is this difference: the first [is found] generically in all things which at the same time and once for all have been made in [their] effects, of which in particular the fabric of

this world is woven. To this mode belongs the reasoning which considers the potentiality of seeds, whether in animals or in trees or in plants. For during the time when the potentiality of the seeds is latent in the recesses of nature, because it is not yet manifest it is said not to be; but when it has become manifest in the birth and growth of animals or of flowers or of the fruits of trees and plants it is said to be.

4. The fourth mode is that which, not improbably according to the philosophers, declares that only those things which are contemplated by the intellect alone truly are, while those things which in generation, through the expansions or contractions of matter, and the intervals of places and motions times are changed, brought together, or dissolved, are said not to be truly, as is the case with all bodies which can come into being and pass away.

5. The fifth mode is that which reason observes only in human nature, which, when through sin it renounced the honor of the divine image in which it was properly substantiated, deservedly lost its being and therefore is said not to be; but when, restored by the grace of the only begotten Son of God, it is brought back to the former condition of its substance in which it was made after the image of God, it begins to be, and in him who has been made in the image of God begins to live. It is to this mode, it seems, that the Apostle's saying refers: "and He calls the things that are not as the things that are"; that is to say, those who in the first man were lost and had fallen into a kind of non-subsistence God the Father calls through faith in His Son to be as those who are already reborn in Christ. But this too may also be understood of those whom God daily calls forth from the secret folds of nature, in which they are considered not to be, to become visibly manifest in form and matter and in the other [conditions] in which hidden things are able to become manifest.

[The End of Book 5]

N: We have divided Nature, which comprises God and his creatures, into four parts. The first species consists of and may be defined as the nature which creates and is not created, the second as the nature which is created and creates, the third as that which is created but does not itself create, the fourth as that which neither is created nor creates.

The first and fourth natures can be predicated of God alone: not that his nature can be divided, for it is simple and more-than-simple, but it can be approached by two modes of contemplation: when I consider him as the Principle and Cause of all things, reason convinces me that the Divine Essence, or Substance, or Goodness, or Virtue, or Wisdom, or whatever else may be predicated of God, was created by none, for nothing greater is prior to the Divine Nature, but all things, both the things that are and the things that are not, are created by It and through It and in It and for It. On the other hand when I consider that same Nature as the End of all things and the ultimate Consummation to which all things tend and in which the limit of their natural motion is set, I find that It is neither created nor creating. For just as the Nature which is from Itself can be created of none, so neither does It create anything. When all things which have proceeded from It either through intelligible or sensible generation shall by a miraculous and ineffable rebirth return to It again, when all things have found their rest in It, when nothing more shall flow forth from It into generation, it can no longer be said of It that It creates anything. For what should it be creating when It itself shall be all in all, and shall manifest Itself in nothing save Itself?

Concerning the two intermediate species enough has been said in the preceding books, and by any who study them carefully they can be clearly understood. The one is recognized in the Primordial Causes, the other in their effects. That which consists in the Causes is, on the one hand, created in the Only begotten Son of God, in whom and through whom all things are made; and, on the other hand, creates all things which emanate from it, that is to say, all its effects, whether intelligible or sensible.

But that nature which is constituted in the effect of the causes is only created by its own causes, but does not itself create, for there is nothing in nature which comes after it. And therefore it is for the most part to be found among the sensibles. It is no objection to this that angels and men, whether good or evil, are sometimes thought to create some new thing in this world previously unknown to human experience, for in fact they create nothing, but produce something out of the material creature which has already been created by God in its effects through its Causes; if good, they do this in accordance with the laws and precepts of God, if evil, under the deceitful inducement and the crafty plotting of the subtlety of the Devil. But all things are so ordered by the Divine Providence that no evil exists substantially in nature, nor anything which could disturb the city of God and its polity.

And after we had undertaken this fourfold contemplation of Nature under these four species, of which two belong to the Divine Nature as Beginning and End, and two to the created nature as Cause and Effect, we thought good to adjoin some theories concerning the Return of the effects into their Causes, that is, into the "reasons" in which they subsist. And we found that the nature of this Return was threefold. First, we considered the general Return which consists in the transformation of the whole sensible creature contained within the confines of this world, of all the bodies, that is to say, whether perceptible to the senses or too subtle to be perceived, so that there is no body contained in corporeal nature, whether latently or patently endowed with vital motion only, or enriched in addition with corporeal sense of the non-rational soul, which shall not return through the mediation of its life process into its hidden causes: for among the things which derive their substances from the cause of all things there is nothing which shall be reduced to nothing.

The second aspect of the Return concerns the general Return of the whole of human nature when it has been saved by Christ into the original condition in which it was created, and into the dignity of the Divine Image which is as it were a kind of Paradise which was obtained for it by the merits of One, whose Blood was poured for all mankind in common, so that no man might be deprived of the natural goods in which he was created, whether he has passed this life well or ill. And the goodness and magnanimity of God, which surpasses all speech and understanding shall so pervade the whole of human nature that it shall be punished in nothing which emanates from the Supreme Good.

The third aspect of the Return is concern with those who, besides ascending to the highest point of the nature which is created in them, shall, through the abundance of the Grace of God, which is supplied through Christ and in Christ to his elect, pass beyond all the laws and limitations of nature and on that superessential plane be transformed into God Himself, and shall be in Him and with him One. The path they traverse can, as it were, be divided into seven stages: the first will be the transformation of the earthly body into vital motion; the second of vital motion into sensation; the third of sensation into reason; then of reason into mind, wherein lies the end of every rational creature; then this fivefold unification of the parts of our nature, in which body, vital motion, sensation, reason and mind are no longer five but one, in each case the lower nature becoming absorbed in the higher not so as to lose its existence but to become with that higher nature one, shall be followed by three more stages of the ascent: first the transformation of mind into the knowledge of all things which come after God; secondly, of that knowledge into wisdom, that is into the innermost contemplation of the Truth, in so far as that is possible to a creature; thirdly, and lastly, the supernatural merging of the perfectly purified souls into God himself, and their entry into the darkness of the incomprehensible and inaccessible Light which conceals the Causes of all things. Then shall the night shine as the day, that is to say, the most secret mysteries of God shall in a manner which we cannot describe be revealed to the blessed and enlightened intelligences: then shall the perfect solidity of the supernatural cube, which consists of the number eight be achieved, to which reference is made in the title of the Sixth Psalm: "The Psalm of David for the Octave." And it was for this reason that the resurrection of the Lord occurred on the eighth day, that that blessed life which shall begin with the end of the world when this life shall have run its sevenfold course through its seven ages should be mystically signified, when human nature, as we have said, shall through the eight stages of its ascent return into its Principle. Five of those stages lie within the limits of nature, while three lie beyond nature and beyond being in God himself. Then the fivefold number of the creature shall be united with the threefold number of the Creator, so that in nothing shall it be manifested save as God alone, in the same way as in the most purified air nothing is manifested save the light alone.

Here, then, we complete the matter of this work, which is divided into five books. And if any shall find that I have written in it anything unacceptable or superfluous, let him blame my rashness and carelessness, but in humble contemplation let him pardon with a generous heart a human intelligence which is still burdened with the bonds of the flesh it still occupies. For while we are still in this murky life no part of our studies can be perfect, I think, or entirely free from error: not even the righteous, so long as they are alive are called righteous because they are so but because they desire to be so, and long for the perfect righteousness that is to be: they take their name from their inclinations. For I would not believe that any man so long as he is burdened with his mortal limbs and fleshly senses, save only Christ, could attain to the perfect condition of virtue or the height of contemplation of the Truth, and in this I have the support of John the Evangelist. "If we say that we have no sin we deceive ourselves and the truth is not in us." And the Apostle says: "Now we see in a glass darkly," and in another place: "We know in part and we prophesy in part."

But if there is in this work anything of value and contributive to the building of the Catholic faith, let it be attributed to God alone, who alone unlocks the things that are hidden in darkness and brings to himself those that seek him and are not deceived by any error, but are cured from all error; and to the Universal Cause of all good things, without which we can do nothing, let all, with one mind in the charity of the spirit, give thanks with us, not tempted by the allure of hostile criticism or consumed with the fire of envy, the one vice above all others which strives to loosen the bond of love and friendship. In peace, however, with all those who receive what we have written kindly and have the keenness of intellect to grasp it, or spitefully reject it and condemn it without first finding out what it is they condemn, I dedicate this book in the first place to God, who has said: "Ask and it shall be given unto you, seek and ye shall find, knock and it shall be opened unto you," and in the second place to you, Wulfadus [the abbot of Saint-Médard and later archbishop of Bourges], most beloved brother in Christ, and collaborator in my studies, entrusting to you the examination and correction of it. For it was begun under your encouragement, and was brought to its close, such as it is, with the help of your knowledge. But if, taking note of those matters which I was compelled to omit from the text of this work because of the weight of the material I had to deal with and the number of doctrines I had to expound; and of those matters too of which at some time or another I promised to expound, never mind how briefly, you shall prove to be a stern collector of your dues, when the work has been read and the promises discovered, I shall deal with them together rapidly, point by point as far as I can. But in the meantime I beseech my readers to be content with what they have already, considering that the powers of my poor intellect are weak, if they can be said to exist at all, and my capacity for enquiring into the things of God is negligible, howbeit devout. Support me not less by the strength of your own most subtle mind than the labors of my imperfect contemplation, and if not in the company of my rivals at least in that of my friends and the searchers after truth. This, I think, will not be a great labor for you: for when such things fall into the hands of true philosophers, provided that the subjects they treat are of interest to them, they not only attend to them gladly but embrace them as their own. If, however, they fall into the hands of those who take more delight in attacking than in understanding, no great effort should be made to refute them. Let every man hold what opinion he will until that Light shall come which makes of the light of the false philosophers a darkness and converts the darkness of those who truly know into light.

Questions: What emphasis does Eriugena lay upon reason and rationality in human nature? Is he a theologian or a philosopher? What does he mean by 'Nature'? What are the stages of creation and where do humans figure in them? Does evil exist according to Eriugena? What is the Return?

63. Eriugena's Homily

Although for centuries attributed to Origen, we now know that this complex and philosophical sermon was written by Eriugena towards the end of his career and perhaps delivered to King Charles the Bald in some monastery such as Saint-Germain of Auxerre. It reflects in compressed and almost mystical form the thoughts that Eriugena had laid out with prolixity and refined argument in the 'Periphyseon'. The work is a deep exegesis of the first half chapter of the Gospel of John. Some of the imagery derives from the fact that the symbol of the evangelist John was an eagle, but the persistent intellectual, Neoplatonic, and sophisticated tone is Eriugena's. One has to wonder how much of this homily the king or monks, men like Wulfadus, would have understood. Still Eriugena represents in many ways the culmination and finest expression of the revival of letters that had begun a century earlier under Charlemagne.

Source: trans. J.J. O'Meara, in O'Meara, Eriugena (Oxford: Clarendon Press, 1988), pp.158-176.

1. The voice of the mystical eagle [the evangelist John] sounds in the ears of the church. Let our exterior sense catch the sound that passes; let our mind within penetrate the meaning that abides. This voice is the voice of the high-flying bird, not he that flies above the material air and aether and the limits of the whole sensible world, but he that transcends all contemplation, beyond all the things that are and all the things that are not. He does this with the swift-flying wings of profound theology, the glances of clear and lofty contemplation. By the things that are, I mean the things that do not altogether escape the perception of either man or angel although they are inferior to God and do not exceed the number of the things that were created by the one cause of all; by the things that are not, I mean those that are altogether beyond the range of all intelligence. The holy theologian John, then flies above not only the things that can be understood and spoken, but is borne aloft even to those things that surpass all intelligence and meaning and is raised aloft beyond all things, by an ineffable flight of the mind, to the secrets of the one Principle of all. He clearly perceives the incomprehensible unified superessentiality and distinct supersubstantiality of that Principle and Word, that is, of the Father and the Son, and begins his Gospel, saying "in the Principle was the Word."

2. O holy John, it is not without reason that you are called John. John is a Hebrew name. Its meaning in Greek is ᾧ ἐχαρίσατο, but in Latin, 'to whom a grace has been given'. To which of those skilled in the knowledge of God has the grace been given that has been given to you, namely to penetrate the hidden mysteries of the highest good and to make known to human minds and senses what has been revealed and made clear to you? Tell me, to whom was such and so great a gift given? Perhaps someone will say: "to the great head of the Apostles, Peter, I mean, who, when the Lord asked him whom he thought he was, replied, 'You are the Christ, the Son of the living God'." But one could say, I think, without rashness that in saying this Peter typified faith and action rather than knowledge and contemplation. Why? For the reason that Peter is proposed as the model of action and

faith, whereas John follows the model of contemplation and knowledge. The latter reposed on the breast of the Lord, which signifies contemplation. The former often floundered, the symbol as it were of fear and action. For action on the divine commandments—until it has arrived at a stable disposition—sometimes discerns the pure types of the virtues, and sometimes its judgment, clouded over with carnal thoughts, is deceived. But the glance of profound contemplation, once it has penetrated to the face of truth, can never be beaten back, can never be deceived, can never be blinded by any darkness.

3. Both, however, run to the tomb. The tomb of Christ is the divine Scripture in which the mysteries of his divinity and humanity are enclosed by the weight of the letter, as the tomb was by a stone. John runs ahead before Peter. For contemplation, altogether purified, penetrates the profound secrets of the divine Scriptures more acutely and more quickly than action which has yet to be purified. Nevertheless Peter is the first to enter the tomb, and then John. And so both run, and both enter. For Peter symbolizes faith, John signifies intelligence. And so, since it is written "unless you believe you will not understand," faith must precede into the tomb of the holy Scripture; then follows intelligence, whose entry is prepared by faith.

In recognizing Christ as God made man in time and declaring, "You are the Christ, the Son of the living God," Peter flew, so to speak, very high. But he who understood that the same Christ was God, generated from God before all time, declaring, "in the Principle was the Word," flew higher still. Let no one think that we prefer John to Peter. Who would do this? Which of the Apostles is higher than him who is called their head? We do not prefer John to Peter, but we compare contemplation with action, the perfectly purified spirit to one yet to be purified, virtue that has arrived at a stable disposition to virtue that is still ascending. We are not now considering the dignity of the persons of the Apostles; rather are we investigating the beautiful diversity of the divine mysteries.

Therefore, Peter, that is, action in the exercise of the virtues, recognizes the Son of God, encompassed in the flesh in a marvelous and ineffable manner. He does this through the virtue of faith and action. But John, that is, the highest contemplation of truth, marvels at the Word of God as he was before taking flesh, absolute and infinite in his Principle, that is, in his Father. Peter, guided by divine revelation, looks upon the eternal and the temporal made one in Christ. John brings only the eternal to the notice of faithful souls.

4. The mystical bird, who flies fast and looks upon the face of God—I mean John, the 'theologian'—rises above every visible and invisible creature, soars over all understanding, and, deified, enters into God who deifies him. O holy Paul, you were caught up, as you yourself say, to the third heaven, to paradise, but you were not caught up above every heaven and every paradise, that is, every human and angelic nature. In the third heaven, O chosen vessel and master of the Gentiles, you heard words which it is not allowed for man to hear. But John, examining truth at its most profound, heard one word through which all things were made—beyond every heaven in the paradise of paradises, that is, in the Cause of all. And it was allowed to him to

proclaim that word and preach it to men, in so far as it can be preached to men, and in all confidence he declares, "In the Principle was the Word."

5. John was, therefore, not just a man, but more than a man, when he rose above himself and all things that are and, raised aloft by the ineffable virtue of wisdom and the pure keenness of the mind, entered into those things that are beyond all things, the secrets, that is, of the one 'essence' in three 'substances' and three 'substances' in one 'essence.' For he could not otherwise ascend to God, without first becoming God. Just as the ray of our eyes cannot perceive the forms and colors of sensible things until it has coalesced with the rays of the sun and becomes one in and with them, so the spirit of the saints cannot receive the pure knowledge of spiritual things that surpass all understanding unless it first becomes worthy to participate in truth that is beyond understanding. And so the holy 'theologian' transmuted into God, participating in truth, declares that the Word subsists in God the Principle, that is, that God the Son subsists in God the Father: "In the Principle," he says, "was the Word."

Look upon the heaven revealed, that is, the mystery of the great and holy Trinity and Unity manifested to the world. See the divine angel ascend above the Son of man, announcing to us that he is the Word in the Principle before all things, and soon descending over the same Son of man and calling out, "And the Word was made flesh." He descends declaring in his Gospel that the Word was made man, supernaturally among all things, from the Virgin. He ascends proclaiming that the same Word was generated from the Father beyond all 'essence' before and beyond all.

6. "In the Principle," he says, "was the Word." One should note that here by the word 'was' the holy evangelist intimates a meaning not related to time, but to substance. For its 'positive' form, that is, *sum* [I am], from which 'was' derives in irregular conjugation, has two meanings: sometimes it signifies that the thing of which it is predicated subsists without reference to any temporal motion, and so it is termed a substantive verb; and sometimes it indicates temporal motions on the analogy of other verbs. In the case when he says, "In the Principle was the Word," it is as if he said plainly, "the Son subsists in the Father." For what wise man could say in all sanity that the Son ever subsisted temporally in the Father? Where there is a question of immutable truth alone, there one must think of eternity alone.

And lest anyone should think that the Word subsisted in the Principle in such a way that one would understand that there was no difference of 'substance' there, he immediately added: "And the Word was with God." That is, the Son subsists with the Father in unity of 'essence' and distinction of 'substances.'

And again, lest such poisonous contagion should creep upon one to the effect that the Word was only in the Father and only with God, but that the Word in itself did not subsist as God substantially and coessentially with the Father—for this error invaded the perfidious Arians—he added immediately: "And the Word was God."

Anticipating also that there would be those who would contend that the evangelist did not write of one and the same Word: "In the Principle was the Word" and "the Word was God," but that he meant one thing in "Word in the Principle" and another in "Word was God," he closely added, annihilating this heretical belief: "This was in the Principle with God." As if he said: "This Word, which is God with God, is the same as and not other than what was in the Principle." The meaning can be seen more clearly in the Greek manuscripts. There the term αὐτός is written, that is, 'he himself,' and this can refer to both, that is, to the Word and to God; for these two nouns *theos* and *logos*, God and Word, are masculine gender in Greek. And so for this reason one can in this way understand: "and the Word was God, he was in the Principle with God," as if he said more clearly than light: "this God-Word with God is the same of whom I said: 'In the Principle was the Word'."

7. "All things were made by him." All things were made by the God-Word himself or by the Word-God himself. And what is the meaning of "All things were made by him" except: in his being born before all things from the Father, all things were made with him and through him. For his generation from the Father is itself the creation of all causes and the working and making of all things that proceed from the causes into the genera and species. All things were made by the generation of the God-Word from the God-Principle. Hear the divine and ineffable paradox, the secret that one cannot unlock, the deep that one cannot fathom, the mystery that one cannot understand. By him who was not made, but generated, all things were made, but not generated.

The Principle from whom are all things is the Father. The Principle through whom are all things is the Son. In the Father speaking his Word, that is, in the Father generating his Wisdom, all things are made. The Prophet says: "You made all things in Wisdom." And elsewhere, representing the Father as speaking in person, "My heart has uttered." And what did his heart utter? He himself explains: "I say a good word," I speak a good Word, I generate a good Son. The heart of the Father is his own 'substance,' from which is generated the Son's own 'substance.'

The Father precedes the Son not by nature but by cause. Hear the Son himself saying "The Father is greater than me," his 'substance' is the cause of my 'substance.' The Father, I say, precedes the Son by cause; the Son precedes all the things that were made through him by nature. The 'substance' of the Son is coeternal with the Father. The substance of the things which were made through him began to be in him before secular times, not in time, but with the times. For time was made among the other things that were made, not made before, not manifested before, but made at the same time.

8. And what is the result of the word which the mouth of the Highest spoke? For the Father did not speak in vain, not without fruit, not without great effect; for even men speaking among themselves effect something in the ears of those who are listening. Three things, therefore, we ought to believe and understand: the Father speaking, the Word pronounced, and the things that are made through the Word. The Father speaks, the Word is generated, and all things are made. Hear the Prophet: "For he spoke and they were made."

That is: he generated his Word through which all things were made.

And lest, perhaps, you should think that of the things that are, some indeed were made through the Word of God himself, but others were either made apart from him or existed through themselves, so that not all the things that are and are not refer to the one Principle, he adds as a conclusion of the whole of the preceding 'theology': "And without him nothing was made"— that is, nothing was made outside of him, for he embraces all things within himself, containing all; and there is nothing that can be conceived to be coeternal with him or consubstantial or coessential except his Father and his Spirit that proceeds from the Father through him.

This is easier to understand in the Greek. Where the Latins say, *sine ipso* [without him], there the Greeks say, χωρὶς αὐτοῦ [outside of him]. Likewise the Lord himself says to his disciples: "Outside of me you can do nothing." You who could not be made through yourselves outside of me, what can you do outside of me? For here too the Greeks write not ἄνευ, but χωρίς, that is, not *sine* [without], but *extra*, [outside of]. I said, however, that it was easier to understand the Greek precisely because, when one hears 'without him,' one can understand 'without his counsel and help,' and on this account fail to attribute everything, all things, to the Word. But when one hears 'outside of,' one leaves nothing at all that is not made in him and through him.

9. "That which was made in him was life." After the holy evangelist, having left all reason and understanding far behind him, has revealed to us the divine mysteries, namely the God-Word in the God that speaks, leaving to those who contemplate the divine Scripture the perception of the Holy Spirit in both [Father and Word]—for just as he who speaks necessarily emits a breath in the word that he speaks, so God the Father at one and the same time generates his Son and produces his Spirit through the Son generated— and after he has established that all things were made through the Son and that nothing subsisted outside him, he started as it were from another beginning the sequence of his theology, saying "That which was made in him was life." He had earlier said, "All things were made through him," and, as if he had been asked by somebody, concerning the things which were made through the God-Word, how and what were the things in him which were made through him, he replies and says: "That which was made in him was life."

This sentence can be punctuated in two ways. It can be divided as: That which was made, in him was life. It can also read: That which was made in him, was life. With these two punctuations we contemplate two different meanings. For the idea that "what was made, separated in times and places, distinct in genera, forms, and numbers, combined or separated in sensible or intelligible substances, all this was life in him" is not the same as that which declares that "that which was made in him was nothing other than life"; so that the sense is that "all the things that were made through him are life in him and one in him." For they were, that is, they subsist, in him causally before they are as effects in themselves. For the things that are made through him are under him in one way, whereas the things that he is are in him in another.

10. All things, therefore, that have been made through the Word live in him unchangeably and are life; none of them ever existed or will exist in him according to times or places; but beyond all time and place they all are one in him and subsist universally, visible things and invisible, corporeal and incorporeal, rational and irrational; and, simply, heaven and earth, the depths and whatever is in them, live in him and are life and eternally subsist. And the things which seem to us to be devoid of all vital motion live in the Word. But if you ask how and in what way all the things that were made through the Word subsist in him in life and as one and causally, take examples from the nature of creatures; get to know the Maker from the things that were made in him and through him: "For his invisible things," as the Apostle says, "are perceived by the intelligence through the things that were made."

See how the causes of all the things which the sensible globe of this world embraces subsist together and as one in the sun, which is called the great luminary of the world. For from it proceed the forms of all bodies, as does the beauty of the diversity of colors and whatever else that can be predicted of sensible nature. Consider the multiple and infinite power of seeds, how a great number of grasses, shrubs, and animals are contained all together in each of the seeds, how from them arises a beautiful and innumerable multiplicity of forms. Look with the interior eyes how many rules in the art of the artist are one and live in the spirit of him who arranges them; how the infinite number of lines subsist as one in one point. Examine examples of this kind from nature. Raised aloft above all things by these examples, as it were by the wings of the contemplation of nature, you will be able with the eye of your mind to see into the secrets of the Word and, in so far as it is given to us in seeking God with human arguments, to see how all things that were made through the Word live in him and are life. "For in him," as the divine mouth has said, "we live and move and are." And as the great Dionysius the Areopagite says, "the being of all things is the Divinity that is beyond being."

11. "And the life was the light of men." O holy theologian, the Son of God, whom you earlier called the Word, you now call life and light. And it was not without reason that you changed the names, in order that you would convey to us differing significations. You called the Son of God the Word because through him the Father spoke all things: "For he spoke and they were made." But you also called him light and life of all things that were made through him. And what does he illumine? Nothing other than himself and his Father. He is, therefore, the light and illuminates himself, makes himself known to the world, and shows himself to them that do not know him.

The light of divine knowledge left the world when man deserted God. In two ways, therefore, the eternal light makes himself known to the world, by Scripture and by what is created. Not otherwise is divine knowledge renewed in us except by the writings of Scripture and the sight of the creature. Learn the divine words and understand them in your spirit: there you will recognize the Word. Look with the bodily sense at the forms and beauty of sensible things: in them you will perceive the Word of God. In all of these the truth will manifest nothing other to you than him who made all things, outside of whom you will contemplate nothing, for he is all things. For in all the things that are, he himself is whatever is. As there is not substantial good, so there is no essence or substance except him.

"And the life was the light of men." Why did he add "the light of men," as if the Word were specifically and properly the light of men, whereas he is the light of angels, the light of the created universe, the light of all visible and invisible being? Perhaps the Word that gives life to all is said specifically and properly to be the light of men because it was in man that he manifested himself not only to men, but also to angels and every created thing capable of participating in the divine knowledge. For he revealed himself to angels not through an angel, nor to men through an angel, but to men and angels through a man, not in appearance, but in true humanity itself, which he took wholly to himself in the unity of his 'substance,' and gave knowledge of himself to those that knew him. The light of men is, therefore, our Lord Jesus Christ, who manifested himself in human nature to every rational and intellectual creature and revealed the hidden mysteries of his divinity by which he is equal to the Father.

12. "And the light shone in the darkness." Hear the Apostle: "You were," he says, "once darkness, now however, you are light in the Lord." Hear Isaiah: "A light has risen to those that sit in the region of the shadow of death." Light shines in darkness. The whole human race was in darkness because of original sin—not in the darkness affecting our external eyes by which we perceive the forms and colors of sensible things, but in that beauty of things intelligible; not in the darkness of this clouded air, but in the darkness of the ignorance of truth; not in the absence of the light which reveals the corporeal world, but in the absence of the light which illumines the world incorporeal. After his birth from the Virgin, light shines in the darkness, in the hearts, that is, of those who know him.

But since the whole human race is divided as it were into two parts, into those whose hearts are illumined by the knowledge of truth and those who still remain in the deep darkness of impiety and perfidy, the evangelist added: "And the darkness did not comprehend it." As if he said clearly: the light shines in the darkness of faithful souls and shines more and more, beginning with faith and tending towards vision; but the perfidy and ignorance of impious hearts did not know the light of the Word of God shining in the flesh. "For their foolish heart," as the Apostle says, "was darkened and calling themselves wise they became fools." That at any rate is the 'moral' sense.

13. The 'physical' meaning of these words is as follows: human nature, even if it did not sin, could not of its own proper resources shine; for according to its nature it is not light, but partakes of light. For it is capable of wisdom, but is not wisdom itself, by participation in which it can become wise. Just as the air that surrounds us does nothing through itself but is called 'darkness,' yet can participate in the light of the sun, so our nature, considered in itself, is a kind of dark substance, but is capable of participating in the light of wisdom. And as the said air, when it participates in the rays of the sun, is not said to shine of itself, but the splendor of the sun is said to appear in it so that it does not lose its own natural darkness and receives the light

coming upon it, so the rational part of our nature, when it possesses the presence of the Word of God, does not through itself know things intelligible and its God, but does so through the divine light established in it. Hear the Word himself: "It is not you," he says "who speak, but the Spirit of your Father who speaks in you." With this one sentence he wished to teach us to understand this same thing in everything else, and that it should be heard in the ear of our heart in an ineffable way: it is not you who shine, but it is the Spirit of your Father who shines in you—that is, it is he who shows that I shine in you, because I am the light of the intelligible world, of created nature, rational and irrational; it is not you who understand me intellectually but I myself understand myself intellectually in you through my Spirit, for you are not substantial light, but the participation of light subsisting through itself.

The light, therefore, shines in darkness, because the Word of God, the life and the light of men, does not cease to shine in our nature which, examined and considered in itself, is found to be a certain darkness without form; nor has that light wished to abandon it, although it sins, nor has it ever abandoned it: it forms it, containing it through nature; it reforms it, deifying it through grace. And since the light itself is incomprehensible to every creature, "the darkness did not comprehend it." For God surpasses all sense and intelligence and alone has immortality. His light because of its excellence is called darkness, for no creature understands what or of what kind it is.

14. "There was a man sent by God whose name was John." Behold the eagle, descending from the highest top of the mountain of theology, in his smooth flight to the deepest valley of history, loosening the wings of lofty contemplation, as he descends from heaven to the earth of the mystic world. For the divine Scripture is a certain intelligible world made up of its four parts, as it were four elements. Its earth, as it were in the middle and lowest place, like a center, is history; around this, like waters, the abyss of the moral exegesis, which the Greeks are wont to call ἠθική, is poured. Around these two, I mean history and the ethical, as it were the two lowest parts of the said world, is wrapped the air of the science of nature, which—I mean the science of nature—the Greeks call Φυσική. But outside and beyond all is the encircling aethereal and fiery burning of the scorching heaven, that is, of the lofty contemplation of the divine nature, which the Greeks call theology; beyond that no intellect proceeds.

The great theologian, I mean John, touching, in the beginning of his Gospel, the highest peaks of theology, penetrating the secrets of the heaven of the mystical heavens, rising above all the historical, the ethical, and the physical, turns his intelligible flight, as it were towards some earth, to narrate according to history the things that happened shortly before the Incarnation of the Word, and says: "A man was sent by God."

15. And so John introduces John into his own theology. "The abyss calls on the abyss in the voice" of the divine mysteries. The evangelist tells the history of his precursor. He to whom was given the grace to recognize the Word in the Principle tells us of him to whom was given the grace to precede the

Word incarnate. *Was*, he says. He did not say simply, "*one* was sent by God," but, "A man was"—so as to distinguish the man, who shared in humanity alone, who preceded, from the man who brought together and unified divinity and humanity, who followed: to separate the passing voice from the Word that remains always and unchangeably; to indicate one as the morning star appearing at the rise of the kingdom of the heavens, and to proclaim the other as the Son of justice that succeeded him. He distinguishes the witness from him concerning whom he bears witness, the one sent from the one who sends, the flickering lamp from the bright light that fills the world and destroys the darkness of death and sin of the whole human race. The precursor of the Lord was man, not God; but the Lord; whose precursor he was, was at the same time both man and God. The precursor was a man who would become God through grace. He whom he preceded was God by nature, who was to become man through humility and the will for our salvation and redemption.

"A man was sent." By whom? By the God-Word whom he precedes. His mission was to precede. Calling aloud he brings forth his voice: "The voice of one calling in the wilderness." The messenger prepares the coming of the Lord. "Whose name was John"—to whom was given the grace to become the precursor of the King of kings, to make manifest the incarnate Word, to baptize him as a spiritual son, and to bear witness to the eternal light by his voice and by his martyrdom.

16. "He came for testimony, to bear testimony concerning the light," that is, Christ. Hear his testimony: "Behold the Lamb of God, behold him who takes away the sins of the world." And again: "He who comes after me was made before me." The Greek reading is clearer: ἔμπροσθέν μου , that is, he was made before me, before my face. As if he said openly: he who in the order of times was born in the flesh after I was born, him, while I was still in the womb of my sterile mother, I saw, before my eyes in a prophetic vision, conceived in my sight and made man in the womb of the Virgin.

"He was not the light, but was to give testimony concerning the light." Take account of what has already been said and understand this as follows: he was not the light, but he *was sent* to bear testimony concerning the light. The precursor of the light was not the light. Why then is he called a 'burning lamp' and 'the morning star'? He was a burning lamp, but he did not burn, lit with his own fire; he did not give light with his own light. He was the morning star, but he did not receive his light from himself. The grace of him whom he preceded burned and shone in him. He was not the light, but he participated in the light. That which shone in him and through him was not his. As we said earlier, no rational or intellectual creature is through itself and substantially light, but it participates in the one and true substantial light, which shines intelligibly everywhere and in all things.

That is why there is added: "But the true light was that which enlightens every man that comes into this world." The true light he calls the Son of God subsisting through himself, generated before all the ages by God the Father subsisting through himself. The true light he calls the same Son become man among men on account of men. He is the true light who says of himself: "I am the light of the world. He who follows me does not walk in darkness, but he will have the light of eternal life."

17. "The true light was that which enlightens every man that comes into this world." And what does "that comes into the world" mean? And who is "every man that comes into the world?" And from where does he come into the world? And how does he come? If you take the text to refer to those who through generation in time and place came into this world from the hidden recesses of nature—what enlightenment can they receive who are born but to die, who grow but to be corrupted, who are composed but to be dissolved again, who fall from the quietude of silent nature into the inquietude of tumultuous misery? Tell me, please, what true and spiritual light is in those who are born into this life, transitory and false? Is this world a suitable habitation for those who are separated from the true light? Is it not justly called the region of the shadow of death, the valley of tears, the abyss of ignorance, the earthly habitation that oppresses the spirit of man and that blocks off the eyes of the soul from seeing the true light?

It is not, therefore, to those who emerge from the hidden causes of seeds into corporeal species that we should apply the words *that which enlightens every man that comes into this world*, but to those who spiritually come into the invisible world through the regeneration of grace, which is given in baptism; who, contemning birth according to the corruptible body, choose birth according to the spirit; who put under their feet the world below, ascend to the world that is above, leave behind them the shadows of ignorance and death, seek the light of wisdom and of life, cease to be sons of men, begin to become sons of God, put behind them and destroy in themselves the world of the vices, put before the eyes of their mind the world of the virtues, and long to ascend to it with all their strength. Them, therefore, the true light enlightens, who come into the world of the virtues, not them who rush into the world of the vices.

18. "He was in the world." Here he calls 'world' not only the sensible creature in general, but especially the substance of the rational nature that is in man. In all of these and, to speak unrestrictedly, in the created universe, the Word was the true light, that is, it subsists and always exists, because it never ceases to subsist in all things. Just as, when one who speaks ceases to speak, his voice ceases and is gone, so, if the heavenly Father ceased to speak his Word, the effect of the Word, that is, the created universe, would not subsist. For the speaking of the Father, that is, the eternal and unchangeable generation of his Word, is the substance and permanence of the created universe.

One can also with reason apply to this sensible world alone the following sentence: "He was in the world and the world was made by him." Lest anyone who shares in the Manichaean heresy should think that the world perceptible by the senses was created by the Devil and not by the Creator of all things visible and invisible, the theologian adds: "he was in the world," that is, he who contains all subsists in this world. "And the world was made by him"—the Creator of the universe does not dwell in the works of others, but in his own that he has made.

19. Notice that the holy evangelist has mentioned the word 'world' four times. Nevertheless we should understand that there are three worlds. The first is that which is filled with the invisible and spiritual substances of the virtues alone: the man who comes into this world possesses the full participation of the true light. The second world is diametrically opposed to the first, for it is made up of things visible and corporeal alone. Although it is at the lowest level of the universe, the Word was in it and through the Word it was made. It is the first step for those who wish to ascend to the knowledge of truth through the senses, for the spectacle of visible things draws the reasoning mind to the knowledge of invisible things. The third world is that which, because of its position in the middle, joins together in itself the upper world of spiritual things and the lower world of corporeal things and of the two makes one. It is perceived only in man in whom all creation is joined as one. For man is composed of body and soul. He gets his body from this world, but his soul from the other, and makes of them one beautiful arrangement. The body possesses all corporeal, but the soul possesses all spiritual, nature; these, brought together in one joining, constitute the whole harmony that is man. And so man is called 'all,' for every creature is amalgamated in him as in a workshop. Hence the Lord himself ordered his disciples who were going to preach, "Preach the gospel to every creature."

This world, then, that is, man, did not know his Creator; nor, held by the bonds of carnal thoughts, did he wish to know his God through either the symbols of the written Law or the signs of the visible creation. "And the world did not know him." Man did not know the God-Word, either before he became man, when he was naked in divinity alone, or after he became man, when he was clothed only in the flesh. When he was invisible he did not know him; when he was visible he denied him. He was unwilling to seek for the one seeking him; he was unwilling to hear him when he called; he was unwilling to worship the one who deified him; he was unwilling to receive the one who received him.

20. "He came to his own," that is, to the things which were made through him and, for this reason, are not improperly called his. "And his own did not receive him." His are all men whom he wished to redeem and did redeem.

"To as many, however, as received him, believing in his name, he gave the power of becoming sons of God." Here there is a division not in the humanity of the rational world, but in its will. Those who receive the incarnate Word are separated from those who reject him. The faithful believe in the coming of the Word and willingly receive their Lord. The impious deny him and stubbornly refuse him, the Jews through envy, the pagans through ignorance. To those who receive him he gave the power of becoming sons of God: to those who do not receive him he still gives time to do so. No one is deprived of the possibility of believing in the Son of God and the possibility of being his son: this depends on the free will of man and his co-operation with grace. To whom did he give the power of becoming sons of God? To those who receive him and believe in his name. Many receive Christ. The Arians receive him, but do not believe in his name; they do not believe that the only begotten Son of God is consubstantial with the Father.

They deny that he is ὁμοούσιος, that is, coessential with the Father. They say that he is ἑτερούσιος, that is, of a different essence from the Father. And so it is of no profit to them to receive Christ, while they try to deny his truth. But they who receive Christ, true God and true man, and believe this firmly, are given the possibility of becoming sons of God.

21. "They who are born not from blood, not from the will of the flesh, nor from the will of man, but from God" (in the old Greek manuscripts "who are born not from blood, but from God" only is written). "Not from blood," he says, that is, not from corporeal procreation are born those who gain adoption as the sons of God through the merit of their faith; they are born from God the Father through the Holy Spirit to be co-heirs with Christ, that is, to share the sonhood of the only-begotten Son of God.

"Not from the will of the flesh, nor from the will of man." Here are introduced the two sexes through whom the number of those born in the flesh are carnally procreated. By the term 'flesh' the evangelist signified the female sex, and by the term 'man' he signified the male.

But you may say: "it seems impossible that mortals should become immortal, that the corruptible should not be subject to corruption, that simple men should be the sons of God, that temporal creatures should possess eternity." Here following, then, is an argument *a fortiori* which will allow you to believe what you doubt. "And the Word became flesh." If what is something greater has already without doubt been accepted, why should it seem incredible that what is less could follow? If the Son of God became man—which no one, of those who receive him, doubts—why should it seem wonderful that a man who believes in the Son of God will become the son of God? For this purpose did the Word descend into the flesh, that the flesh, that is, man, believing through the flesh in the Word, should ascend to him; that many should become adopted sons through him who was the only begotten Son by nature. The Word did not become flesh for his own sake, but for us, who could not be transmuted into sons of God except through the flesh of the Word. He descended alone, he ascends with many. He who made a man from God makes gods of men.

"And he dwelt among us," that is, he possessed our nature so as to make us share in his nature.

22. "And we saw his glory, the glory that he has from the Father as the only-begotten." Where, O holy theologian, did you see the glory of the incarnate Word, the glory of the Son of God made man? When did you see it? With what eyes did you look upon it? I believe you saw it with your corporeal eyes at the time of the transfiguration on the mountain. For then you were the third person present as a witness of the divine glorification. You were present, I think, in Jerusalem and heard the voice of the Father glorifying his Son, saying, "I have glorified him and I shall glorify him again." You heard the crowds of children shouting out, "Hosanna to the Son of David." What shall I say of the glory of the resurrection? You saw him rising from the dead when he came to you and the other disciples through closed doors. You saw his glory as he ascended to the Father, when he was taken up into heaven by the angels. And this above all you have contem-

plated with the deepest gaze of your mind—the Word in the Principle with his Father. There you saw his glory that he has "from the Father as the only-begotten."

23. "Full of grace and truth." The meaning of this phrase is twofold. It can be understood of the humanity and divinity of the incarnate Word, so that the plenitude of grace is referred to the humanity, and the plenitude of truth to the divinity. For the incarnate Word, our Lord Jesus Christ, received the plenitude of grace according to his humanity, since he is the head of the church and the first-born of the universal creatures, that is, of universal humanity, which is in him and through him cured and restored. "In him," I say, because he is the greatest and principal example of the grace by which, without any previous merit, man becomes God, and in him this example is manifested in a primordial way. "Through him," I say, because "we have all received from his plenitude" the grace of deification in exchange for the grace of faith, by which we believe in him, and action, by which we keep his commandments.

The plenitude of the grace of Christ can also be understood of the Holy Spirit. For the Holy Spirit is wont to be called 'grace' since he is the distributor and operator of the gifts of grace. The sevenfold operation of this Spirit filled the humanity of Christ and reposed in him, as the prophet says: "And the spirit of wisdom and intelligence will repose in him, the spirit of counsel and fortitude, the spirit of knowledge and piety; and the spirit of the fear of the Lord will fill him." If, then, you wish to understand of Christ himself the phrase "full of grace," know that it refers to the plenitude of his deification and sanctification according to his humanity. By his deification I mean how man and God are united as one in the unity of the one 'substance'. By his sanctification I mean how he was not only conceived of the Holy Spirit but also was filled with the plenitude of his gifts, and how the lamps of grace, placed as it were on top of the mystical candelabrum of the church, shine in him and from him.

But perhaps you prefer to understand the plenitude of grace and truth of the incarnate Word in connection with the New Testament, as our Evangelist later seems to understand—for he says: "The Law was given by Moses, grace and truth, however, were given by Jesus Christ." In that case you can reasonably say that the plenitude of grace of the New Testament was conferred by Christ, and that the truth of the symbols of the Law was fulfilled in him, as the Apostle says: "In whom the plenitude of divinity dwells bodily." He calls the mystical senses of the shadows of the Law the plenitude of divinity. Christ coming in the flesh taught and manifested that these mystical senses resided in himself corporeally, for he is the spring and plenitude of graces, the truth of the symbols of the Law, and the end of the visions of the prophets. To whom be glory with the Father and the Holy Spirit for ever and ever. Amen.

Questions: What is Eriugena's manner of presentation and reasoning? Since he was employed by Charles the Bald, can we infer from Eriugena's interests what the interests and fascinations of the king and his palace school were like? What are the several senses of Scripture which Eriugena employs?

64. Wulfadus's Library

Wulfadus had been the abbot of Saint-Médard of Soissons and there may have housed the so-called palace school of Charles the Bald for a time. He was the keeper of Charles's rebellious and tonsured son Carloman and a governmental minister of the king. It is not impossible that Eriugena himself stayed at Saint-Médard for a time while Wulfadus was abbot in the early 860s, for Eriugena said that Wulfadus had encouraged him to write the 'Periphyseon' and he presented it to him for correction. Most likely it was in 866 as Wulfadus prepared to leave Saint-Médard to take up his new post as archbishop of Bourges that he had a list of the books in his personal library inscribed in one of his manuscripts (another work of Eriugena) which still survives in Paris. Wulfadus's library cannot have been typical, for aside from containing works and translations of Eriugena (nos. 5-6, 16-17, 30, 31) it also held a rare copy of Petronius's 'Satyricon'.

Source: trans. P.E. Dutton, from M. Cappuyns, "Les 'Bibli Vulfadi' et Jean Scot Erigène," Recherches de théologie ancienne et médiévale," 33 (1966), pp.137-138.

The Books of Wulfadus

1. Histories of Josephus
2. The History of Hegesippus
3. The Tripartite History [of Cassiodorus]
4. The Book of Paterius [compiled from the writings of Gregory the Great]
5. [The Works] of Saint Dionysius the Areopagite [as translated into Latin by Eriugena]
6. More of the Same [author]
7. The Letters of Gregory [the Great] from the Register
8. From The Confessions and On the Trinity by Augustine
9. Origen on the Epistle of Paul to the Romans
10. Likewise [Origen] On Genesis, On Exodus, On Leviticus, On Luke, On [the Book of] Joshua, son of Nun
11. An Excerpt from the Sayings of Saint Gregory on Job [from the Moralia in Job]
12. The Discourses of Cyprian in the first part.
13. The Same [author], the second part to Various [people]
14. Twenty-five Homilies of John Chrysostom on Matthew
15. Synodal Acts
16-17. Two [volumes, books, or copies] of the Periphyseon
18. Ambrose, On the Duties [of the Clergy]
19. Ambrose, On Psalm 118
20. [A Volume of] the Letters of Ambrose
21a. The Pastoral [Care of Gregory the Great]
21b. On the Spirit and the Letter [of Augustine]
22. Canons
23. The Interpretation of Hebrew Names by Jerome
24. Ambrose on Joseph
25. The Explanation of Daniel by Jerome
26. Various Homilies of John

27. Ambrose On the Pride of the Flesh
28. Petronius
29. The Letters of John to Gregory in the Palace
30. The Scholiae of Maximus [the Confessor, the *Quaestiones ad Thalassium*, as translated by Eriugena]
[31. The Ambigua to John of Maximus, as translated by Eriugena—this is the manuscript in which the library list is preserved].

Questions: Since so many of these works are compositions of Eriugena, what does this suggest about the nature of Wulfadus's library? Was he buying manuscripts or employing the services of scribes to copy them for him? In a personal library filled with Christian books, why did Wulfadus bother to place a copy of Petronius? Is there a scheme of organization evident in the order of the books?

65. Wulfadus Goes to Court

Wulfadus may have been the friend of Eriugena and a minister of Charles the Bald, but his daily business like that of all high ecclesiastics forced him to fight for and promote his church's property rights. In the court case below he went so far as to supply Merovingian charters to attest to his church's claim over the villa of Perrecy. Wulfadus may have hoped that his good relations with the king and the fact that the judge of the case, Adalard, was a relative would give him an advantage over Count Eccard. But, though the account below is incomplete, it is clear from the will of Eccard that Wulfadus lost the case. Ironically Eccard donated the land, on his death, to the monastery of Saint-Benoît-sur-Loire (Fleury).

Source: trans. J.L. Nelson, "Dispute Settlement in Carolingain West Francia," in The Settlement of Disputes in Early Medieval Europe, ed. W. Davies and P. Fouracre (Cambridge: Cambridge University Press, 1986), p.53; reprinted with permission.

Bishop Leudo and Count Adalard, *missi dominici* in the county of Autun, came to the villa called Mont, and they caused to come there by the command of the lord king the more noble men of the county and many other men of the said county. And they held an inquiry between Bishop Wulfadus [of Bourges] and Count Eccard [of Mâcon] by means of those whom Wulfadus there named, and others, through the oath which they had sworn to the lord King Charles [the Bald], and through the profession which they had sworn in baptism. They promised that they would speak the truth about the villa of Perrecy, which Wulfadus said ought to belong to his church [of Bourges].

Wulfadus therefore showed charters there, and had them read out, from the times of Kings Childebert and Chilperic, and one from the times of King Pepin [the Short] in the name of Nibelung, which recorded a *precaria* [a charter granting land], to the effect that, by means of the consent of good men and by the wish of the bishop of Bourges the said Nibelung had held [Perrecy] as a *precaria* and paid three pounds on the Feast of Saint Mary [each year].

Eccard there presented a charter of the lord Emperor Louis [the Pious] to be read out, and also his own record of a judgment by which, in a general assembly of our lord Charles [the Bald], against the claims of John, he had recovered property, part of that granted in the [precarial] document, which had been taken away from him.

Then through these men, inquiry was made of Leutbald, Ildric, Suavo, Girbald, John, Ildebod, Eriulf, Wulfadus, another Leutbald, Honesteus and others, on their oath to tell the truth, whatever truth they knew concerning this case.

Then [Eccard's witnesses] unanimously declared, "We have never heard our antecedents say, nor have we ourselves ever heard or seen it told as truth, that the villa had been otherwise than belonging to the fisc of the lord Pepin [the Short] and the lord Charles [the Great] and the lord Louis the emperor, without any dues or any render or any mark of lordship, until the lord emperor gave it by his charter to Eccard."

Then inquiry was made of Leutbald and Jacob, at whose instance Wulfadus had come to that assembly, as to what they knew about the case. They stated that (sic), "We have seen that Eccard had that villa, and we have heard it said that it ought to belong to the church of Wulfadus," and that "many have been hearing this just now since this case was raised, but [they have] not [been hearing] about what truth there ever was in this [claim]."

Then inquiry was made of Guntfrid, and he said that, "I have seen [that] Hildebrand [Eccard's father] had it from the royal fisc and then Eccard [had it] as an allod [a free holding]." And he had "heard it said that it belonged to Wulfadus's church."

Then inquiry was made of Mauronus and he said that Suavus (sic) came to him saying that he had spoken with Odalric his lord and [suggested that] he [Odalric] should acquire that villa and give it to him [Suavus], but in [Odalric's] view there was no case for doing that and he dismissed the idea. Then he spoke with Winfred, another of his lords, and he took the view that there was no case for doing that and likewise dismissed the idea. And then he [Mauronus] heard that Suavus came to Count Odo on that same business, but he did not know what he [Odo] said about it, and he knew nothing further.

Questions: Are any substantial grounds given here to support Wulfadus's claim? Are written records as important as witnesses in the disposition of this case?

66. Charles the Bald Grants a Benefice

Charles the Bald was crowned emperor on Christmas Day 875 in Rome by Pope John VIII. The imperial title appears prominently in all the documents of the last two years of his life. Here he is granting a benefice to one of his men, but he has extended the grant to Hildebertus's son as well. Before long this property would be listed as an allod or free holding.

Source: trans. D. Herlihy, A History of Feudalism (New York: Harper & Row, 1970), pp.105-106; reprinted with permission.

[17 July 876]

In the name of the holy and undivided Trinity, Charles by the mercy of almighty God august emperor. If we give our assent to the just and reasonable petitions of our faithful subjects, we familiarize them with the works of our imperial majesty, and from this we make them more faithful and more devoted in the service of our majesty. Therefore let it be known to all the faithful of the holy Church of God and to our own, present and to come, that one of our faithful subjects, by name of Hildebertus, has approached our throne and has beseeched our serenity that through this command of our authority we grant to him for all the days of his life and to his son after him, in right of usufruct and benefice [*usufructuario et jure beneficiario*], certain estates which are both of them called Cavaliacus, in the county of Limoges. Giving assent to his prayers for reason of his meritorious service, we have ordered this charter to be written, through which we grant to him the estates already mentioned, in all their entirety, with lands, vineyards, forests, meadows, pastures, and with the people living upon them, so that, without causing any damage through exchanges of diminishing or lessening the land, he for all the days of his life and his son after him, as we have said, may hold and possess them in right of benefice and usufruct. And in order that this command of our authority may obtain, in the name of God, fuller and firmer vigor of strength. . . [conclusion omitted].

Audacher the notary in place of Gazlinus recognizes [validates] this act.

Done on the sixteenth Kalends of August, the thirty-seventh year of the reign of Charles most glorious emperor in Francia, and the sixth year in succession to Lothar [II], the first year of his reign as emperor. Done at Ponthion in the palace of the emperor. In the name of God, happily. Amen.

Questions: Did kings like Charles the Bald not recognize the danger in granting lands to several generations of a family? If so, why would he have granted this land to Hildebertus and to his son after him?

67. The Capitulary of Quierzy, 877

In 877, the Emperor Charles the Bald was, at the behest of an importunate pope, about to march back to Italy to defend the church against the Saracens. At Quierzy he made arrangements for the maintenance of the kingdom in his absence, and granted certain concessions to his nervous nobles.

Source: trans. D. Herlihy, A History of Feudalism (New York: Harper & Row, 1970), pp.106-107; reprinted with permission.

[14 June 877]

9. If a count whose son is with us should die, our son should with our other faithful men appoint, from among those who were his most intimate friends and closest neighbors, someone who shall watch over this county, with the servants of the county and of the bishop, until the news shall have reached us. If, however, the deceased count should leave a son of tender years, this administrator, with the servants of the county and the bishop in whose diocese he may be, should look after the same county until the news comes to our attention.

If he had no sons, our son, together with our other faithful men, should designate a person who, with the servants of the county and with the bishop in whose diocese he may be, should look after the same county until the news comes to our attention.

If he has no sons, our son, together with our other faithful men, should designate a person who, with the servants of the county and with the bishop, shall administer the county until our decision is made known. Let no one become angered for the reason that we may give the county to a person of our own choice rather than to him who has administered it. The same procedure should be followed in relation to our vassals. We wish and we expressly order that the bishops, as well as the abbots and the counts, and equally our other faithful men, should observe the same procedures in regard to their own vassals....

10. If any of our faithful men, after our death, should wish to renounce the world, leaving a son or a close relative able to perform meritorious service to the commonwealth, he should be allowed to convey to him his office [*honores*]. If he should wish to live peacefully on his allodial holdings, no one should presume to oppose him, or demand anything from him, saving only that he come to the defense of the fatherland.

Questions: If we assume that Charles's nobles were pressing for these changes, what was it that they wanted? Were some of these measures an attempt to recruit soldiers for the Italian campaign?

68. The Death of Charles the Bald

Charles's last campaign was a disaster, since not only were his nobles and bishops less than committed to the imperial cause, but his nephew Carloman was rushing with an army to Italy to attack his uncle. Hincmar's portrayal, in the Annals of Saint-Bertin, of the campaign and the emperor's death is acerbic and deflating.

Source: trans. P.E. Dutton, from Annales de Saint-Bertin, ed. F. Grat, J. Vielliard, and S. Clémencet (Paris: Klincksieck, 1964), pp.211-217.

877. [Charles] was recovering [from a fever that had nearly killed him] and he proceeded by way of Quierzy to Compiègne. While he delayed there, his son, who was born along the way before [Empress] Richildis could come to Anthénay, fell ill. The boy who was named Charles was received at the baptismal font by his uncle Boso, but he died and was taken for burial to the monastery of Saint Denis.

The Emperor Charles spent Lent at Compiègne and celebrated Easter [7 April] there. He received Bishop Peter of F ssombrone and Bishop Peter of Senigallia, the ambassadors of Pope John [VIII], through whom verbally and by letters Pope John called [the emperor] to rescue and protect the holy church of Rome, as he had promised he would, from the pagans who were [then] attacking it.

On the Kalends of May [1 May] [the emperor] called together the bishops of the province of Rheims and other provinces at Compiègne. There, in his own presence and that of the ambassadors of the apostolic see, he arranged for the church, which he had built in the same chapel with its many liturgical goods, to be consecrated by those same bishops [the famous church of Compiègne whose foundation charter survives]. After that he held a general assembly on 1 July at which he established through a capitulary [see doc. 67] how his son Louis [the Stammerer] along with his faithful followers and the chief men of the kingdom should govern Francia until his return from Rome. He also set down what taxes he received from the kingdom of Francia before the death of Lothar [II] and what should be demanded from Burgundy. That is, that from every lordly manse [should be paid] 1 *solidus*, from every freely held manse 4 *denarii* from the lord's levy and 4 *denarii* from the resources of the tenant, from servile manses 2 *denarii* from the lord's levy and 2 *denarii* from the resources of the tenant. Every bishop should receive from the priests of his diocese what it is possible for them to pay: from each priest the bishops should receive something between 5 *solidi* at most and 4 *denarii* at least and they should return this to the *missi dominici*. To pay this tax [money] was taken from church treasuries according to how much existed there. 5000 pounds of silver in weight was the sum of this tax. Those bishops and others who live beyond the Seine River in Neustria undertook to return [still another] tribute—wherever they could raise it and as large as was imposed upon them—to those Northmen who were staying on the Loire.

The lord Emperor Charles traveled from Quierzy to Compiègne and from there went via Soissons to the city of Rheims, and from there to Ponthion and Langres via Châlons. With him as he traveled from Francia to Italy went his wife [Richildis] and a vast amount of gold, silver, horses, and other resources. Passing the Jura [mountains] he met, at Orbe, Bishop Adalgar [of Autun] whom he had sent in February to Rome to participate in a synod [called] by Pope John. The same Adalgar carried forward to the emperor as a magnificent gift a written record of the synod. The main points of the same synod, after many and manifold praises of the emperor, were these: that the election and rise to the imperial scepters celebrated at Rome in the past year should from that time forward and in perpetuity remain fixed and firm. If anyone is inclined to tamper with or to infringe upon that, no matter his standing, his dignity, or his profession, he is to be anathematized for all time until he renders satisfaction. Those who do and those who urge this infringement, if they are clerics are to be deposed; if lay people and monks, they are to be permanently anathematized. [This is invoked] so that by it he [the emperor] should have influence everywhere, because the synod held the past year at Ponthion had been of no use [to him] at Andernach [where Charles had lost an important battle in 876 as he invaded his nephew Louis's kingdom]. Adalgar came to the emperor [with news that] Pope John would meet him at Pavia. Thus the emperor sent in advance Odacer, the notary of the second cabinet, Count Goiramnus, and Pepin, and Heribert to take care of the needs of the pope. The emperor himself hurried forward and encountered the pope in the city of Vercelli, and, when he had been received with the highest honor, they traveled together to Pavia. There it was reported to them with some certainty that Carloman, the son of [Charles's] brother Louis [the German], was descending upon them with a great army. For that reason, they departed from Pavia and went to Tortona where Richildis was consecrated empress by Pope John; not long afterwards she took flight, with the treasury, back towards Morienna. The emperor, however, stayed with Pope John in the same place for a time. He was waiting for the chief men of his kingdom—Abbot Hugh, Boso, Count Bernard of Auvergne, and Bernard, the March lord of Gothia—who he had ordered to accompany him. [Instead], plotting against him, they had conspired with all but a few of the chief men and bishops of the kingdom. When [Charles] learned that these magnates were not about to come and when he and Pope John discovered that Carloman was approaching, the emperor took flight in the direction of Richildis. Pope John hurriedly rushed back towards Rome. The Emperor Charles sent to the holy apostle Peter, through John's hands, a sculpture of the Savior, made with much gold and adorned with precious gems, who was nailed to the cross. Carloman heard from a misguided messenger that the emperor and Pope John were marching on him with a huge army and [so] he too took flight back the way he had come. And so God by the exercise of his mercy dissolved that meeting [of armies].

But Charles, now laid low with fever, drank a powder which his doctor, a Jew by the name of Sedechaias whom he loved and relied upon too much, gave to him to free him, with that potion, from his fever. Having consumed the fatal poison, [the ailing emperor] was carried over Mont Cenis [the pass through the Alps] and arrived in the place that is called Brios, from which he sent for Richildis who was at Morienna to come to him, and so she did. On the second Nones of October [that is, 6 October], the eleventh day after he drank the poison, [Charles the Bald] died in a vile and common hut. The people who were with him opened him up and removed his innards. They filled his insides with wine and perfume as best they could and placed [the body] in a casket. They began to carry him towards the monastery of Saint Denis, where he had ordered that he be buried. But not being able to carry [him] because of the reeking odor, they put him in a barrel covered inside and out with tar and wrapped with leather stips, but nothing would take away the stench. Whence they came with great trouble to a cell of the monks of the bishop of Lyons at Nantua and [there] they entrusted that body in its barrel to the earth.

Questions: Why would the bishops and nobles of Francia not support Charles's imperial obligations? What steps did the emperor take before leaving for Italy? What was Hincmar's attitude towards Emperor Charles the Bald?

CHAPTER SIX

THE TIME OF CHARLES THE FAT

(878–888)

Charles the Bald

An eighteenth-century drawing [after Montfaucon] of Charles the Bald taken from the Bible of San Paolo Fuori le Mura. Above the king, the Virtues are personified. To his right side stand two armed retainers, while to the left stand Charles's queen and a lady-in-waiting. The scene may celebrate the wedding of Charles to Richildis in late 869.

69. The Annals of Saint-Vaast for the Years 882 to 886

When Hincmar died in 882, the Annals of Saint-Bertin ceased. Thus, the Annals of Saint-Vaast, which was written at that monastery not far from Corbie, becomes our best window on the last twenty years of the ninth century in western Francia. This set of annals is particularly concerned with the activities of the Northmen. The reader should examine closely the formulaic nature of the annalist's description of Norse violence, for though the Vikings are often blamed for the collapse of Carolingian civilization one has to wonder how much damage they actually did. Moreover our best sources for the later ninth century give us a telescoped and, perhaps exaggerated, view of the importance of the Vikings as agents of destruction. One might make the case that the Vikings actually energized western civilization and redistributed wealth.

Source: trans. P.E. Dutton, from Annales Xantenses et Annales Vedastini, ed. B. von Simson, in Monumenta Germania Historica: Scriptores Rerum Germanicarum in Usum Scholarum (Hanover, 1909), pp.51-61.

882. The [eastern] Franks raised an army against the Northmen, but at once turned and ran, and there Walo, the bishop of Metz, died. The Danes set that most famous palace of Aachen on fire and [also some] monasteries. They also set cities on fire—the most noble city of Trier and Cologne—also the palaces of kings and villas, with the inhabitants of the place having been killed. The Emperor Charles [the Fat] raised a huge army against them and besieged them at Elslo [in the Netherlands]. King Godefrid came over to [Charles] and the emperor gave him the kingdom of the Frisians which Rorik the Dane once held. He gave Gisela, the daughter of King Lothar [II by Waldrada] to him in marriage and he made the Northmen depart from his kingdom.

King Louis [III of west Francia] sought out the Northmen on the Loire and hoped to eject them from his kingdom and to receive Hasting as his friend, which he did. But because Louis was young, he [one day] chased after a certain girl, the daughter of Germund. That girl fled into her father's house, but the king on horseback chased her for the fun of it. He smashed his shoulders on the lintel of the door and his chest on the saddle of the horse and he fell hard. After this he grew ill and was carried to Saint-Denis. On the Nones of August [5 August] he died, causing great sadness among the Franks, and he was buried in the church of Saint Denis. They sent for and summoned his brother Carloman who quickly came into Francia. Also a certain Bernard coming from Italy did not permit the tyrannical Boso to remain peaceful.

In the month of October the Northmen established themselves at Condé and bitterly ruined the kingdom of Carloman. King Carloman and his army resided on the Somme at Barleux, but the Northmen did not stop their robbery and all the inhabitants of that place who remained fled to the other side of the Somme. Whence with their forces making a trip through La Thiéarche they crossed over the Oise. King Carloman pursued them and he caught up with them at Avaux. A battle broke out and the Franks were superior; almost a thousand Northmen died there. But this battle in no way tamed them. Carloman went to the palace of Compiègne, while the Northmen took to their boats and returned to Condé. From there they devastated with fire and sword the entire kingdom up to the Oise. Defenses were pulled down, monasteries and churches were demolished, and the servants of the [Christian] religion were killed by the sword or by hunger or they were sold abroad, and the inhabitants of the countryside were killed. No one resisted them.

Abbot Hugh [of Saint-Martin of Tours], hearing of these things, raised an army and came to the king. The Northmen were returning from the region of Beauvais where they had been plundering. Hugh and the king chased them into the woods of Vicogne [near Condé], but the Northmen scattered here and there and, few of them having been killed, they returned to their ships. At about this time [that is, 21 December] Hincmar, the archbishop of Rheims, a man worthily praised by all, died.

883. Fulk, an admirable man in all things, succeeded Hincmar in the episcopal see [of Rheims]. After this the Northmen set the monastery and church of Saint Quentin afire. At the same time they set fire to the church of the Mother of God in the city of Arras. Again Carloman pursued the Northmen, but he did nothing either successful or useful [against them]. At this time Rotgarius, the bishop of Beauvais, died and was succeeded by Honoratus. In the springtime the Northmen departed from Condé and sought out lands along the sea. Remaining there through the summer, they forced the Flemings to flee from their own lands. All around they furiously laid waste to things with their swords and with fire. Around autumn, in order to protect the kingdom, King Carloman established his army in the region of Vithmau at the villa of Miannay [near Abbeville] opposite to Lavier. At the end of October, the Northmen came to Lavier with cavalry and infantry and supplies. Ships also entered the Somme by the sea and forced the king and all his army to flee and made them pass over the Oise. Then the Northmen prepared to winter at the city of Amiens. Next, with no one resisting them, they devastated all the land up to the Seine and around the Oise and they burned both the monasteries and churches of Christ. Then the Franks, seeing that things grew ever better for the Northmen, sent a certain Christian Dane by the name of Sigfried, who carefully worked to save the kingdom, to [the Northmen]. He came to Beauvais and then proceeded to Amiens to do the business enjoined upon him.

884. Then Engelwin, the bishop of Paris, died and Abbot Gauzelin replaced him. The Northmen did not stop from capturing and killing Christians or from destroying churches, pulling down fortifications, or putting villas to fire. The corpses of clerics, laymen, nobles, women, young people, and children were lying in every street. There was no street or place in which the dead did not lie and lamentation and sadness filled everyone, seeing that Christians were massacred.

Meanwhile, because the king was still a young man, all the magnates gathered in Compiègne to determine what they should do. After they had discussed the matter, they sent Sigfried, the Danish Christian, who was loyal to the king and the nephew of Rorik, [to the Northmen]. He was supposed to deal with the chiefs of his people to see if they would accept tribute and leave the kingdom. He undertook to fulfill the assignment given to him and went to Amiens. [There] he repeated his mission to the chiefs of his people who were present. After a lengthy discussion, delayed in part by much back and forth activity, by repeating now these things, now those, in the end [the Northmen] imposed on the king and the Franks a tribute of 12,000 pounds of silver calculated according to their way of weighing things. Once hostages had been exchanged, those who lived beyond the Oise began to feel safer. Thus from the day of the Purification of Saint Mary [2 February] until the month of October [884] this freedom from attack was granted to them.

But the Northmen, raiding as usual beyond the Scheldt, devastated with fire and sword churches, monasteries, cities, and villages, and slaughtered people. After holy Easter [19 April] the [people] began to pay the tribute. Churches and church properties were ruthlessly stripped [of wealth]. Finally, when the tribute had been paid, the Franks gathered together to resist the Northmen in case they intended to break their agreement. The Northmen burned down their camps and withdrew from Amiens. The king and the Franks pursued them on a slow march beyond the Oise. The Danes on their journey came to Boulogne-sur-Mer and there deliberated about what they should do. A group of them crossed the sea, another group came to Louvain in the kingdom that once belonged to Lothar and there they set up camps in order to spend the winter. The Franks who were with Carloman returned to their own land; a few young men remained with him to hunt in the Bezu forest. A man by the name of Bertold wanted to help the king kill a boar, but he accidentally wounded the king in the shin. Having received that wound, the king survived for more than seven days and then died in the same place on [12] December. He was around eighteen years old. His body was carried to the monastery of Saint Denis and was there buried. The Franks took council and sent Count Theoderic to Italy to the Emperor Charles [the Fat] [to invite him] to come to Francia.

885. The Emperor Charles, having received the news, made a rapid march and came to Ponthion, and there all the men who lived in Carloman's kingdom came to him and placed themselves under his rule. Thus the Emperor Charles returned to his own land, ordering those men who lived in the kingdom that was formerly Lothar's and those who lived in the kingdom [that was formerly] Carloman's to proceed to Louvain to fight the Northmen. On the agreed upon day both armies came together at that place, except Abbot Hugh, who held back from this outing because of a foot ailment. But [these armies] accomplished nothing successful there, and returned to their own lands in great shame. The Danes laughed at the Franks who came from Carloman's kingdom: "So why did you come to [see] us? It was not necessary. We know who you are and [what] you want, so let us visit you. Let us do that [for you]."

At the same time [in May] Godefrid the Dane, because he was undertaking to break his pledge with the crafty help of his vassal Gerulf [of Frisia], was killed by Duke Henry. Hugh, the son of King Lothar [II, by Waldrada], was blinded on the orders of the emperor who was acting on the advice of Duke Henry. On the eighth Kalends of July [24 June] [the Northmen] with their entire army entered Rouen and the Franks pursued them to the same place.

Since their ships had still not come there, they crossed the Seine in ships found along the river and then they fortified a camp there. While this was taking place, all those who lived in Neustria and Burgundy assembled and, when an army had been raised, they approached as if to make war upon the Northmen. But, though they should have fought, [when] Ragnold, the duke of Le Mans, fell with a few of his men, they all returned to their own lands in great sadness, having accomplished nothing useful.

Then the Northmen began to rage with fire and to thirst for slaughter. They killed and captured Christians, demolished churches, and no one resisted them. Once again the Franks prepared themselves to resist, not in war, but rather by constructing fortifications to impede the progress of their ships. They constructed a castle on the river Oise at a place [now] called Pontoise, and they entrusted Aletramnus with guarding it. Bishop Gauzelin built fortifications at Paris. But, in the month of November, the Northmen set out upon the Oise and surrounded with a blockade the castle at Pontoise. They stopped those who were shut up in the castle from drawing water from the river, for they had no other water to draw upon. But those who were in the castle began to be pressed by their lack of water. Need I say more? They sued for peace, seeking only to leave there alive. Once hostages were exchanged on both sides, Aletramnus and his men set out for Beauvais. The Northmen set fire to the castle and stole everything that was left there, for those who abandoned the castle left everything there except their arms and horses. It was under this condition that they had been allowed to leave.

Wildly excited by their victory, the Northmen approached Paris and, with great energy, immediately attacked a tower. They thought that they could take it without any great delay, because it was not yet fully strengthened. But Christians defended it with great vigor and the battle lasted from morning till evening. Night interrupted the battle and so the Northmen, that night, returned to their ships [26 November]. Bishop Gauzelin and Count Odo labored all through the night with their men to fortify the tower in preparation for [the coming] battle. The following day [27 November] the Northmen again rushed back to the battle at the same tower and a fierce battle went on until sunset. But the Danes, having lost many men, returned to their ships. Then they set up a camp for themselves opposite to the city and they laid siege to the city, constructed machines [of war], employed fire, and used all their ingenuity to capture the city. But the Christians fighting bravely against them were superior in everything.

886. On the eighth Ides of February [6 February] a grave crisis arose for the inhabitants of the city, since a very serious rise in the water level of the river smashed the smaller bridge [running to the south from the Ile de la Cité]. When the bishop learned of this event, he selected some strong and noble men to guard the tower that night so that, in the morning, they might restore the bridge. None of this was hidden to the Northmen. They rose before dawn with all their men and rushed to that tower and laid siege to it and they began to attack before help from the city could arrive. Those men in the tower resisted bravely and the shouting of the multitude [of them] lifted up to heaven. The bishop stood on the wall of the city with everyone who was in the city crying intensely because they could not come to the assistance

of their people and because there was nothing they could do [to help]. [Gauzelin] entrusted them to Christ's care. The Northmen approached the gate of that tower in [full] force and tried to set fire to it. Those men inside the tower, worn down by wounds and defeated by fire, and to the dishonor of Christians, were killed in various ways and their bodies were flung into the river. Then the Northmen demolished the tower. After these things [had occurred], they did not cease their attack upon the city.

The bishop's heart was broken over this grave loss. He sent letters to Count Herkenger [of Melun], commanding him to go as quickly as he could to eastern Francia and to search out Henry, the duke of Austrasia, so that he might come to the assistance of the bishop and the Christian people [as a whole]. What was commanded, Herkenger at once carried out and he convinced Henry with his army to come to Paris, but Henry accomplished nothing there and returned to his own territory. But Gauzelin, who was anxious to help his Christian people in every way, reached a cordial understanding with Sigfried, the king of the Danes, to free [Paris] from the siege.

While these things were taking place, the bishop fell gravely ill, died [on 16 April], and was buried in the city. His death was not a secret to the Northmen who, before the fact was known to the citizens [of Paris], shouted from outside the city that he was dead. The people, touched by the death of their bishop and by the siege, were immensely depressed, but the illustrious Count Odo fortified them with his encouraging words. Nevertheless the Northmen daily attacked the city and many people on both sides were killed, many were laid low with wounds, and food began to grow scarce in the city.

Then [on 12 May] Hugh, the venerable abbot, died and was buried in the monastery of Saint Germain of Auxerre. But Odo, seeing the people fall into despair, went out of the city secretly to seek help from the chief man of the kingdom and to send word to the emperor that Paris would soon perish if it did not receive assistance. Returning to Paris after his absence, Odo discovered a great deal of sadness, but he did not enter the city without an astonishing incident, for the Northmen, knowing in advance of his return, blocked off the gate of the tower to him. But even with his horse dead, Odo slashed at his enemies left and right and, entering the city, made his sad people happy. No one can count the dead, what great dangers they faced there, how many thousands of people on both sides fell there in various skirmishes. For, without any cessation, those [warriors] struck that city with a varying complement of arms, machines [of war], and battering rams. But with great persistence they begged God [for help] and were delivered. But in the eight or so months before the emperor could come to [Paris], the struggle continued in various ways.

Questions: What phrases and formulas does the annalist repeat when describing the destruction caused by the Northmen? What is the nature of Norse activity in these years and what strategies of resistance have the Franks discovered? Does the annalist blame anyone for the invasions and does he have a hero who might save the day?

70. The Song of Louis: *Ludwigslied*

Carolingian kings did have triumphs over the Northmen, though annalists seem to have been better recorders of the defeats they suffered. The 'Ludwigslied' is a poem written in Old High German that celebrates the victory of a King Louis, the son of another King Louis, over the Northmen. It has long been accepted that the poem refers to the success of Louis III, son of Louis the Stammerer, over the Northmen in the Battle at Saucourt in 881. The poem is an example of the kind of rousing royal song that must have stirred the hearts of Frankish warriors as they set out to resist the Northmen. Why a poem for a west Frankish king should be written in German and why a fairly minor battle in a protracted conflict should occasion such celebratory praise are questions worth considering.

Source: trans. J.K. Bostock, in Bostock, A Handbook of Old High German Literature, 2nd ed. revised by K.C. King and D.R. McLintock (Oxford: Clarendon Press, 1976), pp.239-241; reprinted with permission.

I know a king—his name is Hluduig—who serves God zealously: I know He rewards him for it. As a young man he became fatherless [Louis III was at most sixteen years old when his father Louis the Stammerer died]. This was at once made good to him: the Lord took him and became his guardian. He gave him forces, a lordly following, and the throne here among the Franks. Long may he enjoy it! This he then at once divided, the number of the enjoyments, with Carloman his brother.

When this was all accomplished, God desired to prove him [to see] whether he could endure hardships so young. He let heathen men [Northmen] journey across the sea to remind the Frankish people of their sins. Some at once perished, some were chosen. He who had formerly lived amiss suffered punishment. He who was then a thief and survived took to fasting; later he became a good man. One was a liar, one a robber, one full of licentiousness, and he mended his ways.

The king was far off, the realm all in disarray. Christ was angered: alas, it paid for this. Yet God took pity on it: He knew all the distress. He bade Hluduig ride thither at once: "Hluduig, my king, help my people. The Northmen have them hard pressed." Then said Hluduig: "Lord, I will do all that thou commandest, unless death prevents me."

Then he took leave of God, raised the standard, and rode thither into Francia to meet the Northmen. Those who were waiting for him thanked God. They all said: "My lord, we have waited for thee so long." Then Hluduig the Good spoke loudly: "Take comfort, comrades, my companions in adversity. God has sent me hither and commanded me himself, if it should seem advisable to you, that I should fight here and not spare myself until I have saved you. Now I desire all God's servants to follow me. Our life here is allotted for as long as Christ wishes; if He wishes our departure hence, over that He has authority. Whoever does God's will here with courage—if he comes out alive—I will reward him for it; if he does not survive, (I will reward) his family."

Then he took up shield and spear. Courageously he rode. He wanted to demonstrate the truth to his adversaries. Then, it was not long before he found the Northmen. He rendered praise to God: he sees what he has longed for. The king rode bravely and sang a holy song, and all together they sang "Kyrie eleison." The song was sung, the battle was begun, blood shone in cheeks, the Franks romped there. There every warrior fought, but none like Hluduig: swift and brave—that was in his blood. This one he hewed through, that one he ran through. He at once poured out bitter drink for his enemies: so woe to them for ever!

Praised be the power of God! Hluduig was victorious. And thanks to all the saints! His was the triumph. Hail again to Hluduig, [our] fortunate king. As ready as he has always been whenever there has been need of it, may the Lord in his mercies save him!

Questions: How does the poet's attitude differ from the annalist's? What virtues does he appreciate most in King Louis? Why might this poem in Old High German have been written for a west Frankish king?

71. Abbo's Account of the Siege of Paris by the Northmen

Abbo was a monk of Saint-Germain-des-Prés in Paris and wrote his poem on the Norse assaults on Paris in 885-886 and 896 at the end of the ninth century. The Latin of his poem with its three books may be difficult to read, but the author's sentiments are clear as he celebrates noble men like Gauzelin, Odo, and Ebolus who stayed with Paris during its dark days. Abbo did not, however, think much of Charles the Fat who turned from being the savior of Paris into its betrayer almost over night in late 886. As such there may at the end of the ninth century be a shift away from the mood of predominant royalism that had existed among learned men and women for most of the century and towards a newer enthusiasm for nearby and protective nobles.

Source: trans. F.A. Ogg, A Source Book of Mediaeval History: Documents Illustrative of European Life and Institutions from the German Invasions to the Renaissance (New York: American Book Company, 1908), pp.168-171; revised.

885. [The Northmen] came to Paris with 700 sailing ships, not counting those of smaller size which are commonly called barques. At one stretch the Seine was lined with the vessels for more than two leagues, so that one might ask in astonishment in what cavern the river had been swallowed up, for nothing was visible there, since ships covered that [river] as if with oak trees, elms, and alders. On the second day after the fleet of the Northmen arrived under the walls of the city, Sigfried, who was then king only in name but who was in command of the expedition, came to the dwelling of the illustrious bishop. He bowed his head and said: "Gauzelin, have compassion on yourself and on your flock. We beseech you to listen to us, in order that you may escape death. Allow us only the freedom of the city. We will do no harm and we will see to it that whatever belongs either to you or to Odo shall be strictly respected." Count Odo, who later became king, was then the defender of the city. The bishop replied to Sigfried, "Paris has been entrusted to us by the Emperor Charles, who, after God, king and lord of the powerful, rules

over almost all the world. He has put it in our care, not at all that the kingdom may be ruined by our misconduct, but that he may keep it and be assured of its peace. If, like us, you had been given the duty of defending these walls, and if you should have done that which you ask us to do, what treatment do you think you would deserve?" Sigfried replied: "I should deserve that my head be cut off and thrown to the dogs. Nevertheless, if you do not listen to my demand, on the morrow our war machines will destroy you with poisoned arrows. You will be prey to famine and pestilence and these evils will renew themselves perpetually every year." So saying, he departed and gathered together his comrades.

In the morning the Northmen, boarding their ships, approached the tower and attacked it. They shook it with their engines and stormed it with arrows. The city resounded with clamor, the people were aroused, the bridges trembled. All came together to defend the tower. There Odo his brother Robert, and the Count Ragenar distinguished themselves for bravery; likewise the courageous Abbot Ebolus, the nephew of the bishop. A keen arrow wounded the prelate, while at his side the young warrior Frederick was struck by a sword. Frederick died, but the old man, thanks to God, survived. For many this was their last moment of life, but they inflicted bitter blows on many of the enemy. At the last the enemy withdrew, carrying off a vast number of Danish dead. Now Apollo, having followed Olympus, turned towards the west, to furthest Thule and the southern regions.

No longer did the tower appear as fine as it once did, but its foundations were still solid and it delighted a little in the windows that had been opened up to the sun. The people spent the night repairing the holes with boards. By the next day, on the old citadel had been erected a new tower of wood, a half higher than the former one. In the morning the sun and the Danes fell on the tower together. They engaged the [Christians] in violent skirmishes. On every side arrows sped and blood flowed. With the arrows mingled the stones hurled by catapults and war-machines; the air was filled with them. The tower which had been built during the night groaned under the strokes of the darts, the city shook with the struggle, the people ran hither and thither, the bells jangled. The warriors rushed together to defend the tottering tower and to repel the fierce assault.

Among these warriors two, a count and an abbot [Ebolus], surpassed all the rest in courage. The former was the redoubtable Odo who never experienced defeat and who continually revived the spirits of the worn-out defenders. He ran along the ramparts and hurled back the enemy. On those who were secreting themselves so as to undermine the tower he poured oil, wax, and pitch, which, being mixed and heated, burned the Danes and tore off their scalps. Some of them died; others threw themselves into the river to escape the awful substance....

Meanwhile Paris was suffering not only from the sword outside but also from a pestilence within which brought death to many noble men. Within the walls there was not enough ground in which to bury the dead.... Odo, the future king, was sent to Charles, emperor of the Franks, to implore help for the stricken city.

One day Odo, powerful with his arms, suddenly appeared on Montmartre in splendor in the midst of three bands of warriors. The sun made his armor glisten and greeted him before it illuminated the country around. The Parisians saw their beloved chief at a distance, but the enemy, hoping to prevent his gaining entrance to the tower, crossed the Seine and took up their position on the bank. Nevertheless Odo, his horse at a gallop, got past the Northmen and reached the tower, whose gates Ebolus opened to him. The enemy pursued fiercely the comrades of the count who were trying to keep up with him and get refuge in the tower...[The Danes were defeated in the attack.]

Now came the Emperor Charles [the Fat], surrounded by soldiers from many lands, even as the sky is adorned with resplendent stars. A great throng, speaking many languages, accompanied him. He established his camp at the foot of the heights of Montmartre, near the tower. He allowed *Fatty's* the Northmen to have the country of Sens to plunder; and in the spring he *concessions* gave them 700 pounds of silver on condition that by the month of March they leave France for their own kingdom. Then Charles returned [home]; he was not to live long.

Questions: Who are Abbo's heroes? How does his account differ from the annalist's? Is his language as formulaic?

72. Hincmar of Rheims, *On the Governance of the Palace*

With Charles the Bald dead, Hincmar of Rheims tried once again to elevate himself to a central role in the west Frankish kingdom, but it was dissolving even as he tried to remake it. Louis the Stammerer died in 879 and his son Louis III, under unusual circumstances, in 882. It was in 882 that Hincmar composed the following treatise on royal government for Carloman, Louis III's younger brother. The work was Hincmar's attempt to restore Carolingian royal government to the form it had under Louis the Pious. The reader will have to decide whether it is a nostalgic or realistic attempt. Since it is often claimed that Carolingian royal government failed because it lacked a sophisticated administrative system with which to govern such a vast territory, the reader might like to weigh the strengths and weaknesses of that government as it is described by the archbishop.

Source: trans. D. Herlihy, A History of Feudalism (New York: Harper & Row, 1970), pp.209-227; reprinted with permission.

The Admonition of Hincmar, archbishop of Rheims,
to the bishops and King Carloman, arranged in chapters.
Hincmar, bishop and servant of the people of God.

1. You have called upon my feeble powers, good and holy men, who are younger than am I in count of years and duration of holy orders. I was present at the deliberations concerning the church and palace, when the realm flourished in size and unity, and I then heard the counsels and the wisdom both of those who ruled the holy Church in sanctity and justice and of those who felicitously in these past times presided over the strength of the empire. By their instruction I learned the customs of our ancestors.

Moreover, after the death of the lord Emperor Louis [the Pious], I stayed in the service of those who sought for peace among his sons, who were at that time our kings. I worked for this as my puny strength allowed, in frequent journeys, addresses, and writings. You ask now that I should describe for the instruction of this young man, our new king, as well as for the restoration of the honor and the peace of the church and the kingdom, the governance of the church and the administration of the royal household within the sacred palace, as I heard of it and saw it. Thus, in his inexperience our king may advance in learning, and in governing the kingdom, he may please God, rule happily in this world, and from the present kingdom attain an eternal one. For we know by experience that a new vase once filled with savor and smell retains it for a long time. Just as a wise man [Horace] has said: "Once a new jug is imbued with a smell it holds it for long."

We have also read how Alexander in his youth had a tutor by the name of Leonidas, who was known for his loose morals and disorderly behavior. These faults the young boy absorbed from him like bad milk. Thus, in adulthood, the wise and brave king blamed himself and sought to mend his ways, but as the story relates, although he conquered all kingdoms, in this he was unable to conquer himself.

2. Therefore, the lord king should understand to what office he has been elevated, and he should pay close heed to the admonitions and the warning of the King of kings, who says to him as to other rulers: "And now, O ye kings, understand: receive instruction, ye who judge the earth. Serve ye the Lord with fear and rejoice unto him with trembling. Embrace discipline: lest at any time the Lord be angry, and you perish from the just way." As we have read that many who have ignored this admonition and warning have perished, so we read that it has happened even in our own days. He should also listen carefully to Holy Scripture which commands him, "Love justice, ye who are the judges of the earth. Think of the Lord in goodness and seek him in simplicity of heart. For wisdom will not enter into a malicious soul, nor dwell in a body subject to sins."

3. In response to the duty placed upon me and to your good and reasonable request, I therefore undertake the task you have set for me. I rely neither on my intelligence nor on my style but, as I said above, on the tradition of our ancestors, recalling the words of the Lord to the prophet: "And thou shall hear the word out of my mouth and shall tell it to them from me." From Me, he says, and not from you, because, as He says, "He that speaketh of himself seeketh his own glory." Holy Scripture imposes upon every official in every order and profession the obligation that he understand all that he says. If he understands the origin of the office which he occupies, he will want even more solicitously to render an accounting for the "talent" of the administration entrusted to him. We shall all stand before the tribunal of Christ, so that each of us will relate what we did in the flesh, both good and evil. May the king not hear from the just judge what the Lord, as told in the Gospel, said to the bad and lazy servant. Rather may he hear: "Well done, good and faithful servant, because thou hast been faithful over a few things, I will place thee over many things. Enter thou into the joy of thy

lord."

4. We read in Holy Scripture, in the Old Testament, that David, who was at once king and prophet, and who prefigures our Lord Jesus Christ, Who alone could have become both king and prophet, established two orders among the priests: that is the supreme pontiffs and the priests in lower orders, who now fulfill the office of priesthood. He made this provision in order that when any of the pontiffs departed this life, whosoever among the priests was considered the best should succeed him. And in the New Testament, our Lord Jesus Christ from the multitude of his disciples, as we read in the Gospel, chose twelve whom he named apostles. The place of these apostles the bishops hold in the church, as both Holy Scripture and the Catholic doctors demonstrate. He also designated seventy-two others who under the twelve apostles prefigure priests, that is, the ministers of the second rank. Thus, when bishops die, according to the sacred canon inspired by the Spirit of God and consecrated by the reverent observance of the entire world, persons from among these priests of second or of lower rank are elevated to the height of supreme priesthood in place of the departed bishops. This, Holy Scripture, in the Acts of the Apostles, clearly illustrates. Thus Peter, after the death of Judas, who was counted among the apostles and had received the apostolic commission, addressed his brethren: "Wherefore," he said, "it is fitting that he be among these men who have accompanied us all the time that the Lord Jesus came in and went out among us." The divine election singled out Matthias, who was counted with the eleven apostles.

5. And in the holy Book of Kings, we read that the chief of the priests anointed the kings to their office by holy unction. They set the crown signifying victory on the kings' heads and placed the book of the laws in their hands. Thus, they might know how to rule themselves, correct the wicked, and direct the good along the path of righteousness. As the blessed Pope Gelasius proved from the Holy Scripture to the Emperor Anastasius, and as was stated in the acts of the council recently held at the tomb of Saint Macra, there are two powers by which this world is principally ruled. Certain things are specifically given to the rule of one or the other. These are the sacred authority of the priests and royal power. Just as the names of the two orders are different, so also are the duties which the offices impose on those persons who hold them. Therefore, each should diligently pay heed in his order and his profession to the name by which it is known, and strenuously seek that in his office he act consistently with its name. First of all, as the blessed Cyprian said, the bishop should inquire after the meaning of the name of the office, the dignity of which he holds. "Bishop," a Greek name, means "watchman." The responsibility of a watchman, and what is required of him, were revealed by the Lord himself when, in the person of the prophet Ezekiel, he announced to the bishop the purpose of his office in these words: "I have made thee a watchman to the house of Israel." By his office the watchman incessantly proclaims by word and example to the people committed to him how they ought to live. Thus it is written concerning Christ, who commands that we follow, that is, imitate him: "These things Jesus began to do and to teach." The watchman ought, therefore, to pay close attention to the life

and the morals of those committed to him. After he has observed, he should try, if he can, to correct them by word and deed, and if he cannot, he ought to drive away, according to the evangelical rule, the perpetrators of iniquities.

6. The king ought to maintain within himself the dignity of his own name. For the name "king" intellectually signifies that he should fulfill the office of "corrector" for all his subjects. But how can he who does not correct his own morals be able to correct others when they are wicked? It is by the justice of the king that the throne is exalted, and by truth that the governments of people are strengthened. What the justice of the king is, the same blessed Cyprian abundantly showed in his treatise "Concerning the Twelve Abuses of the World" in regard to the ninth abuse.

7. The sacerdotal order possesses, to be sure, divinely promulgated laws indicating how a man may arrive at the height of government, that is, the episcopal office; how he who justly attains it ought to live; how he who lives well should teach; how he who teaches well ought to recognize his own weakness daily by much meditation; how he ought to rule the ministers placed under him; finally, with what pure intention he ought to confer the sacred ecclesiastical orders and with what discretion he ought to bind and loose his subjects. These same laws say concerning their own nature: "To no priest is it permitted to be ignorant of the canons or to do anything against those rules which the Fathers established." For there is no less guilt in violating holy tradition than in injuring the Lord himself. Since this is the case, as the sacred authority demonstrates, schism and heresy are related. In other words, the schismatic offends no less when by the denial of the holy rules he contemptuously separates himself from the unity of the holy church, which is the body of Christ, than does the heretic, who holds wrong opinions concerning God, the head of the church.

8. We have already said concerning the ecclesiastical laws that "to no priest is it permitted to be ignorant of the canons or to do anything against those rules which the Fathers established." Thus, it is ordained by sacred laws that no one may licitly remain ignorant of the laws or scorn what has been established. When it is said that no one may licitly remain ignorant of the laws or scorn what has been established, no person in any particular secular status is exempt; all are bound by this sentence. For the kings and the ministers of the commonwealth have made laws, which those acting in various provinces ought to apply. The rulers have established the capitularies of the Christian kings, their ancestors, which, with the general consent of their subjects, they have ordered to be lawfully maintained. Concerning these laws blessed Augustine says: "Although men may exercise a judgment concerning these things at the time they were enacted, nonetheless, once they are established and confirmed, it is not allowed to judges to judge concerning them, but only according to them."

9. It is even less permissible for a king than for anyone else, no matter what his station, to act contemptuously against the divine laws. Therefore, the prince of the land ought strenuously to provide and secure that God be not

offended in those persons who chiefly maintain the Christian religion and who keep others from offending. The king by divine judgment has received ecclesiastical property to defend and protect. Therefore, men should be elevated to the episcopal office with his consent, by the election of the clergy and people, and with the approval of the bishops of the province, without any intervention of money. For the Lord says in the Gospel: "He that entereth not by the door into the sheepfold but climbeth up another way, the same is a thief and a robber." In every respect, without obstinacy, he should honor the ecclesiastical laws, if he does not wish to offend the King of kings. The bishops and the king thus ought to make sure that a bishop is chosen by consideration of nothing save God alone, that is, not for reason of any gift or any human favor or kinship or friendship or temporal service or any consideration which is opposed to truth or to divine authority. So also the king, as Saint Augustine has shown, should take care lest by gifts or the praises of some scoundrel he is wheedled or deceived by flattery. Nor, out of any consideration of blood relationship or of carnal affection, should he spare those who act wickedly against God, the holy church, or the commonwealth. The spirit of God said through David and the prophet: "Have I not hated them, O Lord, that hated thee: and pined away because of thy enemies. I have hated them with a perfect hatred: and they are become enemies to me." To hate the enemies of God with a perfect hatred is to love the purpose of their creation but to condemn what they do, to repress the morals of the wicked, and thus to contribute to their salvation.

10. The king ought to appoint such counts and, under them, judges who hate greed and love justice. The counts and justices should conduct their administration in the same manner and appoint similar officials under them. Whoever, in every order and profession, is set in a position of power and is called a lord ought to possess the virtue of command with the assistance and help of God, as Saint Cyprian demonstrates in his tract "Concerning the Twelve Abuses of the World" in regard to the sixth abuse:

"It profits nothing to have the authority of commanding, if the lord himself does not have the strength or virtue. But this strength of virtue does not require external might, although this also is necessary to secular lords, but rather inner spiritual power. It ought to be practiced along with good morals. For often the power of commanding is lost by weakness of spirit. Three things are necessary for those who rule: fear, obedience, and love. For unless the lord is equally loved and feared, his commands will avail little. Through favors and friendliness, let him seek to be loved, and through just punishments, not for injury to himself but violations of the law of God, let him strive to be feared. Moreover, because many are dependent on him, he himself should adhere closely to God, who established him in his position of leadership and who, so to speak, fortified him to bear the burdens of many persons. For a peg, unless it is very strong and attached to something stronger than itself, quickly falls with everything hanging upon it. Thus also the prince, unless he tenaciously adheres to his Creator, will quickly perish and all that he supports."

Let a lord also know that, as he has been made first among men in leadership, so he will earn for himself in the future world unremitting punishment unless upon this present earth he corrects the sinners placed under him.

11. The acts of the council held at the tomb of Saint Macra which we have mentioned—salubrious, if they are respected and followed—contain briefly arranged by chapter the decrees of the Fathers of the church made in accordance with Holy Scripture, and the laws of the Christian kings, which concern the honor and the vigor of the holy church and her rulers, and those things which are relevant to the strength and maintenance of the king and kingdom, and likewise the administration of the royal household. Nonetheless, the Samaritan (that is, the true guardian of the human race) gave two pennies (that is, the Old and New Testaments) to the innkeeper (that is, the pontifical order), to whose care he committed the wounded man. He told him, "Whatsoever thou shalt spend over and above, I, at my return, will repay thee." In like manner, I shall seek to add what follows to the above acts, as if in additional payment beyond what has already been given in this book.

12. In my youth I knew Adalhard [see doc.32], an old and wise man, a relative of the Emperor Charlemagne, and abbot of the monastery of Corbie, who was first among the emperor's chief councillors. I read and I copied his work "On the Governance of the Palace." Among other things, it mentioned that the government of the entire kingdom rested chiefly on two principal divisions, excepting, of course, the eternal and ubiquitous judgment of almighty God. The first division, he said, assured the constant and unfailing rule and governance of the king's palace. The second by zealous attention assured the government of the entire realm, in its various aspects.

13. In that which concerns the first division, the palace of the king was organized in the following fashion, to the honor of the entire government. Excepting the king and the queen with their most noble family, the palace at all times was ruled both in spiritual and in secular or material things through these officers. First, there was the *apocrisiarius*, the one responsible for ecclesiastical affairs. This office took its origins from the time when the Emperor Constantine the Great became a Christian. He wished to give testimony of his love and respect for the saints Peter and Paul, through whose teaching and ministry he had come to obtain the grace of the sacrament of baptism. He therefore by edict granted his capital, that is, the city of Rome, to Pope Silvester [see doc.5]. He built his capital in that other city, adding his name to what was formerly called Byzantium. Thus, officers of both the see of Rome and the other principal sees from that time served continuously in the palace, holding the charge of ecclesiastical affairs.

14. The Apostolic See exercised this office sometimes through bishops and sometimes through deacons. Saint Gregory, when he was in the deaconate, held this office. The other principal sees similarly filled the office with deacons, as the sacred canons required. In these cisalpine regions, Saint Remi by his preaching converted Clovis to Christianity and on the vigil of Holy Easter baptized him together with three thousand Franks. Afterward, under succeeding kings, holy bishops left their sees at suitable times, stayed at the palace, and assumed this office. From the time of Pepin [the Short] and

Charles, this office was given at times to priests and at times to bishops, but by royal authority and with the consent of the bishops, priests filled it more frequently than bishops. For bishops are required to exercise a continuing supervision over their flocks and to guard them by example and word. According to the holy canons, they may not remain absent from their people for long.

15. According to the regulations promulgated from the sacred canons by Saint Gregory, bishops may not pointlessly stay in attendance at the praetorial palace, which today is more usually called the royal palace. They would thus incur condemnation, in acting against the canons entrusted to them at their ordination, and would lose their ecclesiastical office. Let us now give examples of both licit and illicit practice. At the time of Pepin and Charles, the priest Fulrad filled this office with the consent of the bishops; at the time of Charles, the bishops Engelramnus and Hildibold; at the time of Louis [the Pious], the priest Hilduin and, after him, Fulco, also a priest; finally, the bishop Drogo.

16. The *apocrisiarius*, whom we today call the chaplain or the guardian of the palace, had under his supervision and direction all the clergy of the palace. Associated with him was the archchancellor, who formerly was called *a secretis*. Under him were wise, intelligent, and faithful men, who were to record in writing the imperial commands without excessive desire for payment and would faithfully keep the royal secrets. Under these officers, the sacred palace was administered through these officials: the chamberlain, the count of the palace, the seneschal, the wine steward, the constable, the master of lodgings [*mansionarius*], four chief hunters, and one falconer.

17. Under them or associated with them were other officials, such as the porter, keeper of the purse, dispenser, and keeper of the utensils. Also some of these latter had subordinates or deacons, or others associated with them, such as wardens of the forest [*bersarii*], keepers of the kennels, hunters of beavers, and others in addition. Although each of these had a function in the palace according to his specialty, nonetheless, it was not upon them that the strength of the entire realm was dependent. Rather, as is stated below, the strength of the realm rested upon the other officers, in regard to the matters both great and small which occurred daily, whenever they were gathered at the palace. The great officers themselves were not equally useful, because of the diversity of their charges, their competence, and circumstances. Nevertheless, as has been stated, none of them was able to or wished to remove himself from the service of the king, in the interest of preserving true faith to the king and to the realm. Concerning these persons and their offices, much could be said; you have here at least the principal things.

18. First of all, according to the type or the importance of the office, the minister was to be chosen from among those of noble mind and body, stable, intelligent, discreet, and sober. Moreover, since by the grace of God the realm is formed by many regions, if it was possible, care was taken to select these officials from different regions, whether they were chosen for the first

or second rank or for any level. Access to the palace was thereby facilitated for all subjects, since they recognized that members of their own families or inhabitants of their own region had a place in the palace.

19. Since we have briefly discussed how the officials mentioned above were selected and appointed, now it is necessary to turn to the rank of the same ministers and their functions, that is, how their offices were carried out. Each of these officials of whom we have spoken held chief authority over his office. He was responsible to no one and acted for no one, unless it was for the king alone or, in some instances, for the queen and for the king's glorious family. Still, in matters which were not part of their responsibility or which concerned other persons, all of them did not have equal access to the king, but each was content with his own measure of functions and authority. When or where reason required it, they sought the help of another. At the highest rank, there were two officials. One was the apocrisiarius, whom we call the chaplain or the custodian of the palace. He had the constant supervision over all ecclesiastical matters and all ministers of the church. The other was the count of the palace, who had the care of all secular matters and decisions. Thus, neither clerics nor laymen needed to disturb the king unless they had the approval of these two. The officers would determine if the matter ought to be brought before the king. If the matter was secret and it was proper that the king be informed of it before anyone else, these officers arranged to give the interested party an opportunity for speaking. They would inform the king in advance so that he could receive the statement according to the status of the person, whether with honor or patience or also pity.

20. The *apocrisiarius* had supervision over everything which concerned the practices or the constitution of the church. He considered disputes relative to the canonical or monastic life, and questions of every sort regarding ecclesiastical affairs which reached the palace. He saw to it that only those external issues were brought to the king which without him could not be adequately settled. Further, he had responsibility over those things which especially concerned the honor or the services of the church within the palace. Moreover, whoever in the entire palace sought any spiritual consolation or advice found it without fail with him, as necessity required. If he discerned that anyone who did not request help of him still had need of it, he strove to rescue him from wicked thoughts and works and to turn him to the way of salvation, according to the station of the person. Other spiritual problems which had to be settled or anticipated and which arose among those who lived continuously in the palace or among visitors—it would be lengthy to enumerate them—whether regarding God or the world, pertained especially to his supervision. We do not mean to say that no one else, either of the palace or a visitor from outside, illuminated in wisdom and true devotion by the grace of God, contributed nothing in this regard. But it was the firm custom that no one did what was to be done without the participation, or at least the agreement, of the *apocrisiarius*, lest someone should by chance bring useless or unworthy matters before the king.

21. The count of the palace, among his other nearly innumerable duties, held chief responsibility for the just and reasonable settlement of all disputes which, although arising elsewhere, were brought to the palace for equitable decision. In the interest of equity, he also reversed bad judgments. By this he earned favor among all—with God for reason of his justice and among men for his observance of the laws. If a case was presented which the secular laws had not anticipated in their decrees or for which pagan custom demanded a crueller punishment than Christian rectitude or holy authority allowed, this was brought to the consideration of the king. Together with those conversant in both sacred and profane law, who feared the statutes of God more than those of human making, the king would make a decision which, if possible, would respect both laws. If this was not possible, the secular law would properly be suppressed and the justice of God respected.

22. The good management of the palace, and especially the royal dignity, as well as the gifts given annually to the officers (excepting, however, the food and water for the horses) pertained especially to the queen, and under her to the chamberlain. According to the circumstances, they always took care at an appropriate time to prepare for future events, lest something should be lacking at the time it was needed. The gifts given to the various legations were under the chamberlain's supervision, unless the matter was one which, by the king's command, was appropriate for the queen to handle together with the chamberlain. They gave attention to these and to similar things for this purpose, in order that the king, in so far as it could be accomplished reasonably and appropriately, might be freed of all concern for the household or the palace. Thus, continuously placing his hope in almighty God, he could keep his mind ever intent on the governance and preservation of the state of the entire realm.

23. To three officers—the seneschal, the wine steward, and the constable—each according to the function and importance of his office, fell this responsibility: by common agreement and according to their separate duties, they were not to be remiss in informing all local officials, as soon as possible, concerning the times, places, and seasons of the king's arrival, and the duration of his stay, so that they could collect and prepare what was needed. Otherwise, if the local officials learned of this too late and performed their duties at an impropitious time or with excessive haste, the royal party by such negligence might have been unnecessarily inconvenienced. Although these responsibilities fell upon both the wine steward and the constable, nevertheless the seneschal was chiefly concerned with them, since all other matters except water or fodder for the horses were his responsibility. The master of lodgings shared these duties with them. As his name indicates, his office had the supervision over, and the chief responsibility for informing, the local officials mentioned above and those known as "receivers" [*susceptores*], so that they would know at a suitable time, well in advance, when and in what place the king would arrive among them, in order that they might prepare the lodgings. Otherwise, if they learned too late, they would either sin through making excessive demands from their own dependents or, because of an unworthy reception, which occurred in spite of their wishes, they would still offend the

king, not by will but by performance.

24. Similarly, the four hunters and the fifth falconer, with the same unanimity, according to the season, had to arrange that those things which pertained to the spheres of their respective ministries were considered at an appropriate time and not too late. They had to determine how many hunters were to be kept at the palace at various times, when all should be present or all dismissed, and how many should be sent, in accordance with the usual custom, to be supported for a time outside the palace. They also at an appropriate time assigned men to designated places for the purpose equally of carrying on the hunt and nourishing themselves. Both the one duty and the other, that is, within the palace and outside, were to be done with moderation and prudence, so that what was profitable would be accomplished and what was not profitable would be omitted. In these offices, it is not possible easily to determine the appropriate number of men or of dogs or of falcons. Therefore, on their judgment rested the decision of determining how many and of what sort these men and animals should be.

25. In all these arrangements the purpose was that officials of sufficient number and type to take care especially of these and other needs and functions should never be missing from the palace. First of all, although these major officials or some of the minor ones might leave the palace for general, special, or private matters, nonetheless at all times the palace was to be adorned with worthy councillors and never deprived of them. Without a suitable number of such officials, it could not function reasonably and appropriately. Furthermore, legations of any sort which came to see the king or to submit to him might be appropriately received. Finally, a first councillor might provide just advice; a second the consolation of pity and kindness; and the language of a third might offer a correction to dishonesty or imprudence. From every part of the entire realm, anyone desolate, impoverished, oppressed by debts, overwhelmed by unjust accusations, or in similar situations which would be too long to enumerate, but especially widows and orphans, of both great men and small, each according to his need or situation, were always to have access to the mercy and the pity of the senior officers. Through one of the councillors, each person might hope to gain the pious ears of the prince.

26. Similarly, there were those who deserved reward for lengthy service, and arrangements were made that none of these needy persons was left entirely destitute. They were to be brought to the attention of the prince not by pleading with him directly but by calling upon the faith and duty of those officers mentioned above. This was to be done for them, first, because, the officers would please God with their justice and mercy. Second, the officers would assure among those remaining in the royal service a most steadfast fidelity and constancy in faithfully fulfilling their duties. Finally, they would make joyous and happy even those who lived at great distances within the borders of the realm. And if any of these officers or councillors died, a suitable and competent person was found to replace him.

27. In order that the large numbers which always had to be present in the

palace might be maintained without fail, they were divided into three classes. In the first class were found those servants who were without special responsibilities. The kindness and concern of the senior officers provided them with food or clothing or gold or silver, sometimes too with horses or other gifts, both on particular occasions, as time, reason, and propriety allowed them, and also at regular intervals, which was the more usual custom. Thus, these servants never lacked support, and they always held even closer to their hearts the royal service, because the chief officers rivaled one another by daily inviting now some servants, and then others, to their houses. There the chief officers sought to establish close relations with them, not by feeding their hungry stomachs but by sentiments of friendship and love, according to their ability. Because of the officers' zeal in this regard, rarely was there found a servant who remained one week without receiving from anyone an invitation.

28. The second class consisted of those young men in the various offices who, closely following their master, both honored him and were honored by him. Each of them, according to circumstances, might gain encouragement in his post by the observation of and conversation with the lord. The third class consisted of those young servants or vassals [*pueris vel vasallis*], whom both the greater and lesser officials zealously sought to have, to the extent that they were able to manage them and support them without sin, that is, without plunder or robbery. In these classes we have mentioned, even apart from those who were always coming to and going from the palace, there was this satisfaction. Their numbers were always adequate for any need which at times might unexpectedly occur. Finally, as we mentioned above, the greater part of them, because of the favors to them already described, always remained cheerful, quick to smile, and intellectually alert.

29. This is the second division, by which the status of the entire realm was maintained, as much as pertained to human reason, always and everywhere excepting the judgment of the omnipotent God. At that time the custom was followed that no more than two general assemblies were to be held each year. The first assembly determined the status of the entire realm for the remainder of the year. No turn of events, saving only the greatest crisis which struck the entire realm at once, could change what had been established. All the important men, both clerics and laymen, attended this general assembly. The important men came to participate in the deliberations, and those of lower station were present in order to hear the decisions and occasionally also to deliberate concerning them, and to confirm them not out of coercion but by their own understanding and agreement. Moreover, all classes were present in order to provide gifts [to the king].

30. The other assembly was held with the important men only and the principal councillors. This assembly began the consideration of the affairs of the coming year. It deliberated over some matters which seemed likely to occur and which called for consideration and action, or over the events of the past year which might require decision or further attention. For example, if the margraves in some part of the realm had made treaties lasting a certain time,

what should be done immediately after the period of the treaties had expired? Should they be renewed or terminated? If war or peace involving certain areas was imminent, and if attacks had to be launched or withstood here and there in some regions, peace was to be established in other areas, as reason might then demand. These same men held council and determined well in advance what the actions or the policy of acting in the future was to be. Once the decision was reached, it was to be kept in silence and to remain thoroughly unknown to all others until the second general assembly, just as if the decision had been discussed by no one. Thus, if perchance a decision had been reached concerning affairs within or without the realm, and certain persons in their foreknowledge might wish to overturn it or to render it fruitless, or through any other ruse obstruct its execution, they were in no way capable of doing this. In such instances, in the second general assembly, whether to satisfy the remaining important persons or to placate or to arouse the spirits of the people, the decision was taken again, with new deliberations and with the consent of the participants, just as if nothing had been settled earlier concerning it. Thus, with the participation of the important persons and under the leadership of God, the policy would be carried. At the end of the first year, the ordinances for the second were to be enacted in the manner described above.

31. In so far as was possible, councillors, both clerical and lay, were chosen from those who, each according to his character and office, showed a fear of God. They were also to have such fidelity that, with the exception of eternal life, they valued nothing more than the king and the realm, neither friends nor enemies, nor relatives, nor those who offered gifts, nor flatterers, nor those who made threats. They were to be wise, not in a misleading or deceptive fashion, nor according to the wisdom exclusively of this world, which is an enemy to God, but they were to be learned in that wisdom and intelligence which might enable them not only to repress those who placed their hopes in the human trickery mentioned above but to confound them entirely in their own just and right wisdom. Those councillors agreed among themselves and with the king that whatever they had discussed in confidence, whether it concerned the state of the realm or any particular person, ought not to be mentioned by any of them to a servant or to any other individual, without their consent, not for one day or two days or more or a year but forever. For it frequently happens in these matters that in order to advance or preserve the general good, the discussion sometimes touches upon a particular person, who when learning of it is either greatly disturbed or, what is more serious, falls into despair or, worst of all, turns to treason. The knowledge thus renders useless for all profit a person who perhaps could have done countless services; he would not, however, have been the least upset if he had known nothing concerning the discussion. What may happen concerning a single man may also occur concerning two or a hundred or a greater number or an entire family or even a whole province, if great precaution is not taken.

32. The *apocrisiarius*, that is, the chaplain or the guardian of the palace, and the chamberlain were always present at the councils, and they therefore were

chosen with the greatest care or, once chosen, were so instructed that they could participate with profit. If a person was found among the other officials who manifested such qualities that by learning and later by giving advice he might sooner or later replace the great officers mentioned above, he was ordered to be present at all the deliberations and to concentrate with the greatest attention upon what was done, keeping to himself what was told him, learning what he did not know, and preserving what was ordained and established. Thus, if by chance an event occurred either within the realm or beyond its borders, or something unforeseen was announced, for which no plans had been made, rarely was it necessary that the matter be treated in the general assembly; moreover, time might not allow that the great men be summoned. Then the palatine officials, by the mercy of God, relying on their close acquaintance both with public councils and with similar discussions, answers, and consultations within the household, might act with dispatch, in accordance with the nature of the affair or the time. They might either fully determine what ought to be done or at least settle how the affair might be postponed or held in suspense without any loss for a determined period. These things regard the major affairs.

33. Concerning minor affairs or those which especially concerned the palace—not, as we have said, regarding the realm in general but touching especially those particular persons who were attached to the palace—the lord king was clearly to arrange with the palatine officials that no loss would be suffered or, if loss had occurred or was imminent, it might be lessened, entirely extinguished, and eradicated. If, however, the case was one which demanded speed, but which might by some means and without sin or prejudice be held in suspense until the general assembly, they were to advise on the means of suspending it, in a manner similar to that use in important matters. Imitating the wisdom of the great men, they were in the meantime to give recommendations which would be pleasing to God and beneficial to the realm. The policy of the great men when they were summoned to the palace was directed toward this especially, that they would not deliberate concerning special or private cases, no matter what they were or who were the persons involved, nor did they hear appeals in contests which were brought concerning facts or law, but they first settled with the mercy of God those things which pertained to the general welfare or the state of the king and the realm. When this was finished, they then considered whatever had been reserved for them, upon order of the king, which the count of the palace or the other officials in whose competence the cases fell could not themselves settle without the aid of their careful consideration.

34. Whether in one or the other of the general assemblies mentioned above, lest it appear that they were summoned needlessly, the important persons and the senior advisors of the realm were given by royal authority, for their discussion and consideration, the decisions which the king through the inspiration of God had made, and the information which he had learned from every quarter since their last meeting. These documents [capitularies] were titled and arranged in chapters. Having received the chapters, the great men deliberated sometimes one day, sometimes two, three or more days, according

to the importance of the affair. With the aid of messengers chosen from the servants of the palace mentioned above, they proposed questions to the king and received responses on all matters which seemed appropriate to them. However, no stranger joined them until the individual matters, concerning which a decision had been made, were related to the king and placed under his sacred eyes and until all had agreed with whatever he chose to do in the wisdom given him by God. This then is the way in which one, or two, or any number of chapters were handled until, by the mercy of God, all questions which the times had posed were settled.

35. Meanwhile, while these things were being done in the absence of the king, he himself was occupied with the remaining throng, receiving presents, greeting important persons, chatting with those rarely seen, sympathizing with the aged, rejoicing with the young, and engaging in similar activities, in regard to both spiritual and temporal affairs. Nevertheless, as often as those withdrawn in council wished it, the king would go to them and remain with them for as long as they desired. They then in all friendliness told him how they had found individual matters; they frankly related what they had discussed on one side and the other, in disagreement or argument or friendly rivalry. It should also be noted that if the weather was pleasant, the assembly was held out of doors. If it was held indoors, different places were designated where the important persons could gather in sufficient number and could hold their meetings, separate from the remaining throng; other, less important persons were then unable to participate in the deliberations. In either case, however, the meeting place of the great men was divided into two sections. In the first, all the bishops, abbots, and more exalted clerics could meet without any lay participation. Similarly, the counts and the princes of comparable rank could honorably gather in the morning apart from the other throng, for the time needed, in either the presence or the absence of the king. Thus the great men in the accustomed manner were summoned, the clerics to their own designated hall, the laymen to their own hall, both of which were suitably furnished with seats. When the great men were separated from the other, they had the power of deciding when they should sit together and when separately, as the nature of the case dictated, whether it concerned spiritual or secular or mixed issues. So also it was in their discretion to summon outsiders, as for example, when they wished provisions or when they wanted to pose questions. Once answers were received, those summoned would depart. This is what happened when those matters which the king above wished to have considered were presented to them.

36. The second interest of the king was to interview persons coming from all parts of the realm, to learn if they brought with them information worthy of consideration. Not only was this allowed, but it was also strictly enjoined upon the participants. Before coming, each was to inquire with the greatest diligence into both internal and external affairs. Each was to collect information concerning any relevant matter not only from his own people but from strangers and from both friends and enemies, with no attention paid or close consideration given to the type of person from whom the information was gained. If the people in any part, region, or corner of the realm ap-

peared agitated, he was to learn the cause of the disturbance, and also if the people were grumbling or the sound of any other upset was echoing, or if similar events were happening which might require the attention of the general assembly. Concerning foreign affairs, he was to make inquiry whether any subjugated people was rebelling or a rebellious people had surrendered or a people not yet conquered seemed to be preparing an attack against the realm or if any other similar occurrence had taken place. He was especially to discover in all matters which presented a certain danger what were the causes for these or other disturbances.

37. In devoted obedience to your request I have offered to you these remarks concerning the governance of the palace and the rule of the kingdom, for the instruction of our king and his ministers and officers of the realm. As I learned them from the writings and words of my elders, and as I myself personally observed them in my youth, I have given them as a supplement to those stipulations collected from the decrees of our ancestors and offered to King Louis [III], recently deceased. It shall be your responsibility to find the persons who, through their moral stature and high qualities, may restore those institutions which now have decayed. I know that no one is now alive of those whom I saw serving as officers of the palace and of the realm in the days of the lord emperor Louis [the Pious]. However, I do know that sons were born to replace these fathers from their own families, although I am unfamiliar with their morality and their qualities. May they seek not to be deficient in morals, virtue, wisdom, and the liberal arts, as their years and the times may allow. Thus they may deservedly fill the places and positions of their fathers. In assuming those places let them prudently take care, lest, as Saint Gregory says, those placed at the pinnacle of honor should be corrupted by the close touch of glory, just as Saul, a humble man before his elevation to a post of honor, later deserved reprimand because of his swollen pride.

Questions: Could one, based on Hincmar's treatise, make a chart of the officers of Louis the Pious's palace and the way in which power and responsibility flowed? Hincmar describes the palace structure of the 880s as having suffered utter decay, yet only forty years before (and perhaps a mere ten under Charles the Bald) it had been vigorous and efficient. What would explain this collapse? Who were the most important officers in the Carolingian palace? If a subject had a grievance how did he or she take it to the king?

73. Notker the Stammerer Addresses Charles the Fat

Notker was a monk of Saint-Gall and a poet. He was commissioned by Charles the Fat to narrate the deeds of Charlemagne, but the emperor seems to have wanted to hear how Charlemagne had dealt with a demanding episcopate. Notker's book, although it provides some novel information on Charlemagne, also tells us a great deal about the expectations of Charles the Fat and his time. Notker tugs at the emperor's heart-strings when he alludes to Charles's desire for a legitimate heir, since in 884 when Notker was writing Charles still had only an illegitimate son Bernard. Notker casts a wry eye on the past, even while recounting Charles the Fat's family history.

Source: trans. P.E. Dutton, from Notker der Stammler, Taten Kaiser Karls des Grossen, ed. H.F. Haefele, in Monumenta Germaniae Historica: Scriptores Rerum Germanicarum, nova series, vol. 12 (Berlin, 1959), pp.1, 22, 47, 68, 74, 78, 80-81.

1.1. The almighty Arranger of all things and the Orderer of kingdoms and times, when he had smashed to bits the iron and clay feet of that wonderful statue among the Romans, erected a golden head by means of glorious Charlemagne on another, no less wonderful statue among the Franks [the image is biblical].

1.18. I greatly fear, O lord Emperor Charles [the Fat], lest, while I want to fulfill your command, I manage to offend all the ecclesiastical orders, particularly the higher priests [that is, the bishops]. But, nevertheless, all these [critical] churchmen do not concern me, so long as I have your protection.

1.34. I am by nature rather indolent and slower than a turtle, since I have never journeyed to Francia [proper]. [Still] I saw the radiant chief of the Franks [Charles the Fat in 883] in the monastery of Saint-Gall. From his thighs two golden-haired flowers poked out. One of these rose up to equal his height. The other, rising up gradually, adorned the peak of his body with greatest glory and covered him as he passed by [me].

2.11. To the gentiles all around [Charlemagne] became more and more formidable than any of his ancestors, and worthily so, of course, since he never [went back] on his word in judgment and never stained his hands with Christian blood except once out of necessity [perhaps Notker is thinking of Charlemagne's slaughter of the Saxons, but they were not Christian at the time]. I am unwilling to tell that story before I see some little Louis or Charles standing beside you.

2.12. I shall not finish telling the story [of the destruction of the monastery of Prüm] before I see your Bernard [Charles's illegitimate son] wearing a sword on his thigh [that is, when he had reached manhood].

2.14. Let this never come to pass [an attack of the Northmen as Charlemagne had once helplessly witnessed.] Let the guardianship of our Lord Christ prevent it. Let your [own] sword, hardened with Norse blood, resist it. Let the blade of your brother Carloman, soaked in Norse blood, be joined with yours. Now, not because of fear, but because of a lack of prosperity and a want of lands for your most faithful [Arnulf], Carloman's sword is turning to rust. All the same by the command and the will of your power it should not be so difficult for that sword to be brought back sharp and shining. Aside from that tiny splinter Bernard [his son], only one small bough [Arnulf] now sprouts, under the solitary treetop of your protection, from that once most bountiful root of Louis [the German]. Meanwhile let me introduce something concerning your [great]-great-grandfather Pepin [the Short] into this history of Charlemagne, so that, with the clemency of God granting it, sometime soon a future little Charles or little Louis of your own might imitate it.

2.16. Indeed, O august emperor, I had proposed to unravel a short little narrative of your great-grandfather Charlemagne—all the things he did are [now] known to you. But since the occasion presented itself, it seemed necessary to say something about your glorious and illustrious father Louis [the German], and something about your most religious grandfather, Louis the Pious, and something about your most warlike [great]-great-grandfather Pepin the Younger [the Short]. About these men there has been a thundering silence, because of the laziness of modern writers, but I believed that it would be execrable to leave all of those deeds [of theirs] unmentioned.

Questions: Why did Charles the Fat want to hear funny stories about bad and duplicitous bishops? Does Notker suspect that time is running out for Charles and the Carolingian line? What images express his sense of finality?

74. The Saxon Poet's Thoughts on Charlemagne

The Saxon Poet wrote his metrical life of Charlemagne around 888. He drew primarily from Einhard's biography, but at the end of his work he reflected on his own time and on his own people. The cult of Charlemagne that had been building throughout the ninth century reached a crossroads in the 880s as Notker remembered a playful, popular Charlemagne and the Saxon Poet recalled the august perfection of Einhard's Charlemagne. Still the very fact that a Saxon, whose people had been pagan and entirely Germanic until Charlemagne conquered them, could have written a Christian Latin poem a century later is tribute in itself to the penetration of the Carolingian educational reform and to the achievements of Carolingian civilization.

Source: trans. M.E. McKinney, The Saxon Poet's Life of Charles the Great (New York: Pageant Press, 1956), pp.85-86, 103-104; reprinted with permission.

[from Book 5]

Heart-torn muses, compose now a song of mourning, for this year is worthy of many tears. Covering the preceding forty-three years what has been written except the prosperity of Charles? Of that period it was fitting to write with a happy pen his annual exploits and various triumphs. But now logical order and sequence of time compel us, even though sorrowing, to tell about the death of so great a man. Here elegies in the true sense of that word make their plaintive note; it is not necessary to compose some sad fiction; the very subject matter itself has its own appeal to our emotions. Who, when he reflects what kind of a person Charles was, would not mourn and grieve that such splendor as he represented would now be gone from the world? But the following fact is the sole comfort of the faithful whom death has ever robbed of their own loved ones; they believe happily that these departed ones, by virtue of their own just acts, are sharers of the heavenly kingdom. Therefore, it is pleasing for us to sing of the good that Charles wrought, in return for which we think that he is living with Christ.

My bold barbarian language takes up this great subject with the strength of slender genius; but great love, which is the true author of this poem, does not permit me to be silent, even though I do not know how to express it. I owe Charles an ever-ardent love and a perpetual homage, for it was he who caused my nation to know the light of faith and to cast off the darkness of perfidy, by his battles over how long a period, by suffering how many dangers, by what hard work, and by what zealous watching! Almost all the peoples of Europe remember his great effort even to this day, because they shared in it. Indeed he assembled all the forces of his kingdom to draw us away from pagan religion. What man could subdue fierce barbarism by the address of exhorting dogma? The good God brought this to pass through the agency of Charles; and it could not have been accomplished otherwise. Charles, by using a twofold method, persuaded the stony hearts of the Saxons to yield to the Lord; now frightening them with war, now enticing them with gifts, being very magnanimous in the former, and very generous in the latter. He did not give up until all Saxony had thrown away her idols and become faithful. What thanks are we Saxons as a nation able to express, according to his own little measure? If no little spark of letters or any tiny knowledge or art illumines my mind, shall I not justly give to Charles a eulogy of praise, since it was through him that I was privileged to acquire this good? Our parents were unacquainted not only with the documents of faith, but were totally ignorant in respect to all writings. Recently through Charles the integrity of this life and the hope of eternal life has been given us....

Therefore, you who read the wonderful acts of Charles, cease to marvel at the histories of the ancients. Neither the Decii nor the Scipios were greater than Charles; not Camillus not Cato not Caesar. Neither Pompey nor the Fabian family ready to die for native land is ranked ahead of Charles in merit. Perhaps they had earthly glory equal to his, but now Charles holds the pinnacle of celestial honor. He has great distinction for the virtue that David, Constantine, and Theodosius exemplified. David rejoiced because he conquered the ancient enemy and snatched many from his snares; Constantine and Theodosius rejoiced that thousands of souls had been saved through the presence of the same virtue, by thy grace, O Christ! Who can say how many souls Charles returned to the Lord, when he caused the Saxons to believe in Him? As many as are the churches that now shine where the ancients used to worship pagan temples; as many as are the monasteries that have been built; as many as are the praises and prayers that are offered up by the faithful in these buildings; just so many will be the rewards, O Christ, which Thou shall give to Charles! When the final day of the great judgment comes, when Thou, Christ, will render to each one his due reward, O how happy will he be when he presents the talents entrusted to him, now increased many times with great gain. No one will be able to be nearer to the apostolic band than Charles, as the fact itself proves. Peter will advance followed by the Jewish throng, whose dogma he believed; Paul, if one dare say it, will lead the nations of the whole earth, saved through his spoken message. Andrew will lead forth in his train the Greek people; John will present the churches of Asia; Matthew, the Ethiopians made white as snow by baptism; Thomas will lead the horde of Indians to heaven; then the throng of rejoicing Saxons will follow Charles, a glorious source of eternal joy to him. O may I follow at the end of the procession of all of those of our people who were saved. And if, O Christ, by virtue of Thy pity Thou art willing, transferest Thou me, a goat, from the left to join me with the sheep on the right, in order that I may there sing the lays of no mortal song to Thee, but may be able to voice thy eternal praise.

Questions: Why would a Saxon poet sing such praise of his people's conqueror? What does he personally thank Charlemagne for?

75. The Vision of Charles the Fat

In 886-887, after his disastrous performance in Paris, Charles the Fat retreated to eastern Francia. There he plotted to divorce his barren wife and attempted to adopt Louis of Provence, the son of Boso and Ermengard. Indeed Ermengard was herself the daughter of Louis II, the emperor of Italy. But, in 887 Arnulf of Carinthia, the illegitimate son of Carloman of Bavaria, Charles the Fat's brother, perhaps worried by Charles's latest move to remake his family, deposed the emperor. In 888, stripped of power and privilege, Charles the Fat, the last of Charlemagne's legitimate and mature line, died. The Vision of Charles the Fat was probably composed not long afterwards at Rheims in the circle of Archbishop Fulk. In it there is what must seem to the modern reader to be a rather desperate attempt to uphold and preserve a beleaguered royal line.

Source: trans. P.E. Dutton, from Visio Karoli, ed. G. Waitz, in Monumenta Germaniae Historica: Scriptores, vol. 10 (Hanover, 1852), p.458.

In the name of highest God, King of kings, I, Charles the emperor, by the grace of God, king of the Germans, patrician of the Romans, and emperor of the Franks.

On the holy night of the Lord's day, after celebrating the divine service of the evening hours, when I went to bed for some rest and wanted to snatch some sleep, a voice [suddenly] called out, saying: "Charles, your spirit will now leave you [that is, your body] and you will see the just judgments of God and some predictions meant for you. After no little time has passed, however, your spirit will again return to you."

At once I was seized in spirit and he who took me away was brilliantly white and he held in his hand a ball of thread emitting a ray of the purest light, just as comets do when they appear. He began to unravel that thread and said to me, "Take a thread of this shining ball and [first] wind it and [then] tie it firmly to the thumb of your right hand, since by it you are to be led through the labyrinthine punishments of the lower regions." Having said this, he proceeded before me, rapidly unravelling the brilliant ball of thread. He led me into the deepest, fiery valleys, which were full of pits burning with tar, sulphur, lead, wax, and oil.

There I found bishops of my father and of my uncles. In horror I asked them why they were suffering such awful torments. They responded: "We were the bishops of your father and of your uncles, but rather than preach and admonish them and their people about peace and concord, as we should have, we sowed discord and promoted evil. For that reason we are now burning in this infernal punishment, we and other lovers of murder and rapine. To this place too will come your bishops and the people of your ministers, who likewise even now love to do these things."

While I overheard these things, shaking in fear, demons all black in color swept down and with iron hooks tried to grab hold of the thread of that ball which I held in my hand and to drag me towards them, but they were not able to latch onto that thread with its bouncing rays of light. Next, they ran behind my back and tried to hook me, and throw me over into those sulphurous pits. But my guide, who held the [main] ball of thread, threw a thread of the ball around my shoulders, doubled it, and with force dragged me after him.

Then we climbed up tremendously high mountains raging with fire, from which marshes and rivers burning and boiling with all kinds of metal flowed. There I discovered the countless souls of the men and magnates of my father and my brothers thrown in, some up to their hair, others up to their chins, and others up to their waists, and they cried, screaming: "While we lived, we loved with you, your father, your brothers, and your uncles to engage in war and to commit murder and rapine in the name of earthly greed. Thus we now suffer these torments in these rivers boiling with all sorts of metals."

While I, full of fear, listened to these words, I heard behind me souls crying out, "The powerful suffer powerfully in punishment." As I looked back, I saw upon the banks of that boiling river furnaces with tar and sulphur that were overflowing with great dragons, scorpions, and snakes of all kinds. There I also saw some of my father's magnates, some of my uncles', some of my brothers', and some of my own. They said to me, "Alas for us, Charles, you see what awful punishment we suffer because of our evil and our pride, and because of the wicked advice we gave to our kings and to you, all for the sake of greed." While they were groaning sadly [as they suffered] these torments, dragons, with their jaws wide open and full of fire, sulphur, and tar, flew towards me and tried to swallow me. But my guide tripled the thread of the ball around me even more tightly. Those fiery mouths were overwhelmed by the rays of that pure light and [my guide] pulled me out very forcefully.

Then we descended into a valley that was dark on one side, but hot as if a furnace of fire [burned there]. The other side was so pleasant and splendid that I am unable to describe it. I turned towards the dark side which spewed flames, and there I saw some kings of my [royal] line suffering in great torment. Seized by an overwhelming fear, I thought that I was to be thrown into that torment then and there by some great black giants who set that valley aflame with every kind of fire.

I was trembling a great deal, but I saw—since the light of that ball of thread shone before my eyes—a light briefly illuminate one portion of the valley. There I saw two fountains flowing, one extremely hot, the other clear and mild. There I saw two large vessels. When I went there, the thread of that ball leading the way [in the dark], I looked upon the vessel containing the boiling water, and there I saw my father, Louis [the German] standing up to his thighs. Louis, overcome with immense pain and disturbed by anguish, said to me: "Have no fear, my lord Charles. I know that your spirit will again return to your body and that God has allowed you to come to this place to see for what great crimes I and those others you have seen endure these torments. For one day I stand in this vessel of boiling bathwater, and on the next I pass over into that other vessel filled with the gentlest water. This happens because of the prayers of Saint Peter and Saint Remi, under whose patronage our royal line has hitherto reigned. If you, my faithful bishops and abbots, and the whole ecclesiastical order will come to my assistance with Masses, offerings, psalms, vigils, and charity, I will soon be released from this vessel of boiling water. For my brother Lothar and his son Louis [II] were freed from these punishments because of the prayers of Saint Peter and Saint Remi, and they have already been led over to the joys of God's paradise." Then he said to me, "Look to your left." When I did, I saw two very tall vessels filled with boiling water. "Those," he said, "have been prepared for you in case you do not change and fail to perform penance for your wretched sins."

Then I began to shake violently. When my guide saw my spirit in such grave terror, he said to me, "Follow me to the right side, to that most radiant valley of paradise." As we went, I observed sitting among other glorious kings placed in the brilliant light my uncle Lothar who was seated upon an immense topaz rock and crowned with a precious diadem. Close to him sat his son Louis similarly crowned. Seeing me close by, [Lothar] called me over and said in a great kind voice: "Come here, Charles. You are the third successor to me in the empire of Romans. I realize that you came through the place of punishment where your father, my brother, is placed in those warm baths set out for him. By God's mercy he will very shortly be released from that punishment as we [already] have been because of the merits of Saint Peter and the prayers of Saint Remi, to whom God gave great office over the kings and the whole population of Franks. If [Remi] does not support and assist the remnants of our family, our [royal] line will soon cease having power in the kingdom and in the empire. Thus, you should know that the power of the empire will soon be removed from your hand and that you will live but a very short time." Then Louis turned towards me and said, "Louis, the son of my daughter [Ermengard] should receive, by hereditary right, the empire which you have held till now." After he said this, the little boy Louis seemed to appear before me instantly. Then his [great]-grandfather Lothar looking upon the boy, said to me, "This child is like the one our

Lord set down in the midst of his disciples, and said, 'The kingdom of heaven belongs to such children. I say unto you that angels there always behold the face of my Father who is in heaven'. Through the thread of the ball that you hold in your hand, return the power of the empire to that child." Untying the thread from the thumb of my right hand, I gave him, by means of that thread, the whole government of the empire, and immediately the entire brilliant ball rolled up in his hand as if it were a ray of the sun. After this wondrous event, my spirit was returned to my body in an extremely fatigued and frightened condition.

Therefore let everyone know, whether they are willing to hear it or not, that the entire empire will pass into the hands of that boy according to the design of God. Know also that I am unable to act on his behalf, since the moment of my death is almost upon me. God who rules the living and the dead will complete and confirm [that translation of power], for his kingdom is eternal and sempiternal and will remain without end throughout the ages. Amen.

Questions: How is the dream text structured and what is the nature of its language? For whose benefit must it have been written? Why would the author choose to support a transfer of power through a dream text?

76. Last Thoughts

One has the feeling that at the end of the ninth century, some annalists and observers of the time recognized that the Carolingian order was passing and they tried to express their recognition of these changed conditions. If the contemporary annalist of Fulda merely summarizes the changing players on the scene, he knows that royalty itself was by 888 a diminished thing. Regino of Prüm, writing in the first decade of the tenth century, goes further: he makes a historical judgment on the passage of Carolingian power. In both cases, these men thought about the end of Carolingian royal power when they thought about the passing of Charles the Fat.

1. The Annals of Fulda on the New Political Order in 888

Source: trans. P.E. Dutton, from Annales Fuldenses sive Annales Regni Francorum Orientalis, ed. G.H. Pertz and F. Kurze, in Monumenta Germaniae Historica: Scriptores Rerum Germanicarum in Usum Scholarum (Hanover, 1891), p.116.

At that time many kinglets rose up in Europe in the kingdom of Arnulf's cousin Charles [the Fat]. For Berengar, son of Eberhard, makes himself king in Italy. Rudolf, son of Conrad, determined to hold on to upper Burgundy by himself in the fashion of a king. Louis [of Provence], son of Boso, and Wito, son of Landbert, therefore, decided to hold the Belgian parts of Gaul and also Provence like kings. Odo, son of Robert, usurped for his use the land up to the Loire River or the province of Aquitaine. Ramnulf [of Aquitaine] thereafter set himself up as king.

2. Regino's Reasons for the End of the Carolingian Line

Source: trans. P.E. Dutton, from Reginonis abbatis Prumiensis Chronicon, ed. F. Kurze, in Monumenta Germaniae Historica: Scriptores Rerum Germanicarum in Usum Scholarum (Hanover, 1890), p.129.

After Charles [the Fat's] death, the kingdoms which had obeyed his will, as if devoid of a legitimate heir, were loosened from their bodily structure into parts and now awaited no lord of hereditary descent, but each set out to create a king for itself from its own inner parts. This event roused many impulses towards war, not because Frankish princes, who in nobility, strength, and wisdom were able to rule kingdoms, were lacking, but because among themselves an equality of generosity, dignity, and power increased discord. No one so surpassed the others that they considered it fitting to submit themselves to follow his rule. Indeed Francia would have given rise to many princes fit to govern the kingdom had not fortune in the pursuit of power armed them for mutual destruction.

Questions: What was wrong with self-made kings and 'kinglets'? Is there any truth to Regino's opinion about the reasons for the demise of the Carolingian line?

A drawing [after Vétault] of the statue made in 1867 by Louis Rochet for the Universal Exposition in Paris. The piece stands today near the Cathedral of Notre-Dame in Paris. The grizzled Charlemagne belongs to The Song of Roland and to legend, but even by 900 the legends of Charlemagne and the Carolingians were already beginning to take shape in the European imagination.

Index of Topics

Topics are listed by document number and, in some instances, by books and sections or chapters within that document. Thus 41.12 is a reference to document 41, which is the correspondence of Einhard, and to letter 12. If the topic surfaces several times within a document, no section or chapter number is given. Thus 41 is a simple reference to Einhard's letters.

Acknowledgement of Sources in Copyright

CHAPTER ONE

1. A List of Superstition and Pagan Practices, beginning on page 3 is taken from: trans. J.T. McNeil and H.M. Gamer, *Medieval Handbooks of Penance* (New York: Columbia University Press, 1938). pp. 419-21, reprinted with permission.
2. The Correspondence of Boniface, Missionary and Martyr, beginning on page 4: trans. E. Emerton *The Letters of Saint Boniface* (New York: Octagon Books, 1973), pp.43-45, 47, 78-83, 157-79; reprinted with permission.
4. The Reanointing of Pepin in 754 , beginning on page 12: trans. B. Pullan, *Sources for the History of Medieval Europe from the Mid-Eighth to the Mid-Thirteenth Century* (New York: Barnes & Noble, 1966), pp.7-8; reprinted with permission.

CHAPTER TWO

11. The Lateran Palace of Pope Leo III , beginning on page 50: trans. C. Davis-Weyer, *Early Medieval Art, 300-1150*, in Sources & Documents in the History of Art, ed. H.W. Janson (Englewood Cliffs, New Jersey: Prentice-Hall, 1971), pp.88-92; reprinted with permission.
13.2. The General Capitulary for the *Missi* from 802, beginning on page 61: trans. D. Herlihy in *The History of Feudalism* (New York: Harper & Row, 1970), p.87; reprinted with permission.
13.4. Relating to Vassalage, beginning on page 74: trans. D. Herlihy in *The History of Feudalism* (New York: Harper & Row, 1970), p.87; reprinted with permission.
15. The Iconodule Controversy in Francia, beginning on page 84: trans. C. Davis-Weyer, *Early Medieval Art, 300-1150*, in Sources & Documents in the History of Art, ed. H.W. Janson (Englewood Cliffs, New Jersey: Prentice-Hall, 1971), pp.100-103; reprinted with permission.
18. Theodulf of Orléans: Precepts for the Priests of his Diocese, beginning on page, 94: trans. G.E. McCracken with A. Cabaniss in *Early Medieval Theology*, vol. 9 of The Library of Christian Classics (Philadelphia: Westminster Press, 1957), pp.382-399; reprinted with permission.
19. Letters of Alcuin, beginning on page 106: trans. S. Allott in *Alcuin of York, c. A.D. 732 to 804* (York: William Sessions, 1974), pp.11-13, 36-38, 72-73, 78, 80-82, 91-92, 120-121, 123-126; reprinted with permission.

CHAPTER THREE

25. Thegan's *Life of Louis*, beginning on page 141: trans. by J.R. Ginsburg in collaboration with D.L. Boutelle, in D.L. Boutelle, "Louis the Pious and Ermoldus Nigellus: An Inquiry into the Historical Reliability of *In honorem Hludowici*," (Ph.D. diss.: University of California, Berkeley, 1970), pp.309-334; revised and printed with permission.
26. Benedict of Aniane: His Life and Times, beginning on page 156: trans. Judith R. Ginsburg with Donna L. Boutelle, from *Vita Benedicti Abbatis Anianensis et Indensis auctore Ardone*, ed. G. Waitz, Monumenta Germaniae Historica: Scriptores, vol. 15.1 (Hanover, 1887), pp.200-220; revised and printed with permission.
27. The *Ordinatio Imperii* of 817 , beginning on page 176: trans. B. Pullan in *Sources of the History of Medieval Europe from the Mid-Eighth to the Mid-Thirteenth Century* (New York: Barnes & Noble, 1966), pp.38-42; reprinted with permission.
33. A Royal Judgment of Pepin in 828, beginning on page 197: trans. J.L. Nelson, "Dispute Settlement in Carolingian West Francia," in *The Settlement of Disputes in Early Medieval Europe*, ed. W. Davies and P. Fouracre (Cambridge: Cam-

bridge University Press, 1986), p.49; reprinted with permission.
35. Claudius of Turin's Complaint, beginning on page 247:
trans. A. Cabaniss, in *Early Medieval Theology*, ed. G.E. McCracken and A. Cabaniss, in The Library of Christian Classics, vol. 9 (Philadelphia, Westminster Press, 1957), pp.241-248; reprinted with permission.
36. The Penitential of Halitgar , beginning on page 251:
J.T. McNeil and H.M. Gamer, trans., *Medieval Handbooks of Penance* (New York: Columbia University Press, 1938), pp.297-314; reprinted with permission.
37. Saint-Riquier (Centula): Its Precious Goods , beginning on page 264:
trans. C. Davis-Weyer, *Early Medieval Art, 300-1150*, in Sources & Documents in the History of Art, ed. H.W. Janson (Englewood Cliffs, New Jersey: Prentice-Hall, 1971), pp.95-96; reprinted with permission.
38. The Emperor Louis's Palace at Ingelheim, beginning on page 265:
trans. C. Davis-Weyer, *Early Medieval Art, 300-1150*, Sources & Documents in the History of Art, ed. H.W. Janson (Englewood Cliffs, New Jersey: Prentice-Hall, 1971), pp.84-88; reprinted with permission.
39. The Astronomer's Account of the Rebellions , beginning on page 267:
trans. A. Cabaniss, *Son of Charlemagne: A Contemporary Life of Louis the Pious* (Syracuse, New York: Syracuse University Press, 1961), pp. 89-103; reprinted with permission.
40. Paschasius Radbertus's Defense of Wala , beginning on page 275:
trans. A. Cabaniss, *Charlemagne's Cousins: Contemporary Lives of Adalard and Wala* (Syracuse, New York: Syracuse University Press, 1967), pp.160-164, 191-196; reprinted with permission.
42. Rudolf of Fulda: The Life of Saint Leoba , beginning on page 311:
C.H. Talbot, in *The Anglo-Saxon Missionaries in Germany: Being the Lives of SS. Willibrord, Boniface, Sturm, Leoba and Lebuin, together with the Hodoeporicon of St. Willibald and a Selection from the Correspondence of St. Boniface* (New York: Sheed and Ward, 1954), pp.205-226; reprinted with permission.
43. The Final Days and Death of Louis the Pious, beginning on page 326:
trans. A. Cabaniss, *Son of Charlemagne: A Contemporary Life of Louis the Pious* (Syracuse, New York: Syracuse University Press, 1961), pp.120-125; reprinted with permission.

CHAPTER FOUR
44. Nithard's History , beginning on page 333:
trans. B.W. Scholz with B. Rogers, in *Carolingian Chronicles: Royal Frankish Annals and Nithard's Histories* (Ann Arbor: The University of Michigan Press, 1970), pp.129-174; reprinted with permission.

CHAPTER FIVE
52. Sedulius Scottus, *On Christian Rulers*, beginning on page 402:
trans. E.G. Doyle, in Sedulius Scottus, *On Christian Rulers and the Poems*, Medieval & Renaissance Texts & Studies, vol. 17 (Binghamton: State University of New York at Binghamton, 1983), pp.51-61; reprinted with permission.
54. Otfrid of Weissenburg on Old High German , beginning on page 419:
trans. F.P. Magoun, Jr., "Otfrid's Ad Liutbertum," *PMLA* 58 (1943), pp.872-889; reprinted with permission.
56. Letters of Lupus of Ferrières , beginning on page 425:
trans. G.W. Regenos, *The Letters of Lupus of Ferrières* (The Hague: Martinus Nijhoff, 1966); reprinted with permission.
57. The Wandering Monks of Saint-Philibert, beginning on page 434:
trans. D. Herlihy, *The History of Feudalism* (New York: Harper & Row, 1970), pp.8-13; reprinted with permission.
58. A Judicial Dispute in the Loire Valley , beginning on page 437:
trans. J.L. Nelson, "Dispute Settlement in Carolingian West Francia," in *The Settlement of Disputes in Early Medieval Europe*, ed. W. Davies and P. Fouracre (Cambridge: Cambridge University Press, 1986), pp.56-57; reprinted with permission.

59. A Charter of Immunity from Charles the Bald , beginning on page 440:
trans. D. Herlihy, *The History of Feudalism* (New York: Harper & Row, 1970), pp.126-128; reprinted with permission.
60. Saint Remi's Protection of People and Property, beginning on page 441:
trans. D. Herlihy, *The History of Feudalism* (New York: Harper & Row, 1970), pp.122-124; reprinted with permission.
61. The Coronation of Charles the Bald as King of Lotharingia, beginning on page 443:
trans. D. Herlihy, *The History of Feudalism* (New York: Harper & Row, 1970), pp.128-131; reprinted with permission.
62. Eriugena's *Periphyseon: the Beginning and End*, beginning on page 445,:
trans. I.P. Sheldon-Williams, revised by J.J. O'Meara, in Eriugena, *Periphyseon (The Division of Nature)*, (Montreal: Bellarmin, 1987), pp.25-30, 710-715; reprinted with permission.
63. Eriugena's Homily, beginning on page 453:
trans. J.J. O'Meara, in O'Meara, *Eriugena* (Oxford: Clarendon Press, 1988), pp.158-176.
65. Wulfadus Goes to Court , beginning on page 467:
trans. J.L. Nelson, "Dispute Settlement in Carolingain West Francia," in *The Settlement of Disputes in Early Medieval Europe*, ed. W. Davies and P. Fouracre (Cambridge: Cambridge University Press, 1986), p.53; reprinted with permission.
66. Charles the Bald Grants a Benefice , beginning on page 469:
trans. D. Herlihy, *A History of Feudalism* (New York: Harper & Row, 1970), pp.105-106; reprinted with permission.
67. The Capitulary of Quierzy, 877 , beginning on page 470:
trans. D. Herlihy, *A History of Feudalism* (New York: Harper & Row, 1970), pp.106-107; reprinted with permission.

CHAPTER SIX
70. The Song of Louis: *Ludwigslied* beginning on page 482:
trans. J.K. Bostock, in Bostock, *A Handbook of Old High German Literature*, 2nd ed. revised by K.C. King and D.R. McLintock (Oxford: Clarendon Press, 1976), pp.239-241; reprinted with permission.
72. Hincmar of Rheims, On the Governance of the Palace, beginning on page 485:
trans. D. Herlihy, *A History of Feudalism* (New York: Harper & Row, 1970), pp.209-227; reprinted with permission.
74. The Saxon Poet's Thoughts on Charlemagne, beginning on page 501:
trans. M.E. McKinney, *The Saxon Poet's Life of Charles the Great* (New York: Pageant Press, 1956), pp.85-86, 103-104; reprinted with permission.

PRINTED IN CANADA